American Social Welfare Policy

American Social Welfare Policy

A Pluralist Approach

FOURTH EDITION

Howard Jacob Karger
University of Houston

David Stoesz
Virginia Commonwealth University

Allyn and Bacon
BOSTON • LONDON • TORONTO • SYDNEY • TOKYO • SINGAPORE

Series Editor, Social Work and Family Therapy: Patricia Quinlin
Editor-in-Chief, Social Sciences: Karen Hanson
Series Editorial Assistant: Alyssa Pratt
Editorial-Production Service: Omegatype Typography, Inc.
Composition and Prepress Buyer: Linda Cox
Manufacturing Buyer: Suzanne Lareau
Cover Administrator: Linda Knowles
Electronic Composition: Omegatype Typography, Inc.

Library of Congress Cataloging-in-Publication Data
Karger, Howard Jacob
   American social welfare policy : a pluralist approach / Howard Jacob Karger, David Stoesz.—4th ed.
     p. cm.
   Includes bibliographical references and index.
   ISBN 0-8013-3311-3
   1. Public welfare—United States.   2. United States—Social policy.   3. Welfare state.   I. Stoesz, David. II. Title.
HV95 .K354 2002
361.973—dc21
                                    2001022694

Dedication

For my children, Aaron, Rafi, and Saul

—H. J. K.

For Marc, Darcy, and Tim

—D. S.

Contents

Part Three: The Government Sector

chapter **8**

The Making of Governmental Policy   205

chapter **9**

Tax Policy and Income Distribution   233

chapter **10**

Social Insurance Programs   251

chapter **11**

Public Assistance Programs   271

chapter 15

Child Welfare Policy 415

chapter 16

Housing Policies 438

chapter 17

The Politics of Food Policy and Rural Life 464

Part Four: The American Welfare State in Perspective

chapter **18**

The American Welfare State in International Perspective   488

Glossary   511

Index   521

Preface

The advent of a new century finds conservatism hegemonic in U.S. domestic policy. Now beginning their third decade of dominance in social policy, conservatives have found new ways to place their imprimatur on public philosophy, in the process vanquishing liberals, many of whom are social welfare professionals. The most conspicuous illustration of the conservative triumph in public affairs is, of course, the "election" of George W. Bush to the presidency. That Al Gore won the popular vote, and might perhaps have won the Electoral College as well, may leave human service professionals with a false sense that a resurgent liberalism is latent within the U.S. populace.

Nothing could be farther from the truth.

Since the "revolution" that installed Ronald Reagan in the White House, the ideological right has defined the discussion of social policy. The Clinton interregnum, afforded by the leveraging of the Democratic party to the center by means of the Democratic Leadership Council (DLC), was an accommodation to regnant conservatism. Aside from his peccadilloes, Clinton will be remembered as a centrist president, one who behaved more like a moderate Republican than like a liberal Democrat. The DLC interlude, however, did witness two classically liberal initiatives—and both failed spectacularly. The first was the effort to pass a Health Security Act, an attempt to universalize health care in the United States, the only industrial country without such a health policy. Despite being drafted in a manner that appeased the health industry, the measure failed. The second was the Gore presidential campaign. Despite unprecedented economic prosperity that should have made for certain victory, an incumbent vice president running a campaign heavily laden with liberal themes was trumped by a second-term governor of Texas.

While liberal human service professionals have continued to lick their ideological wounds, conservatives have made serious inroads into the U.S. welfare state. To date the hallmark has been the 1996 Personal Responsibility and Work Opportunity Reconciliation Act, which terminated the 60-year entitlement to family assistance, converting the welfare system to a block grant program devolved to the states. Federal welfare reform may serve as prelude for more Draconian ventures under the presidency of George W. Bush, who has advocated "privatizing" Social Security and "reforming" Medicare. Although such conservative designs on the bedrock of the welfare state may well be blocked by Senate Democrats, the message should be clear: Not only have liberals lost the public support undergirding welfare programs, but they have watched the foundation of social insurance erode as well.

The irony is that the current policy environment could offer social welfare advocates multiple opportunities, if they were willing to shed their insistence on federal entitlements as a basis for social policy. Consider several of the conservative themes that are driving public philosophy:

- "Privatization" has long been part of human services in the United States, as is amply evident in nonprofit organizations as well as private practitioners.
- "Devolution" is familiar to providers of child welfare, mental health, and corrections—traditionally state-controlled programs—to say nothing of professionals who have served as elected officials in state and local governments.
- "Faith-based social service" has been a cornerstone of the nonprofit sector, evident in such agencies as Catholic Charities, the Salvation Army, and Jewish community services, among others.

As these examples suggest, advocates of social justice *already have* substantial expertise in domains that conservatives have appropriated; this expertise could be mobilized to enhance the public interest, and social work would benefit as a result.

Several changes will be required, however, if human service professionals are to reclaim a prominent role in social policy. Foremost, "compassionate conservatism" must be taken seriously along with traditional liberal prescriptions in social affairs. Markets have been a primary means of distributing goods and services to the nonpoor, and the application of market dynamics to low-income families should be evaluated on merit, not discarded out of ideological preference. State and local politics have been important as arenas for introducing innovations in social welfare as well as for providing social workers a first step on the ladder of public service; such opportunities should be celebrated, not dismissed.

Essential as a reorientation is if social work is to reassert its role in public policy, by itself such a reorientation will be insufficient if the profession is to be an influential player. The currency of the realm in public policy is power, and power occurs in three basic forms: money, votes, and networks. These resources have been the staple of politics, but the information age has introduced a higher level of sophistication. Money means access to capital and various means for increasing its value; votes are massaged by constant polling; networks are identified and modified depending on the objective at hand. In a postindustrial policy environment, influence is a function of a player's facility in manipulating these three resources. To be competitive, one must have command of information systems, large data sets, and complex decision menus.

If social work can educate students about these methods and begin to insert them into the policy environment, the profession will become an influential force in social policy. On the other hand, if the profession rests on the laurels of the New Deal and the War on Poverty, all the while

denigrating the rapacity of "special interests," it will remain a bit player. Such an eventuality would essentially waste the quite substantial assets that social work brings to social affairs: a distinguished legacy, the altruism of the young, and a unique moral imperative. Just as the foundation of the conservative juggernaut can be attributed to the anguish of young Republicans in the aftermath of the 1964 presidential election, so the rebirth of Progressivism may be found in the dismay of the 2000 presidential election. Social workers can be among the catalysts in this rebirth.

This fourth edition of *American Social Welfare Policy* attempts to provide the information necessary for the reemergence of social work in social policy, nationally and internationally. In addition to discussing the basic concepts, policies, and programs that have typified the U.S. welfare state, the text includes separate chapters on the voluntary nonprofit sector and the for-profit corporate sector. A new chapter on tax policy directs attention to a new strategy in social policy: tax expenditures. The final chapter examines the influence of global capitalism, a development that not only weds the developed nations with the undeveloped nations but also, in the process, shifts capital and jobs in unprecedented volumes.

In writing the fourth edition, we owe many debts. The reviewers of this and previous editions have provided an invaluable service in identifying deficiencies. We would like to thank the reviewers of the fourth edition for their insightful comments and suggestions: Jay Bishop, University of Maryland, Eastern Shore; Pat Brownell, Fordham University; Katharine Byers, Indiana University; Edward Gumz, Loyola University, Chicago; Mark Hanna, California State University, Fresno; Sue Henry, University of Denver; Richard Holody, Lehman College; Martha Raske, University of Southern Indiana; Todd Rofuth, Southern Connecticut State University; Elizabeth H. Ruff, University of New England; Deborah Schild Wilkinson, University of Kansas; and Jennifer Stucker, Eastern Washington University. In addition, we would also like to thank our student assistants, including Kari Miller, who provided research for select chapters. We owe a huge debt to Krupa Parikh for doing the crucial and tedious job of proofing the chapters and endnotes. Finally, thanks to our families for suffering our many absences with patience. In anticipation of a fifth edition, comments by students and faculty are welcome.

chapter 1

Social Policy and the American Welfare State

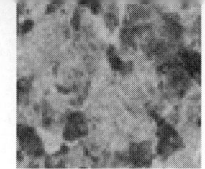

This chapter provides an overview of the American welfare state. In particular, it examines various definitions of social welfare policy, the relationship between social policy and social problems, and the values and ideologies that drive social welfare in the United States. In addition, the chapter examines the effects of ideology on the U.S. welfare state, including the important roles played by conservatism and liberalism (and their variations) in shaping welfare policy. The chapter also explores the political economy of welfare in this country, including the roles played by the Keynesians, free market economics, socialism, and communitarianism, among others.

American social welfare is in transition. Starting with the Social Security Act of 1935, liberals argued that federal social programs were the best way to help the disadvantaged. Now, after 70 years of experimenting with the **welfare state,** a discernible shift has occurred. The conservatism of U.S. culture—so evident in the Reagan, Bush, and even Clinton presidencies—has left private institutions to shoulder more of the welfare burden. For proponents of social justice, the suggestion that the private sector should assume more responsibility for welfare represents a retreat from the hard-won governmental social legislation that provided essential benefits to millions of Americans. Justifiably, these groups fear the loss of basic goods and services during the transition in social welfare.

A pluralistic mix of private and public services is an overriding feature of U.S. social welfare. As in other realms, such as education, in social welfare private institutions coexist alongside those of the public sector. American social welfare has a noble tradition of voluntary citizen groups' taking the initiative to solve local problems. Today, private voluntary groups provide important services to patients with acquired immune deficiency syndrome (AIDS), the homeless, and refugees.

Social welfare is also big business. During the last 25 years the number of human service corporations—for-profit firms providing social welfare through the marketplace—has increased dramatically. Human service corporations are prominent in long-term nursing care, health maintenance, child day care, psychiatric and substance abuse services, even corrections. For many welfare professionals the privatizing of social services is troubling, occuring as it does at a time when government has reduced its commitment to social programs. Yet human service corporations will likely continue to be prominent players in shaping the nation's social welfare policies. As long as U.S. culture is democratic and capitalistic, entrepreneurs will be free to establish social welfare services in the private sector, both as non-profit agencies and as for-profit corporations.

The **mixed welfare economy** of the United States, in which the voluntary, governmental, and corporate sectors coexist, poses important questions for social welfare policy. To what extent can voluntary groups be held responsible for public welfare, given their limited fiscal resources? For which groups of people, if any, should government divest itself of responsibility? Can human service corporations care for poor and multi-problem clients while continuing to generate profits? Equally important, how can welfare professionals shape coherent social welfare policies, given the fragmentation inherent in such pluralism? Clearly, the answers to these questions have much to say about how social welfare programs are perceived by human service professionals, their clients, and the taxpayers who continue to subsidize social programs.

The multitude of questions posed by the transition of social welfare in this country is daunting. The interaction of ideological, political, social, and economic factors has so exacerbated the problem that the idea of "the welfare mess" has become a fixture in contemporary folklore. Yet past advocates of social justice such as Jane Addams, Whitney Young Jr., and Wilbur Cohen, to name a few, interpreted the inadequacy of social welfare provision and the confusion of their times as an opportunity to further social justice. It remains for another generation of welfare professionals to demonstrate the same imagination, perseverance, and courage to advance social welfare in the years ahead. Those accepting this challenge will need to be familiar with the various meanings of social welfare policy, differing political and economic explanations of social welfare, and the multiple interest groups that have emerged within the American social welfare system.

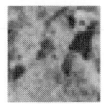 # Definitions of Social Welfare Policy

The English social scientist Richard Titmuss has defined **social services** as "a series of collective interventions that contribute to the general welfare by assigning claims from one set of people who are said to produce or earn the national income to another set of people who may merit compassion and charity."[1] Welfare policy, whether it is the product of governmental, voluntary, or corporate institutions, is concerned with allocating goods, services, and opportunities to enhance social functioning.

William Epstein defines social policy as "social action sanctioned by society."[2] Social policy can also be defined as the formal and consistent ordering of human affairs. **Social welfare policy,** a subset of social policy, regulates the provision of benefits to people to meet basic life needs, such as employment, income, food, housing, health care, and relationships.[3]

Social welfare policy is influenced by the context in which benefits are provided. For example, social welfare is often associated with legislatively mandated programs of the **governmental sector,** such as **Temporary Assistance for Needy Families (TANF).** In the TANF program, social welfare policy consists of the rules by which the federal and state governments apportion cash benefits to an economically disadvantaged population. TANF benefits are derived from general revenue taxes (often paid by citizens who are better off). But this is a simplification of benefits provided to those deemed needy. Benefits provided through governmental social welfare policy include cash, but also noncash or in-kind benefits, including personal social services.[4] Cash benefits can be further divided into social insurance and public assistance grants.

In-kind benefits (provided as proxies for cash) include benefits such as food stamps, Medicaid, housing vouchers, Women, Infants, and Children (WIC) coupons, and low-income energy assistance. Personal social services are services designed to enhance relationships between people as well as institutions, such as individual, family, and mental health treatment; child welfare services, rehabilitation counseling, and so forth. While complicated, this classification reflects a common theme; namely, the redistribution of resources from those who are better off to those who are disadvantaged. This redistributional aspect of social welfare policy is generally accepted by those who view social welfare as a legitimate function of the state. Governmental social welfare policy is often referred to as "public" policy, because it is the result of decisions reached through a legislative process that is intended to represent the entire population.

But social welfare is also provided by nongovernmental entities, in which case social welfare policy is a manifestation of "private" policy. For example, a nonprofit agency with a high demand for its services and limited resources may establish a waiting list as agency policy. As other agencies in similar circumstances adopt the same strategy for rationing services, clients begin to pile up on waiting lists. Eventually, some clients are denied services because of the waiting lists. Hence, the policies of independent private agencies have a significant impact on the welfare of clients. Or consider the practice of "dumping," a policy that has been used by some private health care providers that abruptly transfer uninsured patients to public hospitals while they are suffering from traumatic injuries. Some patients have died as a result of private social welfare policy.

Because U.S. social welfare has been shaped by policies of governmental and nonprofit agencies, confusion exists about the role of for-profit social service firms. The distinction between the public and private sectors was traditionally marked by the boundary between governmental and nonprofit agencies. Profit-making firms are also "private," being nongovernmental entities; but they differ from the traditional private voluntary agencies in that they operate on a for-profit basis. Consequently, within private social welfare it is important to distinguish between policies of for-profit and policies of nonprofit organizations. A logical way to redraw the social welfare map is to adopt the following definitions: *Governmental social welfare policy* refers to decisions made by the state; *voluntary social welfare policy* refers to decisions reached by nonprofit agencies; and *corporate social welfare policy* refers to decisions made by for-profit firms.

Social Problems and Social Welfare Policy

Social welfare policy often develops in response to social problems. The relationship between social problems and social welfare policy is not linear, however; not all social problems result in social welfare policies. In many instances, too, social welfare policies exist but are funded at ineffectual levels. For example, the Child Abuse Prevention and Treatment Act of 1974 was designed to ameliorate the problem of child abuse, yet underbudgeting left Child Protective Service (CPS) workers in a catch-22 situation. The act required CPS workers to promptly investigate child abuse reports, but agencies had inadequate staff resources to deal with the skyrocketing number of complaints. Caught in a resources crunch, many CPS workers were unable to properly investigate allegations of abuse. As a result, many children died or were seriously injured.

Social welfare is not merely an expression of social altruism; it contributes to the maintenance and survival of society. In this respect, social welfare policy helps hold together a society that may fracture along social, political, and economic stress lines. Social welfare policy is also useful in enforcing social control, especially as a proxy for other coercive measures such as law enforcement and the courts.[5] When their basic minimum needs are met, the disadvantaged are less inclined to revolt against the unequal distribution of resources. Social welfare policies also subsidize the private employment sector, because welfare benefits supplement low and nonlivable wages. Hence, social welfare policies subsidize employers who would otherwise have to raise salaries. Social welfare also supports important industries, such as agriculture, housing, and health care. Indeed, if social welfare benefits were eliminated, a segment of U.S. business would collapse. Without such social benefits, fundamental questions would also arise about the moral, spiritual, and ethical nature of U.S. society. Social welfare policies also relieve the social and economic dislocations caused by the uneven nature of economic development. Finally, social welfare policies are a means for rectifying past injustices. For example, affirmative action was designed to remedy the historical discrimination that has denied large numbers of Americans access to economic opportunities and positions of power.

Social Work and Social Policy

Social work practice is driven by social policies, which dictate how the work is done, with whom, for how much, and toward what ends. For example, a social worker employed in a public mental health center may have a caseload of well over 200 clients. Given that caseload size, it is unlikely that a worker can engage in any kind of sustained psychotherapeutic intervention with clients; caseload constraints permit little more than superficial case tracking. Or consider the JOBS (Jobs Opportunities and Basic Skills) worker required to find employment for mothers on public assistance who are about to lose benefits because of the imposition of time limits but who are unlikely to find adequate work because of high unemployment in their area. In these instances, social, ideological, and economic factors contribute to policies that determine the ability of the social worker and the agency to accomplish their mission.

Since 1980, an ideological preference among policymakers for private sector social services has resulted in less funding for public agencies. A conservative emphasis on cutting taxes has led to reductions in public revenues, which, in turn, has been translated into reductions for social programs. As a result of diminishing revenues, public agencies are taking predictable measures to adjust, including reductions in the number of qualified staff (the staff does more with less), the introduction of short-term or group interventions designed to process more clients (thereby allowing more new intakes and a shorter waiting list), and reductions in pay or benefits for professional staff. All of these strategies conspire to shape an agency geared to processing more clients rather than to helping clients in any real sense. Thus, what a trained social worker is able to accomplish depends, in part, on the available resources within the agency.

Although this may not be obvious at first glance, the same is true for many social workers in private practice who depend on managed care plans for reimbursement. Specifically, managed care plans dictate how much a social worker can be paid and how often the social worker will see a client; accordingly, care management dictates the kinds of interventions that will be practical in the allotted time. The rationing of client services by managed care companies has become a volatile issue. Thus, social policy and its components—ideology and values—greatly influence social work practice. In fact, they have as much impact upon clients and social workers

as do the microlevel theories that otherwise guide much of social work.

 # Values, Ideology, and Social Welfare Policy

Social welfare policies are shaped by a set of social and personal values that reflect the preferences of those in decision-making capacities. According to David Gil, "Choices in social welfare policy are heavily influenced by the dominant beliefs, values, ideologies, customs, and traditions of the cultural and political elites recruited mainly from among the more powerful and privileged strata."[6] Charles Prigmore and Charles Atherton list no fewer than 15 values that influence social welfare policy: achievement and success, activity and work, public morality, humanitarian concerns, efficiency and practicality, material comfort, equality, freedom, external conformity, science and secular rationality, nationalism and patriotism, democracy and self-determination, individualism, racism and group superiority, and belief in progress.[7] How these values are played out in the realm of social welfare is the domain of the policy analyst.

Despite the best of intentions, social welfare policy is often not based on a rational set of assumptions and reliable research. One view of a worthwhile social policy is that it should leave no one worse off and at least one person better off, at least as that person judges his or her needs. In the real world of policy that is rarely the case. More often, the policy game is played as a zero-sum game, in which some people are advantaged at the expense of others. In fact, it can be argued that major social policies are based on values, not on the careful consideration of alternative policies.

Of course, there are serious consequences when social welfare policy is determined to a high degree by values. Since the late 1970s, social welfare policy has been largely shaped by values that emphasize individualism, self-sufficiency, work, and the omniscience of the marketplace. Because policymakers expected disadvantaged people to be more independent, supports from government social programs were cut significantly. Although these reductions saved money in the short run, most of the beneficiaries whose supports fell to the budget ax were children. Eventually, cuts in social programs may well lead to greater expenditures, as the generation of children who have gone without essential services begin to require programs to remedy problems associated with poor maternal and infant health care, poverty, illiteracy, and family disorganization. As Silvia Ann Hewlett poignantly observed, "Although the United States ranks No. 2 worldwide in per capita income, this country does not even make it into the top ten on any significant indicator of child welfare."[8]

Social values are organized through the lens of ideology. Simply put, an **ideology** is the framework of commonly held beliefs through which we view the world. It is a set of assumptions about how the world works: what has value, what is worth living and dying for, what is good and true, and what is right. For the most part, these beliefs are rarely examined and are simply assumed to be true. Hence, the ideological tenets around which society is organized exist as a collective social consciousness that defines the world for the society's members. All societies reproduce themselves, in part, through reproducing ideology; in this way, each generation accepts the basic ideological suppositions of the preceding generation. When widely held ideological beliefs are questioned, society often reacts with strong sanctions. Ideological trends influence social welfare directly when adherents of one orientation hold a majority in decision-making bodies, such as a state or national legislature.

Ideology strongly influences social welfare policy during periods of social and economic instability. The continuity of American social history has been intermittently shattered when certain oppressed groups have asserted their rights in the face of mainstream norms. Such periods of social unrest strain the capacity of conventional ideologies to explain social problems and offer solutions. Sometimes social unrest is met with force, as during the period of the great labor strikes of 1877. In other instances, such as the Great Depression, social unrest is met with the expansion of social welfare programs.

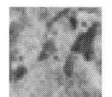

The Political Economy of American Social Welfare

The term **political economy** refers to the interaction of political and economic institutions in a society. The political economy of the United States has been labeled **democratic capitalism;** that is, in this country an open, representative form of government coexists with a market economy. The interaction of political and economic institutions is frequently irregular, however, and social welfare functions make society more stable. The main function of social welfare is to modify the play of market forces and to moderate the social and economic inequities that the market generates.[9] To that end, two sets of activities are necessary: state provision of social services (benefits of cash, in-kind benefits, and personal social services) and state regulation of private activities to alter (though not necessarily improve) the lives of citizens. In short, social welfare bolsters ideology by helping to remedy the problems associated with economic dislocation, thereby allowing society to remain in a state of more or less controlled balance.

Although Americans are assured of their political rights by a constitution that mandates a representative democracy, there is no corresponding document guaranteeing economic rights. Such a document would be undesirable in a free market society, because it would allow government to interfere in the operations of the marketplace. In the absence of any guaranteed economic rights, large numbers of Americans find the economy unresponsive to their needs, and the political system is the only vehicle through which to seek redress. But because access to the political system often presupposes wealth and status, it is a less than optimal method for achieving social justice for many citizens. To some extent, social welfare programs compensate for deficiencies in the U.S. political economy by appeasing dissident groups.

It is important to understand the political economy in order to comprehend the intense disagreement around the optimal way to enhance the general welfare. Yet there is little common understanding of how this nation's political economy works or how it should work. Instead, several competing schools of thought purport to explain how the political economy functions and how best to deploy it to solve new problems. The stakes are high: Major institutions—government, corporations, organized labor, and the social welfare industry—stand to lose or gain considerable power based on how the political economy should be defined. Invariably, any given explanation of the political economy will benefit some institutions more than others. Because social welfare is advantaged or disadvantaged based upon which school of political economy holds sway at any given moment, policy analysts pay close attention to important schools of thought.

As noted earlier, the U.S. welfare state is driven by political economy. While ideally the political economy of the welfare state should be viewed as an integrated fabric of politics and economics, in reality some schools of thoughts or movements contain more political than economic content, and vice versa. For example, most economic schools of thought contain sufficient political implications to qualify them as both economic and political dogmas. Conversely, most political schools of thought contain significant economic content. It is therefore often difficult to separate political from economic schools of thought. For the purposes of this chapter, though, we will organize the political economy of American welfare into two separate categories: (1) predominantly economic schools of thought, and (2) predominantly political schools of thought. The careful reader will find a significant overlap among and between these categories.

 # The U.S. Economic Continuum

In large measure, economics forms the backbone of the political system. For example, we would not have the modern welfare state without the contributions of economist John Maynard Keynes. Conversely, we would not have the conservative movement without the contributions of classical or free market economists such as Adam Smith or Milton Friedman. Virtually every political movement is in some way or another grounded in economic thought. The three major schools of economics that have traditionally dominated American economic thought are Keynesian economics; classical or free market economics; and, to a lesser degree, democratic socialism.

Keynesian Economics

Keynesian economics is the engine that drives liberalism and most welfare state ideology. Albeit indirectly, John Maynard Keynes was the economic architect of the modern welfare state, and all welfare societies are built along his principles. Sometimes called demand or consumer-side economics, this model emerged from Keynes's book *The General Theory of Employment, Interest and Money*, published in 1936.

An Englishman, Keynes took the classical model of economic analysis (self-regulating markets, perfect competition, the laws of supply and demand, etc.) and added the insight that macroeconomic stabilization by government is necessary to keep the economic clock ticking smoothly.[10] He rejected the laissez-faire idea that a perfectly competitive economy tended automatically toward full employment and that the government should not interfere in the process. Keynes argued that instead of being self-correcting readily able to pull themselves out of recessions, modern economies were recession prone and had problems providing full employment.

According to Keynes, periodic and volatile economic situations that cause high unemployment are primarily caused by an instability in investment expenditures. The government can stabilize and correct recessionary or inflationary trends by increasing or decreasing total spending on output. A government can accomplish this by increasing or decreasing taxes, thereby increasing or decreasing consumption, and by the transfer of public goods or services. For Keynes, the "good" government is an activist government in economic matters, especially when the economy gets out of a full employment mode. Keynesians hypothesize that social welfare expenditures are investments in human capital that eventually increase the national wealth (e.g., through increases in productivity) and thereby boost everyone's net income.

Keynes's doctrine emerged from his attempt to understand the nature of recessions and depressions. Specifically, Keynes saw recessions and depressions as emerging from businesses' loss of confidence in investments (e.g., a focus on risk rather than gain), which in turn causes hoarding of cash. The loss of confidence eventually leads to a shortage of money as everyone tries to hoard cash simultaneously. Keynes's answer to this problem is that government should make it possible for people to satisfy their economic needs without cutting their spending, which will prevent the spiral of shrinking incomes and shrinking spending. Simply put, the government should print more money and get it into circulation.[11]

Keynes also understood that this policy alone would not suffice if a recession were allowed to get out of control, as in the Depression of the 1930s. In a depression businesses and households will not increase spending regardless of how much cash they have. To help an economy exit this "liquidity trap," government must do what the private sector will not; namely, spend. This spending can take the form of public works projects (financed by borrowing programs) or of direct governmental subsidization of demand (welfare entitlements). To be fair, Keynes saw public spending only as a last resort to be employed if monetary expansion failed. Moreover,

he sought an economic balance: Print money and spend in a recession, but stop printing and stop spending once it's over. Keynes understood that too much money in circulation, especially when production is active and there is full employment, leads to inflation. Although relatively simple, Keynes's theories represent one of the great insights of twentieth-century economic thought.[12] Keynes's ideas also form the economic basis for the modern welfare state.

Conservative or Free Market Economics

Whereas liberalism is guided by Keynesian economics, the conservative view of social welfare is guided by free market economics. The ascendence of the conservative economic (and social) argument accelerated after 1973, when the rise in living standards began to slow for most Americans. Conservatives blamed this economic slowdown on governmental policies; specifically, deficit spending, progressive taxes, excessive regulations, and monetary policies.[13]

Milton Friedman, sometimes considered the father of modern conservative economics, was one of Keynes's more ardent critics. In opposition to Keynes, Friedman argues that using fiscal and monetary policy to smooth out the business cycle is harmful to the economy and worsens economic instability.[14] Unlike Keynes, Friedman contends that the Depression did not occur because people were hoarding money; rather, there was a fall in the quantity of money in circulation. He argues that Keynesian economic policies should be replaced by simple monetary rules (hence the term *monetarism*). In effect, Friedman believes that the role of government should be to keep the money supply growing slowly and steadily at a rate that is consistent with stable prices and long-term economic growth.[15]

Friedman's analysis counsels against active efforts to stabilize the economy. Instead of pumping money into the economy, government should simply make sure that enough cash is in circulation. He calls for government to be relatively inactive in economic affairs and not try to manage or intervene in the business cycle. Under

Friedman's framework the case for Keynesian demand-side economics is diminished, and welfare spending would exist only for altruistic rather than economic reasons.[16] To the right of Milton Friedman is Robert Lucas, 1994 Nobel Prize winner and developer of the "theory of rational expectations." Lucas argues that Friedman's monetary policy is still too interventionist and will invariably do more harm than good.[17]

Developing outside of conventional economics, **supply-side economics** enjoyed considerable popularity during the early 1980s. Led by Robert Barth, editorial page head of the *Wall Street Journal*, supply-siders were journalists, policymakers, and maverick economists who argued that demand-side policies and monetary policies were ineffective.[18] They maintained that the incentive effects of reduced taxation would be so large that tax cuts would dramatically increase economic activity—to the point where tax revenues would rise, not fall. (Former president George Bush referred to this as voodoo economics in 1980.[19]) Specifically, supply-siders argued that tax cuts would lead to a large increase in labor supply and investment and therefore to a large expansion in economic output. The budget deficit would not be problematic, because taxes, increased savings, and higher economic output would offset the deficit. In the early 1980s supply-siders seized power not only from the Keynesians, but also from more mainstream conservative economists, many of whom believed in the same things but wanted to move more slowly.[20]

Although some supporters preferred to think of supply-side economics as pure economics, the theory contained enough political implications to qualify as a political as well as an economic approach. Popularized by supporters such as Jack Kemp, Arthur Laffer, and Ronald Reagan, supply-side economics provided the major rationale for cuts in social programs executed under the Reagan administration.

Despite their popularity in the early years of the Reagan administration, supply-side ideas fell out of favor when it became evident that massive tax cuts for the wealthy and corporations did not result in increased capital formation and economic activity. Instead, the wealthy spent their tax savings on luxury items, and corporations used their tax savings to purchase other companies in a merger mania that took Wall Street by surprise. In addition, many corporations took advantage of temporary tax savings to transfer their operations abroad, further reducing the supply of higher-paying industrial jobs in the United States. For these and other reasons, during the Reagan administration the budget deficit grew from about $50 billion a year in the Carter term to $352 billion a year in 1992.[21]

Conservative economists argue that large social welfare programs—including unemployment benefits and public service jobs—are detrimental to the society in two ways. First, government social programs erode the work ethic by supporting those who do not work. Second, public sector social welfare programs divert money that could otherwise be invested in the private sector, because they are funded by taxes. These conservative economists believe that economic growth helps everyone; because overall prosperity creates more jobs, income, and goods, and these will eventually filter down to the poor. For conservative economists, investment is the key to prosperity and the engine that drives the economic machine. Investment in capital creates economic growth that results in more jobs, income, and goods. Accordingly, many conservative economists favor tax breaks for the wealthy, on the premise that such breaks will result in more disposable after-tax income freed up for investment. High taxes are an impediment to economic progress because they channel money into "public" investment and away from "private" investment. A validation of the conservative economic position on a low-tax and investment-driven economy is claimed in the $2 trillion federal surplus that is predicted to occur in the early 2000s.

In the neoconservative paradigm, opportunity is based on a person's relationship to the marketplace. Thus, legitimate rewards can occur only through marketplace participation. In contrast to liberals who emphasize mutual self-interest, interdependence, and social equity, conservative economists argue that the highest form of social good is realized by the maximization of self-interest. In the conservative view the best society is one in which everyone actively pursues his or her own good. Through a leap of faith, the maximization of self-interest can be transformed into a mutual good. In that sense, conservatives occupy the opposite end of the philosophical continuum from liberals.

Conservative economists maintain not only that high taxation and government regulation of business serve as disincentives to investment, but that individual claims on social insurance and public welfare grants discourage work. Together these factors lead to a decline in economic growth and an increase in the expectations of beneficiaries of welfare programs. For conservatives the only way to correct the irrationality of government social programs is to smash them completely. Charles Murray, in his much celebrated *Losing Ground,* suggested that the entire federal assistance and income support structure for working-aged persons (Medicaid, the former AFDC, food stamps, etc.) should be scrapped. This would leave working-aged persons no recourse except to actively engage the job market or turn to family, friends, or privately funded services.[22]

Many conservative economists argue that economic insecurity is an important part of entrepreneurial activity. Unless people are *compelled* to work, they will choose leisure over work. Conversely, providing economic security for large numbers of people through welfare programs leads to diminished ambition and fosters an unhealthy dependence on the state. Conservatives further argue that self-realization can occur only through marketplace participation. Hence, social programs harm rather than help the most vulnerable members of society. This belief in the need for economic insecurity forms the basis for recent welfare reforms that include a maximum time limit on welfare benefits.

Many conservative economists are influenced by "public choice" theory. The **public choice school** gained adherents among conservative analysts as faith ebbed in the supply-side school. Not widely known beyond academic circles until its major proponent, James Buchanan,

was awarded the Nobel Prize for economics in 1986, the public choice model states that there are strong incentives for interest groups to make demands on government, in that the resulting concessions flow directly to the group while their costs are spread among all taxpayers. Initial concessions lead to demands for further concessions, which are likely to be forthcoming so long as the interest group is vociferous in its demands. Under such an incentive system, different interests are also encouraged to band together to make demands, because there is no reason for one interest group to oppose the demands of others. But while demands for goods and services increase, revenues tend to decrease. This happens because interest groups resist paying taxes directed specifically toward them and because no interest group has much individual incentive to support general taxes. The result of such a scenario is predictable: Irresistible demands for government benefits accompanied by declining revenues lead to government borrowing to finance programs, which results in large budget deficits.[23] Adherents of public choice theory view social welfare as a series of endless concessions to disadvantaged groups that will eventually bankrupt the government. On the other hand, it would be logical also to apply public choice analysis to interest groups related to the defense industry, which make similar demands on government while not paying corresponding taxes. Despite such contradictions, the public choice school is likely to remain influential and may continue to shape social welfare policy by calling for further reductions in public expenditures for social programs.

Democratic Socialism

Democratic socialism (as opposed to the old Soviet-style socialism) is based on the belief that radical economic change can occur within a democratic context. While eschewing capitalism, democratic socialists, such as the late Michael Harrington, maintain a fundamental belief in the democratic process.

Democratic socialism differs from both Keynesianism and conservative economics in an important way. Specifically, Keynesians have a basic faith in the market economy but want to shape it to make it more responsive to human needs. They want to retain capitalism, albeit with economic reforms that would smooth out the economy's harsher side. Most conservatives, on the other hand, believe that the economy should be left alone except for a few minor tweaks, such as regulating the money flow. Other conservative economists believe that the market should be left totally alone. On balance, however, both Keynesians and economic conservatives have a basic faith that capitalism can advance the public good and is not antithetical to meeting human needs. In that sense, Keynesianism and economic conservatism have more in common with each other than with a radical leftist perspective.

In contrast, proponents of **socialism** argue that the fundamental nature of capitalism is anathema to advancing the public good. They contend that a system predicated on the pursuit of profit and individual self-interest can lead only to greater inequality between the haves and have-nots. The creation of a just society requires a fundamental transformation of the economic system, and democratic socialists argue that the pursuit of profit and self-interest should be replaced by the collective pursuit of the common good. Not surprisingly, democratic socialists rebuff Keynesianism because of its inherent belief that economic problems can be fixed by simple technicalities as opposed to major institutional change. They dislike conservatism for more obvious reasons, such as the primary importance it places on markets, its belief in subordinating individual interests to market relations, and its overall social conservatism.

Socialists see social problems as a logical consequence of an unjust society.[24] Left-wing theorists maintain that the failure of capitalism has led to political movements that have pressured institutions to respond with increased social welfare services. They believe that real social welfare, in contrast, must be structural and can be accomplished only through a redistribution of resources. In a just society—a society in which all goods, resources, and opportunities were made available to everyone—all but the most

specific forms of welfare (health care, rehabilitation, counseling, and so forth) would be unnecessary. In this radical worldview, poverty is inextricably linked to structural inequality. People need welfare because they are exploited and denied access to resources. In an unjust society, welfare functions as a substitute, albeit a puny one, for social justice.

For some socialists, social welfare is an ingenious arrangement on the part of business to have the public assume the costs caused by the social and economic dislocations inherent in capitalism. According to these theorists, social welfare expenditures "socialize" the costs of capitalist production by making public the costs of private enterprise. Thus, social welfare serves both the needs of people and the needs of capitalist expansion and production. For other socialists, social welfare programs respond to human needs in a way that supports an unjust economic system, which in turn continues to generate problems requiring social programs.

Radicals maintain that social welfare programs function like junk food for the impoverished: They provide just enough subsistence to discourage revolution but not enough to make a real difference in the lives of the poor. Within this radical framework, social welfare is seen as a form of social control. Frances Fox Piven and Richard Cloward summarize the socialist argument:

> *Relief arrangements are ancillary to economic arrangements. Their chief function is to regulate labor, and they do that in two general ways. First, when mass unemployment leads to outbreaks of turmoil, relief programs are ordinarily initiated or expanded to absorb or control enough of the unemployed to restore order; then, as turbulence subsides, the relief system contracts, expelling those who are needed to populate the labor markets.*[25]

In place of liberal social welfare reforms, the radical vision proposes that the entire system—social, political, and especially economic—undergo a major overhaul. In short, the radical position is that real welfare reform—including a complete redistribution of goods, income, and services—can occur only in the context of a socialist system.

 # The U.S. Political Continuum

Various understandings of the political economy produce differing conceptions of the ultimate public good. Competition among ideas about the public good and the welfare state has long been a knotty issue in the political economy of the United States. Because any shift in government policy is driven largely by an ideologically determined view of the public good, any analysis must be based on whose definition is being examined. In a democratic capitalist society, beliefs about the public good often vary depending on each proponent's position in the social order.

The major American ideologies, (neo)liberalism and (neo)conservatism, hold vastly different views of social welfare and the public good. Conservatives believe that the public good is best served when individuals and families meet their needs through marketplace participation. Accordingly, conservatives prefer private sector approaches over governmental welfare and advocate for smaller government social welfare programs. Conservatives are not *anti*welfare per se; they simply believe that government should have a minimal role (i.e., serve as a "safety net") in ensuring the social welfare of citizens. Traditional liberals, on the other hand, view government as the only institution capable of bringing about a measure of **social justice** to millions of Americans who cannot fully participate in the U.S. mainstream because of obstacles such as racism, poverty, and sexism, among others. Traditional liberals therefore view governmental social welfare programs as a key component in promoting the public good. One of the major differences between conservatives and liberals lies in their differing perceptions on how the public good is enhanced or hurt by the welfare state.

The definition of "the public good" is lodged in the political and ideological continuum that makes up American political economy. An appreciation of this continuum requires an understanding of the interaction of schools of political thought and how they evolved. These ideological tenets also shape the platforms of the major political parties. These political movements can be divided into two categories: (1) liberalism and left-of-center movements, and (2) traditional conservatives and the far right.

Liberalism and Left-of-Center Movements

Liberalism. Since Franklin Delano Roosevelt's **New Deal,** advocates of **liberalism** have argued for advancing the public good by promoting an expanding economy coupled with the growth of universal, non-means-tested social welfare and health programs. Traditional liberals used Keynesian concepts as the economic justification for building the welfare state. As such, the general direction of policy from the 1930s to the middle 1970s was for the federal government to assume greater amounts of responsibility for the public good.

American liberals established the welfare state with the passage of the Social Security Act of 1935. Harry Hopkins—a social worker, the head of the Federal Emergency Relief Administration, a confidant of President Roosevelt, a coarchitect of the New Deal, and a consummate political operative—developed the calculus for American liberalism: "tax, tax; spend, spend; elect, elect."[26] This liberal approach was elegant in its simplicity: The government taxes the wealthy, thereby securing the necessary revenues to fund social programs for workers and the poor. This calculus dominated social policy for close to 50 years. In fact, this approach was so successful that by 1980 social welfare programs accounted for 57 percent of all federal expenditures.[27]

By the late 1960s the welfare state was an important fixture in the social landscape of the United States, and politicians sought to expand its benefits to more constituents. Focusing on the expansion of middle-class programs such as FHA home mortgages, federally insured student loans, Medicare, and veterans' pensions, liberal policymakers secured the political loyalty of a middle class that directly benefited from these programs. Even conservative politicians understood voter support for the middle-class welfare state; not surprisingly, the largest expansion of social welfare spending occurred under Richard Nixon, a Republican president.

Yet the promise of the U.S. welfare state to provide social protection similar to that prevailing in industrialized European nations never materialized. By the middle 1970s the hope of traditional liberals such as Ted Kennedy, Tip O'Neill, and George McGovern—to build a welfare state like those of northern Europe—had been replaced by an incremental approach that narrowly focused on consolidating and fine-tuning the programs of the Social Security Act. One reason for this failure was the ambivalence of many Americans toward centralized government. "The emphasis consistently has been on the local, the pluralistic, the voluntary, and the business-like over the national, the universal, the legally entitled, and the governmental," observed policy analyst Marc Bendick.[28] Public ambivalence about social programs was further exploited by the Reagan administration. Having lost the public policy debate, liberals were in a poor position to press for additional programs to serve vulnerable populations that remained unprotected by the "reluctant" U.S. welfare state.[29]

Liberalism also lost ground because of the way this country's welfare state was structured. The Social Security Act of 1935—the hallmark of American liberalism—was essentially a self-financing social insurance program that rewarded working people. Public assistance programs—which contained less political capital and were therefore a better measure of public compassion—were rigorously means tested, sparse in their benefits, and designed to be operated by the less than generous states. For example, although Social Security benefits were indexed to the cost of living (through COLAs) in the mid-1970s, AFDC benefits deteriorated so badly that the program lost about half its value from 1975 to 1992. Social Security reforms reduced the elderly poverty rate by 50 percent, but the plight of poor families worsened.

Neoliberalism. The liberal belief that the welfare state was the best mechanism to advance the public good was in retreat by the late 1970s. What remained of traditional liberalism was replaced by a **neoliberalism,** which was more cautious of government, less antagonistic toward big business, and more skeptical of the value of universal entitlements.

At a time when traditional liberals and most Democrats still viewed government as the best institution for bringing social justice to millions of disenfranchised Americans, the defeat of Jimmy Carter and the election of a Republican Senate in 1980 forced many liberal Democrats to reevaluate their party's traditional position on domestic policy. This reexamination, which Charles Peters christened "neoliberalism" in order to differentiate the new ideology from both old-style liberalism and neoconservatism, attracted only a small following in the early 1980s.[30] By the middle 1990s, however, most leading Democrats could be classified as neoliberal. Randall Rothenberg charted signs of the influence of neoliberalism on the Democratic domestic policy platform as early as 1982, when he observed that the party's midterm convention did not endorse a large-scale federal jobs program, did not endorse a plan for national health insurance, and did not submit a plan for a guaranteed annual income.[31]

In the late 1980s a cadre of prominent mainstream Democrats, among them Paul Tsongas, Richard Gephardt, Sam Nunn, and Bill Bradley, established the Democratic Leadership Council (DLC). In part, their goal was to wrest control of the Democratic Party from traditional liberals (who were presumably easily exploited by the Republican Party) and to create a new Democratic Party that was more attuned to the beliefs of the traditional core voters. In 1989 the DLC released *The New Orleans Declaration: A Democratic Agenda for the 1990s*. This declaration promised that Democratic Party politics would shift toward a middle ground combining a corporatist economic analysis with Democratic compassion. Two of the founders of the DLC were Bill Clinton and Al Gore. In fact, Bill Clinton chaired the DLC just before announcing his candidacy for presidency.[32]

Compared to traditional liberals, neoliberals were more forgiving of the behavior of large corporations and were opposed to economic protectionism. Adherents of realpolitik, neoliberals viewed the New Deal approach (with the exception of Social Security) as too expensive and antiquated to address the current mood of voters and the new global realities. To reestablish the credibility of the Democratic Party, neoliberals distanced themselves from the large-scale governmental welfare programs associated with Democrats since the New Deal. Like their neoconservative counterparts, they called for reliance on personal responsibility, work, and thrift as an alternative to governmental programs. Accordingly, their welfare proposals emphasized labor market participation (workfare), personal responsibility (time-limited welfare benefits), meeting family obligations (child support enforcement), and frugality in governmental spending ("reinventing government"). As a substitute for comprehensive welfare reform, neoliberals argued for reduced governmental spending while encouraging businesses to assume more responsibility for the welfare of the population.

Former Secretary of Labor Robert Reich, a former Harvard professor and advisor to the Democratic Leadership Council, advocated a postliberal formulation that replaced social welfare entitlements with investments in **human capital.** Public spending was divided into "good" and "bad" categories: "Bad" was consumption, such as unproductive expenditures on welfare and price supports; "good" was investments in human capital, such as expenditures on education, research, and job training.[33] In a 1983 book Reich anticipated that a significant part of the present welfare system would be replaced by government grants to businesses that agreed to hire the chronically unemployed; he also made these further predictions:

> Other social services—health care, social security, day care, disability benefits, unemployment benefits, relocation assistance—will become part of the process of structural adjustment. Public funds now spent directly on these services will instead be made available

> to businesses, according to the number of people they agree to hire. Government bureaucracies that now administer these programs to individuals will be supplanted, to a large extent, by companies that administer them to their employees. Companies, rather than state and local governments, will be the agents and intermediaries through which such assistance is provided.[34]

Neoliberalism altered the traditional liberal concept of "the public good." Instead of viewing the best interests of large corporations as antithetical to the best interests of society, neoliberals argued for free trade, less regulation of corporate activity, and a more laissez-faire approach to social problems. And neoliberals viewed longtime Democratic Party supporters such as labor unions with caution. For example, when labor unions fought to stop NAFTA (the North American Free Trade Agreement), President Clinton continued to endorse it, despite labor's threats to oppose his reelection bid in 1996. The same was true for the GATT (General Agreement on Tariffs and Trade) agreement. In both instances Clinton was firmly aligned with conservative Democrats and Republicans. Traditional liberal Democrats found themselves alone, bereft of support from the first Democratic White House in 14 years. The new shapers of the public good had systematically excluded key actors of the old liberal coalition.

The neoliberal view of the public good reflects a kind of postmodern perspective. For neoliberals, the public good is elusive, and the form it takes is fluid; definitions change as the social order evolves and new power relationships emerge. Thus, neoliberals do not define the public good as tethered to industrial era allegiances but look to a postindustrial society composed of new opportunities and new institutional shapes and forms.

Neoliberalism, then, is more a political strategy and pragmatic mode of operation than a political philosophy embodying a firm view of the public good. This is both its strength and its weakness. Specifically, the strength of neoliberalism lies in its ability to compromise and therefore to accomplish things. Its weakness is that when faced with an ideological critique (such as the Republicans' Contract with America), neoliberals are incapable of formulating a cogent ideological response. When President Reagan argued for staying the course in the early 1980s, voters knew exactly what he meant even if they disagreed with him. When Clinton argued for staying the course in 1994, the public was uncertain as to what the course was.

In first the American and later the British context, neoliberalism represents a "third way." In *The Third Way* Anthony Giddens has offered a coherent philosophical rationale for neoliberalism: "We should speak of a *positive welfare*, to which individuals and other agencies beside government contribute—and which is functional for wealth creation. The guideline for investment is *human capital* wherever possible, rather than the direct provision of economic maintenance. In place of the welfare state we should put the *social investment state*, operating in the context of a positive welfare society."[35]

The Greens/Green Party. A loosely knit national organization that is part of a worldwide movement that began in Germany, **Greens** promote ecological awareness, social justice, grassroots democracy, and nonviolence. In the United States Greens are organized into state Green parties and Green locals. By 1996 the Green Party had run Senate candidates in Alaska, New Mexico, and Maine and candidates for the House in Alaska, California, New Mexico, Massachusetts, New York, and Rhode Island. Running as the Green Party's 2000 presidential candidate, Ralph Nader made it onto the ballot in many states.[36]

As their fundamental orientation, U.S. Greens have adopted 10 values: ecological wisdom, grassroots democracy, nonviolence, social justice, decentralization, community-based economics, feminism, respect for diversity, personal and global responsibility, and future focus. In addition, Greens argue for policies that promote economic and environmental sustainability. Greens encourage their members to live green lifestyles and to organize local Green groups in urban and rural areas; work on community issues such as toxic dumping, homelessness, equal rights and recycling; field ballot initiatives and referendums and challenge restrictive election laws; work for or against legislation; and take nonviolent direct action.[37]

Communitarianism. Sometimes known as civic republicans,[38] communitarians represent a loose-knit group of intellectuals who propose a "third way." In part, **communitarianism** arose as a response to the lacuna that emerged when the political center began to erode in the late 1970s and the United States moved markedly to the right. Groups that were once considered fringe, such as the Christian fundamentalist right, now found themselves in mainstream positions of power. At the same time, there was an uneasy sense among certain intellectuals and political leaders that the moral and social fabric of the nation was unwinding along with its political center.

According to Peter Steinfels, "Communitarians essentially staked out political territory somewhere between the liberal advocates of the welfare state and civil liberties entrenched in one corner, and conservative devotees of laissez-faire and traditional values on the other."[39] Communitarians generally agree with liberals on issues of individual rights, equality, and democratic change. They argue, however, that none of these values can be preserved unless basic communities and institutions (e.g., families, schools, neighborhoods, unions, local governments, religious institutions, and ethnic groups) succeed in rebuilding individual character and promoting the virtues of citizenship.[40]

Communitarians are concerned with rebuilding communities. For them, radical individualism is responsible for the breakdown of society. In addition, they advocate for strong two-parent families (although they do acknowledge that some single-parent families succeed), which they view as the main conduit for socialization and good citizenship. In communitarian philosophy, the family is where each new generation acquires its moral anchor.[41]

Communitarians attempt to balance conservatism with liberalism. On the one hand, communitarians—like traditional conservatives—fault liberals for consistently citing economic and political forces as the causes of poverty, drug abuse, crime, and urban problems while neglecting the importance of personal responsibility. On the other hand, they blame conservatives for overemphasizing the value of the free market and for promoting the pursuit of self-interest as the answer to social problems. Conservatives, as communitarians see it, ignore the corrosive effects of the market and the subsequent economic pressure it places on family life and community spirit. Communitarians take no positions on abortion or gay rights.[42]

On the surface, communitarians appear more conservative than traditional liberals. They argue for adolescent curfews, work requirements for welfare, family values, "drug-free" zones, more emphasis on public safety, less access to legal redress for criminals, and the need for government to create more obstacles to divorce. Communitarians also reject the view that Americans are so divided over basic values that teaching moral education is impossible. They argue that moral education and character building should be part of curricula from kindergarten to college. Although communitarians advocate the protection of basic rights, they also call for "sensible limits on freedom," including driver sobriety checkpoints and mandatory drug testing for those in public jobs. Echoing anti–federal government sentiment, communitarians call for shifting power out of Washington and into the private sector and local government. But, lest communitarians sound too conservative, they also advocate European-style child allowance benefits, extended paid and unpaid parental leaves, and flexible working hours. Communitarians also call for national service and an end to private gun ownership.

Communitarians maintain that the terms *liberal* and *conservative* are antiquated. Amatai Etzioni argues that "When it comes to freedom of speech, enforcement of law, public safety, the family and schools, we find it better to talk about authoritarians who want to impose their moral solution on everybody, libertarians who oppose any voice other than that of the individual, and communitarians who want new moral standards reached through consensus."[43] Evidence of the bridging effects of communitarianism was reflected in an agenda developed in the early 1990s that was endorsed by leaders from across the political spectrum, among them Democrats Daniel P. Moynihan and Al Gore and Republicans David Durenberger and Jack Kemp.

The Self-Reliance School. A perspective that is gaining adherents in economically distressed areas of the United States as well as in Third World countries is the **self-reliance school** of political economy.[44] This school maintains that industrial economic models are irrelevant to the economic needs of poor communities and are often damaging to the spiritual life of people.[45] Adherents of self-reliance repudiate the emphasis of Western economic philosophies on economic growth and the idea that the quality of life can be measured by the material acquisitions of citizens. These political economists stress a balanced economy based on the real needs of people, production designed for internal consumption rather than for export, productive technologies that are congruent with the culture and background of the population, the use of appropriate and manageable technologies, and a small-scale and decentralized form of economic organization.[46] Simply put, proponents of self-reliance postulate that more is less and less is more. The objective of self-reliance is the creation of a no-poverty society in which economic life is organized around issues of subsistence rather than around trade and economic expansion. Accepting a world of finite resources and inherent limitations to economic growth, proponents argue that the true question of social and economic development is not what people think they want or need but what people require for survival. The self-reliance school accepts the need for social welfare programs to ameliorate the social and economic dislocations caused by industrialization, but it prefers low-technology and local solutions to social problems. This contrasts with the conventional wisdom of the welfare state, which is predicated on a prescribed set of programs on a national scale, administered by large bureaucracies using sophisticated management systems.

Classical Conservatives and the Far Right

Classic Conservativism. Former political leaders Nelson Rockefeller, Richard Nixon, and Barry Goldwater were a few representantives of traditional **conservatism.** Virtually no traditional conservatives now occupy important leadership positions in the Republican party, however; most have been replaced by cultural conservatives.

On one level, all U.S. conservatives agree about important values relating to social policy. They are anti-union, oppose aggressive governmental regulations, demand lower taxes and less governmental spending, want local control of public education, oppose extending civil rights legislation, and believe strongly in states' rights. Beneath this agreement, however, important differences exist among various conservative groups.

Older, traditional conservatives diverge with the newer cultural conservatives on a range of social issues. First, as strict constitutionalists, traditional or classical conservatives believe strongly in the separation of church and state. They see matters such as prayer and religion as personal choices in which government has no legitimate right to intervene. Second, although both classical conservatives and cultural conservatives advocate a less powerful federal government, cultural conservatives also demand that the federal government use its power to implement their domestic agenda in areas they consider amoral, including abortion and homosexuality.

Third, classical conservatives are more socially liberal than cultural conservatives. For example, the late Barry Goldwater, a conservative former U.S. senator and 1964 presidential candidate, stated that "I have been, and am still, a traditional conservative, focusing on three general freedoms—economic, social, and political. . . . The conservative movement is founded on the simple tenet that people have the right to live life as they please, as long as they don't hurt

anyone else in the process."[47] Goldwater's outspoken support of homosexuals in the military was in direct opposition to the principles of neoconservatives. Regarding reproductive freedom, classical conservatives challenge neoconservatives on various measures to limit or ban abortions.

During the Reagan–Bush presidencies, factions within the conservative movement became more pronounced. Old-style conservatives such as Nelson Rockefeller, Barry Goldwater, and William Cohen, who were more concerned with foreign policy than with domestic issues, were replaced by a new breed of radical cultural conservatives: Dick Armey, Newt Gingrich, Phil Gramm, and others. These cultural conservatives were adamant about reversing a half century of liberal influence in social policy. How the cultural conservatives have shaped social policy warrants elaboration. First, it is important to examine the forerunners of cultural conservatism, the neoconservatives.

Neoconservativism. Before the 1970s, conservative thought held that business activity and governmental programs were essentially independent of one another. Accordingly, conservatives seemed content merely to snipe at welfare programs, reserving their attention for areas more in line with traditional conservative concerns: the economy, defense, and foreign affairs. By the mid-1970s, younger conservative intellectuals recognized that this classically conservative stance vis-à-vis social welfare was no longer tenable: Welfare had become too important to be dismissed so lightly. Consequently, **neoconservatism** emerged—a movement that sought to contain the growth in governmental welfare programs while at the same time transferring as much welfare responsibility as possible from government to the private sector.[48] Neoconservatives faulted government programs for a breakdown in the mutual obligation between groups; the lack of attention to efficiencies in the way programs were operated and benefits awarded; the dependency of recipients on programs; and the growth of the welfare industry and its special interest groups, particularly professional associations.[49] To counter the liberal goals of full employment, national health care, and a guaranteed annual income, neoconservatives maintained that high unemployment was good for the economy, that health care should remain in the private marketplace, and that competitive income structures were critical to productivity. Neoconservative economists argued that income inequality was socially desirable, contending that social policies that promote equality encourage coercion, limit individual freedom, and damage the economy.[50]

The neoconservative attack on the welfare state was particularly pointed because of the fact that many neoconservatives, among them Irving Kristol and Norman Podhoretz, were former liberals who had developed such misgivings about the welfare state that they joined the conservative movement. These neoconservatives served an important role in critiquing the welfare state, in large measure because they were so familiar with its philosophical origins. Despite their opposition to the welfare state, hoewever, they found their new home in conservatism anything but tidy. Born out of an urban environment, neoconservatives fashioned themselves as cosmopolitan intellectuals and free thinkers. Social issues such as abortion, school prayer, and the like were not a hot button for the neoconservative movement. As a whole, the intellectual fabric of the neoconservative movement was more urban and sophisticated than that of the cultural conservatives.

By the late 1970s, however, the position that the neoconservatives occupied in the conservative movement began to be usurped by the emerging cultural conservatives. The neoconservatives had provided the intellectual wedge that fractured the liberal consensus around the welfare state, but it was cultural conservatives such as Trent Lott and Tom DeLay who attained the leadership positions necessary to take down what was left of the institutional structure of liberal public philosophy. Properly understood, neoconservatism is at odds with the culturally conservative social agenda promoted by the Republican Congress since 1994.

Cultural Conservativism. The neoconservative assault on liberal social policy was soon taken over by cultural conservatives, who raged against governmental intrusion in the marketplace while simultaneously attempting to use the authority of government to advance their social objectives in the areas of antiwelfare planks, sexual abstinence, school prayer, abortion, and anti–gay rights proposals. Cultural conservatives cleverly promoted a dual attitude toward the role of government. Mimicking their classical conservative predecessors in demanding a laissez-faire approach to economics, they steadfastly refused to translate that orientation to social affairs. Instead, cultural conservatives argued for social conformity and a level of governmental intrusion into private affairs that made most classical conservatives gag. In contrast to the classical conservative skepticism about blending religion and politics, cultural conservatives opportunistically embraced the rising tide of fundamentalist religion. As a measure of their success, this cobbled-together coalition of economic conservatives, right-wing Christian ideologues, and opportunistic politicians had by the early 1990s virtually decimated what remained of Republican liberalism (those Republicans who were conservative on economic and defense concerns but relatively liberal on domestic issues). Liberal Republicans had gone the way of liberal Democrats—both had become endangered species.

The conservative view of "the public good" differs dramatically from the liberal view. For liberals, the state represents the best vehicle for achieving the public good and is an ally in promoting social change. In contrast, cultural conservatives view the state as the cause of rather than the solution to social problems. They argue that the very existence of the state is antithetical to the public good, because government interferes with the maximization of individual self-interest. Hence, the conservative posture toward the state is adversarial, except when conservatives endeavor to use the state to further their social agenda. In theory, cultural conservatives see the primary role of government as protecting people, property, and those who own property (policing and defense). On the surface, these conservatives argue for a minimalist state that does not interfere with individual self-interest or the market economy. But cultural conservatives have been willing to compromise these libertarian tenets by adopting the agenda of traditionalists in myriad social issues such as school prayer, abortion, sexual orientation, and drug testing.

In terms of social welfare, the conservative agenda in the 1980s was fourfold: (1) End the liberal hegemony in social policy, (2) reroute public policy through the private sector, (3) stop costly social programs that allegedly lessen the profits and global competitiveness of corporations, and (4) preclude the possibility of a resurgence in social programs. In tandem with this agenda, the Reagan administration crippled social programs, using multiple strategies such as tax policy and federal budget deficits, thus effectively prohibiting the future growth of the welfare state.

Despite important victories, cultural conservatives were unable to construct a programmatic alternative to the welfare state. By the end of the 1980s, after a decade of hammering away at social programs, they had accomplished relatively little in terms of replacing liberal social policies. The U.S. welfare state remained intact, if a little battle-worn. As an example, costs for social insurance and entitlement programs such as Social Security, Medicare, and Medicaid continued to soar. In the end, cultural conservatives had underestimated three important variables: (1) the resiliency of the welfare state, (2) the continued support (however ambivalent) the welfare state enjoyed among the middle class, and (3) the difficulty of translating rhetoric into viable reform proposals. Overall, the most enduring legacy of the Reagan and Bush administrations was the $4.5 trillion federal debt left in the wake of rash tax policies coupled with increased military spending.

Nevertheless, in 1994 frustrated and fearful voters seemed ready to offer the right a second chance by giving them control of the Senate and the House. Cultural conservatives learned from past mistakes. Instead of toying with incremental policies, they proposed bold new social initiatives. These reform measures emerged in their most sophisticated form in the Contract with America, a document signed by more than 300 House Republicans in 1994. The contract was designed to define the legislative debate and alter most of the safety net programs within a two-year period.[51] The most important victory of the conservative movement occurred with the passage of the Personal Responsibility and Work Opportunity Reconciliation Act (PRWORA) in 1996.

Traditionalism. Proponents of **traditionalism** have a Christian religious orientation to social policy and emphasize a moral relationship between politics and religion. Although similar to cultural conservatives, they are even more extreme in their beliefs. Traditionalists are characterized by evangelical groups such as the Moral Majority. According to traditionalists, God's laws must be translated into politics, and "higher laws" must become the laws of the state. Because traditionalists presume the United States to be a Christian nation, they see the separation between church and state as unnatural. Apart from its belief in a strong military defense, this movement emphasizes the Christian value of hard work and proposes little welfare, except for the most needy.

Traditionalists are highly critical of governmental social programs, which they associate with a liberal social philosophy (secular humanism) that is eroding traditional social institutions, particularly the family and the church. Lightning-rod issues for traditionalists are abortion, prohibition of prayer in school, affirmative action, and school integration—all of which traditionalists associate with the increasing liberalism of society.

Libertarianism. **Libertarians** reflect another perspective. This increasingly influential group believes in virtually no government regulation. According to the libertarian plank:

> We, the members of the Libertarian Party, challenge the cult of the omnipotent state and defend the rights of the individual. We hold that all individuals . . . have the right to live in whatever manner they choose, so long as they do not forcibly interfere with the equal right of others to live in whatever manner they choose. We . . . hold that governments . . . must not violate the rights of any individual: namely,

(1) the right to life—accordingly we support the prohibition of the initiation of physical force against others; (2) the right to liberty of speech and action—accordingly we oppose all attempts . . . [at] . . . government censorship in any form; and (3) . . . we oppose all government interference with private property. . . .[52]

Libertarians argue that smaller government is better, because government invariably grows at the expense of individual freedom. They also believe that the only proper role for government is to provide a police force and a military (and that the military should possess only defensive weapons). Libertarians are highly critical of taxation, recognizing that government is dependent on tax revenues. Aside from advocating minimal taxation earmarked for defense and police activities, libertarians oppose the income tax. Because of their emphasis on individual freedom (and therefore individual responsibility), libertarians advocate the decriminalization of narcotics. They also believe that government should only intercede in social affairs when the behavior of one individual threatens the safety of another. The Libertarian Party critique of social welfare is based on the belief that the state should not be involved in social and economic activities, except in very limited and extreme circumstances.

The Welfare Philosophers and the Neoconservative Think Tanks

Many welfare professionals of the twentieth century built their careers around a vision of a U.S. welfare state that was European in origin.[53] Most welfare philosophers treated governmental programs (the basis of the welfare state) as synonymous with social welfare. This vision was shared by virtually every social welfare scholar writing in the late 1960s and early 1970s.[54] In turn, most

social workers adhered to a liberal welfare philosophy based on a system of national social programs that would be deployed as more citizens demanded greater services and benefits. The vision behind the expansion of the government-driven welfare state was the European model, especially the Scandinavian variant that spread health care, housing, income benefits, and employment opportunities equitably across the population.[55] This vision led Richard Titmuss to hope that the welfare state, as an instrument of government, would eventually lead to a "welfare world."[56]

For welfare philosophers in the United States, government programs designed to ameliorate the caprices of capitalism were both desirable and inevitable. In their classic *Industrial Society and Social Welfare,* Harold Wilensky and Charles Lebeaux suggested that "under continuing industrialization all institutions will be oriented toward and evaluated in terms of social welfare aims. The 'welfare state' will become the 'welfare society,' and both will be more reality than epithet."[57] Accordingly, from the New Deal through the Johnson administration's Great Society initiatives, the belief that government should be the primary institution for promoting social welfare was a persistent theme among American welfare philosophers.[58]

For decades this explanation of the role of social welfare in U.S. society was accepted by welfare professionals who took jobs with governmental agencies or in voluntary sector organizations that were heavily dependent on governmental contracts. In fact, the combination of government bureaucracy and agency casework became so prevalent that Wilensky and Lebeaux concluded that "virtually all welfare service is dispensed through social agencies . . . and virtually all social workers operate through such agencies."[59] For most social welfare professionals, the welfare state was not a philosophical abstraction but the basis of their livelihood.

Despite this widespread acceptance of the vision of liberal welfare philosophers, an alternative vision arose—a vision that questioned the fundamental nature of welfare and social services. Throughout the 1970s and 1980s, conservatives of all ilk relished in making proposals on welfare reform—especially the right-wing **think tanks,** or conservative policy institutes. In fact, no policy institute on the right could prove its mettle until it produced a plan to clean up "the welfare mess." The Hoover Institution of Stanford, California, helped shape the early neoconservative position on welfare. "There is no inherent reason that Americans should look to government for those goods and services that can be individually acquired," argued Hoover's Alvin Rabushka, who listed four strategies for reforming welfare: (1) letting users pay, (2) contracting for services, (3) funding mandated services through the states, and (4) emphasizing private substitution.[60] Martin Anderson, a Hoover senior fellow and subsequent domestic policy adviser to the Reagan administration, elaborated the neoconservative position on welfare in terms of the need to (1) reaffirm the need-only philosophical approach to welfare and state it as explicit national policy; (2) increase efforts to eliminate fraud; (3) establish and enforce a fair, clear work requirement; (4) remove inappropriate beneficiaries from the welfare rolls; (5) enforce support of dependents by those who have the responsibility and are shirking it; (6) improve the efficiency and effectiveness of welfare administration; and (7) shift more responsibility from the federal government to state and local governments and private institutions.[61]

Another conservative think tank, the American Enterprise Institute (AEI), commissioned sociologist Peter Berger and theologian Richard John Neuhaus to prepare a theoretical analysis of U.S. society. Berger and Neuhaus's *To Empower People: The Role of Mediating Structures in Public Policy* identified the fundamental problem confronting the culture as the growth of megastructures (big government, big business, big labor, and professional bureaucracies) and the corresponding diminution in the value of the individual. The route to empowerment was to revitalize "mediating structures," among them the neighborhood, family, church, and voluntary associations.[62] In a subsequent analysis an AEI scholar recategorized the corporation from a megastructure to a mediating structure, thus leaving the basic institutions of liberal social reform—government, the professions, and labor—as the sources of mass alienation.[63]

Not to be outdone by AEI, the Heritage Foundation featured *Out of the Poverty Trap: A Conservative Strategy for Welfare Reform* by Stuart Butler and Anna Kondratas.[64] Following along the same lines, the Free Congress Research and Education Foundation proposed reforming welfare through "cultural conservatism"; that is, by reinforcing "traditional values: delayed gratification, work and saving, commitment to family and to the next generation, education and training, self-improvement, and rejection of crime, drugs, and casual sex."[65]

A handful of other works also served as beachheads for the conservative assault on the liberal welfare state. George Gilder's *Wealth and Poverty* argued that beneficent welfare programs represented a "moral hazard," insulating people against risks essential to capitalism and thus contributing to dependency.[66] Martin Anderson contended that the poverty-line figure should include the cash equivalent of in-kind benefits—food stamps, Medicaid, and housing vouchers—and that this would effectively lower the poverty rate by 40 percent.[67]

As a collection, these works, ideas, and theories provided conservatives with a potent critique of liberal governmental welfare programs. Unlike classical conservatives of an earlier generation, neoconservatives not only did their homework on social welfare policy but also prepared serious proposals for welfare reform.

 # Conclusion

John Judis and Michael Lind argue that "Ultimately American economic policy must meet a single test: Does it, in the long run, tend to raise or depress the incomes of most Americans? A policy that tends to impoverish the ordinary American is a failure, no matter what its alleged benefits are for U.S. corporations or for humanity as a whole."[68] To this we would add: "What are the effects of an economic policy on the social health of the nation?" Researchers at Fordham University's Institute for Innovation in Social Policy contend that the nation's quality of life has become unhinged from its economic growth. "We really have to begin to reassess this notion that the gross domestic product—the overall growth of the society—necessarily is going to produce improvements in the quality of life."[69] Constructing an Index for Social Health that encompassed governmental data from 1970 to 1993, researchers found that in six categories—children in poverty, child abuse, health insurance coverage, average weekly earnings adjusted for inflation, out-of-pocket health costs for senior citizens, and the gap between rich and poor—"social health" hit its lowest point in 1993.

Consistent with the wide range of ideas reflected in the various approaches to political economy, social welfare in the United States is characterized by a high degree of diversity. U.S. social welfare is not a monolithic, highly centralized, well-coordinated system of programs. Rather, a great variety of organizations provide a wide range of benefits and services to different client populations. The vast array of social welfare organizations contributes to what is commonly called "the welfare mess." As the phrase suggests, different programs serving different groups through different procedures have engendered an impenetrable tangle of institutional red tape that often functions poorly for administrators, human service professionals, and their clients.

The complexity of U.S. social welfare policy can be attributed to several cultural influences, some of which are peculiar to the American experience. The U.S. Constitution outlines a federal system under which the states vest certain functions in the national government. Although the states have assumed primary responsibility for social welfare through much of the history of the United States, this changed with the New Deal of Franklin Delano Roosevelt, which ushered in a raft of federal programs. Over subsequent decades, federal social welfare initiatives took on a dominant role in the nation's social welfare effort. Still, states continued to manage important social welfare programs, such as mental health, corrections, and social services. Over time, the relationship between the federal government and the states has changed. From the New Deal of the 1930s through the Great Society of the 1960s, federal welfare programs expanded, forming the American version of the "welfare state." During the 1980s, however, the Reagan administration sought to return more of the responsibility for welfare to the states, a process called devolution.[70] This process was further promoted by the Clinton administration with the signing of the PRWORA.

A second confounding element can be attributed to the relatively open character of U.S. society. Often referred to as a melting pot, the national culture is a protean brew of groups that have immigrated to the United States and then competed with one another to become an established part of national life.[71] An enormous influx of Europeans in the late nineteenth century gave way to waves of Hispanics and Asians entering the United States a century later.[72] Historically, social welfare programs have played an important role in the acculturation of these groups. At the same time, many ethnic groups bring with them their own fraternal and community associations, which not only provide welfare benefits to members of the community but also serve to maintain its norms. Other groups that have exerted important influences on U.S. social welfare are African Americans, the aged, women, and Native Americans. The very pluralism of U.S. society—a diverse collection of peoples, each with somewhat different needs—contributes to the complexity in social welfare.

The economic system exacerbates the complexity of social welfare in this country. With important exceptions, the economy of the United States is predominantly capitalist, with most goods and services being owned, produced, and distributed through the marketplace. In a capitalist economy people are expected to meet their basic needs through the marketplace and by participation in the labor market. When groups are unable to participate fully in the labor market because, like the aged or the handicapped, they are unable to work or because, like women and African Americans historically, they do not earn enough as a result of discrimination, "social" programs are deployed to support these groups. These programs take various forms. Many are governmental programs mandated by legislation. Private sector programs often complement those of the public sector. Within the private sector, two organizational forms are common—nonprofit organizations and for-profit corporations. Often these private sector organizations coexist, proximate to one another.[73] For instance, in many communities, family planning services are provided by the public health department, a governmental agency; by Planned Parenthood, a private nonprofit agency; and by a private for-profit health maintenance organization.

Finally, various religious or faith-based organizations are strongly influencing social welfare in the United States. This is seen most clearly in the range of faith-based agencies that offer services in most large cities: Jewish Family Services, Lutheran Social Services, Catholic Charities, and the Salvation Army, among others. Given the American tradition of the separation of church and state, these religious-based agencies are vehicles to provide services to groups that would not otherwise receive them. However, this is not to say that no relationship exists between the government and faith-based agencies. During the 1970s the federal government experimented with contracting out some services to the private sector, and faith-based agencies frequently competed for these contracts. Today many faith-based agencies receive federal funds for specific services they provide to the public. It is likely that this trend will grow with the Bush administration.

The pluralism of this nation's culture is of increasing interest to social welfare policy analysts as the influence of the federal government in social policy diminishes. In light of reductions in many federal social programs and calls for the private sector to assume more responsibility for welfare, the prospect of molding the diverse entities involved in American social welfare into one unified whole under the auspices of a central authority—the federal government—seems remote. This vision of a unified whole is implicit in the proposals of advocates for nationalized programs that ensure basic goods and services such as food, housing, education, health, and income as a right of citizenship. But although programs of this nature have been integral to the welfare states of northern Europe for decades, there is a serious question as to how plausible they are for the United States, which already has so much complexity built into its social welfare system.[74]

Questions about the proper role of the federal government in social welfare reached a fever pitch by the late 1980s. Proponents of a strong federal role conceded that the U.S. welfare state was, by European standards, incomplete. For these analysts the "reluctant welfare state"[75] or the "semi-welfare state"[76] required further elaboration through social programs in primary areas of need—income, health, and employment. The principle that social welfare should be a "national effort on behalf of those in need," noted Robert Reich, has been central to American social welfare for a half-century. According to Reich, "The theme permeated Roosevelt's New Deal, Truman's Fair Deal, Johnson's Great Society: America is a single, national community, bound by a common ideal of equal opportunity and generosity toward the less fortunate. E Pluribus Unum."[77] To proponents of more state intervention in social welfare, the growth of nongovernmental initiatives represented the abandonment of the most effective method for assuring the protection of vulnerable populations. "Conservatives," some observed, "continually assert that many social services in the public sector can be transferred to the voluntary sector."[78]

Advocates of more nongovernmental activity in social welfare trace their argument to the Colonial era in America. Daniel Boorstin, former librarian of Congress, has written passionately about the unique role played by voluntary organizations in the United States. Boorstin maintains that voluntary organizations "have many unique characteristics and a spirit all their own." Voluntary organizations are no less than "monuments to what in the Old World was familiar neither as private charity nor as governmental munificence. They are monuments to community. They originate in the community, depend on the community, are developed by the community, serve the community, and rise or fall with the community."[79]

But can the problems of the postindustrial nation be addressed adequately without massive federal social programs? Daniel Patrick Moynihan, a former U.S. senator and an authority on welfare, claims that there is no choice but to begin to think about new ways to solve social problems. According to Moynihan, "The issues of social policy the United States faces today have no European counterpart nor any European model of a viable solution. They are American problems, and we Americans are going to have to think them through by ourselves."[80] To the extent that Moynihan is correct, future welfare initiatives are increasingly likely to reflect the diversity of American social welfare.

The complexity of social welfare in the United States helps account for changes in welfare policies and programs. Since 1980, for example, a convergence of social, political, and economic forces has led to a reappraisal of welfare. Both liberal and conservative scholars have questioned the dominance of government programs in welfare provision. At the same time, a firestorm of fundamentalism has swept across the nation, attracting the allegiance of groups associated with evangelicalism. The traditionalist movement flexed its muscles through the elections of

Ronald Reagan and George H. W. Bush, the installation of a Republican Senate in the early 1980s and a conservative House of Representatives in 1994, and an effective grassroots mobilization that challenged government policies on issues ranging from the family to affirmative action. By the mid-1990s, social conservatism had begun to influence leaders of the Democratic Party, a traditional supporter of government welfare programs. In order to reestablish credibility in an increasingly conservative political milieu, liberals distanced themselves from the large-scale government welfare programs with which they had been associated with since the New Deal. In place of these programs, many liberals called for a reliance on personal responsibility, work, and thrift. The Clinton administration partly realized these values by emphasizing "civic liberalism" in social policy, by engineering class-mixing situations such as AmeriCorps, and by extending child support enforcement to ensure a minimum benefit for all children.

Conservative public sentiment toward social welfare serves as a backdrop for the debate on the future of welfare policy.[81] Unfortunately, the consequences of the conservative movement in social policy have been felt most acutely by marginal groups. Government programs that benefited African Americans, women, and the poor have been severely cut, leaving these groups more vulnerable. As we enter the new millennium, welfare professionals face a formidable challenge: How can basic goods and services be brought to vulnerable populations within a context of such complexity and uncertainty?

 # Discussion Questions

1. According to the authors, American social welfare is undergoing a transition. Which ideologies, schools of political economy, and interest groups within social welfare stand to gain most from this transition?

2. Ideology tends to parallel schools of political economy. From a sample of current social welfare issues—for example, health care, long-term care of the aged, and substance abuse—how would classical conservatives and liberals ad-

dress these problems? How would neo-conservatives and neoliberals diverge from traditional conservatives and liberals in their proposals?

3. Among the schools of political, social, and economic thought discussed in this chapter, which one would come closest to being moderate? Why?

 # Notes

1. Richard Titmuss, *Essays on the Welfare State* (Boston: Beacon Press, 1963), p. 16.
2. Contained in personal correspondence between David Stoesz and William Epstein, April 2000.
3. Education would logically be included here, except that in the American experience it has been treated separately.
4. See Alfred Kahn, *Social Policy and Social Services* (New York: Random House, 1979).
5. Frances Fox Piven and Richard Cloward, *Regulating the Poor* (New York: Vintage, 1971).
6. David Gil, *Unraveling Social Policy* (Boston: Shenkman, 1981), p. 32.
7. Charles Prigmore and Charles Atherton, *Social Welfare Policy* (Lexington, MA: D.C. Heath, 1979), pp. 25–31.
8. Silvia Ann Hewlett, *When the Bough Breaks* (New York: Basic Books, 1991), p. 12.
9. Claus Offe, *Contradictions of the Welfare State* (Cambridge, MA: MIT Press, 1984).
10. John Maynard Keynes, *The General Theory of Employment, Interest and Money* (London: Macmillan, 1936).
11. Paul R. Krugman, *Peddling Prosperity: Economic Sense and Nonsense in the Age of Diminished Expectations* (New York: W. W. Norton, 1994).
12. Ibid.
13. Ibid.
14. Milton Friedman, *Money Mischief: Episodes in Monetary History* (New York: Harcourt Brace, 1992).
15. Milton Friedman, *Capitalism and Freedom* (Chicago: University of Chicago Press, 1962).
16. Ibid.
17. Robert E. Lucas, *Studies in Business Cycle Theory* (Cambridge, MA: MIT Press, 1981).
18. Krugman, *Peddling Prosperity*.
19. Ibid.
20. Ibid.
21. Congressional Budget Office, *The Economic and Budget Outlook: Fiscal Years 1993–1997* (Washington, DC: Congressional Budget Office, 1992), p. 28.
22. Charles Murray, *Losing Ground* (New York: Basic Books, 1984), pp. 227–228.
23. *Privatization: Toward More Effective Government* (Washington, DC: U.S. Government Printing Office, 1988), pp. 233–234.
24. Jeffry Galper, "Introduction of Radical Theory and Practice in Social Work Education: Social Policy." Mimeographed paper, Michigan State University School of Social Work, ca. 1978.
25. Piven and Cloward, *Regulating the Poor*, pp. 3–4.
26. Harry Hopkins, *Spending to Save: The Complete Story of Relief* (Seattle: University of Washington Press, 1936).
27. Neil Gilbert, Harry Specht, and Paul Terrell, *Dimensions of Social Welfare Policy* (Englewood Cliffs, NJ: Prentice-Hall, 1993).
28. Marc Bendick, *Privatizing the Delivery of Social Welfare Service* (Washington, DC: National Conference on Social Welfare, 1985), p. 1.
29. Bruce Jansson, *The Reluctant Welfare State* (Belmont, CA: Wadsworth, 1988).
30. Charles Peters, "A New Politics," *Public Welfare* 41, no. 2 (Spring 1983): pp. 34, 36.
31. Randall Rothenberg, *The Neoliberals* (New York: Simon & Schuster, 1984), pp. 244–245.
32. David Stoesz, *Small Change* (New York: Longman, 1995).
33. Robert Reich, *The Next American Frontier* (New York: Times Books, 1983).
34. Ibid., p. 248.

35. Anthony Giddens, *The Third Way* (Cambridge: Polity Press, 1999), p. 117.

36. Politics Now. Retrieved 2000 from the World Wide Web: http://www.politicsnow.com/campaign/wh_house/green/index.htm

37. Nationwide Green Organizations in the USA. Retrieved 2000 from the World Wide Web: http://www.greens.org/usa/

38. Michael J. Sandel, *Democracy's Discontent* (Cambridge, MA: Belknap Press/Harvard University Press, 1996).

39. Peter Steinfels, "A Political Movement Blends Its Ideas from Left and Right," *The New York Times* (May 24, 1992), p. B16.

40. Amitai Etzioni, *The Spirit of Community: Rights, Responsibilities, and the Communitarian Agenda* (New York: Crown, 1993).

41. Amitai Etzioni (ed.), *New Communitarian Thinking: Persons, Virtues, Institutions, Communities* (Charlottesville and London: University Press of Virginia, 1995).

42. Katha Pollitt, "Subject to Debate," *The Nation* (July 25/August 1, 1994), p. 118.

43. Richard Benedetto, "A New Approach to Nation's Problems. Interview with Amitai Etzioni," *USA Today* (April 23, 1992), p. 13A.

44. Bruce Stokes, *Helping Ourselves: Local Solutions to Global Problems* (New York: W. W. Norton, 1981).

45. Sugata Dasgupta, "Towards a No-Poverty Society," *Social Development Issues* 12 (Winter 1983), pp. 85–93.

46. Some of these economic principles were addressed by E. F. Schumacher in *Small Is Beautiful* (New York: Harper & Row, 1973).

47. Barry M. Goldwater, *The Conscience of a Conservative* (New York: Putnam, 1960), pp. 109–110.

48. See Peter Steinfels, *The Neoconservatives* (New York: Simon & Schuster, 1979).

49. Interview with Stuart Butler, Director of Domestic Policy at the Heritage Foundation, October 4, 1984.

50. Alan Walker, "The Strategy of Inequality: Poverty and Income Distribution in Britain 1979–89," in I. Taylor (ed.), *The Social Effects of Free Market Policies* (Sussex, England: Harvester-Wheatsheaf, 1990), pp. 43–66.

51. Kristen Geiss-Curran, Sha'ari Garfinkle, Fred Knocke, Terri Lively, and Sue McCullough, "The Contract with America and the Budget Battle," unpublished manuscript, University of Houston, Spring 1996.

52. The Libertarian Party, "Statement of Principles," The Libertarian Party, 2600 Virginia Ave, NW, Washington, DC, 1996.

53. Daniel Patrick Moynihan, *Came the Revolution* (New York: Harcourt Brace Jovanovich, 1988), p. 291.

54. See Harold Wilensky and Charles Lebeaux, *Industrial Society and Social Welfare* (New York: Free Press, 1965); and Mimi Abramovitz, "The Privatization of the Welfare State," *Social Work* 31 (July–August 1986), pp. 257–264.

55. R. Erikson, E. Hansen, S. Ringen, and H. Uusitalo, *The Scandinavian Model* (Armonk, NY: M. E. Sharpe, 1987).

56. Richard Titmuss, *Commitment to Welfare* (New York: Pantheon, 1968), p. 127.

57. Wilensky and Lebeaux, *Industrial Society and Social Welfare*, p. 147.

58. Abramovitz, "The Privatization of the Welfare State."

59. Wilensky and Lebeaux, *Industrial Society and Social Welfare*, p. 231.

60. Alvin Rabushka, "Tax and Spending Limits," in Peter Duignan and Alvin Rabushka (eds.), *The United States in the 1980s* (Stanford, CA: Hoover Institution, 1980), pp. 104–106.

61. Martin Anderson, "Welfare Reform," in Peter Duignan and Alvin Rabushka (eds.), *The United States in the 1980s*, pp. 171–176.

62. Peter Berger and John Neuhaus, *To Empower People: The Role of Mediating Structures in Public Policy* (Washington, DC: American Enterprise Institute, 1977).

63. Michael Novak, *Toward a Theology of the Corporation* (Washington, DC: American Enterprise Institute, 1981), p. 5.

64. Stuart Butler and Anna Kondratas, *Out of the Poverty Trap: A Conservative Strategy for Welfare Reform* (New York: Free Press, 1987).

65. William Lind and William Marshner, *Cultural Conservatism: Toward a New National Agenda* (Washington, DC: Free Congress Research and Education Foundation, 1987), p. 83.

66. George Gilder, *Wealth and Poverty* (New York: Basic Books, 1981), p. 118.

67. Anderson, "Welfare Reform," p. 145.

68. John Judis and Michael Lind, "For a New Nationalism," *The New Republic* (March 27, 1995), p. 26.

69. Mitchell Landsberg, "Nation's Social Health Declined in '93," *Houston Chronicle* (October 16, 1995), p. 1C.

70. Domestic Policy Council, *Up from Dependency* (Washington, DC: White House Domestic Policy Council, December 1986).

71. For a classic description of the assimilation phenomenon, see Nathan Glazer and Daniel Patrick Moynihan, *Beyond the Melting Pot* (Cambridge, MA: MIT Press, 1970).

72. Thomas Muller et al., *The Fourth Wave* (Washington, DC: Urban Institute, 1985).

73. The three auspices of social welfare in the United States have been termed the mixed economy of welfare. See Sheila Kamerman, "The New Mixed Economy of Welfare," *Social Work* 28 (January–February 1983), pp. 43–50.

74. Marc Bendick, *Privatizing the Delivery of Social Welfare Service* (Washington, DC: National Conference on Social Welfare, 1985).

75. Jansson, *The Reluctant Welfare State.*

76. Michael Katz, *In the Shadow of the Poorhouse.* (New York: Basic Books, 1986).

77. Robert Reich, *Tales of a New America* (New York: Vintage, 1987), p. 11.

78. Robert Schilling, Steven Schinke, and Richard Weatherly, "Service Trends in a Conservative Era: Social Workers Rediscover the Past," *Social Work* 33 (January–February 1988), p. 7.

79. Daniel Boorstin, *Hidden History* (New York: Harper and Row, 1987), p. 194.

80. Daniel Patrick Moynihan, *Came the Revolution* (New York: Harcourt Brace Jovanovich, 1988), p. 291. Emphasis original.

81. For further details, see David Stoesz, "The Functional Conception of Social Welfare," *Social Work* 34 (March 1989), pp. 86–91.

chapter 2

Social Welfare Policy Research: A Framework for Policy Analysis

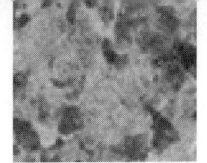

This chapter examines one of the major tools used by the policy researcher, a structured framework for policy analysis, as well as the common components of such policy frameworks. We also propose our own model for policy analysis.

Policy analysts engage in the systematic investigation of a social policy or a set of policies. Thus, policy analysts can be employed in a variety of settings, including federal, state, and local governments; think tanks (on both the left and the right); universities; social justice groups, public interest groups, or community organizations; and larger social agencies. The goals of policy analysis can range from pure research to providing information to legislators (as is done by congressional researchers) to advocacy research.

The previous chapter examined how ideology, economic theories, and political ideas influence the social welfare state. It also indicated that concepts such as social justice and equity play a central role in the formation of social welfare policy. A **policy framework**—in other words, a systematic means for examining a specific social welfare policy or a series of policies—is one means analysts use to evaluate the congruence of a policy with the mission and goals of the social welfare state. We can also employ policy frameworks to assess whether key social welfare values (e.g., social justice, redistribution, equity) are incorporated within a given policy. Moreover, policy frameworks help us determine whether a policy fits within the theoretical guidelines of social welfare activities and whether a policy is consistent with established social welfare foundations; that is, with the historical precedents that guide social welfare initiatives. For example, let us consider the proposal that foster care should be abolished and that all children suspected of being abused or neglected should be placed in orphanages. The use of a policy framework would show that this proposal represents a clear break with the general drift of child welfare policy at the beginning of the twenty-first century and, moreover, that it repudiates general social

welfare values that stress self-determination, justice, equity, and compassion. In addition, a systematic analysis would reveal that this policy is not feasible—economically, politically, or socially.

Apart from examining a given policy, an analytic framework is also useful for comparing existing policies. For example, comparing the mental health policies of Missouri with those of Massachusetts and Minnesota would yield valuable information for all three states. A comparative analysis of the health systems of the United States, Canada, and Sweden would also provide useful information for decision makers. Lastly, analytic frameworks can be used to evaluate competing policies. Given alternative policies, an analytic framework can help the analyst make a recommendation as to which policy would most effectively solve a problem or remedy a need.

Policy analysis frameworks can be useful for social work practitioners on several different levels. For one, policy analysis can be done on the agency as well as on statewide or national levels. Social work practitioners can look at agency policies around issues such as flextime, merit pay, agency-based day care services, job shifting, and so forth. Child welfare workers can use policy analysis to evaluate impending state or federal legislation and the concomitant fiscal allocations. Social workers in health care can analyze managed care policies in terms of equity, effectiveness, and a wide range of other issues. Agency or other policies dictate what a social worker will do, with whom, and for how long. Policies define who is (or is not) a client and what services will be provided for clients. Social work practice is clearly influenced—if not driven—by social policy.

Policy analysis is also useful in the environmental scanning activities of nonprofit and for-profit agencies. Specifically, as the delivery of social services becomes more grounded in the rules of the marketplace, social agencies are forced to replicate successful private sector corporate behavior. This includes being on top of changing demographic trends (doing market analyses) and monitoring new legislation. In some social welfare sectors, events change so rapidly that agencies must quickly modify their operations if they are to remain viable. Data-based environmental scanning allows agencies to make long- and short-range plans based on changing demographics, new forms of competition, and the effects of present and impending legislation. Environmental scanning also allows agencies to discover new markets and to protect their existing ones.[1]

Social welfare policies and programs are complex phenomena. For example, it is easy to propose a social policy such as mandatory drug testing for all governmental employees. On the surface, the policy may appear simple: Drug users are to be discovered by the tests and then forced to seek treatment. On closer scrutiny, however, the hidden issues appear more problematic. Is it constitutional to require drug treatment if a positive result is found? Is occasional use of marijuana sufficient grounds for requiring drug treatment? Because alcohol is a legal substance, drug tests do not detect drinking. Is alcohol less debilitating than marijuana? Can the policy of mandatory drug testing be misused by supervisors to harass employees? Will the policy produce the intended results? Although these questions must be addressed, without a systematic way to analyze the effects of an intended policy, decisions become arbitrary and may produce side effects worse than the original problem.

All well-designed policy frameworks are characterized by eight key elements:

- Policy frameworks attempt to analyze a social policy or program *systematically.*
- Policy frameworks reflect an understanding that social policy is not created in a vacuum but is context sensitive, and policy options usually contain a set of competing priorities.
- Policy frameworks employ rational methods of inquiry and analysis. The evidence used for the analysis of a policy must be derived from scientific inquiry, and all data must be collected from reliable and legitimate sources. Data should be interpreted and analyzed as objectively as possible.

- Although open to interpretation, the analytic method is explicit, and all succeeding analysts should be able to approximate the same conclusion.
- The objectives of policy analysis reflect a commitment to deriving the largest possible social benefit at the least possible social cost. A good social policy is one that benefits at least one person (as that person perceives his or her own self-interest) while at the same time hurting no one. In the real world of finite resources—and of proliferating claims upon them—that goal is rarely achieved. Nevertheless, analysts should strive to realize that aim.
- Policy frameworks should take into account the unintended consequences of a particular policy or program.
- Policy frameworks examine a particular policy in the context of alternatives; that is, they consider alternative social policies or alternative uses of the resources allocated to a given policy.
- Policy frameworks examine the potential impact of a policy (or a series of policies) on other social policies, other social problems, and the public.

In the end, the analysis of a social policy—often through utilization of a policy framework—provides decision makers and the general public with information, an understanding of the possible ramifications of the policy on the target problem as well as on other problems and policies, and a series of alternative policies that could be more effective in dealing with the problem. Untoward costs and injuries are more likely to result when a systematic framework for policy analysis is not used.

History is replete with examples of well-intentioned policies that proved to be catastrophic. For example, in 1919 the U.S. Congress enacted a law prohibiting the manufacture, sale, or transport of alcohol in an effort to cut down on crime, familial instability, unemployment, and other social problems. Proponents of Prohibition, including many social workers, touted the end of alcohol as a major step forward in the social evolution of the United States. However, when Prohibition was repealed 13 years later in 1932, most of the original supporters did not argue vigorously for its continuance. Despite the hopes of its backers, Prohibition did not decrease crime or familial instability or encourage social order; instead, Prohibition encouraged the growth of an organized crime industry that fed the ongoing taste of Americans for alcohol. Instead of eliminating alcohol-related nightlife, Prohibition fostered the growth of illegal but well-attended speakeasies. Even many supporters conceded that alcohol was almost as abundant as before Prohibition. Had a systematic analysis of the prohibition policy been undertaken, good policy analysts might have demonstrated the futility of the measure.

A similar argument can be made for the current policy of drug interdiction and enforcement. After almost a century of vigorous drug enforcement, heroin, cocaine, and other drugs continue to be readily available. The latest round of drug enforcement has resulted not in less drug use but in a doubling of the prison population from 1980 to 1996 (more one million people are now incarcerated). The "war on drugs" has also resulted in the added public expense of new prison construction, the creation of international drug cartels whose wealth and power rival that of many national governments and multinational corporations, a dramatic increase in the homicide rate associated with drugs, and the deterioration of inner city neighborhoods racked by a gang warfare rooted in the lucrative drug culture. Moreover, although drug enforcement policies have not led to the diminished use of drugs, they have fostered the creation of a drug industry that includes governmental officials, contractors, private correctional corporations, police departments, and large parts of the legal and judicial system. These groups have a vested interest in maintaining a status quo drug policy, regardless of its efficacy. In short, a social problem led to a social policy; but the policy, in turn, has led to a powerful industry that depends for its very existence on the continuation of that ineffective policy.

As this example suggests, social policy is often driven by politics and rarely, if ever, systematically analyzed. Policy analysis often occurs only after a bill or policy is enacted. As a result, analysts are often asked to perform an autopsy to determine why a specific bill or policy failed.

The purpose of a policy framework is to provide the analyst with a model—a set of questions—for systematically analyzing a policy.[2] The choice of a framework, then, must fit the requirements of the project as well as the resources of the analyst. Every policy framework can be either fine-tuned or substantially modified. In fact, the best policy framework may result from a synthesis of existing models. In short, a policy framework is simply a set of questions that analysts systematically ask about a past, present, or future policy in order to determine its desirability or viability.

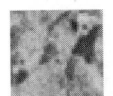 # A Proposed Model for Policy Analysis

The policy analyst is expected to evaluate a policy and make recommendations. To succeed in this charge, the analyst must accept his or her own values while, at the same time, basing the analysis on objective criteria. The policy framework that we propose here is divided into four sections: (1) the historical background of the policy, (2) description of the problem(s) that necessitated the policy, (3) description of the policy, and (4) the policy analysis (see Figure 2.1).

Historical Background of the Policy

Understanding the historical antecedents of a particular policy is important to the policy analyst for two reasons. First, for the sake of continuity, the analyst needs to identify the problems that led to the original creation of the policy and the historical background of the policy under consideration. Questions might include: What historical problems led to the creation of the policy? How important have these problems been historically? How was the problem previously

FIGURE 2.1   A Proposed Model for Policy Analysis

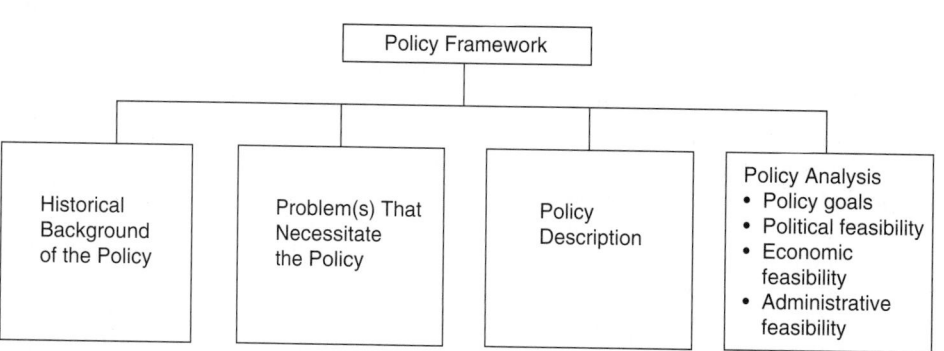

handled? What is the historical background of the policy? When did the policy originate? How has the original policy changed over time? What is the legislative history of the policy (e.g., what similar policies have been discussed and debated in the House and the Senate)? In addition, the policy analyst must examine similar policies that were adopted in the past and how they fared.

Second, beyond providing continuity, a historical analysis helps to curb the tendency of decision makers to reinvent the wheel. Policies that were previously unsuccessful may continue to be so; or the analyst may come to realize that circumstances have changed, thus creating a climate in which a previously failed policy might now be viable. In addition, a historical analysis helps the analyst to understand the forces that were previously mobilized to support or oppose a given policy. In short, a historical analysis locates a particular policy within a historical framework, thus helping to explicate the evolutionary nature of a specific social policy or series of policies.

Problem(s) That Necessitate the Policy

The second step in analyzing a policy addresses the problem(s) that led to the creation of the policy. In order to assess the ability of a policy to successfully remedy a social problem, the analyst must understand the parameters of the problem. Furthermore, the analyst must be familiar

with the nature, scope, and magnitude of the problem and with the populations affected by it. In this way, the policy analyst will be able to discern early the appropriateness of the policy for tackling the problem it is expected to remedy. Specific questions that the policy analyst might ask include: What is the nature of the problem? How widespread is it? How many people are affected by it? Who is affected and how? What are the causes of the problem?

Policy Description

The next step in this policy framework is to describe the policy. This section requires a detailed explanation of the policy, including a description of (1) how the policy is expected to work; (2) the resources or opportunities the policy is expected to provide (power, cash, economic opportunity, in-kind services, status redistribution, goods and services, and so forth); (3) who will be covered by the policy and how (e.g., universal versus selective entitlement, means testing, and so forth); (4) how the policy will be implemented, including coordination; (5) the expected short- and long-term goals and outcomes of the policy; (6) the administrative auspices under which the policy will be lodged, including the roles of the private sector and of local, state, and federal governments in its development; (7) the funding mechanism for the policy, including short- and long-term funding commitments; (8) the agencies or organizations with overall responsibility for overseeing, evaluating, and coordinating the policy; (9) the formal or informal criteria that will be used to determine the effectiveness of the policy; (10) the length of time the policy is expected to be in existence—for example, is it a "sunset law" (a law designed to end at a certain date)? and (11) the knowledge base or scientific grounding on which the policy rests.

Policy Analysis

In this section, the heart of any policy analysis, the analyst goes beyond a simple description of the policy and engages in a *systematic* analysis of the policy.

Policy Goals. The goals of the policy are the criteria by which all else is measured. Oftentimes the goals of a policy are not overtly stated, and the analyst must conjecture on the overall goals of the policy. The following questions can help to explicate the goals of a particular policy.

- Are the goals of the policy legal?
- Are the goals of the policy just and democratic?
- Do the goals of the policy contribute to greater social equality?
- Do the goals of the policy positively affect the redistribution of income, resources, rights, entitlements, rewards, opportunities, and status?
- Do the goals of the policy contribute to a better quality of life for the target population? Will the goals adversely affect the quality of life of the target group?
- Does the policy contribute to positive social relations between the target population and the overall society?
- Are the goals of the policy consistent with the values of professional social work (self-determination, client rights, self-realization, and so forth)?

Other, perhaps more difficult, questions should also be asked. Analysts must understand the value premises of the policy as well as the ideological assumptions underlying it. To this end, several questions should be addressed: What are the hidden ideological suppositions contained in the policy? How is the target population viewed in the context of the policy? What social vision, if any, does the policy contain? Does the policy encourage the status quo, or does it represent a radical departure? Who are the major beneficiaries of the policy? In whose best interest is the policy? Is the policy designed to foster real social change or only to placate a potentially insurgent group? Uncovering the hidden ideological dimensions of a policy is frequently the most difficult task for the policy analyst.

Despite the good intentions of a prospective policy, its goals must be achievable for it to be successfully implemented. U.S. history is littered with worthy goals that were simply not viable at the time they were proposed. For example, during the middle 1930s (at the height of the Great Depression), a California physician named Francis Townsend proposed that all citizens over the age of 65 be given a flat governmental pension of $200 per month. Although in more prosperous times this proposal might have been given at least a cursory hearing, in the midst of one of the greatest depressions in history, policymakers summarily dismissed the proposal as not viable. The overall feasibility of a policy is based on three factors: political feasibility, economic feasibility, and administrative feasibility.

Political Feasibility. The political feasibility of a particular policy is always a subjective assessment. In order to evaluate a policy, the analyst must assess which groups will oppose and which groups will support a particular policy and must estimate the constituency and power base of each group. In U.S. politics, however, the size of the constituency base and its relative power are sometimes unrelated. For example, despite its relatively small numbers, the American Medical Association (AMA) is a powerful lobby. Conversely, although more than 30 million Americans are poor, their political clout is negligible. Thus, the analyst must carefully weigh the political strength of each side in the policy struggle.

The political viability of a policy is always subject to the public's perception of its feasibility.

In other words, for a policy to be feasible, it must be *perceived* as being feasible. For example, although some observers maintain that a sizable portion, if not the majority, of the public would like to see some form of national health care, none exists. In part, a national health care program does not exist because of the power of the health care industry; but in part, such a program has not been enacted because the public believes that it cannot happen. Therefore, the United States lacks a national health care policy not because people reject it, but because they believe that it cannot occur. Thus is born a public myth around what is possible and impossible. Many good policies fail to be enacted because of public mythology about what is feasible.

To assess the political feasibility of a policy, the analyst must examine the public sentiment toward it. Is a large segment of the public concerned about the policy? Do people feel that they will be directly affected by the policy? Does the policy address a problem that is considered to be a major political issue? Does the policy threaten fundamental social values? Is the policy compatible with the present social and political climate? What is the possibility that either side will be able to marshal public sentiment for or against the policy? The answers to these questions help the policy analyst determine the political feasibility of the policy.

The question of political feasibility also encompasses a smaller, but no less important, dimension. In order to do a thorough assessment, the analyst must understand the relationship between the policy and external factors in agencies and institutions. For example, which social welfare agencies, institutions, or organizations support or oppose the policy? What is the relative strength of each group? How strong is their support of or opposition to the policy? What are the major federal, state, or local agencies that would be affected by the policy? How would these agencies be affected? The world of social policy is heavily political, with some governmental and private social welfare agencies having political power on a par with that of elected decision makers. Groups of institutions often coalesce around

issues, problems, or policies that directly affect them, and through their lobbying strength they have the ability to defeat legislation. In cases in which they cannot defeat a policy outright, these administrative institutions can choose to implement a policy in such a way as to ensure its failure. The analyst must therefore take into account whether these administrative units support or oppose a proposed or existing social policy.

Economic Feasibility. Many, if not most, social policies require some form of direct or indirect funding. In assessing the economic feasibility of a policy, the analyst must ask several hard questions: What is the minimum level of funding required for the successful implementation of the policy? Does adequate funding for the policy currently exist? If not, what is the public sentiment toward funding the policy? Is the funding called for by the drafters of the policy adequate? What are the future funding needs of the policy likely to be?

Given the current political and economic climate in the nation, it appears unlikely that new social policy initiatives requiring large additional revenues will be successful. Perhaps new policy legislation requiring additional revenues will be based on the reallocation of existing resources (budget-neutral policies) rather than on new revenue sources. This approach—taking money away from one program to fund another—is referred to in Congress as **pay-go** funding. The inherent danger in this approach is that thinning out fiscal resources among many programs may mean that none will be adequately funded. The analyst must therefore decide whether a new policy initiative should be recommended regardless of the funding prospects. The parameters of this decision are complex. If a new policy is recommended despite insufficient resources, the chances of its failure are greater. If a policy is not recommended, however, the possibility exists that adequate fiscal resources may be allocated in the future. Therefore, many policy analysts lean toward incremental approaches, tending to recommend policies in the hope that suitable funding will become available in the future.

Administrative Feasibility. The analyst must also be concerned with the administrative viability of the policy. Regardless of the potential value of the policy, responsible administrative and supervisory agencies must possess the personnel, resources, skills, and expertise needed to implement the policy effectively. If the requisite personnel are lacking, agencies must have the fiscal resources to hire qualified employees. In addition, directors and supervisors must be sympathetic to the goals of the policy, have the expertise and skill necessary to implement or oversee the policy, and possess an understanding of the fundamental objectives of the policy. The analyst must focus on two key aspects of administrative feasibility: (1) effectiveness and (2) efficiency and alternative policies.

Effectiveness. The question of effectiveness has to do with the likelihood that the policy can accomplish what its designers intended. The answer to this question encompasses other questions: Is the policy broad enough to accomplish its stated goals? Will the benefits of the policy reach the target group? Will the implementation of the policy likely cause new or other social problems? What ramifications does the policy have for the nontarget sector (e.g., higher taxes, reduced opportunity, diminished freedom, or fewer resources)?

An important question facing policy analysts involves the nature and extent of the unintended consequences of a policy. Virtually all policies have certain consequences that are unforeseen. An example of this can be seen in the case of methadone, a drug legally administered to addicts as a substitute for heroin. When introduced in the 1960s, methadone was thought to be a safe way to wean addicts away from heroin. By the mid-1970s, however, health experts realized that methadone was almost as addictive as heroin and that some addicts were selling their methadone as a street drug. Despite this outcome, some addicts were able to withdraw from heroin and, in hindsight, the methadone program was probably a positive development. Because policy analysts cannot see into the future, they make their recommendations on the basis of available data. Nevertheless, an attempt must be made to try to predict possible adverse future consequences.

Efficiency and Alternative Policies. The policy analyst must also look closely at efficiency—the cost-effectiveness of the proposed policy compared to that of alternative policies, of no policy, or of the present policy. Social policy always involves a trade-off. Even in the best of economic times, societal resources are always inadequate compared to the breadth of human need. For example, virtually everyone could benefit from some form of social welfare, whether it be counseling services, food stamps, or free health care. But because resources are finite, society must choose the primary beneficiaries of its social allocations. Publicly financed services are often awarded on the basis of two criteria: (1) the severity of the problem, with services going to those who most require the allocation; and (2) means, with services provided to those who can least afford them. As a result of finite resources, the adequate funding of one policy often means denying or curbing allocations to another. This is the essential trade-off in social welfare policy. When analysts evaluate a policy, they must be cognizant that promoting one policy means that needs in other areas may go unmet. Thus, a significant question remains: Is this policy important enough to justify the allocation of scarce resources? Moreover, are there other areas where resources could be better used?

The policy analyst is concerned with the cost-effectiveness of a given policy compared to the cost-effectiveness of alternative policies. Given the additional expenditures, will the new policy provide results that are better than either the present policy or no policy at all? Would it be advantageous to enlarge or modify the present policy rather than creating a new one? Could an alternative policy provide better results at a lower cost? What alternative policies could be created that would achieve the same results? How would these alternative policies compare with each other and with the proposed policy?

These questions must be addressed in any thorough policy analysis.

In summary, the policy analyst must address several key questions: Is the proposed policy workable and desirable? What, if any, modifications should be made to the policy? Does the policy represent a wise use of resources? Are there alternative policies that would be preferable? How feasible is the implementation of the policy? What barriers, if any, are there to the full implementation of the policy? These questions represent the core of policy analysis.

Researching and Analyzing Social Policies

There are two major hurdles in policy analysis. The first is finding and focusing on a manageable social policy to analyze, and the second is finding or generating information relevant to it.

One of the most difficult tasks the analyst faces is choosing the actual policy. In order to do a careful policy analysis, the analyst must select a policy that is both discrete and specific. For example, it would be difficult, if not impossible, to do an exhaustive analysis of child welfare policy in the United States. For one thing, the United States does not *have* one specific child welfare policy. Policies on child welfare are composed of myriad programs that constitute a patchwork quilt of social policies. Given the limitations of time and resources, the question then becomes *which* policy will be analyzed. Second, the differences among child welfare policies on the national, state, and community levels make such a policy analysis even more daunting. Thus, defining and narrowing a specific and manageable social policy constitutes a formidable task.

A second task involves locating relevant information on a specific social policy. There are seven major avenues for finding information. First, policy analysts may choose to generate their own data through primary research, including surveys, opinion polls, experimental research, longitudinal studies, and so forth. Although this method can yield a rich body of information, time and cost constraints may prove an impossible obstacle. Moreover, the same research may already exist in other places, in which case the replication of the effort would be unwarranted.

Second, governmental or agency records are often fruitful sources of relevant data on a specific policy. These records can include archives, memos, and the minutes of meetings of boards of directors, governmental officials, and staff. This research method can also include an examination of policy manuals, departmental records, and minutes of public meetings. A surprising amount of this information can be found online in government or agency websites.

A third avenue for policy research involves the records and published minutes of legislative bodies and committees. On the federal level these sources include the *Congressional Record* and the minutes of the various House and Senate committees and subcommittees (many of which can be accessed online). All state legislatures have similar record-keeping procedures, and most of these legislative records can be found in regional or university libraries or online.

A fourth source of information is found in governmental publications. For example, the U.S. Government Printing Office maintains catalogues of all government documents published. Other documents include the Census Bureau's population studies (many of which are updated annually); publications of the Departments of Labor, Commerce, Housing, and Health and Human Services; and the *Green Book* of the House Committee on Ways and Means, a yearly publication containing the most comprehensive information available on social programs and participants. Many of these publications can be found in regional and university libraries and online.

A fifth source of policy-relevant information is available through think tanks, advocacy organizations, and professional associations. All think tanks (many of which also function as advocacy organizations) employ research staff who evaluate and analyze social policies. Examples of these include the Brookings Institute, the American Enterprise Institute, the Heritage Foundation, the Hoover Institute, the Urban Institute, the Center on Budget and Policy Priorities, the Reason Foundation, the Hudson Institute, the Progressive Policy Institute, the Economic Policy Institute, and the Independent Sector. Again, at least some of the information can be accessed through the Internet. Most, if not all, of these think tanks are affiliated with particular political ideologies, however; so their evaluation of data and their policy recommendations must be viewed critically.

Many national advocacy organizations retain research staff and publish reports that may be helpful to the policy analyst. Some of these organizations are the Urban League, the NAACP, the Children's Defense Fund, the National Farm Organization, and the National Organization for Women. Many professional associations, such as the American Medical Association, the American Public Human Services Association, and the American Psychological Association, also publish policy-relevant information. A listing of these organizations can be found in any major library. Updated lists can also be found through Internet search engines.

A sixth procedure used by policy analysts is to consult professional journals, books, and monographs. Articles or books on specific policy areas can be found in various places, including the *Social Science Index* and the subject headings in library catalogues, online library systems, and electronic databases, which are becoming increasingly common in the larger professional associations. Electronic databases such as Nexus are also becoming common commercial ventures.

Lastly, policy-relevant information can be gathered from interviews with principals in the policy process, advocates, recipients of services, and government officials. Personal interviews may help the analyst determine the background of the issue, assess the opposition or support for a particular policy, or gauge the public reaction to a policy. Taken together, these sources can be a gold mine for the policy analyst.

 # Conclusion

The choice of a policy analysis framework depends upon several considerations, including (1) the kind of problem or policy that is analyzed; (2) the resources available to the analyst, including time, money, staff, facilities, and the availability of data; (3) the needs of the decision maker requesting the analysis; and (4) the time frame within which the analysis must be completed.

Because it is impossible to discover *all* of the data (data are essentially infinite) and to ask *all* of the possible questions, no policy analysis is ever complete or perfect. Policy analysis is always an approximation of the ideal, and therefore decisions are inevitably made on the basis of incomplete data. How incomplete the data are and how close an approximation to a rational decision is provided to decision makers will depend on the skills of the analyst, the available resources, and the time allotted for the project.

Despite its reliance on an analytic framework, social policy analysis in the real world is to a large degree subjective. Because a policy is analyzed by human beings, it is always done through the lens of the analyst's value system, ideological beliefs, and his or her particular understanding of the goals and purposes of social welfare. Subjectivity may be evident in the omission of facts or questions or in the relative weight given to one variable over another. Other forms of subjectivity include asking the wrong questions of the policy, evaluating it on the basis of expectations that it cannot meet, or expecting it to tackle a problem it was not designed to remedy. Finally, political pressure can be put on the policy analyst to come up with recommendations that are acceptable to a certain interest group. Regardless of the causes of subjectivity, policy analysis is always an approximation of the ideal and always involves an informed hunch as to the effects of a policy or a set of policies.

Discussion Questions

1. What are the main advantages of using a systematic framework for social policy analysis? Describe the benefits of using such a framework. What, if any, are the potential drawbacks?

2. Although by definition the unintended consequences of a social policy are unpredictable, what specifically can a policy analyst do to minimize the risks of a policy's producing harmful unintended consequences? Describe a recent social policy that has produced unintended consequences that were either positive or harmful.

3. Is it possible for a policy researcher to neutralize his or her personal values when conducting a policy analysis? If so, describe ways in which this can be done.

4. What specific components could be added to the proposed policy framework presented in this chapter? Which of the components provided in this framework are the most important, and why?

5. Are most social policies analyzed thoroughly and rationally? If not, why not? Describe the factors that stand in the way of a systematic and rational analysis of social policy in U.S. society. How much value do decision makers place on social policy research before reaching a decision?

6. Because any analysis of social policy is by nature incomplete, should decision makers therefore not rely heavily on policy studies? What alternatives, if any, can be used in lieu of a thorough and systematic policy analysis?

 # Notes

1. Thanks to Brene Brown, Assistant Professor at the University of Houston Clear Lake and doctoral student at the University of Houston Graduate School of Social Work, for her ideas on environmental scanning. Ms. Brown has repeatedly pointed out that environmental scanning is a concept that successful agencies must adopt.

2. Many social policy writers have developed excellent policy frameworks, among them Elizabeth Huttman, *Introduction to Social Policy* (New York: McGraw-Hill, 1981); Neil Gilbert and Harry Specht, *Dimensions of Social Welfare Policy,* 2nd ed. (Englewood Cliffs, NJ: Prentice-Hall, 1986); Gail Marker, "Guidelines for Analysis of a Social Welfare Program," in John E. Tropman et al. (eds.), *Strategic Perspectives on Social Policy* (New York: Pergamon Press, 1976); David Gil, *Unraveling Social Policy* (Boston: Shenkman, 1981); and Charles Prigmore and Charles Atherton, *Social Welfare Policy* (New York: D. C. Heath, 1979).

chapter 3

Technology and Social Policy

The Internet and attendant communication technologies have expanded the opportunities for citizens to access and disseminate information. These technologies have allowed users to access a growing list of information on health and mental health, diseases, services, products, political and economic ideas, cultural trends, and almost every other imaginable topic. The growth in the Internet is so explosive that it is estimated that 25,000 new sites are added each month to the World Wide Web.[1] Approximately 3.4 trillion e-mail messages were delivered in the United States in 1998, and about 2.1 billion U.S. e-mail messages are sent daily.[2]

The Internet is also a social technology through which people with common interests can find each other and talk, listen, and sustain communication over time. In large measure, the Web is redefining communication between and among groups and individuals. Virtual meetings are popular; America Online alone has more than 350 and Prodigy more than 400 ongoing virtual meetings. These range from organized special interest groups to informal discussion groups. Whether in a website, a virtual meeting, a bulletin board forum, or one of the more than 35,000 Usenet newsgroups, almost every possible interest is covered on the Internet. Even people with obscure interests can find some camaraderie in the United States or in the world.

The Internet and related information technologies represent a major technological breakthrough of our time. However, there are also important policy concerns arising from the use of electronic communication technologies, including the delicate balance between social well-being and the free flow of information in a democracy. For those with access, the Internet is fast becoming a marketplace of ideas as well as a market for a wide range of goods and services. But this technology is also leaving some people behind, especially the poor. This chapter will address the effects of technology on social policy. We will focus particularly on the digital divide,

political advocacy and the Internet, and policy-oriented Internet research.

The Digital Divide

The term *digital divide* addresses the information "haves" and "have-nots"—the differential access to technology that exists along income, class, and racial lines. It is a term used to describe an individual's or a community's lack of access to computers and online resources.

The digital divide in the United States is quickly becoming one of the most important social equity issues of the twenty-first century. It is also an important civil rights issue, in that it makes a political, economic, and moral statement about the role of communications technology in fostering a more egalitarian society. For example, those with telecommunications services, such as a home telephone and a personal computer with Internet access, can effectively engage the global economy, participate in political debates, and interact within the "global village." People without this access risk being left behind, disconnected from the global community, the political system, and the information-driven market economy.

People use the Internet and related technologies for many different purposes. Among those accessing the Internet at home, 77.9 percent use it for e-mail (and 93.6 percent of e-mail users communicate mainly with family and friends). A majority of home users (59.8 percent) also use the Internet for information searches. More than half of unemployed persons (53.9 percent) use home-based Internet access to search for jobs. Using the Internet at home for "job-related tasks" is far more common for those making above $25,000. Pursuing online courses and school research is also popular inside and outside the home (36.1 percent and 38.8 percent, respectively). Outside the home, more than 65 percent of those making under $25,000 use e-mail to communicate with family and friends.

Internet access across the country is soaring, with more than 26 percent of U.S. households having home access. This is an increase of almost 41 percent since 1997, when just over 18 percent of households had home access. Moreover, access is up for all demographic groups, with an increase of 52.8 percent for white, 52 percent for black, and 48.3 percent for Hispanic households.

However, certain groups still cannot access the Internet and are therefore unable to benefit from its growing list of uses.[3] Although greater numbers of people are enjoying the World Wide Web, the disparity in access continues to widen along racial, ethnic, and class lines. The significant growth in computer ownership and usages has occurred to a large extent within key income levels, demographic groups, and geographic areas. In fact, the digital divide between certain groups of Americans has actually increased since 1994. For example, there is a widening gap between those at upper and lower income levels. Additionally, although all racial groups now own more computers than in 1994, African Americans and Hispanics now lag farther behind non-Hispanic whites in their levels of PC ownership and online access (Table 3.1). The following represent some of the significant findings of the National Telecommunications and Information Administration report, *Falling Through the Net: Defining the Digital Divide:*[4]

- Although PC ownership rates have grown by 10 to 13 percent since 1994, central city rates of PC ownership (32.8 percent) and online access (17.3 percent) lag behind the national averages, as do rural areas (34.9 percent and 14.8 percent). Urban areas are slightly higher than the average in PC ownership (37.2 percent) and in home Internet access (19.9 percent). The urban areas in the West have the highest rates of PC ownership (43.9 percent) and online access (23.14 percent); the Northeast's central cities have the lowest penetration rates (24.7 percent and 12.6 percent). If income is kept constant, no significant differences exist between rural, urban, and central city areas in computer penetration, although rural areas have a lower rate of online access (see Table 3.2).

- Households earning below $35,000 a year have fewer PCs (36.6 percent) and less online access (26.3 percent) than the national averages. Rural households earning between $5,000 and $10,000 account for the lowest penetration rate for computers (7.9 percent) and for online access (2.3 percent). Not surprisingly, urban households earning more than $75,000 a year have the highest PC ownership rates (76 percent) and online access rates (50.3 percent).

TABLE 3.1 ■ Percentages of U.S. Households with a Computer by Race/Origin and by Rural, Urban, and Central City Areas

	U.S. 1994	U.S. 1997	RURAL	URBAN	CENTRAL CITY
Non-Hispanic White	27.1	40.8	36.7	42.5	41.5
Non-Hispanic Black	10.3	19.3	14.9	19.9	17.1
Other Non-Hispanic	32.6	47.0	35.8	48.4	43.5
Hispanic	12.3	19.4	19.2	19.4	16.2

Source: National Telecommunications and Information Administration, *Falling Through the Net: Defining the Digital Divide.* Retrieved July 1999, 2000 from the World Wide Web: http://www.digitaldivide.gov

TABLE 3.2 ▪ Percentages of U.S. Households with a Computer by Income and by Rural, Urban, and Central City Areas

	U.S.	RURAL	URBAN	CENTRAL CITY
Under $5,000	16.5	15.0	16.9	16.4
$5,000–$9,999	9.9	7.9	10.5	11.0
$10,000–$14,999	12.9	11.0	13.5	13.2
$15,000–$19,999	17.4	17.0	17.5	17.8
$20,000–$24,999	23.0	20.9	23.7	24.4
$25,000–$34,999	31.7	31.7	31.7	31.0
$35,000–$49,000	45.6	45.0	45.9	46.4
$50,000–$74,999	60.6	59.6	60.9	60.0
$75,000+	75.9	75.3	76.0	73.9

Source: National Telecommunications and Information Administration, *Falling Through the Net: Defining the Digital Divide.* Retrieved July 1999, 2000 from the World Wide Web: http://www.digitaldivide.gov

▪ Although all income groups are more likely to own a computer now than in 1994, the penetration levels for those with higher incomes have grown more rapidly. As a result, the gap in computer ownership levels between higher- and lower-income households has widened.

▪ Although PC ownership rates for minority groups has grown since 1994, African Americans and Hispanics still lag behind the national average. In 1997 African Americans in rural areas had the lowest PC ownership rates (14.9 percent), followed by African Americans and Hispanics in central cities (17.1 percent and 16.2 percent, respectively). Online access is also the lowest for black households in rural areas (5.5 percent) and in central cities (5.8 percent), followed by Hispanic households in central cities (7.0 percent) and rural areas (7.3 percent). In contrast, white households are almost 41 percent more likely to own a PC than black or Hispanic households. This divide cuts across all income levels. For example, whites earning $75,000 a year are more likely to have PCs (at 76.3 percent) than African Americans (64.1 percent). Similarly, the rate for online access is nearly 3 times as high for whites (21.2 percent) as for African Americans (7.7 percent) or Hispanics (8.7 percent). America's digital divide is fast becoming a racial divide.

▪ The households most likely to own a PC are those headed by people in the 35- to 44-year-old age bracket.

▪ The higher the educational level, the greater the likelihood that a person will own a PC and have online access. Those with a college education are 10 times more likely to own a PC (63.2 percent) than those without a high school diploma (6.8 percent). This difference is even more striking in rural areas: 64.7 percent versus 5.3 percent. The most striking differences, however, are in online access among those with a college degree (38.4 percent), those with a high school diploma (9.6 percent), and those without any high school education (1.8 percent).

▪ Married couples with children are roughly twice as likely to own PCs (57 percent) and to have online access (29.4 percent) than single-parent female-headed households (25 percent, 9.2 percent).

As access to computer technology becomes increasingly important to economic and social success, the above data illustrate that many people in central cities and in isolated rural areas are failing to acquire the necessary skills as rapidly as the more affluent members of society.

Addressing the Digital Divide

The crisis of the digital divide has occupied policy discussions in national legislative bodies, state capitals, industry boardrooms, and grassroots community organizations since 1998. These discussions, and the media attention paid to them, are causing society to become increasingly aware of the detrimental effects of a lack of access to the Internet for e-commerce, civic engagement, political organization, and the like. Several organizations such as Jesse Jackson's Rainbow/PUSH, the Benton Foundation, and most notably the National Telecommunications and Information Administration (NTIA) of the U.S. Department of Commerce have identified the digital divide as a problem and are working toward solutions.

Other organizations have announced stepped-up initiatives to address the digital divide. These efforts are often sweeping collaborative exercises between nonprofits and industry members. Many of these efforts, such as the Steve and Jean Case Foundation's PowerUp and the Bill and Melinda Gates Foundation's Millennium Scholarship program, have increased the visibility of the digital divide in relationship to youth, libraries, and minority populations.

The NTIA was designated by the Clinton administration as the agency responsible for spearheading federal efforts to narrow the digital divide. Those efforts accounted for the tripling of the agency's budget to $225 million by fiscal year 2001. The increase includes funds for a wide variety of programs, including a $50 million Home Internet Access Initiative designed to provide low-income and minority Americans with lower-cost Internet connections, training, and support. On December 9, 1999, Commerce Secretary William M. Daley hosted a Digital Divide Summit, a national conference that brought together 800 technology industry leaders, government officials, and representatives of minorities and civil rights groups to discuss ways of narrowing the digital divide.

In addition to the NTIA efforts, the federal government has initiated the E-Rate program, which is designed to provide schools and libraries with lower-cost Internet access and other telecommunication services. By 1999 E-Rate had funded more than 45,000 schools with more than $2.5 billion in telecommunications subsidies in order to connect these institutions to the Internet. Despite these efforts, the digital divide between low-poverty schools and high-poverty schools still exists. In 1998 51 percent of all classrooms nationally were wired to the Internet, but only 39 percent of schools with high levels of poverty were online. In contrast, 62 percent of schools with low levels of poverty were wired.

Despite the data, the question remains whether the extent of the digital divide is real or exaggerated. Ekaterina Walsh found that technology does not divide people, and she argues that diversity is alive and well on the Internet. She points out that Internet use numbers would be higher if they included those who use computers outside the home. The NTIA began to measure such use in its latest report, acknowledging that blacks and Hispanics often turn to access outside the home. By excluding from its statistics those who use computers and the Internet at the library, and so on, the government has artificially widened the digital divide among groups.[5] Nevertheless, although a large percentage of poor people and minorities do use public centers for Internet access, a library or after-school program does not afford the same leisure and privacy as Web access at home. This effectively creates second-class citizens in terms of technological access. Use of the Internet exclusively at work is generally not sufficient to meet the information, educational, and entertainment needs of a family.

Regardless of its causes, the digital divide is a serious problem in low-income and rural communities. A concerted effort will be required to ascertain what is needed by communities and individuals, and then to make readily available the appropriate resources. Strong government policies and private initiatives should be put into action to ensure that the new information tools do not widen already existing social divisions based on socioeconomic status and geography. There is a great deal at stake, including the ability of individuals to acquire the skills essential for success in today's job market (the Department of Commerce estimates that 60 percent of jobs require technological skills[6]), improvements in educational opportunities (online courses and training, etc.), and provision of the technological tools and access that low-income communities need in order to thrive.

Some proposals for narrowing the digital divide include helping churches, recreation centers, and other organizations to band together to negotiate a less expensive Internet infrastructure and access. In addition, national cooperatives could be developed that would facilitate less expensive Internet access and lower-priced computers. Specifically, these initiatives could put computers in the homes of low-income, rural, urban, and underserved and minority areas. Through the aggregate demand of a local community organization, a family could purchase a personal computer and Internet access, paying only a small amount of money per month. Because of the aggregated demand, a community could purchase computers cheaply from manufacturers and thereby pass along those savings; families could then purchase a PC, online access, and technical support from their local community organization. This goal could be accomplished through a partnership joining unions, colleges and universities, tribal councils, faith-based organizations, rural and agricultural organizations, and other kinds of community-level organizations.[7]

Political Advocacy and the Internet

The Internet has opened up countless opportunities and possibilities for political advocacy. Almost every national and state advocacy organization has a Web presence highlighting its position, its mission statement, and often research related to its goal. (See the advocacy-oriented websites contained in the Internet Supplement.) In addition, there are even advocacy organizations related to technology, such as the Center for Democracy and Technology. The Internet is a fertile ground for promoting an advocacy organization, finding new members, storing organizational information, developing online brochures, and disseminating research and other information.

The Internet contains remarkable opportunities for both large and small advocacy organizations. These organizations can use the Internet to set up mailing lists, newsgroups, surveys, even the election of board members. Members can be notified of meetings and be made instantly aware of legislative or judicial changes related to organizational issues. Instead of waiting for materials to be printed and then posted, an organization can immediately disseminate this information to members worldwide, and at a significantly lower cost than mailings. In general, what can be accomplished through a hard copy paper medium can be done at a far lower cost through the Internet.

Advocacy organizations can also use the Internet for carrying out lobbying efforts (most legislators have posted e-mail addresses), for retrieving government documents, for corresponding via e-mail with government officials, even for recruiting new members and soliciting donations through mailing lists shared with other organizations.

One community organization that is effectively using the Internet is the Association of Community Organizations for Reform Now (ACORN). Founded in 1970 by a group of Arkansas welfare mothers, ACORN has grown into the largest low- and moderate-income organization in the country, with a membership of more than 125,000 African American, white, and nonwhite Latino families. It is composed of more than 500 neighborhood chapters working on local, citywide, and national campaigns. ACORN has pioneered multiracial and multi-issue organizing and has introduced strategies to confront corporate targets, worked in electoral organizing, and developed direct action tactics like squatting. In recent years, ACORN has founded labor unions, helped to build a progressive radio and television network, and worked to provide affordable housing and to revitalize deteriorating neighborhoods.[8] On its website (www.acorn.org) ACORN provides a wide range of organizational information, including its accomplishments; its program, philosophy and platform; its organizational history; a list of member council organizations; and a list of chapters and officers and their e-mail addresses. The website also includes a "rapid response" page that will contact website visitors about events in their area, solicit donations, and provide job information. Lastly, ACORN's website contains an e-mail page focusing on predatory lending practices. Specifically, the page contains a simple interface with a sample letter that can be automatically generated and sent to the appropriate legislator in the visitor's home area. Despite ACORN's efforts, however, the potential of the Internet to foster the growth of progressive advocacy organizations will depend in large measure on the ability of society to narrow the digital divide.

Hate Groups and the Internet

Just as the Internet has the potential for increasing social justice efforts, it also has the potential to exacerbate social differences and increase the reach of hate groups. Hate crimes in the United States and elsewhere are a serious problem. In 1998 there were 7,755 hate crimes reported to the FBI by 10,730 law enforcement agencies in 46 states and the District of Columbia. (For an overview of U.S. hate crimes, see Figure 3.1.)

Hate groups are increasingly using the Internet as a tool to spread propaganda.[9] In fact, the number of hate sites increased from 1 in 1995 to more than 400 in 2000.[10] According to Tom Metzger, founder of the White Aryan Resistance, a California-based white supremacy group, "We use the Internet extensively. It's one of the greater phenomenons I've ever seen."[11] Hate-oriented websites recruit people ripe for the message, and almost anyone looking for validation of their ideas can find it online. Moreover, hate groups use the Internet for the same reasons as other

groups—it's fast, it's cheap, and it allows them to reach across the country and the world.

Some online hate sites are becoming more sophisticated, posting essays about white pride in formats that read like college papers, complete with footnotes and full bibliographies. To the uninitiated these essays can appear legitimate and authoritative. These "reports" are made to seem even more convincing by their use of references from mainstream journals and newspapers. Increasingly, hate sites are developing niche marketing, offering links to women's pages, kids' pages, and singles pages, all promoting their hate message. The goal of these websites is to create a virtual community where people who feel disenfranchised can feel at home. Such virtual communities can be a powerful draw for those who are full of rage and on the margins of society. Moreover, these virtual communities often become physical communities as members make plans to get together.

Other hate sites don't sugarcoat the message. Some websites offer a version of the video game Doom, called White People's Doom, which viewers can download free. The hero is white and the villains are minorities. One recently defunct website included a version of the word game Hangman that showed an African American man hanging when the player won. The Southern Poverty Law Center categorizes hate groups under the following headings: Ku Klux Klan groups; Neo Nazis; Skinheads; Christian Identity; Black Separatists; and Others.[12] A group that has received much press is the Christian Identity movement.[13] This group encompasses many subgroups, including the violent militia and patriot movements. The virulently anti-semitic and racist Christian Identity movement promotes the "Israel Message," which is grounded in the belief that whites are the true Israelites. Other races (including Jews and people of color) are referred to as "Beasts of the Field," "Children of Satan," or "Mud People." The Christian Identity movement believes that the non-white races will be destroyed in an apocalyptic battle in which whites will emerge victorious. To encourage the inevitable, the militia part of the movement is committed to instigating a race war that will speed things up. Both Timothy McVeigh

---

FIGURE 3.1   U.S. Hate Crimes, 1998

Of the 7,755 hate incidents reported in 1998, 4,321 were motivated by racial bias; 1,390 by religious bias; 1,260 by sexual orientation bias; 754 by ethnicity/national origin bias; 25 by disability bias; and 5 by multiple biases. The 7,755 incidents involved 9,235 separate offenses, 9,722 victims, and 7,489 known offenders. Seventy percent of the incidents involved only one individual victim; 97 percent involved a single offense type.

Crimes against persons made up 68 percent of the 9,235 offenses. Intimidation was the most frequently reported hate crime, accounting for 38 percent of the total. Destruction/damage/vandalism of property accounted for 28 percent, and simple and aggravated assault accounted for 18 percent and 12 percent, respectively. Thirteen persons were murdered in 1998 in hate-motivated incidents. Racial bias motivated 8 of the murders; sexual orientation bias, 4; and ethnicity/national origin bias the remaining one. In racially motivated incidents, 2,084 of the 3,573 antiblack offenses involved white offenders; 567 of the 989 antiwhite offenses involved black offenders.

In 8 out of 10 of the 9,722 reported hate crimes, the victims were individuals; the remaining were businesses, religious organizations, or various other targets. Sixty-five percent of the 9,722 victims in 1998 were targets of crimes against persons. Nearly 6 of every 10 victims were attacked because of their race, with bias against blacks accounting for 38 percent of the total.

About 7,489 known offenders associated with the 7,755 incidents were recorded in 1998. Of the known offenders, 66 percent were white and 17 percent black. Law enforcement officials identified only 536 offenders in connection with 1,390 religious bias incidents in 1998.

Source: U.S. Department of Justice, Federal Bureau of Investigation, *Hate Crime Reports–Hate Crimes, 1998.* Retrieved June 15, 2000, from the World Wide Web: http://www.fbi.gov/ucr/hatecm.htm

of the Oklahoma City bombings and Buford Furrow (who shot several children and adults in a Los Angeles Jewish Community Center in August 1999) were affiliated with this movement.

One of the more virulent hate groups is the World Church of the Creator, now led by Reverend Matt Hale. This "church" claims to have 24 regional and local branches and members all over the world. Their logo is explained on their website:

> The "W", of course, stands for our White Race, which we regard as the most precious treasure on the face of the earth. The Crown signifies our Aristocratic position in Nature's scheme of things, indicating that we are the Elite. The Halo indicates that we regard our Race as being unique and sacred above all other values.

Symbolism of our Flag:

(A) *The blood-red color of our flag symbolizes our struggle for the survival, expansion and advancement of the White Race.*

(B) *The triangle on the end of pure white color symbolizes the emergence of a Whiter and Brighter World out of our struggle.*

(C) *The center of the flag is adorned with the WCOTC logo, which symbolizes our unique White Racial Religion—CREATIVITY: the Beacon of Hope and Salvation for the White People.*

> We Creators say: to hell with the J.O.G. flag, which has become a symbol of race mixing; we Creators now have our own flag, which proudly proclaims—WHITE PEOPLE AWAKE! SAVE THE WHITE RACE! Our battle flag is the flag of a Whiter and Brighter Future, so let us make sure that it will be flying over all of Planet Earth by the year 2000.

Other hate groups are equally pernicious. Perhaps the most homophobic hate group in the United States is the Westboro Baptist Church, led by pastor Fred Phelps. Phelps is known for picketing the funerals of AIDS victims (including the service for Matthew Shepard, who was murdered in Wyoming) with antigay signs that read: "God Hates Fags," "Thank God for AIDS," and "AIDS Cure Fags."[14] The main page of the group's website includes the following:

> PICKETING MINISTRY—Schedule of picketing events, dates and, if available, times
>
> FAG CHURCHES—Why churches that support homosexuality and other sins are the most evil institutions on earth
>
> FAG COMPANIES—Companies that support sodomy
>
> FAG FACTS—Facts and statistics about fags—do not read this if you have a weak stomach. Fags live filthy, unhealthy, dangerous, unhappy, and in many cases, violent lives; fags prey on children; the fag agenda; the true number of fags; fags aren't discriminated against in employment, so why should they be a protected class?; sexual orientation.

The goal of these hate sites and virtual communities is not to recruit the "weekend warrior" but to reach his or her children. Specifically, there's an explicit drive to enlist bright young people in order to ensure a cadre of future leadership. The Internet is especially useful in this strategy, because it naturally attracts college-bound kids. According to Tom Metzger of the Aryan Nation, "Everybody wants to reach kids. Nobody goes around recruiting 80-year-old people."[15] Young people are easier to reach because they are impressionable, feel a need to belong, and tend to see things in black and white. Many youths attracted to hate movements do poorly in school and in sports, have a bad family situation, and are generally angry people. Ironically, however, Congress appears more concerned about protecting children from pornography than from the message of hate provided in these websites.

There are more than 35,000 Usenet newsgroups, and most Internet users around the world have access to them. For the most part, newsgroups or Usenet groups are nonmoderated forums. Under the alt. requirements of the Usenet guidelines, these groups are easy to start. As a result, alt. forums have proliferated, many of them started by hate groups or individual hatemongers. Some examples include alt.fan.ernst-zundel (Zundel is the historical revisionist who vehemently denies the existence of the Holocaust); alt.flame.niggers; alt.flame.whites; alt.music.white-power; alt.politics.nationalism.black; alt.politics.nationalism.white; alt.politics.nationalism.white.announce; alt.politics.white-power; alt.revisionism; alt.revolution.counter; and alt.skinheads.

The influence of online hate groups extends beyond the borders of the United States. In general, Europeans are not accustomed to the sweeping rights to free speech guaranteed to U.S. citizens by the First Amendment. For example, in Germany it is illegal to incite hatred or racism, and sales or public displays of symbols such as Nazi swastikas are outlawed. Hate literature such as *Mein Kampf* and *The Protocols of the Elders of Zion* are banned in Germany and in most European Union countries. On the other hand, European right-wing extremists can find a virtual community and purchase banned goods on the U.S. information highway. Moreover, although hate groups and their online presence are banned in most of western Europe, these same websites can resurface from the safe haven of the United States, where they are protected by the First Amendment.[16] To further extend their reach, many hate-oriented U.S. websites provide translations of their sites in German and Spanish.

In response to the growth of online hate sites, some European leaders (e.g., Switzerland's European Nuclear Physics Laboratory [CERN], where the Internet was developed) are calling for registration of websites and their authors. They argue that no one questions a car rental agency's right to demand a driver's license and that the same should be expected for Internet users. U.S. Internet leaders take the opposite position, arguing against anything that interferes with free speech protections. According to Michael Vatis of the FBI's counterterrorism division, "In the United States, we make a fundamental distinction between hate speech and hate crimes. The answer to hateful speech is not to prohibit it but to approach it head on and fight it with rational speech."[17] Unfortunately, for people like Richard Baumhammers (charged with killing five people in a shooting spree targeted at immigrants), Buford Furrow, or Timothy McVeigh, there is a permeable line between hateful speech and hateful acts.

Despite concerns about such issues as the digital divide, free speech, and the encampment of hate groups in the virtual community, the Internet and its associated technologies are here to stay. Given this, policy analysts must learn to use and master these communication technologies. One of the most effective ways that policy analysts can use the Internet is to conduct and review social policy–oriented research.

Social Policy Research and the Internet

The use of e-mail, listservs, the Internet, the World Wide Web (WWW), gopher protocols, and FTP (File Transfer Protocol) sites has made the job of the policy analyst immeasurably easier, more efficient, and even more fun. More importantly, by narrowing the distance between policy analysis and policy research (through shortening the period between the acquisition of data and the publication of a policy), technology has created a minirevolution in policy analysis. No longer do policy analysts (or students doing policy research) have to wait months before their library receives the report or data they are seeking; no longer does the analyst have to contend with lost, misplaced, or checked-out documents, or wade through large stacks filled with dozens of feet of government reports. Instead, with the touch of a finger the policy analyst can download reams of the newest government data, legislative reports, and governmental bills. The Internet has created a virtual library of millions of sources for the policy analyst, sources that can be accessed even from the comfort of home.

An unparalleled range and diversity of global online resources are available through the Internet. One obvious benefit of conducting Internet research is that it can be done any time of the day or night. Moreover, this research can complement, or even mitigate the limitations of, library holdings. The Internet can help meet the research needs of policy analysts by providing access to materials residing in more extensive collections.

Policy analysts engage in different types of research activities, of course. Although the Internet can provide access to vast stores of information, the degree to which it will facilitate your particular type of research will vary. It is helpful at the outset to know your research needs and how the Internet can help.

Journals and Online Research

Although titles, tables of contents, and article abstracts of many professional journals can be found online, the full text is typically not available electronically. Full library searches remain the most fruitful way to conduct research when the full texts of print journals are required. Many professional journals are beginning to convert their text into an electronic format, but this remains a costly and time-consuming process. Moreover, because journals provide income for their publishers, there is little incentive to give away free what journal subscribers must pay for. Still, when research requirements involve locating the most current information available, the Internet is a good starting place. This is especially true in that all major newspapers and news services are now online.

Some of the major guides for professional referred journals relevant for human service professionals include Psych Journal Search (http://www.cmhc.com/journals/); MedWeb (http://www.gen.emory.edu/MEDWEB/keyword/electronic-publications.html); and Electronic Journals and Periodicals (http://psych.hanover.edu/Krantz/journal.html).

Although the full texts of many journal articles are generally not made available online, there are online databases that do provide these services. These vary in cost. Some are free, but the majority involve a competitive range of pricing schedules with charges for an initial sign-up; an annual maintenance fee; charges for time spent searching the database; and a charge for each full article or research abstract that is viewed or downloaded.

Online Data Collection

For research requiring more formalized qualitative and quantitative data collection, recruiting subjects and collecting data online has several advantages:

- Posting messages on e-mail lists or newsgroups to recruit and interview subjects is more efficient and less costly than traditional forms of data collection such as mailing questionnaires or using field researchers.
- Research costs are lowered, as data obtained online do not require transcription.
- Research participants anywhere in the world can respond to data collection efforts at their convenience.
- The actors in the research process can quickly and conveniently communicate with one another to clarify aspects of the research, provide feedback, and share reactions to the findings. After data have been prepared for analysis, they can be imported immediately into a qualitative or quantitative software program.[18]

Conversely, there are also disadvantages in using the Internet for data collection. The pool of people available for the researcher are limited to those who possess

- sufficient education to enable them to express themselves in written form
- the ability to operate a computer and Internet software
- adequate financial resources to maintain a home Internet account, or access through their place of employment
- physical access to the Internet through a telephone line
- the inclination to use the Internet and to participate in research[19]

It is important for researchers to determine whether the Internet is the appropriate venue to access the necessary samples for certain types of research, such as surveys or qualitative studies. Otherwise, the danger exists that convenience and cost will dictate a sample and that as a result, it will be biased.

Ethical Concerns Related to Online Research Involving Human Subjects

Just as copyright and fair use laws dictate the use of online information sources, ethical principles of research also apply. Two major areas that demand vigilance on the part of researchers who study human subjects are confidentiality and informed consent.

The protected rights of research subjects have been codified into laws and codes of professional ethics. Violating these rights puts the researcher at risk of incurring not only professional sanctions but also legal ones. At the heart of such protection is informed consent. The fundamental ethical principle underlying informed consent is respect for subjects' autonomy: their right to make an informed decision about whether or not to participate in research based upon their understanding of the procedures, risks, and benefits.

Confidentiality around the subjects and their responses is another hallmark of ethical research. Challenges to confidentiality arise in online research when identifying information on the subjects and/or their responses is published on any type of online forum. There are obviously no guarantees that all forum users will be professionals who honor professional codes of ethics. E-mail presents similar concerns, as there is no way to ensure that the person accessing the e-mail is indeed the research subject. Opportunities for research abound on the Internet; many individuals openly discuss personal information in public forums such as chat rooms or newsgroups, some of which may be of interest to researchers. But there are reports of some researchers who have opportunistically exploited this situation, conducting naturalistic studies by observing a support mailing list or newsgroup.[20] This kind of research is a clear violation of the informed consent rule guiding professionals who engage in responsible human subjects research.

Finding and Accessing Online Information

The task of searching for information on the Internet may initially appear to be daunting, especially given that Internet traffic is doubling every hundred days and more than 100 million people are now online.[21] Fortunately, tools for searching the Internet allow users to quickly locate and access the data they need. These include (1) search engines, (2) subject directory guides, and (3) meta–search engines. The ease with which users can engage in an Internet search is enhanced by an understanding of the differences among these tools.

- *Search engines* collect and index all of the online data. They are easy to use, and the information is returned ranked by percentage of relevancy to the search topic. There are many search engines; a few well-known ones are AltaVista (http://www.altavista.digital.com/), Excite (http://www.excite.com/), HotBot (http://www.hotbot.com/), and Lycos (http://www.Lycos.com/). One drawback of search engines is that all online data are included and indexed, thereby forcing the user to sort through mounds of irrelevant responses. Without a specific search concept and words, search engines may not be an efficient way to locate information.[22]

- *Subject directory guides* are helpful when the user knows the broad topic but has not yet decided a narrower subtopic. The information obtained will be an index of the World Wide Web's contents by subject category, with the results provided in a subject directory. Information found in this type of search tool reflects efforts by editors who have searched for information and reviewed its contents. As with search engines, information retrieved by this search will be ranked by percentage of relevancy. Because of editorial review of all of the material in these databases, the user will obtain more highly relevant responses than search engines provide. There will also be a smaller quantity of information available, which limits the total number of responses. Examples of subject guides include the Library of Congress World Wide Web home page (http://lcweb.loc, gov), the Argus Clearinghouse (http://www.clearinghouse.net/searching/find.html), Mental Health Net (http://www.cmhc.com/), Yahoo! (http://www.yahoo.com/), and Medical Matrix (http://www.medmatrix.org/Spages/Psychiatry.asp).

- *Meta–search engines* inquire about your search across all the other online search engines. While this search yields a vast amount of information, the advantage of meta–search engines is that they will collate the results, remove duplications, remove links that are outdated or no longer valid, and then rank order the results. Examples of meta–search engines include Metacrawler (http://www.metacrawler.com/), SavvySearch (http://www.cs.colostate.edu/~dreiling/smartform.html), and Inference Find (http://m5.inference.com/ifind/).

Each type of search engine has advantages and disadvantages. It is helpful to remember that new information is being constantly added to the Internet. Because of the large volume of information being generated and the time it takes to synthesize, review and index it, there will be a time lag until information is available to these engines.

Citing and Documenting Information Obtained Online

Correct citation of sources is as important for online information as it is for print references. Moreover, intellectual property rights (copyright and trademark laws) apply to online material in almost the same way as to printed material. Electronic information technologies may have transformed the movement of information, but they have not changed our prior concepts of intellectual property ownership. Copyright and trademark laws are considered fully adequate for defining property boundaries in cyberspace, with small adjustments being made to accommodate the new technologies. Over the past 100 years, intellectual property laws have been revised in response to changes in business, society, and technology. These copyright laws now cover online public messages, collections of messages called message threads, e-mail, computer program files, text files, image files, sound and MIDI files, and electronic databases and trademarks. Shareware, freeware, and public domain software are the only types of software that can move through online systems and networks without potentially violating anyone's copyrights.[23] In short, when writing reports or research papers, carefully cite online sources in order to avoid plagiarism.

Evaluating Reliable and Legitimate Internet Sources

We all are familiar with the sayings "caveat emptor" and "don't believe everything you read." These timeless warnings certainly apply to information obtained online. The following are important to keep in mind.

- The Internet is home to an abundance of bogus "professionals" and websites with information of unknown validity. Obviously, information obtained from these sources is questionable and should not be cited. Because of its speed, the Internet is the perfect vehicle for propagating unfounded rumors.
- Certain types of legal or technical information obtained online may be inappropriate because the website or the person giving out the information is in a different country and subject to different jurisdictions.[24]
- The quality of online information varies widely, from the most up-to-date research from leading policy institutes to out-of-date or inaccurate research.
- The Internet poses great challenges to human service professionals and society at large because of the mismatch between the speed with which new data can be disseminated and the length of time required for careful peer review.[25]

Efforts are currently under way to mitigate the potential liabilities arising from online infor-

mation. One strategy is to develop innovative yet peer-reviewed approaches to Internet publishing. As well, providing Internet researchers with guidance on the best available sources of relevant information may help prevent their utilizing inaccurate or outdated sources.

Electronic Journals: An Increasingly Popular Venue

Online journals are becoming increasingly popular. There are two types: the print journals with a website and the electronic journal that has no print counterpart.[26] Increasingly, online journals are seen as a way to address problems that libraries are having with their print journal collections—such as storage, preservation, accessibility, and cost. In addition, having journals available online facilitates research by making the materials available electronically regardless of business or academic schedules. One major project that has facilitated the online availability of journals is Journal Storage (JSTOR), a not-for-profit organization of approximately 200 libraries, including those of Columbia, Harvard, Princeton, and Yale. JSTOR (http://www.jstor.org/about) has digitalized all or some of more than 52 core journal titles in 12 disciplines, including economics, political science, sociology, higher education, Asian studies, and anthropology.

Online Publishing

As with any research endeavor, online information must meet the criteria for validity and reliability. The fact that information is distributed electronically does not make it any less subject to these standards. These are important concepts to keep in mind when considering whether to publish online. For example, publishing research or an article on an Internet mailing list does not carry any formal academic recognition. Peer-reviewed journals that appear in print are still considered the venue in which to achieve such distinction. However, if you have published a report electronically, many print journals will not subsequently accept it, because prior "publication" has already occurred. For policy analysts who need to formally document their publications, then, online publishing may be a problem.

Fortunately, there are a growing number of legitimate online publications. One way to discern whether an online journal is peer reviewed and legitimate is to see whether there is a masthead listing an editor, an editorial board, and guidelines for submission and review. Also, an online journal that is a professional endeavor will have been issued an International Standard Serial Number (ISSN) through the Library of Congress or other official agency.[27]

In summary, the Internet facilitates a wide range of research activities. These range from conducting literature searches to publishing in online journals. Search tools available to help the researcher locate information include search engines, subject directory guides, and meta–search engines. Each kind of tool has unique features that support varying types of research activities, from very broad to specific information searches. Just as we adopt a critical stance when evaluating the credibility and quality of print sources, it is important to maintain a critical perspective when evaluating information obtained online.

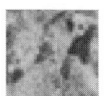 # Conclusion

The emergence of the information superhighway is transforming U.S. society in manifold ways. For example, the ability to enjoy the full rights of citizenship is rapidly being tied to the ability to utilize information technology. Access to legislators and governmental bodies, to the most up-to-date information, and even to the best deals on goods and services is becoming increasingly dependent on the ability to employ technology. Unfortunately, many Americans, especially poor people, are being left behind. The gap between computer users and nonusers is called the digital divide. The question, however, remains whether the digital divide is a new social phenomenon that requires new approaches or whether it is simply another manifestation of poverty. Regardless, the reality is that a large segment of U.S. society is not sharing in the technological advances and will find it increasingly difficult to obtain well-paying employment in the new global marketplace.

The rules of engagement in the marketplace of ideas have changed almost overnight. The world of cyberspace that includes Internet access, faxes, photo transmittal services, and online reference libraries is providing direct information access to millions of homes and educational institutions worldwide. The more farsighted progressive organizations are actively using these new technologies in exciting and innovative ways. But it is not surprising that hate groups, long frustrated by the inability to deliver their message in a consistent and attractive format, have also rushed to embrace the new technologies. In fact, the Southern Poverty Law Center counts more than 400 hate-related Internet sites.[28] With unlimited access to the Internet, the scope of hate-group activities is rapidly expanding.

What can be done to arrest the growth of online hate groups? The Internet currently provides stealth technology for hatemongers. Although in the United States hateful speech is "protected speech," there is no reason why a recipient of an unsolicited and threatening message (including nonthreatening spam e-mail) coming from the superhighway should not have the right to instantly know the source of the message. Accountability should replace anonymity as the operative principle.

Regardless of the inherent problems in the new information age, it has become a permanent fixture of this country's social landscape. Therefore, social policy analysts must learn not only how to master the new technologies but how to use them to their fullest potential. One important avenue for utilizing the Internet and its associated technologies is through social policy research.

Discussion Questions

1. Does the digital divide exist? Why?
2. How can the digital divide be narrowed? What are some realistic policy strategies that could be used to narrow the divide?
3. How can community organizations and other progressive groups best use the Internet? Give specific examples of how organizations can make optimal use of this technology.

4. Because of its long reach and low costs, the Internet is the perfect breeding ground for the growth of hate groups. Should legislative controls be placed on the Internet to limit its use by hate groups?
5. Describe the value of the Internet in policy research. What are some of its strengths and possible pitfalls?

 # Notes

1. S. Berglund, "Legal Issues in Healthcare and the Internet," *Medicomputer Perspective: Supplement to Computers & Medicine* 26, no. 1 (1997), pp. 16–21.
2. L. Sproull and S. Faraj, "Atheism, Sex, and Databases: The Net as a Social Technology," in B. Kahin and J. Keller (eds.), *Public Access to the Internet* (Cambridge, MA: MIT Press, 1995), pp. 62–81; J. Grohol, "Best Practices in E-Therapy: Confidentiality & Privacy." Retrieved 1999, from the World Wide Web: http://www.ismho.org/issues/99901.htm; Howard Karger and Joanne Levine, *The Internet and Technology for the Human Services* (New York: Addison Wesley Longman, 1999).
3. National Telecommunications and Information Administration, "Fact Sheet: Americans Using Internet for Many Tasks," in *Falling Through the Net: Defining the Digital Divide.* Retrieved July 1999 from the World Wide Web: http://www.ntia.doc.gov/ntiahome/ digitaldivide/factsheets/usage.htm
4. Ibid.
5. Ekaterina Walsh, Shelley Morrisette, and Nicky Maraganore, "The Digital Melting Pot," *The Forrester Review.* Retrieved March 3, 1999, from the World Wide Web: http://www. forrester.com/ER/Research/Brief/Excerpt/ 0,1317,5703,FF.html

6. PowerUP, "About the Digital Divide." Retrieved 2000 from the World Wide Web: http://www.powerup.org/digitaldivide.html
7. Teresa E. Anderson and Alan Melchior, "Assessing Telecommunications Technology as a Tool for Urban Community Building," *The Journal of Urban Technology* 3, no. 1 (1995), pp. 101–116.
8. Association of Community Organizations for Reform Now (ACORN). Retrieved 2000 from the World Wide Web: http://www.acorn.org.
9. We will not provide the URL addresses of the websites discussed in this section, as we don't want to inadvertently promote traffic to these sites. If readers want to explore these hate sites they can be accessed through HateWatch (a group that monitors the online activity of hate groups) at http://www.hatewatch.org
10. Marisol Bello, "Hate Groups Use Internet to Attract Followers," *Tribune-Review.* Retrieved May 7, 2000, from the World Wide Web: http://www.triblive.com/news/rhat0507.html
11. Quoted in Bello, "Hate Groups."
12. Southern Poverty Law Center. Retrieved 2000 from the World Wide Web: http://www.splc.org
13. The examination of white power groups is complicated because of the many different factions, some of which are in competition with others. Some groups are highly violent, whereas others (at least on the surface)

disavow violence. A good discussion of the differences among white power groups is offered
by the Southern Poverty Law Center
(http://www/splc.org)

14. HateWatch. Retrieved 2000 from the World
    Wide Web: http://www.hatewatch.org

15. Quoted in Bello, "Hate Groups."

16. Carol J. Williams, "Cyber-Hate Panelists Duel
    over Line between Free Speech, Racism. Ger-
    many: A Media Giant Learns That Laws
    against Extremism Aren't Stopping Misuse of
    the Internetgame," *Los Angeles Times* (June 27,
    2000), p. 6.

17. Quoted in Williams, "Cyber-Hate Panelists."

18. R. Lakeman, "Using the Internet for Data Col-
    lection in Nursing Research," *Computers in
    Nursing* 15, no. 5 (1997), pp. 269–275.

19. Ibid.

20. Grohol, "Best Practices in E-Therapy: Confi-
    dentiality & Privacy."

21. E. Weise, "Net Use Doubling Every 100 Days,"
    USA Today (April 16, 1998), p 6.

22. J. Yaffe, *Quick Guide to the Internet for Social
    Work* (Needham Heights, MA: Allyn & Bacon,
    1998).

23. L. Rose, *Netlaw: Your Rights in the Online
    World* (Berkeley: McGraw-Hill, 1995).

24. P. Parkin and D. Stretch, "Facilities on the
    Internet May Be Abused," *British Medical
    Journal* 313, no. 4 (November 11, 1997),
    pp. 67–69.

25. E. Coiera, "The Internet's Challenge to Health
    Care Provision," *British Medical Journal* 312,
    no. 3–4 (January 6, 1996), pp. 8–16.

26. J. Grohol, *The Insider's Guide to Mental Health
    Resources Online* (NY: Guilford Press, 1997).

27. Ibid.

28. The Southern Poverty Law Center. Retrieved
    2000 from the World Wide Web: http://
    www.splc.org

chapter 4

Discrimination in American Society

Discrimination and poverty are inextricably linked in the fabric of social welfare in the United States. Economic, social, and political discrimination often leads to poverty for its most vulnerable victims; poverty, in turn, results in the need for the creation of income maintenance and other programs. Realizing that discrimination encourages poverty, some policymakers have attempted to address this cycle of misery by attacking discrimination. These policymakers hope that when discriminatory practices and attitudes are curtailed, vulnerable populations will be given equal opportunities for achievement and success. This chapter probes discrimination based on race, gender, sexual orientation, disability, and age.

Discrimination

The causes of discrimination in U.S. society are complex. A range of literature explores the motives for discrimination. Broken down, the main theories fall into three broad categories: psychological, normative–cultural, and economic.

Psychological interpretations attempt to explain discrimination in terms of intrapsychic variables.[1] A theory called the frustration–aggression hypothesis, formulated by J. Dollard, maintains that discrimination is a form of aggression that is activated when individual needs become frustrated.[2] According to Dollard, when people cannot direct their aggression at the real sources of their rage, they seek a substitute target. Thus, relatively weak minority groups become an easy and safe target for the aggression and frustration of slightly stronger discontented groups. For example, poor whites have often been thought one of the more outwardly racist groups in Southern society. Exploited by the rigid economic and social class system of the old South, they often focused their rage on African Americans, a group even weaker than themselves. African Americans

therefore served a twin function for poor whites: On the one hand, they formed a lower socioeconomic group, making poor whites feel better about their own standing; on the other, they functioned as a scapegoat for the frustrations of poor whites. Women, racial minorities, homosexuals, and other disenfranchised groups can serve the same function for those on a slightly higher social rung.

Another psychological approach, the "authoritarian personality" theory developed by Theodore Adorno and other psychoanalytic authors, posited that discriminatory behavior is determined by personality traits that involve a reaction to authority.[3] Persons who exhibit the traits of irrationality, rigidity, conformity, xenophobia, and so forth are more likely to discriminate against minorities than are people lacking those traits. Other authors, such as Wilhelm Reich, argued that discriminatory attitudes arise from a sense of insecurity, self-hatred, deepseated fears, and unresolved childhood needs and frustrations.[4]

The normative–cultural explanation suggests that individuals hold prejudicial attitudes because of their socialization. That is, through both overt and covert messages, a society teaches discrimination and rewards those who conform to prevailing attitudes and behaviors. Because of strong societal pressures to conform to established norms, resistance to discriminatory practices becomes difficult.[5] For example, special opprobrium in the old South was reserved for liberal whites who broke the norms governing interactions with African Americans. Often, societies are more tolerant of outsiders who break the norms than they are of insiders who "betray" the group. This theory suggests that as social and institutional norms supporting discriminatory practices change, individual attitudes should follow suit.

Among economic approaches, one argument contends that dominant groups discriminate in order to maintain their economic and political advantages. This theory is based on the belief that relative group advantages are gained from discrimination. For example, male workers may discriminate against female workers because they perceive them as encroaching on their employment prospects. These males may fear that they will be replaced by a female worker who will accept lower wages. And employers themselves may uphold discriminatory attitudes because as long as women workers are stigmatized, they will command a lower salary and thereby serve as a cheap labor pool. In that sense, the increasing racial tensions in U.S. society can be understood partly as reflecting the job advancements made by minority groups: Whites may fear losing employment opportunities, upward mobility, or even their jobs.

A more Marxian economic analysis sees sexism, racism, homophobia, and other forms of discrimination as economically useful to the capitalist class. According to Marxists, capitalism requires a marginal and unskilled labor pool willing to take jobs refused by economically enfranchised groups. Specifically, industrialization requires a mobile labor force willing to relocate freely for available employment. In this framework, discrimination has helped force disenfranchised groups to relocate (usually westward) to flee persecution based on ethnic, religious, or racial differences. There are various levels of stigma, and not all out-groups experience it with the same intensity. In the extreme, however, stigma can reduce the economic currency of whole populations and thereby create an underclass forced to take whatever jobs are available at whatever wages are offered. By threatening relatively well-paid workers with replacement by a stigmatized group, employers are able to force wage concessions. Also, by manipulating stigmatized groups against each other, employers can keep the wage demands of these groups relatively low. Moreover, because stigmatized groups are often employed in unstable jobs, they can be moved around as the economy requires it. Paradoxically, the lowered economic currency of disenfranchised groups increases their value to the economic order. To put it bluntly, societal discrimination determines who will flip the burgers and supersize the drinks.

To maintain an air of legitimacy, discrimination must have moral, social, and theological

underpinnings. To that end, some have used the Bible to explain the inferiority of women, the "sin" of homosexuality, and the necessity of separating the races. To augment or replace biblical interpretations, spurious scientific explanations have been developed that are rooted in quasi-psychoanalytic theory, Social Darwinism, and pseudoanthropological "insights" concerning the attributes of stigmatized groups. For example, some people maintain that menstrual cycles cause severe mood swings that make women incapable of holding positions of power. Others believe that African Americans are descended from Ham and have therefore committed biblical sins that justify discrimination. Some members of the Ku Klux Klan claim that African Americans are racially inferior; they argue on the basis of theories grounded in shaky anthropological research undergirded by even more dubious intelligence testing. Some white supremacist groups believe that Jews are descendants of Satan and that the "true Israelites" (in the form of the lost tribes of Israel) are Aryans. These stereotypes have little to do with reality. Moreover, it is difficult to imagine that marginalized skinheads or those living in white supremacist enclaves are the hope of the white race or the "true Israelites." Without the legitimation offered by moral, religious, social, and "scientific" sources, discrimination is devoid of social validity and becomes naked exploitation.

Social stigma and discrimination can lead to the transformation of disenfranchised groups into a lower socioeconomic class. Alternatively, as in the case of gays, lesbians, and the aged, social stigma and discrimination can result in social marginalization without triggering statistically observable economic discrimination. For example, although the individual incomes of gays and lesbians (and the assets of the elderly) are higher than the national averages, people in these groups often experience economic discrimination in the form of constricted career choices, including forced occupational clustering, limited access to upper managerial positions, discrimination in hiring practices, forced retirement, and so forth. In addition, discrimination can also turn violent. For example, from

1990 to 1996 there were more than 243 attacks against religious institutions—black churches and white churches, synagogues and mosques. About 78 percent of all suspicious black church fires during that period occurred in the Southeast. In response, Congress passed the Church Arson Prevention Act of 1996, which broadened the ability of the federal government to seek criminal penalties in cases involving vandalism or destruction of religious buildings.

The following sections will examine some core components of discrimination and social stigma, including racism, sexism, homophobia, ageism, and discrimination against people with disabilities.

Racism

For purposes of analysis, U.S. society is often divided between whites and people of color. Today, however, clumping white Americans into a single category is as misleading as not understanding the important cultural differences among people of color. For example, in 1850 it was relatively easy to describe white Americans; in all probability they were Protestant and of Anglo-Saxon or Teutonic background. But after the Civil War vast numbers of immigrants began to arrive from southern and central Europe. They were not Protestant, they were not Anglo-Saxon, and they had different languages and cultures from those who preceded them. It is now difficult to describe a white American. About 200 million Americans can trace at least some of their ancestry back to the following groups (in descending size order): English, German, Irish, French, Italian, Scottish, Polish, Dutch, Swedish, Norwegian, Russian, Czech, Slovakian, Hungarian, Welsh, Danish, and Portuguese.[6] In addition, there are many white Americans of Hispanic background. Although all of these white groups have generally assimilated into American life, many still maintain some of the characteristics that have contributed to the particular attributes

of white American society. It is not surprising that the field of white studies is becoming popular at schools such as the University of California at Berkeley, Northwestern University, Harvard University, and the University of Massachusetts.[7]

The term **racism** refers to discrimination against and prejudicial treatment of a racially different minority group. This prejudicial treatment may take the form of differential hiring and firing practices and promotions, differential resource allocations in health care and education, a two-tier structure in transportation systems, segregation in housing policies, discriminatory behavior of judicial and law enforcement agencies, and/or stereotypical and prejudicial media images. A pattern of racial discrimination that is strongly entrenched in a society is called institutional racism.

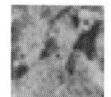

Discrimination against African Americans

The nation's African American population was estimated in 1999 at 34.9 million, or 13 percent of the total population. Between 1990 and 1999 the African American population increased by 4.4 million people, or 14 percent; meanwhile, the total U.S. population grew by 10 percent. According to projections, the African American population may increase to 59 million by 2050, a 70 percent rise. The black population is young, with almost 33 percent under age 18 in 1999. This compares with 24 percent of the white population. In 1998, the median African American age was 30, 5 years younger than for the U.S. population as a whole. Conversely, 8 percent of African Americans were 65 years old and over, versus 14 percent of whites.[8]

African Americans are concentrated in the South (55 percent resided there in 1999). They are also more likely to live in metro areas (86 percent versus 78 percent for whites). More than 55 percent of African Americans live in central cities. The 10 states with the largest African American populations in 1998 were New York (3.2 million); California (2.5 million); Texas (2.4 million); Florida (2.3 million); Georgia (2.2 million); Illinois (1.8 million); North Carolina (1.7 million); and Maryland, Louisiana, and Michigan (1.4 million each).[9]

African American Gains

Many African Americans have not only improved their socioeconomic position in recent years, but have done so at a relatively faster rate than whites. The most noticeable gains have occurred in the areas of professional employment, incomes (including two-earner family incomes), higher education, and home ownership. The following illustrates some of the advances.

African Americans in Poverty. The number of poor African Americans dropped from 9.7 million in 1996 to 9.1 million in 1997, while their poverty rate decreased from 28.4 to 26.5 percent. For African American families, the number and percentage in poverty fell from 2.2 million to 2.0 million and from 26.1 to 23.6 percent, respectively, from 1996 to 1997. African Americans accounted for 60 percent of the decline in the number of poor persons in the United States between 1996 and 1997. Similarly, about 400,000 fewer families were poor in 1997 than in 1996, and more than half of families rising out of poverty were African American. African American families with a female head of household and no husband present experienced a significant drop in both the number and percentage of families who were poor: 1.6 million and 39.8 percent in 1997, down from 1.7 million and 43.7 percent in 1996. Although the 1998 poverty rate for African Americans was 26.1 percent (or 9.1 million people), it remained statistically unchanged from 1997 and represented the lowest rate since the Census Bureau began collecting poverty data in 1959.[10]

Black Family Income. The typical black family income in 1995 was $3,000 more than in 1992.[11] In that year, African Americans were the only group whose inflation-adjusted median income exceeded that of 1989, the year before the last recession. In 1995 black married couples earned 87 percent as much as white married couples, up from 79 percent in 1989.[12] For two-earner black couples between 24 and 35, average annual income was less than $3,000 lower than that of white couples, a significant improvement over earlier decades. The black median household income in 1998 was $25,351, remaining at an all-time high first reached in 1997. **Per capita income** increased 3.3 percent between 1997 and 1998, to $12,957. Nearly one-third (28 percent) of African American families reported total money income in 1998 of $50,000 or more; for African American married-couple families, that percentage was 48 percent.

Black Businesses. Black businesses increased in number 46 percent (from 424,165 to 620,912) between 1987 and 1992. (The nation's total number of firms increased only 26 percent in that same period.) Receipts for black firms increased by 63 percent, from $20 to $32 billion.[13]

African American Employment. The number of African Americans in technical, professional, and managerial positions increased in number 57 percent from 1973 to 1982. By 1999 17 percent of African American men and 24 percent of women worked in managerial and professional specialty occupations.

Home Ownership. Blacks recorded a 47 percent increase in home ownership during the 1970s compared to 30 percent for whites.[14] By 1999 46 percent of black households owned their own homes, an increase of 5 percent since 1995.

Education. African American youngsters recorded a substantial gain in SAT scores from 1976 to 1989, scoring 19 percent higher in verbal and 32 percent higher in math scores. By comparison, white SAT scores dropped by 5 and 2 percent, respectively.[15] In 1998 83 percent of blacks aged 25 to 29 were high school graduates. There is now no statistical difference in high school graduation rates between the two racial groups. By 1999 about 77 percent of African Americans 25 years old and over had at least a high school education; about 15 percent had at least a bachelor's degree. More than 800,000 African Americans have an advanced degree. A slightly higher percentage of black women than men aged 25 and over have earned at least a bachelor's degree (16 percent versus 14 percent). The number of African Americans under 35 enrolled in college in 1998 (1.7 million) was 50 percent higher than the number enrolled a decade earlier.

Homicide Rates. Between 1985 and 1995, the homicide rate for African Americans dropped by 17 percent.[16]

The "Diswelfare" of African Americans

Despite these relative improvements, millions of African Americans did not experience progress during the 1990s; instead, they experienced a significant erosion in living standards. The effects of discrimination are illustrated by key socioeconomic indicators in the areas of poverty, family structure, African American businesses, labor force participation and income, crime, housing, health, education, and welfare dependency.

Poverty. Even with the significant decrease in black poverty rates, these rates continue to be much higher than for non-Hispanic whites. In 1997 some 8.6 percent of whites were poor, a rate less than one-third that for blacks. Similarly, median household income in 1997 was more than 50 percent higher for non-Hispanic whites than for blacks. The 1997 poverty rate remained high among blacks in a year in which the national unemployment rate averaged 4.9 percent, its lowest level in 24 years. Moreover, the black poverty rate in 1997 was at about the same level as it was in 1987 through 1989, years in which unemployment averaged between 5.3 and 6.2 percent. The 1997 poverty rate was substantially higher than the poverty rates for every year of the 1970s, even though the unemployment rate was close to or above 6 percent for more than half of the 1970s. Although poverty among black children fell in

1997 to its lowest level in decades (40 percent), the rate remains high.[17]

Family Structure. In 1999 47 percent of African American families were married couples, 45 percent were single female–headed households, and 8 percent were households headed by men only. African American families are larger than non-Hispanic white families: Sixteen percent had five or more members, in contrast to 11 percent of white families. (Larger family sizes result in lower per capita income.) Four million African American children (36 percent) resided with both parents in 1998. In 1997 36 percent (1.4 million) of all children living in a grandparent's home were African American.[18]

African American Businesses. As mentioned earlier, black-owned businesses grew 46 percent between 1987 and 1992, and business receipts grew at the same rate as for white firms. However, receipts in black-owned businesses constituted only about 1 percent of total U.S. business receipts in 1992. Receipts for black-owned firms averaged $52,000 per firm, compared with $193,000 for all U.S. firms. Fifty-six percent of black-owned firms had receipts of under $10,000, and less than 1 percent had receipts of $1 million or more.[19]

Labor Force Participation and Income. Discrimination continues in the areas of employment and wages. Although laws and regulations addressing racial discrimination in employment have had some success, they have not adequately prevented widespread discrimination against African Americans. The Urban Institute compared the experiences of comparable African American and white male job seekers. Using hiring audits, the study found that black applicants were subject to unfavorable treatment during the application process 20 percent of the time, compared with 7% for white applicants. Unfavorable treatment included (1) not advancing to the next level of the hiring process; (2) encountering more questions or resistance before receiving an application form; (3) being steered toward less desirable positions than white counterparts; (4) being forced to wait longer for interviews; (5) receiving only cursory interviews; (6) hearing discouraging or derogatory remarks; and (7) being turned down for a position when it was offered to a white applicant.[20]

Despite the narrowing of some important economic indicators, the unemployment rate for blacks is still more than twice that of whites. Although unemployment among black men fell in 1997 to 8.6 percent, the lowest in 23 years, it was still twice the jobless rate for white men (about 4.4 percent).[21]

Discrimination carries into income. Not surprisingly, the lowest income gap is found between blacks and whites without a high school diploma. The more education people attain, the greater the income gap. In 1997 white males with master's degrees earned $70,706 a year; African American males, $42,125. This $28,500 difference translates into a salary differential of almost 70 percent. In varying degrees, the same salary gap is evident between minority and white women. (See Table 4.1.)

Jared Bernstein offers several explanations for the African American wage gap. These include discrimination in employment (aided by the lax enforcement of antidiscrimination laws); more frequent employment in vulnerable sectors of the labor economy; a combination of regional,

TABLE 4.1 ■ 1997 Salary and Educational Attainment for Workers over Age 25

	ALL RACES		WHITE	
	Men	*Women*	*Men*	*Women*
No H. S. Diploma	$21,992	$15,203	$22,374	$15,293
H. S. Graduate	30,665	21,291	31,195	21,602
Some College	36,677	27,206	37,164	27,195
Assoc. Arts Degree	46,255	33,432	47,220	33,896
B.A. Degree	57,553	41,856	60,081	41,884
Master's Degree	70,706	50,758	71,423	52,653
Ph.D./Prof. Degree	78,290	54,528	80,951	60,003
	BLACK		HISPANIC	
	Men	*Women*	*Men*	*Women*
No H. S. Diploma	$19,033	$14,944	$17,674	$12,886
H. S. Graduate	25,790	19,993	24,021	19,247
Some College	30,249	23,769	29,569	22,932
Assoc. Arts Degree	31,474	26,758	30,090	24,322
B.A. Degree	35,762	31,010	37,725	31,993
Master's Degree	42,125	40,589	44,702	*NA
Ph.D./Prof. Degree	NA	NA	NA	NA

*NA: Sample size too small for accurate calculation.

Source: American Council on Education (ACE), Division of Governmental and Public Affairs, "ACE Fact Sheet on Higher Education" (Washington, DC: American Council on Education, November 2, 1999).

industrial, and occupational choices; lower rates of unionization in the labor market; and the general erosion of worker rights.[22] Another explanation suggests that as middle-class African Americans advance, greater unemployment occurs among those with less education and skills. But this explanation does not address the large African American/white unemployment differential among college-educated men, a disparity that is greater in central cities of the East and North. According to Franklin Wilson, the cause of this discrepancy can be found in two factors: (1) the decline during the 1980s in the number of jobs traditionally filled by college-educated African American men (e.g., public sector jobs dealing with affirmative action, social welfare, and criminal justice); and (2) the inability of educated African Americans to penetrate the professional/technical occupations that entail managerial or supervisory responsibilities. Not surprisingly, these positions usually involve higher salaries and more job security.[23] Also, personnel cutbacks in federal and state governments are likely to exacerbate the income differential of African Americans, because one of the major opportunities for their employment has been in the governmental sector. Regardless of the causes, African Americans continue to earn less than whites, irrespective of household composition, education, region, or religion.

Crime. Black males (28.5 percent) are about six times more likely than whites (4.4 percent) to be incarcerated during their lifetime. Among women, 3.6 percent of blacks and 0.5 percent of whites will enter prison at least once. Based on current rates of incarceration, an estimated 7.9 percent of black males (compared to 0.7 percent of white males) will enter state or federal prison before they reach age 20, and 21.4 percent of black males (versus 1.4 percent of white males) will be incarcerated before age 30. Some important factors influence these numbers. About 62 percent of first-time offenders admitted to federal prison and 31.1 percent of those admitted to state prison are sentenced because of drug offenses. About 12 percent of drug users are black, but blacks make up nearly 50 percent of all drug

possession arrests in the United States.[24] Moreover, of the 3,219 prisoners on death row in 1996, 42 percent (1,384) were black. Given that African Americans make up only 13 percent of the U.S. population as a whole, blacks were overrepresented on death row by more than three times their number in the population.[25]

Although the homicide rate for males in the United States has fallen significantly in recent years, the rate remains unacceptably high. For African American males, the probability of being murdered before age 45 in 1995 was 2.21 percent, compared to 0.29 percent for white males. In Washington, D.C., 1 in 12 black 15-year-old males (about 8 percent) will be murdered before age 45. By comparison, the death rate for U.S. soldiers serving in the military during World War II was 2.5 percent; during World War I, it was 2.4 percent; and during the Vietnam War, 1.2 percent.[26]

Housing. Housing patterns reflect the economic gulf between African Americans and whites. Minority (African American, Hispanic, and Native American) households are both poorer and more likely to be renters than white households. This encourages a home ownership rate of only 46 percent for African Americans compared to about 70 percent for non-Hispanic whites.[27] In 1995, 78 percent of poor black renters paid more than 30 percent of their income for housing; 54 percent paid more than 50 percent. Only 49 percent of poor black households received housing assistance. Nineteen percent of poor black families live in physically deficient housing (e.g., in substandard structures, or in overcrowded or doubled-up housing), and 21 percent of poor black households have affordability problems *and* live in physically deficient housing.[28]

Health. The effects of racism can also be seen in health issues. The black infant mortality rate in the United States in 1997 was 13.7 per 1,000 live births, more than twice that of whites (6.0 deaths). Taken by itself, the U.S. black infant mortality rate ranks high internationally (see Table 4.2). The rate of sudden infant death syndrome (SIDS) among African Americans was 143.2 deaths per 100,000 live infant births in

TABLE 4.2 ▪ Infant Mortality Rates (Deaths per 1,000 Live Births) and Ranks: Selected Countries, 1994

RANK	COUNTRY	RATE	RANK	COUNTRY	RATE
1	Japan	4.3	20	Spain	6.7
2	Singapore	4.3	21	New Zealand	7.2
3	Hong Kong	4.3	22	Israel	7.8
4	Sweden	4.5	23	Greece	7.9
5	Finland	4.7	24	Czech Republic	8.0
6	Switzerland	5.1	*	U.S. (overall)	8.0
7	Norway	5.2	25	Portugal	8.1
8	Denmark	5.5	26	Belgium	8.2
9	Germany	5.6	*	U.S. (Native American)	8.7
10	Netherlands	5.6	27	Cuba	9.4
11	Ireland	5.9	28	Slovakia	11.2
*	U.S. (white only)	6.0	29	Puerto Rico	11.5
12	Australia	6.1	30	Hungary	11.6
13	Northern Ireland	6.1	31	Chile	12.0
14	England & Wales	6.2	32	Kuwait	12.7
15	Scotland	6.2	33	Costa Rica	13.7
16	Austria	6.3	*	U.S. (black only)	13.7
17	Canada	6.3	34	Poland	15.1
18	France	6.5	35	Bulgaria	16.3
19	Italy	6.6	36	Russian Federation	18.6

Sources: Adapted from March of Dimes, "Infant Mortality Rates and Ranks: Selected Countries, 1994." Retrieved 2000 from the World Wide Web: http://www.modimes.org/healthlibrary2/factsfigures/mortal.htm and Centers for Disease Control, Health Statistics, "Infant Mortality Rates Vary by Race and Ethnicity." Retrieved June 10, 2000, from the World Wide Web: http://www.cdc.gov/nchs/releases/99facts/99sheets/infmort.htm

1997 compared to 64.8 for whites. Blacks had a coronary death rate in 1997 of 136.2 per 100,000 compared to 97.7 for whites. The black death rate for strokes per 100,000 population in 1997 was almost double that of whites (42.5 versus 24.0). For HIV/AIDS the black infection rate in 1998 per 100,000 population was almost 10 times that for whites (84.7 compared to 9.9). The pediatric AIDS rate for African American children under age 14 in 1998 was 3.2 per 100,000, compared to 0.2 for white children.[29] Not sur-

prisingly, life expectancy is lower for African Americans. In 1996 black males had a life expectancy of 66.1 years compared to 73.9 years for white males. For African American women the life expectancy was 74.2 years compared to 79.7 years for white women.[30]

A major factor affecting infant mortality is low birth weight. Although the cause is unknown, low birth weight (less than 5.5 pounds) increases the chances of infant death during the first month by 40 percent.[31] In 1993, 7.2 percent of all babies in the United States were born at low birth weight; for African American babies it was 13.3 percent.[32] Moreover, less than half of all African American children in 1985 had been fully immunized against measles, rubella, diphtheria, polio, and mumps.[33]

Education. As a high school diploma becomes less valuable in the marketplace, only educational upgrading can protect workers' incomes. In fact, on the average, college graduates earn around 75 percent more than male high school graduates. As an example, between 1979 and 1987 the annual wage of a high school graduate fell 8.6 percent while the income of a college graduate rose by 9.2 percent.[34]

By 1997, continuing an upward trend in black educational attainment that began in 1940, there was no statistical difference in high school completion rates between African American and white students (around 86 percent). Although the high school dropout rate is now relatively low, it is still significant—because the failure to complete high school is strongly correlated with poverty. According to the American Public Human Services Association, in 1989 nearly half of all female heads of families and 60 percent of parents receiving welfare in 36 of the previous 60 months did not finish high school.[35] Furthermore, an estimated 85 percent of juveniles appearing in court are functionally illiterate.[36]

Although the same proportions of black and white students graduate from high school, college completion rates differ. In 1997, of the over-25 age group, about 25 percent of whites were college graduates (as were 42 percent of Asian and Pacific Islanders), but only 13 percent of African Americans completed college.[37] The strong correlation between higher education and higher salaries suggests that the disparity between African American and white college completion rates will have a long-term impact on the economic well-being of these groups. In addition, fewer minority college graduates have gone on to obtain advanced degrees. For example, in 1986–87 whites made up 81 percent of all undergraduates: They received 88 percent of the bachelor's degrees, 88 percent of the master's degrees, and 89 percent of all doctorates.

By contrast, African Americans accounted for 9 percent of all undergraduates but received only 6 percent of the bachelor's degrees, 5 percent of the master's degrees, and 4 percent of the doctorates.[38]

Welfare Dependency. Welfare dependency is another indicator of racism. Although African Americans make up only 13 percent of the U.S. population, they make up roughly 41 percent of all public assistance recipients, 35 percent of all food stamp recipients, 31 percent of Medicaid recipients, and 25 percent of SSI (Supplemental Security Income) beneficiaries.[39]

 # Hispanic Americans

Although the history of race relations in the United States is older than the nation itself, the issue is rising in importance with the coming of a "minority majority"—the name given by some to the changing demographics expected in U.S. society over the next 50 years. There are "two Americas." One is the aging, white society that is still found in smaller metropolitan areas, smaller towns and rural areas; the second is a younger, more multicultural society that is growing rapidly in the most visible cultural centers of the country.

The Demography of Hispanic Americans

There are approximately 31 million people of Hispanic origin living in the United States—close to 12 percent of the total population. The U.S. Census Bureau estimates that by the year 2005 Hispanics will constitute the largest minority group, at more than 13 percent of the total population). By 2050, one of every four Americans will be Hispanic. By comparison, the non-Hispanic white population now makes up about 72 percent of the total population; by 2050 it will represent just 53 percent. These demographic changes are already evident in urban centers such as Miami, New York, and Los Angeles. In

Los Angeles County, for example, Hispanics are already the largest ethnic group.[40]

The use of the umbrella term *Hispanic* masks a rich diversity within this group. U.S. Hispanics have roots in 22 different countries; their family histories are from Mexico, Puerto Rico, Cuba and other Caribbean islands, and Central and South America as well as the United States. Some 60 percent of Hispanics in the United States are more comfortable speaking Spanish, 20 percent speak mostly English, and nearly 20 percent speak both. And, although U.S. Latinos pump $300 billion into the U.S. economy, 40 percent of Latino children live in poverty. Of those living below the poverty line in 1996, nearly 28 percent were Mexican American, 33 percent were Puerto Ricans living on the U.S. mainland, 12.5 percent were Cuban Americans, and 19 percent were from Central and South America. These figures compare to 6.5 percent of people living below the poverty line who were whites and 26 percent who were African Americans.[41]

Because of the large number of undocumented workers coming from Central America and Mexico, the Hispanic population of the United States is difficult to accurately measure. Although some estimates of the number of undocumented workers in the United States (most of them from Spanish-speaking countries) are in the 12 million range, other researchers have estimated this population to be 3 to 6 million.[42] Nevertheless, it is known that the total Hispanic population is growing rapidly. For example, in the years 1987–94 this population grew by 96 percent.[43] The Hispanic population is also geographically concentrated, with 65 percent living in just three states: California, Texas, and New York. Eighty-eight percent of all Latinos live in nine states, and 88 percent live in urban areas (a figure 13 percent higher than the national average).[44]

Hispanic Poverty and Income

The poverty status of Hispanics worsened in the 1980s and 1990s in relation to other groups, including African Americans. For example, the overall poverty rate for African Americans declined slightly from 1992 (33 percent) to 1995 (29.3 percent); during those same years the poverty rate for Hispanics rose to 30.3 percent, surpassing the black poverty rate for the first time.[45] The median household net worth for Latino households between 1995 and 1998 fell 24 percent, from $12,170 in 1995 to $9,200 in 1998. This drop may have been a result of the continuing immigration of poor and unskilled workers.

In 1979 28 percent of Hispanic children were below the poverty line; by 1990 that number had risen to 38 percent (well over twice the 16 percent poverty rate for white children) and was still rising. By 1990 some 2.8 million Hispanic children were living in poverty, the highest level ever recorded since the Census Bureau began to keep data on Latinos in 1973.[46] The high poverty rate for children is clearly correlated with the 48 percent of Hispanic female-headed families that fell below the poverty line in 1990, a number significantly higher than the 25 percent of non-Hispanic white female-headed families in this category, and slightly above the 47 percent of African American female-headed families in poverty.[47]

The median earnings of Hispanic males are also low. In 1988 they were $21,697, lower than the earnings of African Americans ($23,374). (Almost the same wage differential existed between Hispanic and African American women— $16,860 versus $17,811.) These earnings levels represented a fall in relative income for both Hispanic men and women; in 1978 Hispanics had earned slightly more than African Americans.[48] By 1995 Hispanics replaced African Americans as the most impoverished group in the United States. Scott Barancik sums up the economic position of Hispanics:

> *Hispanics account for a disproportionately large share of the American households with low incomes and a disproportionately small share of those with high incomes. Census Bureau data show that of all the households in the top income fifth in 1987, just over three percent were Hispanic. By contrast, nine percent of those in the bottom fifth were Hispanic, meaning that Hispanics were about three times as likely to be among the poorest fifth of U.S. households as among the wealthiest fifth.[49]*

Traditionally, Hispanic women have had high fertility rates. In 1992 the Hispanic fertility rate was 3.04 births per woman, compared with 1.94 for non-Hispanic white women. Since 1980 Hispanic fertility has risen by about 20 percent while white fertility has risen by less than 7 percent. The increase in teenage fertility is even more dramatic. Between 1980 and 1992 Hispanic teen birthrates increased by 30 percent while white teen rates increased by only 6 percent.[50]

Diversity in the Hispanic Population

Although for statistical purposes the Hispanic population is often considered as a single group, the various Latino subgroups have distinct social and historical backgrounds. For example, Cubans living in Florida may have little in common historically or politically with Mexican Americans living in California, and Puerto Ricans living in New York may have little understanding of the culture of either Cuban Americans or Mexican Americans. These sociocultural differences are also reflected in the significant differences in incomes and family patterns among these groups. One study noted that

> Latina mothers displayed patterns that fell intermediate to the patterns of Anglo and Black mothers, though there was no single pattern that characterized all Latino subgroups. Puerto Rican mothers stand out as being considerably worse off than other groups: they are less likely to be married, less likely to be living with parents or other adults, more likely to be living in poverty and more likely to be receiving welfare. Cuban mothers stand out in the opposite way, with the highest household incomes of any group and the lowest rates of receiving welfare. Mexican and Central and South American mothers look more like Anglos than any other group in terms of their marriage patterns and living arrangements, although their poverty rates are much higher.[51]

These differences are also reflected in males' earnings. Two in three U.S. Hispanics, or 17.1 million people, are of Mexican origin. The average earnings of Mexican men were $17,700 in 1994, down 8 percent from 1987 (in constant 1994 dollars). The average earnings of all Hispanic men also dropped 8 percent over the same period, to $19,100. Cuban American men, however (4 percent of the Hispanic population), saw their income increase 12 percent, to $31,400 in constant 1994 dollars.[52]

Mexican Americans constitute about 63 percent of all Hispanic Americans in the United States and are the fastest growing Spanish-speaking subgroup. For example, according to the Bureau of the Census, there were about 13 million Mexican Americans in the United States in 1989, a 100 percent increase over the 1970 census.[53] In part, the poverty of Mexican Americans is correlated to deficits in educational attainment. Although Mexican Americans have made educational gains, in 1980 their median attendance in school was 9.8 years, the lowest of any Hispanic subgroup.[54] Moreover, they have the highest dropout rate in the United States. In 1980 more than 62 percent of Mexican Americans between the ages of 25 and 64 had less than a high school education, and only 4.4 percent had some college.[55]

Puerto Ricans constitute 12 percent of all Hispanics and less than 1 percent of the total U.S. population. Since the early 1960s, Puerto Ricans have steadily lost ground in labor force participation and in earnings of family heads. In 1988 Puerto Ricans' average family income was one of the lowest among minority groups in the United States—$18,932.[56] From 1960 to 1984 Puerto Rican family income dropped relative to other minority groups, and more than 43 percent of Puerto Rican families lived below the poverty line in 1984.[57]

Although Hispanic incomes have dropped relative to those of other minority groups, the number of Hispanic businesses increased 76 percent (from 490,000 to 862,600) between 1987 and 1992. Receipts for Hispanic businesses increased by 134 percent during this period.[58]

The economic data on Hispanic communities suggest two subgroups with very different characteristics. For example, while average household worth fell, the Latino community's total wealth rose. This fact is explained by the increasing numbers of poor households on the rich–poor spectrum and by the increasing wealth on the rich end. In 1998 home ownership increased over 1995, and the median indebtedness of Latino households decreased—both of which are positive signs.[59] Between 1997 and 1998, the median U.S. household income rose 3.5 percent while Hispanic households experienced a 4.8 percent increase.[60] Overall, however, the economic data clearly suggest a worsening picture for America's Hispanic communities.

 # Native Americans

Oppression and exploitation are by no means limited to African Americans and Hispanics. Native Americans, in some ways the most destitute group in the United States, experience the same level of oppression as other disenfranchised populations.

Although there are 504 federally recognized tribes (including 197 Alaskan Native groups) and 304 Indian reservations, there is no single definition of a Native American. The Bureau of Indian Affairs (BIA) considers someone to be an American Indian if the person is a member of a recognized Indian tribe and has one-fourth or more Indian blood. The Bureau of the Census uses self-identification.

The history of Native Americans is marked by hardship, deprivation, and gross injustice. Before the arrival of Christopher Columbus, the Indian population in the territorial United States was somewhere between 900,000 and 12 million.[61] The indigenous Indian population was dramatically reduced as a result of the westward expansion of whites and the wars and genocidal policies that followed. By 1880 the census reported the existence of only 250,000 Indians.[62] Moreover, Native Americans were not granted citizenship until 1924, and New Mexico did not allow them to vote until 1940.[63]

The economic landscape of the American Indian is similar to those of other at-risk minority populations. In 1990 more than 16 percent of Indian males living on the reservation were unemployed compared to 6.4 percent of the total population. In that same year 33 percent of the American Indian population lived below the poverty line compared to 14.5 percent of whites. Sixty-five percent of Indians on reservations were high school graduates compared to 75 percent of the general population. Median household income in 1990 was about $20,000 a year compared to $30,000 for the general population.[64] Housing was and remains a major problem. Sixteen percent of Native American homes are without electricity; the U.S. average is only 0.1 percent.[65]

From 1970 to 2000, the reported Native American population grew from 574,000 to more than 2 million. This population rise was due to a lower infant mortality rate, a high birthrate, and the fact that more individuals of mixed Indian descent were reporting their race as Indian. This last factor may be partly correlated with the resurgence of Native American pride that began in the 1970s. According to BIA estimates, about 1.5 million Indians live on or near Indian reservations and about another 356,000 live in urban areas.[66]

Most health indicators for Native Americans are disturbing. Roughly 43 percent of Native Americans who live beyond infancy die before age 55; this compares to slightly more than 16 percent for the general population. Many of these deaths are attributable to accidents. For example, in 1984 the Native American death rate from accidents was 81 per 100,000, of which 42 were related to motor vehicles (and frequently involved alcohol). This figure is much higher than the 1984 age-adjusted death rate for all races—35 per 100,000.[67]

Native Americans also have a maternal death rate 20 percent higher than the national average; the death rate for tuberculosis is six times higher than that for the population as a whole; for chronic liver disease it is four times the norm; for diabetes, influenza, and pneumonia, two times; and suicide rates are twice the national average, with rates tending to be highest among young people. Moreover, Native Americans have the highest rate of alcoholism of any ethnic group in the United States.[68] Poor education, alcoholism, gambling, and high suicide rates plague many Native American urban and reservation communities.

Caught in the paternalistic and authoritarian web of the Bureau of Indian Affairs, Native Americans continue to struggle for their identity. Having been robbed of their land, murdered indiscriminately by encroaching white settlers (as well as by the U.S. Cavalry), and treated alternately as children and pests by the federal government, for many years Native Americans were further oppressed by having their children taken away by welfare officials. This widespread abuse by welfare workers, who evaluated Native American child-rearing practices as neglectful in the context of white middle-class family values, was partially remedied by the **Indian Child Welfare Act of 1978,** which restored child-placement decisions to the individual tribes. As a result of this act, priority in placement choices for Native American children was given to tribal members rather than white families. In an attempt to remedy historical injustices, the Indian Self-Determination Act of 1975 emphasized tribal self-government; self-sufficiency; and the establishment of independent health, education, and welfare services. Despite these limited gains, the plight of Native Americans serves as a reminder of the mistakes made by the United States in both its past and its present policies toward disenfranchised minority groups.

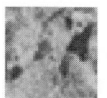

Asian Americans

The 1990 census reported more than 20 Asian/Pacific subgroups in the United States, including Chinese, Filipino, Japanese, Asian Indian, Korean, Vietnamese, Laotian, Thai, Cambodian, Polynesian (Hawaiian, Samoan, and Tongan), Micronesian (Guamain), and Melanesian (Fijian). The five largest Asian population groups in

the United States are Chinese (1.6 million), Filipino (1.4 million), Japanese (850,000), Asian Indian (815,000), and Korean (800,000).[69] In 1970 there were 1.5 million Asians living in the United States; by 1980 there were 3.7 million; and by 1990, 7.3 million. This growth represented an astounding 475 percent increase over 20 years and made Asians the fastest growing group in the U.S. population. Demographers predict that this growth will continue into the twenty-first century because of above-average birthrates and accelerating legal and illegal immigration. If these predictions are correct, by 2080 Asians will constitute 12 percent of the U.S. population, compared to 3 percent in 1990.[70]

While the social and economic data on Asian Americans are mixed, perhaps the most striking feature is that Asian Americans as a group had the highest median family income in the United States in 1995 (see Figure 4.1). Economic and social data also point to a population that has made great strides, especially in the educational area. For example, in 1990 82 percent of Asians were high school graduates compared with 78 percent of non-Hispanic whites, 65 percent of blacks, and 51 percent of Hispanics.[71] In 1989 college-bound Asian seniors had a high school grade point average of 3.25/4.0 versus 3.08/4.0 for all other students.[72] In 1992 the nation's most elite universities reported Asian American enrollment of 14 percent, almost five times this group's representation in the general population.[73] Although Asians made up only 3 percent of the population in 1990, they represented 12 percent of the students at Harvard University; 20 percent at Stanford; and 30 percent at the University of California, Berkeley.[74] In 1986 all five top scholarships of the Westinghouse Science Talent Search scholarships went to Asian Americans.[75] In 1998 26.5 percent of all males in the United States had completed college—and of that number 27.3 percent were non-Hispanic whites, 13.9 percent blacks, 11.1 percent Hispanics, and 46.4 percent Asian Americans.[76]

In 1990 Asian Americans had approximately the same unemployment rate (4.6 percent) as non-Hispanic whites (4.5 percent),[77] and median earnings for Asians with four years of college was

FIGURE 4.1   Median Family Income, 1995

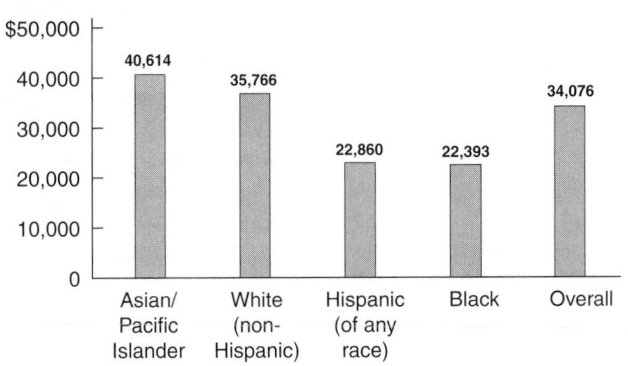

$34,469 compared to $36,134 for whites. Japanese Americans earned 37 percent more than the median family income for all Americans.[78] From 1987 to 1992 the number of Asian businesses grew 61 percent (from 439,271 to 705,672). Receipts from Asian businesses increased 163 percent in that same period, from $36.5 to $96 billion.[79] Census data indicate that Asian poverty levels range from less than 5 percent for Japanese Americans to 35 percent for newly arrived Southeast Asian immigrants.[80]

Impressive as these economic statistics are, they conceal several things. First, most Asians live in expensive urban areas where salaries are higher than the U.S. average. Second, economic statistics for Asian Americans obscure the problems of many low-wage recent immigrants who work in sweatshops in urban Chinatowns. For example, in 1980 the average suburban Chinese household earned $16,790 compared to $9,059 for the average Chinatown household.[81] Third, although many Chinese and Japanese Americans have achieved economic success, Southeast Asians are at higher risk of poverty than whites. Fourth, Asians are underrepresented in the higher-salaried public and private career positions. Fifth, although a large number of Asian immigrants have become successful entrepreneurs and own and operate their own small retail businesses, for some this role was forced on them as a result of discrimination.

Asian Americans have been stigmatized in U.S. society in several ways. Most dramatic was the internment of Japanese Americans in detention camps during World War II. However, Asians in this country have also experienced more subtle forms of discrimination. For example, because of their economic and educational achievements, Asians are often thought of as a "model minority." Because of this status many Asians experience pressure from the white majority as well as from other minority groups. An example of this tension is evident in the hostility between Korean shopkeepers and inner-city African American residents. Asians have also been the victims of hate crimes, some motivated by mudslinging that goes on periodically between Japan and the United States over recurrent trade problems. Specifically, the U.S. trade deficit with Japan and the resulting displacement of blue-collar workers in this country have often been blamed on Japan. In addition, some Asian Americans complain that they are discriminated against in colleges and universities because of their superior academic performance.[82] Facing this backlash, some Asians are redoubling their efforts to become mainstream members of U.S. society—to be in the center of the society rather than on the margins as "hyphenated Americans." They also want to bolster their clout in the political arena by helping to shape U.S. public policy.

Many Asians point to contributions to U.S. society that results from the input of Oriental cultural values. For example, Asian culture often includes a sense of frugality that leads to environmental conservation, greater consideration for the feelings of others, and a sense of balance between group and individual welfare. According to sociologist Tu Weiming, the less individualistic culture of Asians, their lower sense of self-interest, their less adversarial nature, and their less legalistic approach to society may have important applications for the United States.[83] After all, the cross-fertilization of cultures is an important factor that has made the United States strong and resilient.

Immigrants and Immigration

Immigration, one of the knottiest social and legal issues to reemerge in the 1990s, has long had a major economic and social impact on U.S. society. A 1992 Urban Institute study estimated that 3.4 million illegal immigrants lived in the United States, with 86 percent settling in just seven states. Critics point out that these seven states paid $4 billion in benefits and incarceration for illegals while illegal immigrants paid only $1.9 billion in taxes. Although poverty rates are higher for immigrants, naturalized citizens have lower poverty rates (10.5 percent) than native-born Americans (14.5 percent).[84] Moreover, a significant portion of Hispanic poverty is attributable to the large numbers of illegal immigrants entering the United States and to the low-paying menial jobs they occupy. Asian Americans have also felt the backlash from mainstream Americans who are worried about the consequences of admitting non-Europeans into U.S. society.

Legal immigration to the United States has undergone several distinct changes since the mid-1980s. From 1985 to 1988 the total number of immigrants into the United States remained relatively constant; it then rose sharply from 1988 to 1991. The sharp rise after 1988 was due to the impact of the Immigration Reform and Control Act of 1986 (IRCA), which granted legal status to undocumented immigrants who had been in the United States continuously since 1982 or had worked in agriculture. In 1995 the total number of immigrants admitted to the United States was 720,461, less than half of the 1,827,167 admitted in 1991.[85]

Major changes have occurred in the structure of U.S. immigration from the 1950s onward. According to the Immigration and Naturalization Service (INS), the most notable change was the shift of immigration from Europe and Canada (almost 52 percent of all immigrants to the United States in 1964) to Asia (36.4 percent of all immigrants in 1994). In other words, while the proportion of immigrants coming from Europe and North America declined by more than 50 percent from 1964 to 1994, the immigration rate of Asians rose by about five times, from 7.4 percent to 36.4 percent. This reversed a trend of nearly two centuries. By 1995 Asian immigration was highest, at 37 percent, followed by North American immigration at 32 percent and European immigration at 17.8 percent. On the other hand, total immigration from Europe more than doubled from 63,043 in 1985 to 160,916 in 1994. This change was due largely to the impact of the Immigration Act of 1990, which revised the numerical limits and preferential categories used to regulate immigration. Specifically, the Act increased the level of employment-based immigration and allotted a higher proportion of visas to highly skilled immigrants, a preference that resulted in a rise in immigration from most European countries.[86] In addition, special provisions were granted to the Irish, including special executive orders that gave permanent residency to Irish individuals already residing in the United States.[87] Contrary to popular misconceptions, immigration from South and Central America, Mexico, and the Caribbean remained relatively constant from 1964 to 1994 (see Figure 4.2). Most immigrants to the United States (66.6 percent) choose to settle in just seven states: 23.1 percent in California, 17.8 percent in New York, 8.6 percent in Florida,

FIGURE 4.2　Immigrants by Place of Origin, 1994

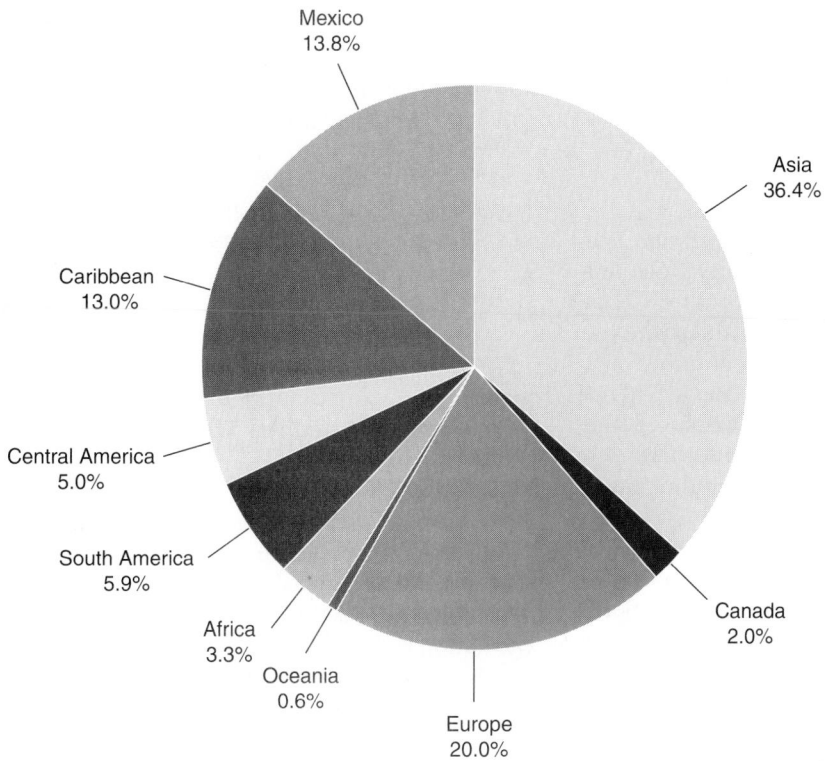

Source: U.S. Department of Justice, Immigration and Naturalization Service (Washington, DC, 1996).

6.9 percent in Texas, 5.5 percent in New Jersey, and 4.7 percent in Illinois.[88]

Groups such as the Federation for American Immigration Reform (FAIR) have promoted exclusionary messages in both national and international forums. These groups see immigration as a time bomb that threatens a negative impact on the U.S. economy and on the interests of American workers. Moreover, this hostility is also rooted in some people's fear of losing an already vaguely defined American identity. In 1999 independent presidential candidate Pat Buchanan made immigration policy a major plank in his bid for the presidency. According to Buchanan,

> . . . the onset of mass immigration in the 1960s overwhelmed the great American melting pot. Cultural institutions already under assault by liberals who despise our heritage were unable to assimilate the 30 million immigrants who flooded into the U.S. over the past three decades. Exploding crime statistics, swamped social services, and the rise of ethnic militancy tell the sad story.
>
> This year, 1.3 million more immigrants will pour into the U.S.—400,000 of them illegal aliens. If America is to survive as "one nation," we must take an immigration "time out" to mend the melting pot.
>
> As President, I will:
>
> - Halt illegal immigration by securing our porous borders and strengthening internal enforcement.
> - Stand with the three-in-four Americans who agree that mass legal immigration

> *must be reduced by restoring the 20th century average of 250,000 to 300,000 immigrants per year.*
> - *Support a national campaign of assimilation to teach newly adopted Americans our culture, history, traditions, and English language. To do otherwise cripples American cohesion and keeps the newest members of the American family from full participation.*[89]

In 1996, Congress passed the **Personal Responsibility and Work Opportunity Reconciliation Act (PRWORA).** The most comprehensive welfare reform legislation passed since the New Deal of 1935, the 900-page bill contained profound implications for both legal and illegal immigrants (PRWORA will be discussed more fully in Chapter 11).[90] Specifically, the PRWORA disentitled most legal immigrants (including many who had been living in the United States for years but had not elected to become citizens) from food stamps, Aid to Families with Dependent Children (AFDC), and Supplemental Security Income (SSI). (Illegal immigrants were never entitled to these benefits.) Based on the PRWORA, the only immigrants still entitled to benefits were (1) those who had become citizens or who had worked in the United States and paid Social Security taxes for at least 10 years; and (2) veterans of the U.S. Army who were noncitizens. In addition, the bill gave states the option to deny Medicaid benefits to immigrants. In Texas alone the PRWORA was expected to disqualify 187,000 legal immigrants from food stamps, 22,000 from AFDC benefits, and 53,000 from SSI.[91] Although some of the provisions were later rescinded, the sentiment that fueled the bill remains.

In September 1996 Congress revisited immigration, this time voting to double the size of the Border Patrol, stiffen penalties for document fraud and immigrant smuggling, bar illegal immigrants from qualifying for Social Security benefits or public housing, give states the right to deny illegal immigrants drivers' licenses, and slightly increase the earnings requirements for U.S. residents wishing to sponsor foreign family members.[92]

Immigration policies have been questioned on other fronts. For one, the current focus on Latino immigration distorts the diversity of illegal immigrants. For this reason, these policies have failed to address the largest single source of immigration—people who overstay their visas. For example, 107,000 Poles, 106,000 Filipinos, 79,000 Italians, and 78,000 Canadians overstayed their visas in 1996. Nevertheless, as a result of U.S. immigration policies, the steepest sustained drop in immigration since World War II occurred in 1995.[93]

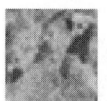 # Women and Society

Sexism is a term that denotes the discriminatory and prejudicial treatment of women based on their gender, and sexism is a problem that U.S. society has wrestled with since the beginning of the nation.

Sexism can manifest itself in a variety of ways. It can be social, as when women are kept out of military academies, private clubs, and certain sports. It can take the form of occupational boundaries that keep women from operating heavy construction machinery, being involved in skilled trades such as bricklaying, or flying commercial or military jets. It can take political forms, like appointing or electing token women to offices or cabinet positions or creating "special appointments" to placate feminist groups.

Violence and Sexism

Sexism can also manifest itself in crime and family violence. According to the U.S. Department of Justice (DOJ):

- Approximately 1.9 million women are physically assaulted annually in the United States. Women are more likely than men to be injured during an assault
- Violence against women is primarily partner violence.[94]

- Approximately 1.3 million women and 834,700 men are raped and/or physically assaulted annually by intimate partners.
- Approximately 1 million women are stalked annually in the United States.[95]

In response to this violence, Congress passed the Violence against Women Act (VAWA), which was signed into law by President Bill Clinton in 1994. VAWA reflects a comprehensive approach to domestic violence and sexual assault, combining a broad array of legal and other reforms. Specifically, it was designed to improve the response of police, prosecutors, and judges to these crimes; force sex offenders to pay restitution to their victims; and increase funding for battered women's shelters. VAWA establishes the nationwide enforcement of protection orders entered in any court and provides penalties for crossing state lines to abuse a spouse or violate a protection order. VAWA also prohibits anyone facing a restraining order for domestic abuse from possessing a firearm.[96] The act provides grants for training police, prosecutors, and judges in domestic abuse; provides grants for battered women's shelters; assists victims of sexual assault, including providing educational seminars, hotlines, and more programs to increase awareness (as well as targeted efforts to underserved racial and ethnic minority communities); provides grants for safety-related improvements to public transportation, national park systems, and public parks; funds efforts to prevent youth violence; assists funding for rape crisis centers; and allocates funds for the treatment and counseling of youth subjected to or at risk of sexual abuse (e.g., runaways, homeless youth, and street people).[97]

In addition to VAWA, the Clinton administration created a toll-free national Domestic Violence Hotline (1-800-799-SAFE) that has responded to as many as 10,000 calls a month. President Clinton also initiated legislation that reauthorized VAWA and toughened penalties for those who commit violent crimes in the presence of children. The DOJ established various measures to combat violence against women, and in FY 1999 $21.9 million of Civil Legal Assistance grant funds were distributed to strengthen legal assistance for domestic violence. Lastly, in 1999 the DOJ equipped universities and colleges in 21 states and territories with $8.1 million in grant funding to address domestic violence and stalking on campuses.

The Feminization of Poverty

Sexism also has an economic face. Women's wages are lower than those of men, and women more often have to resort to public welfare programs. The term **feminization of poverty** was coined by Diana Peirce in a 1978 article in *Urban and Social Change Review* in which she argued that poverty was rapidly becoming a female problem and that women accounted for an increasingly large proportion of the economically disadvantaged.[98] Advocates maintain that the feminization of poverty is illustrated by the demographics of poverty.

The U.S. Census Bureau indicates that the feminization of poverty is showing signs of abating. According to the Census Bureau, although 24 percent of females were below the poverty line in 1997, that number decreased to 22.6 percent in 1998. The Census Bureau also noted that 31.6 percent of female-headed households were poor in 1997 but that the number decreased to 29.9 percent in 1998.[99]

Despite this trend, the effects of female poverty is staggering. For example, in the United States in 1992 there were 12 million families maintained by women—a figure that had more than doubled since 1970, when there were only 5.6 million such families.[100] Not coincidentally, the poverty rate for female-headed households was 32 percent in 1995.[101] Moreover, the number of poor families headed by women increased 54 percent from 1970 to 1981, while at the same time the number of poor families headed by men dropped by nearly 50 percent. Two out of three poor adults are women.[102] Not surprisingly, this leads to a strong dependence of poor women on the welfare system, which is illustrated by the huge increase in the welfare rolls from 1960 (3 million) to 1992 (13.5 million).[103]

The causes of the feminization of poverty are complex. When women are deserted or divorced, many have to find jobs immediately or go on welfare. According to Ann Withorn, women generally enter the welfare system after exhausting other possibilities for income maintenance.[104] Those who choose welfare are held in poverty by the low benefits; those who opt to work are kept in poverty by the low wages that characterize service jobs, the most rapidly expanding sector in the U.S. labor market. Low-paying service employment, such as jobs in fast-food outlets and retail stores, make welfare benefits seem attractive because at least staying at home involves no child care costs.

Women and Low-Income Work

Women frequently enter the workforce through the service and retail trades, doing clerical jobs, cleaning, food preparation or service, personal service work, or auxiliary health service work. These occupations are characterized by low pay, a low level of union organization, little status, meager work benefits, and limited prospects for job advancement. Thus, much of the increase of women in the workforce is in the "secondary labor market" (see Chapter 5), a marginal area of employment. When economists cite the creation of millions of jobs in the 1980s and 1990s, much of what they refer to was in the secondary labor market, the underbelly of the work world. For example, of the 18.8 million jobs created between 1979 and 1989, 14.4 million were in retail trade and in services (i.e., business, personal, and health services), the two lowest-paid economic sectors.[105]

The economics of low-wage service work are gloomy. For example, if a single mother[106] with one child in day care chooses to avoid the stigma of welfare and finds work at near the minimum wage, her prospects for economic survival are bleak. The mock budget in Table 4.3 illustrates the dilemma of a single mother who finds full-time employment at $6.00 an hour (85 cents an hour above the minimum wage).

Work at or slightly above the minimum wage is problematic, limiting the economic choices for the unskilled female household head. Moreover, the National Commission on Children estimates that the typical family spends about $6,000 an-nually on expenses associated with raising a child.[107] This would mean that, excluding a mother's personal expenses, having two children requires a minimum income of $12,000 per year. According to the National Commission on Children, "If a single mother with two children moved from welfare to a full-time, minimum wage job in 1991, her net income would have increased by only about $50 per week."[108] The stagnancy of the minimum wage combined with the effects of inflation to make a single mother's plight even more dire in the year 2000. In short, neither welfare nor low-income work provides single female–headed households with viable economic choices.

Indeed, single-mother families in the United States fare worse than their counterparts in many European industrial nations. In a study of the relative economic well-being of single-mother families in eight nations, Yin-Ling Wong, Irwin Garfinkel, and Sara McLanahan found that compared with two-parent families, single mothers in the United States are considerably worse off financially than single mothers in the eight countries surveyed. The United States ranked last, surpassed by Canada, Australia, France, Germany, Norway, Sweden, and the United Kingdom.[109]

Inequities in **public transfer programs** also exacerbate the economic problems of low-income women. For example, Social Security and public assistance are often the only viable options for women, and about 8 out of 10 poor female–headed families rely on public cash transfers through public welfare programs.[110] Although median transfers to women are lower than to men, they constitute a higher share of the recipients' total income: about one-third for female–headed households as compared with one-tenth for male–headed households. Moreover, Social Security is the only source of income for 60 percent of elderly women; in 1990 some 15 percent of these women were in poverty compared with 8 percent of elderly men. Like other public transfer programs, Social Security is riddled with pitfalls. In large part, many problems with Social Security are based on the assumptions that all families are nuclear and that fami-

TABLE 4.3 ■ Monthly Budget for a Working Mother with One Child in School and One Infant in Day Care

Gross Monthly Income for a Full-Time Worker @ $6.00 an hour: $960	
Expenses	
Day care for 1 child	$ 442.00[1]
Rent	$ 450.00[2]
Health care	$ 93.75[3]
Utilities	$ 60.00[3]
Food	$ 234.00[4]
Clothing	$ 62.00[1]
Transportation	$ 200.00[3]
Entertainment	$ 50.00[3]
Sundry (soap, cleaners, repairs, sheets, blankets, etc.)	$ 100.00[3]
Total Approximate Cost	$1,691.50[3]
Monthly Deficit between Income and Budget	–$ 731.50[3]

1. Child care costs are calculated based on the average of the most and least expensive cities for child care according to the Runzheimer International survey of childcare costs. Retrieved from the World Wide Web: http://www.relojournal.com

2. Rent is calculated on the basis of the average of HUD-determined fair market rents in the lowest-cost metropolitan areas in a state. The average rent of all these states totaled $450.00. See U.S. House of Representatives, Committee on Ways and Means, *Overview of Entitlement Programs, 1998 Green Book* (Washington, DC: U.S. Government Printing Office, 1998).

3. This amount is based on figures provided in John E. Schwartz and Thomas J. Volgy, "A Cruel Hoax upon the Poor," *The San Diego Union Tribune* (November 9, 1992), p. 5.

4. The amount for food is based on the maximum food stamp allocation that this mother would receive in 2000 if she had no countable income.

lies with young children need more per capita income than aged couples or single individuals. Women have cited some of the inequities in Social Security:

■ Because women's wages are lower than men's, their retirement benefits are also lower.

■ Married female workers fare better on Social Security than single women. Married individuals who never worked can benefit from Social Security payments made by a spouse.

■ Couples in which one worker earned most of the wages may fare better than couples in which the husband and wife earned equal wages.

■ Homemakers are not covered on their own unless they held a job in the past. Widows do not qualify for benefits unless they are 60 years old or have a minor in the house.

■ Regardless of the length of the marriage, divorced women are entitled to only one-half of their ex-husband's benefits. If this partial payment is the divorced woman's only income, it is usually inadequate.

Furthermore, divorced women must have been married to the beneficiary of Social Security for at least 10 years to qualify for his benefits.

■ Because women, owing to child care responsibilities, are likely to spend less time in the workforce than men, their benefits are usually lower.[111]

As result of the Social Security amendments of 1983, several sex-based qualifications were eliminated: Divorced persons can qualify for benefits at age 62 (even if the ex-spouse has not yet claimed benefits), and divorced husbands can claim benefits based on the earnings records of their ex-wives.[112] Although these changes are important, they have led to only minor improvements in the system. Other reforms under discussion include an earnings-sharing option that would equally divide a couple's income between husband and wife (thereby eliminating the category of a primary wage earner and a dependent spouse) and a double-decker option in which everyone would be eligible for basic benefits regardless of whether they contributed to the system (individuals who contributed to the paid labor force would receive a higher benefit). These options are only in the discussion phase, but given the current problems with Social Security, their adoption seems unlikely in the near future.

Women and Work

Myths abound in attempts to explain why women consistently earn less than men. These myths include:[113]

Myth 1. A working mother's wages are not necessary to her family's survival; her job is a secondary activity that usually ceases with marriage or childbirth.

Fact. Most families require two paychecks to maintain the same standard of living as their parents. Twenty percent of working mothers are heads of households; two out of three working mothers report that they cannot decrease their working hours be-

cause of economic need. In 1984, one-third of women who worked had a spouse who earned less than $15,000 per year.[114] Moreover, 18 percent of all working women bring home larger paychecks than their husbands. Sixty-six percent of working African American women provide more than half of the median African American family income.

Myth 2. A working mother is unreliable, because her family is her primary concern.

Fact. Although some working mothers choose the "mommy track" (work affording flexible and/or shorter hours), others are forced into it by a lack of affordable quality day care. (Parenthetically, many men would choose the family as their first priority if they were forced to make the decision. However, they are usually not asked to make that choice.) Seventy-five percent of mothers return to work within a year after childbirth. Even without family assistance programs, most working mothers continue to maintain employment.

Myth 3. Large numbers of working women leave the workforce to return home to raise their children.

Fact. Statistics show that an opposite trend is occurring. In 1978 mothers of infants had a labor force participation rate of 35.7 percent; by 1988 it had risen to 50.8 percent. The choice of mothers to become full-time homemakers is the exception, not the rule (see Figure 4.3).

Myth 4. The cost to business of providing benefits to working mothers is prohibitive. Small businesses cannot afford to provide benefits and services such as child care, maternity leave, and flextime. For large businesses, such costs decrease their international competitiveness.

Fact. Family assistance programs raise productivity, increase worker loyalty, decrease turnover, and curb absenteeism costs. The majority of employers report no change in costs owing to family leave legislation.[115]

FIGURE 4.3 Who Is in the Work Force?

There were 103 million women age 16 and over in the United States in 1995. Of that 103 million, a record 61 million were in the civilian labor force. In 1999 the Women's Bureau of the U.S. Department of Labor noted that 62 million women were working, 75 percent full time and 25 percent part time. Nearly 60 percent of women age 16 and over were in the labor force. Women between the ages of 20 and 54 had labor force participation rates of at least 70 percent. More than half of teenage women ages 16 to 19 were labor force participants. In 1990 nearly 40 percent of the 56.6 million workers in the United States were mothers, an increase of 4.4 million since 1980. Women's labor force participation grew from almost 38 percent in 1960 to 48 percent in 1995, a rise that accounted for 60 percent of the total growth in the workforce. Almost 67 percent of mothers with children under 18 worked in 1990, compared with 56.6 percent in 1980. When broken down, almost 50 percent of women with children under age one were in the labor force in 1990. Of the total female labor force, nearly 75 percent are married, and 81 percent of divorced women with children under age 18 (2.6 million) work. African American women are more than three times as likely to be single heads of families than white women, and those with children under 18 have the same labor force participation rates as their white counterparts.

In 1999 black women had a workforce participation rate of 63.5 percent; non-Hispanic white women participated at 59.6 percent, and Hispanics at 55.9 percent. There were 3.4 million self-employed women in nonagricultural industries in 1999. In 1998, 3.7 million women were multiple job holders compared to 4.2 million men.

Source: U.S. Department of Labor, Women's Bureau, *20 Facts on Women Workers*. Retrieved 2000 from the World Wide Web: http://www.dol.gov/dol/wb

Myth 5. Women are doing better economically. In fact, they are rapidly closing the wage gap and are forging ahead of men.

Fact. The wage gap between men and women is shrinking, but slowly. In 1979 women made 64 percent of a male wage; by 1993 the ratio had grown to 71 percent; and by 1999 it had risen to 76.5 percent of the male wage. A study by the Economic Policy Institute, covering the years from 1973 to 1993, showed that after adjusting for inflation the typical worker's wages fell 7.5 percent. But whereas wages for males dropped by 12 percent, female workers' pay rose during that period by 6 percent in general, and by 16 percent for women in upper-level jobs.[116] This might seem like a step forward for women, but the increase in female wages may have been a result more of declining male wages than of increasing female wages. For example, from 1994 to 1995, although household wages rose 2.7 percent, women's wages fell by $255.[117]

Income and Job Disparities between Men and Women

Some of the income disparity between men and women can be traced to **occupational segregation.** Occupations such as cashier, receptionist, and home health aides are traditional women's jobs in which 75 percent or more of the workers are women. But they are also typically among the lowest paying jobs. And although women have gained ground in acquiring more managerial and professional positions, the clerical and teaching fields are still among the most likely female occupations.

There are about 100 employment categories in which women's participation is slight. For example, fewer than 25 percent of truck drivers, geologists, aircraft engine mechanics, airplane pilots and navigators, firefighters, and automobile mechanics are women. In 1999 the largest category of women workers were teachers (3.9 million, not including faculty members in colleges and universities), and women secretaries numbered 2.7 million.[118]

About half of all working women are in occupations in which 80 percent of coworkers are women.[119] In fact, 97 percent of secretaries are women, 93 percent of bookkeepers, 93 percent of nurses, and 82 percent of administrative/clerical staff. In 1988 only 9 percent of women worked in occupations classified as nontraditional (i.e., in which 75 percent of employees are men). In 1995 women still made up only 3 percent of firefighters; 8 percent of state and local police officers; 1.9 percent of construction workers; 11.8 percent of college presidents; and 3 to 5 percent of senior-level management positions in corporations.[120] (See Table 4.4.) In the 1980s and 1990s the greatest increase in women entering nontraditional jobs took place in the professional sphere. From 1983 to 1995 the proportion of female attorneys increased from 15 to 20 percent; female physicians rose from 16 to 20 percent; and marketing and advertising managers from 22 to 32 percent.[121]

The women with the highest earnings in 1999 were those employed as pharmacists, lawyers, electrical engineers, computer system analysts, teachers in colleges and universities, and physical therapists. In the 20 leading occupations of employed women in 1998, the ratio of women's to men's earnings was highest in the category of registered nurses (94.8 percent) and lowest in Managers and Administrators (66.9 percent). When women work in the same occupations as men, they usually earn less. And women's wages lag behind men's even in female-dominated professions (see Tables 4.5 and 4.6). For instance, in 1997 male computer system analysts earned $952 weekly compared to $850 for women. Even women therapists, who outnumber men three to one, have average weekly earnings of $686 compared to $733 for men.[122] Moreover, female attorneys earn at only 63 percent of the level of their male counterparts; female sales representatives earn between 62 and 72 cents of every dollar earned by a male in the same position; and female social workers earn only 73 cents for each dollar earned by a male social worker.[123]

Employment and earnings rates rise with educational attainment for both males and females. Among all labor force participants age 25 years and over in 1995, women were more likely than men to have completed high school. Ninety-one percent of female labor force participants held at least a high school diploma, compared with 88 percent of men. A slightly lower percentage of female labor force participants than men were college graduates—27 percent compared to 29 percent. Despite this, as Table 4.7 illustrates, earnings are considerably lower for females with the same education as males.[124]

TABLE 4.4 ■ Employed Women by Occupational Group

OCCUPATION	NUMBER EMPLOYED (MILLIONS)
Total	57.5
Management and professional specialty	16.9
Technical, sales, and administrative support	24.1
Service occupations	10.2
Precision production, craft, and repair	1.2
Operators, fabricators, and laborers	4.4
Farming, forestry, and fishing	0.7

Source: U.S. Department of Labor, Bureau of Labor Statistics, *Employment and Earnings* (Washington, DC: U.S. Department of Labor, January 1996).

TABLE 4.5 ▪ Salary Survey, 1996

JOB CATEGORY	WOMEN	MEN	TOTAL
Accounting auditor	$28,340	$37,648	$32,032
Advertising CEO	100,800	126,800	123,160
Art director	45,600	50,700	48,609
Computer systems analyst	39,572	45,760	43,992
Computer operator	19,084	26,000	21,268
College dean of arts and sciences	106,428	104,030	106,088
College professor, public institution	56,050	63,000	62,000
Teacher, secondary school	34,528	37,856	35,880
Engineering, 10–14 yrs experience	64,108	63,520	64,000
Engineering, 3–4 yrs experience	44,000	45,577	45,000
Financial services salesperson	26,936	48,932	37,366
Food service supervisor	15,288	19,344	16,848
Medicine health manager	30,212	44,200	32,396
Insurance salesperson	30,160	36,660	31,772
General counsel	291,096	304,658	297,877
Attorney	84,200	89,500	88,862
Lawyer (overall)	47,684	64,324	58,032
Orthopedic surgeon	222,478	298,444	292,000
Internist	119,258	138,240	133,581
Psychiatrist	115,297	143,739	132,929
Family practitioner	109,000	125,333	122,000
Registered nurse	35,360	36,868	35,464
Pharmacist, chain	56,577	56,844	59,176
Real estate salesperson	24,908	37,960	30,836
Retail/personal sales	12,584	19,032	14,712
Executive travel services	30,800	38,600	32,500
Frontline travel agent	22,000	27,200	22,700
Mixed animal vet	35,500	40,900	39,700

Sources: *Working Woman,* "Working Woman's 1996 Salary Survey," cited in DeWayne Peebles, Susan Robinson, Dorothy Rogers, and Fiona Stephenson, "Scorecard of Women's Issues in 1996," Unpublished paper, University of Houston Graduate School of Social Work, Houston, TX.

The Glass Ceiling. Upward mobility is a key factor in male–female wage discrepancies. In 1995 a 21-member bipartisan Glass Ceiling Commission was created under the Civil Rights Act of 1991. The task of the commission was to study ways to eliminate barriers to advancement by minorities and women. Its recommendations included the enforcement of existing antidiscrimination laws

TABLE 4.6 ■ Median Weekly Earnings, Selected Traditionally Female Occupations, 1995

OCCUPATION	WOMEN	MEN
Registered nurses	$693	$715
Elementary school teachers	627	713
Cashiers	233	256
General office clerks	360	389
Health aides, except nursing	285	345

Source: U.S. Department of Labor, Bureau of Labor Statistics, *Employment and Earnings* (Washington, DC: U.S. Department of Labor, January 1996).

TABLE 4.7 ■ Median Income by Educational Attainment and Sex: Year-Round Full-Time Workers, 1994

LEVEL OF EDUCATION	WOMEN	MEN
9th to 12th grade (no diploma)	$15,133	$22,048
High school graduate	20,373	28,037
Some college, no degree	23,514	32,279
Associate degree	25,940	35,794
Bachelor's degree or more	35,378	49,228

Source: U.S. Department of Commerce, Bureau of the Census, *Income, Poverty, and Valuation of Noncash Benefits: 1994* (Washington, DC: U.S. Department of Commerce, 1995).

and suggestions that businesses should more actively use affirmative action policies, that they should initiate work/life and family-friendly policies, and that CEOs should demonstrate greater commitment to the process of equal opportunity.[125]

The commission reported that 97 percent of senior managers of Fortune 1000 and Fortune 500 companies were white and that 95 to 97 percent were male. They also found that if women or minorities did achieve top jobs, they did not receive the same paycheck.[126] In a separate 1997 study, the journal *Catalyst* looked at proxy statements from each Fortune 500 company. What they found was that the highest-paid female corporate executives earned 68 cents of every dollar earned by the highest paid men.

Catalyst later found, in a 1999 study, that women represented 11.9 percent of corporate officers in the 500 largest U.S. companies, a 37 percent increase since 1995. The *Catalyst* study also showed a 28 percent increase in the number of companies with two or more women officers. Despite this, men still hold 93 percent of the high-profile jobs with profit-and-loss responsibility. Many women in executive or management level positions are in "staff" positions such as human resources or public relations.[127] And women still hold only 1 in 10 board seats. At the current rate of progress, it will take 475 years for women to reach equality with men in upper management positions.[128]

Many women face extraordinary challenges in finding and securing adequate employment for fair wages. Some of the obstacles faced by working women include the difficulty of finding high-quality and affordable day care, the existence of limited family leave policies, inflexible working conditions, inadequate health insurance, and problems of sexual harassment.

Day Care: A Barrier to Female Employment

A major barrier to female employment involves day care and subsidized child care leaves. For many working families child care is a necessity. A 1982 Census Bureau survey found that 45 percent of single mothers would seek employment if affordable quality child care were made available. But infant and toddler care is more expensive than care for preschoolers, and care provided in a center is more expensive than family day care.

According to one study, in 1947 only 12 percent of women with children under age six were in the workforce; by 1996 that number had increased to 62 percent.[129] A Census Bureau survey found that 34.5 percent of children under age five of full-time employed mothers and 22.6 percent of children under age five of part-time employed mothers were cared for in organized day care settings.[130] A 1997 study by the Institute of Applied Research found that because of the lack of accessible and affordable child care, only 25 percent of low-income working mothers left their children in an organized child care setting.[131] On the other hand, a 1998 study by the U.S. Department of Health and Human Services found that more than two-thirds of low-income parents reported that they had no problems in finding child care centers.[132]

The availability of day care has increased rapidly, both in the number of vacancies and in the number of available day care centers. In the early 1990s there were three times as many child care centers as in the mid-1970s, and four times as many children were enrolled in such programs.[133] In 1996 the Children's Foundation reported that there were 93,221 regulated day care centers in the United States offering 5.3 million slots. Of that number, approximately 4.2 million were for preschool-aged children and 1.1 million were for school-aged children. The study also found that on average, 88 percent of the available spaces in day care centers were filled.[134]

In a given city, child care can cost between $3,600 and $10,000 a year. According to the Runzheimer International research group, the monthly cost of full-time child care ranges from under $300 a month to more than $700 per month, depending on the city. This expenditure can put a tremendous financial strain on both single- and two-parent families. As shown in Table 4.8, a single mother in Boston earning $6.00 an hour would have to spend her entire salary just to pay for day care for one child.

The Title XX Social Services Block Grant program first instituted in the 1970s is the largest federal program for child care services. In 1990 the U.S. Congress passed additional important legislation that increased the supply of child care and expanded early childhood education. Through child care and development block grants and amendments to Title IV-A of the Social Security Act, Congress provided new funds to help families with child care costs and to help states improve the quality and supply of child care services.[135]

The lack of subsidized child care leaves poses a major problem for working women in the United States, however. Sheila Kammerman reported on a study of working mothers in five industrialized countries—Sweden, East and West Germany, Hungary, and France.[136] In all those countries except West Germany, a higher proportion of women were employed than in the United States. All nations, except the United States, provided a tax-free family allowance that ranged from $300 to $600 yearly. Guaranteed maternity leave (in Sweden the leave also pertains to fathers) ranged from 14 weeks in West Germany to eight months in Sweden. In most places, guaranteed maternity leave also included full pay. Although the 1993 Family and Medical

TABLE 4.8 ■ Cities with the Most and Least Expensive Monthly Child Care Costs, 1998

MOST EXPENSIVE CITIES	
Boston, Mass.	$718
New York, N.Y.	661
Manchester, N.H.	631
Chicago, Ill.	545
San Francisco, Calif.	543
Wilmington, Del.	540
Minneapolis, Minn.	536
Milwaukee, Wis.	533
Portland, Ore.	527
LEAST EXPENSIVE CITIES	
Tampa, Fla.	260
New Orleans, La.	311
Casper, Wyo.	312
Billings, Mont.	317
Little Rock, Ark.	319
Mobile, Ala.	319
Jackson, Miss.	325
Springfield, Ill.	332
Columbia, S.C.	338
Albuquerque, N. Mex.	321

Source: Runzheimer International. Retrieved 2000 from the World Wide Web: http://www.runzheimer.com

Leave Act (FMLA) allows for maternity leave, it is unpaid maternity leave.

In brief, the child care system in the United States is two-tiered. Those with adequate incomes can afford to purchase first-rate child care or, if they desire, can stay at home; those with low wages are at the mercy of the ebb and flow of political support for publicly supported day care.[137]

Women in Uniform

The downsizing of the U.S. military in recent years has reduced the actual number of women in the armed forces, but the proportion of women has not changed. In 1998 the army had the largest number of women, but the air force had the highest percentage (18 percent). Conversely, the Marine Corps had the lowest percentage of women (6 percent).[138] By 1999 women constituted 14 percent of those on active duty, only a slight increase from the early 1990s. The percentage of women officers has remained steady at around 13 percent. In 1997 the three O-8 level women and the two O-9 level women (lieutenant general/ vice admiral) represented less than 2 percent of all O-8 and O-9 officers. The highest percentage of women officers (17.5 percent) was at level O-2 (first lieutenant/lieutenant junior grade).[139]

The growth of women in law enforcement has followed a similar trajectory to that in the armed forces. Specifically, the proportion of women in law enforcement leveled off at around 14 percent in 1998, representing only a 3.2 percent increase from 1990. Law enforcement agencies that report no women in top command posts have increased from 20 to 30 percent.[140] At the present rate of advancement, women will not achieve equality in the military or in law enforcement in the near future. Moreover, progress has been made only when people took legal action to fight discrimination in hiring and promotion practices.[141]

Other Obstacles Faced by Working Women

Apart from low wages and difficulties in securing child care, many working mothers also require flexible family leave arrangements. Although 30 states had some form of parental or medical leave law in the past, no such law existed on the national level until 1993. In 1992 former President George Bush vetoed the Family and Medical Leave Act after it had passed the House and Senate for a second time. With the election of President Bill Clinton, the FMLA was rushed through Congress and was signed into law on February 5, 1993.

The FMLA requires public employers, and private employers with 50 or more workers, to offer job-protected family or medical leave for up to 12 weeks to qualifying employees (those who worked at least 1,250 hours for the employer in the previous year) who need to be absent from work for reasons that meet the terms of the law. For example, the reasons include an employee's illness (including maternity-related disability), or the need to care for a newborn or an ill family member. The law does not require employers to provide paid leave, but it does mandate that employers who provide health coverage continue to do so during the leave period. Should a worker use the leave, he or she is guaranteed the same or a comparable job upon returning to work. Those who work in firms with fewer than 50 employees are not protected by the FMLA. Unfortunately, many workers cannot afford to take advantage of the law, because it provides only for unpaid leave.

Another issue affecting working women is health insurance. Women working in traditionally female occupations (the largest share of working women) have the highest uninsured rate. More than 15 million women of childbearing age in the United States have no public or private medical coverage for maternity care, even though the average cost of having a baby is more than $4,300. Half of all women earning $6.00 an hour or less are without health care, and divorced and separated women are twice as likely to be uninsured as married women. Of the 4 million births each year in the United States, 500,000 are not covered by any health insurance plan. About 5 million women of reproductive age have private insurance policies that don't cover maternity care. Moreover, health insurance frequently does not cover important women's health services, such as family planning, long-term care, reproductive care and elective abortions, and maternity care and childbirth.[142] If women are to participate more fully in the labor force, health care insurance must be available to everyone.

Still another issue affecting working women is sexual harassment, an issue brought to the foreground by Anita Hill in the 1990 Senate confirmation hearing of Supreme Court Justice Clarence Thomas. Sexual harassment is defined as unwelcome sexual behaviors, including jokes, teasing, remarks, questions, and deliberate touch-

ing; letters, telephone calls, or materials of a sexual nature; pressure for sexual favors; and sexual assault. Although sexual harassment is against the law (Title VII of the 1964 Civil Rights Act has been interpreted as prohibiting sexual harassment), it remains all too common in the workplace. Women in nontraditional jobs are at greater risk of sexual harassment.[143]

Finally, a major obstacle faced by many working women is the inflexibility of work. Because women frequently take on the major responsibility for child care, elder care, and home management, they often forgo educational or training opportunities. To help working women balance family and work responsibilities, options such as flexible hours, job sharing, and part-time work with benefits need to be expanded.

Fighting Back: The Equal Rights Amendment and Comparable Worth

The Nineteenth Amendment to the U.S. Constitution gave women the right to vote in 1920. That, however, did not seem to lessen their economic and social plight, and shortly after winning the vote the Women's Party proposed the first **Equal Rights Amendment (ERA)** to the Constitution. Although it seemed a good idea at first, progressive social workers such as Jane Addams, Florence Kelley, and Julia Lathrop saw the ERA as endangering the hard-fought protection won for women workers. For example, reformers had successfully fought for a maximum weight limit on lifting for women workers, the establishment of maximum workday laws in many states, and mandatory work breaks. These social workers saw the ERA as potentially eradicating protective legislation for women workers. Moreover, these reformers saw the ERA as mainly benefiting middle-class professional women at the expense of poor, working-class women.

In 1972, Congress passed a newly drafted ERA and set a 1979 date for state ratification. When the ERA had not been ratified by 1978, Congress extended the deadline to June 30, 1982. Despite the endorsement of 450 organizations representing 50 million members, opponents of the ERA were able to defeat the amendment in

1982, just 3 states short of the 38 required for ratification.

The ERA of the 1970s read as follows: "Equality of rights under the law shall not be denied or abridged by the United States or any other State on account of sex.... The Congress shall have the power to enforce, by appropriate legislation, the provisions of this article.... This amendment shall take effect two years after the date of ratification."[144]

The ERA would not have nullified all laws on the basis of gender; instead, it would have required men and women to be treated equally. Most alimony, child support, and custody laws would not have been invalidated, although laws giving preference to one gender would have been struck down. On the other hand, special restrictions on the property rights of married women would have been invalidated, and wives would have been free to manage their own separate finances and property. Again, contrary to popular myth, the ERA would have affected only public employment; private employment practices would not have been changed. In the areas of military service and jury duty, women would have been subject to participation under the same conditions as men.[145]

The battle for women's rights has also been fought around the issue of **comparable worth**— the idea that workers should be paid equally for different types of work, if those jobs require the same levels of skill, education, knowledge, training, responsibility, and effort. The desire to equalize incomes through comparable worth is based on the belief that the **dual labor market** has created a situation in which "women's work" (e.g., secretarial work, teaching, social work, nursing, child care) is automatically less highly valued than traditional male occupations.

An illustration of the debate around comparable worth is provided in Table 4.9, which lists average wages for jobs typically occupied by women and men. Although the policy is controversial, 20 states have passed laws making comparable worth a requirement or goal of state employment. Comparable worth is a good idea in theory, but it brings up a difficult question: What criteria should be used to determine the compa-

TABLE 4.9 ■ Comparable Worth: Average Annual Wages, 1997

OCCUPATION	1997 AVERAGE ANNUAL WAGE
Barber	$20,910
Hairdresser	$17,800
Child care worker	$14,830
Refuse and recyclable materials helper	$22,270
Receptionist or information clerk	$18,710
Carpenter's helper	$20,560
File clerk	$17,350
Machine or repairer helper	$19,930
Waiter or waitress	$12,750
Medical secretary	$22,270
Butcher or meat cutter	$23,880
Auto mechanic	$28,830
Auto body repairer	$29,050

Source: Bureau of Labor Statistics, "Employment Statistics, 1997, Occupational Employment and Wage Estimates." Retrieved March 24, 2000, from the World Wide Web: http://stats.bls.gov/oes/national/1997/oesnat97.htm

rability of different jobs? Moreover, some critics have rejected the idea of full-scale enforcement of comparable worth on the grounds that the economic costs would be catastrophic.

In 1963 Congress passed the Equal Pay Act, which required employers to compensate male and female workers equally for performing the same job under the same conditions (not all jobs were covered by the bill). Another protective measure was Title VII of the Civil Rights Act of 1964, which prohibited sex discrimination in employment practices and provided the right of redress in the courts. In 1972, Presidential Executive Order 11375 mandated that employers practicing sex discrimination be prohibited from receiving federal contracts. Title IX of the Educational Amendments of 1972 prohibited discrimination in educational institutions receiving federal funds. Finally, the Equal Credit Act of 1975 prohibited discrimination by lending institutions on the basis of sex or marital status.

Abortion and Women's Rights

Feminists often point to the abortion debate as another area in which women's rights are threatened. Specifically, pro-choice advocates argue that where abortion is concerned, some male legislators and judges (with the exception of the nine male judges who decided on *Roe v. Wade*) have promulgated laws and regulations to control the behavior of women by denying them reproductive freedom. They argue that the choice of an abortion is a personal matter involving only a woman and her conscience. Antiabortion forces claim that life begins at conception and that therefore abortion is murder. Moreover, they point to the 32.5 million legal abortions performed in the United States from 1973 to 1999, while at the same time pointing to the scarcity of adoptable infants.[146] This argument becomes even more pronounced when abortion statistics are examined: In 1987 59 percent of those having abortions were younger than 25; 65 percent of them were white; 58 percent had experienced no previous abortion; and 82 percent were unmarried.[147]

In 1973, Sarah Weddington, a young attorney from Austin, Texas, argued *Roe v. Wade* before the U.S. Supreme Court. Though her client had long since relinquished her child for adoption, Weddington argued that a state could not unduly burden a woman's right to choose an abortion by making regulations that prohibited her from carrying out that decision. The Court ruled in favor of Weddington, and abortion was legalized in the United States, thereby nullifying all state laws that made abortion illegal during the first trimester of pregnancy. (Before 1970, four states—New York, Alaska, Hawaii, and Washington—had already made abortion legal contingent upon the agreement of a physician.) Within a decade after *Roe v. Wade,* almost 500 bills were introduced in Congress, most of which sought to restrict abortions by promoting a constitutional amendment outlawing abortion, by transferring the power to regulate abortion decisions to the states, or by limiting federal funding of abortions.[148]

The abortion issue has been marked by several key issues: (1) clinic access, (2) fetus viability testing, (3) parental consent for minors, (4) waiting periods, (5) insurance regulations, (6) public funding, and (7) partial birth abortions (abortions beyond the first trimester). The abortion debate has also been marked by Byzantine maneuvers and complex twists. In 1977 the Hyde Amendment prohibited the federal government from funding abortions except to save the mother's life. Also in 1977, however, the federal government lifted its ban on funding abortions for promptly reported cases of rape and incest and in cases where severe and long-lasting harm would be caused to a woman by childbirth. The 1980 Supreme Court decision in *Harris v. McRae* upheld the constitutionality of the Hyde Amendment. In 1981 the government again reversed its position, this time cutting federal funding of abortions except to save the life of the mother.[149] By 1990 federal funds paid for only 165 abortions, a dramatic drop from the almost 300,000 federally funded abortions in 1977.[150] In 1994, the Freedom of Access to Clinic Entrances Act was signed into law. This bill expanded the civil liberty of persons to have unobstructed access to any abortion or reproductive health services clinic. Any person or group that interferes with the right of such persons is subject to legal penalties, which range from a high fine to imprisonment.

The strategy of the antiabortion movement is to whittle away at *Roe v. Wade* by attempting to restrict abortions on the state level. For example, in Akron, Ohio, rules were promulgated that required a minor to receive parental consent for an abortion and that imposed a one-day moratorium between a woman's signing the consent form and the actual performance of the abortion. In 1986 the Supreme Court struck down a Pennsylvania law designed to discourage women from obtaining abortions. Yet in a 1989 landmark decision, the Supreme Court upheld a Missouri law that prohibited public hospitals and public employees from performing an abortion (except to save the life of the mother), required physicians to determine whether a woman who is at least 20 weeks pregnant is carrying a fetus able to survive outside the womb, and declared that life starts at conception.[151] During its 1990–1991 term the Court ruled in *Rust v. Sullivan* that the United States can prohibit federally financed family planning programs from giving out abortion information. On January 22, 1993, President Bill Clinton's second day in office, he signed a bill overturning this "gag rule"; on the same day, in another blow to anti-abortion advocates, Clinton overturned the federal ban on using fetal tissue matter gained from abortions in scientific experiments.

Since 1973, the abortion issue has proved to be one of the most divisive issues in public life in the United States. The public itself is ambivalent: Although nearly three out of four voters polled believe that abortion should be legal, 56 percent oppose the use of federal money to fund abortions for women who cannot afford them.[152] This highly charged issue has led to murder, fire-bombings of abortion clinics, large demonstrations on both sides of the issue, and widespread civil protest.

Sexual discrimination operates in all areas of social, political, and economic life. Like racism and other forms of discrimination, it is omnipresent, although often hidden from view. Another form of discrimination that has occupied the public agenda in recent decades is the stigma associated with gays and lesbians.

Gays and Lesbians: Two Populations at Risk

In today's "culture wars" one of the most intense controversies rages around the issue of whether homosexuality is an acceptable lifestyle and, if so, whether those who are openly gay and lesbian should enjoy protected minority status under civil rights laws. Only 40 years ago, few in public or religious sectors even dared to raise the possibility that it might be acceptable to be openly gay in the United States. For example, in 1960, all 50 states maintained laws criminalizing sodomy by consenting adults. In 1970, 84 percent of respondents to a national Gallup poll agreed that homosexuality was "social corruption that can cause the downfall of a civilization." Two-thirds of those polled thought homosexuals should not be allowed to work as schoolteachers, church pastors, or even government employees.

Recent decades, however have seen slow but dramatic shifts in public attitudes toward homosexuality. After years of concerted pressure by gay activists, in 1993 the American Psychiatric Association removed homosexuality from its *DSM-III* list of "objective disorders" and declared it "a normal, if divergent lifestyle." Throughout the 1970s and 1980s, laws forbidding sodomy were repealed in state after state. By 1995, 29 states had rescinded laws that criminalized consensual sodomy, 9 states had statewide gay rights laws in force, and more than 100 local communities had placed gay rights ordinances (recognizing sexual orientation as a protected minority status) on the books. In a landmark vote in 1992, Oregonians rejected by 55 percent to 45 percent a referendum that would have branded gays and lesbians as "abnormal and perverse" and would have required schools to teach that homosexuality is wrong. The referendum would also have barred antidiscrimination protection for gays and lesbians.[153] Some 75 percent of Americans polled nationwide in the early 1990s felt that homosexuals should not be discriminated against in employment, housing, or public accommodations.[154] These policies and polls reflect a significant shift in public opinion about homosexuality.

Despite these limited successes, many homosexuals continue to be forced to live in the "closet," concealing their sexual orientation in order to survive in a hostile world. Often the objects of ridicule, homosexuals have been denied housing and employment, harassed on the job, beaten, assaulted, and even killed because of their sexual orientation. In many states homosexuality is still considered a criminal or felony offense, and in some of these states the police systematically raid homosexual bars and ran-

Nevertheless, the self-perception of gays and lesbians has undergone a dramatic shift since the 1960s. Gays and lesbians have begun to identify themselves as members of an oppressed minority, similar to other oppressed minority groups. As gays and lesbians have become more visible, they have organized support groups; religious groups such as Dignity (Roman Catholics), Integrity (Episcopalians), Mishpachat Am (Jews), and Lutherans Concerned; social service organizations; subchapters of professional associations; and political action groups. The political power of gays and lesbians has grown, and in 1984 activists succeeded in inserting a gay civil rights plank in the Democratic Party platform. These changing attitudes have encouraged some political leaders to court the gay vote openly by supporting gay issues. The Clinton administration was the first to endorse gay rights openly (albeit erratically). For example, Clinton's administration backed the Employment Non-Discrimination Act (a gay civil rights bill); appointed more than 100 openly gay and lesbian persons to administrative jobs; nominated the first-ever open lesbian to the U.S. District Court; helped defeat antigay initiatives in Oregon, Maine, and Idaho; mandated that all federal agencies add sexual orientation to their affirmative action policies; stopped the practice of denying security clearance based on sexual orientation; granted political asylum to people at risk of persecution in their home countries based on their sexual orientation; and increased public health spending on AIDS.[184]

Gays and lesbians continue to face discrimination in social and economic areas. This discrimination is manifested in the absence of gay and lesbian rights in employment and employment benefits, housing, immigration and naturalization, insurance, custody and adoption, and neighborhood covenants that bar home sales to nonrelated couples.[185] Moreover, social service agencies routinely refuse to allow foster care in gay or lesbian homes; insurance companies deny workers the right to cover same-sex partners under health insurance; and gays and lesbians are often refused the right to name their partner as next of kin in medical emergencies.

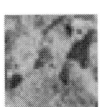

Ageism

Ageism is an important problem in a consumer-oriented society that idolizes youth. Like other minority groups, the aged face significant social and economic barriers. For example, workers over 50 often find it difficult to find equivalent employment if they lose their jobs. The aged in the United States are seldom revered or respected for their wisdom and experience; nor do they occupy elevated social positions protected by tradition. Instead, once they have lost their earning potential, the aged are often perceived as a financial albatross around the neck of an economically productive society. Socially isolated in retirement communities, low-income housing, or other old-age ghettos, the aged often become invisible.

For the first 99 percent of human history, the average life expectancy was approximately eighteen years. Over the past 100 years, life expectancy rose from 47 in the year 1900 to 76 in 1999.[186] Over the same century, the percentage of the U.S. population over age 65 more than tripled—from 4.1 percent in 1900 to 12.7 percent in 1998. The over-65 population in the United States totaled 34.4 million in 1998.[187]

In addition to the increase in the elderly population, there is an increase in the number of very elderly people, those over age 85. In 1998, more than 3 million of the 34 million elderly were over age 85. It is estimated that by the year 2030, 85 million people in the United States will be over age 60, and 9 million will be over age 85.[188] This trend will have important consequences for health care costs, because disabilities increase with age. Whereas only 9 percent of people aged 65 to 69 need help with daily activities such as eating, bathing, and dressing, 45 percent of those over age 85 need assistance with daily activities.[189] Similarly, although only a small percentage (4.2 percent) of all elderly people live in nursing homes, these numbers vary dramatically with age. For example, in 1996 only 1.1 percent of people aged 65 to 74 lived in nursing homes, compared with 19.8 percent of those over age 85.[190]

In 1997 more than 59 percent of people over age 65 were women, and among people over 85 there were 2.5 women for every man.[191] The longer life expectancy of women, combined with the tendency of wives to be younger than husbands, means that on average women outlive their husbands by 10 years, a pattern that results in four times as many widows as widowers.[192]

The Elderly Poor and Social Programs

The percentage of seniors living below the poverty line dropped from 35.2 percent in 1960 to a low of 10.5 percent in 1995. Seniors today receive an average of $22,000 in Social Security benefits and approximately $12,000 in Medicare benefits each year.[193] Despite the drop in poverty, in 1998 elderly women had a higher poverty rate (12.8 percent) than men (7.2 percent), with half of all single women over age 65 having a yearly income of less than $12,000.[194] In that same year the median income for men age 65 and over was $18,166 compared to $10,054 for women.[195]

Women tend to work fewer years than men and earn less in their jobs. Hence, on the average, women receive less Social Security benefits than men. In fact, the average Social Security benefit for a woman is about $600 per month compared to $800 for a man.[196] The lower economic status and greater longevity of women means that they are more likely to require public assistance programs as they grow older.

The great majority (84.7 percent) of elderly seniors are white, a disproportionately high ratio due in part to the ability of non-Hispanic whites to obtain adequate medical care. However, this pattern is changing. It is estimated that by the year 2030 African American elders will increase by 265 percent and the population of Hispanic elders will increase by 530 percent. These numbers compare to a relatively low anticipated 97 percent increase in the number of white elders. Given their lower average incomes, fewer assets, and less access to health insurance programs, it is likely that many minority elderly will require governmental assistance.[197] Clearly, policymakers must calculate the impact of increasing numbers of minority elderly in determining the future funding needs of health and income-based social programs.

The elderly do not readily fit the stereotypes of poverty, neglect, and despair so often associated with old age. Many of the elderly in the United States are doing well financially and have accumulated considerable wealth and assets. According to one study, "average income and assets for persons over 65 have risen dramatically, from a median per capita income of $3,408 in 1975 to $10,808 in 1993."[198] Controlled for inflation, this rise represented an 18 percent increase in purchasing power. Moreover, some researchers have estimated that the average elderly household has a net worth of $258,000.[199] Seniors represent $66 of every $100 invested in the stock market, and 70 to 75 percent of them own their home, assisted by the previously low cost of homes (the median cost of a home in 1970 was $20,000 compared to $120,000 in 1995).[200]

The elderly, representing about 13 percent of the U.S. population, receive 60 percent of federal social spending. This is four times the amount spent on children and represents more per capita spending than in Japan or in any western European country.[201] Other than the very poor, seniors are the only group with universal health coverage and the only group to receive non-means-tested government assistance. In contrast, today's younger workers earn less on average than their predecessors of 30 years ago. They are also less likely to have health insurance or pension benefits.[202]

There is a feeling among some critics that a nation with around 20 percent of its children living in poverty cannot afford to subsidize financially well-off seniors. The emerging backlash comes from younger workers who feel taken advantage of, resulting in their reluctance to adequately fund elderly-based programs such as Medicare and a growing refusal to fund programs targeted at needy seniors.[203]

Health Care and the Elderly

Despite the relative affluence of U.S. elderly people as a group, 10.5 percent of the elderly still live below the poverty line. Those living in poverty include a disproportionate number of women and minorities. As Judy Ochoa and Barbara Navarro argue, "In reality, both the stereotype from a few years ago of forgotten elders subsisting on dog food and the present day stereotype of 'country club' seniors have some basis in fact, but are only parts of a varied group with varying needs."[204] As the numbers of the very old and the minority elderly increase, we can expect a dramatic increase of seniors who are in financial need.

The implications of these trends for social welfare policy are profound. For one, as the numbers of elderly increase, their demands on society for housing, health, and recreational services will become more pronounced. The stresses put on the health care system by an increasingly aging population are already apparent in the near insolvency of Medicare. For example, in 1989 the elderly accounted for 33 percent of all hospital stays and 45 percent of all days of hospital care. The average stay for older people was 8.9 days compared with 5.3 days for persons under 65. The average length of stay for older people has increased 5.3 days since 1968 and 1.8 days since 1980. Moreover, although the elderly account for about 13 percent of the population, they account for 36 percent of personal health care expenditures. In 1991 these expenditures totaled $162 billion and averaged more than $5,300 a year for each older person. Benefits from Medicare ($72 billion) and Medicaid ($20 billion) covered about 63 percent of those costs in 1987, compared with only 26 percent for persons under age 65.[205] As more of the population ages in the coming decades, and as the group aged 85 and up rapidly increases, the burden of paying for health care will become even more problematic.

With more people living long enough to experience multiple chronic illnesses, disability, and dependency, more relatives in their fifties and sixties will be faced with the responsibility and expense of caring for them. The parent support ratio is a figure denoting the number of persons age 85 and over per 100 persons age 50 to 64. Between 1950 and 1993 the percent support ratio more than tripled, rising 3 to 10. Over the next six decades it will triple again, to 29.

Because elderly women live longer than men and yet have only 56 percent of their income, it is expected that more of elderly women's health care costs will have to be picked up either by the state or by their families, putting increasing burdens on both. In addition, as people live longer and require more care—especially in-home care—more pressure will be put on family members to provide or pay for that care. Because families are already stressed by increasing workloads, other family pressures, and the often large geographic distances between children and parents, the state may ultimately have to provide even more care for greater numbers of elderly.

The elderly vote in large numbers, and over the years their voices have been heard more clearly by politicians than those of African Americans and other minorities. In the 1960s policymakers responded to the needs of the elderly by passing the Older Americans Act (OAA) of 1965. The objectives of the OAA included (1) an adequate retirement income that corresponds to the general standard of living; (2) the promotion of good physical and mental health, regardless of economic status; (3) the provision of centrally located, adequate, and affordable housing; (4) the availability of meaningful employment, with the elimination of age-specific and discriminatory employment practices; (5) the provision of civic, cultural, and recreational opportunities; and (6) adequate community services, including low-cost transportation and supported living arrangements.[206]

Despite the attempts made by the American Association of Retired Persons (AARP) and other advocacy groups such as the Gray Panthers, however, ageism still persists. Negative stereotypes of elderly persons continue to be perpetuated by the media and the film industry. Moreover, the elderly continue to be victimized by crime, abuse by family members, and job discrimination. Perhaps the clearest expression of continuing ageism is seen in employment policies. The 1967 Age Discrimination in Employment Act (ADEA) protects most workers aged 40 to 69 from discrimination in hiring, job retention, and promotion. However, for most workers the protection of the ADEA stops when they reach age 70. Legislation to remove the "70 cap" has consistently failed in Congress, as employer lobbies have persuasively argued that they require a free hand in personnel policies. For many of the elderly, especially minorities and women, their economic well-being is precarious. Like race, gender, and sexual orientation, age is a liability that makes older populations vulnerable to injustice.

 # People with Disabilities

People with disabilities represent another group that experiences the effects of discrimination. About 8 to 17 percent of the U.S. population between the ages of 20 and 64 have disabilities that limit their ability to work, and about half that number are disabled to the point that they either cannot work or can work only irregularly.[207]

Disability is a difficult term to define. One medical definition is based on the assumption that a disability is a chronic disease requiring various forms of treatment. Another definition derived from the medical model—a definition used as a basis for determining eligibility in the Social Security Disability Insurance program—characterizes people with disabilities as people unable to work (or unable to work as frequently) in the same range of jobs as nondisabled people.[208] People with disabilities are thus viewed as inherently less productive than the able-bodied. A third model defines disability in terms of what people with disabilities cannot do, seeing the disabled in terms of their inability to perform certain functions expected of the able-bodied population. As William Roth maintains, "The functional limitation, economic, and medical models all define disability by what a person is not—the medical model as not healthy, the economic model as not productive, the functional limitation model as not capable."[209]

A newer definition, the psychosocial model, views disability as a socially defined category. In other words, people with disabilities constitute a minority group, and if the person with disabili-

ties is poor, it is a result less of personal inadequacy than of a discriminatory society. This definition situates the problem of disability in the interaction between the disabled person and the social environment. Therefore, the adjustment to disability is not merely a personal problem but a challenge requiring the adjustment of society to disabled people. This definition requires that society adjust its attitudes and remove the barriers it has placed in the way of self-fulfillment for people with disabilities—through architecture and transportation systems designed for the able-bodied and subtle stereotypes that impugn the competence of people with disabilities. In part, this newer definition of disability was expressed in Section 504 of the Rehabilitation Act of 1973 (PL 93-112).

Although the range of disabilities is great, people with disabilities share a central experience rooted in stigmatization, discrimination, and oppression. Like other stigmatized groups, people with disabilities experience poverty and destitution in numbers disproportionately larger than the general population. Perhaps not surprisingly, rates of disability are greatest among the aged, African Americans, the poor, and blue-collar workers.[210] Compared to the able-bodied, people with disabilities tend to be more frequently unemployed and underemployed and, as a consequence, often fall below the poverty line. Moreover, because disability is often correlated with poor education, age, and poverty, it is not surprising that African Americans are twice as likely as whites to have some level of disability (their representation is even greater in the fully disabled population), and that more women are disabled than men. The problems of low wages and unemployment are exacerbated because people with disabilities often need more medical and hospital care than others, are less likely to have health insurance, and spend three times more of their own money on medical care than do the able-bodied.[211]

Although discrimination continues to exist, major strides have been made in the integration of people with disabilities into the social mainstream. These advances have often resulted from organized political activity on the part of people with disabilities and their families. For example, an outgrowth of this political activity is Title V of the Rehabilitation Act of 1973, which mandates the following rules for all programs and facilities that receive federal funds:

- Federal agencies must have affirmative action programs designed to hire and promote people with disabilities.
- The Architectural and Transportation Barriers Compliance Board must enforce a 1968 rule mandating that all buildings constructed with federal funds—including buildings owned or leased by federal agencies—be accessible to people with disabilities.
- All businesses, universities, and other institutions having contracts with the federal government must implement affirmative action programs targeted for people with disabilities.
- Discrimination against people with disabilities is prohibited in all public and private institutions receiving federal assistance.[212]

The greatest stride was made on July 26, 1990, when former president George Bush signed the Americans with Disabilities Act (ADA) (PL 101-336) into law (see Figure 4.4). This act is the most comprehensive legislation for people with disabilities ever passed in the United States. The ADA lays a foundation of equality for people with disabilities, and it extends to disabled people civil rights similar to those made available on the basis of race, sex, color, national origin, and religion through the Civil Rights Act of 1964. For example, the ADA prohibits discrimination on the basis of disability in private sector employment; in state and local government activities; and in public accommodations and services, including transportation provided by both public and private entities. Some policies of the ADA went into effect immediately, whereas others were to be phased in over several years.[213]

In spite of its loopholes, the ADA represents an important step forward for people with disabilities. Nevertheless, some might argue that although the ADA is a good law in principle, it is being abused to the point of stirring up wide-

spread resistance. Specifically, disability is often defined so broadly that virtually anyone with a problem, regardless of its extent, can claim protection under the ADA. Moreover, some people seek to use this protection to excuse incompetence or inappropriateness on the job or in school. On the other hand, any social policy that attempts to address the widespread needs of a large constituent is inherently vulnerable to abuse.

Federal laws discouraging discrimination notwithstanding, discrimination against people with disabilities is still widespread. For instance, most buildings still do not meet the needs of the physically challenged in terms of access, exits, rest rooms, parking lots, warning systems, and so forth. Many apartment complexes and stores continue to be built without allowance for the needs of people with disabilities. The struggle for full integration remains an ongoing battle.

Legal Attempts to Remedy Discrimination

Concerted attempts to eliminate discrimination are a relatively recent phenomenon. Although the Fourteenth Amendment of the Constitution guaranteed all citizens equal protection under the law, it was also used to perpetuate discrimination on the basis of "separate but equal" treatment. In fact, overt segregation existed in the South until the middle of the twentieth century, and separate but (supposedly) equal public facilities characterized much of the social and economic activity of the United States. The extensive system of Southern segregation included public transportation, schools, private economic activities, and even public drinking fountains. It was only in the middle 1950s that the U.S. Supreme Court overturned the ***Plessy v. Ferguson*** (1896) decision that had formed the basis for the separate but equal doctrine.

In 1954 the Supreme Court, in its landmark decision on ***Brown v. Board of Education of***

FIGURE 4.4   A Summary of the Americans with Disabilities Act (ADA)

I. Employment
  A. Employers may not discriminate against an individual with a disability in hiring or promotion if the person is otherwise qualified for the job.
  B. Employers can ask about someone's ability to perform a job but cannot inquire if the person has a disability; nor can employers subject a person to tests that tend to screen out people with disabilities.
  C. Employers must provide "reasonable accommodation" to employees with disabilities. This includes job restructuring and modification of equipment. Employers are not required to provide accommodations that impose an "undue hardship" on business operations.
  D. All employers with 15 or more employees must comply with the ADA.

II. Transportation
  A. New public transit buses and rail cars must be accessible to individuals with disabilities.
  B. Transit authorities must provide comparable para-transit or other special transportation services to individuals with disabilities who cannot use fixed bus services, unless an undue burden would result.
  C. Existing rail systems must have one accessible car per train.
  D. New bus and train stations must be accessible. Key stations in rapid, light, and commuter rail systems must be made accessible. All existing Amtrak stations must be accessible by July 26, 2010.

III. Public Accommodations
  A. Private entities such as restaurants, hotels, and retail stores may not discriminate against individuals with disabilities.
  B. Auxiliary aids and services must be provided to individuals with vision or hearing impairments, unless an undue burden would result.
  C. If removal is readily achievable, physical barriers in existing facilities must be removed. All new construction and alterations of facilities must be accessible.

IV. State and Local Government
  A. State and local governments may not discriminate against individuals with disabilities.
  B. All government facilities, services, and communications must be accessible, consistent with the requirements of Section 504 of the Rehabilitation Act of 1973.

V. Telecommunications
  A. Companies offering telephone service to the general public must offer telephone relay services to individuals who use telecommunications services for the deaf (TDDs or similar devices).

Topeka, Kansas, ruled that so-called separate but equal facilities in education were inherently unequal. The Court ruled that separating the races was a way of denoting the inferiority of African Americans. In addition, the court stated that segregation hampered the educational and mental development of black children. Although the Supreme Court ruled against officially sanctioned segregation in public schools, **de facto segregation** was not addressed until the *Swann v. Charlotte-Mecklenburg Board of Education* ruling of 1971. This ruling approved court-ordered busing to achieve racial integration of school districts that had a history of discrimination.

The legal gains made by African Americans were won only through considerable, often bitter struggle. Up to the middle 1960s, Southern blacks enjoyed few rights, with total segregation enforced in almost all spheres of social, economic, political, and public activity. Segregation in the North occurred through de facto, or unofficial, rather than de jure, or legal, means, although the net effect was in many ways the same.

In 1955 Rosa Parks, too tired to stand in the "colored" section in the back of a bus in Montgomery, Alabama, sparked a nonviolent bus boycott led by Martin Luther King Jr. Still another protest was begun when African American students in North Carolina were refused service at an all-white lunch counter. The Civil Rights movement grew and resulted in widespread demonstrations (in Selma, Alabama, one march drew more than 100,000 people), picket lines, sit-ins, and other forms of political protest. Gaining international publicity, the protests of the late 1950s and early 1960s attracted Northern religious leaders, students, and white liberals—some of whom would lose their lives. By the time the Reverend Martin Luther King Jr. was assassinated in 1968, many demands of the Civil Rights movement had been incorporated in the Civil Rights Act of 1964. Ironically, Congress exempted itself from complying with the act until 1988. And in U.S. society as a whole, the 1964 Civil Rights Act did not live up to its implicit promise. The balance of racial power did not shift; for the most part, African Americans and other minority groups continued to be disenfranchised economically, politically, and socially. It soon became apparent that other remedies were required. One of these was affirmative action, a set of policies designed to provide equal admissions and employment opportunities for minorities and women.

Affirmative Action

Two basic strategies have been employed to address racial, economic, and other injustices. The first is nondiscrimination, in which no preferential treatment is given to selected groups. The second is **affirmative action,** whose overall goal is to ensure that women and minorities are admitted, hired, and promoted in direct proportion to their numbers in the population. Affirmative action policies and legislation represent an aggressive step beyond the largely reactive stance taken by simple nondiscrimination policies. As such, rigorous affirmative action policies give preferential treatment to minority and female applicants. The ostensible purpose of affirmative action policies is to right past wrongs done to groups of people throughout the country's history.

Federal affirmative action policies began in 1941, when President Franklin Roosevelt issued an executive order barring discrimination against black contractors in the federal government and the war industry. Without staff or enforcement authority, however, the policy was rendered useless. As a response to the Civil Rights movement, Presidents Kennedy, Johnson, and Nixon initiated affirmative plans to move the country toward nondiscrimination. Designed initially to address discrimination against African Americans, affirmative action policies were expanded to address discrimination based on gender, age, and disability.

There are three types of affirmative action programs: (1) Employers and schools can adopt voluntary programs to increase the hiring of minorities and women; (2) the courts can order an employer or school to create an affirmative action plan; and (3) federal, state, and local governments can require contractors to adopt affirmative action plans to remain eligible for government contracts.[214]

As Table 4.10 illustrates, affirmative action and civil rights legislation affect a much wider group of Americans than minorities. Moreover, as the table demonstrates, rulings on affirmative action and civil rights cases have been inconsistent, characterized by two steps forward and one or two steps backward. This has happened partly because civil rights and affirmative action policies have been forged from a blend of often conflicting legislation and court decisions.

Opponents of affirmative action argue that it leads to racial quota systems (employers can use quotas to avoid lawsuits), preferential treatment, and reverse discrimination. They argue that it violates the equal protection under the laws guaranteed in the Fourteenth Amendment. Still others argue that affirmative action policies benefit minority group members who do not need the help and that they place at a disadvantage whites who are innocent of any wrongdoing. These critics maintain that rights inhere in individuals, not in groups. Other conservatives, such as Supreme Court Justice Antonin Scalia, argue

TABLE 4.10 ■ Milestones in Civil Rights and Affirmative Action Rulings

LEGISLATION OR COURT RULING	SUMMARY
Plessy v. Ferguson (1896)	The U.S. Supreme Court established the "separate but equal" doctrine.
Fair Employment Practices Committee (1935)	Employers are directed not to discriminate in hiring based on race.
Brown v. Board of Education of Topeka, Kansas (1954)	The Supreme Court ruled that "separate but equal" facilities in education were inherently unequal.
Equal Pay Act of 1963	Men and women have a right to equal pay for doing the same work.
Civil Rights Act of 1964, including amendments added in 1972, 1978, and 1991	1. Voter registration is a legal right that cannot be tampered with.
	2. It is unlawful to discriminate or segregate based on race, color, religion, or national origin in any public accommodation, including hotels, motels, theaters, and other public places.
	3. The attorney general will undertake civil action on the part of any person who is denied access to a public accommodation. If the owner continues to discriminate, a court fine and imprisonment will result.
	4. The attorney general must represent anyone who undertakes the desegregation of a public school.
	5. Each federal department must take action to end discrimination in all programs or activities receiving federal assistance.
	6. Public or private employers, employment agencies, or labor unions with more than 15 employees cannot discriminate against an individual because of race, color, religion, national origin, or sex. An Equal Opportunity Commission will be established to enforce this provision.
	A 1968 amendment to this act prohibited discrimination in housing.
Age Discrimination Act of 1967	Persons over 40 may not be discriminated against in any terms or conditions of their employment.
Griggs v. Duke Power Co. (1971)	The Court prohibited discriminatory employment practices. It put the burden of proof on the employer to show that hiring criteria have a direct relationship to the job. *Griggs* was overturned by *Wards Cove Packing Co., Inc. v. Atonio* (1989), in which the Court imposed tougher standards for proving discrimination and shifted the burden of proof onto the employee.
Swann v. Charlotte-Mecklenburg Board of Education (1971)	The Court ruled in favor of court-ordered busing to achieve racial integration of school districts with a history of discrimination.
Title IX of Education Amendments of 1972	Institutions receiving federal financial assistance may not discriminate based on sex.

TABLE 4.10 ■ Continued

LEGISLATION OR COURT RULING	SUMMARY
Rehabilitation Act of 1973	Discrimination on the basis of mental or physical disability is prohibited.
Vietnam Era Veterans Readjustment Act of 1974	Employers with federal contracts must take steps to employ and advance qualified disabled veterans.
Milliken v. Brady (1974)	The Court ruled that mandatory school busing across city–suburban boundaries to achieve racial integration was not required unless segregation had resulted from an official action.
Marco DeFunis v. University of Washington Law School (1974)	DeFunis claimed that he was denied admission to law school even though his grades and test scores were higher than those of minorities who were admitted. The Supreme Court ruled in his favor.
Age Discrimination Act of 1975	Employers who receive federal financial assistance may not discriminate based on age.
Regents of the University of California v. Bakke (1978)	The Supreme Court ruled that Alan Bakke was unfairly denied admission to the University of California–Davis Medical School. Like DeFunis, Bakke argued that his qualifications were stronger than those of many of the minority candidates who were admitted.
United Steelworkers v. Weber (1979)	The Court upheld an affirmative action plan to erase entrenched racial biases in employment.
Fullilove v. Klutznick (1980)	The Court ruled that federal public works contracts may require 10 percent of the work to go to minority firms.
Firefighters Local Union No. 1784 v. Stotts (1984)	The Court ruled that an employer may use seniority rules in laying off employees, even when those rules adversely affect minority employees. This ruling was a blow to affirmative action, because it perpetuated the dilemma that minorities are the last to be hired and first to be fired. The Department of Justice used this decision to force Indianapolis and 49 other jurisdictions to abandon their use of hiring quotas.
Wyatt v. Jackson Board of Education (1986)	An affirmative action plan must have a strong basis in evidence for remedial action.
United States v. Paradise (1987)	The Court found that a judge may order racial quotas in promoting and hiring to address "egregious" past discrimination.
Johnson v. Transportation Agency (1987)	The Court permitted the use of gender as a factor in hiring and promotion.
City of Richmond v. J. A. Croson (1989)	The Court imposed standards of "strict scrutiny." Racial or ethnic classifications must serve a compelling interest and be narrowly tailored.
Martin v. Wilks (1989)	The Court imposed tougher standards for Asian Americans to be included in affirmative action plans and made it easier to challenge settlements of those plans.

(continued)

TABLE 4.10 ■ Continued

LEGISLATION OR COURT RULING	SUMMARY
Metro Broadcasting, Inc. v. FCC (1990)	The Court allowed minority preferences to promote diverse viewpoints across the airwaves.
Adarand Constructors, Inc. v. Pena (1995)	The Court ruled that federal affirmative action measures using racial and ethnic criteria in decision making must meet the same standards of strict scrutiny imposed in *Croson.*
Hopwood v. State of Texas (1996 5th Cir.)	The appeals court ruled that the University of Texas's goal of achieving a diverse student body did not justify its affirmative action program, suggesting that achieving diversity does not represent a compelling state interest.
California Proposition 209 (California Civil Rights Initiative) (1996). Now Article I, Section 31 of the California Constitution	Racial or gender preferences in public education, employment, and state contracting are prohibited. In 1997 a three-judge panel of the Ninth Circuit Court of Appeals upheld the referendum passed by California voters. The U.S. Supreme Court refused to consider the appeal.[215] The passage of the CCRI effectively put an end to affirmative action in California.
Washington State I-200 (1998)	"Preferences" in state and municipal hiring and recruitment to the state university system are eliminated. This 1998 ballot measure effectively repealed affirmative action in Washington State.
One Florida Plan (1999)	Racial preferences in university admissions and state contracting are prohibited. In November 1999 Florida Gov. Jeb Bush ordered an end to racial preference programs in agencies under his control. The One Florida Plan replaces race and ethnicity with criteria such as a student's socioeconomic background, geographical diversity, status as a first-generation college student, or preparation in a low-performing D or F school.

Sources: Adapted from ACLU, "Affirmative Action," ACLU Briefing Paper No. 17 (New York: ACLU, n.d.); American Council on Education, "Major Civil Rights and Equal Opportunity Legislation Since 1963," retrieved from the World Wide Web: http://www.berkshire-aap.com/ace; American Council on Education, "The Major Affirmative Action Cases: A Digest of the Record," retrieved from the World Wide Web: http://www.berkshire-aap.com/ace; Winnie Chen, Vilma Hernandez, Erin Townsend, and Carol Wyatt, "Affirmative Action," unpublished class paper, University of Houston Graduate School of Social Work, 1996; and Marjorie Blythe and Anna Conaty, "Affirmative Action and the State of America's Minorities," unpublished paper, University of Houston Graduate School of Social Work, 2000.

that there never was a justification for affirmative action because the Constitution is "colorblind."[216] Moderates such as former president Bill Clinton note that "Affirmative action has been good for America. Affirmative action has not always been perfect, and affirmative action should not go on forever. . . . We should reaffirm the principle of affirmative action and fix the practices. We should have a simple slogan: Mend it, but don't end it."[217]

Yet attacks on affirmative action have also come from liberal quarters. Columnist Roger Hernández argues:

> *Admittedly, affirmative action offers protection from discrimination. But the price it exacts is too high. Affirmative action reinforces the degrading notion that certain cultures are so inferior they render all individuals brought*

up in it [sic]—regardless of their socioeconomic status—into incompetent fools who cannot get along without special attention.

. . . The sense of ethnic inferiority such a philosophy encourages does more harm than the outright discrimination affirmative action is supposed to prevent.

. . . Ending affirmative action attacks the idea that every member of certain ethnic groups is a muddle of social pathologies.[218]

William Julius Wilson, an African American sociologist, criticizes the ability of affirmative action strategies to help the most disadvantaged members of society:

Programs based solely on [race-specific solutions] are inadequate . . . to deal with the complex problems of race in America. . . . This is because the most disadvantaged members of racial minority groups, who suffer the cumulative effects of both race and class subjugation . . . are disproportionately represented amongst the segment of the general population that has been denied the resources to compete effectively in a free and open market. . . .

On the other hand, the competitive resources developed by the advantaged minority members . . . result in their benefitting disproportionately from policies that promote the rights of minority individuals by removing artificial barriers to valued positions. . . . [If] policies of preferential . . . treatment are developed in terms of racial group membership rather than real disadvantages suffered by individuals, then these policies will further improve the opportunities of the advantaged without necessarily addressing the problems of the truly disadvantaged such as the ghetto underclass.[219]

Affirmative action is one of the most controversial issues in American social policy. Moreover, it is open to a whole array of moral conundrums. For example, how much discrimination does a group have to encounter to justify preferential treatment? Although Asian Americans as a group have certainly encountered (and continue to encounter) significant discrimination, their income levels and educational attainment mitigate against the need for preferential treatment. More-

over, if historical social discrimination were a basis for affirmative action, then Jews, Catholics, Irish, Eastern Europeans, and other groups who have historically been squeezed out of the U.S. social mainstream should also be eligible. For example, it is unlikely that a Jew will be elected president in the near future since many people believe that the country is not ready for a Jewish president. Given this reality, should Jews claim affirmative action status? Moreover, poor whites are discriminated against in U.S. society because of their class background. Should they too be covered under affirmative action? Women who grow up in upper-class families and are educated at Ivy League universities are covered under affirmative action by virtue of their gender. Do they experience more discrimination than a poor white Appalachian male who is marked by language, culture, and class background? These are some issues that plague the enforcement of clear and fair affirmative action guidelines.

 # Conclusion

Discrimination takes many forms in America. It can be targeted against African Americans, Hispanic Americans, Native Americans, Asian Americans, women, gays and lesbians, the physically challenged, and poor whites. Because discrimination often leads to poverty, it can result in the creation of income maintenance and poverty programs designed to meliorate its effects. Those who become beneficiaries of income programs soon find themselves with a second handicap—the stigma of being on public assistance.

Some policymakers have tried to reduce the need for long-term and expensive social welfare programs by trying to arrest the cycle of discrimination and stigma. They often undertake this effort by advocating for policies and legislation designed to attack discrimination at its roots. Antidiscrimination programs, policies, and legislation include affirmative action programs, women's rights legislation, city and state gay and lesbian ordinances, and legislation protecting the rights of the physically and mentally challenged. Policymakers hope that by curtailing discrimination, the society can offer vulnerable populations equal opportunities for achievement and success. At best, however, the scorecard on these well-intended programs and policies has been mixed. Despite a strong start, affirmative action programs have not led to widespread economic success for women and minorities. Gays and lesbians continue to be discriminated against, even in places that have passed civil rights ordinances. Although women have made significant gains over the past few decades, they continue to earn less than males in similar jobs.

Out of the insidious brew of discrimination and social stigma comes oppression—the enforcement of discrimination and unequal power relationships. In the final analysis, discrimination and social stigma promote poverty, destitution, and social isolation. It is perhaps a truism that oppression flows from prejudice in the same way that opportunity flows from tolerance. Discrimination is a likely manifestation in a society that breeds an individualistic and competitive ethos, status fears among marginal groups, and the need for visible scapegoats upon which to blame the alienating quality of life.

Discussion Questions

1. The effects of racism take many forms, including overt discrimination, poverty, housing problems, high rates of underemployment and unemployment, wage differentials, family disruption, inferior educational opportunities, high crime rates, and welfare dependency. Moreover, the relationship between racism and poverty is clear. Less clear, however, are the causes of racism. Describe what you believe to be the primary causes of both individual and institutional racism. How are these causal factors nourished or condemned by society?

2. Since approximately 1990 there has been a marked increase in the number of racially based incidents, especially against African Americans, Asian Americans, and gays and lesbians. What are some of the reasons for the rise in such incidents?

3. Over the past three decades, many legal and judicial attempts have been made to eradicate the effects of racism, including the 1964 Civil Rights Act and numerous Supreme Court rulings. Were these legal attempts successful? If not, why not? What, if anything, can be done to eliminate the effects of racism?

4. It is generally acknowledged that sexism is a powerful and pervasive force that permeates much of U.S. society. How is sexism manifested? What strategies, if any, can be employed to lessen the impact of sexism in society?

5. Most women in U.S. society are forced to work either to provide a second household income or as the family's primary wage earner. Describe some of the major obstacles faced by working women. What can be done to eliminate some of them?

6. Gays and lesbians face severe economic and social problems apart from AIDS. What are some of the most important social, political, and economic hurdles standing in the way of full equality for gays and lesbians? What can be done to ameliorate these hurdles?

7. Being elderly in our society is in many ways a social handicap. Describe some key social, economic, and political indicators that illustrate this idea.

8. It is generally agreed that people with disabilities face significant discrimination. What is the evidence, if any, to support this belief?

9. The Americans with Disabilities Act (ADA) is often considered the most important piece of legislation affecting people with disabilities. Why do policy analysts consider the ADA such an important act? What are its loopholes, if any?

10. After reviewing the various causes of discrimination discussed in this chapter, describe what you believe to be the major cause of discrimination today. Why is this cause more important than others? Using this cause as a framework, what can be done to counteract the effects of discrimination?

 # Notes

1. Billy J. Tidwell, "Racial Discrimination and Inequality," *Encyclopedia of Social Work*, 18th ed. (Silver Spring, MD: NASW, 1987), p. 450.
2. J. Dollard et al., *Frustration and Aggression* (New Haven, CT: Yale University Press, 1939).
3. Theodore W. Adorno et al., *The Authoritarian Personality* (New York: Harper & Row, 1950).
4. Wilhelm Reich, *Listen Little Man* (Boston: Beacon Press, 1971).
5. Tidwell, "Racial Discrimination and Inequality."
6. Stephanie Bernardo, *The Ethnic Almanac* (Garden City, NY: Doubleday, 1981).
7. V. Dion Haynes, "Movement Aims to Explain and Deflate White Power," *Daily Titan*. Retrieved 2000 from the World Wide Web: http://dailytitan.fullerton.edu/issues/spring_98/dti_03_04/movementaims.html
8. U.S. Census Bureau, "Census Bureau Facts for Features, African American History Month" (Washington, DC: U.S. Census Bureau, February 14, 2000).
9. Ibid.
10. "Family Income Finally Rises," *The New York Times* (September 27, 1996), p. 18.
11. Ibid.
12. Steven A. Holmes, "Quality of Life Is Up for Many Blacks, Data Say," *The New York Times* (November 18, 1996), pp. A1, A13.
13. U.S. Census Bureau, "Black-Owned Business Firms Up 46 Percent over Five Years, Census Bureau Survey Shows," December 12, 1995. Retrieved 2000 from the World Wide Web: http://www.census.gov/ftp/pub/agfs/smobe/view/b_press.txt

14. William Julius Wilson, *The Truly Disadvantaged: The Inner City, the Underclass, and Public Policy* (Chicago: University of Chicago Press, 1987), p. 109.
15. Lawrence Mishel and David M. Frankel, *The State of Working America* (Armonk, NY: M. E. Sharpe, 1991), p. 251.
16. Holmes, "Quality of Life Is Up for Many Blacks."
17. "Black-White Income Inequalities," *The New York Times* (February 17, 1998), p. 9.
18. U.S. Census Bureau, "Census Bureau Facts for Features, African American History Month."
19. United States Department of Commerce, Bureau of the Census, *Black-Owned Businesses: Strongest in Services*, August 1996. Retrieved 2000 from the World Wide Web: http://www.census.gov/Press-Release/cb98-127.html
20. Jared Bernstein, *Where's the Payoff?* (Washington, DC: Economic Policy Institute, 1995).
21. Ibid.
22. Ibid.
23. Franklin D. Wilson, Marta Tienda, and Lawrence Wu, "Racial Equality in the Labor Market: Still an Elusive Goal?" Institute for Research on Poverty, Madison, WI, 1992, Discussion Paper no. 968–992.
24. Thomas P. Bonczar and Allen J. Beck, "Special Report: Lifetime Likelihood of Going to State or Federal Prison," Publication NCJ-160092, U.S. Department of Justice, Office of Justice Programs, Bureau of Justice Statistics (Washington, DC: BJS Clearinghouse, March 1997).

25. Matthew Klein, "Death Row in Black and White," *American Demographics* (May 1998). Retrieved 2000 from the World Wide Web: http://www.demographics.com/publications/ad/98_ad/9805_ad/ad980522.htm

26. Gareth G. Davis and David B. Mulhausen, "Young African-American Males: Continuing Victims of High Homicide Rates in Urban Communities," Heritage Organization. Retrieved 2000 from the World Wide Web: http://www.heritage.org/library/cda/cda00-05.html

27. Cushing N. Dolbeare, *The Widening Gap* (Washington, DC: Low Income Housing Information Service, 1992), p. 11.

28. Jennifer Daskal, *In Search of Shelter* (Washington, DC: Center on Budget and Policy Priorities, June 15, 1998).

29. The Department of Health and Human Services, Race and Health Home Page. Retrieved 2000 from the World Wide Web: http://raceandhealth.hhs.gov/sidebars/sbinitOver.htm

30. The Centers for Disease Control, *National Vital Statistics Reports* 47, no. 13 (December 24, 1998), p. 1.

31. Children's Defense Fund, *The State of America's Children* (Washington, DC: Children's Defense Fund, 1998), p. 61.

32. March of Dimes, "Leading Infant Health Indicators, 1993," revised March 30, 2000. Retrieved from the World Wide Web: http://www.mod.org

33. Ibid.

34. Mishel and Frankel, *The State of Working America*, p. 219.

35. Children's Defense Fund, *The State of America's Children*, p. 25.

36. Ibid., p. 92.

37. Jennifer Day, "Young African Americans Boost High-School Completion Rate," United States Census Bureau, June 29, 1998. Retrieved 2000 from the World Wide Web: http://www.census.gov/Press-Release/cb98-106.html

38. Mishel and Frankel, *The State of Working America*, p. 253.

39. Diana M. DiNitto, *Social Welfare: Politics and Public Policy* (Englewood Cliffs, NJ: Prentice-Hall, 1991), p. 247.

40. U.S. Bureau of the Census, "Poverty," 1998. Retrieved 2000 from the World Wide Web: http://www.census.gov/hhes/www/poverty.html

41. Ibid.

42. L. Lowell, F. Bean, and R. De La Garza, "The Dilemmas of Undocumented Immigration: An Analysis of the 1984 Simpson–Mazzoli Vote," *Social Service Quarterly* 67 (1986), pp. 118–126.

43. Hispanic News Link, "Hispanics Who Defy Averages," *The Numbers News* (September 1995), p. 1.

44. U.S. Bureau of the Census, *The Hispanic Population in the United States* (Washington, DC: U.S. Government Printing Office, March 1989).

45. See U.S. House of Representatives, Committee on Ways and Means, *Overview of Entitlement Programs: 1992 Green Book* (Washington, DC: U.S. Government Printing Office, 1992), p. 1275; and Barbara Vobjeda and Steven Pearlstein, "Household Income Climbs," *Washington Post* (September 27, 1996), p. A1.

46. U.S. House of Representatives, *1992 Green Book*, p. 1072.

47. Ibid.

48. Ibid., pp. 590–591.

49. Scott Barancik, *Falling Through the Gap: Hispanics and the Growing Income Disparity Between Rich and Poor* (Washington, DC: Center on Budget and Policy Priorities, 1990), p. 3.

50. Joan R. Kahn and Rosalind E. Berkowitz, "Sources of Support for Young Latina Mothers" (Washington, DC: Urban Institute, August 16, 1995).

51. Ibid., p. 6.

52. "Hispanics Who Defy Averages," *Hispanic News Link* (June 1994), p. 2.

53. Guadalupe Gibson, "Mexican Americans," *Encyclopedia of Social Work*, 18th ed. (Silver Spring, MD: NASW, 1987), p. 139.

54. Ibid., p. 140.

55. Marta Tienda, "Puerto Ricans and the Underclass Debate," *The Annals of the American Academy* 501 (January 1989), p. 115.

56. Barancik, *Falling Through the Gap*, p. 25.

57. Marta Tienda, "Race, Ethnicity and the Portrait of Inequality: Approaching the 1990s," *Sociological Spectrum* 9 (1989), p. 32.

58. U.S. Census Bureau, "Number of Hispanic Businesses Up 76 Percent in Five Years, Census Bureau Reports," July 10, 1996. Retrieved 2000 from the World Wide Web: http://www.census.gov/Press-Release/cb96–110.html

59. "Hispanic Income Rises," *Houston Chronicle* (March 25, 2000), p. 9.

60. U.S. Bureau of the Census, "Mean Earnings of Workers 18 Years and Over, by Educational Attainment," revised April 5, 1999, Table A-3. Retrieved 2000 from the World Wide Web: http://www.census.gov/population/socdemo/education/tablea-03.txt

61. H. F. Dobyns, *Native American Historical Demography: A Critical Bibliography* (Bloomington, IN: Indiana University Press, 1976), p. 32.

62. H. E. Fey and D. McNickle, *Indians and Other Americans: Two Ways of Life Meet* (New York: Harper & Row, 1970), pp. 9–12.

63. DiNitto, *Social Welfare,* p. 257.

64. U.S. Department of the Interior, Bureau of Indian Affairs, "Statistical-Abstract-on-the-Web: From the Department of the Interior & Elsewhere." Retrieved June 2000 from the World Wide Web: http://www.doi.gov/nrl/StatAbst/StatHome.html

65. University of Arizona Library, "Contemporary Indian Affairs: A Bibliography of U.S. Government Documents." Retrieved 2000 from the World Wide Web: http://www.lib.ua.edu/indians.htm

66. See Evelyn Lance Blanchard, "American Indians and Alaska Natives," *Encyclopedia of Social Work,* 18th ed. (Silver Spring, MD: NASW, 1987), p. 61; U.S. Bureau of the Census, *Census of Population and Housing Summary* (Washington, DC: U.S. Government Printing Office, 1990), p. 93; and U.S. Department of the Interior, Bureau of Indian Affairs, "Statistical-Abstract-on-the-Web," note 64 above.

67. University of Arizona Library, "Contemporary Indian Affairs."

68. Ibid., pp. 143–144.

69. Margaret L. Usdansky, "Asian Immigrants Changing Face of Rural USA," *USA Today* (September 10, 1992), p. 9A.

70. Felicity Barringer, "U.S. Asian Population Up 70% in 80's," *The New York Times* (March 2, 1990), p. 1.

71. U.S. Bureau of the Census. *Statistical Abstract of the United States: 1994* (111th ed.) (Washington, DC: Government Printing Office. 1994), p. 139.

72. Daniel Goleman, "Probing School Success of Asian-Americans," *The New York Times* (September 11, 1990), p. B5.

73. Arthur Hu, "Hu's on First: Asian Males Lose Again," *Asian Week* (Feb. 12, 1993), p. 15.

74. Goleman, "Probing School Success of Asian-Americans."

75. Ibid.

76. U.S. Bureau of the Census, *Statistical Abstract of the United States: 1998* (Washington, DC: U.S. Government Printing Office, 1999).

77. See Rich Connell and Sonia Nazario, "Affirmative Action: Fairness or Favoritism?" *Los Angeles Times* (September 10, 1995), pp. A1, A26–A28; and U.S. Commission on Civil Rights, "Civil Rights Issues Facing Asian-Americans in the 1990s" (Washington, DC: U.S. Commission on Civil Rights, February 1992), p. 17.

78. U.S. Commission on Civil Rights, "Civil Rights Issues," pp. 16–17.

79. U.S. Census Bureau, "Large Increases in Number of Asian, Pacific Islander, American Indian, and Alaska Native Businesses between 1987 and 1992, Census Bureau Reports," August 1, 1996. Retrieved 2000 from the World Wide Web: http://www.census.gov/Press-Release/cb96–127.html

80. S. B. Gall and T. L. Gall, *Statistical Record of Asian-Americans* (Cleveland, OH: Eastwood Publications Development, 1993), p. 44.

81. Rockefeller Foundation, Research Briefs on Poverty, "Poverty and Asian Americans." Retrieved 2000 from the World Wide Web: http://www.cdinet.com/Rockefeller/Briefs/brief27.html

82. Sussumu Awanchara, "Hit by a Backlash," *Far Eastern Economic Review* 155, no. 2 (March 26, 1992), p. 30.

83. Ibid.

84. Jeffrey Rosen, "The War on Immigrants," *The New Republic* (January 7, 1996), pp. 8–12.

85. U.S. Department of Justice, Immigration and Naturalization Service, "Immigration to the United States in Fiscal Year 1995" (Washington, DC: USDOJ, August 5, 1996).

86. Ibid.

87. Ibid.

88. Ibid.

89. Pat Buchanan for President, The Internet Brigade, 1999. Retrieved 2000 from the World Wide Web: http://www.buchanan.org/000-c-immigration.html

90. HR 3734: Personal Responsibility and Work Opportunity Reconciliation Act (Immigration Provisions)—Conference Committee Version: Title IV, Restricting Welfare and Public Benefits for Aliens (Washington, DC: U.S. House of Representatives, Conference Committee, August 5, 1996), p. 16.

91. Patty Reinert, "Federal Welfare Plan Hits Legal Immigrants," *Houston Chronicle* (August 2, 1996), pp. 1A and 16A.

92. Greg McDonald, "House Passes $600 Billion Spending Bill," *Houston Chronicle* (September 29, 1996), pp. 1A and 32A.

93. U.S. Department of Justice, INS, "Immigration."

94. U.S. Department of Justice, "National Crime Victimization Survey," August 1995. Quoted in U.S. Department of Justice, "The Violence against Women Act," September 23, 1996. Retrieved 2000 from the World Wide Web: http://www.usdoj.gov/vawo/vawafct.htm

95. S. Taylor, "Congress, the Court and Violence against Women," *National Journal* 32, no. 2 (2000), pp. 76–77.

96. U.S. Department of Justice, "National Crime Victimization Survey."

97. Update on VAWA, *National NOW Times* (January 1995). Retrieved 1999 from the World Wide Web: http://www.now.org

98. Diana Pierce, quoted in S. Bianchi, "Feminization and Juvenilization of Poverty: Trends, Relative Risks, Causes and Consequences," *Annual Review of Sociology* 25 (1999), pp. 307–333.

99. U.S. Census Bureau, "Poverty 1998." Retrieved 2000 from the World Wide Web: http://www.censu.gov/hhes/poverty/poverty98/pv98est1.html

100. Women's Bureau, "Women Who Maintain Families," U.S. Department of Labor, June 1993. Retrieved from the World Wide Web: http://bubba.dol.gov/dol/wb/public/wb_pubs/wwmfl.htm

101. U.S. House of Representatives, *1992 Green Book*, pp. 591–596.

102. Ruth Sidel, *Women and Children Last* (New York: Harper, 1984).

103. National Commission on Children, *Poverty, Welfare and America's Families: A Hard Look* (Washington, DC: National Commission on Children, 1992), p. 3.

104. Ann Withorn, quoted in M. A. Jimenez, "A Feminist Analysis of Welfare Reform: The Personal Responsibility Act of 1996," *Affilia* 14 (Fall 1999), pp. 278–293.

105. Mishel and Frankel, *The State of Working America*, p. 105.

106. Although we have stressed single female–headed families here, it is important to acknowledge that single male–headed families are growing even more rapidly. From 1959 to 1989 single male–headed families grew from 350,000 to 1.4 million, compared with 7.4 million mother-only and 25.5 million two-parent households. From 1960 to 1990, the percentage of father-only households increased 300 percent. See Daniel R. Mayer and Steven Garasky, "Custodial Fathers: Myths, Realities, and Child Support Policy," Institute for Research on Poverty, Madison, WI, August 1992, Discussion Paper no. 982–992, pp. 8–9.

107. National Commission on Children, *Poverty, Welfare and America's Families*, p. 3.

108. National Commission on Children, *Beyond Rhetoric: A New Economic Agenda for Children and Families* (Washington, D.C.: National Commission on Children, 1991), p. 90.

109. Yin-Ling Irene Wong, Irwin Garfinkel, and Sara McLanahan, "Single-Mother Families in Eight Countries: Economic Status and Social Policy," Institute for Research on Social Policy, Madison, WI, 1992, Discussion Paper no. 970–992.

110. Winifred Bell, *Contemporary Social Welfare* (New York: Macmillan, 1983), p. 129.

111. Martha N. Ozawa, "Gender and Ethnicity in Social Security," *Conference Proceedings*, Nelson A. Rockefeller Institute of Government, State University of New York at Albany, November 1985, pp. 2–6.

112. Ibid.

113. Much of the following section is based on information found in Wider Opportunities for Women, *Making Both Ends Meet* (Washington, DC: Wider Opportunities for Women, 1991), pp. 4–9.

114. Nina Totenberg, "Why Women Earn Less," *Parade* (June 10, 1984), p. 5.

115. Family assistance was one of the major thrusts of the former Clinton administration. It is also an issue that crosses racial and social class lines.

116. Quoted in D. Harris, "How Does Your Pay Stack Up? *Working Women* (February 1996), pp. 27–28.

117. U.S. Census Bureau, "Income and Poverty 1995," September 26, 1996. Retrieved 1998 from the World Wide Web: http://www.census.gov/hhes/income/income95/prs96asc.html

118. Ibid.

119. Bell, *Contemporary Social Welfare*, p. 126.

120. Feminist Majority Foundation, "Women in Business," 1995. Retrieved 1999 from the World Wide Web: http://www.feminist.org/research/ewb_myths.html

121. National Commission on Working Women of Wider Opportunities for Women, "Women and Nontraditional Work," (Washington, DC: Wider Opportunities for Women, n.d.).

122. U.S. Department of Labor, Women's Bureau, *Equal Pay: A Thirty-Five Year Perspective*, 1998. Retrieved 2000 from the World Wide Web: http://www.dol.gov/dol/wb

123. DiNitto, *Social Welfare*, p. 237.

124. See Nijole V. Benokraitis and Joe R. Feagin, *Modern Sexism: Blatant, Subtle, and Covert Discrimination* (Englewood Cliffs, NJ: Prentice-Hall, 1986); and U.S. Department of Labor, Women's Bureau, "20 Facts about Women Workers," 2000. Retrieved 2000 from the World Wide Web: http://www.dol.gov/dol/wb

125. U.S. Department of Labor, Office of Public Affairs, *The Glass Ceiling Commission Unanimously Agrees on 12 Ways to Shatter Barriers*,

1995. Retrieved 2000 from the World Wide Web: http://www.dol.gov/dol

126. U.S. Department of Labor, Women's Bureau, *Median Annual Earnings for Year-Round Full-Time Workers by Sex in Current and Real Dollars, 1951–98*, 1999. Retrieved 2000 from the World Wide Web: http://www.dol.gov/dol

127. Associated Press, "Glass Ceiling Shows Some Cracks." *The New York Times* (April 23, 2000). Retrieved 2000 from the World Wide Web: http://www.nyt.com

128. Feminist Majority Foundation, "Women in Business."

129. P. Anderson and B. Levine, *Working Paper Series: Child Care and Mothers' Employment Decisions.* (Massachusetts: National Bureau of Economic Research, 1999).

130. U.S. House of Representatives, "Child Care," *Green Book, 1998* (Washington, DC: U.S. Government Printing Office, 1998).

131. Ibid.

132. K. Miller and G. Schultz, "Survey Finds Former Welfare Recipients' Wages Highest in Nation," 1999. Retrieved 2000 from the World Wide Web: http://www.aphsa.org

133. S. Hofferth, "Childcare, Maternal Employment and Public Policy," *Annals of the American Academy of Political and Social Sciences* 563 (May 1999), pp. 20–38.

134. U.S. House of Representatives, *Green Book, 1998*, p. 1123.

135. Children's Defense Fund, *The State of America's Children*, p. 37.

136. Sheila B. Kammerman, "Child Care and Family Benefits: Policies of Six Industrialized Countries," *Monthly Labor Review* 103 (November 1980), pp. 23–28.

137. Sidel, *Women and Children Last*, p. 123.

138. Alliance for National Defense, "Facts and Figures," 1998. Retrieved 2000 from the World Wide Web: http://www.all4nationaldefense.org/factsfigures.html

139. GenderGap, "The Military 'Glass Ceiling': Active Duty Military Personnel by Grade/Rank and Gender, 1997 & 1998." Retrieved 2000 from the World Wide Web: http://www.gendergap.com/military/glasceil.htm

140. National Center for Women & Policing, "Equality Denied: The Status of Women in Policing," 1998. Retrieved 1999 from the

World Wide Web: http://www.feminist.org/policestatus1998.html

141. Ibid.

142. National Commission on Working Women of Wider Opportunities for Women, "Women, Work and Health Insurance" (Washington, DC: Wider Opportunities for Women, n.d.).

143. National Commission on Working Women, "Women and Nontraditional Work."

144. Jim Harris, *The Complete Text of the Equal Rights Amendment* (New York: Ganis & Harris, 1980), p. 7.

145. "Fighting Discrimination," *The Legal Advisor* (Spring 1982), pp. 457–458.

146. Alan Guttmacher Institute, *Facts of Abortion* (Washington, DC: Alan Guttmacher Institute, September 1995).

147. S. K. Henshaw, L. M. Koonin, and J. C. Smith, "Characteristics of U.S. Women Having Abortions, 1987," *Family Planning Perspectives* 23 (March/April 1991), pp. 75–81.

148. Nanneska Magee, "Should the Federal Government Fund Abortions? No," in Howard Jacob Karger and James Midgley (eds.), *Controversial Issues in Social Policy* (New York: Allyn & Bacon, 1993).

149. DiNitto, *Social Welfare*, p. 241.

150. R. B. Gold and D. Daley, "Public Funding of Contraceptive, Sterilization and Abortion Services, Fiscal Year 1990," *Family Planning Perspectives* 23 (September/October 1991), pp. 204–211.

151. DiNitto, *Social Welfare*, p. 241.

152. M. Clements, "Should Abortion Remain Legal?" *Parade* (May 17, 1992), pp. 4–5.

153. Ibid.; see also *Lesbian and Gay Civil Rights in the U.S.* (New York: National Gay and Lesbian Task Force, 1992).

154. Robert Williams, *Just As I Am* (New York: Crown, 1992).

155. Natalie Jane Woodman, "Homosexuality: Lesbian Women," *Encyclopedia of Social Work*, 18th ed. (Silver Spring, MD: NASW, 1987), p. 809.

156. Lambda Legal Defense and Education Fund, "Information Sheet" (New York: Lambda, 1991).

157. A. P. Bell and M. S. Weinberg, *Homosexualities: A Study of Diversity among Men and Women* (New York: Simon & Schuster, 1978), p. 101.

158. See "The Homosexual Numbers," *Newsweek* (March 22, 1993), p. 9; "Homosexual Activity Lower Than Believed, Study Shows," *Springs Gazette Telegraph* (April 15, 1993), p. A18.

159. See "Overcoming a Deep Rooted Reluctance, More Firms Advertise to Gay Community," *Wall Street Journal* (July 18, 1991), p. 48; and "Gay Market a Potential Gold Mine," *San Francisco Chronicle* (August 27, 1991), p. C30.

160. "Gay Market a Potential Gold Mine"; also "For Gays, Ship Charters Are a Boon, Say Two Travel Companies," *Travel Weekly* (August 5, 1991), p. 2; and "Where the Money Is: Travel Industry Eyeing Gay/Lesbian Tourism," *Bay Area Reporter* (September 19, 1991), p. 53.

161. "State of the Union Address 2000," *Washington Post*. Retrieved 2000 from the World Wide Web: http://www.washingtonpost.com/wp-srv/politics/special/states/docs/sou00.htm

162. Federal Bureau of Investigation, "Uniform Crime Statistics: Hate Crimes, 1998," 1999. Retrieved 2000 from the World Wide Web: http://www.fbi.gov/ucr/98cius.htm

163. National Center for Victims of Crimes, "Violence against Lesbians and Gays, 1998." Retrieved 2000 from the World Wide Web: http://www.ncvc.org/

164. "State of the Union Address 2000."

165. DiNitto, *Social Welfare*, p. 109.

166. Kent Kilpatrick, "Oregon Voters Reject Stigmatizing Homosexuals," *The Advocate* (November 5, 1992), p. 2C.

167. American Civil Liberties Union, "Maine Voters Repeal Lesbian and Gay Civil Rights Law; ACLU Vows to Continue 20 Year Fight for Equal Rights," 1998. Retrieved 2000 from the World Wide Web: http://gaylesissues.abvout.com/library/content/blpr021198aclu.htm?rnk=rl&terms=maine+/s+gay+%26+civil

168. Much of the section on gays and lesbians in the military was derived from Rivette Vullo, "Homosexuals in the Military," unpublished paper, Louisiana State University School of Social Work, Baton Rouge, LA, December 4, 1991. See also K. Dyer (ed.), *Gays in Uniform: The Pentagon's Secret Reports* (Boston: Alyson, 1990).

169. Dyer, *Gays in Uniform*, p. xiv.

170. Joseph Harry, "Homosexual Men and Women Who Served Their Country," *Journal of Homosexuality* 10 (1984), pp. 117–125.

171. Dyer, *Gays in Uniform*, p. xv.

172. Conrad K. Harper and Jane E. Booth, "End Military Intolerance," *National Law Journal* 13 (1991), pp. 17–18.

173. Barry M. Goldwater, "Ban on Gays Is Senseless Attempt to Stall the Inevitable," *Los Angeles Times* (September 23, 1993), C7.

174. Servicemembers Legal Defense Network, "Gay Discharge Figures at Highest Level Since 1987," 1999. Retrieved 2000 from the World Wide Web: http://www.sldn.org/scripts/sldn.ixe?page=alert_01_23_99

175. T. R. Reid, "Britain Drops Ban on Gays in Military," *Austin American-Statesman* (January 13, 2000), p. 9.

176. Tony Marco, "What Does the Bible REALLY Say about Homosexual Issues?" Retrieved 1998 from the World Wide Web: http://www.qrd.tcp.com/qrd/religion/anti/CFV/christian.american

177. R. Sneyd, "Same-sex Bill Not about Marriage, Legislators Say," *Patriot Ledger* (March 18, 2000), p. 18.

178. Ibid.

179. J. J. Sampson et al., *Texas Family Code Annotated* (Eagan, MN: West Group, August 1999).

180. N. D. Hunter et al., *The Rights of Lesbians and Gay Men: The Basic ACLU Guide to a Gay Person's Rights*, 3rd ed. (Carbondale & Edwardsville, IL: Southern Illinois University Press, 1992).

181. Centers for Disease Control, "DHAP Basic Statistics," June 13, 1996. Retrieved 2000 from the World Wide Web: http://www.cdc.gov/nchstp/hiv_aids/statisti/exposure.htm

182. Robert Searles Walker, *AIDS: Today, Tomorrow* (Atlantic Highlands, NJ: Humanities Press International, 1992), p. 119.

183. White House, "Clinton Gore Administration Announces New Multimillion Dollar Increase to Combat HIV and AIDS." Retrieved from the World Wide Web: http://www.whitehouse.gov/WH/New/html/20000119_3.html

184. Joann Szabo, Phyllis Tonkin, Veronique Vaillancourt, Philip Winston, and Deidre Wright, "The Clinton Scorecard," unpublished paper, University of Houston Graduate School of Social Work, Houston, TX, April 25, 1996.

185. Norman Wyers, "Is Gay Rights Necessary for the Well-Being of Gays and Lesbians?" in Howard Jacob Karger and James Midgley (eds.), *Controversial Issues in Social Welfare Policy* (Boston: Allyn & Bacon, 1994).

186. K. Dychtwald, *Age Power* (New York: Putnam 1999).

187. American Association of Retired Persons, *A Profile of Older Americans* (Washington, DC: AARP, 1999).

188. C. Adamec, *The Unofficial Guide to Eldercare* (New York: McMillan Press, 1999).

189. C. Cozic (ed.), *An Aging Population: Opposing Viewpoints* (San Diego, CA: Greenhaven Press, 1996).

190. American Association of Retired Persons, *A Profile of Older Americans*.

191. Adamec, *The Unofficial Guide to Eldercare*.

192. Dychtwald, *Age Power*.

193. Ibid.

194. Cozic, *An Aging Population*.

195. American Association of Retired Persons, *A Profile of Older Americans*.

196. D. Olsen, "Testimony in Hearings before the Task Force on Social Security of the Committee on the Budget, House of Representatives, 106th Congress, First Session," May–June 1999. Retrieved from the World Wide Web: http://frwebgate.access.gpo.gov/cg . . . diskb/wais/data/106_house_hearings

197. Adamec, *The Unofficial Guide to Eldercare*.

198. M. Moon and J. Mulvey, *Entitlements and the Elderly: Protecting Promises, Recognizing Reality* (Washington DC: Urban Institute, 1996), p. 9.

199. Ibid.

200. Dychtwald, *Age Power*.

201. Cozic, *An Aging Population*.

202. Ibid.

203. Judy Ochoa and Barbara Navarro, "The State of America's Aged," class paper, University of Houston Graduate School of Social Work, May 2, 2000.

204. Ibid., p. 7.

205. U.S. Census Bureau, "Sixty-Five Plus in the United States," May 1995. Retrieved from the World Wide Web: http://www.census.gov/socdemo/agebrief.html

206. L. D. Haber, "Trends and Demographic Studies on Programs for Disabled Persons," in L. G. Perlman and G. Austin (eds.), *A Report of the Ninth Annual Mary E. Switzer Memorial Seminar* (Alexandria, VA, 1985), pp. 27–29.

207. Ibid., pp. 35–37. See also Bell, *Contemporary Social Welfare*, p. 174.

208. William Roth, "Disabilities: Physical," *Encyclopedia of Social Work*, 18th ed. (Silver Spring, MD: NASW, 1987), p. 86.

209. Ibid.

210. Haber, "Trends and Demographic Studies," p. 32.

211. Bell, *Contemporary Social Welfare*, p. 174.

212. DiNitto, *Social Welfare*, p. 104.

213. Administration on Developmental Disabilities, *Fact Sheet* (Washington, DC: Administration on Developmental Disabilities, n.d.).

214. Kathy Brown, "Mend It, Don't End It," *Outlook* 90, no. 3 (Fall 1996), p. 9.

215. D. D. Gehring (ed.), *Responding to the New Affirmative Action Climate: New Directions for Student Services* (San Francisco: Jossey-Bass, 1998).

216. Brown, "Mend It, Don't End It," p. 11.

217. Bill Clinton, "Mend, Don't End, Affirmative Action," *Congressional Quarterly Weekly Report* 53 (July 22, 1995), pp. 2208–2209.

218. Roger Hernández, "End Affirmative Action, but for the Right Reason," syndicated column, King Features, 1995.

219. Wilson, *The Truly Disadvantaged*, pp. 146–147; emphasis original.

chapter 5

Poverty in America

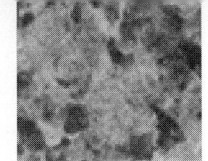

This chapter examines the characteristics of poverty in the United States, focusing particular attention on the wide range of theories that attempt to explain why some people become poor and why many stay there. Also examined are demographic aspects and ways of measuring poverty; family constitution and poverty; child poverty and elderly poverty; the urban and rural poor; and the connections between poverty and work-related issues such as the minimum wage, structural unemployment, dual labor markets, and job training programs. Lastly, this chapter surveys key strategies developed to combat poverty.

Some Theoretical Formulations about Poverty

Poverty is at once a simple and a complex phenomenon. Nevertheless, people living in poverty can be seen as falling into three general categories: (1) those making only minimum wage (the working poor); (2) the unemployed; and (3) those who have poor health or an occupational disability (e.g., a deficit in human capital such as poor education or a low quality and quantity of training and skills).

The word *poverty* can be defined as deprivation—either absolute or relative deprivation. **Absolute poverty** refers to an unequivocal standard necessary for survival (e.g., the calories necessary for physical survival, adequate shelter for protection against the elements, and proper clothing). Those who fall below that absolute standard of poverty are considered poor. **Relative poverty** refers to deprivation that is relative to the standard of living enjoyed by other members of society. Although basic needs are met, a segment of the population may be considered poor if they possess fewer resources, opportunities, or goods than other citizens. For example, if most families in a society have two cars and a family can afford only one, they are relatively poor. Relative poverty

(or deprivation) can be understood as inequality in the distribution of income, goods, or opportunities. Little attention is currently being focused on relative deprivation.

African Americans and Poverty

A question that has plagued contemporary social scientists is, "Why have African, Hispanic and Native Americans remained consistently poor when other groups, such as the Irish, Jews, and Poles, have climbed out of poverty?" The attempts made to answer this question have run the gamut from the alleged genetic deficiency of some minority groups to the difficulty faced by certain minority group members in assimilating because of their color. Cultural, racial, and family explanations have all been put forth over the past 30 years.

One of the most controversial theories offered to explain black poverty was formulated by Daniel Patrick Moynihan, a sociologist and former U.S. senator from New York. In his 1969 book *Maximum Feasible Misunderstanding,* Moynihan stated his argument:

> At the heart of the deterioration of the fabric of Negro society is the deterioration of the Negro family. It is the fundamental source of weakness for the Negro community at the present time. . . . The white family has achieved a high degree of stability. By contrast, the family structure of lower class Negroes is highly unstable, and in many centers is approaching a complete breakdown! . . . the circumstances of the Negro community in recent years have been probably getting worse, not better . . . the fundamental problem, in which this is most clearly the case, is that of family structure . . . so long as this structure persists, the cycle of poverty and disadvantage will continue to repeat itself. . . . A national effort is required that will give a unity of purpose to the many activities of the federal government in this area, directed to a new kind of goal: the establishment of a stable Negro family structure.[1]

Moynihan argued that the bonds holding the black family together had been ruptured both during slavery and at the beginning of the twentieth century, when the large migration of African Americans to the urban areas of the North occurred.[2] Prompted by the intense debate over the Moynihan report, Herbert Guttman demonstrated that the black family was not profoundly disrupted during either slavery or urban migration; instead, the problems of the contemporary African American family were associated with modern forces.[3] In any case, Moynihan's perspective situated the problem of black poverty within the fabric of African American family life. For Moynihan the problem of poverty lay in the matriarchal African American family: The supposed emasculation of the black male by a strong matriarch coupled with the absence of powerful black men as role models for youngsters contributed to an identity crisis for male teenagers, a problem that would play itself out in crime and violence. Outraged by Moynihan's analysis, African American leaders launched an attack on his pseudopsychoanalytic explanation of black family life.

What emerges from the speculation about the causes of black poverty is an understanding that its causes are complex and are rooted in the social, political, and economic realities of the contemporary United States. In some measure, too, Moynihan's theories grew out of the work of the "culture of poverty" school.

The Culture of Poverty

One group of social scientists, the **culture of poverty** (COP) theorists, maintain that poverty and, more specifically, poverty traits are transmitted intergenerationally. These theorists, led by Edward Banfield and Oscar Lewis, argue that poverty involves a way of life passed on from one generation to the next in a self-perpetuating cycle. According to this theory the COP transcends regional, rural/urban, and national differences and everywhere shows striking similarities in family structure, interpersonal relations, time orientation, value systems, and patterns of spending.[4]

Oscar Lewis maintains that the COP flourishes in certain types of societies. In these societies there is a cash economy based on wage labor and production for profit; there is a high rate of under- and unemployment for unskilled workers; low wages are common; there is a failure to provide low-income groups with social, political, and economic organization, either on a voluntary basis or by governmental imposition; a bilateral kinship system rather than a unilateral one exists; and a set of values held by the dominant class stresses the accumulation of wealth and property, the possibility of upward mobility, thrift, and the idea that low economic status results from personal inadequacy.

According to Lewis, the culture of poverty is characterized by hopelessness, indifference, alienation, apathy, and a lack of effective participation in or integration into the social and economic fabric of society. Key COP elements are a present-tense time orientation; cynicism toward and mistrust of those in authority; strong feelings of marginality, helplessness, dependence, and inferiority; a high incidence of maternal deprivation, orality, and a weak ego structure; confusion of sexual identification; lack of impulse control and the inability to defer gratification; a sense of resignation and fatalism; a widespread belief in male superiority; a high tolerance for psychological pathology of all kinds; provincialism coupled with little sense of history; the absence of childhood as a specially protected and prolonged state, and thus early initiation into free sexual unions or consensual (nonlegal) marriages; a high incidence of abandonment of wives and children; a matriarchal family structure containing an emphasis on family solidarity—which is never achieved, because of sibling rivalry and competition for maternal affection; a proclivity toward authoritarianism; and a minimal level of community organization beyond the nuclear or extended family combined with a strong sense of territoriality.

Adherents of this theoretical framework believe that simply being poor does not initiate a person into the culture of poverty. Banfield and Lewis both argue that most people who experience poverty through the loss of a breadwinner, involuntary unemployment, or illness are able to overcome their impoverishment. The poverty that these people endure is not the squalid, degrading, and self-perpetuating kind found among COP victims. Lewis suggests that only 20 percent of those living below the poverty line are actually ensconced in the culture of poverty. Nevertheless, according to Banfield, those who are in the culture of poverty will be poor regardless of their external circumstances, and improvements in their environment will affect their poverty only superficially.

Some opponents of the COP theory argue that this formulation diverts attention from the real factors that cause poverty. These critics maintain that an unjust society encourages the attitudes that Lewis and Banfield have observed. Other critics argue that many of Lewis's observations about the COP theory are also true of the middle and upper classes. For example, the inability to defer gratification underlies many credit card purchases. Free sexual unions and consensual marriages are a common occurrence among the middle classes; they are also well publicized in Hollywood. Provincialism and a lack of community are earmarks of the modern suburb as well as of the slum. The inability to achieve family solidarity is widespread in U.S. culture, and feelings of indifference, helplessness, alienation, and dependence probably afflict middle-class people as often as they do the slum dweller. Consequently, either a culture of poverty does not exist or it has been usurped by the middle classes in the same way that marijuana and jazz have been.

Eugenics and Poverty

Theories based on eugenics and focusing on genetic inferiority have surfaced periodically as explanations for poverty, crime, and disease. In his 1877 book *The Jukes,* Richard Dugdale reported on a study of the New York penal system and found that crime, pauperism, and disease were transmitted intergenerationally and were closely related to prurient behavior, feeblemindedness, intemperance, and mental disorder.[5] A second major book of the eugenics movement was Henry Goddard's *The Kallikak Family,* an account

of a Revolutionary War soldier who had an affair with a feebleminded servant girl before his marriage to a "respectable woman."[6] As part of his analysis, Goddard meticulously listed the disreputable descendants of the servant girl and compared them with the respectable achievers who emerged from the wife's descendants. Dugdale and Goddard's findings were reaffirmed by similar pseudoscientific research that further established poverty as an inherited characteristic. Generations of students were taught the dogma of eugenics.

The eugenics movement went into remission for several decades when it became obvious to what extent racial and genetic theories had formed the groundwork for Hitler's genocidal policies. However, the movement reemerged—albeit in a modified form—with the publication in 1969 of Arthur Jensen's article "How Much Can We Boost IQ and Scholastic Achievement?"[7] Jensen concluded that compensatory education was doomed to failure because 80 percent of intelligence (as measured by intelligence tests) was inherited. He pointed to the fact that the average IQ scores of African Americans were 15 points lower than the scores of their white counterparts, and he concluded therefore that money spent on compensatory education was wasted.[8]

Jensen's theories were taken one step farther by William Shockley, a Nobel laureate in physics who became interested in genetics in 1974. Shockley advocated paying the "unfit poor" (those who paid no income taxes) $1,000 for each point they fell below an IQ of 100, if they agreed to be sterilized. The money they received would be placed in a trust fund and dispensed to them throughout their lives.[9] To encourage the propagation of brilliant people like himself, Shockley invited other Nobel laureates to follow his lead and contribute to a sperm bank.[10]

Richard Herrnstein, a Harvard psychologist and a colleague of Shockley and Jensen, claimed that income and wealth are distributed among Americans on the basis of their abilities, which, in the final analysis, are related to their IQ. Herrnstein argued in 1973 that the United States was becoming a "hereditary meritocracy"; he maintained that the most capable citizens should receive the greatest rewards, which would serve as incentives to them to take the responsibility of leadership.[11]

A more recent book that rekindled the eugenics discussion was Richard Herrnstein and Charles Murray's *The Bell Curve*.[12] The authors argue that socioeconomic inequality in the United States is due not to the effects of capitalism or institutionalized racism but to lack of genetic intelligence. Armed with statistics, tables, and charts, Herrnstein and Murray try to demonstrate that those in the lower socioeconomic strata have lower intelligence, which is reflected in lower IQ scores. Intelligence, they argue, determines success. Much of their discussion focuses on stereotyped groups such as unwed teenage mothers and chronically unemployed males. Herrnstein and Murray claim that whites, and in particular white males, score higher on intelligence tests,[13] which explains why white males control so many of society's institutions. Conversely, the poor have been bypassed by economic opportunity because of lower intelligence. Hence, affirmative action programs run counter to intellectual meritocracy, and expending large sums of money to educate and improve the lot of the poor is a waste given their innate cognitive deficiencies.

Herrnstein and Murray's solution lies in creating policies that better the lives of the poor by removing governmental interference, thus restoring social control to neighborhoods and municipalities. Their proposals include eliminating bureaucratic mechanisms that complicate the lives of the poor. They argue that the best way for society to raise the mean IQ is for smarter, not duller, women to have children. They also argue against what they see as a governmental policy that encourages "the wrong women" to have children.

The scholarship in *The Bell Curve* has been subject to attacks from a wide range of critics in the scientific and educational communities. Herrnstein and Murray's arguments have been compared to those of Nazi eugenicists.[14] Critics also note that they exaggerate IQ as a predictor of job performance by attributing inaccurate validities to IQ test scores and by substituting hypotheticals

for reality. Stephen Jay Gould compares the arguments of Herrnstein and Murray to those of Joseph-Arthur, comte de Gobineau, the "father of all modern racist science."[15]

The theories of Shockley, Jensen, Herrnstein, and Murray have been repudiated by scores of educators, psychologists, sociologists, and anthropologists. Critics claim that IQ scores do not guarantee success in life and point out that many incarcerated criminals have high IQ scores. Moreover, several studies have shown that compensatory education does significantly raise IQ scores.[16] Finally, a variety of studies have found that IQ tests are biased in favor of middle-class and upper-socioeconomic-level students. In short, assertions about genetic inferiority fail to hold up under scrutiny.

The Radical School and Poverty

Radicals define poverty as the result of exploitation by the ruling or dominant class under **capitalism.** According to Marxians, as discussed in Chapter 1, one function of poverty is to provide capitalists with an army of surplus laborers who can be used to depress the wage structure of society. For example, applying the law of supply and demand to the wage marketplace, employers can use an oversupply of workers to pay low wages in the knowledge that there will always be an abundance of takers. Moreover, when there is an oversupply of labor, employers can more easily threaten recalcitrant workers with dismissal, because each worker is aware of the competition for his or her job. The oversupply of workers is inextricably linked to the fabric of poverty, in that the threat of poverty becomes a way to discipline the labor force and thereby force concessions from it.

A second function of poverty is to increase the prestige of the middle class by providing a class directly below it. As long as an underclass exists, the middle class has a group it can feel superior to. The superiority felt by the middle class encourages a bond with the upper class around the issue of social stability, because both classes fear the loss of their social position. The existence of the poor thus obscures the class tensions between the upper and the middle class over the issue of resource distribution. In that sense, an efficient way to defuse a conflict between two potential enemies is to create a third enemy (the poor) that appears to threaten both parties.

According to David Gil, poverty can also be understood in view of status and resource allocations and the division of labor.[17] Most developed societies engage in several universal processes related to these factors. For instance, societies must develop resources—symbolic, material, life-sustaining, and life-enhancing goods and services. They must also develop a division of labor and must assign individuals or groups to specific tasks related to developing, producing, or distributing the resources of the society. The division of labor is used as the basis for assigning statuses to individuals and groups; that is, the more highly a society prizes the function an individual or group is expected to perform, the higher the status and the reward that group or individual will accrue. By manipulating the division of labor, a society is able to assign individuals to specific statuses within the total array of statuses and functions available. These status allocations involve corresponding roles and prerogatives.

Complementing the assignment of status roles is the issue of rights distribution. Higher-status roles implicitly demand greater compensation than lower-status roles, and such rewards come by way of the distribution of rights. Higher-status groups are rewarded by a substantial and liberal distribution of general entitlements and specific rights to material and symbolic resources, goods, and services. Conversely, lower-status groups are denied these resources through formal and informal constraints. The entire process is couched in the language of the marketplace. That is, societies rationalize this form of status and goods allocation by an expressed belief in the omniscience of the marketplace; so as to make the process appear rational, the market is mystically endowed with internal logic. The implicit ideology is so well masked that it often appears fail-safe and is rarely questioned.

Society allocates goods and statuses (often inequitably) because all valuable resources are finite, with their worth judged by the quantity available. For instance, gold is a valuable because its quantity is limited. In that sense, opportunity is a valuable because it, too, is limited. Harvard University is prestigious in part because only a limited number of students are accepted yearly and its admissions policy is stringent. If Harvard University were to adopt an open-door admissions policy, its prestige would likely plummet. High-status occupations and social positions are also scarce commodities that are socially distributed.

The question remains as to how statuses are distributed and how the division of labor is determined. In U.S. society both the division of labor and status allocation—and their by-product, the distribution of rights—are differentially determined by gender, race, and social class. In large part, those occupying high-status positions determine their successors; and, more often than not, the heirs apparent belong to the same social class.

Radicals argue that poverty is a logical outgrowth of an inequitable system of resource, status, and rights distribution. Those who live in poverty have been assigned specific social tasks and roles, and the status of the group often corresponds to the nature of the task. Through the assignment of status, roles, and rights distribution, societies attempt to reproduce themselves and the ideologies that justify their existence. In the end, the main job of any society is to reproduce itself—and in doing so, it reproduces the relations of production and power.

Although on the surface the radicals' argument appears to explain social inequity, it does not necessarily explain poverty. For instance, is it possible for status allocation to be based on the need of a society to reproduce itself, and yet for that society to obviate poverty? Adherents of the radical approach argue that so long as society reproduces itself on the basis of the private ownership of the means of production, poverty will be omnipresent. On the other hand, many radical theorists argue that even though status must be allocated, poverty can still be eliminated through the equitable distribution of goods and resources. But although it may be possible to eradicate poverty and at the same time allocate status, most radicals believe that this cannot be done under the aegis of capitalism. According to radical critics, the social function of the poor in this country cannot be altered without a fundamental rearrangement of the social fabric of U.S. society. In short, poverty is an immutable reality in a society marked by discrimination and the inequitable distribution of resources.

 # Who Make Up the Poor?

The University of Michigan's Panel Study of Income Dynamics (PSID) followed 5,000 U.S. families for almost 10 years (1969–1978). Researchers found that only 2 percent of families were persistently poor (i.e., poor throughout the entire period),[18] a result suggesting that poverty is a fluid rather than a static condition. The data showed that as people gained (or lost) jobs, as marriages were created (or dissolved), or as offspring were born (or left home), people either were pushed into poverty or escaped from it. Moreover, the data showed that most people who were poor in a given year had not been poor for an extended period of time.[19] In fact, about one-third of the individuals who were poor in any given year escaped from poverty the following year, and only about one-third of the poor families in any given year had been poor for at least eight of the preceding years. Changes in family composition, especially divorce or separation, were the leading causes of poverty. Conversely, **spells of poverty** were most often ended by family reconstitution (e.g., remarriage).

U.S. Poverty Highlights

The following statistics from 1999 suggest some important trends in poverty in the United States.

- The poverty rate in 1999 was 11.8 percent (32.3 million people), down from 12.7 percent (34.5 million) in 1998. This was the lowest poverty rate since 1979.

- The poverty rate for children under 18 was 16.9 percent, down from 18.9 percent in 1998. This was the lowest child poverty rate since 1979.

- The poverty rate for people over 65 declined to 9.7 percent, down from 10.5 percent in 1998 and the lowest rate ever recorded.

- Poverty rates also declined for every racial and ethnic group. These rates have fallen below or equaled the lowest recorded rates for each group with the exception of non-Hispanic whites. The poverty rate for blacks was 23.6 percent in 1999, down from 26.1 percent in 1998. Although this was the lowest black rate ever recorded, it was still three times the poverty rate for whites (7.7 percent). The non-Hispanic white poverty rate fell to 7.7 percent, the lowest for this group since 1979. For Hispanics the poverty rate declined to 22.8 percent, down from 25.6 percent in 1998 and not statistically different from the lowest rates ever recorded. The poverty rate for Asians and Pacific Islanders dropped to 10.7 percent in 1999, down from 12.5 percent in 1998. It was the lowest rate since data for this group were first recorded in 1987. The 1997–1999 poverty rate for American Indians and Alaska Natives was 25.9 percent, not statistically different from those of blacks and Hispanics.

- Poverty rates were 10.9 percent in the Northeast and 12.6 percent in the West. In each region the rate represented about a 2 percent drop since 1998. The poverty rates remained the same for the South and Midwest.

- Eighty-one percent of the drop in poverty occurred in metropolitan central cities, where 29 percent of all people but 41 percent of all poor people lived.

- No state showed a significant increase in poverty.[20]

Although these trends are promising, they must be located in several different contexts. First, these data were recorded in the relatively robust economic times of the late 1990s. Poverty was reduced as the size of the economy grew and more economic resources were available. These figures will likely be reversed if the economy experiences a downturn. Second, many of the "lowest" figures are in comparison to 1979, when the economy was far weaker (with higher unemployment and greater inflation than the late 1990s). In light of the strength of the U.S. economy in the late 1990s compared to its weakness in 1979, the reduction in the poverty rate should be significantly greater than it is. For example, the overall poverty rate in 1999 was 11.8 percent; but it was 11.7 percent in 1979 and as low as 11.1 percent in 1973 (also a weak economic period). Finally, although important, the numbers indicating a reduction in poverty are relatively small. From 1989 (a period of economic slowdown) to 1999, the overall poverty rate was reduced only from 12.8 to 11.8 percent. Table 5.1 describes the characteristics and numbers of poor over a 40-year period.

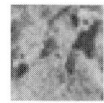 # Measuring Poverty

There are two versions of the federal poverty measure: (1) the poverty threshold and (2) the poverty guideline. The poverty threshold, also called the **poverty line,** is the official federal poverty measure and is used primarily for statistical purposes, such as estimates of the number of Americans in poverty each year. All official population figures are calculated using the poverty threshold. The poverty guideline uses a slightly lower poverty level than the poverty threshold; for example, for a family of four in 1999 the poverty guideline was $16,700 versus $17,029. The poverty guideline is used for determining eligibility requirements for federal programs such as Head Start, food stamps, the National School Lunch Program, and Low-Income Home Energy Assistance Program. Other federal programs, including TANF and Supplemental Security Income, use the poverty threshold.

Set by the Social Security Administration (SSA), absolute poverty in the United States is defined by a poverty line drawn at a given income. The poverty threshold used by the federal government was developed in the mid-1960s; the SSA created it by taking the cost of the least expensive food plan (the Thrifty Food Plan) developed by the Department of Agriculture and multiplying that number by 3. This formula was based on 1955 survey data showing that the average family spent about one-third of its budget on food.[21] Formally adopted by the SSA in 1969, the official measure provides a set of income cutoffs adjusted for the size of the household, the number of children under age 18, and the age of the household head. To ensure the same purchasing power, the SSA adjusts the poverty line yearly, using the Consumer Price Index (CPI).

In 1999 the federal poverty index (poverty line or threshold) for a family of four was $17,029,[22] up from $8,414 in 1980.[23] (See Table 5.2 for a 24-year view of the poverty index). These increases in the poverty index do not represent more liberal standards but are due solely to the effects of inflation. Poverty is assumed to be eliminated when the income of a family exceeds the poverty line.

The poverty index is plagued by a variety of structural problems. In 1995 a National Academy of Sciences (NAS) study panel issued its recommendations in *Measuring Poverty: A New Approach,* a report designed to update the government's traditional method of determining poverty. The NAS study critiqued the following problems in the calculation of the current poverty threshold:[24]

- It excludes in-kind benefits (e.g., food stamps and housing assistance) when counting family income.
- It ignores the cost of earning income when calculating the net income of working families. For example, $5,000 in wage income is treated as the equivalent of $5,000 in welfare benefits, even though work-related income has inherent costs built into it (clothing, transportation, child care, etc.)

TABLE 5.1 ■ Persons below the Poverty Line, Selected Years and Characteristics, 1959–1999 (Numbers in thousands)

YEAR	OVERALL	PEOPLE OVER 65	CHILDREN[1]	INDIVIDUALS IN FEMALE–HEADED FAMILIES[2]	BLACKS	HISPANIC ORIGIN[3]	WHITE
1999	32,258	3,167	12,109	12,687	9,091	7,439	21,922
Rate	11.8%	9.7	18.9	27.8	22.7	22.8	9.8
1995	36,425	3,318	13,999	12,315	9,872	8,574	24,423
Rate	13.8%	10.5	20.2	32.4	29.3	30.3	11.2
1990	33,585	3,658	14,431	12,578	9,837	6,006	22,326
Rate	13.5%	12.2	20.6	37.2	31.9	28.1	10.7
1986	32,370	3,477	12,876	11,944	8,983	5,117	22,183
Rate	13.6%	12.4	20.5	38.3	31.3	27.3	11.0
1980	29,272	3,871	11,543	10,120	8,579	3,491	19,699
Rate	13.0%	15.7	18.3	36.7	32.5	25.7	10.2
1978	24,497	3,233	9,931	9,269	7,626	2,607	16,259
Rate	11.4%	14.0	15.9	35.6	30.6	21.6	8.7
1969	21,147	4,787	9,961	6,879	7,095	NA	16,659
Rate	12.1%	25.3	14.0	38.2	32.2	NA	9.5
1959	39,490	5,481	17,552	7,014	9,927	NA	28,484
Rate	22.4%	35.2	27.3	49.4	55.1	NA	18.1

1. All children, including unrelated children.

2. Does not include females living alone.

3. People of Hispanic origin may be of any race; it is an overlapping category.

Sources: Compiled from Committee on Ways and Means, U.S. House of Representatives, *Overview of Entitlement Programs: 1992 Green Book* (Washington, DC: U.S. Government Printing Office, 1992), Tables 2 and 3, pp. 1274–1275; U.S. Census Bureau, "Poverty 1995," September 26, 1996, retrieved from the World Wide Web: http://www.census.gov/hhes/poverty/pov95/thresh95.html; and Joseph Dalaker and Bernadette D. Proctor, U.S. Census Bureau, Current Population Reports, Series P60-210, *Poverty in the United States: 1999* (Washington, DC: U.S. Government Printing Office, 2000).

- It disregards regional variation in the cost of living, especially the cost of housing.
- When measuring family income it ignores direct tax payments, such as income and payroll taxes.
- It ignores the effects of earned income tax credits.
- It ignores the value of health coverage in determining family income, and ignores medical care costs in determining family consumption needs.
- It has never been updated to account for changing consumption patterns and expenses. For example, although food ac-

counted for one-third of all family expenditures in the 1950s, it now accounts for about one-seventh.[25]

To remedy the inherent problems in calculating the poverty threshold, the NAS panel made three central recommendations:

1. Change the measure of income by adding noncash benefits and by subtracting taxes and work-related expenses, child support payments, and out-of-pocket medical expenses.
2. Create a new poverty threshold that is based on clothing, food, shelter and "a little

TABLE 5.2 ■ Changes in Poverty Thresholds Based on Income and Family Size, 1970–1999

FAMILY SIZE	INCOME, SELECTED YEARS					
	1975	*1980*	*1985*	*1990*	*1995*	*1999*
1	$2,724	$ 4,190	$ 5,250	$ 6,652	$7,763	$ 8,501
2	3,506	5,363	7,050	8,509	9,933	10,869
3	4,293	6,565	8,850	10,419	12,158	13,920
4	5,500	8,414	10,650	13,359	15,569	17,029
5	6,499	9,966	12,450	15,572	18,408	20,127
6	7,316	11,269	14,250	17,839	20,804	22,727
7	9,022	13,955	16,050	20,241	23,552	25,912

Source: Compiled from U.S. Bureau of the Census, *Technical Paper 56,* series P-60, Nos. 134 and 149 (Washington, DC: U.S. Government Printing Office, 1992); U.S. Census Bureau, "Poverty 1995," September 26, 1996, retrieved from the World Wide Web: http://www.census.gov/hhes/poverty/pov95/thresh95.html; and Joseph Dalaker and Bernadette D. Proctor, U.S. Census Bureau, Current Population Reports, Series P60-210, *Poverty in the United States: 1999* (Washington, DC: U.S. Government Printing Office, 2000).

bit more." The panel also suggested new ways of estimating the poverty threshold for families of different sizes and composition, allowing also for geographic variation. They further suggested that annual updates of the threshold be based not simply on inflation but on the growth of median expenditures on basic goods (food, clothing, and shelter).

3. Replace the current use of the March Current Population Survey with data from the Survey of Income and Program Participation, a measure that would change the percentage and distribution of the poor.

In line with the NAS panel recommendations, former Democratic senator Daniel Patrick Moynihan introduced the Poverty Data Correction Act of 1999, which would have required that any data relating to the incidence of poverty be corrected for geographic differences in the cost of living. Moynihan argued that because the current poverty calculations do not allow for geographical differences, they distort the true incidence of poverty.[26] Indeed, one would be hard pressed to argue that the cost of living in Houma, Louisiana,

is equivalent to that in Los Angeles or New York City.

Another problem with the current poverty threshold is its failure to discriminate between levels of poverty. The income deficit for families in poverty (the difference in dollars between a family's income and its poverty threshold) averaged $6,687 in 1999; the per capita family income deficit (the deficit divided by the number of family members) was $1,908. The average income deficit was greater for poor families with no husband present ($7,071) than for poor married couples ($6,293). Moreover, more than 10 percent of all African Americans and 8.3 percent of Hispanics had incomes under 50 percent of the poverty line. Just under 30 percent of African Americans and 31.3 percent of Hispanics had incomes that were 125 percent above the poverty line.[27]

 # Families and Poverty

Family composition is strongly correlated with poverty, and the families at greatest risk of poverty in the United States are those headed by single females. In 1999 the poverty rate for male-present families was 4.8 percent; for female-headed households it was 27.8 percent. When disaggregated, the figures become even starker: families headed by non-Hispanic white women had a poverty rate of 22.5 percent; families headed by African American and Hispanic women had poverty rates of 39.3 percent and 38.8 percent, respectively.[28]

More than one million children see their parents divorce or separate each year in the United States, and more than half of all children will spend some time in a single-parent family. Using six nationally representative data sets tracking more than 25,000 children, Sara McLanahan and Gary Sandefur found that children raised with only one biological parent are disadvantaged in a multitude of ways. Compared to children who grow up in two-parent families, they are (1) twice as likely to drop out of school; (2) 2.5 times as likely to become teen mothers; (3) 1.4 times as likely to be idle—out of work and out of school; (4) likely to have lower grade point averages, lower college aspirations, poorer academic attendance records, and higher rates of divorce in adulthood. These patterns persist even after adjustments for differences in race, the education of parents, the number of siblings, and the child's geographic and residential location.[29]

Child Support Enforcement

A 1995 Census Bureau study reported that slightly more than half of families with an absent parent have child support orders in place. Of those with orders, half received full payment and half received partial or no payment.[30] Federal authorities allege that out of a potential $48 billion, only $14 billion is collected in child support payments. Thus, the supposed gap between what fathers could and actually do pay is $34 billion. Moreover, federal officials claim that if all the money due custodial parents were collected, approximately 800,000 children could be moved off welfare.[31]

The recent attention focused on "deadbeat dads" has taken on distinct political overtones. Some argue that focusing on deadbeat dads has allowed policymakers to blame a variety of social ills, from poverty to high welfare costs to social pathology, squarely on fathers.[32] According to the Census Bureau, 64 percent (6.2 million out of 11.5 million) of custodial parents, including single fathers, do not receive child support. Of the 4.9 million parents that received some support, 76 percent received at least a portion of the amount owed. Although more than 5 million custodial parents went without financial support from their child(ren)'s other parent, about one-third of those chose not to pursue it. Two common reasons given were that (1) they did not want an award or (2) the noncustodial parent was unable to pay.[33] According to Stuart Miller, a significant portion of the child support payments not collected are owed by imprisoned fathers. A high percentage of prisoners have child support obligations, and as many as one-third of the inmates in many county jails are incarcerated because of child support noncompliance. Many of the other delinquent fathers are addicts or alcoholics or are disabled, mentally ill, unemployed, or otherwise unable to pay child support amounts.[34] In 1992 the General Accounting Office found out that 14 percent of fathers who owed child support were dead. The report further stated that 56 percent of fathers who owed child support "cannot afford to pay the amount ordered."[35]

For many years, despite vigorous implementation, child support enforcement (CSE) yielded marginal dividends in relation to the investment. From 1977 to 1997 child support payments for all mothers was flat and remained at about 30 percent; for divorced and separated mothers it went from 36 to 42 percent; for unmarried mothers it rose from 4 to 18 percent.[36] In 1993 $9 billion was collected through CSE, but this cost the government $2.2 billion. Successful collections from 2.8 million families removed 241,880 families, or about 10 percent, from public assistance. For that year, 12 percent of AFDC payments were retrieved through CSE. As a welfare prevention strategy, CSE is available to the nonpoor as well as those on welfare, a feature that obscures the functioning of the program as a welfare reform measure. Thus, of the $9 billion in 1993 CSE collections, most—$6.5 billion—came for families not on public assistance; only $2.4 billion was collected for AFDC families. CSE was a strong performer in overall collections but barely broke even with the welfare population, obtaining only $1.08 in collections for every dollar in program costs.[37]

In 1996, former president Bill Clinton signed into law the Personal Responsibility and Work Opportunity Reconciliation Act (PRWORA). The PRWORA was intended to broadly reform the public assistance system, but it also addressed child support enforcement. Specifically, failure to meet child support obligations could result in revocation of driver's and professional licenses; expanded wage garnishment; liens; and/or denial, revocation, or limitation of passports. Delinquent support obligations could also be collected through unemployment and disability insurance benefits.

By 1998 child support collections totaled a record $14.3 billion, an increase of more than 80 percent over 1992. In addition, jurisdictions collected $1.1 billion in delinquent child support by intercepting the income tax refunds of nonpaying parents. Paternity was established for 1.4 million children; 1.1 million new child support orders were put into effect; 6.5 million noncustodial parents had their income, assets, or employers located; and services were provided in 19.4 million cases.[38]

Much of the variation in child support payments can be attributed to social class: Wealthier absent parents pay more than poorer absent parents. Researchers from the Urban Institute found that in 1990 "60 percent of noncustodial fathers in the highest income quartile paid child support for that year," whereas "only 27 percent of noncustodial fathers in the lowest income quartile paid."[39] Absent fathers who are dropouts who fathered children out of wedlock and who have a new family with children, the study found, are less likely to pay child support. On the other hand, the level of formality of family life is an indicator of paying child support. Noncustodial fathers who were married longer, who recently left a family, and who have a child support court order are more likely to pay support. Absent fathers who move out of state are *more* likely to pay support, presumably because they relocate in pursuit of job opportunities.

Children in Poverty

In 1999 there were 12.1 million poor children in the United States. The poverty rate for children is higher than for any other age group: 16.9 percent in 1999 compared to an overall poverty rate of 11.8 percent. For children under age six, the poverty rate was even higher, at 22 percent (5.2 million children). While high, this rate is eclipsed by the almost 36 percent poverty rate for children under six living in female-headed households.[40] More than 10 percent of children in the United States live in extreme poverty (family incomes below 50 percent of the poverty line). Finally, 40 percent of children live in or near poverty (family incomes below 200 percent of the poverty line). Compared to poverty in later childhood, research indicates that extreme poverty during a child's first five years has especially deleterious effects on his or her future life chances.[41]

In 1999 33.1 percent of African American children were poor, or almost one out of every three black children. For Hispanic children the poverty rate was 30.3 percent, up sharply from 28 percent in 1995.[42] The probability of children growing up poor is strongly correlated with family circumstances. In 1987, for example, the Census Bureau estimated that 61 percent of the children born in that year would spend some part of their childhood in single-parent families, which are five times more likely to be poor than two-parent families.[43] (It should be remembered that although the single female–headed poverty rate is undoubtedly high, it may be somewhat overstated, because the definition of a household used by the U.S. Bureau of the Census counts an unmarried parent living in a consensual union as being a single parent.[44])

Although the child poverty rate is high in every racial and ethnic group, white children account for the highest number of children in poverty, almost 15 million. Poverty rates for white children rose more than 25 percent in the 1980s.[45]

Poverty and the Elderly

On the surface, the poverty picture for the elderly (once the poorest group in the country) seems to be growing less bleak. In 1959 the poverty rate for people over 65 was 35.2 percent; by 1999 it was down to 9.7 percent. Despite this downward trajectory, more than 3.7 million elderly citizens still live in poverty. Moreover, almost 30 percent of the elderly live near poverty levels, at or below 175 percent of the poverty line.[46]

Poverty among people 65 and older is disproportionately experienced by minority group members. Almost 23 percent of African Americans over age 65 were poor in 1999, and more than 49 percent were "near poor" (with incomes less than 175 percent of the poverty line). For African American women those numbers were 26.4 percent and 52.6 percent, respectively. More than 20 percent of elderly Hispanics were poor, and more than 49 percent were near poor. Among women the numbers rose to 25.4 percent and 52.3 percent, respectively.[47]

The federal government's estimates of the numbers of the elderly poor are questionable. At present the poverty line is calculated under two classifications: (1) families headed by persons under age 65, and (2) families headed by persons 65 or older, for whom the poverty line is set lower. For example, in 1998 the poverty line for unrelated individuals 65 or older was $7,818 compared to $8,480 for their younger counterparts—an annual difference of $662 or 8 percent. This difference is based on the belief that the elderly supposedly spend less on food. Arguably, from a physiological perspective, older people generally require more food than younger people to absorb the same amount of nutrients.[48] For example, in 1990, had the poverty line for the elderly been the same as for the rest of the population, their poverty rate would have *exceeded* the rate for the population as a whole, raising by 25 percent the number of elderly people designated as poor.[49]

 ## The Urban and Rural Poor

About 7.5 million people in the United States live in rural poverty. This large segment of the population is generally overlooked because of the national attention directed toward urban poverty.[50] Although rural poverty does not receive significant media attention, many rural centers have poverty rates equal to those of central cities. In 1999 14.3 percent of rural residents had income levels below the poverty line, a rate only 2 points lower than the 16.4 percent poverty rate in central cities.[51]

One-fourth of the rural poor live in the Midwest, one-third live in the South, 14.5 percent live in the West, and 7 percent live in the Northeast. Given that the farm population is only 10 percent of the rural population, the rural poor are mostly nonfarmers. The number of poor rural communities has dropped since 1960, when 2,083 counties had a poverty rate of 20 percent or more. By 1993 the number of persistently poor counties (counties designated by the USDA as having poverty rates of 20 percent or more) had dropped to 500. Although the average poverty rate for persistently poor counties was 29 percent, rates ranged from a low of 20 to a high of 63 percent. Traditionally poor areas include the *colonias* of the Southwest, the Mississippi Delta, Appalachia, and Indian reservations.[52] Most of the low-income counties were in the South, and half were located in just three states—Kentucky, Mississippi, and Tennessee.[53]

Rural ethnic and minority group members are poorer than their non-Hispanic white counterparts. In 1997 more than 30 percent of rural African American, Hispanic, and Indian populations were below the poverty line, compared to about 12 percent of rural white populations. Moreover, rural minority populations are also poorer than their urban counterparts. In 1997 30 percent of rural blacks were poor, compared to 22 percent of the total black population in 1999.[54]

Compared to the urban poor, the rural poor are more likely to be married and working. Poverty populations in rural communities are also more likely than urban poverty populations to be chronic or long-term poor. Though unemployment in general is higher in rural than in urban areas, the rural poor do not rely on public assistance to the same degree as the urban poor.

Lack of information about and access to services, fear of stigma, and reliance on informal employment as a means of earning money may explain some reasons for this difference. The rural poor are also adept at generating income through trade skills and through selling crafts within their community as well as to tourists outside the community.[55]

The family composition of the rural poor is different from that of the poor who live in central cities. The proportion of the rural poor living in two-parent families (61 percent) is much greater than in central cities (42 percent). As mentioned, the rural poor are also more likely than the urban poor to have at least one working family member; and more family heads among the rural poor work full time, year round than do central city family heads. The rural poor are also more likely to be elderly than their urban counterparts.[56]

Multiple factors contribute to chronic rural poverty, including high levels of illiteracy and low levels of education, a shortage of highly trained workers, high numbers of low-skill and low-paying jobs, high levels of underemployment and unemployment, an inadequate infrastructure, and limited access to credit opportunities. Also, inexperienced county and city managers in poor rural areas often find it difficult to attract major industries. As a result, the dearth of economic opportunity and restricted social mobility has resulted in the outmigration of many rural families to urban areas, especially when the primary breadwinner possesses higher-level skills and education. The lure of better-paying jobs in urban areas is also a powerful enticement for younger workers. As the pool of rural professional and skilled workers begins to evaporate, fewer industries are attracted to the area and the economic conditions deteriorate even further. Consequently, poor rural counties begin to experience the same social and economic desperation as poor urban areas. Drug and alcohol abuse climbs, as do theft, numbers of school dropouts, and teenage pregnancy rates. The increased need for mental health and economic development services provides a fertile ground for rural social work activities.

The dearth of nonagricultural rural industries is directly related to rural poverty, as most rural areas rely on nonagricultural industries as a base for the economy. Because of fewer retail outlets and less competition, the costs of commodities and services (e.g., food and gas) in rural areas are frequently higher than in metropolitan areas.[57] In addition, transportation also presents challenges to rural poverty residents. The results of these factors are dwindling or stagnant incomes, rising unemployment, and large numbers of people leaving rural areas.[58]

Work and Poverty

Labor force participation is a key variable in poverty. More than two-thirds of the poor in the United States are children, the aged, or the disabled. But apart from these groups—who are for the most part unable to work—poverty is also widespread within the workforce. The number of working people 22 to 64 who are poor rose more than 50 percent between 1979 and 1991.[59]

A Profile of the Working Poor

As a group, the working poor represent a growing sector of the poverty population. Nevertheless, in 1999 people who worked at any time during the year had a lower overall poverty rate (6.1 percent) than nonworkers (19.9 percent). Of the poor 16 years old and older, 43 percent worked, but only 12 percent worked full time, year round. More than 24 percent of female-headed households with one worker were poor, compared to 68 percent of households in which there were no workers. Not surprisingly, the poverty rate for married couples with one or more workers was 5 percent, compared to 24.4 percent for single female-headed families with one or more workers.[60] The following statistics represent some of the demographics of the working poor in 1998.

- The **working poor** are defined as individuals who spend at least 27 weeks (six months) in the labor force—that is, working or looking for work—but whose family or personal incomes fall below the official poverty threshold. About 7.2 million persons were classified as the "working poor" in 1998, nearly 300,000 fewer than in 1997.

- Among persons in the labor force for 27 weeks or more, the poverty rate for those employed full time was 4.1 percent in 1998, compared with 10.6 percent for part-time workers. The majority of the working poor (63.3 percent) were full-time workers.
- Working wives are less likely than working husbands to be poor, because they are more likely to be in families with a second earner. In 1998 about 2 percent of married women in the labor force for 27 weeks or more were in poverty, compared to 3.7 percent of married men. In contrast, 20.4 percent of families headed by a single woman who was in the labor force for at least six months were in poverty.
- Among those in the labor force for six months or more in 1998, 4.7 percent of non-Hispanic whites were classified as working poor, compared to 10.8 percent of blacks and 12.5 percent of Hispanics.
- Lack of education and poverty are closely related variables for those who work at least half of the year. In 1998 14.5 percent of high school dropouts were among the working poor, more than double the ratio of high school graduates (6.6 percent). The poverty rates were even lower for workers with an associate degree (2.5 percent) and for college graduates (1.4 percent). At all major levels of educational attainment, poverty rates for the working poor are higher for women and blacks than for men and whites.
- In 1998 nearly 12 percent of people who were in the labor force for at least 27 weeks but whose longest job was a service occupation lived below the poverty line. The 2 million working poor in these occupations accounted for nearly 30 percent of all workers living in poverty.
- There is a sizable group of full-time workers who live below the poverty threshold

and who are affected by three primary labor market problems: unemployment, low earnings, and involuntary part-time employment. In 1998 about 83 percent of the working poor who usually worked full time experienced at least one of these major labor market problems, with low earnings the most common problem.[61]

Why Are There Working Poor?

The large number of working poor is attributable to several factors, chief among them the replacement of high-paying industrial jobs with low-paying service jobs. About 20 percent of U.S. jobs will not support a worker and two dependents.[62] Almost 19 percent (23 million) of U.S. workers are employed in part-time jobs at lower hourly wages and with fewer benefits than comparable full-time workers.[63] Data from the 1997 National Compensation Survey shows that economywide earnings for full-time workers averaged $15.77 an hour, versus $8.89 for part-time workers.[64]

This employment trend reflects a clear movement away from higher-paying manufacturing jobs to low-wage service employment. For example, from the 1950s to the 1970s, businesses added about 1.5 million new manufacturing jobs each decade. By the 1980s, however, corporations had eliminated 300,000 manufacturing jobs. Continuing this trend, a million more manufacturing jobs were eliminated during the 1990s. However, these statistics grossly understate the problem. For example, in the 1950s 33 percent of all workers were employed in primary manufacturing industries (e.g., cars, radios, refrigerators, clothing). By 1992 only 17 percent were employed in those industries. While manufacturing jobs have declined, retail service jobs have increased. By 1998 retail trade workers (whose ranks continue to grow) earned $296 a week; manufacturing workers earned $428 a week.[65] At $296 a week a retail worker would have earned $14,208 a year in 1998. Hence, a single mother with two children working full time would have been almost exactly at the 1998 poverty threshold. And as noted earlier, this threshold would not have allowed for her child care costs, transportation, or the wardrobe needed for employment.

The absence of adequate employment opportunities contributes to a variety of psychological and physiological problems, and these in turn have prompted the creation of numerous social programs designed to aid unemployed or underemployed Americans. The history of employment policy in the United States showed a gradual expansion of programs until the policies of the Reagan administration reduced them sharply. Employment policy has become increasingly important for social welfare, as the popularity of TANF workfare programs (see Chapter 11) demonstrates.

At the same time, the lack of high-paying employment opportunities contributes to a growing **underclass.** In a market economy, most people are expected to meet their needs by labor market participation. Work provides income with which to purchase goods and services and benefits that afford security against the costs of health care, sickness, and old age. However, the labor market in capitalist economies is not well synchronized, thus resulting in the failure of employment to provide the basic needs of all people. As a consequence, many people who cannot work must rely on social welfare programs for their economic support. A little more than half—56 percent—of the poor people in the United States are adults of working age.[66]

Underemployment and Unemployment

The failure of the labor market to meet the economic needs of the population has been the source of important distinctions in employment policy. For example, those over 16 who are looking for work are counted by the Department of Labor as unemployed. But the **unemployment** rate does not assess the adequacy of employment. For example, part-time workers who wish to work full time are counted as employed; and workers holding jobs below their skill levels are not identified, even though such workers are **underemployed.** Finally, **discouraged workers** who simply give up and stop looking for work, relying on other methods to support themselves, do not appear in the unemployment statistics because they are not actively looking for work.

A second set of distinctions relates to economic performance. In a robust economy businesses start up and close down in significant numbers, leaving workers temporarily out of work until they find other jobs. Such **frictional unemployment** is considered to be unavoidable, the cost of a constantly changing economy. **Structural unemployment,** in contrast, refers to "deeper and longer-lasting maladjustments in the labor market," such as changes in the technical skills required for new forms of production.[67] Because of swings in economic performance, some unemployment may be cyclical, as when recessions pitch the rate upward; but because certain groups of workers in certain regions have persistent difficulty finding work owing to an absence of jobs, some unemployment may be chronic. Michael Sherraden has examined how these components vary in the composition of the unemployment rate and concludes that structural and frictional factors account for about one-third, **cyclical unemployment** for about one-fourth, and **chronic unemployment** for about one-half.[68]

These distinctions are important because social welfare is connected directly to the employment experience of Americans. When people are out of work, they frequently rely on welfare benefits to tide them over. Thus, welfare programs are often designed to complement the labor market. This has led some observers to refer to welfare as a **social wage;** in other words, the amount the government pays to workers through welfare programs when they are not able to participate in the labor market. Logically, much of welfare could be eliminated if well-paying jobs were plentiful, but such has not been the case in the United States. Policymakers have tacitly accepted an unemployment rate of close to 5 percent, which means that at any given time 5 to 8 million workers are unemployed.[69] Yet in 1978 Congress enacted the Humphrey–Hawkins Full Employment Act, which set an unemployment rate of 3 percent—equivalent to frictional unemployment—as a national goal. Since then, many government programs to aid unemployed, underemployed, and discouraged workers have been reduced or eliminated, leaving many Americans dependent on welfare programs for support.

The absence of employment opportunity contributes to other social problems. Research by M. Harvey Brenner shows that a seemingly small increase in the unemployment rate is associated with an increase in several social problems. During the 1973–74 recession, for example, the unemployment rate increased by 14.3 percent, a change associated with the pathologies shown in Table 5.3. Brenner calculated that the combination of the 1973–74 increase in the unemployment rate, the decrease in real per capita income, and an increase in the business failure rate was related to "an overall increase of more than 165,000 deaths [from cardiovascular disease] over a ten-year period (the greatest proportion of which occurs within three years)."[70] Overall, the total economic, social, and health care costs of this seemingly slight increase in unemployment came to $24 billion.[71]

As noted earlier, underemployment and unemployment constitute a major factor determining poverty. Between 1981 and 1986, 10.8 million workers lost their jobs because of plant shutdowns, layoffs, or other forms of job termination. Five million of these workers had been at their jobs for at least three years.[72] From 1979 to 1984 the Department of Labor conducted a special study of 5.1 million workers whose jobs were abolished between January 1979 and January 1984. This study reported that in 1984, 40 percent of these workers were still unemployed or out of the workforce. Of the remainder, close to half were employed at either part-time jobs or jobs with lower weekly earnings than they had previously received, and the majority experienced significant economic losses for a lengthy time after their jobs were terminated.[73]

The economic data suggest, then, that the private sector is not creating the kinds of jobs necessary to raise large numbers of low-income workers above the poverty line. In order to remedy this situation, the Progressive Policy Institute (PPI) has called for a nonpoverty working wage that would be sufficient to enable any full-time, year-round worker to support a family above the poverty line. This proposal calls for restructuring the earned income tax credit (EITC) so that, in combination with food stamps, the EITC benefit would lift the poor working family

TABLE 5.3 ■ Consequences of Increases in Unemployment

PATHOLOGICAL INDICATOR	PERCENTAGE INCREASE DUE TO RISE IN UNEMPLOYMENT	RISE IN INCIDENCE OF PATHOLOGY
Total mortality	2.3	45,936
Cardiovascular mortality	2.8	28,510
Cirrhosis mortality	1.4	430
Suicide	1.0	270
Population in mental hospitals	6.0	8,416
Total arrests	6.0	577,477
Arrests for fraud and embezzlement	4.0	11,552
Assaults reported to police	1.1	7,035
Homicide	1.7	403

Source: Reprinted from M. Harvey Brenner, *Estimating the Effects of Economic Change on National Health and Social Well-Being* (Washington, DC: U.S. Government Printing Office, 1984), p. 2.

out of poverty. According to the PPI, this proposal would cost $7.8 billion per year ($3.8 billion for increased EITC benefits and an additional $4 billion to accommodate more food stamp beneficiaries), or less than one-half of one percent of the national debt (as of 1996).[74]

Job Training Programs

The failure of the labor market to provide adequate employment opportunities to large numbers of workers has also led to a series of governmental efforts to better prepare the unemployed and underemployed. The first of these was the Manpower Development and Training Act (MDTA) of 1962. Intended as a program to assist workers displaced by technological and economic change, the MDTA was also expected to serve the disadvantaged when the **Office of Economic Opportunity (OEO)** was established in 1964. As one of the primary weapons in the Johnson administration's newly declared War on Poverty or **Great Society** plan, the MDTA grew rapidly, from $93 million in 1964 to $358 million in 1973. In 1973, 119,600 people were enrolled in MDTA programs. Still, the MDTA was only one of several Great Society job programs to aid the disadvantaged, including the Neighborhood Youth Corps (for high school students), the Job Corps (for young adults), and the Work Incentive Program (for AFDC recipients).[75]

By the mid-1970s the proliferation and cost of job training programs prompted the Nixon administration and Congress to consolidate MDTA and other job training programs under the Comprehensive Employment and Training Act (CETA) of 1973. In addition to consolidating federal job training programs, CETA also decentralized program responsibilities to local governments. By 1978 CETA was budgeted at $11.2 billion and enrolled 3.9 million persons[76] (by comparison, in 1978 the unemployed numbered 6.2 million).[77] Yet the nation's most ambitious program for contending with joblessness soon became the center of controversy. The recession of the 1970s placed financial burdens on local governments, at the same time as budget-limiting acts capped the fiscal capacity of local governments. Consequently, strong incentives were created for local governments to use the CETA program to fill civil service positions left vacant because of budget retrenchments. Because many of these jobs required work experience, CETA became a means by which a local government could subsidize its personnel budget—often by hiring relatively skilled persons and neglecting the chronically unemployed. Superseding CETA, the Job Training and Partnership Act (JTPA) of 1982 attempted to focus training on the hard-core unemployed in order to make them economically self-sufficient through private sector employment. Approximately 600 Private Industry Councils were created locally to synchronize training and job opportunities. The Reagan administration initially allocated $2.8 billion for the first year of JTPA, approximately three-quarters of what had been spent on CETA in 1980.[78] But appropriations were reduced in later years, even as the unemployment rate rose above 7 percent. During 1990, 565,200 enrollees were terminated from JTPA; of these, 55 percent found private employment at an average hourly wage of $5.54,[79] on an annual basis considerably below the poverty level for a family of four.

Dual Labor Markets

Despite large enrollments in government employment programs and the substantial expenditures of public funds, the difficulty of elevating people out of poverty through job training programs led several scholars to examine the nature of the work that participants are expected to find. Labor market analysts such as Peter Doeringer, Michael Piore, and David Gordon characterized employers and job seekers participating in job training programs as "a group of low-wage, and often marginal, enterprises and a set of casual, unstructured job opportunities where workers with employment disadvantages tend to find work."[80] These researchers reasoned that the segmentation of the labor market—into better jobs versus disadvantaged jobs—explained much of the problem at the root of government employment programs.

According to Piore, the labor market can be divided into two segments, or "dual labor markets"—**a primary labor market** and a **secondary labor market:**

> The primary market offers jobs which possess several of the following traits: high wages, good working conditions, employment stability and job security, equity and due process in the administration of work rules, and chances for advancement. The other, secondary sector, has jobs which, relative to those in the primary sector, are decidedly less attractive. They tend to involve low wages, poor working conditions, considerable variability in employment, harsh and often arbitrary discipline, and little opportunity to advance. The poor are confined to the secondary labor market.[81]

Piore noted that to the extent that employment is expected to solve the poverty problem, the trick is to see that the poor "gain access to primary employment."[82]

The magnitude of the secondary labor market has been explored in many studies. Researchers calculated that in 1970 36.2 percent of workers fell into the secondary labor market, a modest increase over 1950's 35 percent.[83] By the 1990s, however, two factors increased the proportion of workers in the secondary labor market. First, membership in labor unions—the best security for nonprofessional workers—fell from 30.8 percent of nonagricultural workers in 1970 to about 17 percent in 1996, leaving millions of workers vulnerable to the employment insecurity typical of the secondary labor market.[84] Second, a higher proportion of the new jobs created were in the service sector of the economy, which consists largely of secondary labor market jobs. Between 1979 and 1985, 44 percent of new jobs paid less than $7,400 per year.[85]

For workers in the secondary labor market, social welfare is an important source of support, whether this is in the form of income payments, such as AFDC, or in-kind benefits, such as Medicaid and food stamps. Yet the relationship between public assistance and the secondary labor market is a poor fit. Generally, no state provides benefits to families above the poverty level, even when the cash equivalent of food stamps is added to welfare benefits.[86] Consequently, most families have strong incentives to work in order to supplement their meager welfare benefits. The relatively punitive treatment of earnings under welfare programs encourages families to underreport their income from work. This dilemma is frustrating both for administrators of public assistance programs and for public assistance beneficiaries—especially for those with children, who often resort to deception for purposes of survival. In an investigation of income sources of AFDC recipients, Kathryn Edin and Christopher Jencks found that low AFDC benefits produced a perverse consequence: Virtually every recipient supplemented AFDC with income from other sources, but only one in four reported any portion of this to welfare authorities.[87]

The Minimum Wage and Poverty

The low minimum wage is another factor that explains the growth in numbers of the working poor. In 1999 an estimated 3.3 million hourly workers (4.6 percent of the workforce) earned the minimum wage of $5.15 an hour.[88] Broken down, those figures reveal important workforce trends. Among full-time workers 16 to 24 years old, 10.2 percent earned the minimum wage. That number increased to 12.3 percent for women workers aged 16 to 24. Among African Americans, 5.1 percent of the workforce earned the minimum wage compared to 5.5 percent of Hispanic men and 7.2 percent of Hispanic women. Almost 12 percent of all part-time workers earned the minimum wage.[89]

Further broken down, the following occupations have the highest percentage of minimum wage jobs:

> Private household services (36.8 percent)
> Retail trade—eating and drinking places (24.5 percent)
> Food service workers (23.8 percent)
> All service occupations (14.1 percent)
> Retail trade (11.5 percent)

Personal service workers (10.7 percent)

Farming, forestry and fishing (8.4 percent)

Agriculture (7.8 percent)

Cleaning and building service workers (6.9 percent)[90]

The 1938 Fair Labor Standards Act (FLSA) established the first federal minimum wage at 25 cents an hour. The minimum wage does not increase automatically: Congress must pass a bill and the president must sign it into law for the minimum wage to rise. Minimum wage increases have been signed into law by Presidents Truman, Eisenhower, Kennedy, Johnson, Nixon, Carter, George H. W. Bush, and Clinton. The minimum wage increased to $4.25 an hour by 1991, then remained at that level for more than five years. By 1996 approximately 10 million American workers were earning between $4.25 and $5.14 per hour. In 1997 the federal minimum wage was again raised, this time to $5.15 an hour.

The FLSA applies to employees of enterprises that do at least $500,000 in business a year. It also applies to employees of even smaller firms if the employees are engaged in interstate commerce or in the production of goods for commerce, such as employees who work in transportation or communications or who regularly use the mails or telephones for interstate communications. In addition, the FLSA applies to employees of federal, state, or local government agencies, hospitals, and schools; and it generally applies to domestic workers. Although the minimum wage covers about 90 percent of all nonsupervisory workers, the FLSA contains exemptions that may apply to some workers. For example, the law establishes a subminimum youth wage of $4.25 that employers can pay employees under 20 years of age during their first 90 consecutive calendar days of employment.

In 1950 the minimum wage brought a worker to 56 percent of the median wage. Throughout the 1950s and 1960s, as can be seen from Table 5.4, the minimum wage hovered between 44 and 56 percent of the average wage. By 1980, however, the minimum wage had fallen to 46.5 percent of the average wage, and in 1988 it dropped even farther to 35.7 percent. Overall, from 1979 to 1996 the minimum wage dropped 29 percent. Even the increase to $5.15 an hour in 1997 raised the minimum wage to only 42 percent of the average wage, bringing a family of three to 83 percent of the poverty line.[91] (This was considerably lower than the 120 percent of the poverty level reached by the minimum wage in 1968.[92]) Moreover, in 1997 the minimum wage would have had to be $6.07 (almost $1.00 higher than its current level) to have the purchasing power it did in the 1970s.[93]

From 1981 to 1990, for workers stuck with a frozen $3.35 minimum wage, the drop in earnings relative to the median income was significant in light of the 48 percent jump in the cost of living during that period. This low minimum wage was especially troubling in view of the fact that some 18 million Americans—including 8 million children—lived in a household with a working family member whose income remained below the poverty line.[94] The average share of household income earned by a minimum wage worker is 50 percent; 36 percent of minimum wage workers are sole breadwinners for their households.[95]

The minimum wage has been criticized by both conservatives and liberals. Looking at the persistently high unemployment rate among younger workers—including roughly 35 percent of African American teenagers[96]—some conservatives have argued that the minimum wage deters employers from hiring unproven workers. Lowering (or eliminating) the minimum wage, conservatives suggest, would encourage employers to make more jobs available to the disadvantaged. On the other hand, liberals have contended that the minimum wage is far from adequate. At its present level, a worker employed 40 hours per week would earn approximately $9,888 a year, $4,032 below the 1999 poverty line of $13,920 for a family of three. The controversy surrounding the minimum wage is compounded by the fact that some businesses in the service industry—notably convenience stores and fast-food franchises—have taken advantage of the large number of younger workers by hiring them

TABLE 5.4 ■ Value of the Minimum Wage, Selected Years

YEAR	PERCENTAGE OF POVERTY LINE FOR A FAMILY OF THREE	PERCENTAGE OF AVERAGE WAGE	VALUE OF THE MINIMUM WAGE, 1995 DOLLARS	MINIMUM WAGE NOMINAL DOLLARS
1955	73	44	$3.94	$0.75
1960	88	48	4.75	1.00
1965	103	51	5.59	1.25
1968	120	56	6.49	1.60
1970	107	50	5.92	1.60
1975	101	46	5.71	2.10
1980	98	47	5.76	3.10
1985	81	39	4.76	3.35
1988	73	36	4.33	3.35
1989	71	35	4.13	3.35
1990	79	38	4.44	3.80
1993	75	39	4.50	4.25
1995	72	37	4.25	4.25
1997	83	42	NA	5.15

Sources: Adapted from Isaac Shapiro, *The Minimum Wage and Job Loss* (Washington, DC: Center on Budget and Policy Priorities, 1988), p. 3; U.S. Census Bureau, "Income 1995," September 26, 1996; and Center on Budget and Policy Priorities, "Assessing the $5.15 an Hour Minimum Wage," March 1996, retrieved from the World Wide Web: http://epn.org/cpbb/cbwage.html.

on a part-time basis for limited periods to avoid paying the benefits associated with full-time employment.[97]

According to Jared Bernstein, a rise in the minimum wage also affects the group making just above that wage through a "spillover effect." Workers in this group are more likely to be older (87 percent are adults) and to work more hours (69 percent work full time) than minimum wage workers. Specifically, companies in metropolitan areas experiencing labor shortages use a "real" minimum wage that is often $1 to $2 above the federal level. Increasing the federal minimum wage will consequently influence the wage level above it.

The Living Wage Movement. In 1994, an alliance between labor and religious leaders in Baltimore led to a campaign for a local law requiring city service contractors to pay a living wage. Since then, community, labor, and religious coalitions have fought for and won similar ordinances in St. Louis, Boston, Los Angeles, Tucson, San Jose, Portland, Milwaukee, Detroit, Minneapolis, and Oakland. By 2000, there were more than 75 living wage campaigns under way in cities, counties, states, and college campuses.

The living wage concept is based on the idea that limited public dollars should not be used to subsidize poverty-wage work. When subsidized employers pay workers less than a living wage, taxpayers pay a double bill: the initial subsidy plus taxes for food stamps and the emergency medical, housing, and other social services low-wage workers require to support themselves and their families. Living wage campaigns seek to pass local ordinances requiring private businesses that benefit from public money to pay their workers a living wage. Commonly, these ordinances cover employers who hold large city or county service contracts or receive substantial financial assistance from the city in the form of grants, loans, bond financing, tax abatements, or other economic development subsidies.

Many citywide campaigns have defined the living wage as equivalent to the poverty line for a family of four, although ordinances that have passed stipulate wages ranging from $6.25 to $11.42 an hour, with some campaigns pushing for even higher wages. Increasingly, living wage coalitions are proposing other community standards in addition to a wage requirement, such as health benefits, vacation days, community hiring goals, public disclosure, community advisory boards, environmental standards, and language that supports union organizing.[98]

 ## Strategies Developed to Combat Poverty

Social scientists and policy analysts have identified three basic strategies for combating poverty. The first strategy, used by Lyndon Johnson in the War on Poverty and Great Society programs, was an attempt to apply a curative strategy to the problems of the poor. The **curative approach to poverty** aims to end chronic and persistent poverty by helping the poor to become self-supporting through changes in their personal lives as well as in their environment. By breaking the self-perpetuating cycle of poverty, curative approach strives to initiate the poor into the employment marketplace and, later, the middle class. The goal of the curative approach is rehabilitation rather than relief, and its target is the causes of poverty, not the consequences.

The second strategy is the **alleviative approach to poverty.** This perspective is best exemplified by public assistance programs that attempt to ease the suffering of the poor rather than ameliorating the causes of poverty.

The third strategy is the **preventive approach to poverty,** best exemplified by social insurance programs such as Social Security. In this approach, people are required to save money (via the government) to insure against the costs of accidents, sickness, death, old age, unemployment, and disability. The preventive strategy sees the state as a large insurance company whose umbrella shelters its productive members against the vicissitudes of life.

In 1958 John Kenneth Galbraith, later to become one of John F. Kennedy's principal economic advisers, wrote *The Affluent Society*. In this landmark book Galbraith identified two kinds of poverty: case poverty and area poverty. According to Galbraith, case poverty was a product of personal deficiency, or deficits in human capital. **Area poverty** was related to economic problems endemic to a region. "Pockets of poverty" or "depressed areas" resulted from a lack of industrialization in a region or the inability of an area to adjust to technological change. This kind of poverty was a function of the changing nature of the marketplace.[99]

One example of a case poverty approach is the federal government's attempt to promote education as a means to increase human capital. Poverty is highly correlated with educational deficits, and adolescent parenthood is strongly associated with low levels of basic skills and high dropout rates. For example, youths with the weakest reading and math skills are eight times as likely to have out-of-wedlock children and seven times as likely to drop out of high school as students with above-average skills.[100] To help address these educational deficits, the federal government instituted the Head Start program, which was targeted at poor children aged three to five and their families. The High/Scope Educational Research Foundation's 20-year follow-up study of Head Start (and similar preschools) found that compared to nonparticipants, program graduates were more likely to complete high school, receive additional vocational or academic training, be employed, and be self-supporting; they were also likely to have fewer problems with the law, have lower instances of teenage pregnancy, and not become public assistance recipients.[101]

Area poverty is illustrated by a review of poverty rates on a state-by-state basis (see Table 5.5). The 1998–99 poverty rate for all persons in the United States was 12.3 percent. Some states that were poverty pockets had much higher poverty rates, including New Mexico (20.5 percent), Mississippi (16.9 percent), the District of Columbia (18.6 percent), Alabama (14.8 percent), Louisiana (19.1 percent), West Virginia (16.8 percent), and Texas (15 percent). By contrast, states like New Hampshire (8.8 percent), Alaska (8.5 percent), New Jersey (8.2 percent), and Utah (7.3 percent) had poverty rates below the national average.[102] Depressed states such as Mississippi, Alabama, Louisiana, New Mexico, South Carolina, and West Virginia, among others, typically experience a recession economy regardless of the prosperity enjoyed by the rest of the nation.

The various approaches to poverty are not merely hypothetical formulations; they formed the basis for social welfare policy throughout much of the 1960s and beyond. Between 1965 and 1980, social welfare policies were grounded in the view that public expenditures should be used to stimulate opportunities for the poor. As a result, major social welfare legislation was enacted and billions of dollars earmarked for the remediation of poverty. Beginning with the Reagan administration in 1980 (and later with the first Bush presidency), however, there was a move away from reliance on social welfare expenditures and toward an emphasis on ending poverty through economic growth. Consequently, public expenditures for poverty programs decreased and tax cuts—intended to give people incentives to work and save money—increased. The Reagan approach assumed that it would be more in the interests of the poor to wait for gains realized through increased economic activity than to rely on welfare programs. This perspective assumed that the trickle-down effect of economic growth would benefit the poor more than direct economic subsidies. However, according to analyst Kevin Phillips, "Low-income families, especially the working poor, lost appreciably more by cuts in government services than they gained in tax reductions."[103] Despite the nation's long-standing belief in eradicating poverty through market incomes, the major factors influencing the general decrease in poverty from the 1960s to the late 1970s were governmental cash and in-kind transfers.[104]

Throughout the 1980s and 1990s, experimental work sponsored by the **Manpower Development Research Corporation (MDRC)** served to reinforce a suspicion among social policy analysts that, associated with the deterioration of employment opportunities, a growing number of poor were emerging in the United States. That the life circumstances of the minority poor were being severely attenuated was evident as early as the 1970s. Census tract data indicated that ghettoization was increasing significantly, further isolating poor urban minorities from the U.S. mainstream. That is, as exemplified in Table 5.6, although poverty had deleterious effects in neighborhoods defined as poor (census tracts with 20 percent poor), it considerably worsened social conditions of still poorer neighborhoods (census tracts with 40 percent poor).

Compounding the erosion of income and assets, urban minority communities were further disadvantaged by the exodus of middle-income African Americans to the suburbs and by the disappearance of better-paying manufacturing jobs and growth of low-wage service jobs. The interaction of middle-class flight and technological transformation proved devastating for the minorities residing in older industrial cities. During the 1980s, to be young, African American, and out of school was bad enough; the prospects were even worse for those who lived in the Northeast, particularly as compared with those living in the West. In 1985, 68 percent of young blacks living in the Northeast were unemployed, not in school, or not working, compared with 39 percent of those who lived in the West.

Under these circumstances, it is not surprising that the social and economic status of the minority poor plummeted in the 1980s. In 1983 the median worth of nonwhite and Hispanic families was only $6,900, 12.7 percent of that of white families; by 1989 that had fallen to $4,000, 6.8 percent of the worth of white

TABLE 5.5 ■ Percentage of Persons in Poverty by State, 1998–1999

STATE	AVERAGE PERCENTAGE IN POVERTY 1998–1999	STATE	AVERAGE PERCENTAGE IN POVERTY 1998–1999
United States	12.3	Missouri	10.7
Alabama	14.8	Montana	16.1
Alaska	8.5	Nebraska	11.6
Arizona	14.3	Nevada	10.9
Arkansas	14.7	New Hampshire	8.8
California	14.6	New Jersey	8.2
Colorado	8.7	New Mexico	20.5
Connecticut	8.3	New York	15.4
Delaware	10.3	North Carolina	13.8
District of Columbia	18.6	North Dakota	14.1
Florida	12.8	Ohio	11.6
Georgia	13.2	Oklahoma	13.4
Hawaii	10.9	Oregon	13.8
Idaho	13.5	Pennsylvania	10.3
Illinois	10.0	Rhode Island	10.7
Indiana	8.0	South Carolina	12.7
Iowa	8.3	South Dakota	9.3
Kansas	10.9	Tennessee	12.7
Kentucky	12.8	Texas	15.0
Louisiana	19.1	Utah	7.3
Maine	10.5	Vermont	9.8
Maryland	7.2	Virginia	8.4
Massachusetts	10.2	Washington	9.2
Michigan	10.3	West Virginia	16.8
Minnesota	8.8	Wisconsin	8.7
Mississippi	16.9	Wyoming	11.1

Source: Joseph Dalaker and Bernadette D. Proctor, U.S. Census Bureau, Current Population Reports, Series P60-210, *Poverty in the United States: 1999* (Washington, DC: U.S. Government Printing Office, 2000).

families.[105] By the middle 1990s the poverty rate of African Americans was three times that of whites.[106] But financial data provided only a partial portrait of a social tragedy that was evolving. In 1990 a criminal justice reform organization, the Sentencing Project, reported that one-fourth of all African Americans between the ages of 20 and 29 were incarcerated, on parole, or on probation. Incredibly, Harvard economist Richard Freeman calculated that 35 percent of all African Americans aged 16 to 35 had been arrested in 1989.[107]

TABLE 5.6 ■ Employment Rates in Large Central Cities, 1970–1980

EMPLOYMENT RATE	CENSUS TRACTS WITH 20% POOR			CENSUS TRACTS WITH 40% POOR		
	1970	*1980*	*CHANGE*	*1970*	*1980*	*CHANGE*
All Males, age 16+	63.3%	56.0%	–13%	56.5%	46.0%	–22%
AFDC families	19.8	28.0	+40	30.2	42.0	+40
Black persons	27.2	26.5	–3	6.3	8.3	+32
Poor blacks	28.3	30.5	+8	9.4	13.1	+40

Source: Adapted from Sara McLanahan, Irwin Garfinkel, and Dorothy Watson, "Family Structure, Poverty, and the Underclass," in M. McGeary and L. Lynn (Eds.), *Urban Change and Poverty* (Washington, DC: National Academy Press, 1988), p. 130.

Of the few proposals advanced to reduce poverty, most emphasize employment. New Deal–type job programs were proposed in works that received wide circulation, such as Nicholas Lemann's *Atlantic Monthly*[108] article "The Origins of the Underclass" (later expanded in *The Promised Land*)[109] and Mickey Kaus's *New Republic* article "The Work-Ethic State"[110] (later rewritten as *The End of Equality*).[111] According to William Julius Wilson, increasing job opportunities for the employable poor would have several related payoffs. For example, much welfare dependency among female heads of households can be attributed to the fact that large numbers of young men in poor neighborhoods are not good candidates for marriage because of their poor education, engagement in illicit activities, and unemployment. According to Wilson, employment programs that would make young men more marriageable would reduce not only the social costs of their current status but also those of the women with children who are dependent on welfare.[112]

Experience with employment training programs over at least two decades suggests that the earlier strategy advanced—to solve a substantial portion of the welfare problem by enabling people on welfare to find adequate employment—is not likely to achieve its goals solely through workfare. Although workfare programs may enhance the sense of self-worth of welfare beneficiaries, make for good public relations, and assuage irate taxpayers, these programs—whether coercive or voluntary—have achieved only marginal success in terms of their ability to get welfare beneficiaries into jobs that can make them economically self-sufficient. Given the experience of the MDRC demonstrations, to say nothing of the growing underclass, a more effective strategy would be a national labor policy directed at the secondary labor market. Such a policy would include further raising or supplementing the minimum wage and/or developing a benefit package to complement the minimum wage. In addition, tight labor market policies or the certification of completion of tough government training programs would make disadvantaged workers more desirable to employers. Without a national labor market strategy that addresses the secondary labor market—and therefore the plight of unemployed, underemployed, and discouraged workers—workfare programs are likely to remain punitive and the number of poor is likely to grow.

 **Conclusion**

Poverty is one of the most intractable problems facing U.S. society. Because poverty is both a political and a social issue, the policies surrounding it are often less than objective. For example, one can halve the poverty rate simply by redefining the poverty index. One can also cut poverty rates by placing a high dollar value on in-kind benefits such as food stamps and Medicaid. Conversely, one can swell the ranks of the poor by moving the poverty line upward; that is, by increasing the income level at which people are defined as poor. Like all social policies, poverty-related policies exist in a context marked by political exigencies, public opinion, the economic health of a society, and the complex mask of ideology.

Although various kinds of poverty-related data are available, policymakers remain uncertain as to the precise causes of poverty. What is known is that its causes are complex and involve, among other things, the effects of discrimination; the composition of family life, including the rise in single female–headed families and teenage pregnancies; geographical location; and age. In large measure, the determination of whether a child is poor depends on chance; that is, on the family the child is born into. Policymakers also know that the skewed distribution of income in society and governmental tax and investment policies have major impacts on the numbers of people in poverty and on the extent of their poverty.

Most policymakers agree that employment is the best antipoverty program. Thus, work-related factors such as the value of the minimum wage (especially its relationship to mean in-comes), the level of under- and unemployment, the rise or decrease in family incomes, and the general state of the economy all have a major impact on the level and extent of poverty. The availability of job training programs and the regulation of the dual labor market help determine which workers will make which salaries. Taken together, these factors have caused poverty rates to remain higher in the United States than in many other industrialized nations. They have also helped make poverty seem like an intractable problem with few viable solutions.

Questions of poverty have long plagued social scientists. Specifically, these questions revolve around why some groups are able to rise out of poverty but others appear only to fall deeper into the poverty trap. Although theorists such as Daniel Patrick Moynihan, Oscar Lewis, and others have offered explanations for poverty, none apparently hold up to empirical testing. This is because there is no simple or single answer to poverty. The causes of poverty involve a wide range of social, economic, political, and cultural factors. Poverty is one of the most elusive—if not the most elusive—problems facing U.S. social policy. Theories and strategies that address single explanations or single causes of poverty are doomed to failure, only aggravating a public that is already suspect of most anti-poverty measures.

 Discussion Questions

1. The measurement of poverty is at once both complex and controversial. Nevertheless, the way in which poverty is measured has important implications for the development of social policy in the United States. Describe some of the potential pitfalls in measuring poverty rates and discuss how the calculation of poverty rates affects the creation of social policy.

2. Working families make up an important and growing segment of the poor. What are some of the causes of the increase in the numbers of working poor as a percentage of the total population in poverty? What specific policies could be implemented to reduce the number of working poor families?

3. Several theories have been advanced to explain why some individuals and groups of people are poor while others are not. Theorists who have tried to tackle this problem include Daniel Patrick Moynihan, Oscar Lewis, and Edward Banfield, among others. Although all these theories of poverty have intrinsic flaws, which theory or com-

bination of theories described in this book (or elsewhere) do you think best explains the dynamics of poverty?

4. Many strategies have been developed to fight poverty, including the curative approach, the alleviative approach, and the preventive approach. Of these strategies, which is the most effective in fighting poverty and why? What alternative strategies, if any, could be developed that would be more effective in combating poverty?

5. Policy analysts have traditionally argued that jobs are preferable to welfare and that the lack of employment opportunities results in increasing needs for social welfare. Is this relationship apparent in your community? What is your evidence?

6. A commonly held belief is that government make-work jobs are inferior to pri-

vate sector employment. Yet many New Deal jobs programs have made important contributions to the infrastructure of the nation's cities. What New Deal projects are evident in your community? What were the resources used for these projects? If a new governmental jobs program were initiated, what community needs might it address?

7. The Job Training and Partnership Act has attempted to enhance opportunities for workers in the secondary labor market. What has been the track record of this and other programs in your community? Has one been more successful than another? How would you change these programs to more adequately address the needs of the poor in your community?

 # Notes

1. Daniel Patrick Moynihan, *Maximum Feasible Misunderstanding* (New York: Free Press, 1969), p. 61.

2. Daniel Patrick Moynihan, *The Negro Family: The Case for National Action* (Washington, DC: Office of Policy Planning and Research, U.S. Department of Labor, 1965).

3. Herbert G. Guttman, *The Black Family in Slavery and Freedom, 1750–1925* (New York: Pantheon, 1976).

4. See Edward C. Banfield, *The Unheavenly City* (Boston: Little, Brown, 1966) and Oscar Lewis, *La Vida* (New York: Harper & Row, 1965).

5. Richard Dugdale, *The Jukes* (New York: G. P. Putnam's Sons, 1910).

6. Henry Goddard, *The Kallikak Family* (New York: Arno Publishers, 1911).

7. Arthur R. Jensen, "How Much Can We Boost IQ and Scholastic Achievement?" *Harvard Educational Review* 39 (Winter 1969), pp. 1–23.

8. Winifred Bell, *Contemporary Social Welfare* (New York: Macmillan, 1983), p. 261.

9. William Shockley, "Sterilization: A Thinking Exercise," in Carl Bahema (ed.), *Eugenics: Then and Now* (Stroudsburg, PA: Doidon, Hutchinson & Ross, 1976).

10. Bell, *Contemporary Social Welfare*, p. 263.

11. Richard Herrnstein, *IQ and the Meritocracy* (Boston: Little, Brown, 1973).

12. Richard Herrnstein and Charles Murray, *The Bell Curve* (New York: Free Press, 1994).

13. Winnie Chen, Vilma Hernandez, Erin Townsend, and Carol Wyatt, "Affirmative Action," unpublished paper, University of Houston Graduate School of Social Work, Houston, TX, May 1, 1996.

14. T. Beardsley, "For Whom the Bell Curve Really Tolls," *Scientific American* 272, no. 1 (1995), pp. 14–17; Stephen Gould, "Ghosts of Bell Curves Past," *Natural History* 104, no. 2 (1995), pp. 12–19; and C. Lane, "The Tainted Sources of the Bell Curve," *The New York Review of Books* 41, no. 20 (1994), pp. 14–19.

15. Gould, "Ghosts of Bell Curves Past," p. 14.

16. Bell, *Contemporary Social Welfare*, p. 264.

17. David Gil, *Unraveling Social Policy* (Boston: Shenkman, 1981).

18. Blanche Bernstein, "Welfare Dependency," in Lee D. Bawden (ed.), *The Social Contract Revisited* (Washington, DC: Urban Institute Press, 1984), p. 129.

19. Greg J. Duncan et al., *Years of Poverty, Years of Plenty* (Ann Arbor, MI: Institute for Social Research, 1984).

20. Jospeh Dalaker and Bernadette D. Proctor, U.S. Census Bureau, Current Population Reports, Series P60–210, *Poverty in the United States: 1999* (Washington, DC: U.S. Government Printing Office, 2000).

21. William O'Hare, Taynia Mann, Kathryn Porter, and Robert Greenstein, *Real Life Poverty in America: Where the Public Would Set the Poverty Line* (Washington, DC: Center on Budget and Policy Priorities, and Families USA Foundation Report, July 1990), p. viii.

22. U.S. Census Bureau, "Poverty 1995," September 26, 1996. Retrieved 1996 from the World Wide Web: http://www.census.gov/hhes/poverty/pov95/thresh95.html; Dalaker and Proctor, *Poverty in the United States: 1999.*

23. Committee on Ways and Means, U.S. House of Representatives, *Overview of Entitlement Programs: 1992 Green Book* (Washington, DC: U.S. Government Printing Office, 1992), p. 1272.

24. Institute for Research on Poverty, "Improving the Measurement of American Poverty," *Focus* 19, no. 2 (Spring 1998), p. 2.

25. Ibid.

26. U.S. Senate, Introduction of the Poverty Data Correction Act of 1999. Retrieved 2000 from the World Wide Web: http://www.senate.gov/~moynihan/0119povd.htm p. 1.

27. Dalaker and Proctor, *Poverty in the United States: 1999*, p. xv.

28. U.S. Census Bureau, "Poverty 1995."

29. Sara McLanahan and Gary Sandefur, *Growing Up with a Single Parent* (Cambridge, MA: Harvard University Press, 1997).

30. ACF Press Release, Department of Health and Human Services, Washington, DC, December, 1995. Retrieved 1998 from the World Wide Web: http://www.acf.dhhs.gov/ACFNews

31. Philip D'Amato, Joseph Ekwere, and Gina Vitale, "American Child Support Enforcement: Now and in the Future," unpublished paper, University of Houston Graduate School of Social Work, Houston, TX, spring 1996.

32. Ron Dean, "Myths, Legends and the American Way: Deadbeat Dads," August 15, 1995. Retrieved 1997 from the World Wide Web: Newsgroups: soc.men

33. U.S. Census Bureau, U.S. Department of Commerce, Economics and Statistics Administration, "Who Receives Child Support?" (Washington, DC: U.S. Department of Commerce, May 1995).

34. Stuart A. Miller, "The Myth of Deadbeat Dads" (Washington, DC: American Fathers Coalition, 1996).

35. Quoted in Miller, "The Myth."

36. Elaine Sorensen and Ariel Halpern, "Child Support Enforcement Is Working Better Than We Think," The Urban Institute, Number A-31 in Series "New Federalism: Issues and Options for States" (Washington, DC: Urban Institute, 1998).

37. Ibid.

38. U.S. Department of Health and Human Services, Administration for Children & Families Office of Child Support Enforcement, "Child Support Enforcement Twenty-Third Annual Report to Congress, FY 1998 Program Highlights" (Washington, DC: 1999).

39. Mark Turner and Elaine Sorensen, "Noncustodial Fathers and Their Child Support Payments" (Washington, DC: Urban Institute, 1995), p. 9.

40. See U.S. Census Bureau, "Poverty 1995," and Neil G. Bennett, Jiali Li, Younghwan Song, and Keming Yang, "Young Children in Poverty: A Statistical Update," June 1999 edition, National Center for Children in Poverty (New York: The Joseph L. Mailman School of Public Health of Columbia University, 1999).

41. Bennett, Li, Song, and Yang, "Young Children in Poverty."

42. Dalaker and Proctor, *Poverty in the United States: 1999.*

43. *Congressional Record,* Senate, Vol. 133, No. 120 (Washington, DC: U.S. Government Printing Office, July 21, 1987), pp. S10400–S10404.

44. Sheldon Danziger and Marcia Carlson, "Cohabitation and the Measurement of Child

Poverty," Poverty Measurement Working Papers (U.S. Bureau of the Census, February 1998). Retrieved 2000 from the World Wide Web: http://www.census.gov/hhes/poverty/povmeas/papers/cohabit.html

45. Children's Defense Fund, *The State of America's Children* (Washington, DC: Children's Defense Fund, 1991), pp. 23–24.

46. Dalaker and Proctor, *Poverty in the United States: 1999.*

47. Ibid.

48. Kelly A. Olson, "Application of Experimental Poverty Models to the Aged," *Social Security Bulletin* 62, no. 3 (1999), p. 4.

49. O'Hare et al., *Real Life Poverty in America,* p. 9.

50. Cynthia M. Duncan (ed.), *Rural Poverty in America* (Westport, CT: Auburn House,1992).

51. Dalaker and Proctor, *Poverty in the United States: 1999.*

52. Ibid.

53. Kathryn Porter, *Poverty in Rural America* (Washington, DC: Center on Budget and Policy Priorities, 1989), pp. 7–11; see also Scott Barancik, *The Rural Disadvantage: Growing Income Disparities between Rural and Urban Areas* (Washington, DC: Center on Budget and Policy Priorities, April 1990), pp. ix–x.

54. Porter, *Poverty in Rural America,* pp. 3–11; see also Dalaker and Proctor, *Poverty in the United States: 1999.*

55. Porter, *Poverty.*

56. Porter, *Poverty.*

57. Economic Research Service, "Rural America at a Glance," USDA, Rural Development Briefing Room. Retrieved 1999 from the World Wide Web: http://www.ers.usda.gov/briefing/rural/Ruralecn/index.htm#pov

58. Ohio State University Extension, "Poverty Fact Sheet Series—Rural Poverty," Family and Consumer Sciences. Retrieved 2000 from the World Wide Web: http://ohioline.ag.ohio-state.edu/hyg-fact/5000/5709.html

59. Center on Budget and Policy Priorities, "Number in Poverty Hits 20-Year High, As Recession Adds 2 Million Poor, Analysis Finds" (Washington, DC: Center on Budget and Policy Priorities, September 3, 1992), p. 4.

60. Dalaker and Proctor, *Poverty in the United States: 1999.*

61. U.S. Department of Labor Bureau of Labor Statistics, "A Profile of the Working Poor, 1998," August 2000, Report 944. Retrieved 2000 from the World Wide Web: http://stats.bls.gov/cpswp98.htm

62. Michael Harrington, with the assistance of Robert Greenstein and Eleanor Holmes Norton, *Who Are the Poor?* (Washington, DC: Justice for All, National Office, 1987), p. 10.

63. Michael K. Lettau, "Compensation in Part-Time Jobs versus Full-Time Jobs: What If the Job Is the Same?" Bureau of Labor Statistics, 1994. Retrieved 2000 from the World Wide Web: http://stats.bls.gov/orersrch/ec/ec940080.htmx

64. Bureau of Labor Statistics, "Part-time Workers' Earnings: Some Comparisons," 1999. Retrieved 2000 from the World Wide Web: http://stats.bls.gov/opub/cwc/2000/Summer/art5exc.htm

65. Donald L. Bartlett and James B. Steele, *America: What Went Wrong* (Kansas City, MO: Andrews & McMeel, 1992), p. 18; Bureau of Labor Statistics, "Household Data, Annual Averages, 1999," retrieved 2000 from the World Wide Web: ftp://ftp.bls.gov/pub/special.requests/lf/aat39.txt

66. Michael Novak (ed.), *The New Consensus on Family and Welfare* (Washington, DC: American Enterprise Institute, 1987), p. 58.

67. Michael Sherraden, "Chronic Unemployment: A Social Work Perspective," *Social Work* (September–October 1985), p. 403.

68. Ibid., pp. 404–406.

69. As Sherraden notes, the common understanding that an unemployment rate of 5 is "normal" is not supported by economists, who calculate that structural and frictional unemployment can be reduced to 3 percent through astute social policies.

70. M. Harvey Brenner, *Estimating the Effects of Economic Change on National Health and Social Well-Being* (Washington, DC: U.S. Government Printing Office, 1984), pp. 2–4.

71. Ibid.

72. Harrington, *Who Are the Poor?* p. 10.

73. Center on Budget and Policy Priorities, *Smaller Pieces of the Pie* (Washington, DC: Center on Budget and Policy Priorities, 1987).

74. Robert J. Shapiro, "An American Working Wage: Ending Poverty in Working Families," *Policy Report,* No. 3 (Washington, DC: Progressive Policy Institute, February 1990), p. 1.

75. Sar A. Levitan and Joyce Zickler, *The Quest for a Federal Manpower Partnership* (Cambridge, MA: Harvard University Press, 1974), pp. 1–6.

76. Lawrence Mead, *Beyond Entitlement* (New York: Free Press, 1986), p. 27.

77. U.S. Bureau of the Census, *Statistical Abstract of the United States 1982–83* (Washington, DC: U.S. Government Printing Office, 1983), p. 391.

78. David Rosenbaum, "Federal Job Program Aids the More Able, According to Critics," *The New York Times* (July 22, 1984), p. 9.

79. U.S. House of Representatives, *1992 Green Book,* pp. 1690–1692.

80. Peter B. Doeringer and Michael Piore, *Internal Labor Markets and Manpower Analysis* (Armonk, NY: M. E. Sharpe, 1985), p. 163.

81. Michael Piore, "The Dual Labor Market," in David Gordon (ed.), *Problems in Political Economy* (Lexington, MA: D. C. Heath, 1977), p. 94.

82. Ibid.

83. David Gordon, Richard Edwards, and Michael Reich, *Segmented Work, Divided Workers* (New York: Cambridge University Press, 1982), p. 211.

84. U.S. Bureau of the Census, *Statistical Abstract of the United States 1982–83,* p. 409.

85. Harrington, *Who Are the Poor?* p. 10.

86. National Conference on Social Welfare, *To Form a More Perfect Union* (Washington, DC: National Conference on Social Welfare, 1985).

87. Kathryn Edin and Christopher Jencks, "Reforming Welfare," in Christopher Jencks, *Rethinking Social Policy* (Cambridge, MA: Harvard University Press, 1992), Chap. 6.

88. "House Passes Minimum Wage Increase of 90 Cents," *Houston Chronicle* (March 30, 1996), p. A1.

89. The Bureau of Labor Statistics, Household Data and Averages, "Wage and Salary Workers Paid Hourly Rates with Earnings at or Below Prevailing Minimum Wage by Selected Characteristics," Table 44. Retrieved 2000 from the World Wide Web: http://stats.bls.gov/pdf/cpsaat44.pdf

90. The Bureau of Labor Statistics, Household Data and Averages, "Wage and Salary Workers Paid Hourly Rates with Earnings at or below Prevailing Minimum Wage by Occupation and Industry," Table 45. Retrieved 2000 from the World Wide Web: http://stats.bls.gov/pdf/cpsaat45.pdf

91. Center on Budget and Policy Priorities, "Assessing the $5.15 an Hour Minimum Wage," March 1996. Retrieved 1997 from the World Wide Web: http://epn.org/cpbb/cbwage.html

92. Isaac Shapiro, *The Minimum Wage and Job Loss* (Washington, DC: Center on Budget and Policy Priorities, 1988).

93. Center on Budget and Policy Priorities, "Assessing the $5.15 an Hour Minimum Wage."

94. Center on Budget and Policy Priorities, "Many Black and Hispanic Workers Harmed by Minimum Wage Bill Veto, Analysis Finds" (Washington, DC: Center on Budget and Policy Priorities, June 15, 1989).

95. Democratic National Committee, "America Needs a Raise" (Washington, DC: Democratic National Committee, March 25, 1996).

96. Novak, *The New Consensus on Family and Welfare,* p. 32.

97. Amitai Etzioni, "The Fast-Food Factories: McJobs Are Bad for Kids," *Washington Post* (August 24, 1986), p. 6.

98. Acorn, National Living Wage Resource Center, "Introduction to ACORN's Living Wage Web Site." Retrieved 2000 from the World Wide Web: http://www.livingwagecampaign.org/

99. John Kenneth Galbraith, *The Affluent Society* (Boston: Houghton Mifflin, 1958).

100. Harrington, *Who Are the Poor?* p. 17.

101. Ibid., p. 22.

102. Christine M. Ross, "Poverty Rates by State, 1979 and 1985: A Research Note," *Focus* 10, no. 3 (Fall 1987), pp. 1–5.

103. Kevin Phillips, *The Politics of Rich and Poor* (New York: Random House, 1990), p. 87.

104. Sheldon Danziger, "Poverty," *Encyclopedia of Social Work,* 18th ed. (Silver Spring, MD: NASW Press, 1987), pp. 301–302.

105. Ibid., p. 303.

106. Lawrence Mishel and David Frankel, *The State of Working America* (Armonk, NY: M. E. Sharpe, 1991), p. 171.

107. Jonathan Marshall, "Targeting the Drugs, Wounding the Cities," *Washington Post Weekly* (May 25–31, 1992), p. 23.

108. Nicholas Lemann, "The Origins of the Underclass," *Atlantic Monthly* (June/July 1986), pp. 8–18.

109. Nicholas Lemann, *The Promised Land* (New York: Knopf, 1991).

110. Mickey Kaus, "The Work-Ethic State," *The New Republic* (July 7, 1986), p. 8.

111. Mickey Kaus, *The End of Equality* (New York: Basic Books, 1992).

112. William Julius Wilson, "American Social Policy and the Ghetto Underclass," *Dissent* (Winter 1988), pp. 84–91.

chapter 6

The Voluntary Sector Today

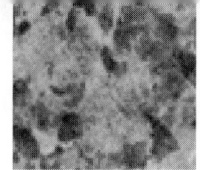

This chapter locates the voluntary sector with respect to the other institutions involved in social welfare in the United States. The heart of the **voluntary sector** is made up of the private, nonprofit organizations that are ubiquitous at the local level. Supporting the voluntary sector are philanthropic contributions that have been an important source of revenues for social service initiatives. The chapter describes the work of prominent human service agencies and examines the role of voluntary agencies in advocating social justice. The fiscal crisis of the voluntary sector is discussed, as are the recession of the early 1980s and the scandal that shook the United Way during the early 1990s, thus further compounding the funding problems of nonprofit service agencies. Finally, the chapter looks at emerging trends in the voluntary sector.

As the twenty-first century begins, welfare professionals are reassessing the capacity of the voluntary sector to meet the nation's social welfare needs. The primary reason for renewed interest in the voluntary sector has been the reluctance of taxpayers and politicians to authorize major new governmental welfare initiatives. As governmental expenditures for social welfare fail to increase in the face of rising demand for human services, the voluntary sector has been called upon to shoulder more of the welfare burden. This shift in responsibilities was stated explicitly by President Reagan, who appealed to the charitable impulses of Americans as a way for the nation to address human needs while reducing federal appropriations to social programs; the idea was restated by George H. W. Bush in his reference to "a thousand points of light" during his 1988 presidential campaign. Although President Clinton made no comparable gesture to the nonprofit sector, his statement that "the era of big government is over" had enormous implications for nonprofit agencies. Finally, the emergence of "compassionate conservatism" and its corollary, "faith-based social services," within the Republican party restates the conservative case for a reinvigorated voluntary sector.

Although many liberals of the 1980s were skeptical about the sincerity of conservatives in championing the virtues of the voluntary sector—suspecting that it was a ruse to gut governmental social programs—other events conspired to focus attention on this sector. A wave of conservatism in the 1980s and 1990s may have stalled the introduction of liberally inspired social legislation, but the conservative imprint on social welfare could be traced as far back as the late 1970s. During the Carter presidency conservatives began to challenge welfare programs on the grounds that they divided the family, eroded the work ethic, and subverted communal norms. A widely distributed monograph by analysts from the American Enterprise Institute criticized social "megastructures" for contributing to alienation among Americans, and called for stronger "mediating structures"—voluntary entities—to empower people.[1] During the 1990s Democrats responded to these conservative trends by jettisoning from their party platform traditional welfare planks that called for major new federal social programs in favor of more pluralist strategies that included the voluntary sector.

Structural Interests within Social Welfare

Organized responses to the needs of Americans have undergone fundamental change since European settlement. In a sense, the voluntary sector is the first modern welfare institution, with a long legacy in American social welfare. Over the centuries the voluntary sector has witnessed the emergence of competing institutions: the state and federal governmental programs of the public sector, the private practices of professional entrepreneurs, and a corporate sector accountable to chief executive officers and stockholders. Reflecting this transformation,

David Stoesz has posited that four groups can be identified within U.S. social welfare: traditional providers, welfare bureaucrats, clinical entrepreneurs, and human service executives.[2] Because these groups have become integrated into the nation's political economy, they are termed *structural interests*.

Traditional Providers

The heart of the voluntary sector consists of professionals and laypersons who seek to maintain and enhance traditional relations, values, and structures in their communities through private, nonprofit agencies. **Traditional providers** hold an organic conception of social welfare, seeing it as tightly interwoven with other community institutions. According to traditional providers, voluntary nonprofit agencies offer the advantages of neighborliness, a reaffirmation of community values, a concern for community as opposed to personal gain, and freedom to alter programming so as to conform to changes in local priorities.

Much of the heritage of social welfare can be traced to early proponents of this structural interest—people such as Mary Richmond of the **Charity Organization Society (COS)** movement and Jane Addams of the settlement house movement. Charity Organization Societies and **settlement houses** were transformed by two influences: the need for scientifically based treatment techniques and the socialization of charity. Together, these factors functioned as an anchor for the social casework agencies in U.S. industrial society. The agency provided the grist for scientific casework that was instrumental in the emergence of the social work profession. The new schools of social work, in turn, relied on casework agencies for internship training, a substantial portion of a professional's education. Once graduated, many professionals elected to work in the voluntary sector, ensuring agencies of a steady supply of personnel.

Voluntary agencies routinized philanthropic contributions by socializing charity. Beginning with Denver's Associated Charities in 1887, the concept of a community appeal spread so rapidly that by the 1920s more than 200 cities had "community chests." The needs of social workers for effective treatment techniques and the economic imperatives for organizational survival functioned together to standardize the social agency. Perhaps the best description of the casework agency is found in the 1923 Milford Conference Report, *Social Casework: Generic and Specific*, which comprehensively outlined the organization through which professional caseworkers delivered services.[3] By the 1940s the social casework agency had become a predominant form of service delivery. Today, much social service provision exists in the form of United Way–subsidized sectarian and nonsectarian agencies, whose member groups collected $3.8 billion in 1999.[4]

Welfare Bureaucrats

Welfare bureaucrats are public functionaries who maintain the welfare state in much the same form in which it was conceived during the New Deal. "Their ideology," according to Robert Alford, "stresses a rational, efficient, cost-conscious, coordinated . . . delivery system."[5] These functionaries view federal government intervention vis-à-vis social problems as legitimate and necessary, considering the apparent lack of concern by the private sector and local governments. Moreover, they contend that federal intervention is more effective than other forms, because authority is centralized, guidelines are standardized, and benefits are allocated according to principles of equity and equality.

The influence of welfare bureaucrats grew as a result of the Social Security Act of 1935. To a limited extent, the larger community chests "exerted a pressure toward rationalization of the professional welfare machinery,"[6] but this did not diminish the effect of the federal welfare bureaucracy, which soon eclipsed the authority of traditional providers. Actually, a unilinear evolution between these interests could have occurred had Harry Hopkins, head of the Federal Emergency Relief Administration in the 1930s, not prohibited states from turning federal welfare funds over to private agencies.[7] Denied the resources to address significantly the massive social problems caused by the Great Depression, private agencies lapsed into a secondary role while federal and state agencies ascended in importance. An array of welfare legislation followed the Social Security Act, including the Housing Act of 1937, the G.I. Bill of 1944, the Community Mental Health Centers Act of 1963, the Civil Rights Act of 1964, the Food Stamp Act of 1964, the Economic Opportunity Act of 1964, the Elementary and Secondary Education Act of 1965, the Medicare and Medicaid Acts of 1965, Supplemental Security Income in 1974, Title XX of the Social Security Act of 1975, and the Full Employment Act of 1978.

The flourishing of bureaucratic rationality concomitant with this legislative activity represented the institutionalization of liberal thought, which sought to control the caprice of the market, ensure a measure of equality among widely divergent economic classes, and establish an administrative apparatus to ensure the continuity of these principles. Confronted with a rapidly industrializing society lacking basic programs for ameliorating social and economic catastrophes, progressives perceived the state as a vehicle for social reform. Their solutions focused on "coordinating fragmented services, instituting planning, and extending public funding."[8] Implicit in the methods advocated by welfare bureaucrats is an expectation, if not an assumption, that the social welfare administration should be centralized, that eligibility for benefits should be universalized, and that social welfare should be firmly anchored in the institutional fabric of society.

The influence of welfare bureaucrats had been curtailed somewhat since the mid-1980s. The Reagan administration all but capped the growth of public social welfare, expenditures of which as a percent of GDP hovered at 18.5 percent through the 1980s until increasing under the Clinton presidency to 21.8 percent in 1994.[9] Even then Democrats still smarting from election losses in the 1980s had begun to amplify

their preference for private sector solutions to social problems. Still, the volume of resources and the number of people dependent on public welfare assure welfare bureaucrats of a dominant and continuing role in the foreseeable future.

Clinical Entrepreneurs

Clinical entrepreneurs are professional service providers, chiefly social workers, psychologists, and physicians, who work for themselves instead of being salaried employees. Important to clinical entrepreneurs in each specialty is the establishment of a **professional monopoly,** the evolution of which represents a concern on the part of practitioners that their occupational activity not be subject to political interference from the state or the ignorance of the lay public. In the United States the professions found that a market economy was conducive to occupational success. In the most fundamental sense, private practice reconciles the professionals' desire for autonomy with the imperatives of a market economy. The transition from entrepreneur to professional monopolist is a matter of obtaining legislation restricting practice to those duly licensed by the state. "Professionalism provides a way of preserving monopolistic control over services without the risks of competition."[10] As an extension of the entrepreneurial model of service delivery, professional monopoly offers privacy in practice, freedom to establish one's worth by setting fees, and the security ensured by membership in the professional monopoly.

The social worker as clinical entrepreneur is a relatively recent phenomenon, and the **National Association of Social Workers (NASW)** did not officially sanction this form of service delivery until 1964. Before that, privately practicing social workers identified themselves as psychotherapists and lay analysts. Typically, they relied on referrals from physicians and psychiatrists, and after World War II they began to establish "flourishing and lucrative"[11] practices. By the 1970s **private practice** in social work was developing as an important form of service delivery, although analysts disagreed about the number of social workers engaged in independent practice. In 1975 NASW estimated that 10,000 to 20,000 social workers were engaged in private practice. By 1983 Robert Barker, author of *Social Work in Private Practice* and a columnist on private practice in *NASW News,* speculated that about 30,000 social workers, or 32 percent of all social workers, engaged in private practice on a full- or part-time basis.[12] By 1985 a large portion of psychotherapy was being done by social workers, and the *New York Times* noted that "growing numbers of social workers are treating more affluent private clients, thus moving into the traditional preserve of the elite psychiatrists and clinical psychologists."[13] Yet in the early 1990s, NASW reported that only about 15,000 of its members—11.1 percent—were in solo or partnership practice as private practitioners, compared to about one-third of NASW members employed in for-profit firms.[14]

Clinical entrepreneurs are an emerging interest in social welfare. Continued growth of this group is likely for several reasons. Through local and state chapters, NASW has been effective in expanding the scope of its professional monopoly. In 1983 31 states had passed legislation regulating the practice of social work; by 1992 all 50 states regulated social work practice. At the same time, professional groups have lobbied for vendorship privileges that allow them more regular income through insurance held by clients. Finally, large numbers of students entering graduate schools of social work do so with the expressed intent of setting up in private practice.[15] Clinical entrepreneurs would be well positioned to become a more influential interest in social welfare in the United States were it not for the incursion of managed care: the attempt of human service corporations to diminish the influence of clinical entrepreneurs.

Human Service Executives

Human service executives share an important characteristic with clinical entrepreneurs: Both groups represent ways of organizing service delivery in the context of the market. However, in some important ways they differ. Unlike clinical entrepreneurs, **human service executives** are salaried employees of proprietary firms and, as such, have less autonomy. As administrators or chief executive officers of large corporations, human service executives advance market strategies for promoting social welfare. Whereas welfare bureaucrats emphasize the planning and regulatory functions of the state, human service executives favor the rationality of the marketplace in allocating resources and evaluating programs. In the present circumstances, human service executives are advocating market reform of the welfare state—the domain of welfare bureaucrats—and thus are in a position to challenge the bureaucratic interest.

For-profit firms became prominent in social welfare in the United States during the 1960s, when Medicaid and Medicare funds were paid to proprietary nursing homes and hospitals.[16] Since then, human service executives have been rapidly creating independent, for-profit human service corporations that provide an extensive range of nationwide services. Human service corporations have established prominent, if not dominant, positions in several human service markets, including nursing home care, hospital management, health maintenance, child care, home care—and even corrections and welfare. Most recently, human service corporations have aggressively exploited the managed care market. In 1981 there were 34 human service corporations, reporting annual revenues above $10 million; by 1985 the number of firms had increased to 66; and by 2000 the number had soared to 268. Of these, 16 corporations reported revenues higher than the total annual contributions to all of the United Way of America.

As the proprietary sector expands to dominate different human service markets, oligopolies emerge and a fundamental change occurs. No longer passively dependent on government appropriations, proprietary firms are in a strong position to shape the very markets they serve, influencing not only consumer demand but governmental policy as well. It is this capacity to determine or control a market that qualitatively distinguishes corporate welfare from the earlier form of business involvement in social welfare; that is, from philanthropic contributions to nonprofit agencies of the voluntary sector. For these reasons, human service executives are now well positioned to challenge the power of welfare bureaucrats.

The structural interests just described can be located in relation to two variables: span of influence and type of economy. As Figure 6.1 indicates, power shifts as a result of significant social influences: privatization and bureaucratization. The consequences of these forces will be evident throughout this book.

Marginal Interests

Social welfare in the United States is also populated by numerous groups that have *not* become as symbiotically attached to the social structure as have the structural interests just described. These marginal interest groups usually represent special populations that have been ignored, excluded, or oppressed by mainstream society. Their number reflects the capacity of U.S. culture to maintain its equilibrium while excluding many groups from full social participation. A partial list of marginal interest groups includes African Americans, poor women, Native Americans, homosexuals, residents of isolated rural areas, and Hispanic Americans. These groups

are of concern to welfare professionals because typically they have not had the same opportunities as mainstream populations; in other words, they have been denied social justice. Within the context of democratic capitalism, elevating marginal interests remains extraordinarily difficult.

The marginal status of many groups relates to the nature of the social welfare industry. In U.S. culture, groups excluded from the mainstream are expected to gather their resources and identify leaders who will mount programs to serve their particular group. Although this expectation is congruent with traditional values such as self-sufficiency and community solidarity, that solidarity approach does not necessarily ensure success. The voluntary sector may be able to accommodate only a limited number of marginal interests because of financial restraints, or it may be unresponsive to groups that violate traditional community norms. Programs to aid victims of domestic violence and the homeless, for example, have often struggled to mount and sustain minimal services, because the United Way often has funding priorities consonant with the needs of clientele more highly regarded in the community.

In a democratic polity, marginal groups can also make claims on the social order by seeking benefits through governmental programs; but to

FIGURE 6.1   Dynamics of Structural Interests

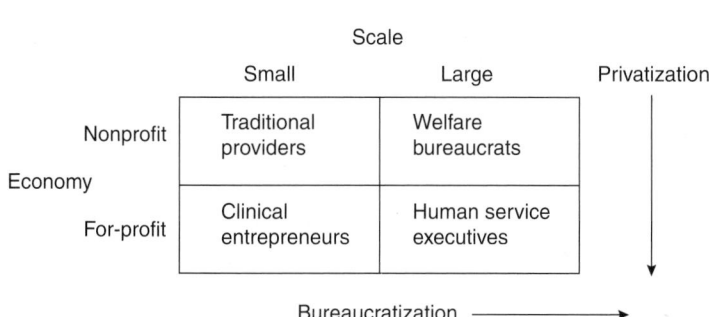

Source: David Stoesz, "A Theory of Social Welfare," *Social Work* (34, no. 2 March 1989), p. 106.

do so presents other problems. Government programs are likely to be managed by welfare bureaucrats, who have their own understanding of what is best for the marginal interest. For a marginal group to get benefits through government programs, its claim must be interpreted, programmed, and monitored by agents of the welfare state, who often have a welfare ideology that differs from that of oppressed groups. The result is likely to be a program that is more consonant with the ideology of the welfare bureaucrats than with that of the marginal group. As an example, the effort to combat AIDS has been plagued by volatile disagreements between gay advocacy organizations and the public health bureaucrats who run the Centers for Disease Control and Prevention.

Despite such obstacles, members of marginal groups have powerful incentives to work within existing structures if their needs are to be met at all. Usually, their success in this regard is mixed. As a result of affirmative action, African Americans have been able to secure positions within the welfare bureaucracy in relatively significant numbers and are now well established among welfare bureaucrats. White women have found independent practice a desirable framework within which to provide services and are well represented among clinical entrepreneurs. In contrast, many marginal groups continue to struggle against a welfare industry that is controlled by structural interests indifferent to minority concerns. The structural interest of human service executives, for example, remains a bastion of white patriarchy. Activists from the African American community struggle to contain gang violence, reduce the number of teen pregnancies, and halt the scourge of illegal drugs, often with inadequate resources. Indeed, one of the most glaring contradictions of American social welfare are state-of-the-art medical centers controlled by human-service executives located right next to inner city ghettos inhabited by the poorest and most neglected Americans. How has the American welfare state come to assure wealth for health and human service executives while generating, at the same time, an underclass?

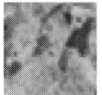 # The Forgotten Sector

As a result of the dynamic expansion of other structural interests over the course of the twentieth century, the voluntary sector lapsed in importance.[17] Following the triumph of the New Deal, leading welfare theoreticians expected government to dominate in the creation and administration of the welfare state. In fact, so complete was the expectation that the government-driven welfare state would dominate social welfare in the United States that references to private voluntary agencies became scant in the professional literature. There was little room within welfare state ideology for a dynamic voluntary sector, and references to private, nonprofit agencies virtually disappeared from discussions of social welfare. When discussed at all, voluntary agencies were viewed as vestiges from an earlier time. Rediscovered during the 1980s, the voluntary sector quickly attracted converts. Perhaps the most notable of the new adherents to the promise of nonprofits was business guru Peter Drucker. Citing the capacity of the "social sector" to address local problems, Drucker recited the virtues of the nonprofit sector in books such as *The New Realities;*[18] in 1990 he even went so far as to establish the Peter F. Drucker Foundation for Nonprofit Management.[19]

To the extent that the voluntary sector has been included as a part of the governmental welfare state, it has been considered a subcontractor of social service. This role was made possible through an amendment to the Social Security Act, Title XX, which allowed for the "purchase of service" from private providers. Under purchase-of-service contracts, government could avoid the costs and responsibilities of administering programs directly. Because of an open-ended funding formula, however, federal costs for Title XX services escalated sharply. Congress later capped Title XX expenditures, initially at $2.5 billion, in order to contain program costs, and still later the Reagan administration was successful in having the program placed under a Social Services

Block Grant, with further funding restrictions.[20] Consequently, in response to Title XX, many voluntary social service agencies secured purchase-of-service contracts, the funding for which allowed nonprofit agencies to expand programs in the late 1960s and early 1970s. Then, when funding was reduced, voluntary sector agencies were heavily penalized. Federal expenditures for Title XX fell from $2.8 billion in 1980 to $2.7 billion in 1992, a significant reduction in that it occurred at a time when demand for service was rising sharply.[21] As a result, voluntary social welfare agencies were hard pressed to maintain services such as home-based care, child day care and protective services, self-support education, and adoption and family counseling services. Although federal funds became critically important to voluntary sector social service agencies, accounting for up to half of agency funding, purchase of service continued to be a relatively minor portion of governmental welfare expenditures. In 1986, for example, Title XX accounted for only about 2 percent of all federal expenditures for welfare programs benefiting low-income people.[22]

Consequently, when policymakers turned to the voluntary sector in the 1980s to compensate for reductions in the governmental welfare effort, little was known about nonprofit social service agencies. Lester Salamon and Alan Abramson, authorities on the voluntary sector, observed that "despite their importance, these organizations have tended to be ignored in both public policy debates and scholarly research."[23] As government assumed a dominant role in U.S. social welfare, the voluntary sector receded in importance. If the Reagan–Bush presidencies rekindled interest in the voluntary sector, the 1994 Republican takeover of Congress created a small firestorm. As part of their Contract with America, congressional Republicans promised to reform welfare as part of an extensive overhaul of the whole welfare state. Government, they argued, had induced the dependency of millions of families on public assistance; welfare programs largely benefited the welfare professionals who worked in them; and all of this diluted the influence of community institutions. Congressional

conservatives had a strategy in mind when they critiqued federal social programs: Replace governmental welfare programs with private, voluntary sector initiatives. "The crisis of the modern welfare state is not just a crisis of government," contended conservative scholar Marvin Olasky. "The more effective provision of social services will ultimately depend on their return to private and especially religious institutions."[24] Suddenly, after half a century of neglect, the "forgotten sector" was being called upon to assume unprecedented responsibilities in caring for the needy.

Beginning in the 1970s, researchers began to investigate the scope of the voluntary sector. Their task has not been an easy one. The voluntary sector is composed of tens of thousands of organizations, many of which are not associated with any national umbrella association. The picture that is emerging from preliminary investigations reveals a sector that, if small by economic standards, is extraordinarily rich socially. Perhaps the most convenient measure of the scale of the voluntary sector is to count the voluntary and philanthropic associations that have received tax-exempt status as social service agencies from the Internal Revenue Service—177,604 in 1996, of which 66,514 are engaged in human services.[25] Despite their proliferation, the voluntary sector accounts for only half of national economic activity attributed to government and one-tenth that of business.[26]

Generally, the expansion of the voluntary sector has paralleled economic growth; for example, between 1960 and 1995 per capita charitable giving increased from $280 to $522 in constant dollars.[27] Charitable giving for 1999 totaled $190 billion, having increased by $15 billion over each of the previous two years. Total donations accounted for 1999 represented 2.1 percent of gross domestic product (GDP). Three-fourths of contributions emanate from individuals, with foundations and corporations accounting for about 10 percent each. Religious institutions receive more than 40 percent of philanthropic contributions, followed by education and health. While human service organizations receive less than 10 percent of donations, their receipts in represented an 8 percent increase over 1998. The American Association of Fund Raising Councils noted that the expansion of giving to human services "is part of a recent pattern of strong performance."[28]

More than its financial significance, the strength of the voluntary sector lies in its incorporation into the social fabric of life in the United States. In 1996 the nonprofit sector employed 7.4 million staff and supervised 4.3 million full-time equivalent volunteers, the volunteer effort representing $128.7 billion in economic activity.[29] This voluntary activity shows a steady increase over the last quarter of the twentieth century: In 1977 26 percent of Americans reported that they were involved in charitable work with the needy; by 1991 that figure had increased to 46 percent.[30] Contrary to popular assumption, the voluntary sector is not bankrolled by wealthy philanthropists and their foundations. Foundations and corporations account for only 10 percent of voluntary sector contributions; "about half of all charitable dollars comes from families with incomes under $25,000."[31]

Nonprofit human service organizations have their share of organizational difficulties, of course. Notably during the Reagan presidency, charitable revenues dropped because of a severe recession, reductions in government assistance, and adverse changes in tax law. The 1980s were hard times for nonprofit organizations, particularly social service agencies. As Table 6.1 shows, federal spending in areas served by nonprofit social service programs was negative for more than a decade, and direct federal support of nonprofit social service agencies was not positive until the early 1990s. Although private giving increased fairly steadily during the late 1980s and early 1990s, it has not compensated for overall federal rescissions.

The data in Table 6.1 provide a poignant answer to the question: Can charitable giving replace federal social welfare? This question has been central to the thinking of conservatives who have criticized the welfare state and advanced the nonprofit sector as an alternative. During the Reagan–Bush presidencies federal social welfare expenditures plummeted, as did federal assistance to nonprofits; and, although private contributions did increase during this period, they were insufficient to compensate for federal cuts. It was not until the Clinton administration that the rise in private giving eclipsed federal cuts in social welfare and the trend in federal aid to nonprofits became positive. Although conservatives were correct in suggesting that there was untapped capacity in the philanthropic sector for social welfare, between 1982 and 1995 this voluntary capacity never made up for federal cuts in benefits to the poor. Eventually, most scholars of the voluntary sector concluded that rather than trying to replace governmental social welfare activities, nonprofit agencies should adopt practices "in support of an expansion of the welfare state."[32]

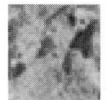 ## Advancing Social Justice

In addition to providing social services, the voluntary sector has been important in U.S. social welfare because it has been the source of efforts to advance the rights of disenfranchised populations. In this respect the voluntary sector is essential to the nation's culture, in that it is a correcting influence to the indifference often shown to marginal populations by governmental and corporate bureaucracies. This case has been argued vigorously by John W. Gardner, former secretary of Health, Education, and Welfare and former chairman of the board of Independent Sector. According to Gardner, the voluntary sector fosters much of the pluralism in the life of this country, taking on those concerns that do not attract the broad spectrum of public support necessary for the legislation that mandates governmental programs, and concerns that do not represent the commercial prospects necessary to attract the interests of the business community. In other words, the voluntary sector serves as the best—and, in some cases, the only—vehicle for

TABLE 6.1 ■ Changes in Federal Spending Compared to Changes in Private Giving (in billions of constant FY 1998 dollars)

	CHANGE FROM FY 1980 LEVELS, EXCLUDING HEALTH AND INCOME ASSISTANCE		
Year	Federal Spending in Areas of Interest to Nonprofits	Federal Support of Nonprofits	Private Giving
1982	–$26.4	–$6.7	–$1.3
1983	–30.1	–7.6	+2.7
1984	–30.9	–7.6	+4.3
1985	–26.1	–6.5	+5.5
1986	–27.2	–6.4	+10.8
1987	–32.0	–6.8	+11.6
1988	–30.1	–5.9	+13.1
1989	–26.5	–4.2	+15.4
1990	–25.0	–4.4	+18.2
1991	–19.4	–2.0	+18.6
1992	–16.7	–0.7	+19.9
1993	–12.7	+1.1	+22.2
1994	–10.9	+2.2	+22.5
1995	–9.3	+3.3	+26.1
Total	–$323.2	–$52.2	+$192.2

Source: Alan Abrahamson, Lester Salamon, and Eugene Steuerle, "The Nonprofit Sector and the Federal Budget," in Elizabeth Boris and Eugene Steuerle (eds.), *Nonprofits and Government* (Washington, DC: Urban Institute Press, 1999), p. 128.

addressing certain social needs. Indeed, much of what Americans would identify as central to their culture can be attributed to organizations of the voluntary sector: hospitals, schools, religious institutions, welfare agencies, fraternal associations, symphonies, and museums, to name of few. According to Gardner,

> *Institutions of the nonprofit sector are in a position to serve as the guardians of intellectual and artistic freedom. Both the commercial and political marketplaces are subject to leveling forces that may threaten standards of excellence. In the non-profit sector, the fiercest champions of excellence may have*

> *their say. So may the champions of liberty and justice.*[33]

Gardner's last reference here is not merely rhetorical but has its basis in history. As Alexis de Tocqueville observed in the 1830s, Americans have long depended on voluntary organizations to solve communal problems. And in addressing these problems, the voluntary sector has compiled an impressive list of positive additions to American life. Those seeking solutions to current problems often find inspiration in voluntary sector initiatives of the past. Gardner noted that "At a time in our history when we are ever in need of new solutions to new problems, the private sector is remarkably free to innovate, create, and engage in controversial experiments." He went on to observe, "In fact, virtually every far-reaching social change in our history has come up in the private sector: the abolition of slavery, the reforms of populism, child labor laws, the vote for women, civil rights, and so on."[34]

Important social welfare initiatives have also originated in the voluntary sector. The inspiration for the **Great Society** initiative—during which new social programs such as Medicaid, food stamps, and the Job Corps were launched—can be traced to Mobilization for Youth, a voluntary sector poverty program in New York City funded by the Ford Foundation. Two champions of community organization, the late Saul Alinsky and the late César Chávez of the United Farm Workers Union, were also influenced by the privately run Industrial Areas Foundation of Chicago. More recently, services to battered women, patients with AIDS, and the homeless have been pioneered by voluntary sector organizations. Given public apathy toward these groups, for many years the voluntary sector was the only source of service for these groups.

That social change begins in the voluntary sector has a particular lesson for human service professionals: The openness of democratic American culture means that anyone is free to organize for purposes of rectifying past injustices. Well within the reach of social welfare professionals are the building blocks of every voluntary sector initiative: recruiting participants, forming a board of directors, filing for tax-exempt status under Internal Revenue Service Code section 501(c)(3) or (4), soliciting contributions, and applying for grants and contracts. Wendy Kopp's Teach for America (TFA) is a good illustration. In 1988, armed with a vision of a Peace Corps–like program for inner cities and rural areas, the then 23-year-old Kopp began to hustle corporate contributions to match idealistic professionals to disadvantaged communities. By 1996 TFA boasted a $5.5 million budget and was graduating 500 volunteers annually.[35] What Wendy Kopp accomplished in New York City illustrates the promise of the voluntary sector in every U.S. community.

Contemporary Nonprofit Human Service Organizations

The voluntary human service sector consists of a large constellation of organizations that are instantly recognizable by most Americans (see Table 6.2).

The United Way

Perhaps the best recognized of voluntary sector organizations is the United Way. Local United Ways, as well as the United Way of America, are nonprofit organizations themselves. The purpose of local United Ways is to raise funds that are then disbursed to nonprofit agencies in the community, most of which are United Way members. Local United Ways also contribute a small percentage of funds to the national headquarters, the United Way of America, which is located in suburban Washington, D.C. Because the United Way is a confederation of organizations, power resides within the local United Ways. The United Way of America provides support services nationwide but has no direct authority over local United Ways.

In 1999 the United Ways in the United States raised $3.77 billion, an amount that, once adjusted for inflation, was comparable to contributions in 1987.[36] As Table 6.3 shows, United Way contributions have oscillated over time, often failing to keep pace with inflation. Two recent events account for marked drops in contributions. First, the recession of the early 1980s, the worst since the Great Depression, accounted for a significant loss in contributions. Second, revelations of managerial improprieties on the part of United Way CEO William Aramony in the early 1990s precipitated another reduction in donations (adjusted for inflation) to United Ways. Thus, while overall charitable contributions actually increased during the early 1990s, donations to the United Way fell. This blow was felt especially acutely by some of the larger metropolitan United Ways. Between

TABLE 6.2 ■ Nonprofit Human Service Organizations, 2000

NAME	BUDGET	AFFILIATES	SERVICES	ISSUES
Alliance for Children and Families	$5 million	350 local	Services ranging from residential care to domestic abuse prevention for more than 5 million people	Serve families and children; formed in 1998 through merger of Family Service America (est. 1911) and the National Association of Homes and Services for Children (est. 1975)
American Foundation for the Blind	$12.9 million	NYC central office and 5 field offices	Information and referral, research and policy research	Encourage independent living; promote technological innovation for the vision impaired
American Red Cross	$2.4 billion	1,300 chapters, 38 blood regions and 8 national testing labs, 15 tissue centers	Disaster assistance, blood services, first aid, and international emergency aid	Maintain quality of blood supply to prevent HIV/AIDS, providing emergency services in the Third World
Arthritis Foundation	$113 million	55 chapters	Information, research, and support for those afflicted with arthritis	Carry out further research on joint disease
Association of Retarded Citizens	$3.2 million (national office)	46 state groups and 950 local chapters	Research, education, and prevention of mental retardation	Eliminate waiting lists for state and city services
Boy Scouts	$499 million	More than 300 local councils	Character and citizenship development	Expand values-based experiences
Camp Fire Boys and Girls	$3.8 million (national office)	42 state chapters and 125 local councils	Clubs, camping, and leadership activities for 629,000 youth	Increase revenues and volunteers to provide necessary services
Catholic Charities	$2.3 million (national office)	1,400 affiliates	Full range of social services and emergency aid	Reduce poverty and empower communities
Child Welfare League of America	$13 million (national office)	5 regional groups; 1,000 member agencies	Program and policy advocacy on a full range of child-related problems	Serve families with incarcerated parents; address substance abuse; reform child welfare and dependency courts
Girl Scouts	$118 million	50 state chapters and 318 local councils	Values-based activities to enhance development of girls	Promote pluralism and prepare girls for leadership roles
Goodwill Industries	$9.7 million (national office)	181 member organizations in North America	Collection and sale of donated goods; job training services	Enhance occupational prospects for the disabled
National Council on Alcoholism and Drug Dependence	$1.3 million (national office)	100 councils	Education and information about substance abuse	Eliminate the stigma associated with substance abuse

(continued)

TABLE 6.2 ■ Continued

NAME	BUDGET	AFFILIATES	SERVICES	ISSUES
National Easter Seal Society	$472 million	400 affiliate and service sites	Rehabilitation and vocational services for children	Facilitate greater independence for program recipients
National Mental Health Association	$9.2 million	Chapters in all states	Promotion of mental health services	Expand services for the mentally ill
National Urban League	$42.4 million	Affiliates in major metropolitan areas	Advocacy of social justice for the minority poor	Increase opportunities for the urban poor
Planned Parenthood Federation of America	$661 million	129 affiliates	Education and services about reproductive health	Promote research on sexuality and preserve reproductive freedom
Salvation Army	$1.8 billion	9,037 units in 107 countries	Full range of Christian programming to those in need	Restore Christian values as a basis for social services
United Jewish Communities	$40 million (national office)	189 federations in North America	Full range of services to the Jewish community	Sustain and renew Jewish values; expand programs
United Service Organizations (USO)	$33 million (national office)	120 world centers, 33 U.S. affiliates	Information and support services to military and their families	Enhance services to military families
Young Men's Christian Association (YMCA)	$61 million (national office)	2,283 YMCAs	Health, fitness, and recreation	Expand and integrate services nationally
Young Women's Christian Association (YWCA)	$81 million (national office)	324 member associations	Services to girls and women	Empower women and fight racism

1991 and 1997, United Way gifts in Los Angeles fell 41.3 percent, San Diego 35.6 percent, Cleveland 29.4 percent, Boston 25.3 percent, Chicago 24.3 percent, Detroit 23.1 percent, and New York 17.5 percent. Meanwhile, contributions to suburban United Ways increased.[37] The consequence was a reduction in funding for services to the poor. In 1970 Giving USA had reported that 13.9 percent of charitable donations went to the poor; by 1998, 9.2 percent were so dedicated.[38]

At the same time, traditional United Way agencies were faced with diminishing revenues as a result of competition from nontraditional organizations that were also seeking charitable contributions. For example, until recently the United Way claimed about 90 percent of all contributions to the Combined Federal Campaign (a campaign directed at federal employees) that were not specifically designated for other purposes. As a result of challenges brought by agencies as diverse as environmental groups and the National Rifle Association, however, nondesignated contributions are now apportioned among a larger number of organizations. Consequently, the United Way receives less than it did in the past from the Combined Federal Campaign.[39]

In response to increased competition for charitable dollars, many United Ways have evolved donor-friendly policies. For example, 76.9 percent of United Ways now offer individuals the option of designating the recipient agency, and 37.7 of United Ways allow the designation of a recipient agency even if it is not a United Way member.[40] But an unintended consequence of

TABLE 6.3 ▪ Amounts Raised by United Ways Nationally

YEAR	BILLIONS RAISED IN CURRENT $	CHANGE FROM PREVIOUS YEAR	BILLIONS RAISED IN CONSTANT $	CHANGE FROM PREVIOUS YEAR
1967	0.677	5.9%	2.026	2.7%
1970	0.787	5.7	2.028	−2.6
1975	1.023	4.5	1.901	−4.2
1980	1.526	7.2	1.852	−5.5
1985	2.330	8.6	2.165	4.9
1990	3.110	4.4	2.380	−1.0
1995	3.148	3.3	2.066	−0.5
1999	3.769	5.4	2.262	3.1

"donor choice" has been the diversion of United Way contributions from urban agencies serving the chronically ill to suburban agencies providing service to a less disadvantaged clientele, as noted above. In Washington, D.C., in 1996, for example, more than 70 percent of United Way contributions were designated to suburban agencies. This, of course, left urban United Way member agencies with fewer resources. Subsequently the Salvation Army withdrew from the United Way on the basis that its services were not adequately valued by contributors.[41]

Revenues of the United Way are derived from multiple sources. As is generally true of charitable contributions, about half of the funds contributed to the United Way are from employees and small businesses. Corporations account for somewhat less than a fourth of United Way revenues. Financial support that the United Way provides to local agencies is also varied. Health, family services, and youth services account for the largest categories of expenditures. Smaller percentages go to agencies providing food, clothing, and housing; day care; public safety; community development; income and jobs support; education; and other kinds of assistance. Of course, the amounts actually allocated in communities vary considerably according to the different priorities of each local United Way.

Elite Philanthropy

The Aramony scandal at the United Way provided a signal lesson in the distinction between "elite" and "bourgeois" philanthropy in the United States. For purposes of simplification, bourgeois philanthropy supports the relatively modest pursuits of the United Ways that dot the nation's landscape. Elite philanthropy, on the other hand, has much grander expectations. "Elite American philanthropy serves the interests of the rich to a greater extent than it does the interests of the poor, disadvantaged, or disabled," argues Teresa Odendahl; it is "a system of 'generosity' by which the wealthy exercise social control and help themselves more than they do others."[42] In 1987, for example, Odendahl calculates that contributions totaling $47 billion, about one-half of all gifts itemized on income tax returns, were made by the wealthy.[43] For what purposes do the rich demonstrate such beneficence? They give to institutions that "sustain their culture, their education, their policy formulation, their status—in short, their interests."[44] In other words, wealthy Americans usually use the tax code to maintain institutions of elite culture, such as private schools, museums, symphony orchestras, and opera companies. These institutions often announce generosity of sufficient magnitude to the public by naming an important structure or endowment after the benefactor, a tradition that is maintained by cultural elites in major U.S. cities. The use of funds that have been withdrawn from public use by the tax code in order to reproduce the social institutions of the rich is unacceptable to Odendahl, who proposes reforms that would require philanthropy to be put to public benefit in different ways.

Indeed, the major philanthropic foundations are identified by the names of the titans of American capitalism. The measure of their considerable clout is the hundreds of millions of dollars in grants awarded annually:[45]

Ten Wealthiest Private Foundations

NAME	YEAR ESTABLISHED	LOCATION	ASSETS ($BILLIONS)	GRANTS ($MILLIONS)
Gates Foundation	1994	Seattle, Wash.	17.1	500
Packard Foundation	1964	Los Altos, Calif.	13.0	440
Ford Foundation	1936	New York, N.Y.	11.4	550
Lilly Endowment	1937	Indianapolis, Ind.	11.1	500
R. W. Johnson Foundation	1936	Princeton, N.J.	8.1	440
Kellogg Foundation	1930	Battle Creek, Mich.	6.2	221
Pew Charitable Trusts	1948	Philadelphia, Pa.	4.8	230
MacArthur Foundation	1978	Chicago, Ill.	4.2	168
Mellon Foundation	1969	New York, N.Y.	3.5	153
Rockefeller Foundation	1913	New York, N.Y.	3.5	175

Because elite philanthropy functions through the same tax code as its more modest cousin, bourgeois philanthropy, insults by the likes of Aramony are acutely discomforting to the more affluent philanthropies. Muckraking journalists reported that Aramony had supplemented his $390,000 annual salary by authorizing excessive perks, including a New York penthouse, limousine service, and European trips on the Concorde. Using United Way funds for seed money, Aramony had also authorized the creation of three independent corporations, which later employed his son.[46] The final chapter in the Aramony scandal was not written until 1995, when a jury found Aramony and two associates guilty of multiple counts of conspiracy, fraud, and filing false tax returns. Aramony was found to have misappropriated $1.2 million in United Way funds, was sentenced to seven years in federal prison, and was fined $522,000.[47]

In late 1995 leaders of major foundations met in New York to survey the damage. Noting that the philanthropic community "seems to have lost a large part of its claim on the sympathies of the American public," Lester Salamon, director of the Johns Hopkins Institute for Policy Studies, suggested the establishment of a special commission that would "rethink the role, function and operation of the nonprofit sector for the next century." Citing "a growing mismatch between the actual operation of the voluntary sector and popular conceptions of what this sector is supposed to be like," Salamon argued that the major philanthropies were vulnerable to "cheap shots and exposés" when a management scam hit the headlines.[48]

The Aramony flap refocused attention on the informal norms of propriety existing within the philanthropic community. In the aftermath of the scandal, *The Chronicle of Philanthropy* surveyed 117 of the nation's largest nonprofits and reported that one-fourth paid chief executives annual salaries of more than $200,000. As examples, Ben Love, chief executive of the Boy Scouts, was being paid $223,375; Robert Ross of the Muscular Dystrophy Association, $284,808; and Dudley Hafner, executive vice president of the American Heart Association, $246,000.[49] Yet even these salaries often paled in comparison to the salaries commanded by the executives of major foundations, as suggested by the examples here:[50]

Compensation for Executives of Selected Foundations

FOUNDATION	EXECUTIVE	1997 SALARY
Lilly Endowment	Thomas Lofton	$450,000
Ford Foundation	Susan Berresford	440,500
Packard Foundation	Colburn Wilbur	272,549
Kellogg Foundation	William Richardson	400,000
R. W. Johnson Foundation	Steven Schroeder	367,000
Pew Charitable Trusts	Rebecca Rimel	339,734
Robert Woodruff Foundation	Charles McTier	270,000

Why are nonprofit executives paid so well? Presumably because, in order to secure charitable contributions, they are expected to associate with the cultural elites who populate the corporate world of the United States. To do so requires a substantial enough salary to cover the entertainment, club memberships, and other incidental costs associated with such socialization. The upscale lifestyle of executives of prominent nonprofits seems to validate this supposition.

The freedom of the voluntary sector to pursue good works should not be dismissed as simply self-serving, however. During the late 1990s Ted Turner announced an unprecedented $1 billion contribution to the United Nations; and this gift was matched by Bill Gates, whose foundation pledged $1 billion for various disease prevention initiatives in the Third World, notably work on HIV/AIDS in sub-Saharan Africa.[51] These contributions were all the more poignant

given the United States government's failure to pay the dues it owed to the United Nations.

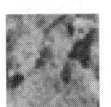

The Future of the Voluntary Sector

Several forces have transformed the nonprofit sector, including the intrusion of commercial firms, the rise of faith-based social services, and the emergence of social entrepreneurship.

Commercialization

The **commercialization** issue is particularly important for financially strapped nonprofit agencies. Faced with static, if not declining, revenues, some voluntary sector agencies have experimented with commercial activities in order to supplement income derived from traditional sources (contributions, grants, and fees). That nonprofit organizations should be allowed to engage in commercial endeavors without restriction is "unfair competition," according to business operators, who note that nonprofits do not ordinarily pay taxes on their income.

Limits on the freedom of nonprofit organizations to engage in commercial activities were highlighted in a celebrated case involving New York University Law School and the Mueller Macaroni Company. Seeking a way to enhance revenues to the law school and thereby lighten the burden of contributing to their alma mater, enterprising alumni acquired Mueller and reorganized it as a nonprofit organization registered in Delaware. Income from the macaroni company was thus redefined as nontaxable income and diverted to the law school as a charitable contribution. This clever arrangement, however, did not go unnoticed by Mueller's competitors, who saw the possibility that Mueller might be able to use its newly acquired tax-exempt status to cut prices and drive other macaroni companies from the market. Further, they argued, what was to prevent any well-endowed non-profit institution from acquiring profitable businesses as a way of supplementing its income while dodging any tax obligation? The situation soon proved so embarrassing to the law school that it sent no representatives to the congressional hearings convened to deliberate on the ethics of the arrangement. Eventually the tax code was altered, making income from commercial activities that are not related to the service function of a nonprofit organization taxable.[52] Since 1950, revenue obtained by nonprofit organizations from commercial activity has been taxable under the unrelated business income tax (UBIT).

Although the tax code revision prompted by the Mueller case served as an adequate measure against gross breaches of business propriety, subsequent developments raised further questions around the commerce issue. For example, a nonprofit hospital association in Virginia attempted to maintain its competitive edge by acquiring several commercial ventures, including an advertising agency, two health clubs, an interior decorating firm, a pharmacy, and a helicopter ambulance service. These acquisitions were criticized by nearby businesses.[53] Even the YMCA has come under fire. In this case, the 1,100-member International Racquet Sports Association complained that Ys held an unfair competitive advantage over for-profit racquet clubs.[54]

These and other conflicts between nonprofit and for-profit organizations were aired during hearings held by the House Ways and Means Committee in 1987.[55] At the hearings representatives of the business community complained that nonprofits were engaging in "unfair competition" with for-profit businesses in two ways. First, they argued, the UBIT is inconsistent in distinguishing between related and unrelated business activities. For example, a nonprofit hospital's pharmacy is considered related to the hospital's mission and is therefore exempt from paying taxes on profit, but a for-profit hospital's pharmacy is part of the business and its profit is therefore taxable. Second, nonprofit organizations benefit from the "halo effect"—that is, the

public's perception that their services are superior because they do not operate from the profit motive. Thus, health spas complain that YMCAs benefit from a philanthropic "halo," and the revenues of the Ys are tax exempt. Yet Ys use many commercial business practices—such as marketing and advertising—to promote their services.

Although complaints of unfair competition on the part of nonprofit organizations appear to be academic, the accusations open the possibility of further restrictions on the revenue base of voluntary sector agencies. For example, some Ys have stopped advertising their programs for fear that local authorities may interpret those programs as commercial and thereby attempt to tax income derived from them. Thus, the unfair competition issue presents some very disturbing questions for administrators of nonprofit organizations. If a nonprofit family service agency bills a client's insurance company for a "usual, customary, and reasonable" fee, a fee comparable to what is charged by a private practice group that must pay taxes on such income, should this income remain tax exempt? Should tax-exempt income be limited to charitable contributions only? Do program outreach and public education activities constitute marketing and advertising? And if so, should they be limited if a nonprofit organization is to retain its tax exemption? Questions like these strike at the heart of the function of the voluntary sector. How these questions are resolved will be of great concern to nonprofit community service agencies, particularly to organizations faced with dwindling revenues.

Faith-Based Social Services

The idea of government's contracting with voluntary sector agencies is not a novel concept; through purchase-of-service agreements dating to the late 1960s, government has negotiated arrangements for delivery of a range of social services, often with sectarian agencies. This liberal mechanism for decentralization, however, has given conservatives an entrée to pose more fundamental questions about the proper role of government in social welfare. Since the 1980s conservative think tanks have, with increasing urgency, sought an alternative to federal social programs. A primary proponent of sectarian nonprofit agencies is Marvin Olasky, a journalist who argues that voluntary religious agencies provided efficient and effective services to the needy before the New Deal and the deployment of the welfare state.[56] Another source of support has come from evangelical Christians, who object to the absence of moral standards that they see as characterizing traditional social service agencies managed by liberal welfare professionals.

During the 1990s conservatives seized on the voluntary sector as an agent of social reform, a possibility facilitated by reassessments of the function of government. A benchmark in the reconsideration of the role of government was the appearance of *Reinventing Government* by David Osborne and Ted Gaebler. A policy analyst who had earlier tracked governors as they struggled to compensate for federal funding rescissions during the Reagan administration, Osborne recognized that institutions other than the federal government represented underused capacity with respect to domestic policy needs. The formulation developed by Osborne and Gaebler was simple: Using the metaphor of a boat, the authors proposed that government might steer the vessel, but that it was up to the private sector to do the rowing. Including multiple examples in which government had successfully contracted with private agencies to serve in the public interest, *Reinventing Government* provided the template for domestic policy for a decade.[57]

By the 2000 presidential election, centrist conservatives within the Republican party found the voluntary sector, and in particular the religious sector, a way to appeal to independent voters. Since its resurgence with the 1980 election of Ronald Reagan, conservatism had been in opposition to liberal social policy; however, it lacked a positive stance with respect to a large segment of the electorate—the middle class, the elderly, and the ill, among others. Invoking the voluntary sector addressed this deficit, an approach that George W. Bush advanced enthusiastically during his 2000 presidential campaign as "compassionate conservatism."

As governor of Texas, Bush had had extensive experience in mobilizing the private sector to address social welfare needs. After passage of the 1996 welfare reform legislation, he had proposed contracting out all of the state's public welfare programming, a deal valued at $500 million annually; but this was vetoed by the Clinton administration. Despite this defeat, in 2000 Bush advanced "faith-based social services" as an alternative to traditional social programs.[58] Proponents of faith-based social services claimed that government programs were too bureaucratic and impersonal to really help those in need, and that secular nonprofit agencies were populated by welfare professionals who failed to infuse services with adequate moral content to be effective. As a presidential candidate, Bush also extended "compassionate conservatism" beyond the parameters of local social services to propose vouchers as an instrument for education reform and private pensions as an alternative to Social Security.[59]

Social Entrepreneurship

Although many theologically inclined liberals endorsed the idea of faith-based social services, others pursued innovations through capital and technology. Concerned about the decline of civic institutions, particularly in urban areas, sociologists proposed "social capital" as a vehicle for revitalization. For Robert Putnam, the term *social capital* referred to "features of social organization, such as networks, norms, and trust, that facilitate coordination and cooperation for mutual benefit. Social capital enhances the benefits of investment in physical and human capital."[60] At the nexus of social capital, community-based nonprofit organizations can facilitate the development of poor neighborhoods providing they exploit new markets and technologies.

An illustration of the social capital approach to community development is the work of former congressman Floyd Flake, pastor of the Allen African Methodist Episcopal Church in Queens.[61] Flake has used his position as church pastor to construct a $23 million network of community development ventures. Seeing the future as a social entrepreneur, Flake recognizes the ideological implications of recent changes in social policy: "Those of us who have made a commitment to stay in an urban community have decided that *this* is our paradise," he observed. "We are going to rebuild that paradise—and we understand that it means some paradigm shifts, even politically, because the majority of statehouses today are in the hands of Republican governors and the majority of the assemblies are in the hands of Republicans. So we can either continue in a protest mode or we find ways to have entrée to deal with who is in power now."[62]

Conclusion

A new generation of social entrepreneurs has emerged as experiments with markets reveal untapped opportunities for program innovation, both locally and nationally. For example, the Ben & Jerry's ice cream company and Working Assets Long Distance (WALD) represent an ethic in which business praxis is inextricably suffused with social consciousness.[63] For 1996 WALD contributed $2.5 million to progressive organizations advocating in several areas: social justice, the environment, civil rights, and international justice.[64] Billy and Debbie Shore have explored even more remote reaches of capitalism, founding Share Our Strength (SOS) and Community Wealth Ventures (CWV), hybrid organizations that profit from their role in niche markets. By the late 1990s, SOS and CWV had a payroll of $2.7 million and contributed $8.5 million to nutrition organizations serving the poor.[65] Although ventures such as SOS and CWV have not yet attained a scale comparable to more prominent organizations, their true value may more accurately be gauged by their pioneering work on the postindustrial frontier. "Charity malls" such as iGive and MyCause.com, Internet intermediaries that divert a portion of sales revenues to nonprofits, are a more recent application of information technology.[66] Arguably the most innovative of Internet sites is thehungersite.com, which allows visitors to click a donation for the Third World; by mid-2000 65 million visitors had donated 17 million pounds of food via this site, all contributed by advertisers.[67]

As commercialization, faith-based social services, and social entrepreneurship indicate, the nonprofit sector has rebounded from the lethargy that characterized it during the middle part of the last century. How the voluntary sector preserves its mission of caring for the disenfranchised without succumbing to the bottom-line ethos of the corporate sector, responds to the range of diverse populations without proselytizing to unbelievers, and adapts the latest innovations in technology while putting forth a human face are the challenges that come with recrudescence.

Discussion Questions

1. What are the most prominent nonprofit human service agencies in your community? Are they members of the United Way? What do agencies perceive to be the advantages of United Way membership? Do they perceive disadvantages to United Way membership?

2. Has the United Way in your community failed to achieve its goals in contributions in recent years? If so, what are the causes? The proposed solutions?

3. What are the newer nonprofit agencies in your community? What populations do they serve? Are these agencies members of the United Way? If not, how do they attract the necessary resources? What is their perception of the United Way?

4. If there are unmet needs in your community, how would you create a nonprofit agency to meet them? Whom would you recruit for your board of directors? Where

would you solicit resources, both cash and in-kind? Whom would you recruit for staff? What would you name your agency? Would your agency focus on providing services or on advancing social change?

5. In response to diminishing resources, many nonprofit social agencies have re-

sorted to entrepreneurial strategies to raise money. What innovative projects have agencies deployed in your community? What entrepreneurial strategies can you think of that might be successful for nonprofit agencies in your community?

 # Notes

1. Peter Berger and Richard Neuhaus, *To Empower People: The Role of Mediating Structures in Public Policy* (Washington, DC: American Enterprise Institute, 1977).

2. David Stoesz, "A Structural Interest Theory of Social Welfare," *Social Development Issues* 10 (Winter 1985), pp. 73–85.

3. National Association of Social Workers, *Social Casework: Generic and Specific* (Silver Spring, MD: NASW, 1974).

4. "National Amounts Raised Highest in 30-Year History" (Alexandria, VA: United Way of America, 2000).

5. Robert Alford, *Health Care Politics* (Chicago: University of Chicago Press, 1975), p. 204.

6. Roy Lubove, *The Professional Altruist* (New York: Atheneum, 1969), p. 197.

7. Walter Trattner, *From Poor Law to Welfare State* (New York: Macmillan, 1974), p. 237; "The First Days of Social Security," *Public Welfare* 43 (Fall 1985), pp. 112–119.

8. Alford, *Health Care Politics*, p. 2.

9. *Social Security Bulletin, Annual Statistical Supplement* (Washington, DC: Social Security Administration, 1999), p. 140.

10. Ibid., p. 199.

11. Trattner, *From Poor Law to Welfare State*, p. 250.

12. Robert Barker, "Private Practice Primer for Social Work," *NASW News* (October 1983), p. 13.

13. A. Goleman, "Social Workers Vault into a Leading Role in Psychotherapy," *The New York Times* (April 3, 1985), p. C1.

14. Per conversation with NASW staff, November 16, 1992.

15. Maryann Mahaffey, "Fulfilling the Promise," *Proceedings* (Fifth Annual Association of Baccalaureate Program Directors Conference, Kansas City, 1987).

16. Donald Light, "Corporate Medicine for Profit," *Scientific American 225* (December 1986), pp. 81–89.

17. Ralph Kramer, "The Future of Voluntary Organizations in Social Welfare," in *Philanthropy, Voluntary Action, and the Public Good* (Washington, DC: Independent Sector/United Way, 1986).

18. Peter Drucker, *The New Realities* (New York: HarperCollins, 1989).

19. Peter Drucker, "It Profits Us to Strengthen Nonprofits," *Wall Street Journal* (December 19, 1991), p. 18.

20. Neil Gilbert, *Capitalism and the Welfare State* (New Haven: Yale University Press, 1983), pp. 6–7; Neil Gilbert and Harry Specht, *Dimensions of Social Welfare Policy*, 2nd ed. (Englewood Cliffs, NJ: Prentice-Hall, 1989), pp. 46–47.

21. Committee on Ways and Means, U.S. House of Representatives, *Overview of Entitlement Programs, 1992 Green Book* (Washington, DC: U.S. Government Printing Office, 1992), p. 830.

22. Ibid.

23. Alan Abramson and Lester Salamon, *The Nonprofit Sector and the New Federal Budget* (Washington, DC: Urban Institute, 1986), p. xi. See also Waldemar Nielsen, *The Third Sector: Keystone of a Caring Society* (Washington, DC: Independent Sector, 1980).

24. Marvin Olasky, "Beyond the Stingy Welfare State," *Policy Review* (Fall 1990), p. 14.

25. Elizabeth Boris, "Nonprofit Organizations in a Democracy," in Elizabeth Boris and Eugene Steuerle (eds.), *Nonprofits and Government* (Washington, DC: Urban Institute, 1999), p. 10.

26. Virginia Hodgkinson and Murray Weitzman, *Nonprofit Almanac* (Washington, DC: Independent Sector, 1996), p. 40.

27. Robert Putnam, *Bowling Alone* (New York: Simon & Schuster, 2000), p. 122. Putnam's figures with respect to the percentage of national income dedicated to charity contradict those of the American Association of Fund Raising Councils.

28. "Total Giving Reaches $190.16 Billion" (New York: American Association of Fund Raising Councils, 2000).

29. Eugene Steuerle and Virginia Hodgkinson, "Meeting Social Needs," in Boris and Steuerle, *Nonprofits and Government*, p. 87.

30. Putnam, *Bowling Alone*, p. 128.

31. Brian O'Connell, *Origins, Dimensions and Impact of America's Voluntary Spirit* (Washington, DC: Independent Sector, 1984), p. 2.

32. Steven Smith and Michael Lipsky, *Nonprofits for Hire* (Cambridge, MA: Harvard University Press, 1993), p. 184.

33. Gardner quoted in O'Connell, *Origins, Dimensions and Impact of America's Voluntary Spirit*, p. 6.

34. John W. Gardner, *Keynote Address* (Washington, DC: Independent Sector, 1978), p. 13.

35. Irene Lacher, "Teaching America a Lesson," *Los Angeles Times* (November 11, 1990), p. E1; personal communication, Teach for America, October 7, 1996.

36. "National Amounts Raised Highest in 30-Year History."

37. David Johnston, "United Way, Faced with Fewer Donors, Is Giving Away Less," *The New York Times* (November 9, 1997), p. 28.

38. Peter Kilborn, "Charity for Poor Lags behind Need," *The New York Times* (December 12, 1999), p. 34.

39. Judith Havemann, "Federal Charity Drive Opened to More Groups," *Washington Post* (January 2, 1988), p. A1.

40. *Designations and Donor Choice in United Way Campaigns* (Fairfax, VA: United Way of America, 1996), Table 1.

41. Tracy Thompson, "United Way Contributors Exercise Their Options," *Washington Post* (September 21, 1996), p. A1.

42. Teresa Odendahl, *Charity Begins at Home* (New York: Basic Books, 1990), pp. 3, 245.

43. Ibid., p. 49.

44. Ibid., p. 232.

45. Sam Verhovek, "Elder Bill Gates Takes on the Role of Philanthropist," *The New York Times* (September 12, 1999), p. 22.

46. David Lauter, "United Way's Chief Quits in Funds Dispute," *Los Angeles Times* (February 28, 1992), p. A1.

47. "Key Dates in the Adjudication of Former Management" (Fairfax, VA: United Way of America, 1996).

48. Karen Arenson, "Woeful '95 Leads U.S. Charities to Introspection," *The New York Times* (December 10, 1995), p. 38.

49. Lynn Simross, "When Sharing the Wealth, Let the Donor Beware," *Los Angeles Times* (April 5, 1992), p. A6.

50. Judith Havemann, "Top Foundations Gave Chiefs a Bountiful Raise," *Washington Post* (July 5, 1998), p. A1.

51. Jean Strouse, "How to Give Away $21.8 Billion," *The New York Times Magazine* (April 16, 2000).

52. W. Harrison Wellford and Janne Gallagher, *Charity and the Competition Challenge* (Washington, DC: National Assembly of National Voluntary Health and Social Welfare Organizations, 1987), pp. 13–15.

53. Michael Abramowitz, "Nonprofit Hospitals Venture into New Lines of Business," *Washington Post* (February 15, 1987), p. C5.

54. Todd Gillman, "Health Clubs Hit YMCAs' Tax Breaks," *Washington Post* (June 30, 1987), p. E2.

55. Anne Swardson, "Hill Taking New Look at Nonprofits," *Washington Post* (June 21, 1987), p. F9.

56. Marvin Olasky, *The Tragedy of American Compassion* (Washington, DC: Regnery, 1992); *Renewing American Compassion* (New York: Fre Press, 1996).

57. David Osborne and Ted Gaebler, *Reinventing Government* (Reading, MA: Addison-Wesley, 1992).

58. Hanna Rosin, "Putting Faith in a Social Service Role," *Washington Post* (May 5, 2000), p. A1.

59. Terry Neal, "Bush Outlines Charity-Based Social Policies," *Washington Post* (July 23, 1999), p. A2.

60. Robert Putnam, "The Prosperous Community," *The American Prospect* 13 (Spring 1993), p. 1.

61. Terry Neal, "Ex-Lawmaker Refuses to Be Boxed In," *Washington Post* (January 10, 1998), p. A8.

62. R. Baker, "The Ecumenist," *The American Prospect* (January 17, 2000), p. 28.

63. Bill Shore, *The Cathedral Within* (New York: Random House, 1999).

64. "Simple Acts, Real Progress" (San Francisco, Working Assets Long Distance, 1997).

65. T. Thompson, "Profit with Honor," *Washington Post Magazine* (December 19, 1999).

66. "High Tech at the Grassroots," *Responsive Philanthropy* (Summer 1999), p. 12.

67. Jonathan Alter, "Charity Begins with a Click," *Newsweek* (June 5, 2000), p. 57.

chapter 7

Privatization and Human Service Corporations

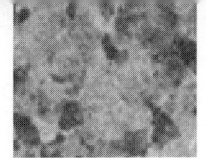

This chapter reviews the privatization of social welfare. Historically, much social welfare has been provided by the private not-for-profit sector. Since the 1980s, however, conservatives have called for downsizing government, in the process shifting service responsibility to the private sector.

In addition, this chapter considers the role of the business community in U.S. social welfare. Historically, some business leaders have made important contributions to the health and welfare of their employees by envisaging utopian work environments and pioneering the provision of benefits to employees. Business leaders were also instrumental in fashioning early governmental welfare policies. More recently, emphasis on the "social responsibility" of corporations has encouraged business leaders to assess the broader implications of corporate activities. Corporations also shape social welfare policy by influencing the political process and subsidizing policy institutes. Proprietary firms have become well established in several **human services** markets: nursing care, hospital management, managed medical care, child care, life/continuing care, and corrections. Finally, the chapter considers collective bargaining as a response to privatization. Health and human service professionals have been reluctant to join unions, primarily because they fear doing so would taint their professional status. Yet continuing privatization means that unions may be the only aggregate defense for professionals who have become employees of profit-making health and human service corporations.

As a function of public dissatisfaction with governmental social programs, increasing reliance on the private sector to finance and deliver social services has emerged as an important theme in U.S. social welfare. **Privatization,** as this idea has been termed, addresses the problem of the proper relationship between the public and private spheres of the national culture. In this case, the concept of privatization has come to involve "the idea that private is invariably more efficient than public, that government ought to stay out of as many realms as possible, and that government should contract out tasks to private firms or give people vouchers rather than provide them services directly."[1] That government should not hold a monopoly on social welfare is not a novel idea. Even liberal policy analysts have entertained ways in which the private sector could complement governmental welfare initiatives.[2] Liberal proponents of welfare programs are often willing to concede a viable role to the private sector—even an innovative role—but insist that government must be the primary instrument to advance social welfare. Conservatives, of course, see the proper balance as one in which the private sector is the primary source of protection against social and economic calamity, and believe that government activity should be held in reserve. According to conservative doctrine, government can deploy the "safety net" of social programs, but these should provide benefits only as a last resort.

A clear articulation of the conservative vision of reinforcing the role of the private sector in social affairs appeared in the 1988 report of the President's Commission on Privatization. "In the United States . . . the growth of government has been based on the political and economic design that emerged from the Progressive movement around the turn of this century," noted the report. "The American privatization movement has represented in significant part a reaction against the themes and results of Progressive thought."[3] Specifically, the report targeted government social programs and the professional administrators who manage them as the undesirable consequences of the progressive state of mind—consequences that could be corrected by privatization. The implications of this analysis are broad: Not only should benefits be removed from government and provided by the private sector, but the administration of social programs should also be removed from the public sector and placed under private auspices. Accordingly, the President's Commission on Privatization identified three "techniques for the privatization of service delivery": (1) selling government assets; (2) contracting with private firms to provide goods and services previously offered by government; and (3) using vouchers, whereby the government would distribute coupons authorizing private providers to receive reimbursement from the government for the goods and services they had provided.[4] Although all these methods had been used to restructure welfare programs at one time or another, the report introduced an unprecedented idea into the debate by characterizing social welfare as a "zero-sum game" in which an advantage to one party is always at the expense of another party. In this case, proponents of privatization suggested that the private sector should assume more responsibility for welfare, but with government social programs reduced. It is this abdication of the government's obligation to ensure the general welfare that makes the current debate on privatization so important.

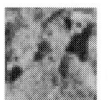 ## Concerns about Privatization

"Governments in the United States spend roughly half a trillion dollars per year paying public workers to deliver goods and services directly," observed John Donahue. "If only one-quarter of this total turned out to be suitable for privatization, at an average savings of, say, 25 percent—and neither figure is recklessly optimistic—the public would save over $30 billion."[5] Such savings could be used to lower taxes or to extend existing programs.

Yet many health and human service professionals have trepidations about privatization. Significant downsizing of government, coupled with the astronomical growth of for-profit health and human service firms, presents a significant challenge to the U.S. welfare state. As a result, many liberal social activists object to privatization, often citing research that identifies risks in relying on the private sector for certain activities. Research on for-profit firms generally confirms liberal doubts about privatizing welfare.

The irony in the critical stance toward privatization assumed by many health and human service professionals is that many of them prefer private practice as a method of service delivery. Thus, private practice on a small scale is condoned, but corporate exploitation of the new health and human service markets is met with considerable skepticism. This issue has become volatile as corporate managed care firms have penetrated markets once controlled by private practitioners. It also raises a profound concern for the social work profession: To the extent that social workers engage in private practice, there are fewer human service professionals in the public sector to work with people presenting more serious disorders. As a result, what limited influence social work has is invested in promoting its self-interest at the expense of the poor—a point underscored by the late Harry Specht and Mark Courtney in *Unfaithful Angels:*

> . . . there has been an increasing tendency of the [social work] profession to use its political power to support licensing of clinical social workers and third-party payments for social workers who are so licensed, to the relative neglect of efforts to improve the lot of social workers employed in the public social services and their clients.[6]

For many human service professionals, then, private practice represents a retreat from a service ethic that transcends self-interest: the public welfare.

Privatizing Public Welfare

The PRWORA allows states to buy welfare services and welfare gatekeepers to determine eligibility and benefits. Faced with a financial crush, states may opt to reduce costs by privatizing the delivery of public assistance benefits, an option that Texas has adopted. While privatization has been going on in child support enforcement and in some sectors of child welfare, it has not been tried in public assistance until relatively recently. Not surprisingly, some corporations stand to make considerable profits from the privatization of public assistance. According to Nina Bernstein, "The new [1996] welfare bill is still a matter of confusion in statehouses and city streets. But to some companies it looks like the business opportunity of a lifetime."[7]

Proponents argue that allowing private companies to run public welfare will prove to be the most cost-effective and humane way for states to face the fiscal demands of the 1996 welfare law. For these supporters, privatization promises to deliver technological efficiency by cutting administrative costs and detecting fraud. Meanwhile, privatized operations will help recipients by offering one-stop shopping for benefits and enrollment. Supporters believe that a profit-making company has the flexibility to reward employees for positive results and to change the welfare system from one that dispenses checks to one that quickly moves people into jobs. Moreover, states that are able to reduce administrative costs will have more money available for child care, transportation, and job training programs. If states overspend, they have no recourse for going to the federal government for a match; if they underspend, it frees up money for other purposes. For state welfare administrators faced with capped block grants and substantial penalties if they fail to move recipients into jobs, a fixed-price private contract has strong appeal.

Driven by a vision of cutting administrative expenses by 20 to 40 percent (mostly by closing offices and eliminating state jobs),[8] Texas was the first state to experiment with letting a private company create and run a system to screen applicants for welfare benefits. In Texas corporations bid to manage the more than $8 billion public welfare system made up of AFDC, food stamps, Medicaid, and more than 25 other programs. The corporate players in this privatization scenario had substantial assets and included such companies as IBM, Lockheed Information Management Services (a nonmilitary division of the $30 billion Lockheed Martin), Electronic Data Systems (a $12.4 billion company formerly owned by Ross Perot), Andersen Consulting (a $4.2 billion company), and Unisys.[9] Even while Texas was serving as the stalking horse for the multibillion-dollar welfare operations in the rest of the nation, similar discussions were under

way in states from Wisconsin to Maryland.[10] Moreover, as a testimony to their commitment to the vast public welfare market, Lockheed hired Gerald Miller, the former director of the Michigan Family Independence Agency and president of the influential American Public Welfare Association. According to Miller, "I see this as the future of welfare reform. The private sector will ultimately run these programs. The era of big government is over."[11] In addition to Miller, Lockheed hired welfare officials from both the states and the federal government to lead its efforts to manage privatized welfare programs.

Opponents argue that if a corporation's profits are linked to reducing the welfare rolls, the incentive to deny aid will be overwhelming. According to Henry Freedman of the Center for Social Welfare Policy and Law, "No company can be expected to protect the interests of the needy at the expense of its bottom line, least of all a publicly traded corporation with a fiduciary duty to maximize shareholder profits."[12] Clearly, corporations will have strong incentives to use the letter of the law to cut people off in an effort to improve their profits and performance.[13] Much of this fiscal incentive will be based on the fixed-price nature of welfare contracts, which will include penalties for a failure to perform. For example, Texas may require a corporation to put up a $250 million performance bond. Given this, states will tend to prefer larger corporations, because they have deeper pockets into which to reach if a penalty is incurred.

Other problems exist with privatizing public welfare. For one, administrative costs for public welfare are already low, overseen to some degree by federal government regulations. To make money managing public welfare, corporations will have to use several strategies. For one, they may have to cut staff and replace long-term welfare workers and managers with inexperienced lower-wage workers. One Texas union estimated that "at least half of the 13,000 state employees who now determine welfare eligibility will be cut out of the new system."[14] Second, as a way to control salaries, corporations may try to dislodge public sector unions where they exist, and to prohibit them where they do not. A third strategy for saving money would be to replace welfare offices and state workers in rural areas with automated kiosks and highly sophisticated voice mail systems, similar to automated banking. All of these corporate strategies would have a major impact on the quality of services delivered. For instance, it is questionable whether automated screening and services coupled with inexperienced welfare workers will be able to provide the same level of service as face-to-face interviews. What of services to people of diverse languages and cultural backgrounds? These and other questions remain unanswered.

Corporations have an established precedent for bailing out of projects they ultimately find to be unprofitable. This is illustrated in IBM's desertion of its OS/2 operating system after an initial investment of billions and in the 1990s divestiture of specific AT&T operations. What will happen if management of the public welfare system proves to be unprofitable or ultimately impossible to administer? Will corporations break their contracts? Even if they complete their contracts, will the state be able to find another corporation to run operations if a company begs out of renewing its contract? This contingency will be especially problematic because states will have disbanded their public welfare bureaucracies and will thus be dependent on corporations to administer public welfare. Indeed, this scenario will put states in a tenuous bargaining position in terms of renegotiating corporate contracts. Moreover, what will happen to needy people if a contractor fails to deliver as promised? Will these people be held hostage as the time-consuming process of litigation is begun? Lastly, there are many precedents involving private corporations that bid on and are awarded defense contracts, only to come back again and again to ask for more money.

Finally, corporations have a long history of establishing monopolistic pricing once they gain a large share of the market. It is conceivable that the bidding process in public welfare will initially produce low bids. In fact, corporations may even underbid—knowing that they will lose money—in order to gain a foothold in a state. If public welfare services were privatized nationally, with only a small group of corporations running the system, these companies soon would be in a strong position to determine their rates of reimbursement. Despite the short-term savings, privatizing public assistance entails significant long-term risks to both recipients and government.

Issues in the Privatization of Health and Human Services

A new question in the debate on the balance between private and public responsibility for welfare was introduced with the recent emergence of health and human service corporations: If government is to divest itself of its welfare obligation, can the business community pick up the slack?

Proponents of privatization have two options for the private provision of social welfare: the nonprofit, voluntary sector (Chapter 6) and the for-profit, **corporate sector.** In the years following President Lyndon Johnson's Great Society programs, government began to experiment with contracting out services through both nonprofit and for-profit providers. The for-profit corporate sector capitalized on the contracting-out provisions of the Medicare and Medicaid programs. At the same time, through the purchase-of-service concept introduced in Title XX, nonprofit agencies became contractors providing a range of social services on behalf of public welfare departments.

Unfortunately, studies comparing the performance of these sectors have been few and their findings debatable.[15] In the absence of definitive results showing the advantages of one sector over another, the privatization debate has become heated. Advocates of *voluntarization*, or reliance on the voluntary sector to assume more of the responsibility for welfare, point to its historical contribution to the national culture, the rootedness of its agencies in the community, and the altruistic motives behind its programs. Proponents of *corporatization,* or dependence on the corporate sector to provide welfare, argue that corporations offer more cost-effective administration, are more responsive to consumer demand, and pay taxes. And whether voluntarists or corporatists prevail in the privatization debate will rest largely on the ability of each party to manipulate the social policy process in its favor. Whatever the outcome, this process is certain to be lengthy and complex, as one might expect with the remaking of an institutional structure that has become as essential as social welfare is in the United States. And whether voluntarization or corporatization defines the future of social welfare, privatization has already highlighted several important issues.

Commercialization

For welfare professionals the idea of subjecting human need to the economic marketplace is often problematic. For example, it is hard to condone health care advertising in view of the fact that the health care industry, notably the Health Insurance Association of America, spent $100 million to defeat the Clinton administration's Health Security Act—even though the United States is still without a universal program for expectant mothers and infants, to say nothing of the 40 million Americans without health insurance.[16] Another example: When research on the AIDS virus led to a diagnostic test, some private physicians exploited the AIDS panic and charged as much as $300 for each test—even though the U.S. Army negotiated a test price of 82 cents.[17] As objectionable as these market-induced practices may be, however, the commercialization of health and human services is a reality that welfare professionals cannot simply dismiss out of a sense of moral indignation.

In one of the earliest treatments of the matter, Richard Titmuss's *The Gift Relationship* explored the differences in the ways nations manage their blood banks. Unlike the practice in the United Kingdom, blood in the United States is "treated in laws as an article of commerce"; that is, rules of the market affect the supply and quality of blood. Titmuss observed the growth of blood and plasma businesses with alarm, because these businesses bought blood from a population that was often characterized by poverty and poor health. Quite apart from the health hazard posed by a blood supply derived from such a population—a hazard highlighted by AIDS—Titmuss was concerned that the profit motive would disrupt the voluntary impulses of community life. "There is growing disquiet in the United States," he observed, that "expanding blood programs . . . are driving out the voluntary system."[18] Indeed, by 1976, 63.3 percent of blood banks in the United States were commercial.[19]

Preferential Selection

If privatization has implications for program administrators, as evident in the commercialization of human services, it also has significant implications for clients. As mentioned earlier, the application of market principles to client service introduces strong incentives for providers to differentiate clients according to their effect on organizational performance. Such selection can be at variance with professional standards, which emphasize the client's need for service over organizational considerations. But the marketplace tends to penalize providers that are imprudent about client selection, at the same time rewarding providers that are more discriminating. The subtle or blatant practice of choosing clients according to criteria of organizational performance—as opposed to client need—is known as **preferential selection.** Under marketplace conditions, providers that do not practice preferential selection are bound to serve a disproportionate number of clients with serious problems and with less ability to pay the cost of care, thereby running deficits. By contrast, providers that select clients who have less serious problems and who can cover the cost of care often claim surpluses. For example, an analysis of psychiatric patients admitted to a public and a private hospital found that the latter selected patients of higher social status. The researchers concluded that "patients in the marginal/uncredentialed social class were comparatively more likely to be admitted to state mental hospitals than to private hospitals."[20]

Preferential selection could be excused, perhaps, as a benign method through which organizations determine which clients are likely to be best served—if it were not for the odious practice of client "dumping." Dumping occurs when clients already being served by an organization (usually a for-profit firm) are abruptly transferred to another organization (usually a nonprofit or governmental agency) because they represent a drain on the institutional resources of the first organization.

Critics of privatization complain that creaming the client population through preferential selection is unethical and should be prohibited. Simply ruling out the practice is, however, easier said than done. Accusations of preferential selection are not new; private nonprofit agencies were accused of denying services to welfare recipients long before proprietary firms became established.[21] Yet recent reports of dumping in instances when life-threatening injuries are evident have drawn the ire of many human service professionals. In some cases, private hospitals have transferred indigent patients with traumatic injuries to public facilities without providing proper medical care, thus contributing to the deaths of several patients.

Incidents of dumping are directly related to the patient's ability to pay for service, and transfers of poor patients have increased as Medicaid has been cut. For example, the transfer of poor patients to the publicly owned Cook County General Hospital in Chicago increased from between 90 and 125 per month to 560 patients in August 1981, one month after Illinois instituted cuts in its Medicaid program.[22] In another instance, researchers at Highland General Hospital, the public health care facility in Alameda County, California, examined the transfer disposition of 458 patients over a six-month period. The researchers concluded that "the transfer of patients from private to public hospital emergency rooms is common, involves primarily uninsured or government-insured patients, disproportionately affects minority group members, and sometimes places patients in jeopardy."[23] In Denver, where public hospitals have sustained heavy deficits by caring for a disproportionate burden of the medically indigent, the problem has become critical. Jane Collins, director of clinical social work for the Denver Department of Health and Hospitals, described public hospitals in the city as having become "social dumps."[24]

Given the market, preferential selection on the part of a large number of providers is likely to be adopted by others who wish to remain in a competitive position. In analyzing the practice in health care, a team of researchers from Harvard University and the American Medical Association noted that "in the same way that competition from for-profit providers leads to reduction in access, the more competitive the market for hospital services generally, the more likely are all hospitals in that market to discourage admissions of Medicaid and uninsured patients."[25] In other words, even nonprofit providers—who are exempt from taxes because they contribute to the community's welfare—are compelled to adopt the discriminatory practices of for-profit providers in a competitive market, unless the nonprofits are willing to underwrite the losses that more costly clients represent to for-profit providers. "When competitive pressures are great," researchers from Yale and Harvard universities have noted, "the behavior of for-profit and nonprofit institutions often converge."[26]

Cost-Effectiveness

Proponents of privatization frequently cite the discipline imposed on organizational performance by a competitive environment as a rationale for market reforms in social welfare. A competitive environment provides strong incentives for organizations to adopt cost-effective practices that reduce waste. This claim has led to a handful of studies of for-profit versus nonprofit service providers. In 1981 Lewin and Associates compared 53 nonprofit hospitals with a matched set of for-profit hospitals in the South and Southwest. They concluded that investor-owned hospitals were more expensive than nonprofit hospitals, largely due to higher **ancillary services** (laboratory, radiology services) and administrative costs. Also, investor-owned hospitals used fewer full-time equivalent staff to provide care than did nonprofit hospitals.[27] This last finding is unsettling because lower staff-to-patient ratios have been associated with higher rates of contagious disease in nursing homes.[28] The Florida Hospital Cost Containment Board released a 1980 analysis comparing 72 proprietary and 82 nonprofit hospitals in that state. With results similar to the Lewin study, the board reported 15 percent higher charges for patient care and an 11 percent higher collection rate by investor-owned hospitals than by their nonprofit counterparts.[29]

In an ambitious study, researchers from the Western Consortium for the Health Professions compared 280 public, private nonprofit, and investor-owned hospitals. The Western Consortium investigators reached conclusions that were even less supportive of a marketplace approach to health care. For example, they suggested that investor-owned hospitals used emergency services and room and board as loss leaders, funneling patients into situations in which higher-cost ancillary services would then be used. Investor-owned hospitals cared for the smallest proportion of patients dependent on Medicaid. The researchers concluded that "the data do not support the claim that investor-owned chains enjoy overall operating efficiencies or economics of scale in administrative or fiscal services."[30]

Significantly, the higher cost of **proprietary,** or for-profit, hospitals cannot be attributed to longer periods of hospitalization, because the average stay at for-profit hospitals, 7.8 days, was (along with the average stay at government institutions) shorter than that of sectarian and other nonprofit institutions.[31] In a comprehensive review of the issue, the Institute of Medicine of the National Academy of Sciences concluded in the mid-1980s that there was "no evidence to support the common belief that investor-owned organizations are less costly or more efficient than are not-for-profit organizations."[32]

More recently, Robert Kuttner summarized analyses conducted by an association of nonprofit hospitals and found that "investor-owned hospitals in 1994 were 13.7 percent more expensive on a charge basis than nonprofit and public hospitals." Again, not only were for-profit hospitals more expensive, but they also provided less care to the poor, admitting only half as many Medicaid patients as nonprofit hospitals. Another analysis of proprietary hospitals by the nonprofit hospital association found that investor-owned hospitals were 30 percent more expensive than not-for-profit hospitals.[33]

Although skeptics of market strategies in welfare use such studies to criticize the supposed economies of corporatization in the human services market, it appears that the practices of for-profit firms are nevertheless influencing nonprofit human service organizations. Many nonprofits have adopted features of for-profit firms—bulk buying, sophisticated information systems, staff reductions—to enhance organizational efficiency. As noted, when nonprofits compete with for-profit firms in the same market, the adoption of competitive practices is inevitable in order to ensure organizational survival. As a result, competitive practices characteristic of human service corporations may become standard organizational procedure, not because they serve the public interest better but because the rules of the marketplace require their adoption.

Nevertheless, the promise of cost containment through privatization has not been borne out, and this presents an enormous problem for the governmental sector. Under a privatized system, government is in a weak position to control the prices charged by contracting agencies unless it is prepared to deploy its own set of public institutions, thereby avoiding the private sector altogether. A good example is provided by the Medicare program. Through Medicare the government subsidizes health care for elderly people, most of which is provided by the private sector. In response to runaway Medicare costs, in 1983 Congress enacted the **Diagnostic Related Groups (DRGs)** prospective payment plan, whereby hospitals are reimbursed fixed amounts for medical procedures. Three years after the

DRG system was in place, the Congressional Budget Office reported that hospitals had increased their surplus attributed to Medicare by 15.7 percent during 1985. This surplus occurred despite a reduction in the number of Medicare patients admitted to hospitals.[34]

Proponents of privatization often claim that noncompetitive markets and governmental regulation, as in the case of the DRG prospective payment system, impose additional costs that must be passed on to consumers. Research, however, does not bear this out. In a study of 6,000 hospitals sponsored by the National Center for Health Services Research and Health Care Technology Assessment, a research team found that "hospitals located in areas with 11 or more neighboring facilities within a 15 mile radius—the most competitive type of hospital market—have admission costs and patient day costs that are 26 percent and 15 percent higher, respectively, than corresponding figures for hospitals with no competitors." Significantly, the hospitals were surveyed before 1983, so governmental regulation through the DRG system could not have contributed to the higher costs.[35]

Standardization

Privatization induces human service organizations to accept an industrial mode of production in which the accepted measure of success is not necessarily the quality of service rendered but the number of people processed. Organizations tend to achieve surpluses, essential for investor-owned facilities, by increasing the intensity of production and lowering labor costs. Because the logic of the market dictates that the goal of production is to process the largest number of people at the lowest possible cost, the **standardization** of services is an important method for lowering organizational costs.

Such uniformity of care has become an issue in the nursing home industry. Because Medicaid regulations stipulate standards of care, providers deriving a large portion of their revenues from Medicaid are induced to standardize care for all patients. Paradoxically, well-to-do patients are unable to purchase better care from a nursing home even if they have the resources to do so. The standardization of care has become a cause for serious concern among nursing home corporations. Richard Buchanan, professor of business administration at Bowling Green State University, noted the social consequences of standardized care:

> The nursing home industry's identical treatment of everyone creates a one-class social system for all patients. This constitutes a denial of the affluent person's rights to purchase the quality of life that had been his or hers until stricken with illness or infirmity. This phenomenon represents creeping socialism of a major order, and creates an atmosphere ripe for either legal or market reprisal.[36]

That standardization of care within an industry dominated by for-profit firms would be equated with socialism is perhaps the best measure of the acuity of the problem.

Under these circumstances, life care—the service offered by the continuing-care retirement community—has emerged as an attractive alternative to the nursing home. Under life care plans, residents can purchase cottages or apartments in self-contained communities that provide a range of human services. In many respects the life care community provides more affluent residents an opportunity to purchase a higher level of long-term care. Many continuing-care facilities boast such amenities as wall-to-wall carpeting, maid service, and designer landscaping. "Already, the facility has shown its first in-house movie . . . and soon residents will be soaking up steam in the saunas, relaxing in the Jacuzzi, exercising on the mechanical bicycles, or browsing in the library," noted a visitor to one facility.[37] Found in the more posh life-care communities are cocktail lounges, billiards rooms, sports facilities, and elegantly furnished restaurants serving continental cuisine. Amenities such as these "provide a lifestyle of grace and activity for seniors with the ability to pay for it," observed an industry reporter.[38] "We sell a style of life," explained David Steel, vice president of Retirement Centers of America Inc., a subsidiary of Avon.[39]

The price of entry into life care communities can be equivalent to that of a new home. Nationwide, in the early 1980s the average entrance fees were $35,000 for a single person and $39,000 for a couple. Monthly fees for medical care, dining and laundry, recreation, and transportation averaged $600 for a single person and $850 for a couple.[40] In more exclusive communities, one- and two-bedroom units sold in the 1980s for $100,000 to $170,000.[41] By the mid-1980s, 275 life care communities were housing 100,000 elders.[42] But this was only the tip of a very large iceberg. Robert Ball, former commissioner of Social Security, estimated that perhaps 15 million elders could afford this type of care.[43] Despite the well-publicized bankruptcies of several life care communities, the prospect of a market of this scale has attracted the interest of several corporations.[44] Beverly Enterprises, the largest nursing home corporation, announced plans to build or acquire several life care communities.[45] Subsequently, Marriott Corporation stated its intention to build several life care communities serving 300 and 400 residents each.[46] Despite the recession of the early 1980s, the interest of brokerage houses in continuing care remained high.[47] By the year 2000, as many as 15 million Americans will need some form of long-term care.[48]

The prospect of extensive proprietary involvement in life care troubles some analysts. Lloyd Lewis, director of a nonprofit life care community, fears that "well-funded proprietary interests" will "drain off the more financially able segment of our older population, widening the gap between the 'haves' and the 'have nots.' "[49] To a significant extent this is already occurring. Robert Ball noted that even life care communities operating under not-for-profit auspices are beyond the means of "the poor, the near poor, or even the low-income elderly."[50]

The accommodation of long-term care facilities to the desire for amenities on the part of affluent residents is likely to produce significant change in how the nation cares for its elderly. As early as 1982, for example, the *New York Times* reported a nationwide shortage of nursing home beds for those "whose nursing care is financed by the government through Medicaid."[51] As human service corporations divert capital to care for those who represent profit margins, economic and political support for the care of those less fortunate diminishes. "Those who cannot gain admission to [a private] institution will be forced into boarding homes . . . or bootleg boarding homes," commented Milton Jacobs, vice president of American Medical Affiliates. "These boarding homes will be filled with what are literally social rejects. We're reverting back to the way the industry was in the fifties and sixties."[52] Left unchecked, this pattern is likely to divide long-term care into two clearly demarcated systems, with the affluent enjoying the generous care of completely—some would say excessively—provisioned life care communities, and the elderly poor dependent on the squalid institutions willing to accept government payment for their care. Ironically, to a great extent dual systems of long-term care will be the outcome of the desire of the affluent to escape the standardization of care associated with the economies of privatization.

Oligopolization

The privatization of human services invites **oligopolization:** the development of oligopolies, or the control of a market by few providers, as organizations seek to reduce competition by buying their competitors. Within the corporate sector three waves of acquisition can be identified: acquisitions affecting long-term care, acquisitions affecting hospital management, and acquisitions affecting health maintenance organizations (HMOs). As firms gain control of major shares of markets, they are in a strong position to leverage influence through trade associations to shape social policy.

The consolidation of proprietary health providers has also encouraged nonprofit providers, driven by the same competitive pressures, to form franchises. Five of the 10 largest hospital systems (in terms of number of beds) are nonprofit. Of these, 3 are operated by religious organizations; one—the New York City Health and Hospital Corporation—is a public conglomerate; and another—Kaiser Foundation Hospital—is a private nonprofit entity. Increasingly, nonprofit health providers are having to join together in order to compete with the aggressive proprietary providers, a trend that has led to oligopolies within the voluntary sector.[53]

Oligopolization of human services presents a daunting specter in that a small number of wealthy and powerful organizations are in a strong position to shape social policy to conform with their interests. Within health care, this development has led Arnold Relman, editor of *The New England Journal of Medicine,* to voice alarm at the growing influence of the "new medical–industrial complex" in defining health policy in the United States.[54] A good illustration of the influence of health providers on public policy was the Clinton administration's ill-fated Health Security Act (HSA).

The HSA was designed to promote for-profit health care providers through regional health alliances, which would compete for members. Even though this plan incorporated the interests of the larger health care firms, it threatened to wipe out many smaller firms. Soon after the HSA was rolled out, the Health Insurance Association of America (HIAA) broadcast $2 million worth of ads, alleging that the HSA would ration health care under socialized medicine.[55] Michael Bromberg, director of the Federation of American Health Systems (FAHS), representing 1,400 for-profit hospitals, announced a preference for a proposal less restrictive than the HSA. Bromberg threatened Hillary Rodham Clinton with an adversarial campaign if the administration did not adjust its plan to accommodate FAHS. The threat was not hollow; FAHS routinely contributed $250,000 apiece to the campaigns of strategically placed Senate and House candidates.[56] Within weeks lobbyists besieged Capitol Hill. Anticipating the 1994 election, health industry interest groups contributed $26 million to congressional campaigns.[57] Eventually, observers would put the price tag on influence peddling around failed health care reform at $100 million.[58]

The Challenge of Privatization

As we have seen, privatization is a disquieting prospect for health and human service professionals. For those committed to increasing government's responsibility for ensuring social and economic equality, privatization is simply a retreat from a century of hard-won gains in social programs. This case is argued cogently by Pulitzer Prize–winning sociologist Paul Starr:

> *A large-scale shift of public services to private providers would contribute to further isolating the least advantaged, since private firms have strong incentives to skim off the best clients and most profitable services. The result would often be a residual, poorer public sector providing services of last resort. Such institutions would be even less attractive as places to work than they are today. And their worsening difficulties would no doubt be cited as confirmation of the irremediable incompetence of public managers and inferiority of public services. Public institutions already suffer from this vicious circle; most forms of privatization would intensify it.*[59]

For defenders of government social programs, the problems inherent in privatization—commercialization, client creaming, inflated costs, standardization, and oligopolization—make it a poor vehicle for advancing social welfare.

Most profoundly, privatization reinforces a tendency in market economies to evolve dual structures of benefits, services, and opportunities: adequate and varied services for the affluent, substandard and uniform services for the poor. As Robert Kuttner has pointed out, "in a purely for-profit enterprise or system, there is no place for uncompensated care, unprofitable admissions, research, education, or public health activities—all chronic money losers from a strictly business viewpoint."[60]

For many human service advocates, the purpose of social welfare is to correct for the inherent tendency of markets to direct resources toward the affluent and away from the poor. From this left-leaning perspective, the idea of privatization of social welfare violates the essential meaning of social welfare. Thus, when Texas proposes to put public welfare out to bid, or when New Jersey plans to privatize child welfare, or when the partial privatization of Social Security is proposed, the left objects.[61]

Yet increased reliance on the private sector at a time when public social programs are under assault is a reality that must be faced by those concerned about social welfare. In the absence of a politically effective left and the diminishing influence of a progressive labor movement, there appears little chance of launching new government social programs—as the demise of health reform during the first Clinton term demonstrated. If the public is unwilling to authorize and pay for new governmental social programs, welfare professionals have little choice but to reconsider privatization as a basis for welfare provision. In seeking to understand the conditions under which privatization may be an appropriate policy response, for example, William Gormley has suggested that privatization is indicated less for "regulation than for distribution of goods, less for social services than for physical services, and less for core services than for auxiliary services."[62]

In some instances, private sector analogues to public services have demonstrated surprising success. Take, for example, job placement of the hard-core unemployed. Traditional public sector approaches to this population include policies realized in the Job Training and Partnership Act and the Family Support Act. Yet in New York and Connecticut an innovative program called America Works has evolved through the private sector:

> *Each year the company finds jobs for more than 700 of the state's hard-core unemployed, 68 percent of whom are (as a result) permanently weaned from the welfare rolls. The company gets paid only after the former wel-*

> *fare recipient has been working for four months and its $5,000 fee is less than half of what it costs New York State to support an average welfare family of three. All told, America Works is saving taxpayers approximately $4.5 million annually and providing many of the state's hard-core unemployed with meaningful work.*[63]

Upon inspection, there are some strong arguments in favor of privatization as a strategy for promoting social welfare. Through commercial loans and issuance of stock, for-profit organizations have faster access to capital than does the governmental sector (which requires a lengthy public expenditure authorization process) or the voluntary sector (which relies on arduous fundraising campaigns) for purposes of program expansion. United American Healthcare, which provides prenatal and primary health care for Medicaid recipients, illustrates how the for-profit sector can be a vehicle for advancing the public good. The private sector has also been the source of important innovations in programs and organizational administration that have often become models for effective administration.[64] It could be argued further that welfare-conscious administrators have missed opportunities for promoting social welfare by ignoring opportunities for professional practice associated with privatization. In this regard, welfare professionals might wonder if patient abuses in the nursing home industry, chronicled in 1974 in *Tender Loving Greed,* would have been lessened had socially conscious administrators managed long-term care facilities.[65] In the late 1980s, after years of lobbying, human service advocates finally secured a regulation that requires "nursing homes with more than 120 beds to employ full-time at least one [undergraduate] social worker"— hardly enough to ensure compliance, considering past abuses.[66]

Privatization will continue to challenge the moral and rational impulses of human service professionals. The President's Commission on Privatization noted in 1992 that "the impact of the privatization movement, broadly understood, is only beginning to be felt. Privatization in this broad sense may well be seen by future historians as one of the most important developments in the American political and economic life of the late 20th century."[67] How health and human service professionals choose to respond to the challenge of privatization—whether reactively or innovatively—will be critical for the future of U.S. social welfare. Privatization may come to be a rallying cry for defenders of established programs that have been discredited as being wasteful and inflexible and currying the favors of special interests; or privatization may ultimately mean discovering new ways to exploit the social carrying capacity of the private sector. As David Donnison has suggested, welfare professionals would be wiser to reconsider their aversion to the private sector and to try to find the "progressive potential in privatization."[68]

Unions and the Private Sector

Unions of health and welfare professionals are one response to privatization. Since the Depression, social welfare professionals have organized collectively in order to obtain better wages and benefits, to enhance working conditions, and improve services to clients. Two pioneers of American social welfare, Bertha Capen Reynolds and Mary van Kleek, vigorously urged social welfare workers to view unions as a vehicle for social justice. Today, members of the Bertha Capen Reynolds Society advocate collective bargaining in order to empower human service professionals.

Social workers in the public sector often hold memberships in unions—most often in the American Federation of State, County, and Municipal Employees (AFSCME), with 55,000 social work members in 1993, or in the Service Employees International Union (SEIU) with 26,000 social work members. Altogether about one in four social workers belongs to a collective bar-

gaining unit.[69] Because of the dispersion of social work activities, however, social workers have been less successful than nurses or teachers in using unions to achieve their ends.

Collective bargaining is the foundation of the union process. Collective bargaining is face-to-face negotiation between unionized employees and management for the purpose of arriving at a union contract. Such bargaining is supposed to be done in good faith, and the legal rights of workers are protected by the National Labor Relations Act. If these rights are attenuated, workers can petition the National Labor Relations Board to address grievances. The ultimate power of unions is to exercise the right to strike when the bargaining process breaks down. Theoretically, both parties have an interest in a successful collective bargaining process, because strikes hurt both union members and their employers.

Collective bargaining can also address professional issues such as caseload size, educational benefits like tuition reimbursement, conference release time and reimbursements, payment for professional dues and subscriptions, and flexible work hours. One union leader noted, "To the professional—the teacher or caseworker—things like class size and caseload size become as important as the number of hours in a shift is to the blue collar worker."[70] In one union organizing campaign, for example, caseload size, career ladders and training, pay equity, and classification downgrading were the primary issues. In a nonprofit mental health clinic, safe working conditions, benefits for part-time workers, workloads, and participation in agency decision making were the focus of organizing efforts.[71]

A significant question before human service professionals has been the extent to which union objectives are consistent with professional values. Despite the constructive influence that unions could potentially exert in response to cuts in public welfare during the Reagan presidency or wholesale privatization of state and local governmental programs, social workers have approached unions with great apprehension. Opponents to collective bargaining contend that (1) unions cost employees money; (2) strike losses are never retrieved; (3) even when they are not purposely kept uninformed by union leadership, members have little voice in union affairs; (4) bureaucratic union hierarchies control the economic destiny of members; (5) union corruption is rampant; (6) union opposition to management attempts to increase productivity arrests organizational growth; (7) union featherbedding results in unneeded employees and unnecessary payroll expenses; (8) union activities foster conflict rather than collaboration; and (9) unions fail to extrapolate the effects of wage increases on future employment, inflation, and taxes.

A fundamental concern among social welfare professionals revolves around the ultimate tactic that unions can bring to employer–employee relations: job actions, particularly strikes. For social workers who have pledged to make client welfare a priority, the prospect of denying services as a result of job actions makes union membership and professional commitment contradictory. In covering a 1984 strike by Local 1199 of the Retail Drug Employees Union that included the social work staffs of more than 50 hospitals and nursing homes, Dena Fisher wrote,

> *Standards for professional practice conflict with the [NASW] Code of Ethics with regard to behavior during a labor strike when the prescribed behavior includes withholding service, failing to terminate clients properly, and picketing activity directed toward consumers. . . . The problem is that participation in a strike is a nonprofessional activity. . . . Standards of professional behavior conflict with union membership requirements.*[72]

Yet proponents of union membership cite ways in which collective bargaining can complement professional objectives. In an attempt to encourage a better relationship with professional social workers, Jerry Wurf, former AFSCME president, stated that

> *AFSCME's involvement [with social issues] is part of a larger commitment to improving public services and programs. But more importantly, these vital efforts prove the true mission of a labor organization to be closely linked to that of social work. AFSCME's growth in the last decade was due in large part to its role as a social missionary. This precious pursuit has undoubtedly been enhanced by the growing number of social workers in our ranks.*[73]

The few studies that have examined the issue have found little incongruity between the loyalties of social workers who belong to unions. Leslie Alexander and his colleagues studied 84 union members with M.S.W. degrees and found that "they view their work as solidly professional and, for the most part, do not see unionism and professionalism as incompatible."[74] Ernie Lightman reported similar findings when studying 121 randomly chosen professional social workers in Toronto. According to Lightman, "the vast majority saw no incompatibility; indeed, many felt unionization may facilitate service goals, offsetting workplace bureaucracy."[75] Reporting on child welfare agencies in Pennsylvania and Illinois, Gary Shaffer found that "workers did not find unionism incompatible with their educational or professional goals."[76]

Such complementarity notwithstanding, the concept of social work "exceptionalism" pervades the debate about professionalism and unions. The exceptionalism premise implies that tasks performed by social workers are more important than those performed by many other workers, especially nonprofessionals, and that normal labor relations principles are therefore not applicable. Proponents of social work exceptionalism must address two matters: First, how is it that other semiprofessionals—teachers and nurses—have reconciled their professional priorities with union activities and become more powerful in the contexts of their work as a result? Are social service activities to be considered more essential than education or health care? Second, does the idea of social work exceptionalism contribute to the powerlessness of social workers? If social work places such value on the empowerment on of clients, why should social workers themselves not also be so empowered? The idea of social work's exceptionalism was put in bold relief in 1991 when members of Canada's Public Service Alliance—many of whom are social workers—

participated in one of the largest strikes in the nation's history, inspired by the government's plan to reduce wage increases.[77] If Canadian human service professionals can reconcile professional and union differences, why is this beyond U.S. social workers?

While social workers in the United States procrastinate about an alliance with unions, events such as privatization and government cuts in funding make the issue ever more urgent. Social workers and unions should be able to collaborate in problem solving, fostering a public debate on social issues and promoting class-aware groupings in an adverse social climate. Facilitating social change is a goal of several organizations, including Jobs with Justice. As Charles Heckscher points out, new approaches to unionization "are still in their infancy . . . [and] the rich variety of innovations being tried today has the potential to restore an essential pillar of labor's strength: the sense among the wider public that employee organization contributes to the general good."[78]

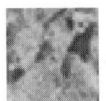

Corporate Welfare

The business community in the United States influences social welfare in several important ways. Benefit packages for employees, which are usually available to dependents, provide important health and welfare benefits to a large segment of the working population. Corporate philanthropy has sponsored important—and, in some cases, controversial—social welfare initiatives. And policy institutes reflecting the priorities of the business community have made substantial changes in U.S. "public philosophy." More recently, the corporate sector has begun to exploit the growing human service markets in long-term care, health maintenance, and corrections. These instances reflect the significant role that the corporate sector has played in U.S. social welfare.

Among welfare theorists, however, corporate activities have tended to be underappreciated. As discussed in Chapter 1, many progressive scholars attributed the cause of much social and economic dislocation to industrial capitalism, and therewith implicated capitalism's institutional representative, the corporation. Thus, the corporation was seen not as a source of relief but rather as the perpetrator of social and economic hardship. As a result, liberal theorists concluded that the government was the only institution capable of regulating capitalism and compensating the victims of its caprices. Welfare state ideology, as it evolved, left little room for the corporation, viewing it as the source of much suffering and as generally unwilling to pay its share of the tax burden to remediate the problems it had spawned. For example, advocacy groups such as the public interest research groups (PIRGs) associated with Ralph Nader and Citizens for Tax Justice regularly criticize the corporate sector for pursuing economic and political self-interest, sacrificing the general welfare in the process. A frequent target of criticism is "corporate welfare," the direct subsidies and tax expenditures granted to businesses in the United States, which total at least $75 billion annually.[79] In his 1996 campaign for the presidency, Ralph Nader contended that corporate influence was unprecedented in public affairs: "Indeed the corporate government's takeover of our political government, so pronounced since 1980, has reached levels of pervasiveness without precedent in modern American history."[80] Notorious examples of the sacrifice of civic values in pursuit of profits have been well chronicled by liberal advocacy groups. These include the disruption, then abandonment, of Love Canal because of improper disposal of toxic waste; the exploitation of Mexican agricultural workers in the Southwest; the extortion of huge sums from New York City housing officials by landlords who provide single-room occupancy lodgings for the homeless; and the deceit of tobacco companies about the harmful effects of smoking. To corporate critics, CEOs flaunt their positions by commanding salaries way out of proportion to their productivity. When superrich CEOs downsize production, lay off thousands of workers, and thereby decimate a local economy,[81] they become cultural pariahs. At the same time, few would doubt that wealth and status are enormously influential when wealthy executives leave private life and run for public office. "It's no accident that the Senate is a citadel of multimillionaires," observed one longtime Washington journalist.[82]

Privileges, power, and wealth notwithstanding, the corporate sector has made contributions to the **commonweal,** or public good, and these are less often recognized. Consider that in 1993 corporate contributions to nonprofit activities totaled $5.2 billion, substantially more than the $3.0 billion contributed to the nation's United Ways. Certainly most Americans would be able to identify the large corporate philanthropies listed in Table 7.1.

Through a variety of activities, from corporate philanthropy to workers' benefits, corporate leadership has made significant contributions to social welfare. Ironically, many welfare advocates who had leveled blanket indictments at the corporate sector during the 1960s found themselves furtively seeking grants from corporate foundations when government funds for new social programs dried up in the 1980s.

At this point many welfare theorists are beginning to reexamine the role of the corporate sector in American social welfare. The concept of the "mixed welfare economy" combines the corporate proprietary sector with the governmental and voluntary sectors as primary actors in social welfare.[83] And the issue of privatization has provoked a vigorous argument about the proper balance between the public and private (including corporate) welfare sectors.[84] Although Neil Gilbert's *Capitalism and the Welfare State* provided a timely review of the issues posed by "welfare capitalism,"[85] empirical investigations of for-profit human service corporations are in their infant stage.[86] Thus, the role of the corporate sector in U.S. social welfare, while expanding, is not well documented.

TABLE 7.1 ■ Twenty Largest Company-Sponsored Foundations by Total Grants, ca. 1994

FOUNDATION	GRANTS
General Motors Foundation	$34,918,915
AT&T Foundation	32,201,548
US West Foundation	23,673,008
General Electric Foundation	23,321,240
UPS Foundation	22,095,097
Shell Oil Company Foundation	20,511,367
Amoco Foundation	20,354,359
Exxon Education Foundation	19,846,586
GTE Foundation	19,496,822
Procter and Gamble Fund	19,146,977
Southwestern Bell Foundation	17,674,280
General Mills Foundation	17,456,689
Ford Motor Company Fund	16,804,535
Prudential Foundation	16,599,151
BankAmerica Foundation	14,854,325
RJR Nabisco Foundation	14,024,533
Wal-Mart Foundation	13,492,280
Merck Company Foundation	12,747,290
Bristol-Myers Squibb Foundation	12,617,655
American Express Foundation	12,436,900

Source: Virginia Hodgkinson and Murray Weitzman, *Nonprofit Almanac* (Washington, DC: Independent Sector, 1996), p. 125.

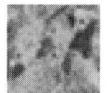 # History of the Corporate Sector

For most of the history of the United States, private institutions have been the basis of welfare provision. During the colonial era, the town overseer contracted out the poor to the resident who was willing to provide food and shelter at the lowest bid. Similarly, communities subsidized medical care for the poor through purchase of physicians' services. Through the eighteenth and nineteenth centuries, this practice contributed to the emergence of private institutions—hospitals and orphanages, among others—that served the needy.[87] Although many of these early welfare institutions were communal efforts and not developed as private businesses, others were precisely that. That is, many early hospitals in the United States were owned and operated by physicians, who became wealthy by providing health care to the community. By 1900 approximately 60 percent of hospitals were privately owned by physicians.[88]

With industrialization, however, the business community took a new interest in the health and welfare of employees. To be sure, certain captains of industry saw employee welfare as a concession to be made as a last resort, sometimes only after violent confrontation with organized workers. Such was not always the case, however. Early in the Industrial Revolution, before government assumed a prominent role in societal affairs, altruistically minded businessmen saw little recourse but to use their business firms as an instrument for their social designs. In some cases their experiments in worker welfare were nothing less than revolutionary. During the early 1820s the utopian businessman Robert Owen transformed a bankrupt Scotch mill town, New Lanark, from a wretched backwater populated by paupers into a "marvelously profitable" experiment in social engineering. Owen abolished child labor, provided habitable housing for his workers, and implemented a system to recognize the efforts of individual employees. Soon New Lanark attracted thousands of visitors, who were as awed by the contrast between the squalor of other mill towns and the brilliance of New Lanark as they were by the substantial profits Owen realized from the venture. A humanist and an irrepressible idealist, Owen believed that the solution to the problem of poverty lay not in the stringent and punitive English Poor Laws but in "making the poor productive." Owen later transported his utopian vision to the United States, where

he attempted to establish a rural planned community in New Harmony, Indiana.[89]

Although Owen's American experiment in local socialism did not survive, business leaders in the United States began to acknowledge that industrial production on a grand scale required a healthy and educated work force. Locating such workers was not easy amid the poverty and ignorance that characterized much of the population of the period. To improve the dependability of labor, several large corporations built planned communities for workers. During the early 1880s, for example, the Pullman Company, manufacturer of railroad sleeping cars, constructed "one of the most ambitiously planned communities in the United States—a company town complete with a hotel, markets, landscaped parks, factories, and residences for over 8,000 people."[90] Although some industries later built communities and facilities as a means of controlling and, in some cases, oppressing workers— as in the "company stores" operated by mining companies to keep miners forever in debt—many expressions of corporate interest in employee well-being clearly enhanced the welfare of the community.

In other instances, businesspeople experimented with alternative forms of business ownership. Current "workplace democracy" and "employee ownership" programs have a predecessor in the Association for the Promotion of Profit Sharing, established in 1892. In 1890 Nelson Olsen Nelson, a founder of this association, set aside a 250-acre tract in Illinois for workers in his company. Naming the village Leclair after a French pioneer of profit sharing, Nelson included in the town plan gardens, walkways, and a school, and he encouraged employees to build residences in the community. Consistent with his philosophy, Nelson offered employees cash dividends as well as stock in the company; and by 1893, 400 of the 500 employees held stock, thus earning 8 to 10 percent in dividends in addition to their wages. Not content with an isolated experiment in industrial socialism, Nelson advanced his ideas in a quarterly journal that promoted profit sharing. Eventually Nelson went so far as to convert his company into a wholly employee-owned cooperative, but overexpansion and irregular earnings led to his ouster in 1918.[91]

It is important to recognize that such experiments in the social function of the business firm were not solely the work of utopian crackpots, nor were they always the product of peculiar circumstances. **Welfare capitalism,** "industry's attending to the social needs of workers through an assortment of medical and funeral benefits, as well as provisions for recreational, educational, housing, and social services," was a popular idea among some business leaders before World War I.[92] Indeed, concern about the optimal purpose and value of business in the national culture was a frequent subject of discussion among the elite of U.S. commerce. Even a staunch capitalist such as John D. Rockefeller took a relatively progressive stance on the corporate role when, in 1918, he asked on behalf of the Chamber of Commerce of the United States:

> Shall we cling to the conception of industry as an institution, primarily of private interest, which enables certain individuals to accumulate wealth, too often irrespective of the well-being, the health and happiness of those engaged in its production? Or shall we adopt the modern viewpoint and regard industry as being a form of social service [emphasis added], quite as much as a revenue-producing process? . . . The soundest industrial policy is that which has constantly in mind the welfare of employees as well as the making of profits, and which, when human considerations demand it, subordinates profits to welfare [emphasis added].[93]

As fortunes, often ill-gotten, accumulated in the hands of the few, some wealthy individuals felt compelled to return a portion of their wealth to the commonweal. In the late nineteenth century, "men who had great fortunes from the massive industrial growth of the post–Civil War period developed a humanistic concern which was manifested in lavish contributions toward social betterment."[94] Andrew Carnegie, who in 1886 had hired "an army of 300 Pinkerton detectives" to put an end to the violent Haymarket strike,[95] wrote seven years later that massive

wealth was a public trust to be put toward the public interest. Carnegie eventually donated some $350 million through foundations for this purpose, most visibly for community libraries (often bearing his name) that began to dot towns across the country. For his part, John D. Rockefeller contributed about $530 million.[96]

Although largely based on the guilt associated with the great fortunes won by a handful of individuals in the midst of cruel circumstances for many, philanthropic foundations also fostered enduring contributions to social welfare. During the 1920s the Commonwealth Fund proved instrumental in the execution of a series of child guidance experiments, and these served as prototypes for today's juvenile service departments.[97] The Russell Sage Foundation funded the publication of important works on the development of social welfare, including the classic *Industrial Society and Social Welfare* as well as a series of volumes that were precursors of the *Encyclopedia of Social Work*.[98]

The Rockefeller Foundation took a leading role in providing health care to a Southern black population that was neglected by state officials.[99] The active role of the Rockefeller Foundation in the eradication of hookworm warrants particular mention. Shortly after the turn of the century, Charles Wardell Stiles was appointed zoologist of the U.S. Department of Agriculture. Hypothesizing that a disease widespread in the South was caused by a parasite, Stiles convinced his superiors to fund a research trip. He succeeded in confirming his theory, but Congress refused to finance an eradication program. So Stiles turned to the Rockefeller Foundation. In 1909 the foundation established the Rockefeller Sanitary Commission for the Eradication of Hookworm Disease, naming Stiles as an officer. By World War I, having diagnosed and treated millions of the rural poor, mostly African Americans, the commission was well on its way to eradicating the disease that had caused such extensive malaise and listlessness among the poor—in the process contributing to one of the most vicious stereotypes about blacks in U.S. culture.[100]

The business community was also involved in early insurance programs designed to assist injured workers. Although court decisions initially absolved employers of liability for injuries incurred by employees, a swell in jury-awarded settlements to disabled workers convinced corporations of the utility of establishing insurance funds to pool their risk against employee suits. Eventually companies realized that they would pay lower premiums through state-operated workers' compensation programs than they had been paying through commercial insurance. Consequently, between 1911 and 1920, all 45 of the then existing states enacted workers' compensation laws.[101] Later, when the Great Depression overtaxed voluntary social welfare agencies and when labor volatility resulting from high unemployment threatened political stability, it is not surprising that politicians, businessmen, and labor leaders drew on their workers' compensation experience in designing the New Deal. Instrumental in creating federal social programs in the Roosevelt era was Gerald Swope, an executive with the General Electric Company. Having envisaged a "corporate welfare state," including "a national system of unemployment, retirement, life insurance, and disability programs and standards," Swope helped fashion the Social Security program from his position as chairman of Roosevelt's Business Advisory Council.[102] The Social Security program clearly bore the imprint of the business community. As the plan was conceived, only workers who had contributed to a "trust fund" would be able to draw benefits; this would ensure that no public funds would be required to operate the program.[103] What became known as the "social security concept" illustrated a public pension program that was in fact modeled on programs of the private sector. As such, it "represented the acceptance of approaches to social welfare that private businessmen, not government bureaucrats had created."[104] The Social Security Act, the crown jewel of the New Deal, meant that the social and economic security of millions of Americans would be underwritten by the state.

Although benefits from programs mandated by the SSA became a staple of the U.S. welfare state, the business community continued to make independent decisions regarding the welfare of workers. Major corporations, such as General Electric, General Motors, and IBM, began to offer "fringe" benefits as supplements to salaries, and these became important incentives in attracting desirable employees. By the standards of the mid-twentieth century, the benefits offered by large corporations were quite generous, including annual vacations, health care, recreation, life insurance, and housing. Business historians Edward Berkowitz and Kim McQuaid have described the conscientiousness with which some corporations cared for their employees and have suggested that it was "almost as if these firms were consciously demonstrating that the true American welfare state lay within the large and progressive American corporation."[105] Private sector activity in health, income maintenance, and education are detailed in Table 7.2. Although private expenditures lagged behind public expenditures, the coporate share of the welfare market increased between 1980 and 1992. During this period public social welfare declined from 68.9 percent of all social welfare expenditures to 63.6 percent; the private sector increased from 34.8 percent to 40.9 percent. This trend continued throughout the 1990s.

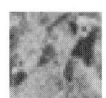 # Corporate Social Responsibility

The corporation has also influenced U.S. social welfare as a result of accusations that it has been insensitive to the needs of minorities, the poor, women, and consumers. During the 1960s criticism of the corporation focused on business's neglect of minorities and on urban blight. A decade later issues relating to affirmative action, environmental pollution, and consumer rip-offs were added to the list. These problems contributed to a public relations crisis, as a leading business administration text noted:

The corporation is being attacked and criticized on various fronts by a great number of

TABLE 7.2 ■ Private Social Welfare Expenditures, by Category and as a Percentage of GDP (in millions)

CATEGORY	1980	1985	1990	1992
Private social welfare expenditures	$255,320	471,223	727,523	824,871
Health	145,000	259,400	410,000	462,900
Personal health care	133,000	232,500	368,900	420,700
Income maintenance	53,564	118,871	164,772	185,724
Private pensions	37,605	98,570	138,114	157,258
Life insurance	5,075	7,489	9,278	10,184
Short-term disability	8,630	10,570	13,680	14,566
Long-term disability	1,282	1,937	2,926	3,143
Supplemental unemployment	972	305	774	573
Education	33,180	54,038	87,864	100,491
Elementary & secondary	11,302	16,782	25,235	27,814
Commercial & vocational	4,661	7,520	15,218	16,832
Higher education	16,042	28,036	43,311	51,245
Welfare & other services	22,776	38,914	64,887	75,756
Percentages of GDP				
Total	27.0	28.8	30.0	33.5
Public	18.6	18.4	19.2	21.3
Private	9.4	11.7	13.1	13.7

Source: Social Security Bulletin, Annual Statistical Supplement (Washington, DC: U.S. Government Printing Office, 1995), p. 151.

political and citizens' organizations. Many young people accuse the corporation of failing to seek solutions to our varied social problems. Minority groups, and women, contend that many corporations have been guilty of discrimination in hiring and in pay scales.[106]

Melvin Anshen, a professor of public policy and business responsibility at Columbia University's Graduate School of Business, bemoaned the fact that "profit-oriented private decisions are now often seen as antisocial."[107]

In order to improve their public image, many businesses established policies on **corporate social responsibility.** Corporations that were reluctant to take seriously the social impli-

cations of their operations ran the risk of inviting the surveillance of public interest groups. As an example, the Council on Economic Priorities (CEP), founded in 1969, developed a reputation for investigating the social responsibility of U.S. corporations. In 1986 CEP released *Rating America's Corporate Conscience,* which evaluated 125 large corporations based on their standing with respect to seven issues: charitable contributions; representation of women on boards of directors and among top corporate officers; representation of minorities on boards of directors and among top corporate officers; disclosure of social information; involvement in South Africa; conventional weapons–related contracting; and nuclear weapons–related contracting.[108] Social responsibility audits such as this one enable consumers to patronize (or boycott) companies according to their own social consciences and thereby create an incentive for companies to follow socially responsible practices.

Although public relations facades frequently gloss over businesses' substantive abuses, specific corporate social responsibility policies have advanced social welfare. During the late 1960s General Electric and IBM instituted strong policies on equal opportunity for and affirmative action toward minorities and women. Under the title Public Interest Director, Leon Sullivan assumed a position on the General Motors board of directors, from which he presented principles governing ethical practices for U.S. corporations doing business in South Africa.[109] U.S. firms' adherence to the "Sullivan principles" contributed to the fall of apartheid in South Africa.

More recently, financial consultants have pioneered the concept of socially responsible investing. The practice of excluding certain industries from mutual fund portfolios because their activities are contrary to those of investors gained considerable ground during the 1980s. An illustration of socially responsible investing is the Domini Social Index (DSI), an investment strategy that screens out businesses in five areas: military contracting, alcohol and tobacco, gambling, nuclear power, and South Africa. After its inception in 1988, the DSI initially performed comparably to the Standard & Poors 500 Index, but by the early 1990s it was generating a return on investment superior to Standard & Poors.[110]

In another instance, Control Data Corporation actually sought out "major unmet social needs, designed means for serving them within the framework of a profit-oriented business enterprise, and brought the needs and the means for serving them together to create markets where none had existed before."[111] These and other initiatives demonstrate that the corporate sector has been willing to undertake significant programs to support troubled communities.[112]

Corporate practices have also been applied directly to social problems. In 1981, in a venture reminiscent of Robert Owen, developer James Rouse established the Enterprise Foundation.

Although this is technically a foundation that supports charitable projects, what makes it different is that within the foundation is the Enterprise Development Company, a wholly owned taxpaying subsidiary. Profits from the Development Company are transferred to the foundation to fund projects. By the late 1980s, this fiscally self-sufficient "charity corporation" had developed innovative projects for low-income housing in dozens of cities.[113] In 1995 the Enterprise Foundation reported that since its inception, $1.7 billion had been committed for loans, grants, and equity investments in order to develop 61,000 new and renovated homes. Following the establishment of neighborhood-based employment centers in 11 cities, the Enterprise Jobs Network aided in employing 26,000 people.[114]

In the early 1980s, recognizing the tendency of community institutions in poor areas to become dependent on government or philanthropy for continuing operations, the Ford Foundation sought contributions from corporations for a program to apply business principles to social problems. By 1983 the Local Initiatives Support Corporation (LISC) had developed investment funds in 24 regions supporting 197 community development projects.[115] LISC projects provided jobs and commodities needed in disadvantaged communities, including a fish processing and freezing plant in Maine, a for-profit construction company in Chicago, and a revolving loan fund to construct low- and moderate-income housing in Philadelphia.[116] Fifteen years after its inception, LISC had helped 1,400 community-based organizations leverage $2.9 billion. LISC contributions were credited with the construction of more than 64,000 homes.[117]

The success of initiatives such as the Enterprise Foundation and LISC have led imaginative social activists to use market strategies to accelerate the upward mobility of the poor. Chicago's South Shore Bank, for example, brought $270 million in new investments to deteriorating neighborhoods and rehabilitated 350 large apartment buildings. By the end of 1990, the bank had increased its assets fivefold and was the exemplar for the community development bank component of the Clinton administration's Empowerment Zone initiative.[118]

By the early 1990s South Shore Bank also was consulting with community development activists in Poland, through collaboration in the Polish–American Enterprise Fund, and in Bangladesh, in partnership with the Grameen Bank, which has pioneered peer lending among poor women and in the process become one of the largest development banks in the world. The concept of providing loans to low-income women in order to encourage self-employment also has been operationalized in the San Francisco metropolitan area through WISE, the Women's Initiative for Self-Employment. Since its inception in 1988, WISE has taught 3,500 poor women about running a business, in the process helping start or expand more than 500 businesses.[119] As South Shore Bank, the Polish–American Enterprise Fund, the Grameen Bank, and WISE indicate, the application of capital to promote social development has spawned a nascent network of international organizations.

In the light of such ventures, some business leaders have become enthusiastic about the activist responses to social problems on the part of the corporation. David Linowes, a corporate leader, foresaw a new role for business in public affairs.

> *Mounting evidence proves that the private sector is uniquely well qualified to fulfill many of the social goals facing us more economically and expeditiously than government working alone. . . . I can visualize a wholesale expansion of existing incentives along with a spate of new reward strategies introduced to America's socio-economic system. Increasingly, I believe, this will help to change the attitude of businessmen regarding social involvement. I look forward to the day, in fact, when competition to engage in government–business programs will be every bit as spirited as competition for the consumer dollar is today.*[120]

As chairman of the President's Commission on Privatization, during the Reagan administration, Linowes worked to define ways in which the private sector could complement the responsibilities of government.[121]

Corporate Influence on Social Welfare Policy

Corporate social responsibility notwithstanding, it would be naive to think that the corporate sector is above self-interest in its orientation toward social welfare. The conservative political economist Irving Kristol stated as much when he wrote that "corporate philanthropy is not obligatory. It is desirable if and only if it serves a corporate purpose. It is expressly and candidly a self-serving activity, and is only legitimate to the degree that it is ancillary to a larger corporate purpose. To put it bluntly: There is nothing noble or even moral about corporate philanthropy."[122] And corporate influence in social welfare is not exerted simply through myriad corporations acting independently. Special interest organizations, such as the National Association of Manufacturers and the United States Chamber of Commerce, have routinely pressed for public policies that clearly reflect the priorities of the business community. The influence that the business community brings to public policy is discussed in greater detail in Chapter 8.

Less well known has been the way in which corporations have funded **policy institutes,** or think tanks, for purposes of shaping public policy. Prominent policy institutes favored by the business community have been the American Enterprise Institute for Public Policy Research (AEI) and the Heritage Foundation. Established as nonpartisan institutions for the purpose of enhancing the public's understanding of social policy, these policy institutes distanced themselves from the special interest connotations of earlier business advocacy groups. At the same time, conservative think tanks served as vehicles through which the business community could take a less reactive stance regarding social policy. Conservative policy institutes, then, addressed the complaint voiced by Lawrence Fouraker and Graham Allison of Harvard's Graduate School of Business Administration: "Public policy suffers not simply from a lack of business confidence on issues of major national import, but from a lack of sophisticated and balanced contribution by *both* business and government in the process of policy development."[123]

The American Enterprise Institute (AEI)

Once noted for its slavish adherence to pro-business positions on social issues, AEI, by the early 1980s, had developed an appreciation for American "intellectual politics."[124] With a budget and staff comparable to that of a prestigious college, AEI was able to recruit an impressive number of notable scholars and individuals and to maintain projects in several domestic policy areas: economics, education, energy, government regulation, finance, taxation, health, jurisprudence, and public opinion. The significance of these activities for social welfare was stated by AEI's then-president, William J. Baroody Jr.:

> The public philosophy that has guided American policy for decades is undergoing change. For more than four decades, the philosophy of Franklin Delano Roosevelt's New Deal prevailed, in essence calling upon government to do whatever individual men and women could not do for themselves.
>
> Today we see growing signs of a new public philosophy, one that still seeks to meet fundamental human needs, but to meet them through a better balance between the public and private sectors of society.
>
> The American Enterprise Institute has been at the forefront of this change. Many of today's policy initiatives are building on intellectual foundations partly laid down by the Institute.[125]

For this ambitious mission AEI empaneled a staff of influential and talented personnel. At the height of its influence, from the late 1970s through the mid-1980s, AEI maintained a stable of more than 30 scholars and fellows *in residence*, who prepared analyses on the various policy areas.[126] The institute's senior fellows included the previously mentioned Irving Kristol; Herbert Stein, an economist and chairman of the President's Council of Economic Advisors in the Nixon administration; and Ben Wattenberg, a veteran public opinion analyst. The AEI "distinguished fellow" was Gerald R. Ford, who had served as thirty-eighth president of the United States.

Michael Novak, director of AEI's project on democratic capitalism, prepared analyses that focused on social welfare policy. Under the direction of Novak, the project on democratic capitalism intended to reform public philosophy by defining the corporation as a promoter of cultural enlightenment rather than as a perpetrator of inequality. "The social instrument invented by democratic capitalism to achieve social goals is the private corporation," he proselytized. "The corporation . . . is not merely an economic institution. It is also a moral and a political institution. It depends on and generates new political forms. . . . Beyond its economic effects, the corporation changes the ethos and the cultural forms of society."[127] At the same time, Novak took careful aim at the public sector, explaining, "I advise intelligent, ambitious, and morally serious young Christians and Jews to awaken to the growing danger of statism. They will better serve their souls and serve the Kingdom of God all around by restoring the liberty and power of the private sector than by working for the state."[128]

Through the late 1970s and early 1980s, AEI laid the groundwork for the conservative revolution in U.S. domestic policy. Much of the conceptual work was done by conservative scholars, but the execution depended on the building of a network between the business community and government. By the election of Ronald Reagan in 1980, that network was in place. This ensured that no social policy proposal would receive serious consideration without first passing the review and comment of AEI.

The Heritage Foundation

In 1986 AEI faltered, and organizational problems led to the resignation of Baroody. With the weakening of AEI, the Heritage Foundation assumed leadership in defining a probusiness and antigovernmental outlook on social policy. Established in 1973 by a $250,000 grant from the Coors family,[129] the Heritage Foundation had a 1983 budget of $10.6 million, already close to those of the liberal Brookings Institution and the conservative American Enterprise Institute.[130] Heritage espoused a militantly conservative ideology; it influenced social policy by proposing private alternatives to establishing governmental programs and by slanting its work to the religious right. By breaking new ground while building mass support for policy initiatives, Heritage complemented the less partisan analyses of AEI.

Heritage social policy initiatives emphasize privatization, which in this case means the transfer of activities from government to business. Implicit in this approach is an unqualified antagonism toward government intrusion in social affairs. Government programs are faulted for breaking down the mutual obligations between groups; for failing to attend to efficiencies and incentives in the way programs are operated and benefits awarded; for inducing dependency in the beneficiaries of programs; and for allowing the growth of the welfare industry and its special interest groups, particularly professional associations.[131]

This critique served as a basis for the aggressive stance taken by the Heritage Foundation in urban development, income security, and social welfare policies. With regard to urban development, Heritage proposed the Urban Enterprise Zone (UEZ) concept, which would enable economically disadvantaged communities to attract industry by reducing taxes, employee costs, and health and safety regulations.[132] The UEZ concept came to the attention of then Congressman Jack Kemp, who convinced the Reagan administration to make it the centerpiece of its urban policy, thus replacing the Economic Development Administration and

Urban Development Action Grant programs through which government had provided technical assistance and funds for urban development.[133] When UEZ legislation stalled in Congress, Heritage changed tactics and targeted states and localities directly. By late 1984, 30 states and cities had created more than 300 UEZs.[134] As secretary of Housing and Urban Development in the first Bush administration, Kemp was well placed to reintroduce the enterprise zone concept as a way of aiding troubled communities; yet this initiative failed to materialize at the federal level.

In the area of income security, the Heritage Foundation—in conjunction with the conservative CATO Institute—prepared an oblique assault on the Social Security program, promoting a parallel system of Individual Retirement Accounts (IRAs). Under the "Family Security Plan" proposed by Peter Ferrara, former senior staff member of the White House Office of Policy Development, the initial IRA provisions of the 1981 Economic Recovery and Tax Act would have been expanded to allow individuals "to deduct their annual contributions to . . . IRAs from their Social Security payroll taxes."[135] Although the idea of substituting IRA investments for Social Security contributions was blocked by liberal politicians, Heritage was clearly banking on future support from workers of the baby boom generation. "If today's young workers could use their Social Security taxes to make . . . investments through an IRA," hypothesized Ferrara, "then, assuming a 6 percent real return, most would receive three to six times the retirement benefits promised them under Social Security."[136] According to this calculus, the interaction of demographic and economic variables would lead to increasing numbers of young workers' salting away funds for themselves, spurred both by high investment returns and by the fear that Social Security would provide only minimal benefits on retirement. The result would be a surefire formula for eroding support for Social Security.

Regarding welfare policy, Heritage was instrumental in scouting Charles Murray, whose *Losing Ground* provided much of the rationale for the conservative assault on federal welfare programs. In 1982 a pamphlet Murray had written for Heritage, entitled "Safety Nets and the Truly Needy," came to the attention of the Manhattan Institute, a conservative New York think tank.[137] Traded by Heritage to Manhattan, Murray elaborated his allegation that government social programs during the War on Poverty had actually worsened the conditions of the poor. Murray's wrecking-ball thesis advocated no less than a "zero-transfer system," which consisted of "scrapping the entire federal welfare and income support structure for working-aged persons."[138] Remembering his earlier sponsor, Murray returned to Heritage on December 12, 1984, to promote his book to a standing-room-only audience at a symposium entitled "What's Wrong with Welfare?"

By the mid-1990s the Heritage domestic policy strategy was coming to fruition. UEZs had become modified and incorporated into the Clinton administration's Empowerment Zone program. The prospect of substituting private pension contributions for Social Security withholding had become a serious policy option in discussions of the restructuring of that program. Most notably, the Personal Responsibility and Work Opportunity Reconciliation Act of 1996 included a five-year lifetime limit on receipt of public assistance, with states having the option of limiting benefits for less than two years.

The conservative triumph in domestic policy was not coincidental. Not long after the Reagan inauguration, Heritage Vice President Burton Pines had likened the conservative cause to a crusade. Pines noted the pivotal role of think tanks in the effort to transform public philosophy and acknowledged a debt to AEI, an organization he described as focusing "primarily on long (sometimes very long) range and fundamental transformation of the climate of opinion." Bringing the conservative Hoover Institution of Stanford into the fold, Pines characterized their work in military terms. "Together," he concluded, "Hoover, AEI and Heritage can today deploy formidable armies on the battlefield of ideas"[139]— forces that were to prove enormously influential in shifting domestic policy to the right.

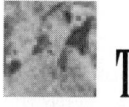

The Future of Corporate Involvement in Social Welfare

Corporations will continue to influence social welfare policy, reflecting the preference of business leaders that the corporate sector assume a primary role in activities of both the voluntary and governmental sectors. Human service advocates, rather than assuming a reactive role in relation to corporate involvement in social policy and programming, should engage the business community proactively. A creative illustration of this kind of engagement appears in the "Decency Principles" proposed in 1988 by Nancy Amidei, a social worker and syndicated columnist. Noting that the Sullivan principles addressed the responsibilities of firms doing business in South Africa, Amidei wondered about the responsibilities of firms doing business in the United States. Her standards for responsible business practices included:

1. *Equitable wages.* Wages should be high enough to allow workers to escape poverty; and there should be comparability across lines of race, age, sex, and handicapping conditions.
2. *Employee rights.* Employees should be provided equal opportunity, the right to organize for collective bargaining, affordable child care, safe working conditions, and health coverage.
3. *Housing.* Businesses should work for more affordable housing and help relocated or migrant workers obtain affordable housing.
4. *Environmental responsibility.* Business practices should include responsible use of resources, sound handling of dangerous substances, and conformance with environmental protection laws.

Amidei suggested that a corporation's adherence to the "Decency Principles" be a basis for government decisions on such matters as providing tax abatements to corporations to attract new industry or awarding government contracts.[140]

At the macroeconomic level, government and industry can collaborate through "industrial policy." In the 1970s and 1980s the idea that government should intervene to aid the business community was reinforced by an increasingly rapid loss of economic advantage to the economies of Japan and Germany, both of which received substantial assistance from their governments. Industrial policy was endorsed by liberal economists such as Lester Thurow, who proposed "the national equivalent of a corporate investment committee" to coordinate economic policy.[141] Thurow argued that subsequent industrialization would provide increased revenues for welfare programs but, more important, create jobs for the unemployed. In the final analysis, further improvement in the economic circumstances of the poor and the unemployed was politically feasible only under conditions of an expanding economy.

Another advocate of fusing social needs and economic requirements was Clinton administration Secretary of Labor Robert Reich. According to Reich, much of the United States' industrial malaise was attributable to underinvestment in human capital. However, human capital investments can be wasteful, leading to nonproductive dependency, when not coupled with the needs of industry. "Underlying many of the inadequacies of American social programs, in short, is the fact that they have not been directed in any explicit or coherent way toward the large task of adapting America's labor force."[142] The attachment of social needs to industrial productivity would fundamentally alter social welfare. "Government bureaucracies that now administer these programs to individuals will be supplanted, to a large extent, by companies that administer them to their employees," suggested Reich. "Companies, rather than state and local governments, will be the agents through which such assistance is provided."[143]

Significantly, industrial policy has attracted conservative adherents as well. Influential analyst Kevin Phillips has proposed a more business-directed version of industrial policy. In Phillips's

"business–government partnership," labor and business would agree to work cooperatively with government so that the United States could regain its dominant role in the international economy. For Phillips, however, industrial policy offers less for social welfare:

> *Political liberals must accept that there is little support for bringing back federal agencies based on New Deal models to run the U.S. economy, and that much of the new business–government cooperation will back economic development and nationalist (export, trade competition) agendas rather than abstractions like social justice or social welfare.*[144]

The primacy of business interests in public policy is not accepted by many social welfare advocates. While "corporatism" may seem plausible to corporate executives, government officials, and labor unions, it offers little to the unemployed or to the welfare or working poor.[145] In fact, some critics of industrial policy suggest that its very emergence signifies the inability of advanced capitalism to ensure the provision of basic goods and services to the economically disadvantaged through the welfare state.[146] If these critics are correct, the rise of industrial policy is an indication of the demise of welfare capitalism rather than a blueprint for enhancing social welfare. Exactly how the relationship among business, labor, and government will be articulated in the future has much to do with the development of public policy. Although the precise nature of such policy must be left to conjecture, the increasing sophistication of the corporate sector in shaping social policy suggests that social welfare policy of the future will show greater congruence with the priorities of the business community.

 # Human Service Corporations

As this chapter has described, continued demand for human services in the postindustrial period has drawn the corporate sector directly into social welfare in the United States. Corporate exploration of the growing human services market has proceeded rapidly, and government welfare programs have failed to keep pace. Heavily dependent on government support and on the contributions of middle-income Americans who have experienced a continual erosion of their economic position, the voluntary sector is unlikely to be able to meet all future service demands. By contrast, relatively unfettered by government regulation and with easy access to capital from commercial sources, the corporate sector has made dramatic inroads into service areas previously reserved for governmental and voluntary sector organizations.

Significantly, the incentives for corporate entry into human services were initially provided through government social programs. Between 1950 and 1991, government expenditures for social welfare increased from $23.5 billion to $1.16 *trillion*, a factor of 50. As a percentage of gross domestic product, public welfare expenditures more than doubled, from 8.8 percent in 1970 to 20.5 percent in 1991. Health care allocations figured prominently in the expansion of public welfare expenditures over this period. In 1970, government spent $24.9 billion on health care; by 1991 that figure had grown to $317.0 billion.[147] The potential profits for corporations entering the rapidly expanding health and human services market were unmistakable.

Concomitantly, public policy decisions have encouraged proprietary firms to provide health and human services. This was the case when Medicaid and Medicare were enacted in 1965. By using a market approach to ensure the availability of health care for the medically indigent and the elderly, Medicaid and Medicare avoided the costs of constructing a system of public sector facilities and, in so doing, contributed to the restructuring of health care in the United States. What had been essentially a haphazard collection of mom-and-pop nursing homes and small private hospitals was transformed, in a short period, into a system of corporate franchises, complete with stocks traded on Wall Street. And almost a decade later, incentives offered through Medicaid and Medicare to encourage the corporate sector to become involved in hospital care were replicated in the health maintenance industry. The

Health Maintenance Organization Act of 1973 stimulated a sluggish health maintenance industry that has since grown at an explosive rate.

Initially dependent on government welfare programs, the corporate sector has developed a life of its own. Exploitation of the nursing home, hospital management, and health maintenance markets has led to corporate interest in other markets. By the 1980s human service corporations had established prominence in child care, ambulatory health care, substance abuse and psychiatric care, and home health care, as well as in life care and continuing care. By the 1990s managed care firms were restructuring health and mental health services so as to fatten corporate profits. Increasingly, proprietary firms were able to obtain funds for facilities through commercial loans or sales of stock, and to meet ongoing costs by charging fees to individuals, companies, and nongovernmental third parties. Insofar as resources for human service corporations are not financed by the state, firms are free to function relatively independent of government intervention.

The Scope of Human Service Corporations

How big is the corporate sector in U.S. social welfare? By the mid-1990s several of the largest firms—Columbia/HCA, CIGNA, and United-Healthcare—reported annual revenues that were far greater than all contributions to the United Way of America.[148] Each of these corporations employed thousands of workers, some more than the number of state and local workers for public welfare programs in any state in the union.[149] Some salient statistics on the larger human service corporations are listed in Table 7.3.

Human service corporations in the United States share several striking features. First, virtually all were incorporated after World War II, the benchmark of the postindustrial era, and the great majority were incorporated after 1960. Second, health and human service corporations have experienced rapid growth. As Figure 7.1 shows, by the early 1980s 34 firms reported annual revenues exceeding $10 million apiece; by the early 1990s the number had risen to 186; and by 2000 it had ballooned to 268. Human service

TABLE 7.3 ■ Prominent Health and Human Service Firms, 1995

FIRM	REVENUES	MARKETS	EMPLOYEES
Columbia/HCA	$20.1 billion	health care	131,600
CIGNA	19.0 billion	health care	44,700
UnitedHealthcare	5.5 billion	health care	28,500
FHP International	3.9 billion	health care	13,000
PacifiCare Health	3.7 billion	health care	4,400
Humana*	3.7 billion	health care	12,000
U.S. Healthcare	3.6 billion	health care	5,000
Tenet Healthcare	3.3 billion	health care	69,000
Wellpoint Health	3.1 billion	health care	3,800
Beverly Enterprises*	3.0 billion	health care	82,000
Wackenhut	748 million	corrections	46,000
Commmunity Psychiatric Centers	507 million	mental health	9,400
Kinder-Care	507 million	child care	22,000

*Earnings for 1994.

Source: Standard & Poor's.

FIGURE 7.1 Human Service Corporations Reporting Annual Revenues above $10 million.

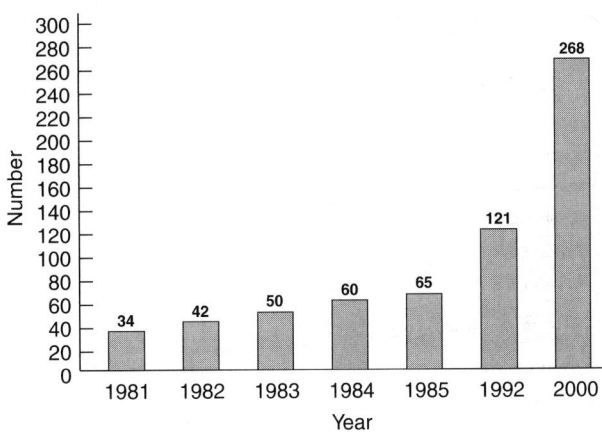

Source: Standard and Poor's, 2000.

corporations seemed immune from the recession of the early 1980s and continued to thrive despite attempts by the Carter and Reagan administrations to contain costs for health and human service programs. Although most of the companies focus on health-related services, many diversify into other service areas; and in some instances, other types of corporations acquire human service firms in order to balance their operations.

Consolidation and Growth in New Human Service Markets

As mentioned earlier, human service corporations have become prominent, if not dominant, in several areas of social welfare: nursing homes, hospital management, health maintenance organizations (HMOs), child care, and home care. More recently, proprietary firms have established beachheads in other markets, notably life and continuing care and corrections.

Nursing Homes

Among corporate initiatives in social welfare, expansion into the nursing home industry is unparalleled. Between 1965 and 1978, expenditures for nursing home care increased 16.9 percent *annually*.[150] By the early 1980s, nursing homes had become a $25-billion-a-year industry, and the number of nursing home beds exceeded those in acute care facilities for the first time.[151] At that time 70 percent of nursing homes were under proprietary management. Market conditions such as these led a writer in *Forbes* magazine to observe, "This is a guaranteed opportunity for someone. How the nursing home industry can exploit it is the real question."[152] Under favorable market conditions, nursing home corporations proliferated. David Vaughan, president of a real estate firm specializing in facilities for the elderly, noted:

> The overall affluence of the over fifty-five population makes investments in special care facilities an extremely attractive venture. The need of capital in meeting the housing needs of this segment of the U.S. population has been so great that we have been able to invest in these facilities with only limited competition.[153]

Guaranteed growth of the nursing home market led to the consolidation of proprietary

firms and the emergence of an oligopoly. As early as 1981, each of the following three corporations held more than 10,000 nursing home beds: Beverly Enterprises, with 38,488 beds; ARA Services, 31,325; and National Medical Enterprises (NME), 14,534.[154] Beverly Enterprises attained first ranking by its 1979 purchase of Progressive Medical Group, which was the eleventh largest chain of nursing homes. NME attained third ranking in 1979 by purchasing Hillhaven, then the third largest operation. ARA Services grew 26 percent in 1979, thereby attaining second ranking, by consolidating smaller operations in Indiana, Colorado, and California.[155] Undeterred by the filing of the first antitrust action in the nursing home industry, nursing home firms continued such acquisitions and mergers.[156] In 1984, using its Hillhaven subsidiary, NME acquired Flagg Industries, which held 12 facilities in Idaho, bringing its total holdings to 339 health care facilities with 42,000 beds. Not to be outdone, Beverly Enterprises acquired Beacon Hill America for $60 million, thereby retaining its top ranking. By the mid-1980s Beverly Enterprises controlled 781 nursing homes with a total of 88,198 beds in 44 states and the District of Columbia.[157]

Given this trend, one industry analyst believed that the industry would eventually fall into the hands of "five or six corporations."[158] A decade later, Beverly continued as the largest corporation focusing on long-term care, managing 703 nursing homes, 30 assisted living centers, 6 hospices, 11 transitional hospitals, and 4 home health centers. Yet Beverly's share of the nursing home market did not go unchallenged. On March 1, 1995, Beverly's primary competitor, NME, merged with American Medical International to form Tenet Healthcare Corporation, a $5.5 billion company.[159]

Hospital Management

The growth of the nursing home industry has been matched by corporate involvement in hospital management. Between 1976 and 1982 the number of investor-owned or investor-managed hospitals increased from 533 to 1,040, accruing gross revenues of approximately $40 billion.[160] Richard Siegrist Jr., a Wall Street analyst, concluded that the future for the industry looked bright, noting that revenues and bed ownership for the five largest companies had roughly tripled between 1976 and 1981. According to this analyst, Humana had doubled its size through an unfriendly takeover of American Medicorp (worth $450 million), gaining 39 hospitals and 7,838 beds. Meanwhile, Hospital Corporation of America (HCA) purchased Hospital Affiliates (worth $650 million), gaining 55 hospitals, 8,207 beds, and 102 hospital management contracts; General Care Corporation (worth $78 million) gained 8 hospitals with 1,294 beds; and General Health Services (worth $96 million) gained 6 hospitals with 1,115 beds. At the same time, American Medical International (AMI) acquired Hyatt Medical Enterprises (worth $69 million), with 8 hospitals, 907 beds, and 26 hospital management contracts, as well as Brookwood Health Services (worth $156 million), with 9 hospitals, 1,271 beds, and 5 hospital contracts.[161]

AMI's strategy of purchasing financially troubled community hospitals proved financially successful. Moreover, in 1984, AMI acquired Lifemark's 25 hospitals and three alcoholism treatment centers through a $1 billion stock transfer.[162] Despite such large-scale growth, AMI continued to rank second behind HCA, which owned 393 hospitals having 56,000 beds.[163] But Humana was to hold the trump card in hospital management. Boldly gambling on its offer to implant artificial hearts in 100 heart patients at no cost, Humana captured the public's attention in 1984. Even though the artificial hearts failed to perform as planned, the project reflected a management strategy that pushed Humana to the head of the pack. By 1993, Humana had forged ahead of its competitors to become the largest health and human service corporation in the world.

The mid-1990s witnessed the largest mergers among health care corporations that had occurred up to that point. As noted above, NME and AMI merged to form Tenet Healthcare Corporation, effectively approximating the market share controlled by Humana. This transaction paled, however, in comparison to the acquisition of HCA by Columbia. The Columbia/HCA merger created a $20 billion behemoth that dwarfed Tenet and Humana. By the mid-1990s the holdings of Columbia/HCA included 292 general hospitals, 28 psychiatric hospitals, and 125 outpatient and auxilliary facilities.[164]

Health Maintenance Organizations

Pioneered by the nonprofit Kaiser-Permanente in California, the concept of **health maintenance organizations (HMOs)** was slow to attract the interest of the corporate sector. However, from 1973 to 1981, the Health Maintenance Organization Act of 1973 authorized funds for the establishment of these membership health plans in a large number of favorable marketing areas. This funding, coupled with the growth in the nursing home and hospital management industries, reversed investor apathy. By 1983, 60 HMOs were operating on a proprietary basis.[165]

An early leader in the HMO industry was HealthAmerica, a for-profit HMO begun in 1980. Within a few years HealthAmerica enrolled almost 400,000 members in 17 locations across the nation, becoming the largest proprietary HMO (second in size only to nonprofit Kaiser-Permanente). Seeking capital for further expansion, HealthAmerica offered stock publicly in July 1983 and raised $20 million for 1.5 million shares. One month later, Phillip Bredesen, chairman and president of HealthAmerica, reported that he anticipated "dramatic growth in the HMO segment of the health care business," and that "HealthAmerica [was] well-positioned with the people and systems that this growth [would] represent."[166]

HealthAmerica's growth did not go unnoticed by Fred Wasserman, founder of Maxicare, another proprietary HMO. Wasserman suspected that Bredesen had stretched his company too thin in an ambitious expansion into new market areas. In November 1986, Maxicare purchased HealthAmerica for $372 million. Coupled with the earlier acquisition of HealthCare USA for $66 million, the purchase of HealthAmerica enabled Maxicare to claim more than 2 million members nationwide and annual revenues approaching $2 billion. After the HealthAmerica takeover, Wasserman spoke optimistically about overtaking Kaiser-Permanente in pursuit of a health maintenance market[167] expected to consist of 30 million members and $25 billion in revenues by 1990.[168] Wasserman's optimism was misplaced, however. The firm proved unable to manage the debt incurred by its appetite for mergers. Maxicare sought protection against creditors, filing for bankruptcy under Chapter 11 in the late 1980s. The collapse of Wasserman's HMO empire was evident in his firm's revenues. Peaking in 1987, Maxicare reported earnings of $1.8 billion; three years later, the firm earned $387 million, less than a fourth of its earlier income.

In the late 1980s managed care became the method of choice for containing health care costs, and the HMO market surged. As business and labor groups attempted to limit the fiscal drain caused by escalating costs of health care, proprietary firms stepped forward to manage care more efficiently. By the mid-1990s more than a dozen managed care companies were reporting hefty revenues. Humana, for example, controlled 17 HMOs as well as the health care provided by some 40,800 physicians, in addition to its 630 hospitals. A rapidly growing competitor, PacifiCare, had established HMOs in six states and enrolled 1.2 million members. The largest firm focusing on health management was United HealthCare Corporation, with facilities in 24 states and Puerto Rico, and enrolling 13.5 million members. FHP International was in second place, reporting annual revenues of $3.9 billion. Yet the insurance giant CIGNA dominated the industry, controlling 46 HMOs in which 3 million people were subscribers.[169]

Child Care

As a human services market, child care is exploited effectively by proprietary firms. In an important study of child welfare services delivery, Catherine Born showed the influence of for-profit providers relative to that of providers in the voluntary and public sectors. She noted:

In the case of residential treatment, among all services purchased, 51 percent was obtained from for-profit firms, 26 percent from voluntary organizations, and 22 percent from other public agencies having contractual agreements with the welfare department. For contracted institutional services, 48 percent was provided by proprietary concerns, 14 percent by voluntary vendors, and 38 percent by other public agencies. The pattern was similar in the case of group home services where 58 percent was proprietarily contracted, 17 percent was obtained from the private, nonprofit sector, and 25 percent was purchased from other public agencies.[170]

The day care market, like its largest provider, Kinder-Care, has expanded rapidly. Begun in 1969, Kinder-Care has demonstrated prodigious growth, claiming approximately 825 "learning centers" representing $128 million in revenue in 1983. The net earnings for Kinder-Care in fiscal year 1983 represented a 68 percent increase over fiscal year 1982. The company executed a five-for-four stock split in November 1982 and a four-for-three stock split in May 1983. Also, during fiscal year 1983, the company entered the market of freestanding immediate medical care by purchasing First Medical Corporation and its 10 facilities for an undisclosed sum.[171] By the second quarter of 1984, Kinder-Care reported that more than 100 new learning centers and 20 new clinics were under construction.[172]

By the early 1990s Kinder-Care's 1,236 centers and annual revenues of $411 million dominated the market, but new competitors were emerging to serve a seemingly infinite need for organized child care. In 1991 Children's Discovery Centers of America claimed 93 centers and $57.2 million in revenues; Rocking Horse Child Care Center of America owned 87 preschool and elementary learning centers and reported earnings of $34.7 million; Sunrise Preschools—the new kid on the block—earned $10.4 million through its 15 preschool programs.

By the mid-1990s, Kinder-Care stood at 1,133 child care centers serving 116,000 children. Yet the smaller Discovery Centers more than doubled the number of its facilities, claiming 193 centers serving 17,500 children. Sunrise Preschools actually lost market share, reporting 1995 revenues of $9.7 million from 29 facilities that cared for 2,700 children.[173]

Home Health Care

Several companies in the **home health care** market have replicated the success of corporations in the nursing home industry. Home Health Care of America, later renamed Caremark, began in 1979. A leader in the field, the company grew particularly quickly. Caremark generated net revenues of $1 million in 1980, $35.8 million in 1983, and $133.2 million in 1986. In 1983 Caremark increased the number of its regional service centers from 10 to 31; despite the costs incurred by this expansion, net income for the year increased 129 percent. By the mid-1990s Caremark was reporting annual revenues of $2.4 billion and claimed health care facilities in Canada, France, Germany, the United Kingdom, the Netherlands, and Japan.[174]

Growth of this magnitude led Elsie Griffith, chief executive officer of the Visiting Nurse Service of New York and chair of the board of the National Association for Home Care, to observe that home health care "is expanding at a phenomenal rate."[175]

Expansion continued during the early 1990s, when home health companies adjusted their services to meet earlier hospital discharges resulting from implementation of Medicare's prospective payment system (discussed in Chapter 12). That is, as patients went home sooner, the need for a range of specialized in-home health services grew. Quickly, home health companies began to offer a variety of these services to patients. In markets where conventional home health companies failed to offer such specialized care, new firms entered the market and expanded rapidly.

Corrections

Among the more ambitious of human service corporations is the Correction Corporation of America (CCA), founded in 1983 by Tom Beasely with the financial backing of Jack Massey, founder of the Hospital Corporation of America. CCA officials noted that many states were unable to contend with overcrowding of prison facilities and proposed contracting with state and local jurisdictions for the provision of correctional services. As CCA acknowledged in its 1986 annual report, court orders to upgrade facilities, coupled with governmental reluctance to finance such improvements, provided strong incentives for jurisdictions to consider contracting out correctional services.

> *Government response to [overcrowding] has been hampered by the administrative and budgetary problems traditionally plaguing public sector facilities. Most systems have suffered a lack of long-term leadership due to their ties to the political process, and many jurisdictions have placed a low priority on corrections funding. The outcome has been a proliferation of out-dated facilities with a lack of sufficient capacity to meet constitutional standards.[176]*

By 1986 CCA operated nine correctional facilities totaling 1,646 beds, and the company was negotiating with the Texas Department of Corrections "to build and manage two minimum security prisons which will provide an additional 1,000 beds."[177]

Most analysts expect that proprietary correctional facilities will continue to grow in popularity as governmental agencies recognize the cost savings of contracting out correctional services. For example, CCA's per diem charge in 1986 was $29.77, about 25 percent less than the cost in public facilities.[178] Texas, Oklahoma, and Arkansas soon put 3,000 correctional "beds" out to bid, an indication of the willingness of states to use proprietary firms on a large scale.[179] The most dramatic example of the possibilities of for-profit corrections dates from 1985, when CCA startled Tennessee state officials by offering to take over the state's entire prison system. As in 30 other states and the District of Columbia, Tennessee's system housed too many prisoners in cramped, archaic facilities and was operating under court supervision. When CCA offered the state a price of $250 million on a 99-year contract, state officials were hard pressed not to give the bid careful consideration. Ultimately, state officials balked at the idea, primarily because of a conflict of interest between CCA and leaders of state government.[180]

Undaunted, CCA moved steadily ahead, capitalizing on the dire need of local and state governments for greater prison capacity. By 1991 CCA managed 17 facilities and reported annual revenues of $67.9 million. Although these earnings were small compared with those of other human service firms, they were astonishing in light of the $7.6 million CCA had earned just six years earlier.

By the mid-1990s CCA reported revenues of $207 million from holdings that had expanded to 49 correctional facilities, totaling 33,153 beds, with plans to develop or expand 16 more. Despite CCA's expansion, the largest for-profit provider of correctional services was Wackenhut, a firm with prisons and detention facilities in the United States, Great Britain, and Australia. For 1995 Wackenhut reported income of $796 million from 24 owned or managed facilities, representing 16,000 beds.[181]

Life Care and Continuing Care

The graying of the U.S. population has led some corporations to construct special residential communities that include health care as a service. As discussed earlier, life care, or continuing care, provides more affluent elders an opportunity to purchase a higher level of long-term care than is ordinarily found in nursing homes. And despite well-publicized bankruptcies of several retirement communities, the potentially enormous market for life care facilities has attracted the interest of several corporations. Beverly Enterprises, the largest nursing home operation, entered the life care business, and subsequently the Marriott Corporation announced plans to have 200 Lifecare Retirement Communities in operation by the year 2000.[182] The investment community has been enthusiastic about life care. Harold Margolin, a vice president of Merrill Lynch, stated that "the financial climate could impact on the growth of the continuing

care segment of the health care industry, but only on the timing. It's going to be a very large industry."[183]

Conclusion: Implications for Health and Human Service Professionals

Despite the proliferation of human service corporations, health and human service professionals have been slow to adopt the corporate sector as a setting for practice. Considering that organizations under traditional auspices—the voluntary and governmental sectors—are limited in their capacity to provide services, however, it is probable that health and human service professionals will discover that corporations are a suitable location for practice.

Actually, for-profit firms can be advantageous for several reasons. Proprietary firms may provide access to the capital needed for expanding social services. As explained earlier in this chapter, a primary explanation for the rapid growth of human service corporations is their ability to tap commercial sources of capital. And human service corporations can reduce the cost of commercially derived capital by depreciating assets and writing off interest payments against income during the first years of operation. This presents obvious advantages for human service administrators who are faced with diminishing revenues derived from charitable or governmental sources. Perhaps the best example of this advantage is the meteoric rise of long-term care corporations, which were almost nonexistent as recently as 1970. By convincing commercial lenders and investors that long-term care was viable, for-profit firms eventually gained control over the industry.[184]

In some instances, too, the corporate sector offers more opportunities for program innovation than are possible under other auspices. Governmental programs must be mandated by a public authority, and this requires a consensus on how to deal with particular concerns. Voluntary sector agencies are ultimately managed by boards of directors that reflect the interests of the community in organizational policy. When human service issues are controversial, welfare professionals can encounter stiff opposition to needed programs. Some of this difficulty can be obviated by a corporate structure that is not so directly wedded to the status quo. An example of how a human service corporation offers opportunities not possible through traditional human service organizations, for-profit correctional companies are able to expand the scope of correctional facilities at a time when government is reluctant to finance new construction and the voluntary sector is unable to raise the necessary capital.

A compelling illustration of the advantages afforded by the for-profit sector is United American Healthcare Corporation, an HMO with 212,000 members. Started in the early 1980s by three physicians (one of them an African American gynecologist, Julius Combs), United American focused on the health care needs of the minority poor, many of whom were on Medicaid. United American targeted the urban poor, offering primary care as well as preventive health care services, such as childhood vaccinations and prenatal care not readily available to Medicaid recipients. For 1994 United American reported revenues of $40 million, $6.5 million above expenses;[185] the next year revenues had jumped to $67 million.[186] Thus, in the span of a decade, by incorporating a health care firm, minority health professionals had enhanced access to and quality of health care for a substantial urban population that had been underserved.

As the example of United American Healthcare suggests, the corporate sector offers greater organizational flexibility than that usually found in governmental agencies and a level of sophistication in managerial innovation not often found in the voluntary sector. To be sure, economic advantages enjoyed by the corporate sector help make this possible; but the track record in organizational experimentation by the corporate sector is undeniable. In fact, ideas that could be of value to traditional welfare organizations are frequently derived from the corporate sector, as such popular books as *In Search of Excellence* and *The Changemasters* attest.[187]

Of course, some human service professionals are skeptical about the prospect of social welfare via human service corporations. According to the critics of proprietary human service delivery, the corporate sector is the organizational manifestation of a capitalist economy that is at the root of much social injustice and human need. For these welfare advocates, professional practice within a corporate context is antithetical to the very idea of "social" welfare. In fact, studies of the organizational practices of human service corporations raise important questions about their suitability for promoting the commonweal. Human service corporations have been found to be less cost-effective than nonprofit and governmental agencies; they engage in discriminatory selection of clients, which penalizes the poor; and they attract clients away from voluntary social service agencies. Despite the undesirable attributes of proprietary human service providers, they are likely to continue to play an active role in defining social welfare. The economy of the United States, after all, is capitalistic, and entrepreneurs are free to establish businesses in whatever markets they consider profitable. Unless government strictly regulates—or prohibits—the for-profit provision of human services, human service corporations will influence U.S. social welfare to an even greater extent in the future.

 ## Discussion Questions

1. Privatization is a hotly debated issue in social welfare. To what extent are some of the major concerns about privatization

(e.g., unfair competition between nonprofit agencies and commercial firms, preferential selection and dumping of clients, superior performance of private providers, the emergence of an oligopoly of private providers) evident in your community? Should human service professionals practice in for-profit firms?

2. Private practice continues to be a focus of students in schools of social work. How many of your classmates are planning to become private practitioners? What are their motives? Do faculty members in your social work program who also have private practices serve as role models to students? Is there an opportunity in your studies to discuss the implications of private practice for social work?

3. How does your state regulate the practice of social work? What governmental unit is responsible for regulating social work? How is it constituted? Does your state have reciprocity arrangements with other states, honoring licenses granted in other jurisdictions? Has your state's social work licensing unit expelled professionals for unethical practices?

4. What is the position of your state chapter of the National Association of Social Workers on regulating professional practice? Are licensing and vendorship still high on the state chapter's priority list? If so, which social workers in your state remain concerned about the regulation of professional practice? Why?

5. What are the main concerns within your professional community about private practice—fees, misdiagnosis, licensing, image, competition with other professionals, vendorship? How are disagreements arbitrated, formally or informally?

6. The debate between private practice and agency-based practice continues as a heated issue within social work. What are the advantages and disadvantages of each? Is there a common base of social work practice? Can you foresee some ways to resolve the issue and bring private practitioners and agency-based practitioners together?

7. Employee ownership is a way for human service professionals to attain control over their practices. Of the prominent social service agencies in your community, which ones might be candidates for employee ownership? If such a transition were accomplished, how would you ensure accountability to consumers? To the community?

8. In order to attain job security, many human service professionals join unions. What is the largest union to which social workers belong in your community? Do issues relating to service delivery figure in the union's negotiations with management? Under what conditions would human service professionals in your community engage in a strike?

9. What are the major corporate philanthropic organizations in your community? What activities have they funded traditionally? To what extent do they incorporate social welfare projects in their funding priorities? Can you determine how priorities and funding decisions are made within these organizations?

10. If you were the director of a nonprofit welfare agency, which sources of philanthropy would you approach in your community to obtain contributions? How would you know which person or persons to approach in the organization? How would you approach them? If a major contribution were secured, how would you recognize the donor?

11. If you were inclined to establish a business providing a human service, what population would you focus on? How would you get capital to start the business? Would you own the business, or would you share ownership with stockholders? How would you market your service? What would you do with the profits—provide stockholders with dividends, enlarge the business, or make contributions to nonprofit agencies? What would be the name of your business?

12. Think tanks exist in Washington, D.C., and in most state capitals. Obtain a copy of the

annual report of a think tank. Who funds the think tank? Is there a relationship between the funding source and the ideological character of reports that the think tank publishes? What is the think tank's track record in social welfare issues?

 # Notes

1. Paul Starr, "The Meaning of Privatization," quoted in American Federation of State, County, and Municipal Employees, *Private Profit, Public Risk: The Contracting Out of Professional Services* (Washington, DC: AFSCME, 1986), pp. 4–5.
2. Charles Schultz, *The Public Use of Private Interest* (Washington, DC: Brookings Institution, 1977); Donald Fisk, Herbert Kiesling, and Thomas Muller, *Private Provision of Public Service* (Washington, DC: Urban Institute, 1978); Harry Hatry, *A Review of Private Approaches for the Delivery of Public Services* (Washington, DC: Urban Institute, 1983).
3. *Privatization: Toward More Effective Government* (Washington, DC: Report of the President's Commission on Privatization, March 1988), p. 230.
4. Ibid., pp. 1–2.
5. John Donahue, *The Privatization Decision* (New York: Basic Books, 1989), p. 216.
6. Harry Specht and Mark Courtney, *Unfaithful Angels* (New York: Free Press, 1994), p. 107.
7. Nina Bernstein, "Giant Companies Entering Race to Run State Welfare Programs," *The New York Times* (September 15, 1996), p. 1.
8. Polly Ross Hughes, "Stakes Are High as State Rushes to Privatize System," *Houston Chronicle* (October 29, 1996), pp. 1A and 10A.
9. Ibid.
10. Judith Havemann, "Welfare Reform Leader Makes Corporate Move," *The Washington Post* (September 17, 1996), p. B6.
11. Ibid.
12. Quoted in Bernstein, "Giant Companies Entering Race to Run State Welfare Programs," p. 1.
13. Ibid.
14. Quoted in Ibid., p. 10A.
15. See Lawrence S. Lewin, Robert A. Derzon, and Rhea Margulies, "Investor-Owned and Nonprofits Differ in Economic Performance," *Hospitals* (July 1, 1981), pp. 65–69; Robert V. Pattison and Hallie Katz, "Investor-Owned Hospitals and Not-for-Profit Hospitals," *New England Journal of Medicine* (August 11, 1983), pp. 54–65; Robin Eskoz and K. Michael Peddecord, "The Relationship of Hospital Ownership and Service Composition to Hospital Charges," *Health Care Financing Review* (Spring 1985), pp. 125–132; J. Michael Watt et al., "The Comparative Economic Performance of Investor-Owned Chain and Not-for-Profit Hospitals," *New England Journal of Medicine* (January 9, 1986), pp. 356–360; Bradford Gray and Walter McNerney, "For-Profit Enterprise in Health Care: The Institute of Medicine Study," *New England Journal of Medicine* (June 5, 1986), pp. 560–563; Regina Herzlinger and William Kradker, "Who Profits from Nonprofits?" *Harvard Business Review* (January–February 1987), pp. 554–562.
16. Douglas Frantz, "Lobbyists, Interest Groups Begin Costly Health Care Battle," *Los Angeles Times* (May 24, 1993).
17. Patricia Franklin, "The AIDS Business," *Business* (April 1987), p. 44.
18. Richard Titmuss, *The Gift Relationship* (New York: Pantheon, 1971), p. 223.
19. Theodore Marmor, Mark Schlesinger, and Richard Smithey, "A New Look at Nonprofits: Health Care Policy in a Competitive Age," *Yale Journal of Regulation* 3 (Spring 1986), p. 320.
20. Charles Muntaner et al., "Psychotic Inpatients' Social Class and Their First Admission to State or Private Psychiatric Baltimore Hospitals," *American Journal of Public Health* 84, no. 2 (February 1994), p. 287.
21. Richard Cloward and Irwin Epstein, "Private Social Welfare's Disengagement from the Poor," in Meyer Zald (ed.), *Social Welfare Institutions* (New York: Wiley, 1965), pp. 628–629.

22. Emily Friedman, "The 'Dumping' Dilemma: The Poor Are Always with Some of Us," *Hospitals* (September 1, 1982), p. 52.

23. David Himmelstein, "Patient Transfers: Medical Practice as Social Triage," *American Journal of Public Health* (May 1984), p. 496.

24. Friedman, "The 'Dumping' Dilemma," p. 54.

25. Mark Schlesinger, "The Privatization of Health Care and Physicians' Perceptions of Access to Hospital Services," *The Milbank Quarterly* 65 (1987), p. 40.

26. Marmor et al., "A New Look at Nonprofits," p. 344.

27. Lewin et al., "Investor-Owned and Nonprofits Differ in Economic Performance."

28. Jerry Avorn, "Nursing-Home Infections—the Context," *New England Journal of Medicine* 305 (September 24, 1981), p. 759.

29. Reported in Arnold Relman, "Investor-Owned Hospitals and Health Care Costs," *New England Journal of Medicine* (August 11, 1983), pp. 370–371.

30. Pattison and Katz, "Investor-Owned Hospitals and Not-For-Profit Hospitals," p. 61.

31. Michael McMullan, personal correspondence, March 7, 1988; "Use of Short-Stay Hospital Services by Medicare Hospital Insurance Beneficiaries by State of Provider and Type of Control: 1985" (Baltimore: Health Care Finance Administration, 1985).

32. Gray and McNerney, "For-Profit Enterprise in Health Care," p. 1525.

33. Robert Kuttner, "Columbia/HCA and the Resurgence of the For-Profit Hospital Business," *New England Journal of Medicine* 335, no. 5 (August 1, 1996), pp. 365–366.

34. "Hospitals' Medicare Profits Up," *San Diego Union* (March 29, 1987), p. A5.

35. "Competition for Doctors and Patients Increases Hospital Costs," *NCHSR Research Activities*, No. 101 (January 1988), p. 3.

36. Richard Buchanan, "Long-Term Care's Pricing Dilemma," *Contemporary Administrator* (February 1981), p. 20.

37. Ann LoLordo, "Life-Care Centers Offer Seniors Worry-Free Living," *Baltimore Sun* (June 4, 1984), p. D4.

38. Carol Olten, "Communities Offering Seniors a Graceful Life," *San Diego Union* (March 13, 1988), p. D5.

39. Anthony Perry, "North County Housing Boom: A Lucrative Shade of Gray," *Los Angeles Times* (March 6, 1988), p. E5.

40. U.S. Senate Special Committee on Aging, *Discrimination against the Poor and Disabled in Nursing Homes* (Washington, DC: U.S. Government Printing Office, 1984), p. 8.

41. Perry, "North County Housing Boom."

42. U.S. Senate, *Discrimination against the Poor and Disabled in Nursing Homes*, pp. 6–8.

43. Ibid., p. 36.

44. The most well-known bankruptcy of a life care community was that of Pacific Homes of California in 1979.

45. "Sun City—with an Add-On," *Forbes* (November 23, 1981), p. 84.

46. Jesse Glasgow, "Marriott to Test Life-Care" *Baltimore Sun* (June 16, 1984), p. C1.

47. "Merrill Lynch: Bullish on Health Care," *Contemporary Administrator* (February 1982), p. 16.

48. Anne Somers, "Insurance for Long-Term Care," *New England Journal of Medicine* (July 2, 1987), p. 27.

49. U.S. Senate, *Discrimination against the Poor and Disabled in Nursing Homes*, p. 25.

50. Ibid., p. 10.

51. Robert Pear, "Lack of Beds Seen in Nursing Homes," *The New York Times* (October 17, 1982), p. 1.

52. Quoted in William Spicer, "The Boom in Building," *Contemporary Administrator* (February 1982), p. 16.

53. Donald Light, "Corporate Medicine for Profit," *Scientific American* (December 1986), p. 42.

54. Arnold Relman, "The New Medical–Industrial Complex," *New England Journal of Medicine* 303, no. 17 (1980), p. 80.

55. Robin Toner, " 'Harry and Louise' Ad Campaign Biggest Gun in Health Care Battle," *San Diego Union-Tribune* (April 7, 1994), pp. 1–5.

56. Sandra Boodman, "Health Care's Power Player," *Washington Post Weekly* (February 14–20, 1994), pp. 18–20.

57. Dana Priest, "The Slow Death of Health Reform," *Washington Post Weekly* (September 5–11, 1994), pp. 6–9.

58. Douglas Frantz, "Lobbyists, Interest Groups Begin Costly Health Care Battle," *Los Angeles Times* (May 24, 1993), p. A7.

59. Paul Starr, "The Limits of Privatization," in Steve Hanke, *Prospects for Privatization* (New York: Proceedings of the Academy of Political Science, 1987), pp. 82–107.

60. Kuttner, "Columbia/HCA," p. 363.

61. Eric Kingson and John Williamson, "Generational Equity or Privatization of Social Security?" *Society* (September/October 1991), p. 90.

62. William Gormley Jr., "Two Cheers for Privatization," in William Gormley Jr. (ed.) *Privatization and Its Alternatives* (Madison, WI: University of Wisconsin Press, 1991), pp. 310–311.

63. Reason Foundation, *Privatization 1992* (Los Angeles: Reason Foundation, 1992), p. 17.

64. David Stoesz, "Human-Service Corporations: New Opportunities in Social Work Administration," *Social Work Administration* 12 (1989), pp. 35–43.

65. Mary Adelaide Mendelson, *Tender Loving Greed* (New York: Knopf, 1974).

66. NASW, "'87 Session of Congress Ends in 11th-Hour Win for NASW," *NASW News* (February 1988), p. 1.

67. Reason Foundation, *Privatization 1992*, p. 251.

68. David Donnison, "The Progressive Potential of Privatisation," in Julian LeGrand and Ray Robinson (eds.), *Privatisation and the Welfare State* (London: George Allen & Unwin, 1984), pp. 211–231.

69. Milton Tambor, "Unions," *Encyclopedia of Social Work* (19th ed.) (Washington, DC: National Association of Social Workers, 1995), pp. 2418–2419.

70. J. Weitzman, *The Scope of Bargaining in Public Employment* (New York: Praeger, 1975), p. 17.

71. Milton Tambor, "The Social Service Union in the Workplace," in H. Karger (ed.), *Social Work and Labor Unions* (New York: Greenwood, 1988).

72. Dena Fisher, "Problems for Social Work in a Strike Situation," *Social Work* 32 (May–June 1987), pp. 253–254.

73. Jerry Wurf, "Labor Movement, Social Work Fighting Similar Battles," *NASW News* 25, no. 12 (December 1980), p. 7.

74. Leslie Alexander et al., "Social Workers in Unions," *Social Work* 25 (May 1980), p. 222.

75. Ernie Lightman, "Professionalization, Bureaucratization, and Unionization in Social Work," *Social Service Review* 56, no. 1 (March 1982), p. 130.

76. Gary Shaffer, "Labor Relations and the Unionization of Professional Social Workers," *Journal of Education for Social Work,* 15 (Winter 1979), p. 82.

77. "Public Service Workers' Strikes Disrupts Life in Canada," *Los Angeles Times* (September 10, 1991) p. A8.

78. Charles Heckscher, "Beyond Contract Bargaining: Partnership, Persuasion, and Power," *Social Policy* 25, no. 2 (1994), p. 29.

79. Stephen Chapman, "Politicians Protect Corporate Welfare," *Richmond Times-Dispatch* (October 23, 1996), p. A13.

80. Ralph Nader, " . . . And What about Corporate Welfare Reform?" *Washington Post Weekly* (October 14–20, 1996), p. 22.

81. Jinlay Lewis, "CEOs' Presence in Bush Party Draws Attention to their Pay," *San Diego Union* (January 13, 1992), p. E3.

82. Fred Barnes, "The Zillionaires Club," *The New Republic* (January 29, 1990), p. 23.

83. Sheila Kamerman, "The New Mixed Economy of Welfare," *Social Work* 28 (January–February 1983), p. 76.

84. Paul Starr, "The Meaning of Privatization," and MDRC Bendick, "Privatizing the Delivery of Social Welfare Service" in *Working Paper 6* (Washington, DC: National Conference on Social Welfare, 1985); David Stoesz, "Privatization: Reforming the Welfare State," *Journal of Sociology and Social Welfare* 16 (Summer 1987), p. 139; Mimi Abramovitz, "The Privatization of the Welfare State," *Social Work* 31, no. 4 (July–August 1986), pp. 257–264.

85. Neil Gilbert, *Capitalism and the Welfare State* (New Haven: Yale University Press, 1983).

86. David Stoesz, "Corporate Welfare," *Social Work* 31, no. 4 (July–August 1986), p. 86; "Corporate Health Care and Social Welfare," *Health and Social Work* (Summer 1986), p. 158; and "The Gray Market," *Journal of Gerontological Social Work* 16 (1989), p. 31.

87. Abramovitz, "The Privatization of the Welfare State," p. 257.

88. Theodore Marmor, Mark Schlesinger, and Richard Smithey, "A New Look at Nonprofits:

Health Care Policy in a Competitive Age," *Yale Journal of Regulation* 3, no. 2 (Spring 1986), p. 322.

89. Robert Heilbroner, *The Worldly Philosophers* (New York: Simon & Schuster, 1967), pp. 98–106.

90. Edward Berkowitz and Kim McQuaid, *Creating the Welfare State* (New York: Praeger, 1980), p. 4.

91. Ibid., pp. 5–10.

92. Gilbert, *Capitalism and the Welfare State*, p. 3.

93. Quoted in Norman Furniss and Timothy Tilton, *The Case for the Welfare State* (Bloomington: Indiana University Press, 1977), p. 156; emphasis original.

94. Murray Levine and Adeline Levine, *A Social History of Helping Services* (New York: Appleton-Century-Crofts, 1970), p. 237.

95. Harold Wilensky and Charles Lebeaux, *Industrial Society and Social Welfare* (New York: Free Press, 1965), p. 88.

96. James Leiby, *A History of Social Welfare and Social Work in the United States* (New York: Columbia University Press, 1978), p. 170.

97. Levine and Levine, *A Social History of Helping Services*, pp. 236–243.

98. Wilensky and Lebeaux, *Industrial Society and Social Welfare*, p. 9; National Association of Social Workers, *Encyclopedia of Social Work*, 18th ed. (Silver Spring, MD: NASW, 1987), p. 781.

99. James Jones, *Bad Blood* (New York: Free Press, 1981), p. 34.

100. Thomas DiBacco, "Hookworm's Strange History," *Washington Post* (June 30, 1992), p. 14 (health section).

101. Berkowitz and McQuaid, *Creating the Welfare State*, pp. 33–36.

102. Ibid., p. 83.

103. Michael Boskin, "Social Security and the Economy," in Peter Duignan and Alvin Rabushka (eds.), *The United States in the 1980s* (Stanford, CA: Hoover Institution, 1980), p. 182.

104. Berkowitz and McQuaid, *Creating the Welfare State*, p. 103.

105. Ibid., p. 136.

106. Michael Misshauk, *Management: Theory and Practice* (Boston: Little, Brown, 1979), p. 6.

107. Melvin Anshen, *Managing the Socially Responsible Corporation* (New York: Macmillan, 1974), p. 5.

108. Steven Lydenberg, *Rating America's Corporate Conscience* (Reading, MA: Addison-Wesley, 1986).

109. Theodore Purcell, "Management and the 'Ethical' Investors." In S. Prakash Sethi and Carl Swanson (eds.), *Private Enterprise and Public Purpose* (New York: Wiley, 1981), pp. 296–297.

110. Lloyd Kurtz, Steven Lydenberg, and Peter Kinder, "The Domini Social Index," in Peter Kinder, Steven Lydenberg, and Amy Domini (eds.), *The Social Investment Almanac* (New York: Henry Holt, 1992), Chap. 25.

111. James Worthy, "Managing the 'Social Markets' Business," in Lance Liebner and Corrine Schelling (eds.), *Public–Private Partnership: New Opportunities for Meeting Social Needs* (Cambridge, MA: Ballinger, 1978), p. 226.

112. Melanie Lawrence, "Social Responsibility: How Companies Become Involved in Their Communities," *Personnel Journal* 61, no. 7 (July 1982), p. 381; James Chrisman and Archie Carroll, "SMR Forum: Corporate Responsibility—Reconciling Economic and Social Goals," *Sloan Management Review* 25, no. 2 (Winter 1984), p. 173.

113. Enterprise Foundation, *Annual Report 1983* (Columbia, MD: Enterprise Foundation, 1983), p. 1.

114. Enterprise Foundation, *Annual Report* (Columbia, MD: Enterprise Foundation, 1995).

115. Brian O'Connell, *Philanthropy in Action* (New York: The Foundation Center, 1987), p. 218.

116. Local Initiatives Support Corporation, *The Local Initiatives Support Corporation* (New York: LISC, 1980); "A Statement of Policy for Programs of the Local Initiatives Support Corporation" (New York: LISC, 1981).

117. Local Initiatives Support Corporation, *Making Change Happen: Annual Report* (New York: LISC, 1995).

118. Joan Shapiro, "Community Development Banks," in Kinder, Lydenberg, and Domini, *The Social Investment Almanac*, Chap. 42.

119. "Would You Like to Be Your Own Boss?" (San Francisco: Women's Initiative for Self Employment, n.d.).

120. David Linowes, *The Corporate Conscience* (New York: Hawthorn Books, 1974), p. 209.

121. *Privatization: Toward More Effective Government* (Washington, DC: U.S. Government Printing Office, 1988), pp. 2–3.

122. Irving Kristol, "Charity and Business Shouldn't Mix," *The New York Times* (October 17, 1982), p. 18.

123. Lawrence Fouraker and Graham Allison, "Foreword," in John Dunlop (ed.), *Business and Public Policy* (Cambridge, MA: Harvard University Press, 1980), p. ix.

124. Peter Steinfels, "Michael Novak and His Ultrasuper Democraticapitalism," *Commonweal* (February 15, 1983), p. 11.

125. William J. Baroody Jr., "The President's Review," *AEI Annual Report 1981–82* (Washington, DC: American Enterprise Institute, 1982), p. 2.

126. Peter Stone, "Businesses Widen Role in Conservatives' 'War on Ideas,'" *Washington Post* (May 12, 1985), p. C5.

127. Ibid., p. 50.

128. Ibid., p. 28.

129. Richard Reeves, "How New Ideas Shape Presidential Politics," *The New York Times Magazine* (July 15, 1984), p. 18.

130. Heritage Foundation, *The Heritage Foundation Annual Report* (Washington, DC: Heritage Foundation, 1983).

131. Interview with Stuart Butler at the Heritage Foundation, Washington, DC, October 4, 1984.

132. George Sternlieb, "Kemp–Garcia Act," in George Sternlieb and David Listokin (eds.), *New Tools for Economic Development* (Piscataway, NJ: Rutgers University Press, 1981), p. 42.

133. Stuart Butler, "Enterprise Zones," in Sternlieb and Listokin, *New Tools for Economic Development*, pp. 73–94.

134. Gilbert Lewthwaite, "Heritage Foundation Delivers Right Message," *Baltimore Sun* (December 9, 1984), p. 2.

135. Peter Ferrara, *Social Security Reform* (Washington, DC: Heritage Foundation, 1982), p. 51.

136. Peter Ferrara, *Rebuilding Social Security* (Washington, DC: Heritage Foundation, 1984), p. 7.

137. Chuck Lane, "The Manhattan Project," *The New Republic* (March 25, 1985), p. 34.

138. Charles Murray, *Losing Ground* (New York: Basic Books, 1984), pp. 226, 227.

139. Burton Pines, *Back to Basics* (New York: Morrow, 1982), p. 254.

140. Nancy Amidei, "How to End Poverty: Next Steps," *Food Monitor* (Winter 1988), p. 52.

141. Lester Thurow, *The Zero-Sum Society* (New York: Basic Books, 1980), p. 95.

142. Robert Reich, *The Next American Frontier* (New York: Times Books, 1983), p. 223.

143. Ibid., pp. 247–248.

144. Kevin Phillips, *Staying on Top: The Business Case for a National Industrial Policy* (New York: Random House, 1984), pp. 5–6.

145. Yeheskel Hasenfeld, "The Changing Context of Human-Services Administration," *Social Work* 29, no. 4 (November–December 1984), p. 524.

146. James O'Connor, *The Fiscal Crisis of the State* (New York: St. Martin's Press, 1973); Ian Gough, *The Political Economy of the Welfare State* (London: Macmillan, 1979).

147. Social Security Administration, *Social Security Bulletin, Annual Statistical Supplement* (Washington, DC: U.S. Government Printing Office, 1994), p. 140.

148. David Stoesz, "Human-Service Corporations and the Welfare State," *Transaction/Society* 16 (1989), pp. 80–91.

149. Bureau of the Census, *Statistical Abstract of the United States, 1986* (Washington, DC: U.S. Government Printing Office, 1986).

150. U.S. Department of Commerce, *1982 U.S. Industrial Outlook for 200 Industries with Projections for 1986* (Washington, DC: U.S. Government Printing Office, 1982), p. 406.

151. J. Avorn, "Nursing Home Infections—the Context," p. 759.

152. J. Blyskal, "Gray Gold," *Forbes* (November 23, 1981), p. 84.

153. D. Vaughan, "Health Care Syndications: Investment Tools of the '80s," *Financial Planner* (December 1981), p. 49.

154. Blyskal, "Gray Gold," p. 80.

155. V. DiPaolo, "Tight Money, Higher Interest Rates Slow Nursing Home Systems Growth," *Modern Health Care* (June 1980), p. 84.

156. National Senior Citizens' Law Center, "Federal Antitrust Activity" (Los Angeles: National Senior Citizens' Law Center, 1982), p. 2.

157. "NME Makes More Health Care Acquisitions," *Homecare News* (February 17, 1984), p. 4.

158. Quoted in W. Spicer, "The Boom in Building," *Contemporary Administrator* (February 1982), pp. 13–14.

159. "Beverly Enterprises" and "Tenet Healthcare Corp," *Standard & Poor's Stock Report* (October 1995), p. 89.

160. B. Gray, "An Introduction to the New Health Care for Profit," in B. Gray (ed.), *The New Health Care for Profit* (Washington, DC: National Academy Press, 1983), p. 2.

161. R. Siegrist, Jr., "Wall Street and the For-Profit Hospital Management Companies," in B. Gray (ed.), *The New Health Care for Profit*, p. 36.

162. American Medical International, *1983 Annual Report* (Beverly Hills, CA: AMI, 1983).

163. "GAO Says Proprietary Hospital Chain Mergers Raise Medicare/Medicaid Costs," *Homecare News* (February 17, 1984), p. 6.

164. "Columbia/HCA" *Standard & Poor's Stock Reports* (October 1996), p. 80.

165. National Industry Council for HMO Development, *Ten Year Report 1971–1983* (Washington, DC, 1983).

166. HealthAmerica, *Company Profile* (Nashville, TN: HealthAmerica, 1983).

167. M. Abramowitz, "Maxicare HMO Soars with Farsighted Founder," *Washington Post* (November 30, 1986), p. 12.

168. National Industry Council, *Ten Year Report*, p. 22.

169. "PacifiCare," "United HealthCare Corp.," and "CIGNA," *Standard & Poor's Stock Reports* (October 1996), 102.

170. Catherine Born, "Proprietary Firms and Child Welfare Services: Patterns and Implications," *Child Welfare* 62 (March–April 1983), p. 112.

171. Kinder-Care, *Annual Report 1983* (Montgomery, AL: Kinder-Care, 1983).

172. Kinder-Care, *Second Quarter Report* (Montgomery, AL: Kinder-Care, March 16, 1984).

173. "Kinder Care," "Children's Discovery Centers," and "Sunrise Preschools," *Standard & Poor's Stock Reports* (October 1996).

174. "Home Health Care of America," *Standard & Poor's Stock Reports* (March 1984, October 1995).

175. "Interview with Elsie Griffith," *American Journal of Nursing* 18 (March 1984), p. 341.

176. "Digest of Earnings Reports," *Wall Street Journal* (August 13, 1987), p. 41.

177. Stephen Boland, "Prisons for Profit," unpublished manuscript, San Diego State University, School of Social Work, 1987, pp. 5–6.

178. Ibid., p. 8.

179. Eric Press, "A Person, Not a Number," *Newsweek* (June 29, 1987), p. 63.

180. D. Vise, "Private Company Asks for Control of Tennessee Prisons," *Washington Post* (September 22, 1985), p. D2.

181. "Correction Corporation of America" and "Wackenhut," *Standard & Poor's Stock Reports* (October 1996).

182. Paul Farhi, "Marriott Corp. Caters to America's Rapidly Aging Population," *Washington Post* (January 2, 1989), p. 5.

183. "Merrill Lynch: Bullish on Health Care," *Contemporary Administrator* (February 1982), p. 16.

184. D. Stoesz, "The Gray Market," p. 45.

185. Udayan Gupta, "United American Healthcare Proves Naysayers Wrong," *Wall Street Journal* (August 22, 1994), p. B2.

186. "United American Healthcare Corporation," *Standard & Poor's Stock Reports* (October 1996).

187. Thomas J. Peters and Robert W. Waterman, Jr., *In Search of Excellence* (New York: Harper & Row, 1982); and Rosabeth M. Kanter, *The Changemasters* (New York, Simon & Schuster, 1983).

chapter 8

The Making of Governmental Policy

This chapter describes the process by which governmental policy is made, exploring the phases of the policy process, examining the influence of various social groups on the policy process, and accounting for the role of key organizations. The public policy process is important because many social welfare policies are established by government, and decisions by federal and state agencies have a direct bearing on the administration and funding of social welfare programs that assist millions of Americans.

In an open, democratic society, it is desirable that **public policy** reflect the interests of all citizens to the greatest extent possible. For a variety of reasons, however, this ideal is not realized. Although many Americans have the right to participate in the establishment of public policy, they often fail to do so. Policy made and implemented by the governmental sector may be perceived as being too far removed from the daily activities of citizens, or too complicated to warrant the type of coordinated and persistent efforts necessary to alter it. Moreover, many Americans with a direct interest in governmental policy are not in a position to shape it, as in the case of children and the emotionally impaired, who must rely on others to speak on their behalf. Consequently, governmental policy does not necessarily reflect the interests—or, for our purposes, the welfare—of the public, even though it is intended to do so. The discrepancy between what is constitutionally prescribed in making public policy and the way decisions are actually made leads to two quite different understandings of the policy process. For welfare professionals concerned with instituting change in social welfare, a technical understanding of how policy is made is essential. It is equally important for them to recognize that the policy process is skewed to favor powerful officials and interests rather than the interests of the uninfluential. Because both social workers and their clients tend to be comparatively powerless, a critical analysis of the policy process is all the more important.

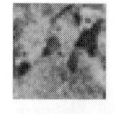 # Technical Aspects of the Policy Process

Public policy in the United States is made through a deliberative process that involves the two bodies of elected officials that make up a legislature. This applies both to the federal government and to the states—with the singular exception of Nebraska, which has only one deliberative body, a unicameral legislature.

At the federal level, a policy concern of a legislator is first developed into a legislative proposal and usually printed in the *Congressional Record*. Because every legislator has a party affiliation and a constituency, legislators' proposals tend to reflect their individual priorities. Usually, several legislators will prepare proposals that are important to similar constituencies, a phase that ensures that all sides of an issue are aired. Through a subtle interaction of ideas, the media, and legislative leadership, one proposal—usually a synthesis of several—is presented as a policy alternative. Other legislators are asked to sign on as cosponsors, and the measure is officially introduced. After the proposed bill is assigned to the appropriate committee, public hearings are held, and the committee convenes to "mark up" the legislation so that it incorporates the concerns of committee members who have heard the public testimony. Under propitious circumstances, the committee then forwards the legislation to the full body of the chamber that must approve it. While it is being approved by the full body of one chamber, a similar bill is often introduced in the other chamber, where it begins a parallel process. Differences between the measures approved by the two chambers are ironed out in a conference committee. The proposed legislation becomes law after it is signed by the chief executive—or, if the executive vetoes the bill, passed by a two-thirds vote of each legislative chamber. This process is always tortuous and usually unsuccessful. The eventual enactment of legislation under these conditions is a true testament to legislative leadership. A third branch of government, the judiciary, assesses legal challenges to existing legislation. In the upper levels of the judiciary, members can hold their posts for life. The primary features of the policy process of the federal government are illustrated in Figure 8.1.

There are several critical junctures in a proposal's tortuous passage into legislation—or oblivion. First, most of the details in any proposal are worked out at the committee or subcommittee level. Different versions—an inevitability in virtually every bill—are negotiated and reconciled at the mark-up session, during which committee members and staff write their changes into the draft. This stage offers an important opportunity to inject minor, and sometimes major, changes into the substance of the bill or to alter the intent of the bill's originator(s).

Second, the viability of a proposal depends to a large extent on the numbers and weight of the witnesses who testify as to its merits at subcommittee and committee hearings. Obviously, public testimony will work to the advantage of well-financed interests; such interests can afford to pay lobbyists to do this professionally, whereas advocates for the disadvantaged often rely on volunteers. Nevertheless, the public testimony stage is an important opportunity to clarify for the record the position that welfare professionals may take on a given proposal. Third, budget considerations figure heavily in the likelihood of a bill's passage. Other federal spending priorities, coupled with the unwillingness of elected officials to raise taxes, increase the likelihood that legislation will be underfunded or even passed with no additional funding whatsoever. Innovative revenue "enhancers," such as earmarked taxes or user fees, can make a proposal more acceptable during periods of fiscal belt-tightening. The policy process, then, is not necessarily

FIGURE 8.1   The Steps Necessary in Getting a Policy Proposal Enacted Into Law

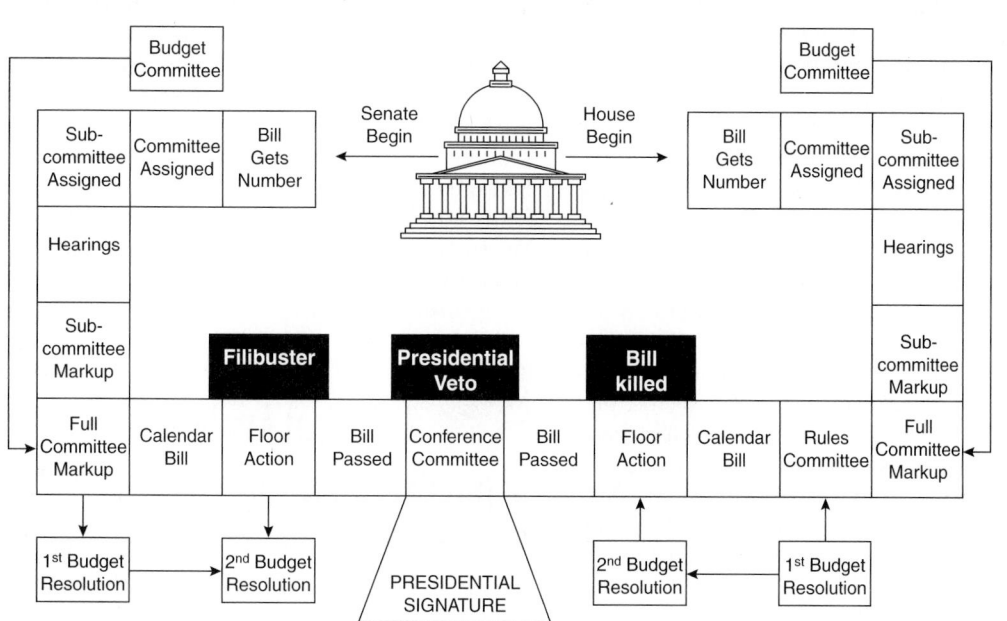

intended to facilitate the passage of a proposal into law. Of some 20,000 bills presented to Congress, in the 1970s and 1980s, for example, only 10 percent were reported out of committee and only 5 percent became law.[1]

Beyond this general outline of the public policy process, multiple variations exist depending on historical and jurisdictional circumstances. In the federal government, all proposals related to taxation must originate in the House of Representatives, a provision the founders of the nation included in the Constitution in order to locate revenue retrieval in the legislative body most representative of the people. Appointments of people for key executive posts, such as cabinet secretaries, ambassadors, and judges, must be ratified through the advice and consent of the Senate, a body less responsive to popular sentiment. States exhibit countless variations within the general outline of the tripartite balance of powers format. California, for example, has experienced chronic budget problems because the state government has been unable to raise sufficient revenue to keep up with mandated expenditures. Since the imposition of Proposition 13 in 1978, a two-thirds majority of the California legislature is required not only to raise taxes but also to establish the state budget; this is a proportion far beyond the simple majority required in other states. Under these conditions, a small number of recalcitrant representatives can easily block the budget process. As these examples suggest, understanding the intricacies of the policy process is an essential step toward mastering public policy.

A few final points regarding the technical aspects of the policy process warrant mention. The decision-making process itself is defined by *Robert's Rules of Order,*[2] a text that lays out in detail the rules for democratic deliberation. Although *Robert's Rules* can appear obtuse, its value should not be underappreciated. Those who have mastered "the means of deliberation" are one step ahead of the rest of the crowd in seeing their ideas become public policy. Social activists who are optimistic that their proposal is working its way steadily through the legislative minefield may find their hopes exploded by an adroit procedural move on the part of an opponent who sidetracks

a bill until the next legislative session. The elaborate rules of decision making, compounded by the traditions of deliberative bodies, may tend to deter citizens from participating in the democratic process. Yet there are means public policy novices can employ to become better acquainted with the ways in which elected officials go about the public's business. Citizen advocate organizations, particularly the League of Women Voters and Common Cause, can be helpful in explaining how public policy is made. Also, Congress and the legislatures of the larger states employ staff members as technical experts to aid them in decision making. Legislative staff are frequently the experts most versed in an area of legislative activity, simply because they work through policy proposals on a regular basis. Staff reports researched as part of committee deliberations can be valuable in that they often provide the most up-to-date data on particular programs or issues. A good example of this type of resource is the "Green Book" used by the U.S. House Ways and Means Committee in its consideration of social programs. Begun in the early 1980s to help committee members comprehend the vast number of social programs under their jurisdiction—Social Security, Medicare, Medicaid, AFDC/TANF, SSI, and unemployment compensation, among others—the volume, *Background Material and Data on Programs within the Jurisdiction of the Committee on Ways and Means,* became essential reading for social program analysts. Because of its convoluted title, the volume became known by its standard-issue green paper cover, hence the Green Book. Fortunately, its popularity led to a (merciful) shortening of its title to *Overview of Entitlement Programs.*[3]

 # A Critical Analysis of the Policy Process

Experience and sophistication notwithstanding, the public policy process often proves frustrating for social activists. Despite the most urgent of needs, the best of intentions, and the most strategic of proposals, the social welfare program output deriving from the legislative process often appears far short of what is required. Yet to conclude from this that public policy simply does not work would be an overstatement. A critical approach to public policy helps explain some of the limitations of the technical approach and suggests ways to make the legislative process a more effective strategy for those concerned with furthering social justice.

From a critical perspective, the policy process consists of a series of discrete decisions, each heavily conditioned by money and connections—in other words, by power. The extent to which governmental policy reflects the concerns of one group of citizens while neglecting those of others is ultimately a question of power and influence. Power is derived from several sources, and these have attracted the attention of philosophers over the centuries. Plato questioned the organization and execution of the civil authority of the state. Machiavelli focused on the limits of discretionary authority exercised by leaders of the state. The social contract philosophers of the Enlightenment—Hobbes, Locke, and Rousseau—considered the moral obligations of the state toward its citizens. Later, as the Industrial Revolution proceeded unchecked, Karl Marx attributed power inequities to control over the means of production, or capital. Subsequently, as governmental authority expanded to ameliorate the economic and social dislocation brought on by industrial capitalism, Max Weber identified bureaucratic administrators as a pivotal group. As the postindustrial era unfolded, such social critics as Marshall McLuhan and Alvin Toffler emphasized how the processing and uses of information can be a source of power and influence.

From these general speculations about social organization, other writers have turned to more specific aspects of social policy as subjects of inquiry. Several schools of thought have emerged. According to the *elitist* orientation, individuals representing a "power structure" control social policy in order to maintain a status quo that advantages them and, in the process, excludes marginal groups. In contrast, a *pluralist*

orientation assumes that social policy in a heterogeneous democratic polity is the sum total of trade-offs among different interest groups, all of which have an equal opportunity to participate. At the program level, *incrementalists* have suggested that the more important questions about social policy are the product of bit-by-bit additions to the public social infrastructure. As counterpoint, other scholars have focused on "paradigm shifts" through which major changes, such as the inception of Social Security in 1935 and the devolution of welfare to the states through the Personal Responsibility and Work Opportunity Reconciliation Act of 1996, have altered the very foundation of social policy. With regard to program evaluation, *rationalists* have used the methods of social science to determine by objective standards to what extent policy changes bring about intended outcomes. By contrast, *social activists* use the political process as the measure of program performance, assuming that the optimum in program assessment is continued recertification and refunding by public decision makers. As might be expected in the investigation of any phenomenon as complex as social policy, a comprehensive explanation is likely to incorporate elements of more than one school of thought.

Underlying these varied approaches to interpreting social policy are assumptions about its very nature. In this regard, two orientations have become prominent. The first orientation might be labeled the *liberal evolutionary perspective*. According to this orientation, social policy reflects steady progress toward a desirable condition of human welfare for all. Most liberal analysts who have promoted the welfare state as an ideal have adopted an evolutionary perspective. Believers in the evolutionary perspective expect that the national government will progressively expand social programs until, eventually, the basic needs of the entire population are guaranteed as rights of citizenship. References to welfare state philosophy appear in many chapters of this book. The liberal evolutionary perspective dominated thinking about the U.S. welfare state from the New Deal until the rise of conservative ideology in the 1980s. The demise of Catastrophic Health

Insurance in 1989 and the devolution of AFDC/TANF to the states in 1996 raise fundamental questions about the validity of this perspective. The liberal evolutionary perspective has been complemented by social systems theory, which assumes that welfare consists of basic institutions and processes that are related and are changed to suit environmental conditions. Reference to "social service delivery systems" was frequent during the 1960s and 1970s, when social programs were expanding, but this approach commanded less credibility when many public programs were thrown into chaos as a result of budget cuts during the 1980s. What had once been coordinated service delivery systems suddenly became disordered and fragmented clusters of agencies struggling for survival.

A competing orientation is the *conflict perspective*, which emphasizes the differences between organized groups that compete for social resources. The conflict perspective views social policy and resultant programs as the product of intense rivalry among various classes and groups. Applied to a capitalist economy and a democratic polity, the conflict approach goes a long way toward explaining the disparate distribution of goods, services, and opportunities within U.S. society. Accordingly, conflict theory is useful in two ways: It accounts for the quite substantial disadvantages experienced by some Americans—the poor, minorities of color, people with disabilities, women; and it shows how such groups can be empowered to achieve a measure of social justice.

Obviously, a conflict perspective accounts for the behavior of for-profit providers of health and human services, which compete intensively for market share, acquire other firms, and lobby public officials to shape policy favorably. The downside of the conflict perspective is that it fails to offer a unifying vision of future social policy.

Questions of governmental decision making often focus on three central aspects: (1) the degree of change in policy represented by a decision, (2) the rationality of the decision, and (3) the extent to which the disadvantaged benefit. First, governmental policies vary in the extent to which they depart from the status quo. Al-

though it can be argued that, in the final analysis, there are no new ideas, there *are* new governmental policies that have enormous implications for certain groups. Few could dispute that the Social Security Act and the Civil Rights Act were radical departures from the status quo and substantially changed the circumstances of older people and African Americans, respectively. On the other hand, such radical departures occur only under fairly unusual circumstances, and therefore rarely. As Charles Lindblom has observed, the great bulk of decision making is "incremental," representing only marginal improvements in social policy already in place.[4] Amitai Etzioni has proposed the term *mixed scanning* to refer to the way decision makers take a quick overview of a situation, weigh a range of alternatives—some incremental, some radical—and ultimately select the one that satisfies the most important factors impinging at the moment.[5] Thus, major shifts in public policy are the exception, rather than the rule. Most social policy changes consist of relatively minor technical adjustments in program administration and budgeting.

Second, social policy does order human affairs, and to that extent the rationality or logic underlying the policy is of great significance. Historically, two basic forms of rationality have served to justify social policy: bureaucratic rationality and market rationality.[6] **Bureaucratic rationality** refers to the ordering of social affairs by governmental agencies. Since Max Weber's work on the modern bureaucracy, this form of rationality has been central to governmental policy and hence to the maintenance of the welfare state. According to bureaucratic rationality, civil servants can objectively define social problems, develop strategies to address them, and deploy programs in an equitable and nonpartisan manner. Bureaucratic rationality takes its authority from power vested in the state, and bureaucracies have become predominant in social welfare at the federal (through the Department of Health and Human Services) and state levels. A characteristic of bureaucratic rationality is a reliance on social planning. Several social planning methods have been developed to anticipate future problems and deal with existing ones. Generally, these can be classified under two headings: technomethodological and sociopolitical.

Technomethodological planning methods emphasize databases from which projections about future program needs can be derived. Such methods place a premium on relatively sophisticated social research methods and work best with programs that can be quantified and routinized, as in the case of cash payments through the Social Security program. **Sociopolitical planning** approaches are more interactive, involving groups likely to be affected by a program. Community development activities, for example, frequently feature planners' bringing together neighborhood residents, businesspeople, and local officials to create a plan that is relevant to the needs of a particular area.[7] Regardless of planning method, it is important to recognize the power and influence that governmental agencies have assumed in social welfare policy, much of it by exercise of bureaucratic rationality.

Market rationality refers to a reliance on the supply of and demand for goods and services as a method of ordering social affairs. While on the surface this may appear to be antithetical to the meaning of rationality, a high degree of social ordering in fact occurs within capitalism. Such organization is implicit in the very idea of a market, entailing a large number of prospective consumers that businesses seek to exploit. In a modern market economy, the success of a business depends on the ability of managers to survey the market, merchandise goods and services, shape consumer preferences through advertising, and reduce competition by buying or outmaneuvering competitors. Of course, market rationality is not a panacea for providing social welfare—because the marketplace is not particularly responsive to those who may not fully participate in it, such as minorities, women, children, and elderly or disabled people. Yet market rationality cannot be dismissed as a rationale for delivering social welfare benefits. Approximately half of Americans get their health and welfare needs met through employer-provided benefits that are ultimately derived from the

market.[8] Since the late 1980s, commercial firms have conducted an ambitious campaign to ration health care benefits through "managed care," an idea that has become anathema to health and human service professionals. Another example of the impact of the market on social welfare benefits is the practice by governmental jurisdictions of contracting out certain human services to private sector businesses, usually with the rationale of reducing costs by taking advantage of efficiencies associated with the market.[9]

The third aspect of governmental decision making addresses disadvantaged populations. It is entirely possible, of course, for social policy to introduce radical change that is based on data but is contrary to the well-being of important groups. The 1996 welfare reform legislation, for example, ended the 60-year entitlement to income for poor families on the basis of evaluations of state welfare demonstrations allegedly showing that states could provide public assistance better if the federal government were not involved. Fearing the consequences of such welfare reform for poor minority children, advocacy groups such as the Children's Defense Fund lobbied ardently against the proposal, but to no avail. Of primary concern among children's advocates was the consequence of **time limits** on the receipt of welfare for poor children. Analysts from public and private research agencies projected that 1 to 4 million children would be terminated from public assistance if a five-year time limit on receipt of aid were imposed. The 1996 welfare reform legislation did include provisions for chronically welfare dependent families—exempting 20 percent of the AFDC/TANF caseload from time limits—but children's advocates claimed these were inadequate. The 1996 welfare reform legislation was not welfare "reform," claimed children's advocates; it was welfare termination. Rather than benefiting poor families, the 1996 Personal Responsibility and Work Opportunity Reconciliation Act would eventually kick millions of poor children out of the safety net and into the underclass.[10]

Clearly, the degree of change represented by any change in public policy, the extent to which it is rational with respect to bureaucratic or market criteria, and the consequences for disadvantaged populations make the social policy process a dynamic and sometimes volatile area of activity. While this process may be intimidating for the uninitiated, it is the primary route to social justice within the governmental sector.

The Policy Process

A critical analysis of the policy process highlights the social stratification of the society, the phases through which policy is formulated, and the organizational entities that have evolved as instrumental in the decision-making process. This section will describe and chart these factors in order to clarify how welfare policy is created in the United States.

Social Stratification

A variety of **social stratification** analyses differentiate groups with influence from those lacking it. The most simple of these schemes consists of a dual stratification: for instance, capitalists and the proletariat, such as Marx used. A stratification familiar to Americans defines three parts: an upper class, a middle class, and a lower class. Placement of individuals in the appropriate class is usually made on the basis of income, education, and occupational status. This three-part stratification is limited in its capacity to explain very much about American social welfare, however. If asked, most Americans identify themselves as middle class, even if by objective criteria they belong to another class. Further, the designation *lower class* is not particularly informative about the social conditions of a large portion of the population with which welfare professionals are concerned.[11]

A more informative stratification was developed by social psychologist Dexter Dunphy, who identified six social groups, which he differentiated according to wealth, internal solidarity, and control over the environment.[12] Dunphy's formulation is adapted in Table 8.1.

As Dunphy's social stratification indicates, some groups—old wealth and executives—are able to influence the environment, but other groups—the working/welfare poor and the underclass—have virtually no influence. This distinction has important implications for social welfare, because those who are of lower status tend to be the recipients of welfare benefits that are the product of a social policy process in which they do not participate. The way in which these various groups influence the social policy process will be discussed in greater detail below.

With these clarifications in mind, the policy process can be divided into four stages: formulation, legislation, implementation, and evaluation. Although these terms are somewhat self-explanatory, during the decision-making process different organizational entities exert their influence, making the process an uneven one that is frequently characterized by fits and starts. Organizations correspond to the stratification groups that figure prominently in their organizational activities and thereby in the policy process.

Formulation

Before the nineteenth century it would have been accurate to state that policy formulation in this country began with the legislative phase. Clearly, this was the situation envisioned by the drafters of the Constitution; but theirs was a largely agrarian society with comparatively little institutional specialization. With industrialization many complexities were injected into the society, and in time special institutions emerged to assist the legislature in evaluating social conditions and preparing policy options. Eventually, even constitutionally established bodies such as Congress lapsed into a reactive role, largely responsive to other entities that formulated policy.[13] Initially institutions of higher education provided technical intelligence to assist the legislative branch, and some still do. For example, the University of Wisconsin Institute for Research on Poverty provides analyses on important welfare policies.[14]

TABLE 8.1 ■ Social Stratification of the Population into Six Groups

NAME OF GROUP	EXAMPLES	CHARACTERISTICS
Old wealth	Upper elites, the independently wealthy, large stockholders	Ownership of resources is the main source of power; control over goals is very high, but control over means is through organizers (executives).
Executives	Top administrators in business; people in government and the military	Organizational solidarity facilitates effective policy implementation; there is some control over goals and a high degree of control over means.
Professionals	Middle-level managers, technical experts, private practitioners, community leaders	Environment encourages limited solidarity; control over means is high, and goal setting can be influenced if collective action is undertaken.
Organized workers	Semiskilled workers; people in civic and political clubs and social action organizations	Environment encourages solidarity; groups have some control over the means by which goals are realized.
Working/welfare poor	Temporary and part-time workers earning minimum wage and who use welfare as a wage supplement	People are in a subjugated position with no control over the environment; frustration is shared and irrational, and explosive behavior can result.
Underclass	Unemployables and illiterates; disabled substance abusers; itinerants, drifters, migrant workers	People are in a subjugated position with no control over the environment; a sense of failure coupled with mobility reduces social interaction and leads to retreatism.

Source: Adapted from Dexter C. Dunphy, *The Primary Group: A Handbook for Analysis and Field Research,* © 1972, pp. 42–44. Reprinted by permission of Prentice-Hall, Inc. Englewood Cliffs, NJ.

That legislators at the federal level, as well as those in the larger states, would rely on experts to assess social conditions and develop policy options is not surprising, given the fact that each legislator must attend to multiple committee and subcommittee assignments requiring expertise in particular matters, while at the same time contending with the general concerns of a large constituency. A typical day in the life of a legislator has been reconstructed by Charles Peters, a longtime Washington observer:

The most striking feature of a congressman's life is its hectic jumble of votes, meetings, appointments, and visits from folks from back home who just drop by. From an 8 A.M. break-

fast conference with a group of union leaders, a typical morning will take him to his office around 9, where the waiting room will be filled with people who want to see him. From 9 until 10:30 or so, he will try to give the impression that he is devoting his entire attention to a businessman from his state with a tax problem; to a delegation protesting their town's loss of air or rail service; to a constituent and his three children, who are in town for the day and want to say hello; and to a couple of staff members whose morale will collapse if they don't have five minutes alone to go over essential business with him. As he strives to project one-on-one sincerity to all these people, he is fielding phone calls at the rate of one every five minutes and checking a press release that has to get out in time to make the afternoon papers in his district.

He leaves this madhouse to go to a committee meeting, accompanied by his legislative aide, who tries to brief him on the business before the committee meeting begins. The meeting started at 10, so he struggles to catch the thread of questioning, while a committee staff member whispers in his ear. And so the day continues.

The typical day . . . usually ends around 11:30 P.M., as the congressman leaves an embassy party, at which he has been hustling as if it were a key precinct on election eve. He is too tired to talk about any but the most trivial matters, too tired usually to do anything but fall into bed and go to sleep.[15]

As a result of competing demands, legislators pay somewhat less attention to the policy process than their public image would have you believe, leaving much of the work to their staffs. Even then, public policy tends to get short shift. Because reelection is a primary concern for legislators, their staffs are frequently assigned to solve the relatively minor problems presented by constituents. In fact, placating unhappy constituents has become so prominent a concern that one legislative observer notes that constituency services—called "casework" by elected officials—have become "more important than issues" for representatives.[16]

Gradually, institutions have begun to specialize in providing the social intelligence necessary for policy formulation. These policy institutes, sometimes called think tanks, now wield substantial influence in the social policy process. Not unlike prestigious colleges, think tanks maintain multidisciplinary staffs of scholars who prepare position papers on a range of social issues. With multimillion-dollar budgets and connections with national and state capitals, think tanks are well positioned to shape social policy. Generally, financial support for these institutes comes from wealthy individuals and corporations with particular ideological inclinations that are evidenced by the types of think tanks they support. Several prominent policy institutes are located on the ideological continuum in Figure 8.2.

Within policy institutes, prominent scholars, usually identified as senior fellows, hold endowed chairs, having often served in cabinet-level positions within the executive branch. For example, when a Republican administration comes into power, large numbers of senior fellows from conservative policy institutes assume cabinet appointments; their Democratic counterparts return to liberal institutes, where senior chairs await them. For junior staffers, an appointment in a think tank can provide invaluable experience in how the governmental policy process actually works. Despite their influence in public policy, however, it is important to recognize that think tanks are private, nongovernmental institutions.

Through much of the twentieth century, a first generation of largely liberal policy institutes, such as the Brookings Institution, contributed to the formulation of governmental welfare policy. Their role was essentially passive, in that they provided technical expertise to legislators and governmental agencies upon request. By the mid-1970s, however, a second generation

---

FIGURE 8.2   Places on the Ideological Continuum of Six Policy Institutes

| Institute for Policy Studies | Urban Institute | Brookings Institution | American Enterprise Institute | Heritage Foundation | CATO Institute |

liberal (left) ←————————————————————————→ conservative (right) of conservative policy institutes, such as the American Enterprise Institute and the Heritage Foundation, moved aggressively forward to shape a public philosophy that was more consistent with their own values. The elections of Ronald Reagan and George H. W. Bush did much to further the influence of these organizations, and the work of scholars from these policy institutes became important to the implementation and continuation of the "Reagan revolution."[17] A third generation of policy institutes emerged later to promote programs for the poor. The Children's Defense Fund and the Center on Budget and Policy Priorities endevor to reassert the needs of the disadvantaged in social welfare policy.[18] The election of Bill Clinton to the presidency in 1992 brought to the forefront the Progressive Policy Institute, a think tank responsible for much of the policy research Clinton used during the campaign, and later influential in establishing domestic policy.

Legislation

The legislative phase involves two primary groups: the legislature and special interest groups that are subclassified as lobbies and **political action committees (PACs)**. Much public policy work is conducted by legislators who are appointed to committees and subcommittees on the basis of their particular interests. An important and often unappreciated component of the legislative phase is the role played by the staffs of committees and subcommittees. Former legislative staffers are definitive experts in the subject area of a committee and are prized as lobbyists for special interest groups.[19] As a result of the increasing complexity of the policy process, the number of legislative staff has multiplied. In the late 1980s, 24,000 staff members served Congress, more than double the number in the late 1970s.[20] Committees are the loci of testimony on issues, and legislative hearings provide an opportunity for the official and sometimes the only input from the public on some matters. Accordingly, representatives of advocacy groups make it a point to testify before certain committees in order to ensure that their

views are heard. At the federal level, the primary committees dealing with social welfare in 2000 are the following:[21]

Senate

Finance Committee. Subcommittees: Medicaid and Health Care for Low-Income Families; Medicare, Long-Term Care, and Health Insurance; Social Security and Family Policy

Agriculture. Subcommittee: Research, Nutrition, and General Legislation

Appropriations. Subcommittee: Labor, Health and Human Services, Education

Labor and Human Resources. Subcommittees: Aging; Children and Families; Disability Policy

Special Aging.

House of Representatives

Ways and Means. Subcommittees: Health; Human Resources; Social Security

Economic and Educational Opportunities. Subcommittees: Early Childhood, Youth, and Families; Employer/Employee Relations; Postsecondary Education, Training, and Lifelong Learning; Workforce Protections

Appropriations. Subcommittee: Labor, Health and Human Services, and Education

The procedure by which an idea becomes legislation was described earlier, in the discussion on technical aspects of the policy process. Throughout the process, representatives of special interests attempt to shape any given proposal so that it is more congruent with priorities of their members. Special interests can be classified according to the nature of their activities: Before elections, interest groups can influence the composition of legislatures by establishing PACs; in between elections, interests can exert pressure strategically through lobbying. As special interests learned to skirt federal campaign regulations, increasing amounts of "soft money" (nonregulated donations) influenced election activity.[22] As Tables 8.2–8.4 indicate, substantial

TABLE 8.2 ■ PAC Contributions to Federal Candidates, 1999–2000

PAC SECTOR	NUMBER OF PACS	TOTAL CONTRIBUTIONS
Labor	203	$25,499,562
Finance, insurance, and real estate	434	20,240,275
Health	186	9,787,568
Miscellaneous business	309	8,889,215
Energy and natural resources	268	8,370,040
Transportation	147	8,352,784
Communications/Electronics	130	7,589,715
Agribusiness	242	7,576,433
Lawyers and lobbyists	147	5,589,421
Construction	101	4,101,135
Defense	47	3,656,200

TABLE 8.3 ■ "Soft Money" Contributions to Political Parties, 1999

	REPUBLICAN PARTY		DEMOCRATIC PARTY	
Rank	*Organization*	*Amount*	*Organization*	*Amount*
1	Philip Morris	$2,939,281	AFSCME	$2,756,704
2	American Financial Group	1,630,000	CWA	2,636,250
3	AT&T	1,571,661	SEIU	1,899,700
4	Amway	1,517,500	Peter Buttenweiser	1,533,500
5	RJR Nabisco	1,103,366	Loral Space and Communications	1,356,000
6	Freddie Mac	1,060,500	National Education Association	1,254,800
7	Microsoft	1,046,729	American Federation of Teachers	1,177,200

TABLE 8.4 ■ Top Lobbyists, 1997 and 1998

RANK	FIRM	1997 EXPENDITURES	1998 EXPENDITURES
1	British American Tobacco	$4,060,000	$25,190,000
2	Philip Morris	15,800,000	23,000,000
3	Bell Atlantic	15,672,840	21,260,000
4	U.S. Chamber of Commerce	14,240,000	17,000,000
5	American Medical Association	17,280,000	16,820,000
6	Ford Motor Company	7,343,000	13,807,000
7	Business Roundtable	9,480,000	11,640,000
8	Edison Electric Institute	10,020,000	11,020,000
9	American Hospital Association	7,880,000	10,520,000
10	Blue Cross/Blue Shield	8,761,936	9,171,572

funds are funneled through PACs, "soft money," and lobbying in order to influence elections for the purpose of shaping public policy.

An examination of campaign finance might lead a cynic to conclude that democracy in the United States produces the best politics that money can buy. Yet individual contributions continue to represent the bulk of party revenues. During the 1997–98 election cycle, the Federal Election Commission reported that 71 percent of Democratic Party contributions of $74 million, and 87 percent of Republican Party contributions of $156.3 million, came from individuals.[23] Individual contributions notwithstanding, strategically targeted gifts from organized groups have disproportionate impact; hence the concern about PACs, "soft money," and lobbyists. The Center for Responsive Politics has ranked the major PACs by sector. With the exception of the Labor and Lawyers and Lobbyists sectors, PAC contributions have favored Republicans over Democrats by a factor more than two to one; thus, PACs have tended to reflect conservative influences in social policy.

Soft money funds—funds that are not restricted by federal campaign law—have increased substantially in recent years. For example, soft money contributions to the major political parties roughly tripled from $79.1 million in 1991–92 to $220.7 million in 1997–98.[24] According to Common Cause, 1999 soft money contributions by business eclipsed those of labor by a factor of 10. A ranking of the top 10 soft money contributors to the major parties compiled by Common Cause reveals the typical ideological division: Business contributes to the Republican Party, and labor gives to the Democrats. In anticipation of the 2000 election, labor broke new ground, donating $15 million in soft money, almost all of it to Democratic candidates.[25] For 1999, Common Cause reported that the Democratic Party received $124 million in soft money all told—an amount eclipsed by the Republicans, who received $159 million. As the 2000 election heated up, interest groups donated soft money in unprecedented amounts, rivaling traditional expenditures on the part of lobbyists.

The Center for Responsive Politics ranked the top lobbying organizations for 1997 and 1998, and the magnitude of their influence on Congress is apparent. Foremost, total expenditures by a single firm, such as British American Tobacco, rivals soft money as well as PAC contributions on the part of major sectors of the economy—and swamps most contributors altogether. In addition, major lobbying organizations can shift major amounts of cash depending on their particular needs. In the face of antismoking litigation and legislation, British American Tobacco quintupled its lobbying expenditures in only one year! Note that 3 of the top 10 lobbying organizations represent the rapidly expanding health industry.

In national politics, the key to influence is choreographing the resources of PACs, soft money, and lobbyists to attain party objectives. By way of illustration, having won control of Congress as a result of the 1994 midterm elections, Republicans moved swiftly to divert the flow of PAC money from the Democratic Party. Leading the effort was Representative Dick Armey, house majority leader, who, in April 1995, sent a letter to Fortune 500 CEOs complaining that their contributions to such "liberal" charities as the American Cancer Society were contrary to Republican intentions in social reform. In order to clarify his intentions, Armey's staff let PAC contributors know that contributions to Republican ventures were expected and that those to Democrats would also be tallied. Special interests seeking access to the new Republican leadership should be zeroing out their contributions to Democrats. In the annals of special interest politics, Armey's brazen tactics broke new ground: "By imposing an ideological test on givers they have introduced a new level of coercion," observed journalist Ken Auletta.[26] Yet Armey's strategy violated no laws, and the money rolled in. In the first eight months of 1995 the Republican party received $60 million in contributions, up from just $36 million in 1993.[27]

Compared to business, labor, and lobbyists, social advocacy groups bring few assets to bear on the political process. Limited by meager resources, social advocacy groups usually rely on volunteer lobbyists. In addition to NASW, there are several advocacy groups within social welfare that have been instrumental in advancing legislation to assist vulnerable populations—among them the American Public Welfare Association, the Child Welfare League of America, the National Association for the Advancement of Colored People, the National Urban League, the National Assembly of Voluntary Health and Welfare Associations, and the National Organization for Women. Of these advocacy groups only one, the American Association of Retired Persons (AARP), ranks among the top 100 lobbyists on Capitol Hill. Despite the number of welfare advocacy organizations and their successful record in evolving more comprehensive social legislation, changes in the policy process are making their work more difficult. Increases in the number of governmental agencies as well as in their staffs make it difficult to track policy developments and changes in administrative procedures. Worse, the escalating cost of influencing social policy, evident in the number of paid lobbyists and in the contributions lavished by PACs, is simply beyond the means of welfare advocacy organizations. As one Democratic candidate for the Senate lamented, "only the well-heeled have PACs—not the poor, the unemployed, the minorities or even most consumers."[28] Compared to more affluent interests, human service professionals have little clout. In social work, the PAC that provides assistance to candidates is Political Action for Candidate Election, or PACE, "the political arm of the National Association of Social Workers." PACE uses a variety of tactics to "expand social workers' activity in politics," including voter registration, support for political campaigns, and analysis of incumbents' voting records.[29] For the 1999–2000 election cycle, PACE budgeted total contributions of $225,000 to $240,000 to candidates running for national office,[30] an amount, though not insignificant to candidates who received assistance, pales in comparison to the amounts wielded by more influential PACS.

This is not to say that proponents of social justice have been ineffectual. Despite their disadvantageous status, welfare advocacy groups were able to mobilize grassroots support to beat back some of the more regressive proposals of the Reagan administration. In the early 1980s, for example, scholars from the conservative Cato Institute and the Heritage Foundation proposed cutting the Social Security program. They were trounced by an effective lobbying campaign mounted by the AARP under the leadership of the late Congressman Claude Pepper (who was then in his eighties). Unfortunately, other social welfare programs did not fare as well. At the same time that Social Security was spared budget cuts, social programs for the poor were reduced by significant margins. Among the newer advocacy organizations, the Children's Defense Fund (CDF) hoped to benefit significantly from the election of Bill Clinton; First Lady Hillary Rodham Clinton had been a former chair of its board of directors, and Clinton's Health and Human Services (HHS) secretary, Donna Shalala, had succeeded Rodham Clinton at CDF. CDF did claim a substantial victory with incorporation of the Children's Initiative in the Clinton 1993 economic package, but in 1996 children's advocates were distraught when Clinton signed a the PRWORA that they thought was injurious to poor children.

Implementation

The fact that a policy has been enacted does not necessarily mean it will be implemented. Often governmental policies fail to provide for adequate authority, personnel, or funding to accomplish their stated purposes. This has been a chronic problem for social welfare programs. It is also possible that a governmental policy initiative will not be enforced even after it has been established. Many local jurisdictions have correctional and child welfare institutions now operating under court supervision because judges have agreed with social advocates that these institutions are not in compliance with state or federal law.

Implementation, difficult enough in the normal course of events, is that much more difficult when the public is disaffected with governmental institutions. The episodic nature of public endorsement of governmental institutions has been studied extensively by Albert O. Hirschman. In *Shifting Involvements* Hirschman investigated the relationship between "private interest and public action." According to Hirschman, public endorsement of governmental institutions is a fundamental problem for industrialized capitalist societies, which emphasize individual competitiveness while generating social and economic dislocations that require collective action. "Western societies," Hirschman observes, "appear to be condemned to long periods of privatization during which they live through an impoverished 'atrophy of public meanings,' followed by spasmodic outbursts of 'publicness' that are hardly likely to be constructive."[31] Disenchantment with governmental solutions to social problems makes public welfare programs vulnerable to their critics, leading to reductions in staff and fiscal support, often followed by an escalation in the social problem for which the social program was initially designed. Thus, the episodic nature of public support for programs designed to alleviate social problems further impedes effective implementation.

Evaluation

The expansion of governmental welfare policies has spawned a veritable industry in program evaluation. Stung by the abuses of the executive branch during Watergate and the Vietnam War, Congress established additional oversight agencies to review federal programs.[32] As a result, multiple units within the executive and legislative branches of government have the evaluation of programs as their primary mission. At the federal level, the most important of these include the General Accounting Office (GAO), the Office of Management and Budget (OMB), the Congressional Budget Office (CBO), and the Congressional Research Service (CRS). State governments have similar units. In addition, departments have evaluation units that monitor program activities for which they are responsible. Finally, federal and state levels of government commonly contract with nongovernmental organizations for evaluations of specific programs. As a result, many universities provide important research services to government. The University of Wisconsin's Institute for Research

on Poverty is distinguished for its research in social welfare. More recently, private consulting firms, such as the Manpower Demonstration and Research Corporation, Abt Associates, Maximus, and Mathematica, have entered the field, often hiring former government officials and capitalizing on their connections in order to secure lucrative research contracts. Of course, any politicization of the research process is frowned upon, because it raises questions about the impartiality of the evaluation. Is a former government official willing to assess rigorously and impartially a program run by an agency in which he or she was employed in the past or would like to be employed in the future? Questions about the closeness between governmental agencies and research firms and the validity of evaluation studies have become so common that the consulting firms located near the expressway surrounding Washington, D.C., are often referred to as "the beltway bandits."

Investigations by program evaluation organizations can be characterized as applied (as opposed to "pure") research, the objective being to optimize program operations. As a result of this emphasis on the function of programs, evaluation studies frequently focus on waste, cost-effectiveness, and goal attainment. Owing to the contradictory objectives of many welfare policies, the constant readjustments in programs, and the limitations in the art of evaluation research, evaluations frequently conclude that any given program has mixed results. Rarely does a program evaluation provide a clear indication for future action. Often the results of a single program evaluation are used by both critics and defenders in their efforts to dismantle or to advance the program.

The very inconclusiveness of program evaluation contributes to the partisan use to which evaluation research can be put. It is not uncommon for decision makers to engage in statistical arguments that have a great influence on social welfare policy. Of recent "stat wars," several relate directly to social welfare. One example is the question whether underemployed and discouraged workers should be included in the unemployment rate. Currently, the Department of

Labor defines as unemployed only those who are out of work and actively looking for jobs; and it considers part-time workers as employed. As a result, many African Americans, Hispanic Americans, young adults, and women are not considered unemployed, even though advocates for these groups contend that they are not fully employed. Liberals argue that including underemployed and discouraged workers in the unemployment rate would produce a more accurate measure of the employment experience of disadvantaged groups. Conservatives argue that the employment rate is not a good indicator of employment opportunity anyway, citing the millions of undocumented workers who come to the United States illegally every year to take menial jobs. Further, including underemployed and discouraged workers would increase the unemployment rate by as much as 50 percent and would prove unacceptably expensive, because extensions in the number of quarters for which workers are eligible for unemployment compensation are tied to the unemployment rate. Predictably, evaluations of employment programs vary considerably. Consultants have generated considerable data about the results of state and local welfare-to-work initiatives. Their studies evince a general theme: Although welfare caseloads have dropped as much as 50 percent, heads of households who have found work (1) tend to remain stuck in sub-poverty-level wages but (2) lose benefits such as food stamps and Medicaid—even though they remain eligible—because of efforts at caseload reduction. Such research serves ideological purposes, of course. Conservatives trumpet the reduction in welfare dependency, and liberals worry about the fate of families who continue to be poor despite full-time work.

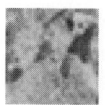 # Non–Decision Making

If the governmental decision-making process is somewhat irregular and irrational, it is also unrepresentative. As Figure 8.3 illustrates, groups in the upper levels of the social stratification population late the institutions through which policy is made. In the case of welfare policy, welfare beneficiaries must adjust to rules established by other social groups.

The primary players in the social policy game are executives and professionals. Old wealth is able to opt out, leaving its social obligations in the hands of executives. Groups lower on the social stratification scale have less and less influence on governmental policy. The interests of these groups are left in the hands of professionals who work through advocacy organizations or "cabals," although occasional unrest on the part of working/welfare poor can result in increased welfare benefits. Thus, the lower socioeconomic groups' lack of influence in the social policy process is virtually built into governmental decision making. The term *non–decision making* has been coined to describe this phenomenon—the system's capacity to keep the interests of some groups off the decision-making agenda.[33] Non–decision making has a long history in the United States; generations of African Americans and women were legally excluded from decision making prior to emancipation and suffrage.

Policymakers' attempts to increase the influence of disadvantaged groups in decision making have not been well received. A classic illustration of this occurred during the Great Society initiative, when poor people were to be assured of "maximum feasible participation" in the Community Action Program (CAP). This stipulation was interpreted to mean that one-third of the members of CAP boards of directors must be poor people—a seemingly reasonable idea—but the militancy of poor people in some cities at the time led to utter chaos in many CAPs. As a result of pressure from mayors and other officials, lawmakers rescinded this requirement in order to make CAPs more compliant.[34] Since then, the representation of lower socioeconomic groups in decision making has been limited, for all practical purposes, to an advisory capacity at best.

The governmental policy process also poses problems for administrators and practitioners. Policies frequently reflect assumptions about the human condition that may seem reasonable to

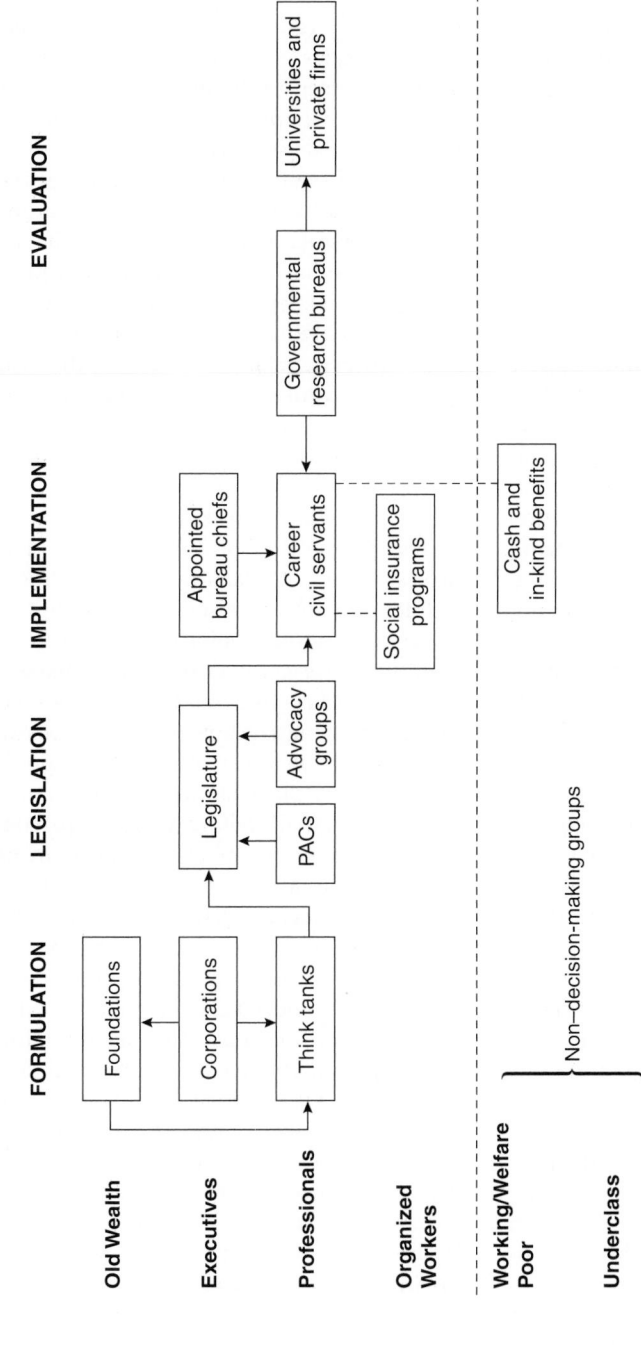

FIGURE 8.3 The Roles Played by Six Social Levels in the Governmental Policy Process

the upper socioeconomic groups that make them but bear little resemblance to the reality of the lower socioeconomic groups that are supposed to be beneficiaries. For example, child support enforcement policy assumes that fathers of children on AFDC/TANF programs have the kind of regular, well-paying jobs that would allow them to meet the amounts of their court orders, whereas often their jobs are intermittent and low-wage. Consequently, support payments to children who are dependent on welfare have been relatively disappointing. An evaluation of Parents' Fair Share, a program designed to increase the child support paid by men whose dependents were on AFDC, resulted in reduced child support payments despite the multiple interventions incorporated in the program.[35] To cite another example, welfare-to-work programs assume that young women want to complete their education and gain meaningful employment—but their socialization often instructs them that school and work are irrelevant and that having a child may be the most meaningful thing they can do. For many years, AFDC/TANF has provided financial support to poor teenaged mothers, a benefit that many conservatives claim has actually induced girls to become pregnant. But an evaluation of New Chance, a teen pregnancy prevention program, resulted in outcomes that were contrary to the intent of the program: Young mothers enrolled in New Chance were more likely to become pregnant again and less likely to participate in the labor market than those in the control group.[36] In sum, the preliminary studies on child support and teen pregnancy suggest that the poor do not necessarily comply with the bourgeois assumptions that are implicit or explicit in social policy.

It is not surprising, then, that welfare programs are not well received by many of the people who depend on them. Instead of being grateful, beneficiaries are frequently resentful. In turn, upper-income taxpayers find this ingratitude offensive and are inclined to make programs more punitive. Ironically, beneficiaries of welfare programs tend to respond to punitive policies with indifference and defiance; because, for many of them, welfare programs have never been particularly helpful. The perception that welfare programs are only minimally helpful is occasionally validated when, under exceptional circumstances, someone from an upper socio-economic group falls into the social safety net and suddenly appreciates the importance of welfare programs for daily survival.

Not all welfare programs are perceived in such a negative light. Generally, programs that benefit persons who are solidly in the working class fare better. The social insurance programs, such as Social Security, unemployment compensation, and Medicare, are usually regarded more highly by beneficiaries. Of course, the insurance programs require people to first pay into the program in order to claim benefits later, so they are designed to be different from the means-tested programs intended for the poor.

A particular consequence of governmental policy making falls on the shoulders of welfare professionals. "Workers on the front lines of the welfare state find themselves in a corrupted world of service," wrote Michael Lipsky in his award-winning *Street-Level Bureaucracy*. According to Lipsky, "Workers find that the best way to keep demand within manageable proportions is to deliver a consistently inaccessible or inferior product."[37] In response to the irrelevance often characteristic of governmental welfare policies, personnel in public welfare offices consequently deny benefits to people who are eligible for them, a process labeled **bureaucratic disentitlement**.[38] It should come as no surprise, then, that public welfare programs mandated by governmental policy have acquired an undesirable reputation within the professional community. The executive director of the California chapter of NASW candidly stated that "Public social services are being abandoned by M. S. W. social workers. It seems to be employment of last resort."[39] Another veteran observer was even more graphic: "To work in a public agency today is to work in a bureaucratic hell."[40] Within the context of public welfare, it is not surprising to find that burnout has become pervasive among welfare professionals. The inadequacy of public welfare policies for both beneficiaries and professionals is an unfortunate consequence of the governmental policy process as it is currently structured.

Making the public policy process more representative is a primary concern of welfare advocates. Since the Civil Rights movement, African Americans and the poor have recognized the power of the ballot, and voter registration has become an important strategy for advancing the influence of these groups. The registration of Hispanic Americans in the Southwest has been the mission of the Southwest Voter Research Institute, founded by the late Willie Velasquez. Under the visionary leadership of Velasquez, Latino voter registration grew steadily and was reflected in an increase in the number of Chicano elected officials. Fifteen years of voter registration campaigning by the institute contributed to a doubling of the number of Hispanic elected officials in the Southwest by the late 1980s.[41]

The most visible example of the political empowerment of people usually excluded from the decision-making process was Jesse Jackson's 1988 campaign to be the presidential nominee of the Democratic Party. Expanding on the grassroots political base built during his 1984 bid for the nomination, Jackson's 1988 Rainbow Coalition demonstrated the support he commanded from a wide spectrum of disenfranchised Americans. Thus, mobilization of the working and welfare poor, as Velasquez and Jackson have shown, can make the policy process more representative.

As the attempts to increase the registration of minority voters suggest, reengaging Americans in the political process is a difficult undertaking. In national elections, only about half of eligible U.S. voters exercise the franchise, the lowest turnout among industrialized nations. Explanations of voter apathy are multiple. Within the voting population, more affluent voters are more than twice as likely to exercise their franchise as are those who are poor: In 1996 65.7 percent of voters with incomes above $50,000 voted in the presidential election, versus only 28.6 percent of those with incomes less than $10,000.[42] A survey conducted by the Pew Research Center for the People and the Press revealed that substantial majorities of respondents agreed with such statements as "government is inefficient and wasteful," "politicians lose touch

pretty quickly," and "government controls too much of daily life."[43] Such perceptions bode ill for the democratic process, of course. Some 30 million prospective voters are inactive, a group made up disproportionately of minorities and the poor.[44] Increasing the involvement of apathetic voters not only would make inroads against non–decision making, but also would make public social programs more responsive to their circumstances.

Social Workers and Social Reform

As a result of non–decision making and voter apathy, advocates of social justice are instrumental in correcting for a skewed political process. Throughout the history of U.S. social welfare, advocates of care for vulnerable populations have been shaping social policies. If we look beneath the surface of policy statements, we find a rich and often exciting account of the skirmishes fought by advocates for social justice. In some respects, social policy innovations can be looked upon as individual and collective biography written in official language. In an age of mass populations that are often manipulated by private and public megastructures, it is easy to forget how powerful some individuals have been in shaping social welfare policy in the United States. Many of these leaders are known because they achieved national prominence; yet some of the more heroic acts to advance social justice were performed by individuals whose names are not widely recognized. As just one example, not to be forgotten in this regard is Michael Schwerner, a social worker who was murdered while working in a voter registration drive in the South during the Civil Rights movement.[45]

Early social welfare leaders emerged during the **Progressive Era**, a period when educated and socially conscious men and women sought to create structures that would advance social justice in the United States. The settlement house gained a reputation as the locus for reform activity, leading one historian to conclude that "settlement workers during the Progressive Era were probably more committed to political action than any other group of welfare workers before or since."[46] From this group Jane Addams quickly surfaced as a leader of national prominence. Through her settlement home, Hull House, she fought not only for improvements in care for slum dwellers in inner-city Chicago, but also for international peace. For Jane Addams, social work was social reform. Instead of focusing solely on restoration and rehabilitation, Addams claimed that there was a superior role for the profession: "It must decide whether it is to remain behind in the area of caring for the victimized," she argued, "or whether to press ahead into the dangerous area of conflict where the struggle must be pressed to bring to pass an order of society with few victims."[47] In that struggle Addams served nobly, receiving an honorary degree from Yale University and serving as president of the Women's International League for Peace and Freedom. In 1931 Jane Addams was awarded the Nobel Peace Prize, a suitable distinction for a social worker who once had herself appointed a garbage collector in order to improve sanitation in the slums around Hull House.

Hull House proved a remarkable institution, and among its residents were women who made lasting and important contributions to the New Deal:

Edith Abbott, president of the National Conference of Social Welfare, dean of the University of Chicago School of Social Service Administration, and participant in the drafting of the Social Security Act of 1935

Grace Abbott, organizer of the first White House Conference on Children, director of the U.S. Children's Bureau, and participant in the construction of the Social Security Act

Julia Lathrop, developer of the first juvenile court and of the first child mental health clinic in the United States, and the first director of the U.S. Children's Bureau

Florence Kelley, director of the National Consumer League, cofounder of the U.S. Chil-

dren's Bureau, and a member of the National Child Labor Committee

Frances Perkins, director of the New York Council of Organizations for War Services, director of the Council on Immigrant Education, and the first Secretary of Labor[48]

The activity around Hull House was never limited to those with a narrow view of reform. A regular participant in the settlement was John Dewey, in his time "America's most influential philosopher, educator, as well as one of the most outspoken champions of social reform."[49]

Settlement experiences crystallized the motivations of other reformers as well. Harry Hopkins, primary architect of the New Deal and of the social programs that made up the Social Security Act, had resided in New York's Christadora House Settlement. Ida Bell Wells-Barnett led the Negro Fellowship League to establish a settlement house for African Americans in Chicago. Lillian Wald, with Florence Kelley a cofounder of the U.S. Children's Bureau, had earlier established New York's Henry Street Settlement, an institution that was to achieve distinction within the African American community. Under the guidance of Mary White Ovington, a social worker, the first meetings of the National Association for the Advancement of Colored People were held at the Henry Street Settlement.[50]

Early social welfare leaders championed causes that improved the conditions of children and immigrants, but they did not always forsake African Americans. When it became apparent that Booker T. Washington's program of "industrial education" was unable to contend effectively with ubiquitous racial discrimination, social reformers Jane Addams, Ida Bell Wells-Barnett, and John Dewey joined W. E. B. Du Bois in the Niagara Movement. The early organizations spawned by the Niagara Movement were later consolidated into the National Urban League, with George Edmund Haynes, a social worker, as one of its codirectors. In 1910 Haynes had been the first African American to graduate from the New York School of Philanthropy, so it is not surprising that an important Urban League program was the provision of fellowships for African Americans to the school.[51] Later, during the height of the Civil Rights movement, the National Urban League, under the direction of social worker Whitney Young Jr., collaborated in organizing the August 28, 1963, march on Washington, memorialized by the ringing words of Martin Luther King Jr., "I have a dream!"[52]

If the New Deal bore the imprint of social workers, the Great Society was similarly marked some 30 years later. Significantly, one leader of the War on Poverty was Wilbur Cohen, a social worker who had been the first employee of the Social Security Board created in 1935. Eventually Cohen was to be credited with some 65 innovations in social welfare policy, but his crowning achievement was the passage of the Medicare and Medicaid acts in 1965. The secretary of Health, Education, and Welfare during the Johnson administration, Cohen was arguably the nation's most decorated social worker, receiving 18 honorary degrees from U.S. universities.[53]

Social Work and Advocacy Organizations

The formulation of social welfare policy in the United States, as this chapter has shown, is a complicated and often arduous process. Much of this can be attributed to the nature of U.S. culture: to the competing interests inherent in a pluralistic society; to the federal system of government, which authorizes decision making on several levels at once; to public and private bureaucracies that serve large numbers of consumers; to economic and technological developments that lead to specialization. Under these circumstances, changing social welfare policy to improve the circumstances of disadvantaged groups can be a daunting task. Regrettably, few welfare professionals consider social policy advocacy an enterprise worthy of undertaking. Most social workers prefer direct service activity, in which they have little opportunity for

direct involvement in social welfare policy. Some social workers do attain important positions in federal and state human service bureaucracies and are close to the policy process. Unfortunately, however, these managers are often administering welfare policies that have been made by legislatures and that do not necessarily represent either clients or human service professionals. Perhaps most troubling, the involvement of social workers in the formulation of social policy has been diminishing in recent years. In a provocative statement, June Hopps, dean of the Boston College School of Social Work and former editor in chief of *Social Work*, acknowledged that "Since the late 1960s and early 1970s, the [social work] profession has experienced a dramatic loss of influence in the arenas where policy is shaped and administered."[54] That this should occur is not only a reversal of the profession's Progressive Era legacy, but also an abnegation of a rapidly expanding service sector.

If one indicator of good social policy is the correspondence between the policy and the social reality of its intended beneficiaries, then social welfare policy should be enhanced by the input of social workers. However, social workers have left much of the decision making about social welfare to professionals from other disciplines. "There are increasing numbers of non–social workers, including psychologists and urban planners," observed Eleanor Brilliant, "taking what might have been social work jobs in service delivery and policy analysis."[55] The consequences of welfare professionals' opting to leave social policy in the hands of others are important. For direct service workers, these consequences can mean having to apply eligibility standards or procedures that, although logical in some respects, make little sense in the social context of many clients. For the public, they may mean a gradual disenchantment with social programs that do not seem to work. The causes of the retrenchment affecting social programs since the late 1970s are complex, of course; but it is worth noting that public dissatisfaction with social programs has escalated as welfare professionals have retreated from active involvement in social welfare policy.

The rebuilding of a role for social workers in social policy will take concerted effort. Individual leadership is a necessary, but no longer sufficient, precondition for this objective. Essential to the undertaking will be social workers' ability to understand and manipulate complex organizations and programs. In fact, this skill may be the most critical for welfare professionals to acquire if they are to advance social justice, for it addresses a question central to the postindustrial era. During the Industrial Revolution, Karl Marx suggested that the central question was "Who controls the means of production?" A mature industrial order and the expansion of civil bureaucracy led Max Weber to ask, "Who controls the means of administration?" The evolution of a postindustrial order, in which primary economic activity occurs in a service sector dependent on processed information, raises a new question: "Who controls the means of analysis?" If social workers are to shape social policy as effectively as they have in the past, they will have to learn to control the means of analysis. This means conducting research on social problems, surveying public opinion about welfare programs, analyzing existing social policy for opportunities to enhance welfare provision, and winning elected office in order to make decisions about proposed social welfare policies.

Advocacy Organizations and the New Policy Institutes

Policy analysis organizations have been instrumental in shaping social policy from as early as the New Deal period. Subsequently, policy institutes have had liberal or conservative labels ascribed to them, with the liberal organizations achieving dominance up until the late 1970s—when, as we have seen, conservative institutes began gaining popularity. The failure of government social programs to expand during the Carter presidency, followed by the profoundly negative impact of the Reagan years and the first Bush administration, led social reformers to look to traditional policy institutes such as the Brookings Institution and the Urban Institute for leadership. But the inability of these organizations to shape the debate on U.S. social welfare policy compelled increasingly impatient reformers to establish a new group of policy analysis organizations.

Children's Defense Fund. Begun by Marian Wright Edelman in 1974, the Children's Defense Fund (CDF) sought to address the health, income, and educational needs of the nation's children.[56] By the mid-1980s CDF had become a major voice in children's policy and had successfully advocated programs at the federal and state levels. In 1984 CDF helped pass the Child Health Assurance Program, which expanded Medicaid eligibility to poor women and children. It also advocated for the 1998 Children's Health Insurance Program (CHIP). CDF is noted for its educational publications, particularly for eye-catching posters depicting injustices inflicted on poor, minority children. Its annual report, *The State of America's Children*, is an authoritative compendium of issues and programs concerning children.

The Center on Budget and Policy Priorities. Established in 1981 by Robert Greenstein, former administrator of the Food and Nutrition Service in the Agriculture Department, CBPP has fought to defend social programs for low-income people against budget cuts. With a modest staff, CBPP distributes its analyses to congressional staffs, the media, and grassroots organizations. Despite its small size, CBPP provided much of the program analysis to refute arguments presented by officials of the Reagan administration in their efforts to cut means-tested social programs. Significantly, CBPP and CDF have developed a close working relationship. CBPP regularly provides data to CDF on the health and income status of children, and Greenstein is a regular contributor to CDF reports.[57]

Economic Policy Institute. In 1986 Jeff Faux convinced labor-oriented liberals to establish a policy institute to represent "the perspective of working families and the poor."[58] During the subsequent decade EPI expanded rapidly and published reports depicting a widening chasm between the economic circumstances of working families and the affluent. Notable among EPI publications is its annual volume *The State of Working America,* which contains current data on income, taxes, wages, wealth, and poverty.

Institute for Women's Policy Research. Created in 1987 by Heidi Hartmann, a social program researcher and director of the Women's Studies Program at Rutgers University, IWPR quickly attained a respected position in Washington, D.C. The IWPR research and advocacy agenda relating to women is extensive, including retirement, family leave, health insurance, welfare reform, and pay equity. In 1994 Hartmann received a MacArthur "genius" fellowship award for her advocacy of gender equity.

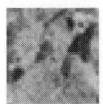 # Political Practice

The capacity of social workers to reassert their role in social welfare policy depends on the willingness of individuals to consider public office as a setting for social work practice. Although many welfare pioneers began their careers advocating for social welfare policy and then assumed administrative positions managing social programs, others used elected office to advance social reform. The first woman elected to the House of Representatives was Jeannette Rankin, who won a seat in 1916 running as a Republican in Montana. As a social worker who had studied under Frances Perkins, Rankin voted for early social welfare legislation and against military expansion. More recently, social workers in **political practice** have included Maryann Mahaffey, a member of the Detroit City Council, and Ruth Messinger, a former member of the New York City Council.

By 2001, six social workers had attained national office:

> Edolphus "Ed" Towns received his Master of Social Work degree in 1973. Elected as a Democratic state committeeman and then as the first African American deputy borough president in Brooklyn's history,

Towns was elected in 1982, with 90 percent of the vote, to serve in Congress as the representative of the 11th Congressional District of New York. Towns's work on congressional committees overseeing government operations, public works, and narcotics directly addresses the primary concerns of his inner-city constituents.[59]

Barbara Mikulski received her M.S.W. degree in 1965 and then served on the Baltimore City Council and in the U.S. House of Representatives. In 1986 Mikulski became the first Democratic woman to be elected to the U.S. Senate in her own right. Through appointments to the powerful Appropriations and Labor and Human Resources Committees, Mikulski is well positioned to advocate programs in health and social services.[60]

Debbie Stabenow was awarded her M.S.W. from Michigan State University, after which she was elected to the Ingham County Commission, the Michigan House, and the Michigan Senate. In 1996 Stabenow ran to represent the 8th Congressional District of Michigan on a platform opposing the extremes of the Republican Congress elected in 1994. Having won election to the House of Representatives, in 1999 Stabenow challenged an incumbent to become the second social worker to be elected to the U.S. Senate in her own right.

Before his election to the House of Representatives in 1997, Ciro Rodriquez earned his M.S.W. from Our Lady of the Lake University. Subsequently, he was elected to the Harlandale, Texas, school board and the Texas House of Representatives. Congressman Rodriquez currently serves on the House Armed Services and Veterans' Affairs Committees as well as on the Congressional Hispanic Caucus.

Barbara Lee was elected in 1998 to fill the House seat of Ron Dellums, a social worker on whose staff she had served. Lee received her M.S.W. from the University of California, Berkeley, and established a

Edolphus "Ed" Towns

Barbara Mikulski

Barbara Lee

Susan Davis

community mental health center while completing her graduate studies. Subsequently she was elected to the California State Senate. Congresswoman Lee now serves on the House Committee on Banking and Financial Services and on the House Committee on International Relations, the Congressional Progressive Caucus, the Congressional Black Caucus, and the Congressional Women's Caucus.

In 2000 Susan Davis defeated an incumbent to represent California's 49th Congressional District. Davis received her graduate degree in social services from the University of North Carolina in 1968; she subsequently moved to San Diego, where she chaired the school board. As a new member of Congress, Davis attained a coveted seat on the Armed Services Committee. Among here primary concerns are education and campaign finance reform.

Conclusion

Perhaps the best indicator of social work's potential future influence on social policy appears at the local level. For example, social workers have lobbied successfully on behalf of nonprofit agencies facing threats to their tax-exempt status,[61] encouraged students to engage in election campaigns and to become more knowledgeable about politics,[62] and managed a campaign for the election of a state senator.[63] In each of these instances, social workers were gaining the kind of experience that is essential to political involvement at higher levels. By 2000 such activity was paying off: More than 200 social workers had been elected to state, county, municipal, and judicial offices. In response to increasing political activity at the state level, social work professor Robert Schneider established the collaborative organization of Influencing State Policy in order to empower human service professionals.[64]

Social workers disinclined to engage in high-visibility activities such as campaigning for public office could make their imprint on politics through legislators' "constituent services." Writing of new developments in Congress, Pulitzer Prize–winning journalist Hedrick Smith observed that members of Congress are increasingly relying on constituent services in place of pork barrel projects as domestic expenditures dry up. Using a term familiar to most social workers, politicians call constituent services "casework"; that is, "having your staff track down missing Social Security checks, inquire about sons and husbands in the armed services, help veterans get medical care, pursue applications for small-business loans."[65] The importance of political "casework" has been noted by political scientists, who attribute up to 5 percent of the vote to such activities, a significant amount in close elections. David Himes of the National Republican Congressional Committee claimed that "our surveys have shown that constituency service, especially in the House, is more important than issues."[66]

The cultivation of practice skills in the political arena at the local level offers perhaps the most promising way for social workers to regain influence in social welfare policy. Such activity can be undertaken by virtually any professional interested in the opportunity. On a volunteer basis, social workers would find few politicians who would turn down their professional assistance in the provision of constituent services. With experience, enterprising social workers might find that political practice could be remunerative, providing that they possessed skills needed by elected officials—such as conducting surveys, maintaining data banks of contributors, organizing public meetings, and keeping current on legislation important to constituents. From another perspective, however, the prospect of political practice should be taken seriously indeed. If social workers are sincere about making essential resources available to their clients—a responsibility stated in the NASW Code of Ethics—then some form of political practice is a professional obligation. "To do less," noted Maryann Mahaffey, "to avoid the political action necessary to provide these resources, is to fail to live up to the profession's code of ethical practice."[67]

Discussion Questions

1. Using a critical approach to welfare policy, select a social welfare program and identify the primary interests that are involved in its creation. To what extent do clients of the program influence the program? To what extent do social workers influence the program? Are there assumptions built into the program that are inconsistent with the assumptions of the clients or social workers who are involved in it? To what extent have classism, racism, sexism, and ageism influenced health and human service programs of interest to you?

2. Politicians elected to the U.S. Congress can be reached through the capitol switchboard: (202) 224–3121. Contact your elected representative and one of your two senators and determine which health and human service committee assignments they have. Do your representatives have committee assignments that could make them influential on issues important to you? Do your representatives have position statements available to constituents about specific social programs?

3. Politicians elected to your state legislature have responsibilities similar to those of congresspeople. Identify your state representatives. Do they have assignments on health and human service committees? Do they have position statements they could send to you on health and human service issues?

4. Select a legislative proposal in a health and human service area of concern to you and follow it through the national or state legislature. Which committees and interest groups supported or fought the proposed legislation? How was the bill changed to make it more acceptable to special interests? Have local interests, such as a major newspaper, endorsed or objected to the proposed legislation? Why?

5. Does your state chapter of the National Association of Social Workers make legislation a high priority for the professional community? What are the legislative goals of the state NASW chapter? How are those goals reflected in the resources allocated? How would you prioritize health and human services in your community?

6. If non–decision making leaves many clients of social programs impotent in the public policy process, how could these people be made more influential? How could the local professional community assist in empowering beneficiaries of social programs? What could you do?

7. Identify social workers who serve in local elected offices. What led them to pursue elective office? What are their future political plans? Could you provide constituent services for these persons or help with their reelection?

 # Notes

1. U.S. Congress, *U.S. Congress Handbook 1992* (McLean, VA: Barbara Pullen, 1992), p. 184.
2. *Robert's Rules of Order* is available from several publishers.
3. The latest annual edition of *Overview of Entitlement Programs* can be obtained through the Government Printing Office in Washington, DC.
4. Charles Lindblom and David Braybrooke, *Strategy of Decision* (New York: Free Press, 1970).
5. Amitai Etzioni, *The Active Society* (New York: Free Press, 1968), pp. 282–288.

6. For a description of these forms of rationality, see Robert Alford, "Health Care Politics," *Politics and Society* 2 (Winter 1972), pp. 127–164.

7. Neil Gilbert and Harry Specht, *Dimensions of Social Welfare Policy* (Englewood Cliffs, NJ: Prentice-Hall, 1986), pp. 206–210.

8. "Nuking Employee Benefits," *Wall Street Journal* (August 29, 1988), p. 16.

9. For example, see Harry Hatry, *A Review of Private Approaches for Delivery of Public Services* (Washington, DC: Urban Institute, 1983).

10. David Stoesz, *A Poverty of Imagination* (Madison, WI: University of Wisconsin Press, 2000).

11. Even Marx, who used a two-part classification, conceded the existence of a *"Lumpenproletariat"* (an uneducated underclass), although he did little to develop the concept.

12. Dexter Dunphy, *The Primary Group* (New York: Appleton-Century-Crofts, 1972), pp. 42–44.

13. Charles Peters, *How Washington Really Works*, rev. ed. (Reading, MA: Addison-Wesley, 1983), p. 112.

14. See, for example, Sheldon Danziger and Daniel Weinberg, *Fighting Poverty* (Cambridge, MA: Harvard University Press, 1986).

15. Peters, *How Washington Really Works*, pp. 101–102, 116.

16. Hedrick Smith, *The Power Game: How Washington Works* (New York: Random House, 1988), p. 152.

17. David Stoesz, "Policy Gambit: Conservative Think Tanks Take On the Welfare State," *Journal of Sociology and Social Welfare* 16 (1989), pp. 8–16.

18. David Stoesz, "The New Welfare Policy Institutes," unpublished manuscript, San Diego State University School of Social Work, 1988.

19. Peters, *How Washington Really Works*, p. 114.

20. Smith, *The Power Game*, p. 24.

21. *Congress at Your Fingertips* (McLean, VA: Capitol Advantage, 1996).

22. First established in 1944, PACs are political organizations that are regulated by federal law: individual candidate contributions are limited to $5,000 per election, contributions to other PACs are restricted to $5,000 annually, and funding of national party committees cannot exceed $15,000 annually. Because of these restrictions, "soft money"—contributions outside the prohibitions of the Federal Election Campaign Act—has become more prominent in federal elections.

23. "15-month Fundraising Figures of Major Parties Detailed" (Washington, DC: Federal Election Commission, June 5, 2000), p. 1.

24. "Overall Campaign Finance Statistics" (Washington, DC: Common Cause, June, 11, 1999).

25. Ruth Marcus and Mike Allen, "Democrats' Donations from Labor Up Sharply," *Washington Post* (July 17, 2000), p. A1.

26. Ken Auletta, "Pay Per Views," *The New Yorker* (June 5, 1995), p. 56.

27. Nancy Gibbs, "Where Power Goes . . . " *Time* (July 17, 1995), p. 21.

28. Smith, *The Power Game*, p. 254.

29. Interview with Toby Weismiller, NASW, Washington, DC, January 11, 1988.

30. Personal communication with Dave Dempsey, NASW, Washington, DC, July 21, 2000.

31. Albert O. Hirschman, *Shifting Involvements* (Princeton, NJ: Princeton University Press, 1982), p. 132.

32. Peters, *How Washington Really Works*, p. 111.

33. Peter Bachrach and Morton S. Baratz, *Power and Poverty* (New York: Oxford University Press, 1979), p. 7.

34. For a review of the CAP experience, see Daniel Patrick Moynihan, *Maximum Feasible Misunderstanding* (New York: Random House, 1973).

35. Dan Bloom and Kay Sherwood, *Matching Opportunities to Obligations: Lessons for Child Support Reform from the Parents' Fair Share Pilot Phase* (New York: Manpower Demonstration Research Corporation, 1994).

36. Janet Quint, Denise Polit, Hans Bos, and George Cave, *New Chance: Interim Findings on a Comprehensive Program for Disadvantaged Young Mothers and Their Children* (New York: Manpower Demonstration Research Corporation, 1994).

37. Michael Lipsky, "Bureaucratic Disentitlement in Social Welfare Programs," *Social Service Review* 33, no. 4 (March 1984), pp. 81–88.

38. Quoted in Robert Kuttner, *The Economic Illusion* (Boston: Houghton Mifflin, 1984), p. 86.

39. Ellen Dunbar, "Future of Social Work," *NASW California News* 13, no. 18 (May 1987), p. 3.

40. Harris Chaiklin, "The New Homeless and Service Planning on a Professional Campus"

(University of Maryland, Chancellor's Colloquium, Baltimore, December 4, 1985), p. 7.

41. "Willie's Vision for Chicano Empowerment," *Southwest Voter Research Notes* 2, no.3 (June 1988), pp. 1.

42. Dale Russakoff, "Cut Out of Prosperity, Cutting Out at the Polls," *Washington Post* (October 24, 2000), p. A12.

43. "Deconstructing Distrust," The Pew Research Center. Retrieved 2000 from the World Wide Web: http://www.people-press.org/trustrpt.htm

44. David Broder, "The 30 Million Missing Voters," *Washington Post* (July 16, 2000), p. B7.

45. Maryann Mahaffey, "Political Action in Social Work," *Encyclopedia of Social Work,* 18th ed. (Silver Spring, MD: NASW, 1987), p. 290.

46. Allen Davis, "Settlement Workers in Politics, 1890–1914," in Maryann Mahaffey and John Hanks (eds.), *Practical Politics: Social Work and Political Responsibility* (Silver Spring, MD: NASW, 1982), p. 32.

47. Allen F. Davis, *American Heroine: The Life and Legend of Jane Addams* (New York: Oxford University Press, 1973), p. 292.

48. Biographical information from *Encyclopedia of Social Work,* 18th ed. (Silver Spring, MD: NASW, 1987).

49. Richard Bernstein, "John Dewey," in Paul Edwards (ed.), *Encyclopedia of Philosophy,* Vol. 2, (New York: Macmillan and Free Press, 1967), p. 380.

50. Mahaffey, "Political Action in Social Work," p. 286.

51. John Hope Franklin, *From Slavery to Freedom* (New York: Knopf, 1979), pp. 319–321.

52. Ibid., pp. 471–472.

53. Charles Schottland, "Wilbur Joseph Cohen: Some Recollections," *Social Work* 32, no. 5 (September–October 1987), pp. 371–372.

54. June Hopps, "Reclaiming Leadership," *Social Work* 31 (September–October 1986), p. 323.

55. Eleanor Brilliant, "Social Work Leadership: A Missing Ingredient?" *Social Work* 31 (September–October 1986), p. 328.

56. For details on CDF see Joanna Biggar, "The Protector," *Washington Post Magazine* (May 18, 1986), p. C4, and *The Children's Defense Fund Annual Report 1984–85* (Washington, DC: Children's Defense Fund, 1985).

57. Information on CBPP was obtained from an interview with David Kahan at CBPP on March 12, 1984.

58. *1998 Annual Report* (Washington, DC: Economic Policy Institute, 1998).

59. Biographical sketch courtesy of Congressman Ed Towns's office, n.d.

60. Biographical sketch courtesy of Senator Barbara Mikulski's office, n.d.

61. Elliot Pagliaccio and Burton Gummer, "Casework and Congress: A Lobbying Strategy," *Social Casework* 69 (March 1988), pp. 321–330.

62. Grafton Hull, "Joining Together: A Faculty–Student Experience in Political Campaigning," *Journal of Social Work Education* 23 (Fall 1987), pp. 116–123.

63. William Whittaker and Jan Flory-Baker, "Ragtag Social Workers Take On the Good Old Boys and Elect a State Senator," in Maryann Mahaffey and John Hanks, *Practical Politics.*

64. For details contact the ISP website: http://www.statepolicy.org/

65. Hedrick Smith, *The Power Game* (New York: Random House, 1988), p. 124.

66. Ibid., p. 152.

67. See Mahaffey and Hanks, *Practical Politics,* Chapter 10, "Political Action in Social Work," p. 284.

chapter 9

Tax Policy and Income Distribution

Form **1040** — U. S. Individual Income Tax Return (2000)

Tax policy, the use of legislation to define how revenues are generated in order to achieve social objectives, is fundamental to the structure of social welfare in the United States. Although tax policy is an instrument of government, its influence is not limited solely to federal and state programs: Through "tax expenditures," or areas exempted from taxation, tax policy provides significant incentives not only for specific industries, as in "corporate welfare," but also for individual behavior, as in the mortgage interest deduction. Tax policy is of increasing interest to advocates of social justice. As support for direct benefits through traditional social programs has waned, social advocates have turned to "targeted tax expenditures"—preferably, refundable tax credits—as a means to advance economic justice. As a vehicle for funding social programs, tax policy is also an important barometer for social equity; and indeed, policy analysts have long used income distribution as an indicator of how fair the economy has been for various groups.

 ## History of U.S. Tax Policy

All governments levy taxes to meet their legislated obligations. Because taxation appropriates income from private parties—individuals and corporations—and puts it to public use, it has been controversial, and at times volatile. Ever since the establishment of the republic, various groups have objected to government taxation, challenging the authority to appropriate private property. Such challenges have been usually sorted out through the courts; but on occasion they have led to violent armed confrontations, as in the Whiskey Rebellion that divided the nation shortly after its creation. Although tax policy has traditionally been of professional interest primarily to the green-eyeshade accountants at the Internal Revenue Service, right-wing militias also have a keen interest in it, because they recognize that tax money is the lifeblood that allows government to function.

Ever since the creation of the welfare state with passage of the Social Security Act of 1935, social program expenditures have grown; and all these programs have been paid for by increasing taxes. The optimal welfare state, as liberals conceived it, would provide essential benefits as a right of citizenship. These benefits would be funded by progressive taxes—taxes that derived their revenues disproportionately from the wealthy. Implicit in this vision was the political calculus that was captured by Harry Hopkins, whose synopsis has become part of welfare folklore: "Tax, tax; spend, spend; elect, elect!" For half a century, this strategy produced solid electoral support for liberal social programs: The wealthy were taxed at higher rates, the revenues were diverted to social benefits for the middle and working classes through social programs, and social program beneficiaries expressed their gratitude by voting Democratic. Ultimately, however, liberal Democratic hegemony in social policy foundered on the shoals of its own success. As working families rose into the middle class, they tended to individualize their achievements, discounting the role of social programs and, in the process, becoming more receptive to conservative proposals to reduce social programs and their tax burden. By the 1980s this scenario led to the election of Ronald Reagan, who had a visceral dislike for federal social programs. The Reagan presidency was revolutionary in several respects, one being profound changes in tax policy.

As a creation of the legislative process, tax policy is most visible in the passage of major bills. Over time these become the basis of the state and federal tax codes, those notoriously confounding labyrinths of accounting rules. Periodically, attempts to reform tax policy emerge, such as the 1986 federal tax reform, which simplified the tax code and eliminated—at least temporarily—provisions for special interests. Indeed, the lobbying around deletion of special tax provisions was so intense that the 1986 tax reform became known as the "showdown at Gucci gulch," after the impeccable dress of the professionals populating the lobbying firms on Washington's K Street.

As this overview suggests, tax policy is dense and at the same time dynamic. Historically, three tax policies have been central to U.S. social policy: the income tax, the withholding tax, and the earned income tax credit.

■ The federal income tax was instituted after approval of the Sixteenth Amendment to the Constitution in 1914. A *progressive tax,* in that the wealthy were taxed at a higher rate, the income tax was initially levied on less than 1 percent of the population and had a top rate of only 7 percent. Today the income tax has five brackets (down from 14 before the 1986 tax reform): 15, 28, 36, 39.6 and 42+ percent. Because a threshold on taxable income has been set, low-income families are exempt from paying the federal income tax.[1]

■ The Social Security withholding tax was established in 1935. For employed workers, the withholding tax was initially set at 2 percent of the first $3,000 in wages; paid equally between employers and workers. Since then Social Security withholding has increased and is now 15.3 percent of the first $68,400 in wages;, the wage cap was established at the outset, under the presumption that Social Security was a public pension plan for workers who would not have recourse to retirement provisions available to the wealthy.[2] The withholding tax is a *regressive tax,* in that lower-income workers pay the same rate as higher-wage employees. Most taxpayers now pay more in Social Security withholding than they do in income taxes.

■ The **earned income tax credit (EITC)** was enacted in 1975 after the failure of a "negative income tax" plan advanced by the Nixon administration. A *refundable tax credit,* the EITC instructs the IRS to send a check to low-wage workers, especially those with children, who have earned income below a certain level. In 1997, for example, a worker with two children could receive a maximum refund of $3,656.[3]

Since the creation of the EITC, other tax credits have been introduced: A child care tax credit allows low-wage workers to deduct the costs of day care, and several states have introduced tax credits for low-income workers, some of which are refundable.

The income tax, Social Security withholding, and the EITC have been primary elements in federal tax policy, but they should not be assumed to be the *sine qua non* of tax policy with respect to social programs. When Maryland advocates of domestic violence prevention were faced with an abrupt reduction in funding from the state in the 1980s, for example, they resorted to a clever solution: associating domestic violence with marriage, they convinced legislators to approve an addition to the marriage license fee—a tax whose additional proceeds would be diverted to services for victims of domestic violence.

Tax provisions fund social programs that exist within an economy that is also shaped by economic policy; thus, economic policy, through tax policy, influences social programs. A classic example was the conservative enthusiasm about "supply-side economics" during the 1980s. As advocated by Arthur Laffer, optimal economic policy would consist of minimal taxation, so as not to impede capital formation and expansion. Given the relatively higher tax rates that preceded his presidency, Ronald Reagan endorsed tax reform that incorporated a one-third cut in the income tax, assuming that the cut would reinvigorate a sluggish economy.[4] But although the tax cut of 1981 jolted the economy out of recession, it also cut off tax revenues to the Treasury, which then had to sell bonds to service the federal debt. Soon the federal government plunged further into debt, the depth of which was unprecedented for peacetime. By 1983 the annual deficit was $207 billion, 6.3 percent of **gross national product,** and growing. Debt service on government bonds grew commensurately, so that by the end of the 1980s, annual interest payments on the debt were $150 billion, the second largest item in the federal budget.[5]

Annual debt service overshadowed domestic policy discussions during the early 1990s. The congressional response was to impose a cap on domestic spending, an effort to stem the hemorrhaging of cash leaving the Treasury during a period when inflowing revenues had been stemmed by tax cuts. Liberal Democrats insisted that entitlement spending for social programs be exempt from the spending cap, with the result that federal budget decisions subsequently penalized discretionary programs disproportionately. Thus, several years after a sharp cut in federal taxes, the effects took the form of pressure to cut discretionary programs, from highway construction to space exploration to student loans.

Looming federal deficits cast a pall over the incoming Clinton administration. After campaigning on a platform that emphasized investments in human capital, President Clinton was confronted with the massive deficits left over from the Reagan and Bush administrations. Clinton's nascent liberal tendencies, evident in his support for public works and national health insurance, were redirected by Alan Greenspan, chair of the Federal Reserve. Greenspan argued that the economy in general, and financial markets in particular, would respond negatively to new social programs that carried high price tags, because such programs would either (1) worsen the federal debt or (2) require significant tax increases. Although Clinton balked at Greenspan's position, economic reality was making short work of the new president's campaign rhetoric. Cornered between forces that advocated social investments and groups demanding deficit reduction, Clinton blew up during a staff meeting, as Bob Woodward recounted in *The Agenda*:

> *"Where are all the Democrats?" Clinton bellowed. "I hope you're all aware we're all Eisenhower Republicans," he said, his voice dripping with sarcasm. "We're Eisenhower Republicans here, and we are fighting the Reagan Republicans. We stand for lower deficits and free trade and the bond market. Isn't that great?"*
>
> *The room was silent once more.*
>
> *He erupted again, his voice severe and loud, "I don't have a goddamn Democratic budget until 1996. None of the investments, none of the things I campaigned on."*[6]

Capitulating to Greenspan's insistence on deficit reduction, Clinton put his social investment plans on hold, a decision that contributed to an unprecedented economic expansion that promised to make possible the eventual elimination of the federal debt by generating a surplus projected at $2 *trillion* over 10 years.

Tax Policy and Special Interests

Tax policy has always contained provisions that benefit specific interests. Bending the tax code in response to lobbying is a long-standing practice in the United States, though today it is most often associated with corporate influence. Actually, the exclusion of pension plans from taxation began in 1921, and these provisions have been updated to include provisions such as Individual Retirement Accounts. Tax expenditures that benefit individuals have now grown to the point that they exceed allocations for many prominent social welfare programs. In 2000, for example, tax expenditures for pension contributions were $348.0 billion, for health insurance $272.7 billion, and for mortgage interest deductions $181.0 billion. By comparison, allocations for Supplemental Security Income were $28.3 billion in 1996, Medicaid $184 billion in 1998, and federal housing programs $26.1 billion in 1997. Even the largest tax credits available for low-income tax payers for 2000 are dwarfed by middle-class tax expenditures: The EITC costs $24.4 billion, child care $20.4 billion, and housing $3.9 billion.[7]

Realizing that the tax code can be manipulated to serve the interests of the affluent, many social justice advocates have targeted "corporate welfare," or the special provisions directed at specific industries, for reform. By the late 1990s corporate welfare had reached such proportions—varying from $87 billion to $150 billion annually, depending on who did the counting—that even prominent Republicans were calling for tax reform. John Kasich, for example, identified a dozen programs for elimination:

- Rural Utilities Services, which subsidizes loans in rural areas: $190 million
- Market Access Program, which facilitates the export of food and wine: $347 million
- Animas–La Plata Project, which diverts water to irrigate farmland: $432 million
- Pyroprocessing Program, which creates new energy from spent nuclear fuel: $100 million
- Appalachian Regional Commission, which builds roads in 13 states: $500 million
- Fossil Energy Research and Development, which encourages new technology for fossil fuels: $1.37 billion
- Timber Roads, which builds roads in remote areas: $100 million
- Clean Coal Technology, which endeavors to lower coal emissions: $500 million
- Overseas Private Investment Corporation, which provides loans to firms investing abroad: $281 million
- General Agreements to Borrow, which funds the International Monetary Fund to avert economic emergencies: $3.5 billion
- Enhanced Structural Adjustment Facility, which aids developing countries: $150 million
- Highway Demonstration Projects, which improves roads as requested by individual lawmakers: $4 billion[8]

Even this list, partial as it is, might rankle many taxpayers; but efforts at downsizing corporate welfare have proved disappointing. As long as there is pork in politics, there is the opportunity to customize tax policy to serve the concerns of individual legislators—who, after all, are often influenced by constituent requests. Thus, tax policy is crafted both to meet the Appalachian Regional Commission's need for roads and to respond to Sonoma Valley vintners' desire to export their products to France.

Tax law also has a significant influence, directly and indirectly, on the revenues of nonprofit organizations. By allowing taxpayers to deduct charitable contributions from taxable income, tax law directly encourages support of philanthropy. Lower tax rates work indirectly, at least in theory, by leaving taxpayers with more discretionary income and assets that they may then donate to nonprofit causes. Comparatively, policy analysts are more confident about the effectiveness of direct support through tax deductions than about indirect support via lower taxation. In 1981, for example, taxpayers who did not itemize their tax deductions were allowed to deduct contributions to nonprofit organizations; at the same time significant reductions in income and estate taxes were instituted. In 1986 legislation removed the deduction for charitable contributions on the part of nonitemizers; concurrently, income and corporate tax rates were reduced sharply, although many tax shelters were also eliminated. The effects on charitable giving proved ambiguous. The disallowal of charitable contributions by nonitemizers affected primarily blue-collar and middle-income families, the families that account for most of the revenues of nonprofit agencies. As a result, charitable contributions by this group of households have declined continuously since 1989. In 1990 tax policy changed the amount of the charitable deduction available to wealthier families, limiting the amount that could be deducted to no more than 3 percent of income for those earning more than $100,000 annually. Thus, incentives for charitable contributions for more affluent families were also diminished. As a result, charitable contributions by itemizers remained relatively constant through the mid-1990s.[9] Yet the charitable impulse of Americans has continued despite changes in tax policy. "Giving as a percent of income has remained remarkably constant in the face of increases in the cost of giving," concluded tax policy analysts.[10]

As discussed in Chapter 6, the story on charitable giving as a function of tax reduction is less unilinear than conservatives might wish. The idea is that as taxes on individual and corporate income are lowered, private wealth increases, creating a larger pool of resources against which nonprofits can lay claim. This, of course, is a mantra that conservatives have chanted since the

1980s—indeed, to the point that some ideologues have proposed that private charity actually replace government activity in social welfare. Deep tax cuts introduced during the 1980s significantly reduced federal social welfare funding; and indeed, until the early 1990s, these were made up for by increases in charitable giving. During the 1990s, however, although both private giving and federal support of nonprofits increased significantly, these sources never compensated for the total revenue losses attributed to direct federal funding cuts.

 # Federal Tax Policy

Tax policy is integral to a president's proposed budget, which identifies not only the expected sources of revenues but also allocations. President Clinton's proposed 2001 budget identified the basic budget categories as follows:[11]

Clinton Proposed Budget for 2001 (in cents per dollar)

TAX REVENUES		PROGRAM EXPENDITURES	
Individual income taxes	$.48	Social Security	$.23
Withholding taxes	.34	Nonmilitary discretionary	.19
Corporate income taxes	.10	Defense	.16
		Medicare	.12
Excise taxes	.04	Nonhealth entitlements	.12
Other	.04	Interest	.11
		Medicaid	.07

Within his proposed $1.84 *trillion* budget, Clinton inserted a $351 billion tax cut over 10 years, as much to assist Vice President Al Gore's presidential campaign as to respond to the more massive tax cut, $1.3 trillion over 10 years, proposed by Republican presidential candidate George W. Bush.[12]

Despite the mammoth size of the federal budget of the United States, it is predicated on a tax base that is minimal compared to those of other industrialized nations. As Table 9.1 shows, not only was the 1995 tax burden of the United States the lowest among industrialized nations; the rate of increase during the preceding three decades was also the lowest.

The relatively low tax rate of the United States largely accounts for the nation's skewed **income distribution.** A tenet of the welfare state has been the progressive taxation of wealth and its redistribution to the poor through social programs. By definition, a welfare state with a low tax rate is unable to generate revenues sufficient to level the differences between rich and poor; thus, the question of income distribution has become integral to the discussion of tax policy. Traditionally, income distribution is calibrated by quintiles, or 20 percent intervals in population; Table 9.2 provides an overview of income distribution in the United States.

During the 1980s and 1990s, the income of the top quintile increased significantly; there was a slight increase in the fourth quintile, but income decreases for the bottom three, a loss particularly striking for the lowest quintile. Despite the lost income for the lowest quintiles, their federal tax rates dropped, most notably during the 1990s. As a result of these factors, the share of family income has changed; the top quintile now claims 54 percent of family income, a sizable increase over 20 years, and that of the lowest quintile has actually declined to only 3 percent. Yet the higher incomes of the top quintile, combined with increasing taxes, have meant that their share of total federal taxes paid increased substantially, rising to 65 percent, while the tax burden of the lowest quintile fell to 1 percent. Table 9.2 is based on pretax income, and the income distribution of after-tax income presents a somewhat different portrait, generally benefiting lower quintiles. Equally important, post–social program benefit income distribution favors lower quintiles even more, as they are the beneficiaries of public assistance as well as the EITC.

As might be suspected, the figures in Table 9.2 provide ample ammunition for ideologues. Liberals are quite correct in noting a deteriorating income distribution with respect to the poorest quintile, which has lost a substantial

TABLE 9.1 ■ Tax Revenue of OECD* Countries as a Percentage of GDP

RANK	COUNTRY	1965	1995	1965–1995 CHANGE
1	Denmark	29.9%	51.3%	21.4%
2	Sweden	35.0	49.7	14.7
3	Belgium	31.2	46.5	15.3
4	Finland	30.3	46.5	16.2
5	France	34.5	44.5	10.0
6	Netherlands	32.8	44.0	11.2
7	Austria	34.7	42.4	7.7
8	Norway	29.6	41.5	11.9
9	Italy	25.5	41.3	15.8
10	Germany	31.6	39.2	7.6
11	New Zealand	24.7	38.2	13.5
12	Canada	25.9	37.2	11.3
13	United Kingdom	30.4	35.3	4.9
14	Spain	14.7	34.0	19.3
15	Switzerland	20.7	33.9	13.2
16	Ireland	25.9	33.8	7.9
17	Portugal	16.2	33.8	17.6
18	Australia	23.2	30.9	7.7
19	Japan	18.3	28.5	10.2
20	United States	24.3	27.9	3.6

*Organization for Economic Cooperation and Development

Source: Adapted from Lawrence Mishel, Jared Bernstein, and John Schmitt, *The State of Working America, 1998–99* (Washington, DC: Economic Policy Institute, 1999), p. 93.

portion of its income during a period when the wealthiest quintile has prospered. As Figure 9.1 demonstrates, since 1977 the wealthiest 1 percent of the population has claimed a significant increase in after-tax income, whereas the lowest quintile has lost almost 10 percent. Conservatives, on the other hand, have validly argued that the wealthiest quintile has been bearing an increasing share of the tax burden while that of all other quintiles has dropped. These differences show how ideologically volatile tax policy can become.

Income is only one component of wealth; another measure of affluence is assets. Al-though considered in discussions of social policy less often than income, assets are important insofar as they are an indication of real wealth. Consisting of savings, real estate, stocks and bonds, and related property, assets not only can be liquidated during periods of adversity, thus offering the owner a buffer against poverty, but also appreciate in value, thus generating additional wealth. The distribution and changes in wealth are depicted in Table 9.3. As that table shows, the distribution of assets is even more skewed than income distribution, with the highest quintile owning more than 80 percent. By contrast, the wealth of the lowest quintile is

TABLE 9.2 ■ Effective Tax Rates by Income Category, 1979–1999*

Income Quintile	AVERAGE PRETAX FAMILY INCOME IN 1995 DOLLARS					
	1979	1983	1987	1991	1995	1999
Highest	$98,300	$99,500	$113,000	$111,000	$120,000	$132,000
Fourth	50,400	48,000	51,100	49,300	49,600	53,000
Middle	36,200	32,800	34,900	33,600	33,300	35,400
Second	23,200	19,800	21,600	20,600	20,100	21,200
Lowest	9,600	8,100	8,700	8,400	8,100	8,400
All	$43,500	$42,000	$45,800	$44,600	$45,700	$49,500
	EFFECTIVE TOTAL FEDERAL TAX RATES IN PERCENTAGES					
Highest	28.5%	24.6%	26.4%	26.2%	29.6%	29.1%
Fourth	22.1	21.0	21.2	21.6	22.5	22.2
Middle	19.2	18.2	18.5	18.9	19.7	18.9
Second	14.9	14.2	15.2	15.1	14.6	13.7
Lowest	8.4	8.5	9.0	7.9	6.0	4.6
All	23.4%	21.4%	22.6%	22.6%	24.7%	24.2%
	SHARES OF FAMILY INCOME					
Highest	48%	50%	51%	51%	53%	54%
Fourth	22	22	22	22	21	21
Middle	15	15	15	15	14	14
Second	10	9	9	9	9	9
Lowest	5	4	4	4	3	3
	SHARES OF TOTAL FEDERAL TAXES					
Highest	58%	58%	60%	60%	64%	65%
Fourth	21	22	21	21	19	19
Middle	13	13	12	12	11	11
Second	7	6	6	6	5	5
Lowest	2	1	2	1	1	1

*1999 figures are estimated.

Source: Adapted from "Preliminary Estimates of Effective Tax Rates" (Washington, DC: Congressional Budget Office, September 7, 1999).

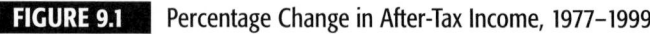

FIGURE 9.1   Percentage Change in After-Tax Income, 1977–1999

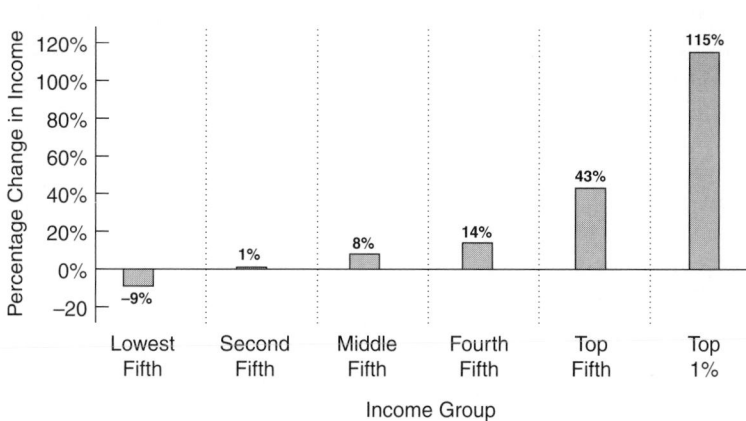

Source: CBPP Analysis of CBO Data. 1999 data are projections.

TABLE 9.3 ■ Changes in Distribution of Wealth, 1962–1997*

Quintile	SHARE OF WEALTH					CHANGE			
	1962	1983	1989	1995	1997	1962–83	1983–89	1989–95	1989–97
Highest	81.0%	81.3%	83.5%	83.7%	84.3%	0.4%	2.2%	0.2%	0.8%
Fourth	13.4	12.6	12.3	11.5	10.8	−0.8	−0.2	−0.8	−1.5
Middle	5.4	5.2	4.8	4.5	4.4	−0.2	−0.4	−0.3	−0.4
Second	0.9	1.2	0.8	0.9	1.0	0.2	−0.3	0.0	0.1
Lowest	−0.7	−0.3	−1.5	−0.7	−0.5	0.4	−1.2	0.8	1.0

*1997 figures are estimated.

Source: Adapted from Lawrence Mishel, Jared Bernstein, and John Schmitt, *The State of Working America, 1998–99* (Washington, DC: Economic Policy Institue, 1999), p. 93.

negative, indicative of debt. As has been the case with income, the distribution of assets has become more skewed during recent decades, the wealthiest quintile controlling more wealth with the lowest remaining in debt. And as with income, the distribution of assets is relatively constant; moderate changes occur, but the distribution pattern remains essentially the same over time. Consider the period following the Great Society efforts of the mid-1960s: Despite a major expansion of social programs for the poor, the lowest quintile still showed negative wealth, remaining mired in debt.

Ownership of assets varies with race and ethnicity. Non-Hispanic whites own disproportionately more than African Americans and Hispanics; conversely, minorities of color experience more debt. Thus, 25 percent of Anglos report sufficient assets to survive at the poverty level, but only 54 percent of Hispanics and 61 percent of African Americans claim such wealth.[13] The capacity to acquire wealth is influenced by tax policy, although changes in wealth are dependent on specific tax legislation. For example, the prosperity of African Americans fluctuated rather significantly between 1983 and 1995, as shown in Table 9.4.

Although discussions of the income and wealth of minorities frequently focus on issues related to poverty, they are equally informative with respect to affluence. For example, 85.2 percent of African Americans with incomes above $75,000 own stock, virtually the same proportion as for Anglos with the same income (86.4 percent); yet the value of stocks owned by this stratum of African Americans is less than one-fourth that of Anglos' portfolios.[14]

State Tax Policy and the Poor

Federal taxes are important in social welfare policy because they subsidize the major social entitlements, but states also levy taxes in order to meet their legislative obligations. Historically, states have held major responsibility in social programs, areas such as mental health, child welfare, and corrections; and to a great degree the adequacy of a state's social programs depends on its tax collections. Unlike federal taxation, which is uniform across the nation, state tax policy varies significantly. By way of illustration, consider the income tax. Whereas the federal income tax is uniform nationwide, 42 states have income taxes, but 18 do

not. State income taxes provide general revenues that can be used for a range of social programs, but this is not the only reason that state tax policy is important. State tax policy can exempt low-income families from any tax liability, thus allowing them to keep more of their income. Of states that levy an income tax, the more progressive jurisdictions have exempted families with low incomes. As Table 9.5 shows, not only do states vary with respect to taxing the poor, but their treatment of poor families changes over time.

States can go one step farther in tax policy by establishing a refundable tax credit for low-income tax filers, essentially replicating the federal EITC. Table 9.6 lists the 42 states with income taxes in 1999. Fifteen of these states exempted a single parent with two children and a poverty-level income from any taxation,[15] but 9 states actually paid rebates that lifted the family income beyond its initial level.

The Efficiency of Tax Policy in Reducing Poverty

In the larger context of social policy, tax policy is one of several strategies that apportion societal resources. Within social welfare, more traditional benefits have consisted of social insurance such as Social Security, cash public assistance (means-tested cash benefits) such as Temporary Assistance for Needy Families (TANF), and non-

TABLE 9.4 ■ Wealth of African Americans (1997 dollars)

	1983	1989	1995
Average wealth	$46,000	$48,600	$43,000
Home ownership rate	44.3%	41.7%	46.8%
Households with zero or negative wealth	34.1%	40.7%	31.3%

Source: Adapted from Lawrence Mishel, Jared Bernstein, and John Schmitt, *The State of Working America, 1998–99* (Washington, DC: Economic Policy Institue, 1999), p. 93.

TABLE 9.5 ■ State Income Tax Thresholds Relative to the Poverty Line, 1991–1999

State	THRESHOLDS			CHANGE		
	1991	*1996*	*1999*	*1991–96*	*1996–99*	*1991–99*
Pennsylvania	$9,800	$15,300	$26,000	$5,500	$10,700	$16,200
Massachusetts	12,000	15,500	20,500	3,500	5,000	8,500
Iowa	9,000	16,400	17,300	7,400	900	8,300
Kansas	13,000	13,000	20,900	0	7,900	7,900
Delaware	8,600	12,500	16,100	3,900	3,600	7,500
Georgia	9,000	11,100	15,300	2,100	4,200	6,300
Indiana	4,000	4,000	9,500	0	5,500	5,500
Missouri	8,900	10,000	13,900	1,100	3,900	5,000
New Jersey	5,000	7,500	10,000	2,500	2,500	5,000
Arkansas	10,700	10,700	15,600	0	4,900	4,900
Hawaii	6,300	6,100	11,000	– 200	4,900	4,700
Oregon	10,100	11,400	14,400	1,300	3,000	4,300
North Carolina	13,000	17,000	17,000	4,000	0	4,000
Michigan	8,400	9,600	11,800	1,200	2,200	3,400
Utah	12,200	14,400	15,500	2,200	1,100	3,300
Oklahoma	10,000	11,800	12,700	1,800	900	2,700
Illinois	4,000	4,000	6,600	0	2,600	2,600
Montana	6,600	8,600	9,100	2,000	500	2,500
West Virginia	8,000	10,000	10,000	2,000	0	2,000
Ohio	10,500	11,500	12,300	1,000	800	1,800
Louisiana	11,000	12,300	12,700	1,300	400	1,700
Kentucky	5,000	5,000	5,200	0	200	200
Virginia	8,200	8,200	8,200	0	0	0
Alabama	4,600	4,600	4,600	0	0	0
Average	8,663	10,438	13,175	1,775	2,738	4,513
Poverty Line	13,924	16,036	17,028	2,112	992	3,104

Source: Adapted from Nicholas Johnson, Robert Zahradnik, and Elizabeth McNichol, *State Income Tax Burdens on Low-Income Families in 1999* (Washington, DC: Center on Budget and Policy Priorities, 2000), p. 30.

cash public assistance (means-tested noncash benefits).

As Table 9.7 demonstrates, these different strategies vary in terms of their efficiency in poverty reduction over time. Table 9.7 reveals a traditional truth as well as a noticeable transformation in poverty reduction strategies. The traditional truth is that social insurance—compulsory contributions to social programs like Social Security and Medicare—makes the biggest dent in

TABLE 9.6 ■ State Income Tax for a Single-Parent Family of Three, 1999

RANK	STATE	POVERTY LINE	TAX	RANK	STATE	POVERTY LINE	TAX
1	Alabama	$13,290	$343	19	Delaware	13,290	0
2	Kentucky	13,290	334	19	D.C.	13,290	0
3	Virginia	13,290	265	19	Idaho	13,290	0
4	Hawaii	13,290	262	19	Iowa	13,290	0
5	Illinois	13,290	250	19	Maine	13,290	0
6	Indiana	13,290	248	19	Mississippi	13,290	0
7	West Virginia	13,290	218	19	Nebraska	13,290	0
8	Michigan	13,290	189	19	North Carolina	13,290	0
9	Montana	13,290	171	19	North Dakota	13,290	0
10	New Jersey	13,290	130	19	Pennsylvania	13,290	0
11	Oklahoma	13,290	113	19	Rhode Island	13,290	0
12	Louisiana	13,290	70	19	South Carolina	13,290	0
13	Oregon	13,290	67	34	New Mexico	13,290	−85
14	Ohio	13,290	51	35	Maryland	13,290	−190
15	Georgia	13,290	23	36	Wisconsin	13,290	−257
16	Utah	13,290	17	37	Colorado	13,290	−310
17	Missouri	13,290	16	38	Kansas	13,290	−364
18	Arkansas	13,290	7	38	Massachusetts	13,290	−364
19	Arizona	13,290	0	40	New York	13,290	−697
19	California	13,290	0	41	Minnesota	13,290	−840
19	Connecticut	13,290	0	42	Vermont	13,290	−910

Source: Adapted from Nicholas Johnson, Robert Zahradnik, and Elizabeth McNichol, *State Income Tax Burdens on Low-Income Families in 1999* (Washington, DC: Center on Budget and Policy Priorities, 2000), p. 30.

poverty, more than twice that of public assistance cash and in-kind benefits combined. Note that each of these traditional means of poverty reduction have experienced declining capacities to accelerate the upward mobility of low-income families. Indeed, the efficiency of all traditional cash transfers in reducing poverty appears to have declined from an apogee during the late 1970s.[16] On the other hand, federal tax policy has shifted from actually exacerbating poverty to alleviating destitution, largely by eliminating the income tax on very low incomes and expanding the EITC. The increasing popularity of tax credits, particularly those targeted at low-income families, sug-

gests an expanding role of tax policy as a strategy in poverty policy.

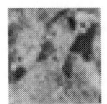 # Tax Expenditures as Poverty Policy

The use of federal tax policy to alleviate poverty and the increase in states' use of tax policy to augment the income of poor families are relatively new features of U.S. social policy. Indeed,

TABLE 9.7 ■ Impact of Safety Net on Poverty Reduction

CATEGORY	1979	1983	1989	1993	1996	1998
Number of poor individuals (in thousands)	43,412	53,187	49,947	60,575	57,476	54,356
Number removed due to						
Social insurance	14,647	15,955	14,939	18,217	17,930	17,588
Means-tested cash benefits	2,693	1,929	2,593	3,093	3,017	2,292
Means-tested in-kind benefits	3,957	3,351	3,912	4,500	4,278	3,976
Federal taxes	−622	−2,010	−1,339	−572	1,734	2,112
Total	20,675	19,225	20,105	25,238	26,959	25,968
Percentage of individuals removed due to						
Social insurance	33.7%	30.0%	29.9%	30.1%	31.2%	32.4%
Means-tested cash benefits	6.2	3.6	5.2	5.1	5.2	4.2
Means-tested in-kind benefits	9.1	6.3	7.8	7.4	7.4	7.3
Federal taxes	−1.4	−3.8	−2.7	−0.9	3.0	3.9
Total	47.6	36.1	40.3	41.7	46.9	47.8
Percentage reduction due to						
Social insurance	6.6%	6.9%	6.0%	7.0%	6.7%	6.5%
Means-tested cash benefits	1.2	0.8	1.0	1.2	1.1	0.8
Means-tested in-kind	1.8	1.4	1.6	1.7	1.6	1.5
Federal taxes	−0.3	−0.9	−0.5	−0.2	0.7	0.8
Total	9.3	8.3	8.1	9.7	10.1	9.6

Source: Adapted from Lynette Rawlings, "Poverty and Income Trends, 1998" (Washington, DC: Center on Budget and Policy Priorities, 2000), p. 105.

the past quarter century has witnessed a significant shift in social welfare policy: Gradually, direct welfare transfers are being augmented with indirect expenditures through tax credits. Although tax expenditures in the form of deductions for families' housing and health insurance costs have been enjoyed by the middle class for more than a half century, it has not been until relatively recently that tax expenditures have been targeted for low-income families. The list of tax credits available to the poor has grown to include credits for earned income, child care, the welfare-to-work transition, care for the elderly and disabled, and adoption expenses. As the number of tax credits targeted to the poor has increased, tax credits have emerged as a contender to replace, at least partially, direct income transfers to aid the poor.

This trend featured prominently in the 2000 presidential campaign, when George W. Bush and Al Gore proposed tax policies that actually competed with respect to benefits to low-income families. As the election came to a close, the presidential candidates pandered to select groups of voters by offering them targeted tax credits. Eventually the targeting mirrored the categorical programming that had become so notorious in public welfare, drawing a sarcastic editorial by Paul Krugman, who figured that Gore's plan was "targeted to a middle-income widow with many children, all about to enter college, who does not receive health insurance from her employer, is enrolled in a training program, drives a fuel-efficient car and is about to inherit a farm."[17]

Although promises of federal tax credits for low-income families were conspicuous during the 2000 presidential campaign, many advocates of social justice had already enjoyed success lobbying state legislatures. Because many state legislatures were controlled by conservatives, a tax credit strategy proved more effective than a traditional appeal for increases in welfare transfers. By 2000 almost a dozen states had complemented the federal EITC with comparable state programs, and several had introduced other tax credits. Notably, Minnesota has enacted a state EITC, a refundable child care credit, a property tax credit for renters, and a subsidized health insurance program. Paul Wilson and Robert Cline note that 27 percent of Minnesotans take advantage of at least one of these programs; the Minnesota array of tax credits thus extends important income and health assistance to families ranging from the welfare poor to the working poor.[18]

As might be expected by a transition of such magnitude, the replacement of welfare transfers with tax credits raises several policy issues:

- Tax and revenue agencies replace welfare departments as the source of benefits, a role that many are either unprepared for or may resist outright.
- Beneficiaries of tax credits must participate in the tax system in order to claim benefits, a status that is unfamiliar for many.
- Because much tax preparation is done by commercial firms, low-income workers may fall prey to unscrupulous preparers, particularly those advancing a refund as a loan.

- Tax credit refunds are almost always paid after the fact, requiring the recipient's willingness to wait, unlike traditional welfare that arrives monthly.
- As tax expenditures, tax credits are no less consequential for the federal and state treasuries than traditional welfare transfers.

Despite these drawbacks, tax credits offer new opportunities in areas historically understood as "welfare." In order to accelerate the upward mobility of the poor, for example, tax credits could be connected directly to asset accrual strategies such as individual development accounts. The tax preparation necessary for people to access tax credits could be one of several basic services—checking, savings, financial planning—offered by community financial services that could replace current welfare departments and serve as alternatives to marginal financial outfits that exploit the poor. Integrated with other capital formation strategies such as electronic benefit transfer, deposits by commercial banks to meet their Community Reinvestment Act obligations, and deposits by government and nonprofit agencies, tax credits could be part of a broad community development initiative that would finance projects in poor neighborhoods, thereby providing jobs to residents. In this respect, tax credits may not only begin to replace traditional welfare transfers, but in so doing may well introduce a new era of basic supports for poor families.[19]

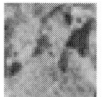 # The Antitax Movement

Proponents of publicly funded social programs assume that tax-generated revenues are prudent investments toward the public good. Within the larger policy context, there are differing views on this assumption, however. It is worth acknowledging that some of the most egregious violations of personal decency, to say nothing of civil rights, have occurred under the auspices of public programs—such as the sterilization of "feebleminded" people during the eugenics movement, the Tuskegee "experiment" on syphilitic African American men, and the warehousing of chronically mentally ill patients as well as of prison inmates.

For conservatives, particularly libertarians, government activities are likely to attenuate individual liberties, a likelihood encouraged by the fragmentation of modern society. The oppressive capacity of the state has long been a concern of political philosophers; in a recent statement of the issue, Jared Diamond notes that all societies try to balance the provision of essential services with measures aimed at thwarting the kleptocratic inclinations of those in power.

> These noble and selfish functions are inextricably linked, although some governments emphasize much more of one function than of the other. The difference between a kleptocrat and a wise statesman, between a robber baron and a public benefactor is merely one of degree: a matter of just how large a percentage of the tribute extracted from producers is retained by the elite, and how much the commoners like the public uses to which the redistributed tribute is put.[20]

To the extent that government enriches the powerful and mistreats citizens, a logical reform strategy is to defund the state by cutting off its tax revenues. By way of illustration, Michael Tanner of the Cato Institute calculates that $3.5 trillion has been spent on poverty programs since the Great Society period, yet with little success. "We are not going to solve our welfare problems by throwing more money at them," he concludes. "It is time to recognize that welfare cannot be reformed. It should be ended."[21]

An equally compelling critique of government taxation can be found in classic liberalism, a philosophic doctrine that emphasizes the freedom of individuals to act in their own best interests. Isaiah Berlin's distinction between "positive" and "negative liberty" was framed within the context of twentieth-century state socialism, in an era when public programs were ascendant. Advocates of public programs justi-

fied them on the basis that they protected the vulnerable from poverty, idleness, and sickness, but Berlin noted that such "positive liberty" invariably strengthened the state. Berlin preferred "negative liberty," because it emphasized the ability of free citizens to act in their own interests.[22] Although dichotomies such as Berlin's may seem to be of limited application in social work practice or, worse, to be a rationale for gutting essential social programs, it is worth noting that a primary ethical value in social work is client self-determination.

The obvious question raised by conservatives is, why tax at all? Beyond central functions of the state, conservatives contend that citizens should be allowed to retain earned income and use it as they see fit. The liberal rebuttal to this suggestion has been that unregulated capitalism inevitably skews the distribution of resources and opportunities, leaving subgroups vulnerable to insecurity with respect to income, employment, and health. The result, liberals have contended, is that specific populations suffer disproportionate and protracted poverty, thus providing the rationale for social programs. For more than a half century, they note, social insurance and public assistance programs have buffered low-income families from poverty.

Recently, economists have examined the concept of "social mobility," in the process raising profound questions about the embeddedness of poverty and thus the necessity for social programs. The policy issue is simple: To the extent that poor people of working age are upwardly mobile, the case for social programs is weakened. Brad Schiller, the author of a standard text on poverty and discrimination, has examined the upward mobility of the poorest Americans and, in its absence, the intractability of the underclass. Using a national data set, Schiller examined the experience of young workers earning the minimum wage and their subsequent earnings, finding that one-third of minimum wage workers had received a raise within a year and that 60 percent were beyond the minimum wage within two years. Of those who entered the labor market in 1980, a recession year, only 15 percent continued earning the minimum wage after three years.[23] Furthermore,

> *the available perceptions of minimum-wage youth seem to dispel the notion that minimum-wage jobs offer low wages and nothing more. Over 85 percent of the minimum-wage entrants stated that they liked their jobs, and over 60 percent felt that they were earning skills that would be valuable in attaining better jobs. Only one out of eight minimum-wage youth perceived a total lack of on-the-job training—a condition compatible with the notion of "dead-end" jobs. Over half (56 percent) of the minimum-wage workers perceived opportunities for promotion with the same employer.[24]*

Seven years after beginning a minimum wage job, the average worker had seen an increase in his or her wages of 154 percent, about 15 percent per year. Although non–minimum wage job entrants were earning more, the minimum wage entrants had closed the gap significantly. Notably, Schiller concluded that race did not appear to retard the wage increases of youth. "The longitudinal experiences of minimum-wage youth . . . refute the notion of a 'minimum-wage trap,' " concluded Schiller. "Youth who started at the minimum wage in 1980 recorded impressive wage gains over the subsequent seven years both in absolute and relative terms."[25]

The upward mobility of low-wage workers thus parallels that of the general population. Daniel McMurer and Isabel Sawhill noted that upward mobility is more pronounced than data on a stagnating income distribution would suggest. Mobility in the United States is substantial, according to the evidence. Large portions of the population move into a new income quintile, with estimates ranging from about 25 to 40 percent in a single year. As one would expect, the mobility rate is even higher over longer periods—it averages about 45 percent over a 5-year period and about 60 percent over both 9-year and 17-year periods.[26]

Mobility is also pronounced among the poor. Reporting on data from the mid-1990s, the Census Bureau found that although 30.3 percent of Americans lived below the poverty line for at least two months during a three-year span, only 5.3 percent were poor continuously for two years. On average, families were below the poverty line for four and a half months.[27]

Using data from the Panel Survey on Income Dynamics, W. Michael Cox and Richard Alm conclude that upward mobility, even of the poorest Americans, is striking.

> *Only 5 percent of those in the bottom fifth in 1975 were still there in 1991. Where did they end up? A majority made it to the top three-fifths of the income distribution—middle class or better. But most amazing of all, almost 3 out of 10 of the low-income earners from 1975 had risen to the uppermost 20 percent by 1991. More than three-quarters found their way into the two highest tiers of income earners for at least one year by 1991.[28]*

Although the research on upward mobility suggests that low-income workers prosper over time, its implications for tax policy are less than direct. After all, the families that make up the aggregate samples that are the basis of the research derive income from social policies, ranging from the minimum wage to family welfare, and these invariably contribute to future income gains. At the same time, the research has a profound implication: If low-income families succeed despite notoriously inadequate welfare programs, they must do so as a result of prudent decision making. If so, the optimal response is not continuing categorical welfare, but converting to tax credits that allow poor families more discretionary income.

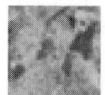 ## Conclusion

Tax policy, often undervalued in discussions of social welfare, serves a vital function, because it provides the revenues through which public programs operate. Increasing fluency in tax policy has significant benefits for advocates of social justice. At the national level, for example, introducing progressive features to the Social Security withholding tax—adjusting the tax rate for income and lifting the cap on taxable income—would generate significant new revenues that could make minimal Social Security benefits more adequate. This could serve a strategic purpose, as well, by providing a counterpoint to conservative contentions that Social Security should be privatized. At the local level, the introduction or expansion of earmarked taxes could be used to fund specific programs such as a children's authority.[29] Modest levies on alcohol products could generate substantial sums for substance abuse treatment.

Leveraging tax policy to advance social justice requires sophistication in social policy, however. The traditional stance of human service professionals has been to take tax revenues for granted and to focus primarily on allocating funding through services and benefits. If social welfare professionals are to enhance their role in the domestic policy debate, they will have to master the financial, procedural, and accounting nuances of tax policy. These are daunting fields, to be sure, but the potential payoff makes the effort worthwhile.

 ## Discussion Questions

1. Why has Harry Hopkins's political calculus, "Tax, tax, spend, spend, elect, elect!" lost its political currency in more recent times?
2. Should the federal government expand its spending on social programs despite the large and ongoing federal debt? What are the effects of increased spending, and what are the effects of stable or even decreasing spending, on social programs?
3. What are the positive and negative effects of increasing corporate taxation? How would it affect the poor in both the short-term and the long-term?
4. Should nonprofit human service corporations be required to pay taxes just as for-profit firms do? What would be the possible consequences of restructuring the tax code to mandate that nonprofits lose their nonprofit tax status?
5. Should the altruism of the population be rewarded by tax codes that permit charitable contributions to be deducted from taxes? Do the long-term effects of this tax deduction encourage or discourage real altruism?
6. Some welfare advocates concerned with income inequality argue that the function of the welfare state is to equalize incomes and assets through social welfare programs. Others believe it is unrealistic to expect that welfare state programs can do more than alleviate human suffering by providing resources to those in need. Should the goal of social welfare programs be to reduce income and asset inequality, or should that function be relegated to tax and labor policy?
7. Has the social work profession been successful in lobbying efforts and in promoting a more just society? If not, why? What strategies should social workers employ to move society toward more equitable income and asset redistribution?

 ## Notes

1. Thomas Dye, *Understanding Public Policy*, 9th ed. (Upper Saddle River, NJ: Prentice Hall, 1998), pp. 242–243.

2. That part of the withholding tax dedicated to Medicare health insurance is levied on all income, whereas that for Social Security has a

cap on taxable income. Committee on Ways and Means, *Overview of Entitlement Programs* (Washington, DC: U.S. Government Printing Office, 1998), p. 58.

3. Committee on Ways and Means, *Overview of Entitlement Programs*, p. 866.

4. Reynolds Farley, *The New American Reality* (New York: Russell Sage Foundation, 1996), p. 85.

5. *The Economic and Budget Outlook: Fiscal Years 1991–1995* (Washington, DC: Congressional Budget Office, 1990), pp. 122, 112.

6. Bob Woodward, *The Agenda* (New York: Simon & Schuster, 1994), p. 165.

7. Committee on Ways and Means, *Overview of Entitlement Programs*, pp. 838–839.

8. David Rosenbaum, "Corporate Welfare's New Enemies," *The New York Times* (February 2, 1997), pp. E1, E6.

9. Virginia Hodgkinson and Murray Weitzman, *Nonprofit Almanac* (Washington, DC: Independent Sector, 1996), pp. 59–63.

10. Alan Abramson, Lester Salamon, and C. Eugene Steuerle, "The Nonprofit Sector and the Federal Budget," in Elizabeth Boris and C. Eugene Steuerle (eds.), *Nonprofits and Government* (Washington, DC: Urban Institute, 1999), p. 122.

11. Stephen Barr, "Clinton Budget Seeks Approval for Buyouts," *Washington Post* (February 8, 2000), p. A14.

12. Charles Babington and Juliet Eilperin, "GOP Hostile to Clinton Budget," *Washington Post* (February 8, 2000), p. A14.

13. Melvin Oliver and Thomas Shapiro, *Black Wealth/White Wealth* (New York: Routledge, 1997), p. 87.

14. Edward Wolff, "Recent Trends in Wealth Ownership" (Avon-on-Hudson, NY: Jerome Levy Economics Institute, 2000), p. 22.

15. To these should be added the 8 states without income taxes, raising the number to 23.

16. Sheldon Danziger, Robert Haveman and Robert Plotnick, "Antipoverty Policy," in Sheldon Danziger and Daniel Weinberg (eds.), *Fighting Poverty* (Cambridge, MA: Harvard University Press, 1986), p. 65.

17. Paul Krugman, "Gore's Tax Problem," *The New York Times* (September 10, 2000), p. WK17.

18. Paul Wilson and Robert Cline, "State Welfare Reform: Integrating Tax Credits and Income Transfers." Paper presented at the 1994 National Tax Symposium, Washington, DC, May 24, 1994.

19. David Stoesz and David Saunders, "Welfare Capitalism," *Social Service Review* (September 1999).

20. Jared Diamond, *Guns, Germs, and Steel* (New York: Norton, 1997), p. 276.

21. Michael Tanner, "Ending Welfare as We Know It" (Washington, DC: Cato Institute, 1994), p. 24.

22. Michael Ignatieff, *Isaiah Berlin* (New York: Henry Holt, 1998), pp. 202–203.

23. Bradley Schiller, "Moving Up: The Training and Wage Gains of Minimum-Wage Entrants," *Social Science Quarterly* 75, no. 3 (September 1994), p. 629.

24. Ibid., p. 627.

25. Ibid., p. 634.

26. Daniel McMurer and Isabel Sawhill, *Getting Ahead* (Washington, DC: Urban Institute, 1998), p. 33.

27. "Poverty Short-Lived for Most, Study Finds," *Richmond Times Dispatch* (August 10, 1998), p. A3.

28. W. Michael Cox and Richard Alm, *Myths of Rich and Poor* (New York: Basic Books, 1999), p. 73.

29. Lela Costin, Howard Karger, and David Stoesz, *The Politics of Child Abuse in America* (New York: Oxford University Press, 1996).

chapter 10

Social Insurance Programs

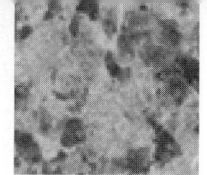

This chapter explores the major forms of social insurance in the United States: Old-Age, Survivors, and Disability Insurance (OASDI), Unemployment Insurance (UI), and Workers' Compensation. In addition, this chapter explores some of the major issues and problems surrounding social insurance programs.

Definition of Social Insurance

Social insurance is the cornerstone of U.S. social welfare policy. Specifically, it is a system whereby people are compelled—through payroll or other taxes—to insure themselves against the possibility of their own indigence, such as might result from the economic vicissitudes of retirement, the loss of a job, the death of the family breadwinner, or physical disability. Based in part on the same principles used in private insurance, social insurance sets aside a sum of money that is held in trust by the government and earmarked to be used in the event of workers' retirement, death, disability, or unemployment. The major goal of social insurance is to help maintain income by replacing a portion of lost earnings. It is a pay-as-you-go system in which the workers and employers of today pay for those who have retired, are ill, or have lost their jobs. Although originally designed to replicate a private insurance fund, the Social Security program has been broadened to include a variety of programs that attempt to provide a minimal level of replacement income. Because the benefits paid to many retired workers exceed their contributions to the system, Social Security has taken on some of the characteristics of an income redistribution and/or public assistance program.

Unlike Social Security, public assistance programs are subject to **means tests** and based entirely on need. The rationale for public assistance is grounded in the concept of *safety nets*, which are designed to ensure that citizens receive basic services and that they do not fall below a given poverty level. Social insurance, on the other hand, requires beneficiaries to make contributions to the system *before* they can claim benefits. Because social insurance affects a larger number of people and benefits are generally higher, expenditures for social insurance are far greater than for public assistance (see Figure 10.1). Social insurance is also universal; that is, people receive benefits as legal entitlements regardless of their personal wealth. Table 10.1 shows federal spending for major social insurance programs. Because the social insurance benefit structure is linked to occupationally defined productive work, most programs tend to be stigmatized little or not at all. In contrast, public assistance recipients are often highly stigmatized. Perhaps this occurs because public assistance programs are financed out of general tax revenues; they are not occupationally linked and not based on a previous work record; and recipients must be determined indigent through means tests.

Although some people complain about the costs of public assistance programs, social insurance programs are financed at a level roughly four times higher than public welfare is. For example, social insurance programs (OASDI, Workers' Compensation, Medicare, and Unemployment Insurance, among others) cost about $634 billion in 1996 compared with about $190 billion for public assistance programs (AFDC/TANF, SSI, food stamps, WIC, and others). Furthermore, social insurance programs accounted for 22.1 percent of the total federal budget in 1993, compared to 3.4 percent for public assistance programs. Finally, the average OASDI beneficiary received $652 a month in 1995, compared with a little over $420 for a mother with two children on AFDC.

The Background of Social Insurance

The first old-age insurance program was introduced in Germany in 1889 by Chancellor Otto von Bismarck. Although that first program was originally intended as a means of curbing the growing socialist trend in Germany, by the onset of World War I nearly all European nations had old-age assistance programs of one sort or another. In 1920 the U.S. government began its own Federal Employees Retirement program. By 1931, 17 states had enacted their own old-age assistance programs, although these often had stringent eligibility requirements. For example, in some cases in which relatives were capable of

FIGURE 10.1   Spending as a Percentage of Gross Domestic Product, 1965–1995

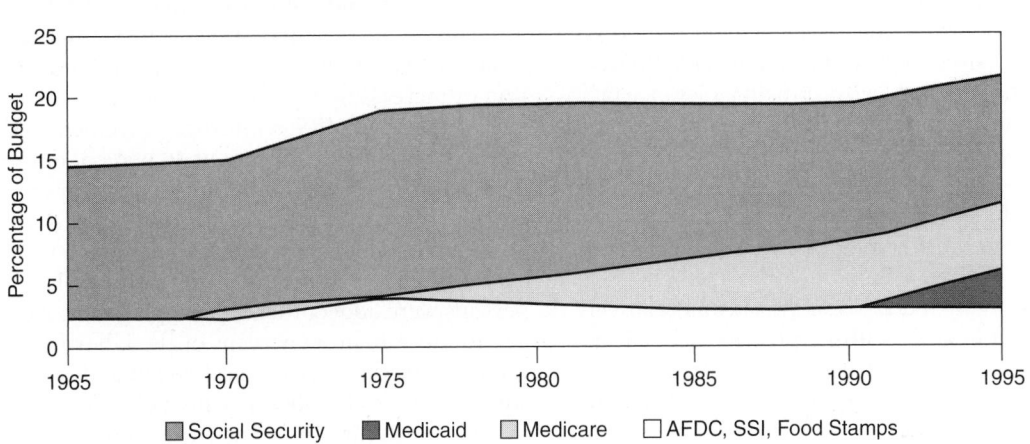

Source: U.S. House of Representatives, House Ways and Means Committee, *Overview of Entitlements, 1994 Green Book* (Washington, DC: U.S. Government Printing Office, 1994), p. 1006.

TABLE 10.1 ■ Past, Current, and Projected Federal Spending for Major Social Insurance Programs, Selected Years (expenditures in billions)

PROGRAMS	1975	1992	1996	2000	2002
OASDI	$65.8	$284.7	$348.1	$421.3	$463.5
Medicare	$14.1	$128.3	$174.7	$252.8	$300.7
Unemployment Insurance	$8.2	$34.6	$23.7	$27.0	$29.2
Total	$90.3	$450.5	$546.5	$701.1	$793.4

Sources: Compiled from various tables in U.S. Bureau of the Census, *Statistical Abstract, 1990* (Washington, DC: U.S. Government Printing Office, 1990), and Committee on Ways and Means, U.S. House of Representatives, *Overview of Entitlement Programs: 1992 Green Book* (Washington, DC: U.S. Government Printing Office, 1992), US Budget, FY 1997, Analytic Perspectives, Review of Direct Spending and Reports, retrieved 1999 from the World Wide Web: http://www.doc.gov/BudgetFY97/spectoc.html

supporting an elderly person, benefits were denied. These state-administered retirement programs were restrictive and often punitive; often elderly people who applied for assistance had to sign over all their assets to the state when they died.[1] Nevertheless, the concept of governmental responsibility for welfare grew during the early part of the twentieth century, and by 1935 all states except Georgia and South Carolina had programs that provided financial assistance to widows and children.[2]

Spurred on by the Great Depression of the 1930s and prompted by the growing rebellion inspired by a California physician named Francis Townsend (who advocated a flat $200 per month for each retired worker), President Franklin Roosevelt championed a government assistance program that would cover both unemployed and retired workers.[3] The result of Roosevelt's efforts was the Social Security Act of 1935, through which the federal government established the basic framework for the modern social welfare state.

The 1935 Social Security Act was relatively modest compared with its present scope. It established categorical assistance to the elderly poor, dependent children, the blind, and some disabled children. Title IV earmarked money for vocational rehabilitation, rural public health, and training for public experts. Two titles covered eligibility and financing for old-age retirement; two others established UI under joint state and federal government auspices. Title VII established a Social Security Board, whose job it was to monitor the fund. Title XI gave the legislature the right to alter any part of the act.[4]

As amended, the Social Security Act provides for: (1) OASDI; (2) UI programs under joint federal and state partnership; (3) federal assistance to aged, blind, and disabled persons under the SSI program; (4) public assistance to families with dependent children under the AFDC program (now TANF); (5) federal health insurance for the aged (Medicare); and (6) federal and state health assistance for the poor (Medicaid). Although all these programs fit under the rubric of the Social Security Act of 1935, not all are social insurance programs (e.g., Medicaid, TANF, and SSI).

The insurance feature of Social Security emerged as the result of an intense debate: Progressives wanted Social Security funded out of general revenue taxes, whereas conservatives wanted it funded solely out of employee contributions. The compromise reached in 1935 was that old-age insurance would be financed by employer and employee contributions of 1 percent on a base wage of $3,000, with a maximum cap for worker contributions set at $30 per year. At age 65, single workers would receive $22 per month; married workers would get $36. In order to allow the program to accumulate reserves, no benefits were paid out until 1940.

The Social Security Act of 1935 has been modified repeatedly, almost always in the direction of increasing its coverage. The original Social Security Act of 1935 afforded retirement and survivor benefits to only about 40 percent of the labor force. Farm and domestic workers, mariners, bank employees, the self-employed, and state and local government employees were excluded. In 1950 farmers and self-employed persons were added, thereby bringing the coverage to more than 90 percent of the labor force. Congress made survivors and dependents of insured workers eligible for benefits in 1939, and in 1956 disability insurance was added to include totally and permanently disabled workers. In 1965 Health Insurance for the Aged (Medicare)—a prepaid health insurance plan—was incorporated into the law. In later years the act was amended to allow workers to retire as early as age 62, provided they agreed to accept only 80 percent of their benefits. In 1977 an automatic cost-of-living index was affixed to benefit payments.

With the amendments of 1939 (extending coverage to widows, elderly wives, surviving children, etc.) Social Security technically became bankrupt, because it was no longer entirely self-financed. As such, the federal government assumed responsibility for any financial shortfalls and thus implicitly assumed responsibility for promoting the general welfare. By 1996 more than 43 million Americans and more than one-quarter of all U.S. households depended on a monthly Social Security check.[5] As Figure 10.2

FIGURE 10.2 Number of Social Security Beneficiaries, by Type of Benefit, August 1996

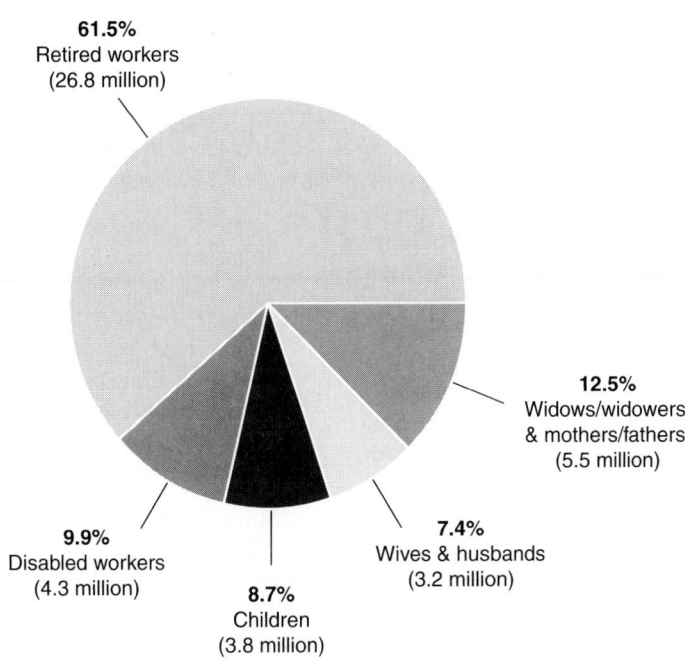

61.5%
Retired workers
(26.8 million)

12.5%
Widows/widowers
& mothers/fathers
(5.5 million)

9.9%
Disabled workers
(4.3 million)

8.7%
Children
(3.8 million)

7.4%
Wives & husbands
(3.2 million)

Source: Social Security Administration, "Number of Social Security Beneficiaries." Retrieved from the World Wide Web: http://www.ssa.gov/research

illustrates, by 1996 only 61.5 percent of Social Security beneficiaries were retired workers.

The Financial Organization of Social Insurance

Covered workers pay taxes into Social Security while they work, and when they retire or become disabled, they (or their family members) collect monthly benefits. Social Security taxes are used to pay for retirement, disability or Medicare benefits. General revenue taxes are used to finance Supplemental Security Income (SSI).

Social Security and Medicare taxes are divided among several trust funds. There are two So-cial Security trust funds: (1) The Old-Age and Survivors Insurance (OASI) trust fund pays for retirement and survivor benefits, and (2) the federal Disability Insurance (DI) trust fund pays benefits to people with disabilities and their families. There are also two Medicare trust funds: (1) The federal Hospital Insurance (HI) trust fund pays for services covered under the hospital insurance (Part A) provisions of Medicare, and (2) the federal Supplementary Medical Insurance (SMI) trust fund pays for services covered under the medical insurance (Part B) provisions of Medicare. The Social Security trust fund accounts are maintained by the Department of the Treasury.

The trust funds are governed by a board of trustees composed of the secretary of the treasury, the secretary of labor, the secretary of health and human services, the commissioner of social security, and two public trustees who serve four-year terms. The board of trustees reports annually to Congress on the condition of the funds and on estimated future operations.

Before 1983 the system was operated on a pay-as-you-go system, with taxes flowing into one end of the pipeline and flowing out the other end. Since 1983 Social Security has operated under a partial reserve system in which it takes in more than it pays out, thereby building up a reserve to help pay benefits to an increasing number of retired workers.

Social Security revenues are deposited daily into trust funds and benefits are paid out. Surplus income (i.e., income not needed to pay benefits) is invested in U.S. government bonds that earn the prevailing rate of interest and whose principal and interest are guaranteed by the federal government. Almost all securities held by the trust funds are "special issue" bonds available only to the funds. The DI trust fund also holds a relatively small number of public issue stocks (marketable securities available to the general public). The OASI trust fund holds no public issue stocks. Unlike marketable securities, special issues can be redeemed at any time at face value. Consequently, investments in special issues provide the trust funds with the same flexibility as having cash. The amount of interest earned is substantial. In 1998 the Social Security trust funds earned $49.3 billion in interest, representing an annual interest rate of 7.2 percent. Contrasting with this stated investment strategy, however, are persistent reports that trust funds are being used for purposes other than Social Security or operational expenses.[6]

Key Social Insurance Programs

OASDI

OASDI is a combination of Old-Age and Survivors Insurance (OASI) and Disability Insurance (DI). OASDI, or what most people refer to

as Social Security, is currently the largest social program in the nation, covering approximately 9 out of 10 workers. OASDI is a federal program administered by the Social Security Administration, which in 1994 became an independent agency headed by a commissioner and a board appointed by the U.S. president for a six-year term.

In many ways, Social Security is a stellar example of a program that has worked:

- Social Security served more than 48 million people in 1999, and 3.9 million people were awarded benefits.
- Social Security accounts for 38 percent of the total income of aged persons.
- In 1999 Social Security kept 39 percent of aged persons out of poverty.
- Women accounted for 58 percent of adult Social Security beneficiaries in 1999.[7]

Moreover, the poverty rate for elderly people was 9.7 percent in 1999, lower than the poverty rate for the general population (12.7 percent). As recently as 1969, before the Social Security **cost-of-living adjustments (COLAs)** took effect, the poverty rate for the elderly was double that of the general population, 25 versus 12 percent.[8] According to the Social Security Administration, in 1996 the poverty rate for the elderly would have been 52 percent without Social Security.[9] In that sense, Social Security has a strong redistributive effect, transferring resources from those with high lifetime earnings to those with low lifetime earnings.

Unlike prefunded private annuity plans, in which a worker draws off money already invested, Social Security benefits are paid by today's workers rather than by the retirees. Benefits under OASDI are entitlement based; that is, they are based on the beneficiaries' earnings, not on the amount of the revenue in the trust fund. If benefits in a given period exceed revenues, the difference is made up from the reserves in the trust funds. OASDI operates in the following manner:

- On an employee's first $76,200 in earnings, the employee and his or her employer each paid an OASDI tax equal to 6.20 percent and a Medicare Hospital Insurance (HI) tax equal to 1.45 percent of earnings in 2000. Employees therefore paid a total of 7.65 percent. Self-employed persons paid 15.3 percent. In general, increases in the wage base are automatic and are based on the increase in average wages in the economy each year. For example, the highest Social Security tax a worker could pay in 1999 was $4,274 (not including the HI tax), with a joint employer/employee tax of $9,448. Self-employed persons had their taxes computed on a lower base (net earnings from self-employment less 7.65 percent), and half of that tax was deductible for income tax purposes.

■ Based on their age at retirement and the amount earned during their working years, workers receive a monthly benefit payment. Retired workers aged 62 receive a reduction of $\frac{5}{9}$ of 1 percent for each month of entitlement before age 65, with a maximum reduction of 20 percent. Benefits are modest; the average retired worker received $798 a month in 1999. The maximum benefit in 1999 for a retired worker at age 65 was $1,536 a month.[10]

■ Under the OASI program, a monthly payment is made to an unmarried child or eligible dependent grandchild of a retired worker or a deceased worker who was fully insured at the time of death, if the child or grandchild is (1) under age 18; (2) a full-time elementary or secondary school student under age 19; or (3) a dependent or disabled person aged 18 or over whose disability began before age 22. A grandchild is eligible only if the child was adopted by the insured grandparent.

■ A lump sum benefit of $255 is payable to a spouse who was living with an insured worker at the time of his or her death.

■ Under the Disability Insurance program (DI), monthly cash benefits are paid to disabled workers under age 65 and to their dependents. The purpose of the DI program is to replace lost income when a wage earner is no longer able to work. Monthly cash benefits are paid and computed generally on the same basis as they are in

the OASI program; that is, they are calculated on the basis of past earnings. Medicare benefits are provided to disabled workers, widows or widowers, or adult children after they have been entitled to disability benefits for 24 months.

■ Almost all people, whether or not they paid into Social Security, are eligible for Medicare benefits. (Medicare is treated in depth in Chapter 12.)

■ Social Security beneficiaries are required to have completed at least 40 quarters of work (10 years) before they are eligible to draw benefits.

Social Security, especially OASDI, has been a heated topic for much of its relatively short history. Political conservatives and laissez-faire economists are troubled because Social Security basically socializes a portion of the national income. Other critics claim that Social Security will lead to moral and economic ruin, because it discourages savings and causes retired people to become dependent on a supposedly fragile governmental system. The Social Security system, on the other hand, is popular with the elderly, who rely on it for much of their income, and with their grown children, for whom it helps to provide peace of mind.

Unemployment Insurance

The first line of defense for workers fired or laid off from their jobs is Unemployment Insurance (UI). Part of the Social Security Act of 1935, UI is a federal/state program whose objectives are (1) to provide temporary and partial wage replacement to involuntarily and recently unemployed workers, and (2) to help stabilize the economy during recessions. Although the U.S. Department of Labor oversees the general program, each state administers its own UI program.[11] The current guidelines of the UI program require employers to contribute to a trust fund, which is then activated if an employee loses his or her job. About 3.3 million workers were on UI in 2000, at a total cost of $4.6 billion. In 2000 the average duration of unemployed workers in the UI program was 14 weeks.[12]

The UI system consists of two basic parts: (1) regular state-funded benefits, generally provided for a maximum of 26 weeks; and (2) a federal/state extended benefits program. The second part provides an additional 13 weeks of benefits to unemployed workers who have used up their regular benefits and are still searching for a job. Extended benefits in the UI system are activated when the level of unemployment insurance claims in a state rises above a specified threshold. The extended benefits program is based on the assumption that when a state's unemployment rate is high, it usually takes longer to find a new job.[13] States pay 50 percent of the benefits provided by the UI extended benefits program.

To be eligible for UI benefits, a worker must be ready and willing to work, be unemployed, be registered for work with the state employment service, and have been working in covered employment during a base eligibility period. Conversely, a worker who is fired for misconduct, quits a job without a legally acceptable reason, fails to register with the state employment service, refuses a job equal to or better than the one previously held, or goes on strike is ineligible for unemployment benefits. States cannot, however, deny benefits to workers who refuse to be strikebreakers or who refuse to work for less than the prevailing wage rate.[14]

Basic decisions concerning the amount of benefits, eligibility, and length of benefit time are made by the states. Benefits are not equal to previously earned income, and average unemployed workers in 2000 received around 46 percent of their previous wage. State unemployment benefits vary widely, ranging in 2000 from a weekly low of $156.19 in Mississippi to a high of $2296.14 in New Jersey. In 2000 the median benefit was $219.18 per week.[15]

Problems in Unemployment Insurance. Congress created the UI system back in 1935, and since then the program has remained essentially the same despite changes in the economy and in the nature of unemployment. There are several problems endemic to the UI program:

1. *Limited coverage.* Throughout most of the 1970s, the majority of unemployed workers received unemployment benefits each month. For example, 75 percent of the jobless received benefits in 1975. By 1986, however, the percentage of unemployed workers receiving benefits had dropped to the lowest levels in the history of the program, with only 32.9 percent of jobless workers receiving benefits in a given month. Although the number of those covered under unemployment insurance rose slightly to 36.8 percent in 1990, 4.3 million of the 6.9 million unemployed workers were not receiving benefits.[16] By 1998, only 38 percent of unemployed persons received benefits.[17]

2. *Benefit decline.* The decline in benefits has followed the decline in unemployment coverage. In 1986 the total UI benefits were 59 percent lower than they were in 1976 (after adjusting for inflation). These figures are complicated by the fact that from 1980 to 1986, the number of long-term unemployed (those looking for work for more than a year) rose from 820,000 to 1.2 million. These factors, coupled with federal budget cuts in 1981 that largely eliminated unemployment benefits for those unemployed for more than six months, contributed to the falling rates of unemployment coverage and a subsequent increase in poverty rates for the unemployed. The median weekly earnings for workers in 2000 was $574; the median UI benefit was $296, or only 51.5 percent of the median wage.

3. *Outdated assumptions about unemployment.* UI was predicated on the assumption that layoffs are temporary and that in most cases employers will recall workers. Now, however, many people are losing their jobs because of long-term structural shifts in the economy. Deepening recessions, corporate downsizing (the number of workers laid off due to corporate downsizing doubled from 1984 to 1995), and increasing numbers of plant closures resulting in permanent displacement (1.5 million factory workers were displaced from 1991 to 1993) have strained the UI system. As a result, the average duration of unemployment has fluctuated widely over recent decades, and periodically large numbers of people have applied for extended benefits. In response, Congress passed the Unemployment

Compensation Amendments of 1993, which required new claimants to be profiled according to their demographic characteristics and work history. Those considered high risk were then targeted for special job search assistance.[18] Tiding people over is no longer helpful when their jobs are permanently gone. Instead, people need the resources and opportunities to retrain for new careers. Unfortunately, the benefits paid out are often not adequate to allow breadwinners to support a family, train for a new career, and find a job.

4. *Mismatched expectations.* UI is based on the belief that workers will find suitable reemployment if given the opportunity to find a job that matches their skills and experience, but those who receive assistance longer than the norm question the underlying assumption that an appropriate fit will be found. In effect, the same principles that apply to the short-term unemployed are extended to the long-term unemployed—which may in fact be a different population. For example, most people laid off find reemployment within 27 weeks. However, one study found that among the long-term unemployed, 38 percent were unemployed for 27 to 40 weeks; 28 percent, 41 to 52 weeks; and 34 percent, 53 to 100 weeks. In contrast, 41 percent of the short-term unemployed were unemployed for 1 to 5 weeks; 37 percent, 6 to 14 weeks; and 22 percent, 15 to 26 weeks. Moreover, the percentage of those considered long-term unemployed rose from 6 percent in 1970 to 19 percent in 1995.[19]

5. *Women and unemployment.* The current system does not accommodate women in the workforce. In the 1930s, when Congress developed the present system, women made up about 30 percent of the workforce; they now make up about half. But because of their role in bearing and rearing children, women still have more intermittent employment patterns than men. For instance, they are employed more often than men in part-time work, and they are more likely to leave and reenter the workforce. UI's eligibility requirements are based on a permanent attachment to the workforce, which puts women at a disadvantage.

6. *Meeting its financial obligations.* UI cannot meet its financial obligations during economic downturns without federal aid or deficit spending. Employers pay into a general fund that is supposed to have adequate financial reserves. Yet many states borrow billions of dollars from the federal government to cover payments made during times of high unemployment. According to the Department of Labor, states have less money in their trust funds today than they did in the 1940s and 1950s, a situation that creates the potential for serious liability problems.[20]

7. *Tightened eligibility requirements.* In recent years many states have tightened UI eligibility requirements. In addition, the UI program often fails to help the states with the most severe unemployment problems. For example, the calculation of unemployment rates is based on a study conducted by the Department of Labor in which 60,000 households are interviewed each month. (Individuals 16 years or older are included in the survey.) Part-time workers in this study are counted as employed, and discouraged workers who have dropped out of the labor force are not counted at all. Although the UI program includes mechanisms that allow states to receive more federal reimbursement when unemployment rates are unusually high, the official state rate is lowered because many of the unemployed are not counted. The consequence is that this artificially low rate of unemployment may not set off the extended benefits mechanism.[21] Furthermore, states with "pockets of poverty" receive no additional help when the overall state unemployment rate is not high enough to set off the triggers.

8. *Equity problems.* The federal unemployment insurance tax rate has been raised only three times since it was initially set at $3,000 in 1935. In 1940 the wage base taxable for UI represented 98 percent of a worker's wages; by 1988 it was just 32 percent. But this is not the only inequity involving UI taxation. For instance, an employer pays the same federal UI tax for an employee who earns $100,000 a year as for an employee who earns only $10,000. Yet the worker with a higher income is eligible for higher unemployment benefits. This tax and benefit structure effectively discriminates against low-wage earners who are at or near the taxable wage base.[22]

Oren Levin-Waldman argues that policy reform of the UI system must be two-tiered. The first tier should reduce the incidence of layoffs; the second tier should help the long-term unemployed develop skills that would make them marketable in today's economy. Among other options, Levin-Waldman suggests implementing work sharing, which involves paying UI benefits to workers as partial compensation for the loss of hours worked. So instead of laying off workers in bad economic times, employers would simply reduce the number of hours each employee worked. Work sharing would avert layoffs by redistributing unemployment within a firm. In better economic times, work sharing would be discontinued. In addition, Levin-Waldman also suggests the development of co-ordinated job retraining programs. Lastly, bonuses (e.g., $500) could be offered to unemployed workers who found reemployment and/or to companies that employed them.[23]

One conservative approach to UI reform transfers the primary responsibility for unemployment insurance to individual workers through the creation of Individual Unemployment Accounts (IUAs). The IUA would be a portable individual trust that belonged to the employee and would work much like an Individual Retirement Account (IRA). IUA holders would be personally responsible for investing and managing their IUA funds. The funds would be created by voluntary tax-free contributions from each worker and/or the employer. The worker would have access to the funds any time he or she was without a job.[24]

Workers' Compensation

The U.S. Bureau of Labor Statistics reported that in 1992, 6,200 workers were killed on the job in fatal traumatic injuries, about 17 workers a day. It also said that there were 6.8 million injuries and illnesses and that about 50,000 workers a year die from workplace-related illnesses.[25]

Workers' Compensation (WC) programs began in 1911 in Wisconsin and New Jersey. By 1948 every state operated some form of WC program. WC programs provide cash, medical assistance, rehabilitation services, and disability and death benefits to persons (or their dependents) who are victims of industrial accidents or occupational illnesses. In the 1990s WC laws protected more than 97 million workers, or 87 percent of the labor force.[26] Although laws vary from state to state, the basic principle is that employers should assume the costs of occupational disabilities without regard to fault.[27]

Not only do the specific laws governing Workers' Compensation vary from state to state; there is little consistency either in benefit levels or in the administration of the programs. For example, some states require employers to carry insurance, other states provide a state-sponsored insurance fund, others allow employers to act as self-insurers, and still others do not require compulsory WC coverage. Some state programs do not cover employees of nonprofit, charitable, or religious institutions. Nevertheless, because of the potential for large claims, most employers transfer their responsibility by purchasing insurance from private companies that specialize in Workers' Compensation.

WC programs are problematic in several ways. First, benefit levels are established on the basis of state formulas and are usually calculated as a percentage of weekly earnings (generally about 66.66 percent). As such, each state sets its own annually adjusted benefit level, and these levels vary widely across states. For example, in 1998 the minimum benefit level ranged from $35 a week in Georgia to $339 in Pennsylvania; the maximum benefit level ranged from $303 a week in Mississippi to $996 in Iowa.[28] Second, the cost to employers for providing WC insurance has been rising rapidly. Employers paid about $43 billion to insure their workers in 1990, a 12.6 percent increase over the 1987 figure of $38.1 billion. The bulk of that money—$28.5 billion—was paid to private insurance carriers.[29] Third, there is great variability among states in the way claims are handled. Workers are often encouraged to settle out of court for attractive lump sums, even though the amounts may not equal their lost wages. Often, benefits are uneven. For example, the price attached to the loss of a body part has been interpreted differently from state to state. Charles Prigmore and Charles Atherton note that in 1978 in Hawaii the loss of a finger was valued at $5,175, more than the courts in the state of Wyoming allowed for the loss of an eye.[30] In addition, there are often long delays between the time an injury occurs and the period in which benefits start. Finally, in some states employers are exempt from the Workers' Compensation tax if they can demonstrate that they are covered by private insurance. Unfortunately, private insurance coverage may prove inadequate after a disability benefit is determined. Even though injured workers or their survivors received $34 billion in benefits and medical payments in 1990, Workers' Compensation may not provide adequate protection for many disabled workers.[31]

The Social Security Dilemma

Because of its widespread public support, Social Security was long perceived by policy analysts and legislators as the third rail of politics—touch it and you die. Besides, the immediate focus of conservative Republicans and Democrats was on the more vulnerable public assistance programs, which enjoyed less public support. In the late 1990s, however, emboldened by the successful passage of the Personal Responsibility and Work Opportunity Reconciliation Act of 1996, conservatives turned their attention to social insurance, the real welfare giant.

Criticisms leveled at the Social Security system had been particularly pointed during the 1980s and 1990s. Opponents argued that Social Security was depressing private savings (and thereby providing less capital for investment) by giving people a retirement check financed by the working population rather than interest on ac-

cumulated savings. Indeed, the average Social Security recipient in 1999 would have needed a savings account of more than $190,000 (at 5 percent interest) to collect interest equal to the average benefit ($9,575) in that year.

Arguments against the Current Social Security System

As in most nations, Social Security in the United States is a pay-as-you-go system; as such, it is an intergenerational wealth transfer scheme based on demographic factors. Birth rate and longevity determine the solvency of pay-as-you-go retirement systems.

The U.S. birthrate at the time of the creation of Social Security was 2.3, but it rose to 3.0 by 1950 and continued to climb throughout that decade. Today it has dropped back to 2.1. The average life expectancy in 1935 was 63; today it is 75. That's bad news for the Social Security Administration. As a result of these demographic factors, the number of workers paying Social Security payroll taxes has gone from 16 for every retiree in 1950 to just 3.3 for every Social Security beneficiary in 1997. That ratio is expected to decline to just 2 to 1 by the year 2025.

Not unexpectedly, the payroll tax has increased continuously over Social Security's history. From an original tax of just 2 percent on a maximum taxable income of $300, the payroll tax has been increased more than 30 times and in 2000 was set at 12.4 percent of a maximum income of $76,200. Moreover, the Social Security payroll tax would have to rise to 18 percent (if Medicare were included, nearly 28 percent) to pay all promised benefits under the current program. Obviously, this payroll tax level will have a negative impact on workers' earnings. Moreover, these tax rates reflect the actuarial estimates of the Social Security system. Historically, the more pessimistic assumptions have proved to be the most accurate. Under those assumptions, the total payroll tax would rise to 44 percent—nearly triple what it is today.

Social Security is helping to exacerbate intergenerational tensions. Younger workers are skeptical about the ability of Social Security to support them when they retire. They are frightened that Social Security will buckle when the baby boomers start retiring around 2010. Some are also anxious because they are saving less than their parents. In short, some younger workers fear that they will be denied Social Security benefits despite having made enormous contributions. Ted Dimig sums up the dilemma: "So, where does this leave my generation? First of all, it leaves us with a huge resentment over the idea that our elders might saddle us with the debt for their retirement; Social Security's 'unfunded liability' currently stands at $2.7 trillion, while shortchanging us on our own retirement."[32]

Although OASDI is an important component of economic security for the nation's retired people, serious problems threaten its future viability. The original strategy of the Social Security Act of 1935 was to create a self-perpetuating insurance fund, with benefits for elderly people being in proportion to their contributions. That scenario did not materialize. For example, in 1992 a single man retiring at age 65 would have received a *maximum* Social Security (OASDI) benefit of $13,056 per year, plus an additional $1,756 yearly in Medicare reimbursements. If the worker had started contributing to the Social Security fund in 1950 and contributed regularly at the maximum level until he retired in 1992, the total contribution would have been about $52,000. Yet in three and a half years this worker would have received his entire contribution back in benefits. If the worker survived to age 72 (the average life expectancy for a male), the benefits he received would be more than $51,300 in excess of his contributions. That amount does not include any cost-of-living increases. Put another way, a man who retired in 1980 could expect to receive Social Security benefits 3.7 times greater than his contributions would have generated had he invested in low-risk government securities. For a similar woman, this ratio was even higher—4.4 times—given her longer life expectancy.[33] These facts call into question the long-term viability of Social Security.

Arguments for the Current Social Security System

The Social Security program serves four main functions. (1) As the nation's preeminent insurance program, it supports 7 million survivors of deceased workers and 4 million disabled Americans. (2) Social Security is the nation's most successful antipoverty program. Largely because of Social Security, the poverty rate among the nation's elderly has fallen over the last 50 years from more than 40 percent to less than 10 percent—this in an era when only 36 percent of elderly Americans have access to private pension plans or annuities. Without Social Security about half of elderly Americans would have incomes below the poverty level. (3) Social Security is of immense value to working as well as retired Americans. Seniors who live decent lives and remain consumers are better for all, including workers and businesses who depend on domestic demand. In addition, given the dispersion of families and current lifestyles, few children of retirees would trade the burden of payroll taxes for that of housing and feeding destitute elderly parents. (4) Social Security is a special kind of "investment" unavailable in the private sector: a lifetime retirement annuity whose benefits rise with inflation. Almost all corporate pensions (many which run out after 20 years) are not adjusted to compensate for the erosion of purchasing power caused by long-term inflation. The belief that the basic protection provided by Social Security is analogous to private savings and would be unnecessary if people just saved more is spurious. And as a disability insurance policy, Social Security provides coverage equivalent to that of a $203,000 policy in the private sector; a similar dependent and survivor policy for a 27-year-old average-wage worker with two children would be equivalent to a $295,000 private sector policy.[34]

Social Security has also been accused of overpaying the elderly, slighting younger workers (who could get a better return if they invested privately), and leading the nation to financial collapse. Merton and Joan Bernstein challenge these criticisms leveled at Social Security. They claim that rather than discouraging private savings, Social Security actually stimulates financial planning for retirement and thus encourages savings.[35] Others counter the overpayment argument by noting that in 1990 60 percent of families over age 65 had total annual incomes under $30,000, while only 16.8 percent had annual incomes exceeding $50,000. Almost 50 percent of elderly nonfamily households (persons living alone or with relatives) had annual incomes below $10,000.[36] These numbers do not suggest an elderly population that is becoming wealthy by exploiting an overly generous Social Security system.

Social Security in Trouble

Social Security began to show signs of fiscal trouble by the mid-1970s. Between 1975 and 1981 the Old-Age and Survivors Insurance fund suffered a net decrease in funds and a deficit in the reserve of between $790 million and $4.9 billion a year. This imbalance between incoming and outgoing funds threatened to deplete the reserve by 1983. Moreover, the prospects for Social Security seemed bleak in other ways. Whereas the ratio of workers to supported beneficiaries (the dependency ratio) was then three to one, estimates at the time indicated that by the end of the century (with the retirement of the baby boom generation) that ratio would be only two to one. In short, the long-term costs of the program would exceed its projected revenues. The crisis in Social Security was fueled by demographic changes (a dropping birthrate plus an increase in life expectancy), more liberal benefits paid to retiring workers, high inflation, high unemployment, and the COLAs passed by Congress in the mid-1970s.

Facing these short- and long-term problems, Congress moved quickly to pass PL 98-21, the Social Security Amendments of 1983. Among the newly legislated changes were a delay in the cost-of-living adjustments and a stabilizer placed on future COLAs. Specifically, if trust funds fall below a certain level, future benefits will be keyed to the consumer price index (CPI) or the average wage increase, whichever is lower. A second change was that Social Security benefits be-

came taxable if taxable income plus Social Security benefits exceeded $25,000 for an individual or $32,000 for a couple. A third change increased the 2027 retirement age to 67 for those wanting to collect full benefits. Although workers could retire at age 62, they would receive only 70 percent of their benefits instead of the current 80 percent. Finally, coverage was extended: New federal employees were covered for the first time, as well as members of Congress, the president and vice president, federal judges, and employees of nonprofit corporations.

In the middle 1990s the Social Security rules were again changed, this time easing the historic Social Security penalty for about one million beneficiaries aged 65 to 67 who are still working. Previously, any earnings that exceeded $11,250 a year would result in $1.00 of benefits lost for every $2.00 earned. The new rules gradually raise the limit to $14,000, then to $30,000 by the year 2002. The new rules also allow those over 70 to continue working without losing Social Security benefits.[37]

The Long-Term Prospects for Social Security

Despite these reforms, the fiscal viability of the OASDI system remains in question. Some analysts suggest that Social Security is on sound footing. They point to the fact that the income and assets reserve in the combined OASDI trust funds reached $900 billion in 2000. By 2025 that amount is projected to peak at $6 trillion.[38] Proponents maintain that the finances of the system will be in close actuarial balance for the next 75 years, with no more than a 5 percent difference between incoming and outgoing revenues.[39] Other analysts point to Congressional Budget Office (CBO) projections that by 2015, when the post–World War II baby boomers retire, OASDI benefit payments will begin to exceed taxes, and trust funds will be exhausted in 2037. At that time, Social Security will be able to pay 73 percent of benefits owed, if no changes are made[40] (see Figure 10.3). The Disability Insurance Fund (DI) will be able to pay full benefits through only 2023 (see Tables 10.2 and 10.3).[41]

FIGURE 10.3 Projected Exhaustion of the Social Security Trust Fund in 2037

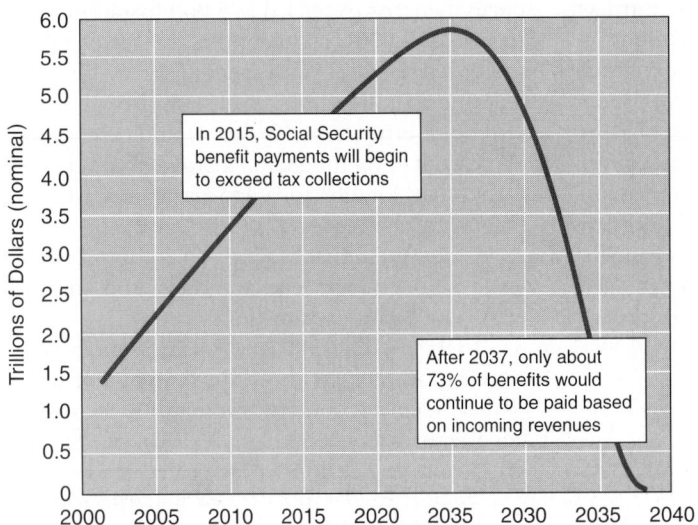

In 2015, Social Security benefit payments will begin to exceed tax collections

After 2037, only about 73% of benefits would continue to be paid based on incoming revenues

Source: Social Security Administration, "The Future of Social Security," Publication No. 05-10055. Retrieved August 2000 from the World Wide Web: http://www.ssa.gov/pubs/10055.html

TABLE 10.2 ▪ Key Dates for the Trust Funds

	OASI	DI	OASDI	HI
First year outgo exceeds income excluding interest	2016	2007	2015	2010
First year outgo exceeds income including interest	2026	2012	2025	2017
Year trust funds are exhausted	2039	2023	2037	2025

Source: Social Security Administration. Retrieved from the World Wide Web: http://www.ssa.gov/OACT/TRSUM/trsummary.html

TABLE 10.3 ▪ Year of Trust Fund Exhaustion Using Social Security Administration Estimates

SET OF ASSUMPTIONS	OASI	DI	OASDI	HI
Alternative I (low cost)	Never	Never	Never	Never
Alternative II (best estimate)	2039	2023	2037	2025
Alternative III (high cost)	2029	2012	2026	2012

Source: Social Security Administration. Retrieved from the World Wide Web: http://www.ssa.gov/OACT/TRSUM/trsummary.html

The Medicare Hospital Insurance fund (HI), which pays hospital expenses, is projected to be able to pay benefits until 2025. This is longer than originally projected because (1) the robust economic growth helped fuel the fund, (2) declining expenditures from the Balanced Budget Act of 1997 slowed spending, (3) health care costs increased more slowly than projected, and (4) efforts to combat fraud and abuse were successful. Despite these promising developments, however, the HI program will likely require additional reforms to ensure its long-term stability. The Supplementary Medical Insurance (SMI) trust fund, which pays doctors' bills and other outpatient expenses, is expected to remain adequately funded into the indefinite future, because current law sets financing each year to meet the next year's expected costs. Despite this funding stability, SMI costs have risen 38 percent over the past five years, or about 5 percent faster than the economy as a whole.

Other critics complain that the federal government is borrowing from the current Social Security surplus to fund other programs and is thereby hiding the real extent of the deficit. Money in the Social Security trust funds was intended to be invested and to be set aside for future years, not to be used to finance other government spending. But in 1990, for example, $65 billion in Social Security surpluses went for non–Social Security spending. As a result, part of every federal program is in effect paid for by the Social Security payroll tax. In that sense, the *real* budget deficit—and the absence of a *real* Social Security surplus to pay for future benefits—has been hidden from the public.[42]

Although some Social Security reforms have provided a short-term solution, structural problems continue to plague the system. As already discussed, one problem is the "graying of America." Since 1900 the percentage of Americans 65 years and older has more than tripled (from 4.1 percent in 1900 to 12.7 percent in 1998), and the absolute number has increased 10 times (from 3.1 million to 34.4 million). Demographic projections suggest that by 2030 the number of persons over age 65 will increase to 65.6 million. In other words, by 2030 the per-

centage of elderly is expected to climb from the current rate of 12.7 percent to more than 21 percent. Furthermore, the elderly are living longer. Between 1900 and 1990 the 75- to 84-year-old group increased 13 times, and the 85-and-over group was 24 times larger.[43] These demographic trends suggest that the **dependency ratio** will significantly increase, as will the pressures on the Social Security system. For example, in 1960 the worker/beneficiary ratio was 5 to 1; by 1980 it had dropped to 3.2 to 1. By 2025 the worker/beneficiary is expected to be 2 to 1.[44] A question exists as to whether two workers in 2040 will be able to support one retired person, and whether the Social Security system—at least as it is now structured—can support more than 20 percent of the U.S. population.

Another problem facing Social Security is the increasing tax burden. Social Security taxes on working families grew more rapidly in the 1980s than at any time since the passage of the Social Security Act in 1935. Between 1983 and 1990 the Social Security tax rate was raised six times, and from 1981 to 1992 the income level subject to the tax almost doubled. As a result, a worker's maximum payroll tax jumped from $1,502 in 1981 to more than $4,000 (including the Medicare portion of the tax) in 1996, an increase of more than 66 percent if inflation is factored in. From 1937 to 1990 the maximum Social Security tax increased 100 times.[45] Social Security taxes now represent the second largest revenue producer for the federal government. The tax burden of Social Security rests on the shoulders of workers and employers and results in a net decrease in both consumption and production.

Proposed Solutions for Social Security

Several solutions have been proposed to address the impending crisis in Social Security. In 1994 President Bill Clinton appointed a Social Security Advisory Council. The mandate of the council was to focus on the fund's future viability. Three distinct proposals emerged from the work of this group, all of which envisioned investing some Social Security funds in private financial markets.

Two of the three recommendations propose the creation of individual investment accounts (over which the beneficiary would have some control) financed with Social Security payroll taxes. The first, proposed by former Social Security commissioner Robert Ball, calls for raising Social Security taxes. In addition, Ball's plan also calls for investing up to 40 percent of trust fund reserves in private capital markets.

The second solution, offered by Edward Gramlich, trims benefits and adds revenues. Gramlich calls for creating a "double deck" plan: Workers would receive a basic benefit based on the number of years they worked, plus a "second deck" or add-on to their benefits equal to 15 percent of their average wages earned over their lifetime. In effect, benefits for low-income workers would remain the same, and benefits for high-income workers would be cut. Under Gramlich's proposal the retirement age would be raised to age 67 in 2027. In addition, Gramlich proposes to exclude benefits awarded to spouses of future retirees. To compensate, workers would be allowed to purchase annuities from the government by setting up defined contribution accounts established within the Social Security system and funded by a 1.6 percent increase in the payroll tax. Participants would have limited investment discretion over these accounts. Finally, Gramlich proposes that the Social Security fund be forced to invest 25 percent of its funds in stocks, which would theoretically yield a higher return over the long term than investing in government bonds.[46] (In down times, it can also yield a lower return.)

The third option, proposed by businessman Sylvester Shieber, would replace Social Security with flat benefits independent of earnings and large mandatory personal retirement accounts. These accounts would be funded by diverting a part of the current payroll tax, and would be held and managed by individuals.[47] There is clearly increasing pressure for at least a partial privatization of the Social Security system.

Projections about the future of Social Security are predicated on the belief that certain economic and demographic factors will be in play for the next 50 years, but economic and demographic shifts could easily invalidate the most earnest predictions, and Social Security could again go into crisis. For example, stagnant industrial productivity, changing demographic trends, an oil crisis, and/or major changes in immigration patterns would all have profound consequences for the future of Social Security. However, there is nothing inviolate about the way Social Security is currently funded. An act of Congress could easily eliminate the insurance feature of Social Security and replace it with general revenue taxation. Given the widespread dependence on Social Security, it seems highly unlikely that policymakers and the public will allow the system to go bankrupt.

Another issue in Social Security involves the competition between public (compulsory) and private (voluntary) pension plans. Some critics argue that private pension plans are preferable to public schemes, because they are based on less dependence on the government and have the potential for yielding higher returns. Private pensions originated as a means of encouraging employee loyalty and as a way of easing out aging workers. However, only about one-third of all workers and one-fourth of current employees are covered under private pension plans. Moreover, only a small fraction of these plans are indexed for inflation.

Critics of private pension plans argue that they are basically unreliable. Employees can switch jobs and thus lose their pension rights, companies may go bankrupt, corporations may attempt to raid pension funds, and corrupt or incompetent managers can wreak havoc on well-endowed pension plans. U.S. pension reserves are currently worth well over $1 trillion and form a major source for investment capital. Despite federal tax subsidies to private pension plans totaling more than $64 billion in 1988, however, coverage under these plans has actually decreased since 1980. Supporters of Social Security argue that unlike the riskier private pension plans, OASDI benefits are portable and indexed for inflation; also, workers are immediately vested in Social Security, and benefits are not contingent on the financial condition of the employer.[48]

Although originally intended to supplement private pension funds and to operate as a pay-as-you-go insurance scheme, OASDI has taken on many characteristics of a public welfare program. That is, as has been discussed, almost all current retirees are realizing benefits far in excess of what they contributed in Social Security taxes over the course of their working lives. (Those who retired in 1993 were the first group of workers to receive less in benefits than they paid in taxes.) The bill for those benefits is paid by the young workers of today.

Given this scenario, should social insurance be modified to reflect social assistance and income redistribution goals? If the answer is yes, then benefits must be structured to reflect the current needs of retired workers rather than their past contributions. Furthermore, if Social Security is viewed as a public welfare program, then its regressive tax structure must be modified along more progressive lines. For example, Social Security is the single largest tax paid by a low-income worker, yet that same worker receives the lowest benefits when he or she retires. Hence, workers hurt most by the tax receive the fewest benefits. Using that same line of reasoning, if Social Security is designed for social assistance, then should everyone, regardless of income, be eligible? More particularly, should the wealthy be allowed to be beneficiaries? Unfortunately, there are no simple answers to these questions.

Should We Privatize Social Security?

Proposals to fully or partially privatize Social Security with individually managed accounts have emerged from several quarters, including the Clinton adminstration. Supporters argue that privatization would provide the individual with control of the Social Security portion of his or her retirement plan, and that successful investors who never touched their accumulations could achieve higher rates of return and higher benefits than Social Security provides.

The question of privatizing Social Security played an important role in the 2000 presidential election. George Bush proposed making per-sonal retirement accounts part of Social Security reform, thereby allowing workers to divert part of their Social Security payroll tax to private investment accounts. He argued that such private accounts could be expected to reap rewards for investors better than meager benefits likely to come to young workers from the dwindling Social Security funds. Bush's proposed plan would convert the 65-year-old OASDI from a program based exclusively on guaranteed benefits into a system in which private markets and investment risk would figure prominently for the first time. In contrast to Bush's carve-out approach, his opponent Al Gore proposed to have the government match contributions made by eligible individuals with tax credits that would vary according to income.[49]

Hans Riemer argues that the privatization of Social Security should be rejected. He cites four reasons:

1. Privatization would end the guaranteed economic security of Social Security (the only economic security Americans currently have) by replacing it with risky stock market accounts. Given current economic trends, future retirees will be forced to rely more on their savings and investments than previous generations. With the erosion of private pension plans and the increased reliance on personal savings and investments, individuals will face much greater risks than in the past—even without privatization of Social Security. Poor investments and/or volatile markets coupled with the elimination or reduction of guaranteed Social Security benefits could potentially lead to the financial ruin of retirees. In addition, unforseen factors such as bad investment advice, poor portfolio performance (resulting from overly conservative or overly aggressive investment strategies), market downturns at retirement time, inflation, and outliving personal savings and investments could be factors in promoting economic insecurity in old age.

2. Privatization would cause stiff tax increases for younger generations, forced market investment, and lower benefits. To institute private accounts, young workers would have to fund both existing Social Security payments and their own accounts for several decades. The alternative would be steep benefit cuts for current retirees. In even a partially privatized system, many younger workers would actually lose money because of the combined effects of steep tax increases, benefit cuts, government borrowing, and high administrative costs.

3. Privatization would undermine the security of those workers who take time out of paid work to care for families, raise children, care for aging parents, or look for new employment. In a system based on individual accounts, any absence from the workforce would directly reduce retirement benefits because they would be tied directly to individual contributions. Unlike a privatized system, Social Security's current benefit formula strengthens families by helping to smooth out the risks associated with absences from work. This is a particularly important concern for women, who already face higher rates of poverty in old age.

4. Under the current Social Security system, working Americans contribute to the Social Security trust fund and collect a base-level pension determined by their total earnings. Lower-wage workers are supported in part by the larger contributions of higher-wage counterparts. Hence, by pooling financial resources the Social Security program is able to reduce the poverty rate for seniors. This is a central democratic feature of Social Security that works only if everyone contributes to the trust fund. Under a fully privatized system, this social contract would be destroyed, as everyone would contribute only to

their individual retirement accounts. The result would be more overall inequality and higher poverty rates for the elderly.[50]

Conclusion

Social insurance programs are replete with both contradictions and difficulties. Nevertheless, social insurance programs, especially OASDI, have become a mainstay of the American social welfare state. Despite the original intent of its architects, Social Security has become a primary source of financial support for elderly people in this country. Moreover, OASDI has demonstrated the ability not only to arrest the poverty rate for its constituents, but actually to reduce it. A majority of Americans have come to view Social Security as a right and to count on its benefits.

Social insurance programs represent a major source of security for both elderly Americans and present-day workers. Over the past 50 years, Americans have come to believe that regardless of the ebb and flow of economic life, Social Security and Unemployment Insurance embody a firm governmental commitment to care for workers and the elderly. Economic gains made by elderly people since the mid-1960s have validated this belief. Because Social Security is clearly linked to past contributions, beneficiaries experience little stigma. This is not true for the highly stigmatized beneficiaries of public assistance programs, and it is to this population that we will turn in the next chapter.

 # Discussion Questions

1. The social insurance programs, especially Social Security, are among the most popular social welfare programs in the nation. Part of the reason for this popularity is that unlike income maintenance programs, social insurance is not stigmatized. What are

other reasons for the popularity of the social insurance programs?

2. There are serious questions about the future of Social Security. Some critics argue that Social Security is doomed, because the trust funds are expected to be depleted by the middle of the next century. Other observers argue that Social Security is sound, because the federal government is backing it. Is Social Security currently on solid ground, and can we expect it to be healthy in the future? If so, why? If not, why not?

What can be done to make the system more stable?

3. The Social Security system is currently plagued by several different problems. What is the most important problem facing the system?

 # Notes

1. Frances Fox Piven and Richard A. Cloward, *Regulating the Poor: The Functions of Public Welfare* (New York: Vintage, 1971).

2. David P. Beverly and Edward A. McSweeney, *Social Welfare and Social Justice* (Englewood Cliffs, NJ: Prentice-Hall, 1987).

3. Piven and Cloward, *Regulating the Poor,* p. 100.

4. W. Andrew Achenbaum, "Social Security: Yesterday, Today and Tomorrow," The Leon and Josephine Winkelman Lecture, University of Michigan School of Social Work, March 12, 1996.

5. Achenbaum, "Social Security."

6. Social Security Administration, "Social Security Trust Funds: Frequently Asked Questions," June 7, 1999. Retrieved 2000 from the World Wide Web: http://www.ssa.gov/OACT/ProgData/fundFAQ.html

7. Social Security Administration, "Fast Facts and Figures," Office of Policy, Office of Research, Evaluation and Statistics (Washington, DC: August 2000).

8. Department of the Census, *Current Population Reports, 1981,* Series P–60, No. 125 (Washington, DC: U.S. Government Printing Office, 1981).

9. Social Security Administration, "Fast Facts: SSI." Retrieved 2000 from the World Wide Web: http://www.ssa.gov:80/statistics/fastfacts/pageii.html

10. Ibid.

11. U.S. House of Representatives, Committee on Ways and Means, *Overview of Entitlement Programs, 1992 Green Book* (Washington, DC: U.S. Government Printing Office, 1992), p. 485.

12. U.S. Department of Labor, "UI Data Summary," 2000. Retrieved 2000 from the World Wide Web: http://www.workforcesecurity.doleta.gov/unemploy/content/data_stats/datasum00/2ndqtr/home.htm

13. Isaac Shapiro and Marion Nichols, *Far from Fixed: An Analysis of the Unemployment Insurance System* (Washington, DC: Center on Budget and Policy Priorities, March 1992), p. viii.

14. Diana M. DiNitto, *Social Welfare: Politics and Public Policy,* 2nd ed. (Englewood Cliffs, NJ: Prentice Hall, 1991), p. 87.

15. U.S. House of Representatives, *1992 Green Book,* pp. 520 and 513–514; U.S. Department of Labor, "UI Data Summary."

16. Center on Budget and Policy Priorities, *Unemployed and Uninsured* (Washington, DC: Center on Budget and Policy Priorities, March 1991), p. 4.

17. William Conerly, "Full Employment Organization." Retrieved from the World Wide Web: http://www.fullemployment.org/familyleaves.html#a6

18. Oren Levin-Waldman, "Reforming Unemployment Insurance: Toward Greater Employment," Working Paper No. 152, The Jerome Levy Economics Institute, Annandale-on-Hudson, NY, December 1995.

19. Ibid.

20. U.S. Department of Labor, "UI Data Summary," 2000.

21. Ibid.

22. Isaac Shapiro and Robert Greenstein, *A Painless Recession* (Washington, DC: Center on Budget and Policy Priorities, February 1991), p. xiii.

23. Levin-Waldman, "Reforming Unemployment Insurance."

24. Stephen M. Colarelli and Lawrence Brunner, "Solving Problems in Unemployment Insurance," Mackinac Center for Public Policy, 1994. Retrieved from the World Wide Web: http://www.mackinac.org/13

25. Joseph Dear, "Partner, Not Problem," *TechNews* 1, no.1 (January/February 1995), p. 1.

26. DiNitto, *Social Welfare.*

27. U.S. House of Representatives, *1992 Green Book,* pp. 1707–1709.

28. U.S. Department of Labor, "State Benefit Compensation Laws," 1998. Retrieved from the World Wide Web: http://www.dol.gov/dol/esa/public/regs/statutes/owcp/stwclaw/table6.pdf

29. U.S. House of Representatives, *1992 Green Book,* pp. 1707–1709.

30. Charles Prigmore and Charles Atherton, *Social Welfare Policy* (Lexington, MA: D. C. Health, 1979), pp. 66–67.

31. W. Joseph Heffernan, *Introduction to Social Welfare Policy* (Itasca, IL: F. E. Peacock, 1979), p. 138.

32. Ted Dimig, "Social Security on the Brink," *Houston Chronicle* (August 4, 1996), pp. 1F and 4F.

33. Joseph F. Quinn and Olivia S. Mitchell, "Social Security on the Table," *The American Prospect* 26 (May–June 1996), pp. 76–81.

34. C. Eugene Steuerle, "Why Are Social Security Benefits Adjusted Every Year?" AARP Webplace, 2000. Retrieved from the World Wide Web: http://www.aarp.org

35. C. Merton and Joan Broadshaug Bernstein, *Social Security: The System That Works* (New York: Basic Books, 1987).

36. American Association of Retired Persons, *A Profile of Older Americans* (Washington, DC: AARP, 1991), pp. 9–10.

37. Michael Doerflein, Angela Garner, Niki Gober, and Stacy Lochala, "Social Insurance," unpublished paper, University of Houston Graduate School of Social Work, Houston, TX, May 1996.

38. Spenser Rich, "Plan Deepens Cuts for Future Retirees," *Washington Post* (May 22, 1995), p. A1.

39. Bernard Gavzer, "How Secure Is Your Social Security?" *Parade* (October 18, 1987), p. 9.

40. Social Security Administration, "The Future of Social Security." Retrieved 2000 from the World Wide Web: http://www.ssa.gov/pubs/100.55.html

41. Social Security Administration, Social Security and Medicare Board of Trustees, "A Summary of the 2000 Annual Reports." Retrieved April 2000 from the World Wide Web: http://www.ssa.gov/OACT/TRSUM/trsummary.html

42. Robert J. Shapiro, "The Right Idea for 1990: Cut Social Security Taxes," *Economic Outlook* 4 (January 29, 1990).

43. American Association of Retired Persons, *A Profile of Older Americans* (Washington, DC: AARP, 1999).

44. U.S. House of Representatives, *1992 Green Book,* p. 109.

45. Social Security Administration, *Social Security Bulletin, Annual Statistical Supplement, 1984–85* (Baltimore, MD: Social Security Administration, April 1986); Shapiro, "The Right Idea for 1990."

46. Doerflein et al., "Social Insurance."

47. Quinn and Mitchell, "Social Security on the Table."

48. Bernstein and Bernstein, *Social Security.*

49. Walt Duka, "A Lot Is at Stake: Bush, Gore Collide over Social Security's Future," *AARP Bulletin* 41, no. 8 (September 2000), pp. 3 and 25.

50. Hans Riemer, "Four Arguments against Social Security Privatization," 2030 Center, May 17, 1998. Retrieved from the World Wide Web: http://www.ourfuture.org/readarticle.asp?ID=197

chapter 11

Public Assistance Programs

This chapter examines key public assistance programs, including the former Aid to Families with Dependent Children (AFDC); AFDC's replacement, Temporary Assistance to Needy Families (TANF); Supplemental Security Income (SSI); and General Assistance (GA). This chapter also investigates and analyzes the problems and issues inherent in public assistance programs.

The American social welfare state is a complex brew of programs, policies, and services. Perhaps few people, including many policymakers, fully appreciate the complexity of the welfare system. One reason is that unlike many European countries, which operate under a comprehensive and integrated welfare plan, the United States possesses a patchwork quilt of social welfare programs and policies. Because of the nation's historical ambivalence about providing public relief, most welfare legislation has resulted from compromises and adroit political maneuvering rather than from a systematic plan. In short, public assistance in the United States is not a coordinated, comprehensive, integrated and nonredundant system of social welfare services; instead, it is a helter-skelter mix of programs and policies.

Public assistance programs are one of the most misunderstood parts of the U.S. welfare state. Although expenditures for public assistance programs are far less than for social insurance programs, they tend to be more controversial. Unlike social insurance, public assistance programs are based entirely on need and are therefore means tested. Figure 11.1 lists the major federal governmental spending areas and the relative expenditures on each.

The rationale for public assistance programs that offer cash, medical, and other forms of assistance is grounded in the concept of *safety nets:* plans designed to ensure that citizens receive

FIGURE 11.1　Where Federal Dollars Go

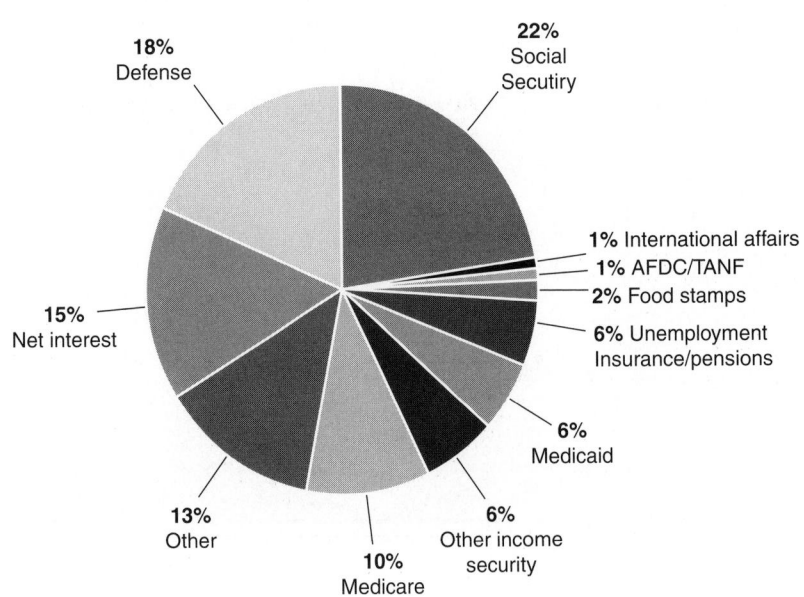

Source: Economic Report of the President, February 1995 (Washington, DC: U.S. Government Printing Office, 1995).

basic services and that they do not fall below a certain poverty level. There are, however, actually 51 separate safety nets—one in each state and one in the District of Columbia. Although federal guidelines help determine the level of aid for the poor, individual states have extensive freedom to fashion their own safety nets. States differ as to benefit levels, and one national study found that the vast majority lack an adequate safety net to help the poor and the jobless.[1] Nevertheless, a major component of the safety net consists of programs designed to ensure that families and individuals receive the resources necessary for survival.

 # Some Assumptions That Underlie Public Assistance

Americans' attitudes toward public assistance are characterized by a mixture of compassion and hostility. This ambivalence plays out in a series of harsh and often conflicting assumptions about public assistance recipients. The struggle over the former AFDC program is symbolic, reflecting the tensions around Americans' ideas about wealth, opportunity and privilege.

On the hostility side, the argument goes like this: If privilege is earned by application and hard work, then people are poor because they lack the desire to elevate themselves out of poverty. In effect, the poor do not apply themselves because they are lazy. To those driven by the intensely competitive spirit of U.S. society, the refusal of the poor to compete appears as a serious character flaw. On the other hand, the reality is that only a few paychecks separate the welfare recipient from the average citizen—thus the compassion. Although the theory of democratic capitalism implies that hard work guarantees success, real life often tells a different story. The tensions and contradictions that characterize contemporary life color people's views about public assistance. The following assumptions, among others, underlie many facets of public assistance: (1) Generous benefits create a disincentive to work; therefore, recipients must always get fewer benefits than they would under the minimum wage. (2) Welfare recipients need prodding to work because they lack internal motivation. (3) Recipients must be forced to engage economic opportunities. (4) Work is the best antipoverty program. (5) Public assistance programs must be highly stigmatized; otherwise people will turn to them too readily. And (6) women receiving public assistance should work, and poor children should not have the luxury of being raised by a full-time homemaker. These assumptions about public assistance—many of which are remarkably similar to those that formed the basis of the Elizabethan Poor Laws—lead to numerous myths and fears.

Myths about Public Assistance

Because there are so many commonly held myths about public assistance, it is important to discriminate between fact and fiction. (In the items that follow, AFDC and TANF are used interchangeably because they served and serve the same clientele.) Several entrenched myths about AFDC/TANF are these:

Myth 1. Many families on the public assistance rolls include an able-bodied father who refuses to work.

Fact. The former Aid to Families with Dependent Children–Unemployed Parent (AFDC–UP) program (322,000 families) accounted for only 12 percent of the total 4.7 million families on AFDC in 1992. About 90 percent of TANF families are headed by one parent—mostly mothers who are unmarried, divorced, widowed, or separated—with only 10 percent of public assistance households being two-parent families.[2] Ninety percent of AFDC children live with their mothers and 10 percent with their fathers. Sixty-six percent of AFDC recipients are children, the remaining recipients being mothers (18.6 percent) and the aged (15.6 percent). Fewer than 1 percent of all welfare recipients are able-bodied males. Among children who were AFDC recipients, almost 60 percent have parents who are not married to each other.[3] Forty-one percent of the fathers of these children cannot be found.[4]

Myth 2. Most poor people are on public assistance, and the number is growing.

Fact. The percentage of poor people receiving welfare has declined since the early 1970s. Although the number of poor people with children rose 50 percent between 1973 and 1989, the number of AFDC families grew by only 20 percent.[5] The TANF rolls decreased from 1996 to 2000 by 47 percent. Moreover, two-thirds of the poor (21.2 million of the 33.6 million poor people in 1991) received *no* money from AFDC, and more than a third do not receive food stamps or medicaid. Public assistance rolls have historically gone up or down depending on the economic conditions in a particular state or locality.

Myth 3. Recipient mothers have more children in order to collect greater benefits; therefore, families on public assistance are large and steadily growing in size.

Fact. TANF families in 1999 included an average of 1.8 children, about the same number as overall U.S. families. About 52 percent of TANF families had only 1 child; 27.6 percent had two or more; and only 7.7 percent had four or more children. Further, the state with the largest number of dependent children in TANF families was Louisiana (2.9 children), which pays one of the lowest benefits.[6] Moreover, slightly less than half of all states have enacted **family cap** legislation, which prohibits TANF families from receiving additional assistance for any child born after the mother has enrolled in the program.[7]

Myth 4. Once on welfare, always on welfare.

Fact. This is now a moot point, because the 1996 TANF regulations instituted a five-year lifetime benefit cap for recipients. Even before TANF, however, more than half of all AFDC recipients left the rolls within one year of going on welfare; by the end of two years, the percentage increased to 70 percent. However, within the first year after leaving welfare, 45 percent returned; almost 66 percent returned by the end of three years. Over the course of seven years, more than 75 percent of those who left welfare returned at some point. From 1968 to 1989, the average total time on welfare was 6.2 years.[8]

Myth 5. Welfare programs create dependency, which is transmitted intergenerationally.

Fact. Although the vast majority of people on AFDC stayed less than four years, those who stayed eight years or more accounted for half the number of people on the rolls at any given point in time.[9]

Research on **welfare dependency** is inconclusive. Robert Moffitt found that the length of welfare spells varied with demographic characteristics, the generosity of the state's public assistance program, and local labor market conditions.[10] P. J. Leahy, T. F. Buss, and J. M. Quane found that previous work experience, age at entry to welfare, and number of children were the best predictors of long-term welfare use.[11] Mary Jo Bane and David Ellwood found that race, education, marital status, work experience, and disability status influenced first-spell durations. These same variables influenced recidivism. Bane and Ellwood also point out that many of the long-term users cycled in and out of welfare, apparently trying to leave but unable to do so permanently.[12] According to Greg Duncan and Saul Hoffman, the total income package received by AFDC families often contained more income from other sources than from welfare, with labor income being mixed with welfare income.[13]

The phenomenon of welfare receipt across generations is not yet fully understood. According to Duncan and Hoffman, only 19 percent of African American and 26 percent of white women coming from heavily dependent welfare homes were heavily dependent on welfare themselves. The 19 percent of second-generation dependent African American women was the same percentage as that of black women heavily dependent on welfare who did not grow up in heavily dependent welfare households. The researchers found that African American men who grew up in heavily dependent welfare households showed no decrease in the average number of working hours; in contrast, white men from heavily dependent welfare homes averaged fewer hours of work per week than did otherwise similar white men.[14]

On the other hand, Peter Gottschalk found a positive intergenerational relationship between welfare use by mothers and daughters.[15] M. Ann Hill and June O'Neill also found persistence in welfare dependency across generations. Looking at data from the National Longitudinal Survey of Youth (NLSY), these researchers found that young white women from welfare families had a 24 percent chance of being on welfare, compared with a 2 percent chance for non-Hispanic white women coming from nonwelfare families. Comparable figures for African Americans were 42 and 15 percent; for Hispanics, 34 and 8 percent.[16] In their study of men's earnings, Mary Corcoran, Roger Gordon, Deborah Laren, and Gary Solon found that "One of our strongest results is the large negative association between a son's outcomes and welfare receipt in his family of origin."[17] Although correlations may exist between welfare receipt and family of origin, the question remains as to whether parental receipt of AFDC was the *cause* of the children's behavior.

Myth 6. Most welfare recipients are African Americans and Hispanic Americans.

Fact. In 1999 non-Hispanic whites constituted 30.8 percent of recipients, African Americans 38.3 percent, and Hispanics 24.5 percent. The remaining recipients were Asian, Native American, or of another ethnicity.[18] Although the percentages of African Americans and Hispanics on the welfare rolls were larger than these groups' representation in the population, this is not surprising, given that people of color are generally poorer than whites.

Myth 8. Public assistance benefits provide a disincentive to work; people on welfare either don't want to work or are too lazy to work.

Fact. In 1999 the nationwide TANF work participation rate was over 38 percent. The rate was above 50 percent in Montana (92 percent), Oregon (97 percent), Illinois (60 percent), Wisconsin (80 percent), and Ohio (54 percent).[19] TANF and AFDC benefits are or have been exceedingly small. In the typical or median state, AFDC benefits in 1992 for a three-person family equaled $372 per month, or 41 percent of the poverty line. Even with the inclusion of food stamps, in every state the combined benefits fell below the poverty line; and in more than half the states the combined benefits of food stamps and AFDC did not equal two-thirds of the poverty line.[20]

Myth 9. Public assistance recipients are doing better than ever.

Fact. The reverse is true. Public assistance recipients are actually doing worse than ever. From 1972 to 1992 AFDC benefit levels did not keep pace with inflation, falling 43 percent (after adjusting for inflation) in the typical state. This decline reflected a benefit loss of $279 per month, or more than $3,300 a year, in 1992 dollars.[21] Maximum benefits were even a little less generous under TANF than under AFDC (mostly because benefit levels were not adjusted for inflation). For the most part, the differences in total income under the two regimes are small, and differences in the work incentives are modest at best.[22]

Myth 10. Unmarried mothers constitute the bulk of welfare recipients.

Fact. Although this is true, according to Duncan and Hoffman, the most important causes for beginning AFDC spells were (1) divorce or separation (45 percent), (2) an unmarried woman's becoming a pregnant household head (30 percent), and (3) a drop in earnings of the female head of the household (12 percent). Conversely, the predominant reasons for terminating AFDC spells were (1) remarriage (35 percent), (2) an increase in the earnings of a female householder (21 percent), and (3) children's leaving the parental home (11 percent).[23]

Myth 11. It is easy to get on public assistance; hence, too many undeserving people are receiving benefits.

Fact. In addition to meeting stringent income and asset guidelines, applicants for food stamps and public assistance recipients must provide extensive documentation and meet verification requirements. Almost 97 percent of Food Stamp Program benefits go to households with incomes at or below the poverty line. More than half those benefits go to households with gross incomes at or below *half* of the poverty line.[24] Moreover, in 1990, for example, 63 percent of all applications for AFDC assistance were denied.[25]

Myth 12. AFDC recipients migrate to states where benefits are high.

Fact. A Wisconsin study showed that only 10 percent of AFDC recipients who had entered the state in a given period were motivated primarily by the availability of higher benefits.[26] Other studies indicate that poor people migrate for a variety of reasons, including proximity to family and friends, the desire for a better life, and the hope of finding work. Although research by the Wisconsin Policy Research Institute concluded that poor people do migrate across state lines to receive higher benefits,[27] the study failed to show that it is high benefits per se that cause migration. According to Henry Freedman of the Center for Social Policy, "Census data on migration show that poor people move in the same direction as those who are not poor, usually toward states with jobs and booming economies rather than those offering higher welfare benefits."[28] At best, the question of whether poor people migrate for higher welfare benefits remains unresolved.

Myth 13. Welfare spending consumes a large portion of state budgets.

Fact. Most states are experiencing significant welfare-related budget surpluses. Specifically, federal TANF funding levels were set at 1994–95 levels, but states are now experiencing a 47 percent reduction in TANF caseloads. In 1999 this surplus reached $400 million in Texas alone. Even before the TANF windfall, in 1991, states spent an average of 3.4 percent of their total budgets on AFDC. Because an amount averaging 1.5 percent of state budgets came from the federal government, states spent only about 2 percent of their budgets on AFDC.[29]

Myth 14. AFDC benefits influence decisions having to do with family structure (i.e., childbearing, marriage, divorce, and living arrangements) by encouraging women to head their own households.

Fact. Under the TANF guidelines, teenage mothers under age 18 are not entitled to benefits unless they are living at home or in a supervised facility. Although some empirical studies found a small correlation between AFDC benefits and the number of women who chose to head households or remarry, most researchers believe that the evidence does not support the hypothesis that the generosity of the welfare system is responsible for the trends in illegitimacy or the growth of single female–headed households. For example, although total welfare benefits have declined since 1975, the number of single female–headed households and the illegitimacy rate have remained relatively constant.[30]

Myth 15. Public assistance caseloads are composed mainly of unwed teenage mothers.

Fact. Although half of recipient mothers began their receipt of AFDC as teenagers (i.e., under age 20), teenage mothers made up only a small portion of the public assistance caseload at any one time. In 1992, 8.1 percent of the AFDC caseload consisted of families headed by a teenage mother. Almost half (47.2 percent) of AFDC mothers were in their twenties, a third (32.6 percent) were in their thirties, and 12.1 percent in their forties.[31]

Aid to Families with Dependent Children

AFDC was the most controversial program in the U.S. welfare system. The ostensible purpose of AFDC was to maintain and strengthen family life by providing financial assistance and care to needy dependent children in their own homes or in the homes of responsible caregivers. Despite these modest goals, the AFDC program has often been used as a symbol in the ideological battle between liberals and conservatives. This has caused AFDC recipients to be victimized in two ways: (1) by their own poverty, and (2) by ideologically motivated assaults against their character and motives.

AFDC was the largest public assistance program. The requirement for receiving AFDC was that a child be deprived of the parental care of one parent because of death, desertion, separation, or divorce. (In the case of the AFDC–Unemployed Parent program, the criterion was deprivation of parental economic support because of unemployment or illness.) In 1992 AFDC served 4.8 million families (about 13.6 million individuals) at a cost of $22.2 billion. Of the 13.5 million recipients, about 67 percent, or 9.2 million, were children. Total AFDC monthly benefits in 1992 averaged $388 per month per family, but benefits varied widely across states. AFDC recipients in 1992 totaled about 5 percent of the U.S. population, and 13 percent of all children in the United States were covered. In 1990, about 60 percent of all children in poverty received AFDC benefits, a significant reduction from the 81 percent of poor children who received them in 1973.[32]

The Evolution of the AFDC Program

Welfare reform has been a heated topic in the United States for several decades. Most presidents since John F. Kennedy have either offered welfare reform proposals or at least given lip service to the need for reform. To understand the broader debate around welfare reform, it is important to examine the history of the AFDC program.

Originally called Aid to Dependent Children (ADC), the AFDC program was part of the Social Security Act of 1935 and was designed to provide support for children by dispensing aid to their mothers. In 1950 the adult caregiver (usually the mother) was made eligible for ADC benefits.[33] Also in the 1950s, medical services paid for in part by the federal government were made available for ADC recipients. In the late 1950s and early 1960s, some critics began to believe that ADC rules led to desertion by fathers, because only families without an able-bodied father were eligible for relief. In 1961 a new component was added that allowed families to receive assistance in the event of a father's incapacity or unemployment. The new program, Aid to Families with Dependent Children–Unemployed Parent (AFDC–UP), was not made mandatory for the states, and until the welfare reform act of 1988, only 25 states and the District of Columbia had adopted it. In 1962 ADC was changed to AFDC to emphasize the family unit.

By 1962 the focus of the AFDC program had shifted to rehabilitating recipients. Policies were enacted that mandated massive casework and treatment services. To increase the chances for success, the social service amendments of 1962 limited the caseloads of social workers to a maximum of 60. Before 1967 all AFDC services were delivered by one worker. As of 1972, federal policy dictated that the AFDC program be divided into social services and **income maintenance programs.** This policy required that one worker be assigned the AFDC paperwork and that the other be responsible for social services.

Despite intensive social services, the number of AFDC recipients grew rapidly throughout the 1960s, then tripled from 1960 to 1970. From 1971 to 1981 that number rose another 50 percent, and in 1992 it reached an all-time high of 13.6 million recipients. In 1950 AFDC recipients had represented 1.5 percent of the population; by 1992 that proportion had reached 5 percent.

One notorious chapter in AFDC history involved the man-in-the-house rule. This policy mandated that any woman with an able-bodied man in the house would be terminated from AFDC—because, regardless of whether the man was the father, it was thought to be his responsibility to support the family. This policy was manifested in "midnight raids" in which social workers made late-night calls to determine if a man was present. Even a piece of male clothing found on the premises could be a reason to cut off aid. In some states the man-in-the-house rule was extended to include rules on dating. In 1968 the U.S. Supreme Court struck down the rule in Alabama, and the Court later reinforced its decision in a California case.[34]

Until the 1996 enactment of the TANF program, the Family Support Act (FSA) of 1988 was one of the most important pieces of welfare legislation since the New Deal. Touted by former congressman Thomas Downey as the first "significant change in our welfare system in 53 years,"[35] the welfare reform bill of 1988 (which was budgeted at only $3.3 billion over a five-year period) attempted to change AFDC from an income support arrangement to a mandatory work and training program. To carry out this goal, the bill established the **Job Opportunities and Basic Skills (JOBS)** program. JOBS required women on welfare with children under age three (or, at state option, age one) to participate in a work or training program. By 1990 each state was required to enroll at least 7 percent of its recipients in a state basic education program, job training, a work experience program, or a job search program. By 1993 that requirement was to rise to 20 percent. As a further incentive, recipients who became employed were to get 12 months of child care assistance and Medicaid benefits after they terminated AFDC.[36]

Adoption of the AFDC–UP program became mandatory for all states, although they could decide to limit enrollment for two-parent families to 6 out of 12 calendar months in a year. Moreover, one family member of an AFDC–UP household was required to participate at least 16 hours per week in a make-work job in return for benefits. In addition, the AFDC reform bill called for mandatory child support payments to be automatically deducted from an absent parent's paycheck. Finally, the FSA allowed states to require a teenage recipient to live with a parent or in a supervised environment in order to be eligible for assistance.[37] Former house member Dan Rostenkowski estimated that an additional 65,000 two-parent families would receive benefits, that 400,000 people would participate in workfare by 1993, and that 475,000 people would be eligible for transitional Medicaid benefits under provisions of the bill.[38]

The FSA's promise soon faded. Instead of declining, AFDC caseloads actually rose by 2.1 million from 1990 to 1992. Federal matching funds to states for the JOBS component of the FSA were capped at $1.1 billion in 1994. Sar Levitan and Frank Gallo wrote that "even if the program expends all the available federal funds, the total work/welfare investment will remain below the [1980] peak level of $3 billion (1992 dollars)."[39] By the end of 1991 the states had spent less than half of the available federal JOBS funds.[40] With limited exceptions, the FSA was a conservative triumph. "By replacing liberal tenets of entitlement, self-determination and federal responsibility with more conservative notions of contract, compulsion, and states' rights," observed Mimi Abramovitz, "welfare reform erodes some of the fundamental principles that support the U.S. welfare state."[41] Underappreciated at the time was the FSA component that permitted states to request waivers to existing AFDC rules. In part, this opened the door for the radical welfare reforms that emerged in 1996.

In his 1992 presidential campaign, Bill Clinton promised to "end welfare as we know it" by instituting a two-year cap on AFDC benefits. In May 1993 Clinton appointed a working group on welfare reform, headed by well-known poverty researchers David Ellwood and Mary Jo Bane and White House advisor Bruce Reed. The Clinton administration welfare reform bill, the Work and Responsibility Act, was completed in June 1994. Among other things, the bill called for expanding the JOBS program to help recipients move from welfare to work. Developing a personal plan, each AFDC recipient would enter into an agreement with a public assistance agency in return for subsidized child care, health care benefits, and other supportive services. Incorporated into this plan was a two-year time limit for parents to receive cash assistance, after which they would be expected to become employed (preferably in the private sector). Parents unable to find employment after two years would leave the JOBS program and enter a subsidized employment program that would provide subsidies to public or private employers to hire recipients in "worklike" positions. Employers would provide a paycheck that equaled the individual's former welfare check in return for the necessary number of working hours at the minimum wage. Participants would have to change jobs every 12 months and be reassessed every two years. In addition, participants would be eligible to receive AFDC benefits if their wages were low enough, and they would continue to receive Medicaid and subsidized child care. The Clinton bill attempted to fight teenage pregnancy by providing grants to up to 1,000 high-risk high schools that proposed innovative teenage pregnancy prevention programs. Lastly, the Clinton bill would have made time limits and work requirements national, but states would have had considerable flexibility for innovation.[42]

While some political insiders believe that the Clinton administration got the policy right, they also believe that the administration introduced welfare reform far too late in the game and with far too little focused effort.[43] Specifically, the Clinton welfare reform bill was introduced in the summer of 1994, when it was forced to compete with a faltering health care bill and a struggling crime bill. By November 1994 the election of the ultraconservative 104th Congress obviated the possibility of passing any welfare reform bill that included liberal components such as subsidized employment.

The Personal Responsibility and Work Opportunity Reconciliation Act of 1996

On August 22, 1996, President Bill Clinton signed the Personal Responsibility and Work Opportunity Reconciliation Act of 1996 (PRWORA) (H.R. 3734), a complex 900-page document that confused even seasoned welfare administrators.[44] The PRWORA was one of the most important pieces of welfare legislation to emerge since the Social Security act of 1935. It fundamentally changed the social welfare system by replacing AFDC, JOBS, and the **Emergency Assistance Program** with the Temporary Aid for Needy Families (TANF) program. The PRWORA was touted as reducing federal AFDC costs by $55 billion over a six-year period.

One of the most radical features of the PRWORA was among the least understood. Under the PRWORA there is no federal **entitlement** to assistance. In contrast, the former AFDC program operated under the principle of entitlement. This meant that states had a responsibility to provide assistance to persons who were eligible under the law. This did not mean that states were required to provide something for nothing. In fact, states could have required the vast majority of those receiving assistance to participate in work, education, training, or job search programs as a condition of receiving aid. The principle of entitlement does mean, however, that states were not permitted to turn away those who qualified under the rules. Under

TANF, in contrast, no family or child is *entitled* to assistance.[45] In effect, the TANF **disentitlement** rescinded the 60-year-old federal entitlement to support for poor children and families. TANF operates in the following manner:

- In order to receive a TANF grant, each state must submit a plan to the Department of Health and Human Services. In turn, HHS determines whether the plan contains the information required by law. Plan requirements are generally limited, and much of the operational detail may be omitted.

- TANF provides lump-sum federal **block grants** to states to run their own welfare and work programs. Each state receives a block grant representing recent federal spending for a **fiscal year (FY)** (generally, the highest of FY 1992–95) for that state for the AFDC program, the JOBS program, and the Emergency Assistance Program. A minority of states receive annual 2.5 percent adjustments in the form of supplemental grants; but for most states the TANF block grant amount is frozen through FY 2002, except for any adjustments due to bonuses or penalties. Under limited circumstances, a state experiencing an economic downturn may qualify for additional federal funding through a contingency fund ($2 billion for 1997–2001). To be eligible to receive funds from the contingency fund in an economic downturn, the state needs to maintain 100 percent of its historic spending level in the year in which the contingency funds are requested. A state may also apply for a loan from the Rainy Day Loan Fund, which provides a $1.7 billion federal revolving loan fund. To be eligible, a state must not have incurred any penalties under the cash block grant. The maximum loan is 10 percent of a state's grant for up to three years, after which the loan must be repaid with interest.

- Maintenance of effort provisions require that in order to receive a full block assistance grant, the state must spend nonfederal funds at no less than 80 percent of a historic spending level based on 1994 spending. This requirement is reduced to 75 percent for a state that meets the act's **work participation rate** (percentage of TANF recipients in the workforce) requirements. A state that does not maintain the required spending level risks a dollar-for-dollar reduction in its block grant funding.

- States are prohibited from using TANF funds to assist certain categories of families and individuals. The most important prohibition involves using TANF funds to assist families in which an adult has received assistance for 60 months or more. (States can, however, choose to pay beneficiaries with their own monies.) States can provide exceptions for up to 20 percent of their caseloads. Although the PRWORA mandates a five-year lifetime limit on cash assistance, it also allows states to set a shorter time limit. Other restrictions include a prohibition on assisting minor parents unless they are attending school and living at home or in an adult-supervised living arrangement (subject to limited exceptions), and a requirement to reduce or eliminate assistance if an individual does not cooperate with child support–related requirements, such as identifying the father.

- The TANF block grant has four specific work requirements. First, unless a state opts out, it must require nonexempt unemployed parents or caregivers to participate in community service after receiving assistance for two months. Second, states must outline how they will require a parent or caregiver receiving benefits to engage in work not later than 24 months after they receive assistance. Third, a state must meet a work participation rate for all families that began at 25 percent in 1997 and has increased to 50 percent in 2002 (see Table 11.1). Fourth, states must meet different participation rates for two-parent families; for example, the rate was set at 75 percent in 1997–98 and at 90 percent in 1999. Failure to comply with the last two work requirements results in the state's paying a penalty of 5 percent the first year and 2 percent thereafter (capped at 21 percent).

- States can spend their block grants on cash assistance, noncash assistance, services, and administrative costs in connection with assistance

TABLE 11.1 ■ TANF Work Participation Rates

ALL TANF FAMILIES	
FY 1997	25%
FY 1998	30%
FY 1999	35%
FY 2000	40%
FY 2001	45%
FY 2002 and beyond	50%
TWO-PARENT TANF FAMILIES	
FY 1997	75%
FY 1998	75%
FY 1999 and beyond	90%

Source: American Public Welfare Association, "The Personal Responsibility and Work Opportunity Reconciliation Act of 1996 (Conference Agreement for H.R. 3734)." Analysis prepared by the American Public Welfare Association, the National Governors' Association, and the National Conference of State Legislatures, August 22, 1996.

to needy families with children. States can also choose to spend up to 30 percent of their TANF funds to operate programs under the Child Care and Development Block Grant and the Title XX Social Services Block Grant (which was cut by 15 percent in 1996). No more than one-third of that amount can be used for programs under Title XX, and the funds must be spent on programs for children or families whose incomes fall below 200 percent of the poverty line. Existing child care provider standards for health and safety are maintained.

■ When parents participate in required work activities, the state may (but is not required to) provide child care assistance. However, a state may not reduce or terminate a family's assistance if a single parent of a child under age six refuses to comply with work requirements based on a demonstrated inability to obtain needed child care.

■ In a departure from the rules under AFDC, TANF recipients are not automatically eligible

for Medicaid. However, states are required to provide Medicaid coverage for single-parent families and qualifying two-parent families with children if they meet the income and resource eligibility guidelines that were in effect in the state's AFDC Program on July 16, 1996. (States may modify these guidelines to a limited extent.)

■ When PRWORA was enacted, most states were in the midst of welfare reform activities through the AFDC waiver process. The PRWORA provides that if a state had a waiver in place before October 1996, it can continue that waiver and will not be required to comply with inconsistent provisions of the act.[46]

■ The TANF program attempted to address the dramatic increase in nonmarital births (especially teen births). First, state TANF plans must demonstrate how they will establish goals and take action to prevent and reduce out-of-wedlock pregnancies, especially teenage pregnancies. Second, states must establish actual numerical goals for reducing their "illegitimacy ratio" for fiscal years 1996–2005. Third, the act provides financial incentives to states to reduce their out-of-wedlock birth rates. On the incentive side, the act authorizes HHS to give $20 million apiece to the five states that show the greatest success in reducing their nonmarital birth rate—while lowering their abortion rate below its 1995 level.[47]

■ The PRWORA also allows states to impose a family cap, which denies assistance to children born into families who are already receiving public assistance.

■ States must permanently deny all Title IV-A cash assistance and Food Stamp Program benefits to individuals convicted of felony drug possession, use, or distribution. Other members of the family can continue to receive benefits. States may opt out of this provision or limit the period of denial by passing legislation.

In addition to TANF, the PRWORA included other reforms:

■ As amended in 1997, the law makes immigrants who arrived in the United States before

August 22, 1996, eligible for Medicaid and SSI benefits. However, immigrants who arrived after that date are barred from all means-tested, federally funded public benefits for the first five years they are in the country. After five years states can, at their option, offer Medicaid to immigrants. Accordingly, aged, blind, and disabled immigrants are not categorically eligible for Medicaid. There are exceptions made for persons who have worked for 40 quarters in covered employment or served in the military. No state can deny coverage of emergency medical services to either illegal or legal aliens.

■ Illegal immigrants are barred from the following federal public benefits: (a) grants, contracts, loans, and licenses; and (b) retirement, welfare, health, disability, public or assisted housing, postsecondary education, food assistance, and unemployment benefits.

■ SSI eligibility was tightened for children. The new standard eliminated the comparable severity standard, the individual functional assessment, and references to maladaptive behavior.

■ The Food Stamp Program retained its structure as an uncapped individual entitlement. However, PRWORA included $27.7 billion in food stamp cuts, accounting for more than half of all non-Medicaid savings. The 1995 Urban Institute report on the anticipated effect of PRWORA estimated that the bill would push 1.1 million children (2.6 million people overall) into poverty and noted that the food stamp cuts were a main factor in those numbers. Under the PRWORA, Food Stamp Program benefits would be cut almost 20 percent in 2002, with average benefits falling from about 80 to 66 cents per person per meal. A substantial portion of these benefit savings would come from across-the-board reductions affecting nearly all recipient households, including families with children, the working poor, the elderly, and the disabled. In addition, Food Stamp Program benefits were limited to three months every three years for unemployed able-bodied single adults aged 18 to 50. An additional three months of eligibility was granted to adults laid off their jobs.

■ Child support collection efforts were strengthened through a number of provisions of the act. First, one condition for receiving assistance is that families must assign child support collection rights to the state.[48] Second, states will have to operate automated centralized collection and disbursement units. Third, noncustodial parents who are $5,000 or more in arrears are subject to passport revocation. Fourth, states must accord full faith and credit to out-of-state child support orders and liens. Federal income withholding, liens, and subpoena forms must be used for interstate cases. Fifth, states must have laws in effect that establish authority to withhold, suspend, or restrict driver's, professional, occupational, and recreational licenses of individuals who owe overdue support or who fail, after notification, to comply with subpoenas or warrants. Other provisions include automated state directories of new hires; expansion of income withholding requirements; access to locator information networks such as that of law enforcement; use of social security numbers on licenses and other government-issued documents; and expedited **establishment of paternity.**[49]

Why was this radical welfare reform bill passed in 1996? The conservatism of the 104th Congress clearly spurred on the bill. The rapidly approaching presidential election also may have played a role, especially in light of the fact that President Clinton had already vetoed a similar welfare reform bill in January 1996. The rhetorical slogans Clinton used in his 1992 presidential campaign, calling for "an end to welfare as we know it" and "two years and off to work," were viewed by the public as endorsements of the popular dislike of AFDC, not as promises to relieve poverty. Frances Fox Piven argues that Clinton's rhetoric created a maelstrom of which he eventually lost control. Moreover, by the time Clinton signed the PRWORA, he had already approved draconian state waivers that were in some cases more punitive than TANF. These factors made it relatively easy for the 104th Congress to usurp the welfare issue that the Clinton administration had already heated up.[50]

State Welfare Reform Waivers

Through state waivers, radical welfare reform was well under way even before the PRWORA became law. In fact, the Clinton administration had granted 43 state waivers during the first term, more than all previous administrations combined. By mid-1996, 43 of the 50 states already had approved or pending AFDC waivers that incorporated many of the TANF reforms. Pointing to the flood of AFDC waivers signed by the Clinton administration, the Enterprise Institute's Douglas Besharov observed, "Based on what happened in the last year, President Clinton can justifiably claim that he has ended welfare as we know it." Besharov, describing the waiver requests as "welfare reform on the cheap without an increase in spending for child care or a penny for job training," concluded that "the revolutionary result is an end to personal entitlement."[51] By 1996, state waivers that included time limits, benefit cuts, and widespread sanctions for disapproved behaviors had already resulted in a 10 percent drop in the AFDC rolls.

Many of the state waivers incorporate several components, including:

- Time-limited lifetime benefits (frequently a two-year cap).
- Enforcement of parental responsibility. Typical provisions include child support; family caps; required immunization of children as part of the benefit process; linkage of benefits to school attendance and grades; and requirements aimed at discouraging teenage pregnancy by obliging teen mothers on public assistance to attend school and live at home or in an approved setting.
- Simplification and efficiency in the delivery of benefits, including the use of **electronic benefit transfers (EBT)** for delivering public assistance benefits; fraud deterrent measures such as the use of debit cards instead of coupons for food stamps; and privatization—subcontracting to the private sector the delivery and management of public assistance programs.

- Measures designed to move people quickly from work to welfare: incentives (often tax breaks) to encourage the private sector to hire recipients; higher limits on earnings and assets (e.g., the value of a vehicle); and job placement and training.
- Measures for promoting personal responsibility: cash-out incentives that offer beneficiaries the cash equivalent of food stamps; offers of one-time lump-sum payments (equaling total benefits for three months to a year) instead of monthly grants; help in the development of asset accounts; termination of cash benefits to those who fail to comply with state welfare rules and regulations; required performance of community service; and the mentoring of recipients.

Because the TANF program allows states with AFDC waivers to continue to function under them until the waiver expires, the vast majority of the states are free to continue with their welfare demonstration projects. The Appendix at the end of this chapter summarizes some of the states' welfare demonstration programs.

Has the PRWORA Worked?

Both Democrats and Republicans have pronounced the PRWORA a success. Specifically, both parties point to the 47 percent drop in public assistance caseloads since the implementation of the bill. Despite this drop, important questions remain. First, caseloads had already begun to drop—from a high of 5 million in 1994 to 4.8 million in 1995, 4.5 million in 1996, and 3.9 million in 1997. These declines occurred in years before the PRWORA was fully in effect. Second, two primary factors explain the more recent caseload changes: the strong labor market and changes in welfare policy. In the late 1990s the nation was in the midst of the longest peacetime expansion in its history, with low unemployment and rising wages. Because of this, gains in employment and wages were experienced by groups who typically had high rates of welfare use. Third, it is difficult to ascertain the success of the PRWORA, because it has been in effect only in a strong economic period. A robust economy may well be masking important program flaws. In addition, the full effect of the federal five-year lifetime cap won't be realized until the 2001 figures are known. The real measure of success for the PRWORA, then, will be its performance in a recessionary period.

Nevertheless, preliminary reports are that most recipients who are leaving public assistance (50 to 60 percent) are taking jobs that are paying just over minimum wage. Because of this, most families continue to receive some form of public assistance. Child care and transportation remain difficult barriers, and some families are finding it increasingly problematic to meet their basic needs for food and clothing. Approximately one-fifth of families leaving welfare return within several months.[52]

Arguably, too much emphasis has been placed on caseload reduction and insufficient attention paid to income and poverty outcomes. For example, a study conducted by the Center on Budget and Policy Priorities (CBPP) found that between 1993 and 1995 the average earnings and overall incomes of low-income female–headed families with children rose substantially as the economy expanded; but from 1995 to 1997, despite continued economic growth, the average incomes of the poorest 20 percent of these families fell. This occurred as welfare changes took effect based on state reforms and the enactment of the 1996 PRWORA.[53]

Specifically, the CBPP study reports that between 1995 and 1997 the annual income of the poorest 20 percent of female–headed families with children, a group that includes 2 million families and 6 million people, fell an average of $580 per family. (The study counts food stamps, housing subsidies, the Earned Income Tax Credit, and other benefits such as income.) Even when all benefits are included, these families have incomes below three-quarters of the poverty line. Among the poorest 10 percent of female–headed families with children, income fell an average of $810 between 1995 and 1997, an average loss of one-seventh of these families' incomes. The average income of these extremely poor families slipped from 35 percent of the poverty line in 1995 to 30 percent in 1997. This income decline wiped out the income gains they secured between 1993 and 1995 and returned average income for this group to the levels of 1993, when unemployment was high. In addition, these income declines had a significant impact on children. The number of poor children fell by 2.4 million between 1993 and 1995, but by only 360,000 between 1995 and 1997. Moreover, those children who remained poor became poorer on average. The CBPP study finds that these disturbing developments were caused largely by sharp reductions in the government cash and food assistance these poor families received. More than three-quarters of the income loss among both the poorest tenth and the poorest fifth of female–headed families with children resulted from declines in assistance provided through means-tested programs, primarily cash and food stamp aid.[54]

In the final analysis, the ultimate test of welfare reform should be not simply how much caseloads fall but whether the well-being of poor children and families has improved.

 # Supplemental Security Income

Supplemental Security Income (SSI) is in some ways one of the more confusing social programs in the United States. In essence, SSI is designed to provide cash assistance to the elderly and to disabled poor people, including children. Although a public assistance program, SSI is administered by the Social Security Administration.

In 2000 the SSI program served 6.6 million people and cost the federal government roughly $30 billion. Unlike OASDI, SSI is a means-tested, federally administered public assistance program funded through general revenue taxes. The basic SSI payment level is adjusted annually for inflation. A portion of elderly people receive SSI in conjunction with Social Security. Age is not an eligibility criterion for SSI, and children may receive benefits under the disabled or blind portion of the act. Among others, the following people are eligible for SSI: (1) mentally retarded individuals, (2) people who are at least 65 years old and have little or no income, (3) those considered legally blind, (4) adults (at least 18 years old) who qualify as disabled because of a physical or mental impairment expected to last for at least 12 months, (5) visually impaired persons who do not meet the criteria for blindness, (6) drug addicts and alcoholics who enter treatment, and (7) children under 18 who have an impairment of severity comparable with that of an eligible adult. In 1999 20 percent of the SSI rolls were made up of eligible low-income seniors and 79 percent of SSI recipients were disabled. Fifty-six percent of SSI recipients were aged 18 to 64; 31 percent were 65 and older; and 13 percent were under age 18.[55]

To qualify for SSI, an applicant must have limited resources. In 2000, SSI applicants were allowed to own resources valued at less than $2,000 for an individual and $3,000 for a couple (excluding, e.g., a house; a car, depending on use and value; burial plots; and certain forms of insurance). SSI benefits are not generous, although they can be higher than TANF benefits. In 1999 the average monthly benefit was $369. The maximum payment for an individual in 2000 was $512 a month; for a couple, $769 a month.[56]

The SSI program began during the Nixon administration. When former president Richard Nixon took office in 1972, he attempted to streamline the welfare system by proposing a Family Assistance Plan (FAP). In this plan Nixon proposed a guaranteed annual income that would replace AFDC, Old Age Assistance (OAA), Aid to the Blind (AB), and Aid to the Permanently and Totally Disabled (APTD). Although Congress rejected the overall plan, the OAA, AB, and APTD programs were federalized in 1972 under a new program—Supplemental Security Income. Basically, the federal government took over the operation of those programs from the state governments. No longer would state governments set eligibility levels, establish minimum payment levels, or administer the programs.

In 1974 there were 3.25 million SSI recipients. By 1999 that number had doubled, to 6.9 million. Concomitantly, SSI expenditures increased from $5 billion in 1974 to more than $29 billion in 2000. In large part these increases resulted from the rapid growth in the numbers of disabled persons receiving SSI, a population that rose from 2.4 million in 1984 to 3.4 million in 1999.[57] Some analysts predict that SSI spending will outpace every social welfare program with the exception of Medicaid.[58]

Two groups of SSI recipients that have shown dramatic growth in their numbers are children with disabilities and adults with disabilities relating to drug addiction and alcoholism. One reason for this growth was the Supreme Court's decision in the *Sullivan v. Zebley* case, which made children eligible for SSI if they had a disability that was comparable to that of an eligible adult. Children are now the fastest growing population on SSI, and by 1999 almost 1 million children were recipients. Of those children, more than 60 percent either have an emotional/mental disorder or are mentally retarded. Moreover, more than 50 percent of adults on SSI either have a mental/emotional disorder or are mentally retarded.[59]

The other group of SSI recipients that have drawn attention are individuals whose drug or alcohol addiction (DAA) is the primary contributing factor in their disability. Between 1980 and 1994, the number of DAA recipients on SSI rose from 23,000 to 86,000, bringing the number to more than 250,000. This group cost the federal government $1.4 billion in 1994.[60]

As a response to SSI's rapid growth, in 1994 Congress passed the Social Security Independence and Program Improvements Act, which, among other things, restricted SSI and Disability Insurance benefits to individuals disabled by drug and alcohol addiction. The new restrictions required SSI beneficiaries with a DAA diagnosis to participate in a substance abuse program. In addition, these beneficiaries (except those for whom treatment was not available) would receive benefits for only 36 months. Beneficiaries removed from the SSI rolls would continue to receive Medicare or Medicaid unless they failed to comply with their treatment program for 12 successive months.[61] In addition, the law also established a Commission on Childhood Disabilities to reevaluate the SSI definition for childhood disability and to look into possible alternative definitions.[62]

Major concerns regarding SSI involve the low level of income and the requirements for eligibility. In fact, 28 states supplement SSI payments with an additional grant, and some states have opted to let the federal government administer that stipend. States may also choose to set their own requirements for supplementary SSI payments, thereby including only certain beneficiaries or limiting disabilities.[63] Stringent eligibility requirements and complex red tape have kept many people off the SSI rolls. For example, the cases of recipients are reviewed every three years (a procedure that usually involves a medical review), and "continuing disability reviews" may be required. Some critics believe that the federal government has purposely made entrance and continued maintenance in SSI difficult in order to discourage participation.

The majority of individuals and couples receiving SSI benefits remain below the poverty line. Historically, only couples receiving a combination of SSI, Social Security, and food stamps were raised to or above the poverty line. In 1999, an aged individual who received SSI was raised to only 75.0 percent of the poverty threshold (see Table 11.2).

General Assistance

General Assistance (GA) consists of cash and in-kind assistance programs financed and administered entirely by the state, county, or locality in which they are located. They are designed to meet the short-term or ongoing needs of low-income persons ineligible for (or awaiting approval for) federally funded cash assistance such as Temporary Assistance for Needy Families (TANF) or Supplemental Security Income (SSI).[64]

Thirty-five states, including the District of Columbia, have state GA programs; that is, programs in which state government has at least some involvement. Twenty-four of those 35 states have statewide GA programs with uniform eligibility rules. The benefit schedule is also generally uniform, although some states adjust their benefits to reflect varying costs of living in different areas. Nine of the 35 states lack uniform state programs but require all counties to provide some form of GA. As a result, eligibility rules and benefit schedules in these states can vary dramatically from county to county. Although Wis-

TABLE 11.2 ■ Supplemental Security Income: Expenditures, Population, Benefits, and Percentages of Poverty Threshold, Selected Years, 1999 Dollars

	1974	1980	1990	1999
Expenditures (in billions)	$18.6	$16.4	$23.8	$32.1
Population (in millions)	4.0	4.1	4.8	6.6
Monthly Benefits, Aged Individuals	$78.48	$112.45	$175.29	$282.37
Percentage of Poverty Line	74.1%	72.3%	73.9%	75.0%
Monthly Benefits, Aged Couples	$93.02	$157.56	$322.82	$642.29
Percentage of Poverty Line	88.1%	86.0%	87.9%	89.3%

Source: Compiled from U.S. House of Representatives, House Ways and Means Committee, *Overview of Entitlements, Green Book, 2000* (Washington, DC: U.S. Government Printing Office, 2000).

consin and Virginia do not provide statewide GA assistance, they do provide supervision and funding for counties that choose to have the program. States lacking governmental involvement in the provision of GA are unlikely to have counties with this program.

Able-bodied adults without children (the population most often associated with GA) are actually the people least likely to be eligible for such assistance. Although the two most populous states, California and New York, provide GA to able-bodied adults without children, few others do. Only 13 states provided GA to this population in 1998, down from 15 states in 1996. In addition, many states that provide assistance to able-bodied adults without children limit the duration of assistance and/or provide in-kind rather than cash benefits. As a rule, GA programs are more likely to provide benefits for the disabled or elderly people, children, or families with children than they are to serve the able-bodied. Thirty-four states provide GA to disabled, elderly, or otherwise unemployable individuals not eligible for (or awaiting approval for) SSI. Twenty-four states provide assistance to children or families with children not eligible for TANF, such as children living with an unrelated adult.

Most states limit GA eligibility to the severely poor. Although income eligibility varies across states, a majority of state GA programs limit assistance to only those with incomes less than half the poverty level. Most states set resource limits between $1,000 and $2,000, regardless of family size. However, states generally disregard some earned income and certain resources (e.g., a home and a car) in determining eligibility.

Nearly all states providing assistance to able-bodied adults require recipients to work in order to maintain benefits. Recipients who fail to comply with the work requirements are often sanctioned, usually losing their entire benefit for a specified period of time.

GA benefits are low and falling. The maximum monthly benefits available to GA recipients are generally set far below the federal poverty level. Among the 27 state GA programs that provide cash benefits to individuals, the average monthly benefit maximum for an individual is only 37 percent of the federal poverty line. GA benefits are also lower than benefits in federal assistance programs. On average, GA monthly cash benefits for disabled individuals are less than 50 percent of maximum state SSI monthly cash benefits, and maximum GA benefits for families are less than 90 percent of the maximum state TANF benefits. Moreover, few states have adjusted their benefits since 1996, with the result that benefits have gradually decreased in real terms. Only 7 states increased benefits in 1998, with 2 states reducing their benefits.

Most states that provide GA also provide medical assistance for GA recipients, although medical benefits are usually less comprehensive than Medicaid. In 5 of the 35 state GA programs, all recipients are eligible for medical assistance under that state's Medicaid program or Medicaid waiver program. Of the remaining 30 state programs, 26 provide medical assistance to some or all GA recipients, either through a formal state or county GA medical program or by providing benefits to cover certain medical expenses. The medical benefits vary widely in the types of services covered, but most provide more limited benefits than Medicaid.

GA caseloads are small compared to those of the major federal assistance programs. Most state GA programs provide benefits to less than 15 percent of the numbers served by TANF. In New York (which has the most extensive GA program) about 8 percent of poor people receive GA—about 232,000 recipients a month. This is less than one-quarter of the number of TANF recipients in New York and about one-third the number of SSI recipients.

Several states have changed their GA programs since 1996, almost always in the direction of tightening nonfinancial eligibility requirements. Connecticut eliminated eligibility for a category of employable persons without children, although it did create an additional category for persons with an impairment that interrupts employment. The District of Columbia eliminated its General Public Assistance program for persons awaiting SSI. Hawaii and Connecticut lengthened the time a person must be disabled in order to qualify for GA as temporarily disabled. Four of the 35 state GA programs established or increased time limits, raising the total number of states with time limits to 10. Three states increased or established durational residency requirements, raising the total number of states with these requirements to 7. Hawaii and Michigan, however, removed time limits for persons with a disability.

PRWORA-related changes to immigrant eligibility have had a significant impact on GA policies. Following the federal lead, 19 of the 35 state GA programs tightened restrictions on assistance to immigrants. New York and Washington, however, have explicitly enabled immigrants no longer eligible for federal benefits to qualify for GA.

Changes to family assistance as a result of PRWORA enabled states to shift some of the burden of providing assistance to the federal government. Nine states transferred from their GA program to their TANF program the responsibility for providing assistance to pregnant women in their first two trimesters and/or two-parent families with little or no work history. Both of these categories of recipients were ineligible for federal assistance under the prior law.[65] The general trend of curtailing and lowering of GA benefit levels puts large numbers of poor people at grave risk.

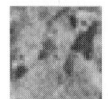

Issues in Welfare Reform

The basic principle underlying the PRWORA was that authority for the design and management of social programs should be transferred from Washington to the states. Promoted early by the Reagan administration, this ideological perspective has been labeled the "devolution revolution" or the "new federalism."[66] Energized by the omnipresent cry of "states' rights," the new federalism trades off long-term and stable federal funding for increased state control in the form of block grants.

The use of social service block grants is not new. The last social program that was block granted and devolved to the states, the Title XX Social Services Block Grant, has been so mismanaged that it is implicated in the deaths from abuse and neglect of 2,000 children annually: almost half of such child deaths are in cases known to state children's agencies, but the agencies are unable to prevent them.[67] States have proven so inept at protecting children that courts have assumed management of child welfare agencies in 21 states and the District of Columbia.[68]

The responsibility of states to care for their poor is also not new. In part, it was the failure of states to meet that responsibility that originally led to the creation of the 1935 Social Security Act, legislation that federalized most public assistance and social insurance programs. Devolving welfare responsibility to the states is neither new nor novel. Nevertheless, the question remains: If states were unable to mount compassionate social welfare programs before 1935, what is the evidence that they will do so today, especially in difficult economic times?

Teenage Pregnancy

Teenage birthrates in this country have declined steadily since 1991. Although this is good news, teen birthrates in the United States remain high, exceeding those in most developed countries. For example, they are twice as high as in England and Wales or Canada, and nine times as high as in the Netherlands or Japan. Nearly 13 percent of all U.S. births in 1997 were to teens (ages 15 to 19), and almost 1 million teenagers become pregnant each year, with about 485,000 giving birth. Consider the following overview of teen pregnancy in the United States:

- Thirteen percent of all U.S. births are to teens. Teens account for 31 percent of all nonmarital births, down from 50 percent in 1970. Each year, almost 1 million teenage women—10 percent of all women aged 15 to 19—become pregnant. Seventy-eight percent of teen pregnancies are unplanned, accounting for about one-quarter of all accidental pregnancies annually. Seventy-eight percent of births to teens occur outside of marriage.

▪ More than half (56 percent) of the 905,000 teenage pregnancies in 1996 ended in births (two-thirds of which were unplanned). Six in 10 teen pregnancies occur among 18- to 19-year-olds.

▪ The fathers of babies born to teenage mothers are likely to be older than the women: About one in five infants born to unmarried minors are fathered by men five or more years older than the mother.

▪ The teenage birthrate is declining. Between 1991 and 1998, the rate fell by 18 percent (from 62.1 per 1,000 women to 51.1). Still, in 1998 about 5 teenage girls in 100 had a baby. Steep decreases in the pregnancy rate among sexually experienced teenagers accounted for most of the drop in the overall teenage pregnancy rate in the early to mid-1990s. Surveys indicate that 20 percent of the decline occurred because of decreased sexual activity; 80 percent was the result of more effective contraceptive practice.

▪ About one out of four teen mothers goes on to have a second baby within two years after the birth of her first baby.

▪ Life often is difficult for a teenage mother and her child. Teens who give birth are much more likely to come from poor or low-income families (83 percent) than are teens who have abortions (61 percent) or teens in general (38 percent). Teen mothers are more likely to drop out of high school than girls who delay childbearing. Only about 64 percent of teen mothers graduate from high school or earn a GED within two years after they would have graduated, compared to 94 percent of teen women who did not give birth. While 7 in 10 teen mothers complete high school, they are less likely than women who delay childbearing to go on to college. With her education cut short, a teenage mother often lacks job skills, making it hard for her to find and keep a job.

▪ A teenage mother may become financially dependent on her family or on welfare. Teen mothers are more likely to live in poverty than women who delay childbearing, and nearly 75 percent of all unmarried teen mothers go on welfare within five years after the birth of their first child. In part because most teen mothers come from disadvantaged backgrounds, 28 percent of them are poor while in their 20s and early 30s; in contrast, only 7 percent of women who first give birth after adolescence are poor at those ages.

▪ Children whose mothers were age 17 or younger when they were born tend to have more school difficulties and poorer health than children whose mothers were 20 to 21 when they were born.

▪ One-third of pregnant teens receive inadequate prenatal care; babies born to young mothers are more likely to be low-birth-weight, to have childhood health problems, and to be hospitalized than are those born to older mothers.

▪ Nearly 4 in 10 teen pregnancies are terminated by abortion. There were about 274,000 abortions among teens in 1996. From 1986 to 1996, abortion rates among sexually experienced teens declined by 31 percent. In 1996, 35 percent of teen pregnancies ended in abortion. Fewer teens are becoming pregnant, and in recent years fewer pregnant teens have chosen to have an abortion. The reasons most often given by teens for choosing to have an abortion are concerns about how having a baby would change their lives, the feeling that they are not mature enough to have a child, and financial problems. Sixty-one percent of minors who have abortions do so with at least one parent's knowledge. The great majority of parents support their daughters' decision to have an abortion. Twenty-nine states currently have mandatory parental involvement laws in effect for a minor seeking an abortion: Alabama, Arkansas, Delaware, Georgia, Idaho, Indiana, Iowa, Kansas, Kentucky, Louisiana, Maryland, Massachusetts, Michigan, Minnesota, Mississippi, Missouri, Nebraska, North Carolina, North Dakota, Ohio, Pennsylvania, Rhode Island, South Carolina, South Dakota, Utah, Virginia, West Virginia, Wisconsin, and Wyoming).

▪ Both non-Hispanic white and black adolescents have experienced declines in pregnancy rates. Among black women aged 15 to 19, the pregnancy rate fell 20 percent between 1990 and 1996; among white teenagers it declined 16 percent. The pregnancy rate among Hispanic teenagers increased between 1990 and 1992 but then fell 6 percent by 1996.[69]

Out-of-wedlock births have grave economic consequences. This is especially true because teenage mothers, regardless of their income, are now more likely to keep their children.[70] The out-of-wedlock birthrate translates into important economic realities. For one, teenage mothers are twice as likely to be poor as nonteen mothers, and a teenage mother earns only half the lifetime wage of a woman who waits until she is 20 to have her first child.[71] Second, as mentioned above, a strong correlation exists between young single motherhood and high welfare dependency. In 1993, 75 percent of unmarried adolescent mothers became welfare recipients within five years of the birth of their first child.[72] Mothers with children age three and under are at the greatest risk of long-term welfare dependency. In 1989, teenage childbearing cost taxpayers almost $40 billion in AFDC, food stamps, and Medicaid costs.[73] Moreover, teen mothers who had grown up on AFDC were more than twice as likely to be welfare reliant themselves.[74] Thus, high rates of teenage pregnancy increase the likelihood of future welfare dependency.

Policymakers and analysts have long struggled with ways to curb teenage pregnancy. Although many programs have been developed to reduce teenage pregnancy, evaluations of these attempts have shown mixed results. One early teen pregnancy prevention program was Project Redirection. From 1980 to 1982, 805 AFDC-eligible mothers aged 17 or younger received intensive services to optimize educational, employment, and life management skills. Evaluation of Project Redirection mothers one, two, and five years after their participation in the program was mixed. Among the five outcomes—education, employment, welfare dependence, childbearing, and parenting/child development—the only area in which Project Redirection participants improved significantly relative to the control group was the last. Project Redirection teens fared no

better than the control group in obtaining a high school diploma or GED certificate. Although participants were more likely to be employed one year after exiting the program, their weekly earnings five years later were only $23 more than those of women in the control group. Five years later, the household income of the control group exceeded that of the Project Redirection group by $19. The effect of Project Redirection on welfare dependence was also ambiguous. Two years after participation, 7 percent of Project Redirection teens were on welfare; five years later, 10 percent fewer of the control group than of the Project Redirection teens were on welfare. Regarding childbearing, Project Redirection teens reported fewer pregnancies in the first and second years after the program; yet five years after the program, they exceeded the control group in their number of pregnancies as well as their number of live births. Researchers noted that many of the improvements of Project Redirection teens had disappeared after two years, leading the evaluators to conclude that "the program impacts were largely transitory."[75]

Even the transitory benefits of Project Redirection were to prove superior to those generated by a larger initiative mounted a few years later. From 1989 to 1992 researchers randomly assigned 2,322 poor young mothers, ages 16 to 22, either to New Chance—a program through which the women received health, education, and welfare assistance coordinated by a case manager—or to a control group that received no special services. At the 18-month follow-up, the experimental group fared worse than the control group in two important respects. First, New Chance participants were more likely to get pregnant again. New Chance mothers were less likely to be using contraception, were more likely to become pregnant, and were more likely to abort their pregnancies than the control group. Second, New Chance mothers were participating less in the labor market. Participants were less likely to be working after entering the program; were earning less; and, during the fourth to the sixth months, were more likely to be on AFDC.[76] To compound matters, New Chance cost $5,073 per participant, excluding child care. (If child care were included, an average of $7,646 was spent on each New Chance mother.)[77] The apparent failure of these prevention programs illustrates how little policymakers understand both the motivation and the behaviors associated with teenage pregnancy. It also illustrates how little is known about the interpersonal, social, and cultural components that promote and encourage teenage pregnancy.

The Underclass

The current discussion of the underclass was started in the 1980s by journalist Ken Auletta, who descriptively identified four groups that make up the underclass: (1) the "passive poor," usually those dependent on welfare; (2) hostile "street predators," often dropouts and addicts; (3) "hustlers," or opportunists, who do not commit violent crimes; and (4) the "traumatized"— alcoholics, bag ladies, and casualties of deinstitutionalization.[78] In the late 1980s William Julius Wilson revived the term, defining the underclass as

> [a] heterogeneous grouping of families and individuals who are outside of the mainstream of the American occupational system. Included . . . are individuals who lack training and skills and either experience long-term unemployment or are not members of the labor force, individuals who are engaged in street crime and other forms of aberrant behavior, and families that experience long-term spells of poverty and/or welfare dependency.[79]

Another description of the underclass is offered by Erol Ricketts and Isabel Sawhill, who define it as a subpopulation characterized by a cluster of behaviors and attitudes that are considered outside of current middle-class social norms.[80]

Relevant social science research has shown that the underclass in the United States increased from 1970 to 1980. Some researchers have estimated that in 1980 between 1 and 2 million people could be characterized as members of the underclass. According to Ricketts and Sawhill, who are considered to have done some

of the best empirical research on the subject, the "underclass" label applies to 1 percent of the U.S. population, roughly one-thirteenth of all people living under the poverty line. Using Ricketts and Sawhill's guidelines, more than 2.4 million people would have been classified as an underclass in 1992.[81]

The seriousness of the underclass phenomenon was underscored in research conducted by David Ellwood and Mary Jo Bane. In an examination of the Michigan Panel Study of Income Dynamics, Bane and Ellwood discovered that although most people are in poverty for short periods of time, a significant number have protracted spells in poverty. Significantly, 18 percent of poverty is long term, and almost 60 percent of the people who are poor at any given time are experiencing a long-term spell of poverty. When the costs of this poverty are borne by minority families, who are disproportionately poor, the consequences are disastrous. Since 1970, poor urban families have been more likely to have poor neighbors, evidence of a continuing deterioration in the socioeconomic condition of poor communities that makes it increasingly difficult to alleviate the pathology of "ghetto culture."[82]

Welfare Behaviorism

The TANF program is predicated on a kind of **welfare behaviorism:** an attempt to reprogram the behaviors of the poor. Current welfare reform efforts, however, are unlikely to deliver on the promises of this approach. Despite data demonstrating the marginal economic benefits of making welfare conditional, conservatives effectively leveraged a moral argument that public policy should change the behavior of the welfare poor. By the mid-1980s, conservative theorists had arrived at a new consensus on poverty; namely, that although the liberally inspired public assistance programs might once have been appropriate for the "cash poor," they were counterproductive with the "behaviorally poor."[83] Rather than alleviating the problems of the behaviorally poor, public welfare exacerbated the "culture of poverty." As poverty programs expanded, conservatives contended, the social dysfunctions of the behaviorally poor metastasized: Beginning as teen mothers, women dominated family life, ultimately becoming generationally dependent on welfare; young men dropped out of school, failed to pursue legitimate employment, and resorted to sexual escapades and repetitive crime to demonstrate prowess; children, lacking adult role models of effective parents at home and capable workers on the job, promised to further populate the underclass.

Conservatives differed in how to respond to behavioral poverty. In *Losing Ground* Charles Murray suggested "scrapping the entire federal welfare and income support structure for working-aged persons."[84] Not long after, Lawrence Mead offered a less draconian measure in *Beyond Entitlement:* Make receipt of public aid contingent on conventional behaviors, particularly work.[85] Eventually, both prescriptions were to be incorporated in welfare policy. Following Mead's admonition, the TANF required recipients to participate in work-related activities. As states secured federal waivers for "experiments," welfare mothers often had to meet a number of other requirements or risk losing aid: Through "Learnfare" children on public assistance had to demonstrate regular school attendance; through the family cap additional assistance for children born after a mother became eligible for assistance would be denied, inducing family planning; the establishment of paternity was required before a child could receive benefits, so as to enable the state to pursue child support; as a method for protecting public health, recipient children were required to have immunizations in order to attend school; to dissuade teenagers from becoming pregnant, states required teen mothers to live with their parents in order to get welfare. In seeking waivers, some states pursued Murray's contention that public assistance be terminated for the able-bodied. As momentum for welfare reform snowballed, the idea of time-limiting welfare benefits was incorporated into newer congressional proposals.[86]

The ending of the 60-year federal entitlement to an income floor for poor families has had extensive political fallout. Die-hard conser-

vatives justified termination of welfare with George Gilder's contention that what the poor needed most was "the spur of their own poverty,"[87] and "compassionate conservatives" found a rationale in "tough love." Either way, welfare reformers conceded that terminating benefits would probably worsen deprivation but argued that that was necessary too. If making welfare conditional worsened poverty, that was the price for combating the underclass. Liberals were aghast. Following Marian Wright Edelman's earlier demand that President Clinton veto welfare reform crafted by the 104th Congress,[88] the *Washington Post* weighed in with an editorial declaring that Clinton's signing the welfare reform plan would be "the low point of his presidency."[89] Citing conservative analysts such as James Q. Wilson, Lawrence Mead, John DiIulio, and William Bennett who had trepidations about the welfare reform plan, Senator Daniel Patrick Moynihan castigated President Clinton for endorsing a bill premised on the belief "that the behavior of certain adults can be changed by making the lives of their children as miserable as possible."[90] Liberal advocacy groups scrambled to convince the president to veto the legislation, but they failed.[91] Cleverly, Clinton had preempted their condemnation by announcing his intention to sign the plan before the conference proposal was voted on by either chamber of Congress. But heat from liberal activists intensified, leading Clinton to promise that he would push ameliorative action on the most controversial features of the welfare reform plan—elimination of benefits for disabled people and legal immigrants—through the incoming 105th Congress.

By mid-1996 evaluation research revealed that the results of state welfare demonstrations were at best problematic. Yet, regardless of what both liberal and conservative policy analysts were coming to conclude about making receipt of welfare contingent on specific behaviors, this research seemed only to accelerate the momentum behind welfare reform. Indeed, the contradictory evidence may well have fueled the palpable urgency that propelled welfare reform through the 104th Congress and on to the White House.

Time Limits. The ultimate in welfare behaviorism is time-limiting public assistance benefits. During his first presidential campaign, Bill Clinton won voters' approval for his pledge to end welfare. As conceived during the campaign, Clinton's prescription for welfare reform included a two-year time limit on receipt of AFDC followed by government-provided employment in the event a private sector job could not be found. In the presidency, however, Clinton was confronted with the cost of his proposal. The provision of a job for welfare recipients would increase welfare costs (perhaps to $10 billion), but the price tag on making similar opportunities available to the working poor was simply unacceptable (between $45 billion and $60 billion).[92] The president's working group on welfare reform finally resolved the matter by applying the two-year time limit, after which public employment would be available only to AFDC recipients born after 1971 (at that time, those under age 25).

Under the leadership of then House Speaker Newt Gingrich, the Republican-dominated 104th Congress presented a much stricter time limit through the Personal Responsibility Act (PRA). In addition to a two-year time limit for any given episode of receipt of welfare, the PRA imposed a five-year lifetime limit on receipt of public assistance. It was clear that Clinton and Gingrich had tapped deep public resentment about welfare. In 1996, Public Agenda, a nonprofit public opinion research organization, surveyed sentiment about welfare. In response to a series of vignettes about families on welfare, respondents approved time limits in the 80- and 90-percentile ranges. Significantly, even respondents who were welfare recipients approved of time limits, although at just slightly lower percentages.[93]

One of the most concise examinations of time-limiting welfare was done by the Urban Institute's LaDonna Pavetti. Using a computer simulation, Pavetti programmed a number of scenarios constructed from the primary features of welfare reform proposals before Congress. Both two- and five-year time limits were simulated; in addition, a series of exemptions were incorporated, including exemptions for having a child under 18 months of age, being disabled, and already having a job. Pavetti then projected the consequences for families who were newly eligible for AFDC as well as for those who were long-term dependents on public assistance. As might be expected, there are many permutations generated by so complex an analysis; however, the major findings were that *(a)* overall, 58 percent of families receive AFDC longer than two years, and more than one-third for longer than five years; *(b)* because welfare rolls are populated by families who have been on AFDC for a long period, at any given time about 70 percent have already received AFDC for longer than two years, and 48 percent for longer than five years; *(c)* exempting recipients because of very young children at home causes the number of families hitting a two-year time limit to drop from 37 percent to 10 percent; and *(d)* exempting recipients who have young or disabled children or who are already working causes the number of families reaching a two-year time limit to fall to 5 percent.

The implementation of time limits without exemptions would cut a swath through public assistance. If exemptions were granted for young children under Pavetti's scenarios, the AFDC termination rate for a two-year time limit would eliminate 207,000 families, including 307,000 children.[94] Yet, Pavetti's numbers may underestimate the casualty rate. Before passage of the PRWORA, the Center on Budget and Policy Priorities cited a Congressional Budget Office (CBO) report stating that "if all states were to adopt a two-year time limit, 5.5 million children would be denied aid by 2006, even assuming that states exempted 20 percent of their caseloads from these state time limits."[95]

Personal and Parental Responsibility. The welfare behaviorism in TANF reflects a belief in the value of personal and parental responsibility. This philosophy harks back to supposedly traditional "main street" values of self-reliance, independence, and individual responsibility. It is based on the idea that this country offers a level playing field replete with abundant economic and social opportunities. It also includes a de facto belief in the limited role of government. For liberals who have advocated expanded social programs, the TANF welfare reforms embody a world that seems at odds with the realities of modern civilization. For liberals, postindustrial capitalism is marked by an interdependence between individuals and government, with human and market needs being inextricably linked. From this perspective, the PRWORA not only is out of sync with the requirements of a postindustrial economy, but also serves to condemn individuals for their own impoverishment, to blame the victim, and to aggravate social injustice.

The view of parental responsibility reflected in the PRWORA focuses on several themes: (1) Fathers who beget children have a responsibility to financially support them; (2) mothers requesting public aid have a responsibility to establish paternity for the purpose of collecting child support; (3) mothers who have physical custody of children have a responsibility to provide for them financially through work efforts; (3) custodial parents have a responsibility to ensure that their children receive and appropriately respond to educational opportunities; and (4) custodial parents have a responsibility to provide basic public health protection for their children, including immunizations. These tenets of parenthood are neither extreme nor especially controversial. In fact, they are in part the glue that holds society together. Controversy arises, then, not on the correctness of these values but in their operationalization. More specifically, significant controversy surrounds the question of whether attempts at engineering appropriate social behaviors are successful or whether they simply function as punishment.

Examples of social engineering as social punishment abound. Learnfare, introduced in Wisconsin in the fall of 1988, targeted teenagers who had more than two unexcused absences from school. Under Learnfare sanctions, such absences would cause the family's AFDC benefits for a dependent teen to be reduced by $77 a month; for an independent teen with a child, the penalty was $190 a month. Wisconsin officials contended that such sanctions would result in the return of 80 percent of teens on AFDC who had dropped out of school. Rhetoric notwithstanding, an independent agency's subsequent

evaluation of the Milwaukee demonstration "did not show improvement in student attendance that could be attributed to the Learnfare requirement." Undeterred, state officials wrote to the evaluators and demanded that they suppress the parts of the study detailing the failure of Learnfare to enhance teen school attendance. When the researchers refused, Wisconsin officials canceled the contract, in the process impugning the professionalism of the evaluators.[96]

In Ohio, meanwhile, another demonstration program promised teens a $62-a-month carrot for good school attendance, coupled with a $62-a-month stick for truancy. Three years after the program's inception, LEAP (Learning, Earning, and Parenting) was heralded as a major victory in the battle against teen truancy. Pundits such as the late William Raspberry trumpeted LEAP's 20 percent increase in teens' rate of high school graduation and 40 percent increase in employment. A closer examination of the LEAP evaluation is less encouraging. The glowing results were reported only for teens currently enrolled in school and excluded those who had dropped out, even though both groups were part of the study's population. Including dropouts, LEAP's outcomes plummet: The number completing high school is not 20 but 6.5 percent; the number employed is not 40 but 20 percent. By comparative measures, LEAP *does* improve teen behavior, but only modestly. And if LEAP generated outcomes that were positive, it also produced negative results. For teens who had already dropped out of school—arguably, those most likely to join the underclass—LEAP produced no discernible effect. Also, because of the benefit reduction sanction levied against truant teens, a significant number of all mothers in the study reported "diminished spending on essentials for their families, especially clothing and food."[97] In their concluding observations, evaluators conceded that changing adolescent behavior is difficult and admitted that LEAP produced some "perverse effects."[98]

Another issue underlying the new welfare reforms involves (re)marriage. According to several studies, no more than a fifth of mothers leave AFDC/TANF as a result of earnings increases; most exits result from a change in marital status.[99] Yet public assistance programs punish marriage in two ways: (1) by how they treat a married couple with children in common, and (2) by how they treat families with stepparents. First, a needy two-parent family with children is less likely to be eligible for aid than a one-parent family. Although the nonincapacitated two-parent family can apply for TANF, many states' restrictions involving work expectation and time limits make the program inaccessible to many poor families. Second, a stepparent has no legal obligation to support the children of his or her spouse in most states. Nevertheless, AFDC/TANF cuts or limits benefits when a woman remarries by counting much of the stepparent's income when calculating the family's countable income, thus jeopardizing the mother's eligibility status.[100] In effect, there is a strong economic disincentive for a low-income woman to marry a man with low earnings. According to the conservative Heritage Foundation's Robert Rector:

> The current welfare system has made marriage economically irrational for most low-income parents. Welfare has converted the low-income working husband from a necessary breadwinner into a net financial handicap. It has transformed marriage from a legal institution designed to protect and nurture children into an institution which financially penalizes nearly all low-income parents who enter into it. Across the nation, the current welfare system has all but destroyed family structure in the inner city. Welfare establishes strong financial disincentives, effectively blocking the formation of intact, two-parent families.[101]

Welfare to Work

TANF is predicated on the belief that recipients should be moved off public welfare and into private employment as quickly as possible, a theme that has permeated welfare reform since the 1960s. Whereas conservatives argue that paid work is the best antipoverty program, some liberals have asserted that child rearing is also a productive form of work. Moreover, these liberals have contended that although it is socially acceptable for middle-class mothers to stay at home with young children, poor mothers are considered lazy and unmotivated if they try to do the same.

Workfare programs have been a constant feature of the welfare landscape since 1967, when new AFDC amendments were added to pressure recipient mothers into working. As part of those new rules, work requirements became mandatory for unemployed fathers, mothers, and certain teenagers. AFDC recipients who were deemed employable and yet refused to work could be terminated.[102] A work incentive program (WIN) was developed to provide training and employment for all welfare mothers considered employable (recipients with preschool-age children were exempt). Day care was made available to facilitate the WIN program. Partly because of a lackluster federal commitment (in 1985 the total federal contribution to WIN was only $258 million), the performance of work programs has generally been disappointing. In addition, many states were reluctant to enact mandatory job requirements, because they believed that enforcing them would cost more than simply maintaining families on AFDC.

Workfare was again resurrected in 1988, when it formed the backbone of the Family Support Act. By the early 1990s, however, the Manpower Demonstration Research Corporation (MDRC) had amassed considerable evidence about the performance of state welfare-to-work programs, and the results fell far short of what conservatives had promised in converting AFDC to an employment-based program. In the best of all welfare worlds, state welfare-to-work programs would show positive outcomes in three ways: (1) Earnings of welfare participants would improve—optimally, enough to make participants economically self-sufficient; (2) welfare expenditures through AFDC would decrease; and (3) states would recover the costs of putting in place welfare-to-work programs. But of 13 welfare-to-work programs evaluated in 1991, most boosted participants' earnings little more than $700 per year. Although most programs also experienced reductions in AFDC payments, these were modest; typically, less than $400 per year. And significantly, in only two programs were AFDC payment reductions greater than the programs' cost per welfare-to-work participant. In other words, in 11 of 13 welfare-to-work programs, the cost of mounting the welfare-to-work program was not recovered initially in welfare savings.[103]

As in most field research, there are important caveats to these findings. First, the welfare-to-work program that most efficiently met the three requirements noted above was Arkansas; for the first year of the program, earnings increased on average $167, and AFDC payments were reduced $145, enough to recover the additional cost of Arkansas's WORK program, $118 per participant. This outcome explains much of former president Clinton's enthusiasm about "ending welfare as we know it." Second, two programs were noted for significantly higher annual earnings ($2,000 plus) as well as welfare savings (more than $700), but in both cases the cost per participant was also high ($5,000 plus). Thus, fostering independence from welfare can entail an acute case of "sticker shock."

Yet these modest accomplishments were not to dampen the fervor of welfare-to-work zealots. They quickly pointed to the Riverside County, California, Greater Avenues for Independence (GAIN) program as an exemplar. Culminating an eight-year investigation of California's GAIN program, the nation's largest welfare-to-work effort, Judith Gueron, head of MDRC, chronicled Riverside County's achievements: a 26 percent increase in the number of AFDC parents working, an average earnings increase of 49 percent, and a 15 percent savings of welfare payments. Over three years, Riverside County GAIN participants' income increased $3,113; welfare savings for the same period were $1,983. In Gueron's words, these were "the most impressive [outcomes] measured to date anywhere."[104] On an annual basis, of course, such figures diminish in significance. Earnings increases on the order of $1,000 a year are unlikely to vault the typical AFDC family off of the program; welfare savings of little more than $600 a year do not raise the specter of

cashiering the welfare bureaucracy. Indeed, commenting on the Riverside experience, Randall Eberts of the Upjohn Institute for Employment Research observed that only 23 percent of participants were still employed and off AFDC three years after beginning GAIN.[105] Also, Riverside County's vibrant economy probably accounted for much of the success that GAIN did achieve, raising the question of how representative the Riverside results were.

To welfare reform researchers, the welfare-to-work bandwagon was less of a star-spangled apparatus than its proponents had made it out to be. Before his assignment to the Clinton working panel on welfare reform, Harvard's David Ellwood admitted as much, writing that the typical welfare-to-work program increased earnings between $250 and $750 per year. "Most work–welfare programs look like decent investments," he concluded, "but no carefully evaluated work–welfare programs have done more than put a tiny dent in the welfare caseloads, even though they have been received with enthusiasm."[106] A similar sentiment was expressed by workfare expert Judith Gueron:

> [Although] welfare-to-work programs have paid off by increasing the employment and earnings of single mothers and reducing their receipt of public assistance . . . MDRC's research also reveals the limits of past interventions. Whether the targeted group were welfare mothers, low-income youth who dropped out of high school, teenage parents with limited prospects, or unemployed adult men, the programs had little success in boosting people out of poverty. . . . Often, welfare recipients who get jobs join the ranks of the working poor.[107]

But perhaps, welfare reform proponents averred, the modest returns in welfare-to-work programs would be amplified over a longer period. If many AFDC recipients had been out of the labor force for so long, they suggested, a two- or three-year assessment of a welfare-to-work program's performance might not reveal more substantial longer-term benefits. Fortunately, in 1995 a five-year assessment of welfare-to-work programs in Virginia, Arkansas, Baltimore, and San Diego examined this possibility. At the end of 5 years, Virginia and Arkansas participants increased earnings a little more than $1,000, and those in Baltimore and San Diego experienced an earnings increase of a little more than $2,000. Welfare savings, on the other hand, varied widely. Baltimore reduced welfare costs $62; San Diego reported the greatest savings, $1,930. Net program costs varied as well, from $118 a participant in Arkansas to $953 a participant in Baltimore.[108] Once annualized, these figures confirmed the shorter-term experience of welfare-to-work programs in other locales. Again, earnings increases were modest, welfare programs savings somewhat less, and the recovery of setup costs questionable.

The long-term study of welfare-to-work provided additional insight that had not been available in previous research. For example, earnings of participants do not continue to increase with each additional year; rather, earnings tend to peak during the second or third year and then fall back toward the range prior to enrollment in welfare-to-work. The only program in which earnings did not fall was in Baltimore, the program with the highest cost per participant.[109] And by definition, higher cost per participant is inconsistent with welfare savings. Hence, a trade-off appears: The objectives of increasing earnings in order to make families independent of welfare and reducing government welfare payments are contradictory.

If the reality of welfare-to-work diverges from the rhetoric of welfare reform, it is because of the mistaken assumption that TANF mothers are so welfare dependent that they have no experience with the labor market. In fact, many mothers have worked and have, as a result, come to see welfare benefits as a form of unemployment or underemployment assistance. To explain the relationship between work and welfare, labor economist Michael Piore splits workers into primary and secondary labor markets. As explained in Chapter 5, workers in the primary labor market hold down salaried jobs that include health and vacation benefits, are full-time, and incorporate a career track. Workers in the

secondary labor market work for hourly wages—often at the minimum wage—in jobs that provide no benefits, are part-time or seasonal, and are not part of a career track.

Other research has captured the erratic relationship between work and welfare for many mothers on TANF. Findings of the Institute for Women's Policy Research revealed that 43 percent of former AFDC mothers were either peripherally attached to the labor market, augmenting welfare with wages, or drifting on and off of welfare depending on the availability of work. When AFDC mothers who were seeking work were coupled to the peripheral and drifting groups, 66 percent of welfare mothers were either participating in the labor market or trying to.[110]

But conditions of the secondary labor market make employment at this level problematic.[111] Given the reality of the secondary labor market, the trick of welfare reform is to catapult TANF mothers beyond the secondary labor market and into the primary labor market. If this could be done, earnings would increase enough to ensure economic self-sufficiency; and welfare savings would be substantial, because families would be unlikely to revert to public assistance in the future. The sticking point is that states need to make substantial investments to achieve such welfare-to-work program performance. But to do so creates two problems. First, a moral hazard emerges, as welfare beneficiaries become recipients of benefits that are not available to the working poor not on welfare. Working people often grumble that the welfare dependent obtain benefits not available to them—but they also suspect that ample benefits induce those who should be working to apply for public assistance. Second, a political hazard is created for any elected or appointed official who expresses a willingness to invest more in welfare recipients than in the working poor. In such circumstances, the prudent politician favors the least costly and most expedient option: to push welfare recipients into the labor market and celebrate doing so with paeans to the work ethic. These moral and political hazards thus prescribe the boundaries of plausibility; and perforce, welfare reform is limited to elevating the welfare poor to the level of the working poor.

Finally, TANF work-to-welfare programs are flawed in another way. Specifically, they fail to take into account barriers to employment. A study of welfare recipients by Sandra Danziger and her colleagues found unusually high levels of some barriers to work, such as physical and mental problems, domestic violence, and lack of transportation, but relatively low levels of other barriers, such as drug or alcohol dependence or a lack of understanding of work norms. Their study also found that recipients commonly have multiple barriers, and that the number of barriers is strongly and negatively associated with employment status. Almost two-thirds of the study respondents had two or more potential barriers to work, and more than one-quarter had four or more. Finally, Danziger and her colleagues found that the expanded model of barriers is a better predictor of employment than traditional models that rely on education, work experience, and welfare history. For example, they found that the number of years of prior welfare receipt is not correlated with current employment, once health and mental health factors, transportation, work skills, and perceived discrimination experiences are taken into account.[112]

The Inadequacy of Public Assistance Benefits

The TANF program is characterized by dramatically different state benefit levels. Over the years, unlike federal programs such as Social Security and SSI, AFDC benefits levels in most states were not automatically adjusted for inflation. In 1992 the combined benefits of AFDC and the Food Stamp Program were below the poverty level in all 50 states. In 41 of the 50 states the benefits were below 75 percent of the poverty line, less than $8,700 for a family of three. In 36 states the monthly AFDC benefit level in 1992 for a three-person family was less than $434, the same benefit as for one recipient in the SSI program. In half of these states the monthly benefit level was below $335. It is this benefit structure that forms the basis for current TANF benefits.

Conclusion: The Evolution of Public Assistance

For a half century, AFDC was a program that did little more than dispense checks; not until relatively recently has recipient behavior been a target for systematic intervention. Because of its lack of direction, AFDC became the source for derogatory colloquialisms such as "welfare mess" and "welfare queen." Instilling some order in welfare was bound to produce some desirable outcomes. It is the extent of positive results that is questionable.

Welfare analysts suspect that most of the improvement in welfare program performance is attributable to those recipients who are relatively well educated, have employment experience, and are upwardly mobile. Such welfare beneficiaries are good candidates for integration with the secondary labor market, and some of them will even find secure employment in the primary labor market, an accomplishment that will inoculate them against future poverty. Of the remaining welfare families, most may be socially mainstreamed with adequate inducements and supports. The welfare behaviorism articulated through initiatives such as welfare-to-work has been testing the malleability of this population. Some of this group will respond positively to incentives and sanctions; some will not. In all likelihood, many—perhaps 20 percent—will fail to negotiate the procedural thicket imposed by the welfare reforms of the late 1990s. While the PRWORA allows states to exempt 20 percent of families from time limits, there is no requirement that those on the lowest social stratum be allowed to stay on aid indefinitely. And indeed, there is no assurance that states will exempt the most troubled families from time limits. It is just as plausible that the savvy state welfare administrator would exempt mothers who are in lengthy educational/training programs, on the basis that they represent a better long-term investment of public resources. Even some conservatives are opposed to the institution of arbitrary time limits. At a 1996 conference on welfare reform, Lawrence Mead stated his opposition to time limits, primarily on the basis that virtually no research had been done to determine the consequences of terminating poor families from public assistance.[113]

Several features of TANF make its full implementation unlikely. A fundamental question is the extent to which states can be expected to comply with the federal work requirements. States must have 50 percent of single parents working at least 30 hours a week by 2002; but to date it is unclear whether most states will meet that target, especially in the event of an economic downturn. The Congressional Budget Office projected that over six years PRWORA grants would fall $12 billion short of the amount necessary to enable states to provide the services and opportunities necessary to meet work requirements; yet the legislation imposes penalties—ranging from 5 to 21 percent of federal funds—for noncompliance on the part of states. In the event of an economic downswing, this will produce an enormous compression effect on the states. Squeezed between static resources and increasing demands for job placement, the initial response will be to remove families from welfare. Whenever possible, states will attempt to transfer the most troubled families to SSI, a program that is entirely federally funded. This, however, will require certification of disability, and the federal government will resist SSI's becoming a dumping ground for the states' welfare reform failures. Indeed, PRWORA tightens the eligibility requirements for SSI in a manner that makes transfers from welfare more difficult. Without the SSI transfer option, states will be induced to reduce the number of cases not in compliance with work requirements. Given difficulties in operationalizing the federal five-year lifetime limit, states will be induced to consider ever shorter limits. Terminating families as soon as possible on the basis of noncompliance will ultimately screen out those families least likely to become employed. Eventually such families will cease seeking aid; and to the extent that large numbers of the more disorganized families disappear from state welfare rolls, states will avoid federal penalties for failing to meet employment requirements. Because disentitlement is a zero-sum game, many members of those families may show up on other rolls, including criminal court dockets.

What will happen to the families dumped from state welfare programs is open to conjecture. Conservative scholars, such as Marvin Olasky, have promised that private, especially religious, agencies will pick up the slack,[114] but this is doubtful. Contributions to nonprofit agencies such as the United Way have stagnated in recent years. Ineligible for state aid and unable to get necessary assistance from the nonprofit sector, former welfare families will turn to metropolitan government as the last resort. Big-city mayors are already dreading the impact that such families will have on their precarious city budgets.[115]

Aside from the possible problems accompanying its implementation, specific incremental benefits of welfare reform must be acknowledged. For example, the welfare reform plan includes $22 billion over seven years for child care in the form of a capped block grant to the states. This should go some distance toward providing the child care that will be needed if so many welfare parents must enter the workforce, although the amount is $1.8 billion short of what the CBO estimates is required. PRWORA allows states to establish Individual Development Accounts (IDAs), a strategy to increase the assets of poor families so as to vault them out of poverty. Unfortunately, the welfare reform plan makes no specific allocations for IDAs, leaving funding the option of state and local governments or philanthropy. PRWORA denies for life benefits to parents convicted of felony drug offenses unless they are participating in a drug treatment program— but family-oriented drug treatment for addicts who are also mothers is generally unavailable. Several of the provisions of PRWORA target teenagers on welfare: Teen mothers are required to live with their parents and stay in school to receive benefits; HHS is mandated to mount a teen pregnancy prevention initiative; and the Justice Department is required to identify older men who impregnate female teenagers and prosecute them for statutory rape. Several provisions address child support, including the requirement that states establish registries for child support and streamline the process for establishing paternity. States are encouraged to be more aggressive in withholding income from noncustodial parents in arrears for child support. Furthermore, more vigorous penalties will be directed at noncustodial parents to encourage them to pay up, such as revocation of professional, driver's, occupational, and recreational licenses.[116]

Given the track record of demonstration programs designed to prevent teen pregnancy and increase child support, the stiff penalties directed at adolescents and deadbeat dads would seem to be more of rhetorical value to elected officials than of practical use to save the public revenues now allocated to welfare programs. Regarding a larger issue, no one seems to have taken the trouble to calculate the ultimate cost of deploying a state-administered welfare apparatus with tracking, surveillance, and sanction capacities designed to reprogram the behavior of the 3.4 million families now on welfare.

Finally, PRWORA includes funding for further research on welfare reform, most of it for the benefit of children. From 1996 to 2002, $6 million has been allocated annually for the study of a random sample of abused and neglected children. The focus of this longitudinal research will be child protection and out-of-home placements. An additional $15 million annually is allocated from 1997 to 2002 to track child poverty rates. If the child poverty rate increases by 5 percent or more for a given year, HHS must prepare a plan for corrective action. Significantly, there are no specific requirements that states study the consequences of deleting families from welfare as a result of time limits, particularly as this action affects children.

Recipients of public assistance programs do not fare as well as those covered under the social insurances. Public assistance programs involve a large dose of stigma, and the character of recipients is often maligned because of their need. Moreover, the relative success of Social Security in arresting poverty among the elderly has not been replicated in public assistance programs. In fact, the reverse is true; the poorest of the poor have endured greater levels of poverty during the 1980s and 1990s than in earlier decades. Indeed, the legacy of welfare reform engineered by the 104th Congress and signed by President Clinton does not bode well for the future prospects of poor people in the United States.

The U.S. welfare system has undergone a dramatic transformation over the past 20 years. Several important themes mark this transformation: (1) the conversion of public assistance policy into labor policy, (2) the conversion of public assistance policy into tax policy, and (3) the increased privatization of social welfare services.

In the first instance, AFDC (the cornerstone of public assistance) was transformed from an entitlement program that guaranteed recipients a minimal level of support to one designed to thrust recipients into the labor market at the earliest possible date. By converting AFDC into workfare (i.e., TANF), the PRWORA eliminated the boundary between public assistance and labor policy. Thus, public assistance policy was converted into a feeder system to supply the secondary labor market with increased manpower. Moreover, public assistance is no longer an alternative to labor policy; it is labor policy. The result is fewer protected islands left for those who cannot compete in the labor market.

The conversion of public assistance policy into labor policy is shored up by tax policy: the expansion of EITC benefits, the only public assistance program that has been purposely enlarged in the past 20 years. In fact, EITC has become the largest public assistance program in the nation. By expanding EITC benefits through the tax code while at the same time eliminating AFDC, the legislature has shifted the focus from the nonworking poor to the working poor, a group more marginally acceptable to conservatives and the larger society. It is no coincidence that the only public assistance programs experiencing growth are EITC and IDA, both of which are tied to labor force participation. Clearly, public assistance payments to the poor will increasingly be routed through tax policy for low-income workers rather than through direct cash or in-kind subsidies for the nonworking poor.

Privatized social services have encroached upon most welfare domains, including health care, public education, mental health and chemical dependency services, nursing home care, corrections, and child care. Many of these markets are already glutted by the influx of corporations seeking to increase their profits and their corporate reach. One of the last remaining frontiers is the delivery of public welfare services, an area virtually untouched by large corporations. In 1996 Texas tended its public welfare services out to public bid. Although the privatization of Texas social services was vetoed by the former

Clinton administration, the concept seems likely to reappear in some form. Administering the multibillion-dollar public welfare apparatus seems too lucrative an area for large corporations to ignore.

This is clearly a difficult time for the American welfare state. Even after huge expenditures on social welfare services, according to Richard Estes, the United States ranks only twenty-third internationally in terms of the adequacy of its social provisions.[117] Given the present economic trend—in which vast numbers of service jobs are produced, many of which are part time, have few if any benefits, and pay the minimum wage—long-term welfare benefit packages will likely be required for an increasing number of citizens. How much these income benefit packages will contain, and at what cost, will be a matter for future discourse in public policy.

Discussion Questions

1. Public assistance programs are arguably the most controversial set of programs in the U.S. welfare state. Critics frequently lambaste them for encouraging everything from welfare dependency to teenage pregnancy. Supporters argue that the programs are poorly funded and barely allow recipients to survive. Why is public assistance so controversial? What, if anything, can be done to make the TANF program less controversial?

2. Many myths have arisen around the AFDC/TANF programs. In your opinion, what myths have been the most harmful to the programs and to recipients? Why?

3. General Assistance is often the hardest hit when states decide to implement cuts in social welfare funding. What accounts for the relative unpopularity of GA? Is the GA budget the most logical place to cut when states are faced with fiscal crises? What, if anything, can be done to strengthen the image of GA?

4. Since the 1970s, most strategies for reforming public assistance have revolved around implementing mandatory work requirements for recipients. This strategy was evident in the programs of Presidents Carter and Reagan and was the centerpiece of the 1988 Family Support Act. More recently, the TANF program mandated that benefits should last for a maximum of five years, after which a recipient would be required to work. Is establishing a mandatory work requirement a viable strategy for reforming public assistance? If so, why? If not, why not? What would be a better strategy for reforming public assistance?

5. TANF benefit levels vary widely from state to state. This situation exists because the federal government has refused to establish a national minimum benefit level. Moreover, there is little federal pressure on states to increase benefit levels and thereby curtail the erosion of public assistance benefits that has taken place since the 1970s.

Should the federal government establish a minimum national benefit level for TANF and compel states to meet that level? If not, why not? If you agree, what should that level be?

6. Public assistance programs are increasingly being designed to change the behavior of poor recipients. Can and should the behavior of poor people be changed through social policy legislation? Will this legislation work? If not, why not?

7. Although administered by the Social Security Administration, the SSI program carries a stigma similar to those of public assistance programs like food stamps or the TANF. Why does this stigma exist? What can be done to diminish it?

Notes

1. Isaac Shapiro and Robert Greenstein, *Holes in the Safety Nets* (Washington, DC: Center on Budget and Policy Priorities, 1988).
2. Ibid., pp. 669–671.
3. Department of Health, Education, and Welfare, *Aid to Families with Dependent Children* (Washington, DC: Social Security Administration, Office of Research and Statistics, 1979), p. 1.
4. Children's Defense Fund, *A Children's Defense Budget* (Washington, DC: Children's Defense Fund, 1986), p. 43; Department of Health, Education, and Welfare, *Welfare Myths and Facts* (Washington, DC: Social and Rehabilitation Service, ca. 1972), p. 1.
5. U.S. House of Representatives, Select Committee on Hunger, "Myths and Realities: Food Stamp and AFDC Recipients" (Washington, DC: U.S. Government Printing Office, April 9, 1992), p. 59.
6. Children's Defense Fund, *The State of America's Children, 1991* (Washington, DC: Children's Defense Fund, 1991), p. 156; U.S. Department of Health and Human Services, "Percent Distribution of TANF Families with No Adult Recipients by Number of Recipient Children October 1998–September 1999," retrieved December 5, 2000, from the World Wide Web: http://www.acf.dhhs.gov/programs/opre/characteristics/fy99/tab03_99.htm
7. Patrick Bresette, "Testimony to the Senate Committee on Health Services On SB 64—Relating to TANF and Medicaid Benefits for Additional Children Born to TANF Recipients," March 9, 1999. Retrieved December 6, 2000, from the World Wide Web: http://www.cppp.org/products/testimony/testimony/tstfamilycap.html
8. "Welfare Reform Issue Paper," Working Group on Welfare Reform, Family Support and Independence, U.S. Department of Health and Human Services, February 26, 1994; Peter Gottschalk, "Achieving Self-Sufficiency for Welfare Recipients—the Good and Bad News," in Select Committee on Hunger, *Beyond Public Assistance: Where Do We Go From Here?* Serial No. 102–123 (Washington, DC: U.S. Government Printing Office, 1992), p. 56.
9. Mary Jo Bane and David T. Ellwood, *Welfare Realities: From Rhetoric to Reform* (Cambridge, MA: Harvard University Press, 1994).
10. Robert Moffitt, quoted in Hillary Hoynes and T. McCurdy, "Has the Decline in Benefits Shortened Welfare Spells," *AEA Papers and Proceedings* 84, no. 2 (May 1994), pp. 43–48.
11. P. J. Leahy, T. F. Buss, and J. M. Quane, "Time on Welfare: Why Do People Enter and Leave the System," *American Journal of Economics and Sociology* 54 (January 1995), pp. 33–46.
12. Bane and Ellwood, *Welfare Realities*.
13. Greg J. Duncan and Saul D. Hoffman, "Welfare Dynamics and Welfare Policy," Unpublished paper, Institute for Social Research, Ann Arbor, MI, 1985.
14. Ibid.
15. Peter Gottschalk, "Is Intergenerational Correlation in Welfare Participation across Generations Spurious?" Boston College,

November 1990, Conference Papers, 1990 ASPE–JCPES Conference on the Underclass (Washington, DC: U.S. Department of Health and Human Services).

16. M. Ann Hill and June O'Neill, "Underclass Behaviors in the United States: Measurement and Analysis of Determinants," City College of New York, March 1990, Conference Papers, 1990 ASPE–JCPES Conference on the Underclass (Washington, DC: U.S. Department of Health and Human Services).

17. Mary Corcoran, Roger Gordon, Deborah Laren, and Gary Solon, "Problems of the Underclass: Underclass Neighborhoods and Intergenerational Poverty and Dependency," University of Michigan, 1991, Conference Papers, 1990 ASPE–JCPES Conference on the Underclass (Washington, DC: U.S. Department of Health and Human Services).

18. Department of Health and Human Services, "Percent Distribution of TANF Families by Race, October 1998–September 1999." Retrieved December 6, 2000, from the World Wide Web: http://www.acf.dhhs.gov/programs/opre/characteristics/fy99/tab06_99.htm

19. U.S. Department of Health and Human Services, "FY 1999 TANF Work Participation Rates." Retrieved December 7, 2000, from the World Wide Web: http://www.acf.dhhs.gov/news/99rate.htm

20. See Michael Harrington, with the assistance of Robert Greenstein and Eleanor Holmes Norton, *Who Are the Poor?* (Washington, DC: Justice for All, 1987), p. 21.

21. Iris Lav and Steven Gold, *The States and the Poor* (Washington, DC: Center on Budget and Policy Priorities, 1993), p. 11.

22. Gregory Acs, Norma Coe, Keith Watson, Robert I. Lerman, The Urban Institute, "Does Work Pay? An Analysis of the Work Incentives under TANF" (Washington, DC: Urban Institute, July 1998).

23. Duncan and Hoffman, "Welfare Dynamics."

24. U.S. House of Representatives, "Myths and Realities," p. 57.

25. U.S. House of Representatives Committee on Ways and Means, *Overview of Entitlement Programs, 1992 Green Book* (Washington, DC: U.S. Government Printing Office, 1992), p. 1606.

26. U.S. House of Representatives, "Myths and Realities," p. 58.

27. Thomas Corbett, "The Wisconsin Welfare Magnet: What Is an Ordinary Member of the Tribe to Do When the Witch Doctors Disagree?" *Focus* 13, no. 3 (Fall/Winter 1991), pp. 2–4.

28. Quoted in Diane Rose, Terri Sachnik, Josie Salazar, Eunice Sealey, and Virginia Wall, "Welfare Reform II," unpublished paper, University of Houston Graduate School of Social Work, Houston, TX, 1996.

29. U.S. House of Representatives, "Myths and Realities," p. 58.

30. Robert Moffitt, "Incentive Effects of the U.S. Welfare System: A Review," *Journal of Economic Literature* 30 (March 1992), pp. 1–61; see also Barbara Vobejda, "Decline in Birth Rates for Teens May Reflect Major Social Changes," *Houston Chronicle* (October 29, 1996), p. 13A.

31. "Welfare Reform Issue Paper."

32. U.S. House of Representatives, *1992 Green Book,* pp. 653–687.

33. W. Joseph Heffernan, *Introduction to Social Welfare Policy* (Itasca, IL: F. E. Peacock, 1979).

34. Elizabeth D. Huttman, *Introduction to Social Policy* (New York: McGraw-Hill, 1981), p. 168.

35. William Eaton, "Major Welfare Reform Compromise Reached," *Los Angeles Times* (September 27, 1988), p. 15.

36. American Public Welfare Association, *Conference Agreement on Welfare Reform* (Washington, DC: American Public Welfare Association, September 28, 1988) pp. 1–3.

37. David Stoesz and Howard Karger, "Welfare Reform: From Illusion to Reality," *Social Work* 35, no. 2 (March 1990), pp. 141–147.

38. Spencer Rich, "Panel Clears Welfare Bill," *Washington Post* (September 28, 1988), p. A6.

39. Sar Levitan and Frank Gallo, *Jobs for JOBS: Toward a Work-Based Welfare System* (Washington, DC: Center for Social Policy Studies, March 1993).

40. Ibid.

41. See David T. Ellwood, "Welfare Reform as I Knew It: When Bad Things Happen to Good Policies," *The American Prospect* 26 (May–June 1996), p. 240.

42. Ellwood, "Welfare Reform as I Knew It."

43. Ibid.

44. "Legal Immigrants to Carry Burden of Welfare Reform," *El Paso Times* (August 3, 1996), p. B1.

45. Mark H. Greenberg, "No Duty, No Floor: The Real Meaning of 'Ending Entitlements'" (Washington, DC: Center for Law and Social Policy, 1996). Retrieved October 8, 1997, from the World Wide Web: http://epn.org/clasp/clduty-2.html

46. Mark Greenberg and Steve Savner, "The Temporary Assistance for Needy Families Block Grant" (Washington, DC: Center for Law and Social Policy, August 1996). Retrieved October 9, 1997, from the World Wide Web: http://epn.org/clasp/clsummry.html

47. Paula Roberts, "Relationship between TANF and Child Support Requirements" (Washington, DC: Center for Law and Social Policy, September 1996). Retrieved October 9, 1997, from the World Wide Web: http://epn.org/clasp/cltcsr.html

48. "Welfare Reform," *NASW News* (September, 1996), pp. 1, 12.

49. NACo Legislative Priority Fact Sheet, New Welfare Reform Law, "The Personal Responsibility and Work Opportunity Reconciliation Act of 1996" (Washington, DC: NACo, 1996).

50. Frances Fox Piven, "Was Welfare Reform Worthwhile?" *The American Prospect* 27 (July–August 1996), pp. 14–15.

51. Quoted in ibid., p. 14.

52. National Governmental Organization, "State Follow-Up of TANF," 1998. Retrieved December 12, 1997, from the World Wide Web: http://www.nga.org/welfare/statefollowup.html

53. Wendell Primus, Lynette Rawlings, Kathy Larin, and Kathryn Porter, *The Initial Impacts of Welfare Reform on the Incomes of Single-Mother Families* (Washington, DC: Center on Budget and Policy Priorities, 1999).

54. Ibid.

55. Social Security Administration, "Fast Facts: SSI," retrieved December 7, 2000, from the World Wide Web: http://www.ssa.gov:80/statisics/fastfacts/pageii.html; Social Security Administration, Office of Research, Evaluation and Statistics, "Fast Facts and Figures" (Washington, DC: Social Security Administration, August 2000).

56. Social Security Administration, Office of Research, Evaluation and Statistics, "Fast Facts and Figures"; Social Security Administration, "A Desktop guide to SSI Eligibility Requirements," August 2000, retrieved December 8, 2000, from the World Wide Web: http://www.ssa.gov/pubs/11001.html

57. See Social Security Administration, Office of Research, Evaluation and Statistics, "Fast Facts and Figures"; and Carolyn L. Weaver, "Welfare Payment to the Disabled: Making America Sick?" *The American Enterprise* (January/February 1995), pp. 61–64.

58. Ibid.

59. Ibid.

60. Ibid.

61. Jeffrey Katz, "Social Security, Conference OKs Bill Creating Independent Agency," *Social Policy* (July 23, 1994), pp. 6–9.

62. Ibid.

63. Ibid., pp. 25–30.

64. Much of the information in this section on General Assistance is taken from the excellent study done by L. Jerome Gallagher, Cori E. Uccello, Alicia B. Pierce, and Erin B. Reidy, "State General Assistance Programs 1998" (Washington, DC: The Urban Institute, April 1999). The study is also available online: http://newfederalism.urban.org/html/ga_programs/ga_full.html#exesum

65. Ibid.

66. Thomas Corbett, "The New Federalism: Monitoring Consequences," *Focus* 18, no. 1 (1996), pp. 3–6.

67. Lela Costin, Howard Karger, and David Stoesz, *The Politics of Child Abuse in America* (New York: Oxford University Press, 1996).

68. Joe Sexton, "Child Welfare Chief Provides a Glimpse at Decentralization," *The New York Times* (September 8, 1996), p. 5.

69. Data compiled from March of Dimes, "Teenage Pregnancy Fact Sheet," retrieved December 9, 2000, from the World Wide Web: http://www.modimes.org/HealthLibrary2/factsheets/Teenage_Pregnancy_Fact_Sheet.htm; Centers for Disease Control, "Teenage Pregnancy Fact Sheet: Facts You Should Know about Teenage Pregnancy, 1999," retrieved December 10, 2000, from the World Wide Web: http://www.cdc.gov/nchs/fastats/teenbrth.htm;

and the Alan Guttmacher Institute, "Teen Births, Sex and Pregnancy," September 1999, retrieved December 10, 2000, from the World Wide Web: http://www.agi-usa.org/pubs/fb_teen_sex.html#tp

70. "Teenaged Childbearing and Welfare Policy," *Focus* 10, no. 1 (Spring 1987), p. 16.

71. Harrington et al., *Who Are the Poor?* p. 12.

72. The Urban Institute, "Welfare Reform: Issues before the Nation" (Washington, DC: The Urban Institute, 1995).

73. Ibid., p. 1100.

74. U.S. House of Representatives, *Overview of Entitlement Programs* (Washington, DC: U.S. Government Printing Office, 1994), p. 448.

75. Denise Polit, Janet Quint, and James Riccio, *The Challenge of Serving Teenage Mothers* (New York: Manpower Demonstration Research Corporation, 1988), Tables 2 and 3, p. 17.

76. Janet Quint, Denise Polit, Hans Bos, and George Cave, *New Chance* (New York: Manpower Demonstration Research Corporation, 1994), Tables 5 and 6.

77. Quint et al., *New Chance*, p. xxxi.

78. Ken Auletta, *The Underclass* (New York: Vintage, 1982), p. xvi.

79. William Julius Wilson, *The Truly Disadvantaged* (Chicago: University of Chicago Press, 1987), p. 8.

80. Erol Ricketts and Isabel Sawhill, "Defining and Measuring the Underclass," *Journal of Policy Analysis and Management* 7, no. 2 (Winter 1988), pp. 316–325.

81. Kathleen Heffernan Vickland, "Is There an Underclass: No," in Howard Jacob Karger and James Midgley (eds.), *Controversial Issues in Social Policy* (New York: Allyn & Bacon, 1994).

82. Christopher Jencks, "Deadly Neighborhoods," *The New Republic* (June 13, 1988), p. 30.

83. Michael Novak, *The New Consensus on Family and Welfare* (Washington, DC: American Enterprise Institute, 1987).

84. Charles Murray, *Losing Ground* (New York: Basic Books, 1984), pp. 227–228.

85. Lawrence Mead, *Beyond Entitlement* (New York: Free Press, 1986).

86. Center on Budget and Policy Priorities, *The New Welfare Law* (Washington, DC: Center on Budget and Policy Priorities, 1996).

87. George Gilder, *Wealth and Poverty* (New York: Basic Books, 1981), p. 118.

88. Marian Wright Edelman, "Say No to This Welfare Reform," *Washington Post* (November 3, 1995), p. A23.

89. "A Children's Veto," *Washington Post* (July 25, 1996), p. A28.

90. Daniel P. Moynihan, "When Principle Is at Issue," *Washington Post* (August 4, 1996), p. C7.

91. Barbara Vobejda and Dan Balz, "President Seeks Balm for Anger over Welfare Bill," *Washington Post* (August 22, 1996), p. B3.

92. Mickey Kaus, *The End of Equality* (New York: Basic Books, 1992), p. 135.

93. Steve Jarkas, *The Values We Live By: What Americans Want from Welfare Reform* (New York: Public Agenda, 1996).

94. LaDonna Pavetti, "Policies to Time-Limit AFDC Benefits" (Washington, DC: Urban Institute, 1994).

95. Center on Budget and Policy Priorities, *The New Welfare Law*, p. 6.

96. Lois Quinn and Robert Magill, "Politics versus Research in Social Policy," *Social Service Review* (December 1994), pp. 83–90.

97. David Long, Judith Gueron, Robert Wood, Rebecca Fisher, and Veronica Fellerath, *LEAP* (New York: Manpower Demonstration Research Corporation, 1996), p. ES6.

98. Ibid., p. ES13.

99. Robert Moffitt, "Incentive Effects of the U.S. Welfare System: A Review," *Journal of Economic Literature* (March 1992) p. 30.

100. Mark Greenberg, testimony before the Domestic Task Force, Select Committee on Hunger, U.S. House of Representatives, April 9, 1992, in *Federal Policy Perspectives on Welfare Reform: Rhetoric, Reality and Opportunities*, Serial No. 102–25 (Washington, DC: U.S. Government Printing Office, 1992), pp. 52–53.

101. Robert Rector, "Strategies for Welfare Reform," Testimony before the Domestic Task Force, Select Committee on Hunger, U.S. House of Representatives, April 9, 1992, in *Federal Policy Perspectives on Welfare Reform: Rhetoric, Reality and Opportunities*, Serial No. 102–25 (Washington, DC: U.S. Government Printing Office, 1992), pp. 67–68.

102. Elizabeth D. Huttman, *Introduction to Social Policy* (New York: McGraw-Hill, 1981).

103. Judith Gueron and Edward Pally, *From Welfare to Work* (New York: Russell Sage Foundation, 1991).

104. Judith Gueron, "Work Programs and Welfare Reform," *Public Welfare* (Summer 1995), p. 10.

105. Randall Eberts, "Welfare to Work," *Upjohn Employment Research* (Fall 1995), p. 4.

106. David Ellwood, *Poor Support* (New York: Basic Books, 1988), p. 153.

107. Judith M. Gueron, "Statement by the President," *Manpower Demonstration Research Corporation, 1991 Annual Report* (New York: MDRC, 1991), p. 2.

108. Daniel Friedlander and Gary Burtless, *Five Years After* (New York: Russell Sage Foundation, 1995), pp. 4–25.

109. Ibid., p. 17.

110. Roberta Spalter-Roth, Beverly Burr, Heidi Hartmann, and Lois Shaw, *Welfare That Works: The Working Lives of AFDC Recipients* (Washington, DC: Institute for Women's Policy Research, 1995), p. 18.

111. LaDonna Pavetti, "Questions and Answers on Welfare Dynamics" (Washington, DC: Urban Institute, 1995).

112. Sandra Danziger, Mary Corcoran, Sheldon Danziger, Colleen Heflin, Ariel Kalil, Judith Levine, Daniel Rosne, Kristin Seefeldt, Kristine Siefert, and Richard Tolman, "Barriers to the Employment of Welfare Recipients," Poverty Research and Training Center, University of Michigan, January 1999.

113. Personal discussion at a conference on welfare reform, the Jerome Levy Economics Institute, Bard College, Annandale-on-Hudson, N.Y., July 12, 1996.

114. Marvin Olasky, "Beyond the Stingy Welfare State," *Policy Review* (Fall 1990), p. 14.

115. Robert Pear, "Giuliani Battles Congress on Welfare Bill," *The New York Times* (July 27, 1996), p. A7.

116. "Personal Responsibility and Work Opportunity Reconciliation Act of 1996," (Washington, DC: National Association of Social Workers, 1996).

117. Richard J. Estes, *The Social Progress of Nations* (New York: Praeger, 1984), p. 109.

Appendix: Highlights of Selected State Welfare Demonstration Projects, 2000

Arizona	EMPOWER (Employing and Moving People Off Welfare and Encouraging Responsibility) establishes a time limit on adult AFDC benefits of 24 months in any 60-month period. Additional AFDC benefits will not be provided for children conceived while a family is on AFDC or, if the family later reapplies for benefits, conceived within 12 months after leaving AFDC. Families can put aside $100 a month in Individual Development Accounts, up to $9,000, for training and education. Transitional child care and Medicaid will be extended from 12 months (as currently allowed) to 24 months after a family leaves AFDC. An additional three-year pilot project will operate in limited areas and will provide work experience by placing participants in subsidized jobs for 9 to 12 months, funded by AFDC grants and cashed-out food stamp allotments.
Arkansas	AFDC parents age 16 or younger will be required to attend school regularly or face reductions in benefits. If appropriate, teenage parents can meet the requirement by attending an alternative educational program. Arkansas will also implement a fam-

ily cap. Family planning and group counseling services focusing on the responsibilities of parenthood will be included in the demonstration.

California — The "Work Pays" demonstration project will encourage teenage AFDC parents to attend school regularly by paying them a $100 cash bonus for maintaining a C average, and $500 for graduating from high school. Averages of D and below can reduce TANF payments by up to $50 a month for two months. TANF families may accumulate $2,000 in assets and $4,500 equity in a car (California counties now have more flexibility in determining equity). Families will be able to deposit $5,000 into savings as long as funds are used to purchase a home, start a business, or finance a child's postsecondary education or training. Recipients who work but receive a low TANF payment may opt out of the program but still remain eligible for health and child care services under Medi-Cal. Participants in both programs can exclude college assistance and work–study funds from the resource limit, and up to $100 in gift income each quarter. The TANF and Food Stamp Compatibility Demonstration project allows recipients with self-employment income to deduct 40 percent of that income when determining eligibility and benefit amount. The Incentives for Self-Sufficiency project provides transitional child care benefits to families no longer eligible for TANF because of marriage. The Assistance Payments Demonstration project includes reductions in cash benefits combined with new work incentives. The Maximum Feasibility Grant will not increase benefits for additional children to those already receiving TANF. Another modification to the original plan encourages minor parents to live at home by disregarding grandparents' income when calculating benefit eligibility.

Colorado — The Personal Responsibility and Employment Program includes several major revisions to the state's former AFDC program. After receiving AFDC benefits for two years, parents who are able to work or able to participate in a training program must do so. Individuals who refuse to participate will lose their TANF benefits. The demonstration will "cash out" food stamps by adding the value of the coupons into the participant's monthly TANF payment. Work is encouraged through a new formula using higher income disregards. Asset levels will allow an individual to own a car regardless of its value or the participant's equity in it. Financial bonuses are provided when participants remain in school and graduate or receive their GED. Financial penalties are assessed when parents fail to have their children immunized.

Connecticut — The Fair Chance initiative is designed to increase supports, incentives, and work expectations for AFDC recipients. There are two components: Pathways and Family Strength. Pathways requires AFDC recipients to work at least 15 hours a week after two years of benefits, 25 hours a week after three years, and 35 hours a week after four years. The program will increase the incomes of families leaving welfare by paying the difference between the noncustodial parent's child support payments and a state-established minimum. Family Strength provisions raise the resource limit for TANF eligibility from $1,000 to $3,000 and extend transitional child care and medical benefits an additional year for a total of two years. Family Strength is implemented statewide; Pathways, in the New Haven and Manchester areas. Reach for Jobs First limits TANF to 21 months for employable adults, with extensions for good faith efforts. Requirements include 12 weeks in job searches; recipients may keep their benefits until they reach the federal poverty line. There is a 50 percent reduction in TANF payments for children born after the receipt of benefits. A recipient who finds work within six months of losing TANF benefits is eligible for transitional child care and Medicaid. Medicaid will continue for 24 months, and child care will exist as long as the family income is 75 percent of the state's Medic-aid income ceiling.

Delaware

The Better Chance program requires all TANF participants to comply with a Contract of Mutual Responsibility. The contract specifies employment-related activities lead-ing to self-sufficiency. There is a time limit of 24 months on cash benefits for able-bodied adults over 19 years old. Teen parents must live in an adult supervised setting, attend school, participate in parenting and family planning education, and immunize their children. High school graduates receive a $50 bonus and 12 months of transi-tional child care and Medicaid benefits. TANF benefits will not increase for children born while a parent is on public assistance. Participants who refuse to cooperate with child support enforcement are denied benefits. The program will operate for seven years before being reevaluated.

Florida

The Family Transition Program limits TANF families to collecting benefits for a maximum of 24 months in any five-year period. Recipients who exhaust their tran-sitional benefits but still are unable to find employment will be guaranteed the op-portunity to work at a job paying more than their TANF grant. Families at high risk of becoming welfare dependent are allotted 36 months in any six-year period. Med-icaid and child care benefits are available. Local community boards oversee the program. Other elements include an increase in the earnings disregard and asset ceilings, as well as a statewide requirement that parents ensure that their children are immunized. In the Family Responsibility Act, children born while parents are receiving TANF will be given 50 percent of the benefit for a first child, and no money will be provided for other children born afterward. Additional children will receive Medicaid, however, and the family's food stamp allocation will increase. Minor parents and children are required to attend school. The failure to attend school will result in the family's being dropped from TANF.

Georgia

The Personal Accountability and Responsibility project (PAR) strengthens federal work requirements. Georgia's welfare agency will exclude from a TANF grant any able-bodied recipient between the ages of 18 and 60 who has no children under 14 and who willfully refuses to work or who leaves employment without good cause. The rest of the family will continue to be eligible for AFDC benefits. The plan also includes a family cap. However, PAR would allow recipients to "earn back" the de-nied benefits through the receipt of child support payments or earnings. Medicaid and food stamps eligibility will continue for all family members. Further, Georgia will offer family planning services and instruction in parental skills to TANF recipi-ents. Further, Georgia requires adults who received TANF payments for 24 of the previous 36 months to work up to 20 hours a month at an assigned job in a local, state, federal, or nonprofit agency. Failure to comply can result in the loss of bene-fits for a period of time. A family may have a vehicle of any value if it is used to commute to and from school or work. The state disregards any earnings of children under 18 who are attending school when calculating the family's eligibility or bene-fit level.

Hawaii

The Creating Work Opportunities program for JOBS families consists of a list of immediately available jobs ready to be filled by recipients. Job-ready JOBS recipi-ents who would otherwise expect to wait at least three months to be placed in a reg-ular education or training activity are required to immediately pursue job leads developed by the JOBS program specialists. The part-time positions (up to 18 hours per week) are private sector jobs at minimum wage, which allow participants to gain work experience, develop their skills, and better target their training needs. The Pursuit of New Opportunities program limits employable adults to five years on TANF, with some exceptions. The maximum grant for nonexempt families is reduced by 20 percent after two full years of eligibility. Earnings disregard and asset limits are increased, and income from minors is excluded, as is one vehicle. To allow two-parent families to remain intact, one parent may work more than 100 hours a month and still be eligible for benefits. Minor parents or those who have not graduated from high school or earned a GED participate in training activities.

Illinois
The Work Pays component (added to the previously approved Project Fresh Start) encourages employment and self-sufficiency by allowing recipients to keep more of their earnings than is normally allowed. The state disregards two of each three dollars earned as long as recipients continue working. Work and Responsibility gets a two-year time limit for benefits when the youngest child is 13 years or older. Income earned by a family member does not count toward the two-year time limit. Recipients unable to find work within the first year are required to accept 60 hours of TANF subsidized work a month. After two years, a family that does not qualify for an extension will not be permitted to reapply for benefits for two years. New recipients with children between ages 5 and 12 must participate in seeking employment; and if they are unable to find a job within six months, they are assigned to community services. There is no increase in benefits for children conceived while a recipient is receiving TANF. School attendance is mandatory, and failure to attend school will result in financial sanctions. TANF recipients are required to name the father and to provide any locating information on him. Recipients are given six months to identify the father before TANF benefits are terminated.

Indiana
The Indiana Manpower Placement and Comprehensive Training (IMPACT) program requires that up to 12,000 job-ready individuals be assigned to a "placement track" and receive help in job search and placement. Once participants are placed on IMPACT, their benefits are limited to 24 consecutive months. Extensions to the time limit include 1 month for every 6 months that a family member is employed. This does not apply to children's benefits. Determinations of eligibility for food stamps will disregard any income earned in the first 6 months of employment. Benefits will not increase for children conceived while the family is on TANF, but the children will be covered under Medicaid. For a family to be eligible for benefits, children must attend school regularly and have full immunizations. Mothers are exempt from working during the first 12 weeks of a child's life. Minor children must live with a parent or guardian, and the income of that family member will be considered in the evaluation of benefit eligibility. Case management and supportive services will continue for a period after TANF benefits end. There are increased sanctions for quitting a job or for failure to comply with program requirements. Subsidies are extended to employers who hire welfare recipients for a maximum of 24 months. IMPACT will operate for seven years.

Iowa
The Family Investment Plan (FIP) establishes a contract with recipients that outlines time frames, activities the family is to participate in, and time limits for benefits. Only parents with a child under six months old at home, those working at least 30 hours per week, and the disabled are exempt. The earnings of a recipient who has never been employed and lacks skills but has found employment are disregarded for four months in terms of the benefits the person can receive. A person unwilling to participate with the agreed-upon terms will have TANF benefits

terminated over a six-month period and will be ineligible to apply again for six more months. Individual Development Accounts allow funds to be deposited, but funds can be withdrawn only to pay for educational training, home ownership, a business start-up, or family emergencies. The allotted asset limit for each TANF participant increases from $1,000 to $2,000, and to $5,000 for the entire family. Vehicle assets have also risen from $1,500 to $3,000. Minor parents must live with an adult or legal guardian, participate in parenting classes, and participate in programs to help them receive a high school education. Parents with children less than three months old are exempt from JOBS, and any income earned by full-time students aged 19 or younger is disregarded in determination of the benefit eligibility of the household.

Kansas   Through Actively Creating Tomorrow for Families, any adult who refuses to attend an interview, refuses a job offer, or quits a job without good cause will lose TANF benefits for three months. Pregnant women will no longer be exempt from participating in JOBS; the only exception will be persons with multiple or severe barriers who are unable to become self-sufficient. Failure to disclose information on the paternity of a child will result in loss of eligibility for the entire family. Income from dependent children attending school will be disregarded from the family's eligibility. In two-parent households one parent is allowed to work more than 100 hours a month without affecting benefits. The value of one vehicle is excluded when benefits are calculated; any other car used at least 50 percent of the time for income is also disregarded.

Maine   Welfare to Work is a contract signed by TANF recipients in which participants agree to commit to work, cooperate with child support enforcement, attend parenting classes, maintain regular health screenings for their children, and have all immunizations up to date. Minor children are required to live in an adult-supervised setting, and their benefits will be issued in the form of a voucher for rent or other expenses the family may incur. Any leftover benefits will be issued to the responsible adult. Recipients who become employed will receive up to one year of transitional Medicaid and child care, effective after a month of employment. Families may own one automobile, regardless of its value; and families who find themselves in a financial crisis may receive up to three months of TANF cash benefits in one lump sum. ASPIRE-Plus looks to the private sector for assistance in job placement. TANF and food stamps will be combined to partially subsidize employment for up to six months. Collected child support will go directly to the family, except for the first $50.

Maryland   The Family Investment Program (FIP) requires able-bodied recipients to participate in employment searches to continue receiving benefits. Failure to comply within six months results in TANF benefit denial for the entire family. Three months of non-cash transitional assistance may be provided for closed cases. Payments go directly to landlords, utilities companies, and so on. If a recipient then participates in a job search for a full month, his or her case can be reopened. Incomes from dependent children attending school full time will not be counted in with the family's total income, and benefits will still be available to 18- and 19-year-olds as long as they are attending secondary school full time. The asset limit is raised to $5,000 for a vehicle. For two-parent families the main financial provider is allowed to work more than 100 hours a month without affecting the household's benefits. Twenty percent of earned income and 50 percent of self-employment income is not counted in determination of eligibility. Pregnant women are not exempt from participating in JOBS unless a medical exemption is provided. Families in a one-time crisis may receive a lump sum equal to three months of benefits. Children born while the family is receiving TANF benefits will be given collected child support, and vouchers for necessities instead of cash benefits. Unmarried minor parents must live in adult-supervised housing, attend parenting classes, attend school on a regular basis, and keep immunizations updated. The state retains all child support collections. Failure to cooperate with child support enforcement will result in loss of benefits for the entire household and in loss of Medicaid for the adult.

Massachusetts   Welfare Reform stipulates that any recipient unable to obtain at least 20 hours per week of employment after 60 days on TANF will perform community service and job searches to earn a cash subsidy. The state will combine TANF and the value of food stamps to be used for 12 months of employment in the private sector. Employers contributing to Individual Asset Accounts will help recipients move from subsidized to nonsubsidized employment. Transitional Medicaid is extended, and earned income and resource limitations are increased. Teen parents without high school diplomas must attend school and live with a parent; there are sanctions for parents who do not ensure regular school attendance or up-to-date immunizations. TANF benefits will not increase for additional children, and sanctions for noncompliance with paternity establishment or lack of cooperation with child support are strictly enforced.

Michigan   The expansion of Michigan's "To Strengthen Michigan Families" welfare demonstration requires AFDC recipients to participate in either the Job Opportunities and Basic Skills training program (JOBS) or Michigan's "Social Contract" activities, which encourage work and self-sufficiency. Michigan is also testing the requirement that TANF applicants participate in job searches by actively seeking employment while eligibility for TANF is being determined. Pre-school-age children must be immunized, and the program disregards the value of one vehicle in determining eligibility. On a limited scale, Michigan will evaluate the use of mediation services to determine if this increases compliance with child support.

Minnesota   The Family Investment program combines TANF, food stamps, and Minnesota's Family General Assistance into one cash grant with a list of rules and regulations. The program increases asset limits and allows two-parent households to remain intact by allowing the primary financial provider to work more than 100 hours a month without affecting benefit eligibility. The Work First program divides recipients into three groups: immediate employment, deferred employment, and a transitional group in which recipients participate in appropriate services for a period of time. There is an eight-week stabilization period for victims of domestic abuse, homeless persons, or persons participating in treatment centers for chemical dependency. TANF benefits are provided in the form of vendor payments for rent and utilities for the family's first six months on the program. Transitional child care, Medicaid, and support services are provided for recipients who have successfully moved from welfare to the workforce. AFDC Barrier Removal does not take the total household income into consideration when determining the eligibility of a minor parent. Income from any dependents or from minor parents who are at school at least part time is excluded when determining eligibility. Any money deposited into an account established for the minor parent or dependent is excluded as income. The family may also own a vehicle up to the amount of the food stamp limit, which is currently $4,600.

Mississippi

Work First has a special fund consisting of recipients' TANF and food stamps to reimburse private sector employers participating in job-ready employment. A savings account is established, and the employer contributes one dollar per hour worked. The state also pays any supplemental income if the recipient's income from work is less than it would have been with TANF and food stamps. The state passes on any child support collected directly to the family. Work Encouragement allows recipients in the workforce to retain TANF and their income by raising the previous earned income limit from 60 percent to 100 percent. The New Direction demonstration project was established as a disincentive for recipients to have more children while receiving TANF. The cash benefit for additional children will not increase, although a newborn will be eligible to receive Medicaid and any child support collected. This does not pertain to firstborn children or to children conceived through rape, sexual assault, or incest. School participation and up-to-date immunization are mandatory for recipients of benefits. Two-parent homes will not have their benefits affected if one parent works more than 100 hours a month. The last incentive to encourage recipients to move from TANF to the workforce is the three-month time limit on Medicaid and child care assistance for TANF recipients.

Missouri

Missouri Families–Mutual Responsibility Plan requires TANF recipients to sign and fulfill a self-sufficiency agreement that establishes a plan for work and places a two-year time limit on benefits. A person may be allowed an additional two years, if necessary, to achieve self-sufficiency. Individuals who are not self-sufficient by the end of the time limit must participate in job search or work experience programs. Those who have received TANF benefits for 36 months or more and have completed their agreement by leaving TANF will not be eligible for further benefits, with certain good cause exceptions. Children's benefits will not be affected. Minor parents must live with their parents or guardians to receive benefits. If they attend school full time and work, they may keep all employment income. In some counties, noncustodial parents who volunteer for the state's JOBS program can receive credit against past-due child support. For two-parent families with at least one parent under 21, the limit is waived on the number of hours the principal wage earner can work. The resource limits are increased for all families; and recipients may own one automobile, without regard to its value.

Montana

Families Achieving Independence has three components: the Job Supplement program, AFDC Pathways program, and Community Services program. The Job Supplement program helps at-risk families avoid becoming welfare dependent by providing a one-time payment of as much as three times the monthly TANF payment the family would otherwise be eligible to receive. Child support collections are passed directly on to the custodial parent. Other TANF applicants must enroll in the Pathways component and sign a Family Investment Agreement that, with some exceptions, limits benefits to 24 months for one-parent families and 18 months for two-parent families. Income disregards and asset limits are raised, and recipients must participate in JOBS, comply with child support enforcement provisions, and obtain medical screenings and immunizations for their children. Adults who do not leave TANF by the end of the time limit must enroll in the Community Services program and perform 20 hours of community work per week. Children's TANF benefits are not time-limited, and children continue to be eligible for Medicaid and food stamps. All participants must also choose between a reduced Medicaid benefit package and a partial premium payment toward a private health insurance policy. Full Medicaid coverage is provided on an emergency basis if certain services are needed for employment purposes.

Nebraska	Under this demonstration project, most welfare recipients are given a choice between two time-limited welfare plans. One offers slightly lower benefits, but enables recipients to retain more benefits when they begin to earn income from work. An alternative plan offers slightly higher benefits, but the level of benefits decrease more quickly when recipients begin to earn employment income. A non-time-limited program remains in place but can be chosen only by recipients exempted by the state from enrolling in one of the time-limited programs. Under all three programs, a recipient must develop a self-sufficiency contract with a caseworker. There is a family cap; resource limits are raised to $5,000; benefits are reduced by $50 for each minor child who fails to attend school; and minor parents who live at home are expected to receive support from their parent(s) if the parent's income exceeds 300 percent of the federal poverty rate. Under the two time-limited programs, cash assistance is provided for a total of 24 months in a 48-month period; food stamps are cashed out; TANF payments are slightly reduced; and all adult wage earners must work or participate in job search, education, or training. Two years of transitional Medicaid and child care are offered for recipients who leave welfare for work.
New Hampshire	The Employment Program requires TANF recipients to participate in job searches while receiving benefits for the first six months, then participate in a work activity for the next six months. New applicants are assessed for employability before receiving benefits. The state is shifting the old concept of welfare to work by combining the New Hampshire Department of Health and Human Service with the Department of Employment Security. A child born while the mother is receiving benefits exempts her from working for 13 weeks. Transitional case management and expanded Medicaid transitional benefits are offered to recipients who leave TANF for the workforce. The resource limit is increased to $2,000, and one automobile is allowed without affecting benefits.
New York	A Jobs First strategy gives applicants alternatives to welfare, provides new incentives for recipients to find work and create businesses, and encourages the formation and preservation of two-parent families. The demonstration gives applicants otherwise eligible for AFDC the option to receive child care or JOBS training program services in place of TANF. The program also provides one-time cash assistance or other services necessary to remedy a temporary emergency that has resulted, or may result, in job loss or impoverishment. The demonstration allows children in AFDC families to receive AFDC for up to two years after a caretaker parent marries and the new spouse's income makes the family ineligible, so long as the household's income does not exceed 150 percent of the federal poverty guidelines. It extends to a full year transitional child care benefits for employed recipients who leave the rolls because of child support payments. In addition, the plan encourages clients to develop their own business enterprises by excluding certain business income and resources, including vehicles.
North Carolina	Work First uses a Personal Responsibility Contract that must be signed by all applicants. Recipients approved to receive benefits must work a minimum of 30 hours a week with a 24-month time limit. The state can also pay one lump sum of cash equal to 3 months of benefits for people in a crisis situation. There are no additional benefits for additional children; minor parents must attend school on a regular basis; immunizations must be up to date; and all recipients must cooperate with child support enforcement. Work Over Welfare is for families with children between the ages of one and five. Recipients must participate in up to 40 hours of

employment or training activities weekly. An Opportunity Agreement is signed outlining employment and training responsibilities; and when the last child reaches six, the recipient immediately is in the Work First program. Benefits are denied to anyone unwilling to sign the agreement. TANF and food stamps are cashed out to subsidize wages paid by private sector employers participating in this program. Benefits are given to any recipient who receives less from employment than she or he would have received from TANF and food stamps.

North Dakota
The federal government and the state will match funds for low-income families during the first six months of pregnancy. However, benefits will not be received until the last trimester. To continue receiving benefits, pregnant individuals must pursue education and training during their first six months of pregnancy and then again after their child is three months old. Training, Education, Employment and Management combines TANF, food stamps, and a low-income Home Energy Assistance Program into one cash benefit. Recipients establish their own time limit, within reason, to be gainfully employed and self-sufficient. New terms help recipients get off welfare, because the family is able to earn and save more money and resources before benefits are affected. A family may own one vehicle, regardless of its value; immunization and health screening must be kept up to date. A stepparent's income will not be counted for the first six months.

Ohio
Through Communities of Opportunity the state and local businesses, industries, and community leaders have generated 2,500 wage-subsidized jobs for the first five years of this project. The minimum wage on these jobs is $8.00 an hour, which allows recipients to move from welfare to the workforce. Any difference between income earned from employment and what TANF and food stamps would pay will be supplemented. Children of Opportunity mandates that children between the ages of 6 and 18 must attend school on a regular basis. Case managers are available to assist families in which truancy is high. Families of Opportunity increases the income two-parent families can earn before benefits are affected. Eighteen months of transitional child care are provided. Learning, Earning and Parenting requires pregnant TANF recipients or parents under age 20 to attend school and receive their GED or high school diploma. LEAP allows recipients to participate in a vocational training or work program if a recipient does not opt for education. A bonus of $62 is given for completing the eleventh grade; $200 is given high school graduates or GED equivalents. TANF is limited to 36 months in any 60-month period, and recipients must seek employment during the application process. The first $250 earned from employment and one-half of income earned above $250 a month is disregarded in calculations of benefits. Two-parent families are able to work more than 100 hours a month and still retain their benefits. Pregnant women must receive prenatal care, and drug treatment if necessary.

Oklahoma
This demonstration seeks to encourage welfare recipients to attend school regularly and ultimately to graduate from high school or an equivalent educational program. The demonstration provides that TANF recipients between the ages of 13 and 18 must remain in school or face a reduction in benefits. The plan applies to teenage parents as well as children. Mutual Agreement—A Plan for Success (MAAPS) increases work incentives by allowing recipients to keep some of their earnings without losing TANF benefits. MAAPS also waives the requirement that the principal wage earner in a two-parent family work fewer than 100 hours per month to qualify for TANF, and it raises the allowance for an automobile from $1,500 to $5,000.

After receiving TANF benefits for three years in any five-year period, recipients still unable to find a job are required to work at least 24 hours a week in a subsidized job. MAAPS also provides intensive case management for three targeted groups: teen parents, long-term recipients, and those with repetitive cycles of dependence on welfare. An agreement between the recipient and the state assesses abilities and outlines rights, responsibilities, and consequences.

Oregon

JOBS PLUS provides subsidized public or private employment at minimum wage for up to 9 months. The state will supplement any income difference between the amount earned from employment and the amount that would have been earned from benefits. Medicaid will still be provided, and workplace mentoring and support services are offered. Any child support received by the state will go immediately to the family. Each JOBS PLUS participant will be given an Individual Education Account, and the employer will deposit one dollar into this account for each hour the recipient worked. Once a person moves from a subsidized position to an unsubsidized job, the funds will be transferred to the State Scholarship Commission and will be available to the immediate family for continuing education or vocational training. Oregon Option is a spin-off from JOBS PLUS that allows TANF recipients 24 months of benefits in a seven-year period. Any money the state saves from its allotted TANF expenditure by getting people established in the work force will be reinvested into longer-term child care and JOBS services. Minor parents are required to live with either their parents or a legal guardian in order to remain eligible for benefits, and they must attend school on a regular basis. Transitional child care is granted for 12 months to recipients whose income remains below a level established by the state. Mothers and fathers can work more than 100 hours a month, and the limit of resources a recipient may accumulate is increased.

Pennsylvania

The Pathways to Independence project provides incentives and support for single- and two-parent families moving from welfare to self-sufficiency. It increases earned income disregards so that recipients can keep more of what they earn before they become ineligible for public assistance. Additionally, it raises TANF resource limits, including the value of a family's vehicle; and it increases the time that transitional child care and Medicaid are provided after a family becomes ineligible for welfare because of earnings. To further aid the transition to work, Pathways extends case management counseling and referral services for up to one year after the family leaves welfare. Families are able to deposit money into retirement savings and education accounts without penalty. After two months of employment, recipient families can choose to receive a cash payment instead of their monthly food stamp benefit.

South Carolina

The Self-Sufficiency and Personal Responsibility Program sets up work requirements and transitional programs to assist recipients going from welfare to the work force. Thirty days are given to a recipient to find employment or vocational training. If unable to secure employment or training, the recipient will be given another 30 days on TANF and the opportunity to find employment in the private sector. A last resort for recipients unable to meet either deadline will be for them to participate in community service to remain eligible for benefits. Medicaid and child care are provided from the beginning of employment, and after 12 months employed recipients will still be eligible to receive Medicaid and child care. Resource limits are $3,000, and the value of an automobile is disregarded. All minor parents and dependents must remain in school on a regular basis and be up to date on immunizations. The Family Independence Act requires recipients to sign an individual plan that outlines employment time limits, training, family skills instruction, and substance abuse treatment, if needed. TANF is limited to two years, and children born 10 or more months after the family is enrolled will not receive an increase in benefits but will receive vouchers that allow the purchase of baby necessities. The state may relocate families from one county to another where better employment possibilities may exist. The state will pay for the move, find child care, and pay the family's first month's rent. There is no 100-hour monthly work limit on two-parent households; the resource limit is $2,500; the value of one automobile may be up to $10,000; and an Individual Development Account for each family may have up to $10,000. Dependent children attending school will have their income disregarded.

South Dakota

The Strengthening of South Dakota Families Initiative encourages welfare recipients to undertake either employment or education activities. The program assigns TANF participants to either an employment or an education track designed to enable them to move from dependency to self-sufficiency. Individuals enrolled in the employment track receive up to 24 months of TANF benefits; those participating in the education track receive up to 60 months of TANF benefits. Upon completion of either track, participants are expected to find employment; failing that, they will be enrolled in approved community service activities. Individuals who refuse to perform the required community service without good cause will have their benefits reduced until they comply. In addition, in conformance with the Food Stamp Program, TANF benefits can be denied to any family in which an adult parent quits a job without good cause. The sanction period will last 3 months, or until the parent acquires a comparable job. The demonstration also enacts new rules pertaining to the employment and earnings of children receiving TANF. The South Dakota demonstration will disregard income earned by children who are attending school at least part time, and children will be permitted to have a savings account of up to $1,000.

Tennessee

Families First sets a time limit for TANF recipients of 18 months in a 60-month period. The state also requires recipients to sign a Personal Responsibility Plan stating their employment or training needs, and promising cooperation with child support enforcement, regular school attendance, and up-to-date immunization. Adults must spend 40 hours a week in employment, training programs, or a job search; but this requirement may be modified if child care is not available. Benefits are not increased for children conceived while a family is already receiving benefits except in cases of rape, incest, or the first child born to a minor. Married couples may work more than 100 hours a month and still remain eligible for benefits. Unmarried minors must remain in school, receive their GED, or participate in some other type of educational or vocational training program. Individual Development Accounts may have up to $5,000 per family; the equity of an automobile may be up to $4,600; and a special account for entrepreneurial activities may have up to $5,000. The Responsible Fatherhood project provides counseling, education, training, employment, and family-related services to fathers to increase their financial support and involvement in their children's lives. Transitional child care and Medicaid may be granted for up to 18 months.

Texas

The Texas plan has a three-tiered system for establishing the duration of benefits. Recipients are eligible for one, two, or three years depending on their work history and level of functional literacy. Time limits begin when a family gets into a work program. The Texas plan has a five-year cap after which recipients cannot receive funds. The five-year cap applies only to adults; children can continue to receive benefits, and the state also can opt to continue to provide assistance to families who reach the cap. Parents are required to sign a Personal Responsibility Agreement stating that they will keep their children in school and off drugs and will provide regular checkups and immunizations for their children. Parents/caretakers will lose benefits if they fail to comply with the agreement. The Texas plan also creates a system of local Workforce Development Boards to oversee all welfare and job training programs. A cash sum of $1,000 may be granted to families in crisis; however, they are barred from applying or receiving benefits for 12 months. Individual Development Accounts may be established by families and can accrue up to $10,000. The money must be spent on education, training, purchasing a home, or beginning a business.

Vermont

Vermont's Family Independence Project (FIP) promotes work by enabling TANF recipients to retain more income and accumulate more assets than is normally allowed. FIP also requires TANF recipients to participate in community or public service jobs after they have received TANF for 30 months or, for families participating in the unemployed parent component of TANF, 15 months. Current child support payments go directly to families.

Virginia

The Welfare Reform Project compiles a list of employers with openings paying $15,000 to $18,000 a year. Transitional child care and health care benefits are available. Families may accumulate up to $5,000 in savings. A stepparent's income is no longer counted in calculations of benefit eligibility. A full-time high school student up to the age of 21 will remain eligible for benefits. Transitional child care and health care for employed persons will remain in effect for 24 months. The Virginia Independence Program offers lump-sum payments of up to 120 days' worth of benefits to discourage recipients from applying for monthly TANF benefits. A minor parent must remain in an adult-supervised living environment, attend school regularly, and have immunizations kept up to date. Children born while the family is already receiving TANF will not increase the value of the benefits. If the family does not cooperate with establishing paternity or locating the father, all benefits may be denied for the entire household. Virginia Initiative for Employment Not Welfare is only for nonexempt adult participants. An agreement of Personal Responsibility is signed, and the time limit to receive benefits is 24 months. If the combined income received from employment and TANF benefits does not exceed the federal poverty guideline, the income will be disregarded. The Full Employment Program allows the state to fund private sector subsidized employment by combining TANF benefits with cashed-out food stamps.

Washington

The Success Through Employment Program reduces TANF benefits monthly after a family receives cash assistance for four years in a five-year period. The program encourages two-parent families to remain together by allowing the primary wage earner to work more than 100 hours a month and still remain eligible for benefits.

Wisconsin

The Work Not Welfare project requires that most TANF recipients either work or look for jobs. The plan provides case management, employment activities, and work experience to facilitate employment. Receipt of TANF benefits is limited to 24 months in a four-year period except under certain conditions, such as a recipient's inability to find employment in the local area because of a lack of appropriate jobs.

Upon exhaustion of benefits, recipients become ineligible for 36 months. With exceptions, a family cap is in effect, although additional children remain eligible for Medicaid benefits and food stamps. Child support is paid directly to the TANF custodial parent in cases in which the funds are collected by the state. All TANF recipients are offered family planning services and instruction in parenting skills.

Wyoming

This reform plan encourages TANF recipients to enroll in school, undertake a training program, or enter the workforce. Wyoming's plan allows TANF families with an employed parent to accumulate $2,500 in assets. Wyoming promotes compliance with work and school requirements through tough penalties: TANF minor children who refuse to stay in school or accept suitable employment can have their monthly benefit reduced by $40; and adult TANF recipients who are required to work or perform community service, but refuse to do so, face a $100 cut in their monthly benefit. Wyoming severely restricts eligibility for adults who have completed a postsecondary educational program while on welfare, and will deny payment to recipients who have confessed to or been convicted of program fraud until full restitution is made to the state. Unemployed noncustodial parents of TANF children who are not paying child support can be ordered by the courts into Wyoming's JOBS program.

Sources: Compiled from Department of Health and Human Services, "State Welfare Demonstrations" (Washington, DC: DHHS, June 1995), and "Speak Out Sheet," Fax Alert for Child Advocates, Children at Risk, Houston, TX, October, 29, 1996.

chapter 12

The American Health Care System

This chapter examines the U.S. health care system—specifically, the organization of medical services; key governmental health programs such as Medicare and Medicaid; the crisis in health care, including attempts to curb health care costs; the large numbers of uninsured people; the impact of the American Medical Association on health care; the growing role of managed care; and the ramifications of the AIDS epidemic in the health care system. In addition, the chapter surveys various proposals designed to ameliorate the problems in U.S. health care and considers how medical services are organized in Great Britain and Canada.

Health care in the United States is marked by several contradictions. On the one hand, Census Bureau data released in 2000 show a small decrease nationally in the number of people without health insurance, a reversal of a 12-year trend. About 1.7 million fewer Americans were uninsured in 1999, with the rate decreasing from 16.3 to 15.5 percent. This decline occurred among all major ethnic groups.[1] On the other hand, although the vast majority of Americans have easy access to a wide range of health care services through employment-based or public insurance programs, more than 42 million people (15.5 percent of the population) are still without coverage. Of that number, 10 million are children.[2]

Who are the uninsured?

- Young adults (18 to 24 years old) are the least likely of any age group to have health insurance coverage. Of poor young adults, 45.4 percent of people above age 18 who are no longer eligible for Medicaid or for the State Children's Health Insurance Program (S-CHIP) lack health coverage.
- Although Medicaid insured 12.9 million poor people during at least a portion of 1999, 10.4 million poor, or 32.4 percent, had no health insurance of any kind during the year.
- The proportion of people without health insurance ranged from 24 percent for those in households with annual incomes of less than $25,000 to 8 percent for those in households with incomes of $75,000 or more.

- Among those 18 to 64 years old in 1999, full-time workers were less likely than their part-time counterparts to be without health insurance (16.4 percent versus 22.4 percent). However, 47.5 percent of poor full-time workers were uninsured in 1999, a proportion not statistically different from the percentage of poor part-time workers without insurance.
- The proportion without health insurance was higher for Hispanics (33.4 percent) than for non-Hispanic whites (11.0 percent). The noncoverage rate for African Americans was 21.2 percent, not statistically different from the 21 percent for Asians and Pacific Islanders. More than 27 percent of American Indians and Alaska Natives were uninsured.
- In 1999, the foreign-born population was more likely than the native population to be uninsured: 33.4 percent versus 13.5 percent. Approximately 42 percent of foreign-born residents—immigrants who are not yet citizens—continue to be without health insurance, and the proportion rises to 60 percent among the poor.
- Employer-based health coverage recently increased in all firms, even small ones. The percentage of workers covered through their employers increased from 53.3 to 55.5 percent between 1998 and 1999. However, although small businesses with fewer than 25 employees increased employee coverage, they were still only half as likely to offer health plans as firms with 100 or more employees.[3]

The relatively high number of uninsured Americans is not surprising, given that family health insurance premiums cost on average $6,350 annually—a large share of income for a family trying to make ends meet. Purchasing affordable, accessible insurance is a particular challenge for many older people, for workers in transition between jobs, and for small businesses and their employees. But lacking health insurance has serious consequences. The uninsured are three times more likely then the privately insured not to receive needed medical care, 50 to 70 percent more likely to need hospitalization for avoidable acute conditions like pneumonia or uncontrolled diabetes, and four times more likely to rely on an emergency room or to have no regular source of care.[4] Approximately 1 million Americans seeking medical care are turned away each year because they cannot pay, and millions more forgo preventive services.[5] This situation exists even though every major city has at least one major medical center with an annual budget of $100 to $200 million.[6]

The Organization of Medical Services

Most health care costs in the United States are paid for by private insurers, public plans, and the direct public provision of health care. Only about 25 percent of health care costs are paid for directly by consumers. The dominant form of health care coverage in the United States is private insurance, which covers about 80 percent of the population (of whom two-thirds are covered by employer-based plans). Many elderly people use private health insurance plans to supplement the coverage offered by Medicare. Medical services in the United States consist of five major components:

1. Physicians in solo practice. These are typically the traditional physicians who may employ a nurse and receptionist. This form of medical organization is becoming increasingly rare in the era of group practices and managed care.
2. Group outpatient settings, including groups of physicians sharing facilities. This setting is becoming more common as physicians are forced to pool resources—capital, equipment, office staff, and so forth—in order to compete in an increasingly difficult health care marketplace. Group outpatient settings may also include health maintenance organizations (HMOs), physicians in industrial Employee Assistance Plan (EAP) settings, or doctors operating under university auspices. During the past few decades, physicians have increasingly worked in group practices or other organized settings. The federal government has strongly supported the development of HMOs.[7]
3. Hospitals—private, nonprofit, or public.
4. Public health services delivered on the state, local, regional, national, or international level. These services include health counseling; family planning; prenatal and postnatal care; school health services; disease prevention and control; immunization; referral agencies; STD (sexually transmitted diseases) services; environmental sanitation; health education; and maintenance of indexes on births, deaths, and communicable diseases. Government-sponsored health services include the Veterans Administration Hospitals (the largest network of hospitals in the United States); Community and Migrant Health Centers; services provided under the Title V Maternal and Child Health Block Grant; and the Title X Family Planning Program.
5. Sundry and corollary health services. This category includes home health services, physical rehabilitation, group homes, nursing homes, and so forth.

Major Public Health Programs: Medicare, Medicaid, and S-CHIP

Health care spending is the second fastest-growing component of the federal budget, overshadowed only by the growth in the public debt. Overall, health care spending accounts for at least 14 percent of total governmental expenditures at the state and federal levels. Eighteen percent of the population are covered by Medicare and Medicaid, which account for about 7 percent of all health care provided in the United States.[8]

Medicare

Medicare, Public Law 89-79, was added to the Social Security Act on July 30, 1965. This program was designed to provide elderly people with prepaid hospital insurance as well as optional medical insurance. Medicare is composed of two parts: compulsory Hospital Insurance (HI), known as Part A; and Supplemental Medical Insurance (SMI), known as Part B. After two years, people under age 65 who receive disability benefits are eligible for Part B.

Part A is a compulsory **inpatient care** (hospital) insurance plan (it also includes some nursing home and home health care), with the premiums coming out of a payroll tax that is part of the Social Security deductions. Most Americans 65 or older are automatically entitled to Part A. Part B is a voluntary supplemental medical insurance plan for any senior who is eligible for Part A benefits. An estimated 96 percent of senior enrollees in Part A also enroll in Part B. Each enrollee pays a monthly Part B premium ($45.50 per person in 2000). Medicare reimbursement to health care providers is subject to maximum rates of payment by level of service, which are often considerably less than some physicians will accept. Patients will sometimes pay the difference between the physician's charge and Medicare reimbursement. Although Medicare provides important services, the gaps in coverage are extensive (see Table 12.1), which is why many seniors opt for HMOs or supplement Medicare with private **medigap** insurance plans.

The Medicare program is the second largest social insurance program in the United States, with 39 million elderly and disabled beneficiaries and total expenditures of $216.6 billion in 1999. Medicare is the largest public payer for health care, financing close to 20 percent of all

health care spending in 2000. Since 1980 Medicare costs have risen at an average of 10 percent yearly. Total Medicare costs more than doubled from 1989 to 1998. In 1970 Medicare spending represented less than 1 percent of the gross domestic product (GDP); by 1994 it had increased to 2.7 percent. In fact, Medicare expenditures are growing so rapidly that the Social Security trust fund is expected to be depleted by 2025 and to run a $53 billion deficit in 2038 (see Figure 12.1). The Medicare program is expected to experience even greater hardships when the baby boom generation begins retiring around 2010.[9]

Medicaid

Before 1965, medical care for those who could not afford to pay for it was primarily a responsibility of charitable institutions and state and local governments. In 1950 the federal government authorized states to use federal/state funds under the Social Security Act of 1935 to provide medical care for the indigent. By 1957, the Kerr–Mills Act provided for a federal/state matching program to provide health care for the elderly and the poor. However, Kerr–Mills was not mandatory, and many states chose not to participate. As a compromise to ward off more far-reaching health policies, President Lyndon Johnson signed the Medicaid and Medicare programs into law in 1965.[10] Replacing all previous governmental health programs, Medicaid became the largest public assistance program in the nation, covering about 13 percent of the population, including more than 15 million children. In 1998 Medicaid served more than 40 million people at a total federal/state cost more than $170 billion. Medicaid expenditures more than doubled from 1990 ($70 billion) to 1998 ($170 billion), and over that period the program accounted for 15 percent of all health care spending.[11]

Medicaid is a means-tested public assistance program. Eligible persons receive services from physicians who accept Medicaid patients (in many places a minority of physicians) and other health care providers. These providers are then reimbursed by the federal government on a per-

TABLE 12.1 ▪ Medicare Benefits and Gaps

MEDICARE PART A HOSPITAL INSURANCE	
Benefits	*Gaps*
Hospital stays: Semiprivate room, meals, general nursing, and other hospital services and supplies.	This does not include private duty nursing, a television or a telephone in the room, or a private room, unless medically necessary. Inpatient mental health coverage is limited to 190 days in a lifetime. For each benefit period, the beneficiary pays a total of $776 for a hospital stay of 1–60 days; $194 per day for days 61–90 of a hospital stay; $388 per day for days 91–150 of a hospital stay; all costs for each day beyond 150 days.
Skilled nursing facility care: Semiprivate room, meals, skilled nursing and rehabilitative services, and other services and supplies (after a 3-day stay).	Beneficiaries pay nothing for the first 20 days. Afterward, beneficiaries pay up to $97 per day for days 21–100; all costs beyond the 100th day.
Home health care: Part-time skilled nursing care, physical therapy, speech/language therapy, home health aide services, durable medical equipment and supplies, and other services.	Beneficiaries pay nothing for home health services, but they do pay 20 percent of the approved amount for durable medical equipment.
Hospice care: Medical and support services from a Medicare-approved hospice, drugs for symptom control and pain relief, short-term respite care, care in a hospice facility, hospital or nursing home when necessary, and other services not otherwise covered by Medicare. Home care is also provided.	Beneficiaries pay up to $5 for outpatient prescription drugs and 5 percent of the Medicare payment amount for inpatient respite care. The amount paid for respite care can change yearly.
Blood: Given at a hospital or skilled nursing facility during a covered stay.	Beneficiaries pay for the first three pints.
MEDICARE PART B SUPPLEMENTAL MEDICAL INSURANCE	
Benefits	*Gaps*
Medical and other services: Doctor's services (except for routine physical exams), outpatient medical and surgical services and supplies, diagnostic tests, ambulatory surgical center facility fees for approved procedures, and durable medical equipment. Also outpatient physical and occupational therapy, including speech/language therapy, and mental health services.	Beneficiaries pay $100 once per calendar year, 20 percent of the approved amount after the deductible (except in the outpatient setting), 20 percent for all outpatient physical and speech therapy services, 20 percent for all outpatient occupational therapy services, and 50 percent for most outpatient mental health services.
Clinical laboratory services	Beneficiary pays nothing.
Home health care: Part-time skilled care, home health aide services, durable medical equipment, and other supplies and services.	Beneficiary pays 20 percent of approved amount for durable medical equipment.
Outpatient hospital services: Services for the diagnosis and treatment of an illness or injury.	Beneficiary pays a set copayment amount (after the deductible).
Blood: Pints of blood needed.	Beneficiary pays for the first three pints of blood, then 20 percent of the approved amount for additional pints.

Source: U.S. Government Medicare Site. Retrieved Oct., 2000, from the World Wide Web: http://medicare.gov/Publications/Pubs/Pdf/2000Preventive.pdf

FIGURE 12.1   Medicare Expenditures

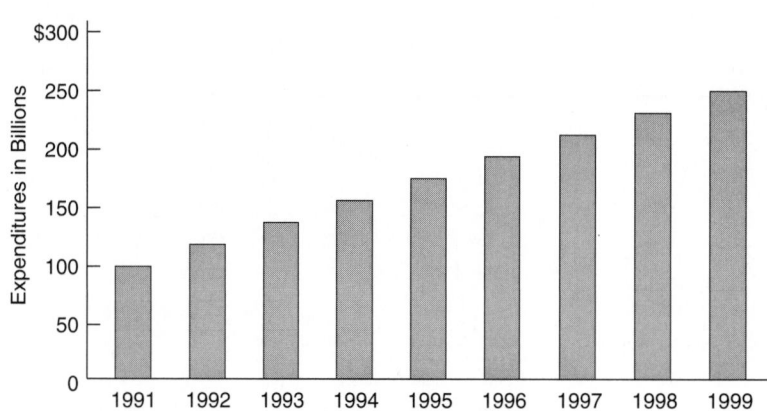

Source: Alex F. Brown and Sons, Inc., *Medicare: Where Do We Go from Here?* (Baltimore, MD, February 16, 1996).

patient basis. Alternatively, several states are requiring Medicaid recipients to enroll in state-contracted HMOs. Medicaid is also a federal/state program. States determine eligibility within broad federal guidelines. Thus, states make many of the key decisions as to where to set income eligibility limits, which groups to cover, what services to cover, and how much to pay for these services. To be eligible for federal funds, states are required to provide Medicaid coverage for most individuals who receive federally assisted income maintenance payments, as well as for related groups not receiving cash payments. Some examples of the mandatory Medicaid eligibility groups are:

- Low-income families with children who meet certain of the eligibility requirements in the state's AFDC plan in effect on July 16, 1996.
- Supplemental Security Income (SSI) recipients.
- Infants born to Medicaid-eligible pregnant women. Medicaid eligibility must continue throughout the first year of life, as long as the infant remains in the mother's house-

hold and she remains eligible, or would be eligible if she were still pregnant.
- Children under age 6 and pregnant women whose family income is at or below 133 percent of the federal poverty level. The maximum mandatory income level for pregnant women and infants in certain states may be higher than 133 percent if the state has established a higher percentage for covering those groups. States are required to extend Medicaid eligibility until age 19 to all children born after September 30, 1983, in families with incomes at or below the federal poverty level. This provision phases in coverage so that by the year 2002, all poor children under age 19 will be covered.
- Recipients of adoption assistance and foster care under Title IV-E of the Social Security Act.
- Certain Medicare beneficiaries and special protected groups; for example, those who lose SSI payments due to earnings from work or increased Social Security benefits.
- States also have the option to provide Medicaid coverage for other "categorically

needy" groups. These optional groups share characteristics of the mandatory groups, but the eligibility criteria are somewhat more liberally defined. Examples of these optional groups are (1) infants up to age 1 and pregnant women not covered under the mandatory rules whose family income is below 185 percent of the federal poverty level; (2) certain targeted low-income children; (3) certain elderly, blind, or disabled adults who have incomes above those requiring mandatory coverage but below the federal poverty level; (4) children under age 21 who meet income and resources requirements for TANF, but who otherwise are not eligible for TANF, (5) institutionalized individuals with income and resources below specified limits; (6) persons who would be eligible if institutionalized but are receiving care under home and community-based services waivers; (7) recipients of state supplementary payments; and (8) TB-infected persons who would be financially eligible for Medicaid at the SSI level.[12] (Table 12.2 shows the numbers and eligibility categories of the Medicaid population.)

The majority of states also extend coverage to the medically indigent—people who are ineligible for public assistance but who cannot obtain medical care or pay a medical bill. More than half the states extend coverage to families in which the breadwinner is receiving unemployment compensation.

Because Medicaid is funded by federal/state matching funds (on average states pay 43 percent of their Medicaid costs), states help to set Medicaid benefit levels. All states are required to provide inpatient and outpatient hospital care, physicians' services, laboratory and X-ray services, skilled nursing home services for adults, home health care, family planning services and supplies, nurse and midwife services, and early periodic screening for children; they also have

TABLE 12.2 ■ Medicaid Recipients by Category, 1972–1998, Selected Years (in thousands)

YEAR	TOTAL	AGE 65 OR OLDER	BLIND/DISABLED	CHILDREN	ADULTS	OTHER
1972	17,606	3,318	1,733	7,841	3,137	1,576
1975	22,013	3,643	2,661	9,598	4,529	1,800
1977	22,831	3,636	2,802	9,651	4,785	1,959
1980	21,605	3,440	2,911	9,333	4,877	1,499
1982	21,603	3,240	2,890	9,563	5,356	1,434
1984	21,365	3,165	2,950	9,771	5,600	1,187
1990	25,255	3,202	3,718	11,220	6,010	1,105
1993	33,432	3,863	5,016	16,285	7,505	763
1997	34,872	3,954	6,129	15,790	6,803	524
1998	40,649	3,964	6,638	18,309	7,908	655

Source: U.S. House of Representatives, Committee on Ways and Means, *Overview of Entitlement Programs, 2000 Green Book* (Washington, DC: U.S. Government Printing Office, 2000), p. 914.

the option of further extending Medicaid benefits to include drugs, eyeglasses, inpatient psychiatric care for individuals under age 21 or over age 65, and so forth. In addition, states have broad administrative powers over Medicaid, including the determination of reimbursement rates. As a result, individual states can discourage Medicaid participation by establishing low reimbursement rates and low state-defined income standards.

States may also restrict the content, scope, and duration of various services. In 1993, for example, the Clinton administration granted Oregon a Medicaid waiver that allowed the state to retreat from the goal of providing all possible health services to a limited number of Medicaid recipients. Instead, Oregon opted to provide more limited coverage to a greater number of persons by establishing a list of medical priorities and then allocating a specific level of dollars according to that priority list. Other care was not provided.[13] The Oregon Medicaid plan covered 120,000 more people (almost everyone under the poverty line) but disallowed certain procedures, including some experimental cancer and AIDS treatments. Other states have modified Medicaid by placing a limit on the number of days of hospital care a patient can receive or by limiting the number of physician visits covered in a year. States are also free to impose limited copayments for some Medicaid services.[14]

Federal law allows states to provide Medicaid benefits to poor children and pregnant women who are ineligible for public assistance. One such option involves the establishment of a Medically Needy component under the state Medicaid program. Under this option, a family whose countable income is greater than the state's Medicaid income eligibility limits but whose medical expenses are so large that the remaining income places the family below the poverty line is eligible for Medicaid. The Medically Needy component allows states to set Medicaid income limits that are up to one-third higher than the state's maximum TANF benefit. This option is particularly important for self-sufficient families who face a medical catastrophe that will deplete their economic resources.

Families whose health insurance limits are exhausted or who have no insurance also may be eligible. Thirty-six states had adopted a Medically Needy program by 1996.[15]

Medicaid was designed as a federal/state program to pay for health care for low-income and disabled citizens. Two-thirds of Medicaid recipients are low-income people who are covered for doctors' visits and hospital stays. Medicaid also pays for one-third of all births. Even so, the greatest single outlay of Medicaid funds goes to the elderly. In 1995 Medicaid paid for more than two-thirds of all people in nursing homes (excluding care for mentally retarded people) at an average annual cost of $18,000 per person.[16] As a result, close to three-fifths of all nursing home expenditures are paid for by the federal government. Not surprisingly, the growth of the nursing home industry parallels the creation of Medicaid. From 1965 (the year Medicaid was created) to 1970, the number of nursing home residents rose by 18 percent. From 1970 to 1975 that number rose another 17 percent; from 1975 to 1980, 14 percent; and from 1980 to 1985, about 12 percent. Because four-fifths of nursing homes are for-profit facilities, Medicaid functions as a de facto subsidy for the nursing home industry.

Despite federal guidelines, four important gaps exist in Medicaid coverage: (1) the low eligibility limits set for Medicaid; (2) the refusal of many states to adopt most or all of the Medicaid options; (3) the gaps in coverage for the elderly and disabled; and (4) the general ineligibility of poor single persons and childless couples for Medicaid unless they are elderly or disabled. The Robert Wood Johnson Foundation noted that Medicaid reached 19 percent fewer poor and near poor families in 1986 than it did in 1976.[17] Although Medicaid covered 12 percent of the population in 1994, only 46 percent of those with incomes below the poverty line were covered.[18]

In 1996, for the first time in almost a decade, Medicaid enrollment for children and their parents began to decline, dropping by 2 percent nationwide from 1995. Individual states reported 1995–98 declines of 12 percent (California), 18 percent (Florida), 19 percent (New York), and 29 percent (Wisconsin). These Medicaid declines were closely associated with dramatic reductions in the number of people receiving welfare. At the national level, welfare rolls declined by 42 percent from 1994 to 1998, with many states reporting decreases of over 50 percent. It appears that many children and their parents who leave welfare do not remain enrolled in Medicaid, even though most would probably continue to be eligible. Medicaid administrative data from California and Florida indicate that at least half of those leaving welfare (including children) lose their Medicaid coverage as well.[19]

For all its shortcomings, the Medicaid program has led to important gains in the nation's health. In 1963, 54 percent of poor people did not see a physician. In that same year, only 63 percent of pregnant women received prenatal care; by 1976 that number had increased to 76 percent. Between 1964 and 1975 the use of physicians' services by poor children increased 74 percent. This increased health care utilization helped bring about a 49 percent drop in infant mortality between 1965 and 1988. For African American infants the drop in mortality was even sharper: Infant mortality dropped by only 5 percent in the 15 years before Medicaid, but by 49 percent in the 15 years after the program began. Ongoing preventive care also cut program costs for Medicaid-eligible children by 10 percent.[20] Medicaid is one of the most important governmental health programs in the United States.

The State Children's Health Insurance Program (S-CHIP)

As part of the Balanced Budget Act of 1997, Congress and President Clinton created the State Children's Health Insurance Program (S-CHIP), a federal–state partnership that allocated $48 billion over 10 years to expand health care coverage to uninsured children. S-CHIP gives each state three options for covering uninsured children: designing a new children's health insurance program; expanding current Medicaid programs; or a combination of both strategies.

Together with Medicaid, S-CHIP provides health care coverage to millions of previously uninsured children—including coverage for prescription drugs, and for vision, hearing, and mental health services. Before S-CHIP Medicaid eligibility was linked to welfare receipt. In large measure, Medicaid-eligible children had to be in an SSI or a TANF family. Perhaps the most important policy initiative in S-CHIP is that it unlinks state-subsidized child health care from welfare receipt. S-CHIP enables states to insure children from working families with incomes too high to qualify for Medicaid but too low to afford private health insurance. Each state with an approved plan receives enhanced federal matching payments for its S-CHIP expenditures up to a fixed state allotment. By July 2000 all 50 states, the District of Columbia, and five U.S. territories had implemented S-CHIPs, covering over 2.5 million children. In addition, the number of children enrolled in Medicaid increased because of statewide outreach and eligibility simplification efforts.

Based on S-CHIP, 15 jurisdictions have created their own separate child health program, 23 have expanded Medicaid, and 18 have developed a combination of a separate state program and a Medicaid expansion program. In addition, many states have already amended their programs to expand eligibility beyond their original proposal. Before S-CHIP only 4 states covered children whose family incomes were at least 200 percent of the federal poverty level (about $33,000 for a family of four). By 2000, 30 states had approved plans to cover children with incomes at that level. Many states have made strong progress in implementing their S-CHIP programs, finding innovative ways to identify and enroll uninsured children in both Medicaid and S-CHIP.

The federal S-CHIP statute requires states to report regularly on their progress toward covering low-income children, and it requires that each state or U.S. territory with an approved child health plan must submit a program evaluation to the secretary of Health and Human Services. Working with the states, the Department of Health and Human Services and the National Academy of State Health Policy facilitated the evaluation process by creating an evaluation framework that enables states to report their findings in a standardized manner.

States report having worked aggressively to simplify their application, enrollment, and reenrollment processes to ensure that eligible families can easily apply, enroll, and remain enrolled. Steps include providing joint Medicaid and S-CHIP mail-in applications and offering presumptive eligibility, retroactive eligibility, and continuous eligibility. In addition, 39 states have eliminated face-to-face interviews for Medicaid and/or S-CHIP. Only 7 states currently require an assets test for children enrolling in Medicaid or the S-CHIP program. Of the 17 states with combination programs, 16 have dropped the assets test in both their Medicaid expansion and their separate state program; while 1 state has dropped it for the S-CHIP program but not Medicaid. Thirteen of the 17 states with Medicaid expansions have dropped their assets test. States have dropped this requirement in the face of mounting evidence that it serves as a barrier to enrollment.

The Balanced Budget Act of 1997 gave states the option to enroll children in S-CHIP and Medicaid for up to 12 months, regardless of changes in income or family circumstances. Thirty-two states—more than 60 percent—have taken advantage of this new authority to ensure that children do not unnecessarily lose their coverage as a result of temporary changes in income or fluctuation in monthly paychecks. Of the 2 million children covered in 1999, states reported that more than 1.2 million children were in new state-designed children's health insurance programs and almost 700,000 were enrolled in Medicaid expansion plans.[21]

The Tobacco Settlement

Occasionally, public policy is made by the court system rather than the legislature. This was the case in the 1998 tobacco industry settlement. For 40 years tobacco companies had won every lawsuit brought against them and never paid out a dime. The long march toward a national tobacco settlement began on April 14, 1994, when repre-

sentatives from seven of the leading American tobacco companies stood before Congress and swore that nicotine was not an addictive substance. The presentation was astounding even in the eyes of many people who were neutral toward cigarette companies. In 1998 the tobacco companies were forced to accept a 600-page Master Settlement Agreement (MSA) requiring them to pay $206 billion to 46 states over a 25-year period. (That amount does not include $40 billion paid in separate settlements reached by four other states.) The MSA was the largest civil settlement in U.S. history. Payments are based on states' shares of the cost of smoking-related illnesses paid for through the Medicaid program. In exchange for the fine levied by the MSA, 39 states with pending individual lawsuits agreed to drop their cases. Lawsuits brought against tobacco companies by individuals, groups, and other government entities were allowed to continue. Some highlights of the MSA:

- Public health initiatives prohibit youth targeting in advertising and promotion; ban the use of cartoon characters in advertising, promotion, packaging, and labeling; restrict sponsorship by brand names; ban outdoor advertising; ban sales of merchandise with tobacco brand names; ban free samples to youth; and set minimum pack size at 20 cigarettes.

- The agreement aims to change corporate culture. Tobacco companies must develop corporate principles committed to compliance with the MSA, such as reducing youth smoking, designating an executive manager to identify ways to reduce youth access, and encouraging employees to identify alternative methods to reduce youth access.

- The MSA disbands tobacco trade associations, including the Council for Tobacco Research, the Tobacco Institute, and the Council for Indoor Air Research. It creates regulations and oversight for any new trade organizations.

- The settlement limits industry lobbying by prohibiting tobacco companies from opposing legislation aimed at restricting youth access and reducing consumption, specifically at the state and local levels.

■ It includes the creation of a $1.45-billion public education fund to carry out a sustained nationwide advertising and education program to counter youth tobacco use and educate consumers about tobacco-related disease.[22]

States will accrue significant revenues from the tobacco settlement: $6.4 billion by 2000, $6.9 billion by 2001, $8.3 billion by 2002, and $8.4 billion by 2003. Contrary to the hopes of many public health advocates, there are no restrictions on the use of MSA funds by the states. According to the National Governors' Association, states spent their settlement money in the following ways in 2000–01:

■ *Health.* At least forty-three states allocated some portion of tobacco settlement monies to health priorities. Thirty-eight states allocated some portion to tobacco use prevention and control; 16 states to programs for the elderly, including prescription drug programs; 13 states to S-CHIP; 12 states to Medicaid; 12 states to research, including biomedical, cancer, and tobacco-related studies; and 10 states to treatment of chronic diseases.

■ *Education.* Twenty states spent some portion of their tobacco settlement on education, including scholarships, school construction, technology, literacy, and other topics.

■ *Natural resources.* Three states allocated monies to natural resources projects, including water projects.

■ *Employment and social services.* Fifteen states devoted money to improving or implementing social service programs; 10 states to substance abuse or mental health programs; 7 states to early childhood development or children's social services; 5 states to improving criminal justice systems, with an emphasis on youth programs.

■ *Economic development and commerce.* Twenty-two states allocated money to economic development, commerce, and information technology; 6 states used MSA funds to assist tobacco growers and quota holders.

■ *Undecided.* Six states—Arizona, Arkansas, Missouri, Oregon, Pennsylvania, and Tennessee—and the District of Columbia had not made spending decisions as of October 2000. Voters in Arizona, Arkansas, Oklahoma, and Oregon considered ballot initiatives on the issue in November 2000.

■ *Finance.* Thirty states deposited their tobacco settlement funds into trust funds; 20 states deposited the money into the general fund; 2 states set up foundations with the money; 5 states used endowments; 13 states have used combinations of these methods for dealing with the money.[23]

Overall, states have allocated about $1.5 billion of the money they received in 2000. According to the National Conference of State Legislatures, 54 percent has gone for health care services, 12 percent for children's programs, 9 percent for education, 8 percent for antismoking initiatives, and 6 percent for senior citizens' programs. Another 11 percent is spread elsewhere, including aid to communities dependent on the tobacco industry.[24] The fear of some health care advocates is that the MSA funds may eventually be absorbed into state treasuries and used for purposes other than health and human services, including state tax cuts. (For some facts on the U.S. tobacco industry, see Figure 12.2.)

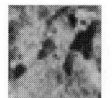 # The Health Care Crisis

Health care in the United States is plagued with problems—notably, eroding coverage, rising costs, **cost shifting**, and many anxious citizens. This and the following sections explore some parameters of the health care crisis, including health care spending and cost efficiency, the effectiveness of the U.S. health care system, attempts at cost cutting, the growing importance of

FIGURE 12.2   Tobacco at a Glance

Cigarettes account for more than 90 percent of spending on tobacco products in the United States; in 1998 Americans smoked 24 billion packs. U.S. spending for all tobacco products totaled about $49 billion in 1995.

Five U.S. companies—Philip Morris, R. J. Reynolds, Brown & Williamson, Lorillard, and Liggett—produce almost all of the cigarettes sold in the United States. Two companies, Philip Morris and R. J. Reynolds, account for more than 70 percent of industry sales. About 36 billion packs of cigarettes were produced by U.S. firms in 1997; about 12 billion packs were exported to other countries, and about 280 million were shipped to U.S. territories and to U.S. armed forces stationed overseas. The rest were consumed by domestic smokers. Smokeless tobacco products are also produced by five domestic manufacturers: U.S. Tobacco, Conwood, Pinkerton, National, and Swisher. More than 120 million pounds of chewing tobacco and snuff were produced in the United States in 1996; in 1995, smokeless tobacco companies posted revenues of $1.7 billion. About 2.5 billion large cigars and cigarillos and 14.2 million pounds of pipe and roll-your-own tobacco were produced by U.S. companies in 1995.

The United States is the second largest tobacco producer in the world, well below China. In 1996, tobacco was grown on over 124,000 U.S. farms, with a crop value of $2.9 billion. The tobacco industry supports more than 600,000 jobs.

Source: CNN, "A Brief History of Tobacco." Retrieved from the World Wide Web: http://www.cnn.com/US/9705/tobacco/history/index.html

managed care, and the impact of AIDS on the health care budget.

Overview of U.S. Health Care Expenditures

U.S. health care cost $1.3 trillion in 2000, up from 73 billion in 1970. This translates into 14.3 percent of the total **gross domestic product (GDP)**. (Health expenditures as a percentage of the GDP measure the proportion of all resources devoted to health care.) In comparison, health care spending in 1970 was only 7.1 percent of the GDP. From 1970 to 2000, per capita health care costs rose from $341 to $4,611, an increase of almost 1,400 percent (see Figure 12.3). National health expenditures are expected to total $2.2 trillion and reach 16.2 percent of the GDP by 2008.[25]

Health care spending consumed 12.5 of the GDP in 1992. In comparison, education was only 7.3 percent of the GDP in that year, and military spending had actually decreased to less than 6 percent.[26] Moreover, the costs of providing health care have risen faster than the rate of inflation. From 1980 to 1992, annual increases in per capita expenditures on health care were approximately 5 points above the yearly rate of inflation. Beginning in 1992, the growth in health care expenditures decelerated somewhat, registering less than 3 points above the rate of inflation[27]—then accelerated again in the late 1990s. But even if health-related expenditures declined, the United States would spend at least 18 percent of its GDP on health care by 2005.[28] Without wide-ranging reforms, health care spending is expected to reach about $1.6 trillion by 2003.[29]

When health care expenditures are broken down, the largest share (33.3 percent) goes to hospitals; in 1999 hospital care alone cost more than $401 billion.[30] (See Figure 12.4.) Increases in the cost of hospital care have been a key factor in driving up health care costs. In 1965 the average daily hospital room charge was $41; by 1994 it had risen to $1,127. In 1965 the average cost per hospital stay was $315; by 1994 the cost had risen to $6,427.[31]

Of the $626 billion spent by private sources for health care in 1998, about 60 percent ($375 billion) was spent on private health care insurance premiums. Premiums increased only 2 percent yearly from 1994 to 1998, but they jumped

FIGURE 12.3 National Health Care Expenditures, Selected Years, 1970–2000

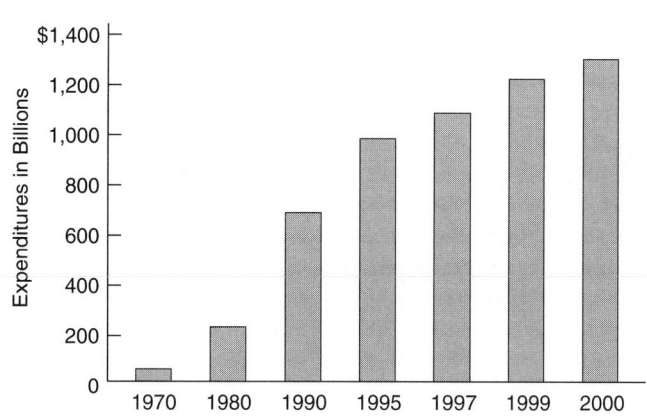

Source: Compiled from Health Care Financing Administration, "Actuarial Products, N.H.E. Projections, Table 1." Retrieved from the World Wide Web: http://www.hcfa.gov/stats/NHE-Proj/

FIGURE 12.4 Where the U.S. Health Care Dollar Is Spent

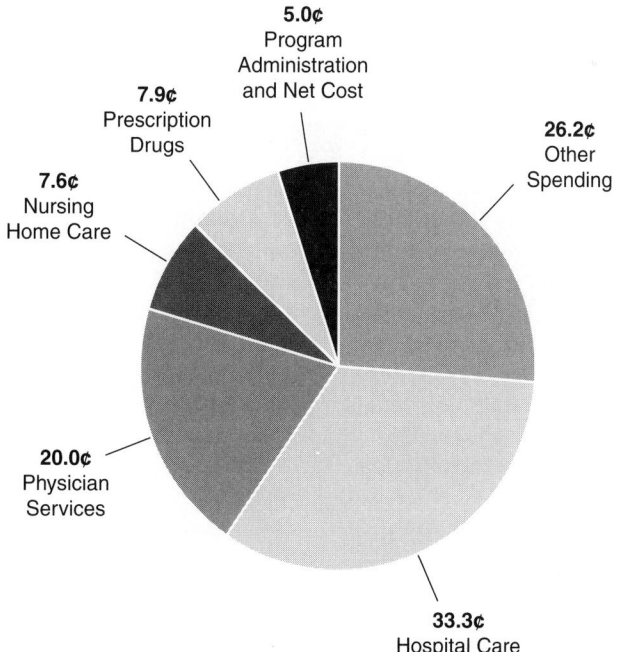

Source: Health Care Financing Administration, Chart 1. Retrieved December 23, 2000, from the World Wide Web: http://www.hcfa.gov/stats/NHE-Proj/

8.2 percent in 1998. For 2001–02 health insurance premiums are predicted to rise 10 to 13 percent for larger employers and 20 percent for smaller ones.[32] Figure 12.5 shows where the U.S. health insurance dollar is spent.

U.S. Health Care in International Perspective

Health care costs considerably more in the United States than in any other industrialized nation.[33] In 1997, for example, per capita spending on all health care services ranged from a high of $4,090 in the United States to a low of $1,347 in the United Kingdom. The median for all 29 member countries of the Organization for Economic Cooperation and Development (OECD) countries was $1,747 (see Table 12.3).[34]

In 1997, the percentage of GDP spent on health care ranged from 13.5 percent in the United States to 6.7 percent in the United Kingdom. The OECD median was 7.6 percent. Although all countries have devoted an increasing percentage of their resources to health care since 1960, the United States experienced the highest total increase: The 5.2 percent of GDP devoted to health services in 1960 rose to 14.3 percent in 1997. During this same period, the percentage of GDP spent on health care in the median OECD country increased by 3.7 percentage points, from 3.9 to 7.6 percent (see Table 12.4).[35] With the exception of Germany and the United States, the majority of developed countries have assured their citizens universal health insurance coverage since 1970. In the United States only 32.9 percent of the population had government-assured health insurance coverage in 1995. Of

FIGURE 12.5   The U.S. Health Insurance Dollar

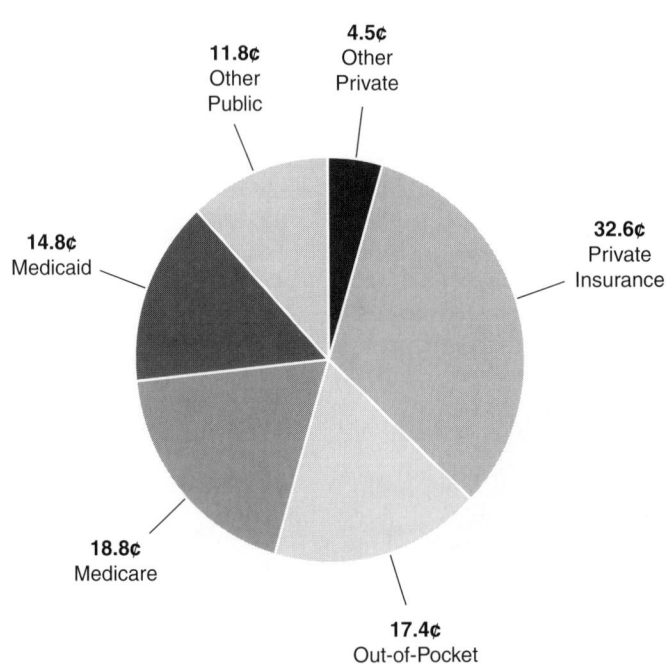

Source: Health Care Financing Administration, Chart 1. Retrieved December 23, 2000, from the World Wide Web: http://www.hcfa.gov/stats/NHE-Proj/

TABLE 12.3 ■ Per Capita Expenditures on Health in 1997 Compared to the OECD Median ($1,747)

COUNTRY	PERCENTAGE DIFFERENCE AND AMOUNT	COUNTRY	PERCENTAGE DIFFERENCE AND AMOUNT
United States	+134% ($4,090)	Australia	+3% ($1,805)
Germany	+34 ($2,339)	Japan	+0 ($1,741)
Canada	+17 ($2,095)	New Zealand	−23 ($1,352)
France	+17 ($2,051)	United Kingdom	−23 ($1,347)

Source: Gerard F. Anderson, "Multinational Comparisons of Health Care," The Commonwealth Fund (October 1998). Retrieved from the World Wide Web: http://www.cmwf.org/programs/international/ihp_1998_multicompsurvey_299.asp#overview

TABLE 12.4 ■ Total Health Care Expenditures as a Percentage of GDP

COUNTRY	1960	1997	PERCENTAGE POINT CHANGE	COUNTRY	1960	1997	PERCENTAGE POINT CHANGE
United States	5.2%	13.6%	8.4	Germany	4.8%	10.4%	5.6
France	4.2	9.6	5.4	Canada	3.0	7.3	5.4
OECD Median	5.5	9.3	4.3	Australia	4.9	8.3	3.4
New Zealand	4.3	7.6	3.3	United Kingdom	3.9	6.7	2.8

Source: Gerard F. Anderson, "Multinational Comparisons of Health Care," The Commonwealth Fund (October 1998). Retrieved from the World Wide Web: http://www.cmwf.org/programs/international/ihp_1998_multicompsurvey_299.asp#overview

the eight major OECD countries, only the United States has more than 1 percent of its population uninsured.

Two indicators of the intensity of services provided during a hospital stay are cost per day and personnel per bed. The United States' cost per day in 1996 was 5 times the OECD median and 2.3 times greater than Canada's, the country with the second highest cost per day. In 1994 the United States also had the most hospital employees per bed, more than double the OECD median.[36] There is also considerable variation in the number of physicians per capita: In 1996 Germany had 3.4 physicians per 1,000 people, the United States had 2.6, and the United Kingdom had 1.6. In addition, average physician incomes differ significantly. In 1991 U.S. physi-

cians' incomes were the highest ($171,000) by a wide margin. Physicians in Germany had the second highest average incomes ($101,640 in 1992). In Australia, France, and the United Kingdom, physicians earned on average less than $70,000 in 1991.

The high cost of health care in the United States is problematic when we compare U.S. health indicators to those of other nations. For example, in 1996 life expectancy at birth for women in the United States was the second lowest in the OECD, at 79.4 years. Life expectancy at birth for women ranged from a high of 83.6 years in Japan to a low of 79.3 years in the United Kingdom. Japan had the longest life expectancy at birth for males (77 years) and the United States had the shortest (72.7 years). From

1960 to 1996, life expectancy at birth for both men and women in OECD countries increased an average of almost 7 years. The greatest increase occurred in Japan (12.6 years), the smallest in the United Kingdom (5.6 years). The increase in the United States was 6.2 years.[37]

Infant mortality rates also illustrate troubling trends. In 1996 the United States had the highest infant mortality rate in the OECD (7.8 per 1,000 live births); Japan had the lowest (3.8 per 1,000 live births). Another health indicator is premature deaths, or deaths that would have been preventable had appropriate medical knowledge been applied or had risky behavior been less prevalent. The United States had the most preventable deaths per 100,000 people, and Japan had the least.[38] In short, the beneficial effects of large U.S. health care expenditures are questionable. Americans neither are healthier nor live longer than people in similar industrial nations where health care spending is lower.[39]

 # Explaining the High Cost of U.S. Health Care

Accounting for the enormous costs of the U.S. health care system is complicated. Some policy analysts attribute at least some of these costs to the following factors.

■ The increasing costs of malpractice suits against health care providers are passed along to consumers directly in higher medical costs and indirectly through the practice of defensive medicine. Medical malpractice costs increased more than 48.6 percent from 1990 to 1994, far outpacing the 16.6 percent increase in overall tort costs in those same years. According to a 1998 Congressional Budget Office (CBO) study, medical malpractice reform could result in savings of $1.5 billion over 10 years.[40] Fearful of malpractice

suits, some physicians behave overcautiously and order overly aggressive diagnostic tests. Some policy analysts estimate that as much as 30 percent of current health care expenditures are consumed by unnecessary services, many of which are related to defensive medicine.[41] The American Medical Association estimates that defensive medicine may account for as much as 14 percent of health care costs.[42] In 1991 the cost of practicing defensive medicine was estimated at $25 billion. The average annual malpractice insurance premium for a general surgeon rose from $9,900 in 1982 to $22,500 in 1991. In 1991 malpractice insurance for physicians cost $5.1 billion.[43]

■ The United States leads the world in the development and use of medical technology, but many of these advances have come at a high price. Between 1980 and 1991 the annual number of coronary bypass operations for men increased from 108,000 to 206,000; diagnostic ultrasounds for women rose from 114,000 to 652,000; and the use of CAT scans increased from 306,000 to more than 1.4 million.[44] Overall, treatment is now available for some diseases that were formerly untreatable, but at a high price. In addition, some technologies are introduced before being sufficiently tested to determine their cost-effectiveness and their superiority to existing technologies.

■ The administrative costs involved in processing millions of insurance claims also add to rising health care expenditures. It is estimated that as much as 25 percent of every health care dollar goes for managing the mountains of paperwork required to run the system.[45] Despite the paperwork, the U.S. General Accounting Office estimated that in 1991 fraud cost $70 billion, or 10 percent of every health care dollar.

■ The treatment of people with AIDS has led to increasing fiscal strains on the health care system.[46] While spending on HIV and AIDS victims has grown faster than all other health care spending, it is still relatively small. Overall expenditures on HIV-positive individuals increased from 1.3 to 1.4 percent of the total health care budget between 1992 and 1995.[47] Federal spending on AIDS in 1999 accounted for $10 billion.[48]

■ Increased longevity has led to growing numbers of elderly people, many of whom have chronic diseases that are often expensive to treat. Although it might seem easy to blame rising health care costs on the elderly, however, the Congressional Budget Office maintains that increases in the aged population accounted for only 5 percent of the increase in per capita health care spending between 1965 and 1990.

Hospital Costs and Physicians' Salaries

Hospital costs account for 33.3 percent of all health care expenditures. The total costs of hospital care reached $401 billion in 1999, up from $28 billion in 1970. From 1980 to 1990, hospital costs rose almost 2.5 times, from almost $103 billion to $256 billion. Although the rise in hospital costs began to slow down in the middle 1990s, it picked up again by 1997. The temporary deceleration of the increase in hospital costs in the middle 1990s is explained by several factors, including cost savings facilitated by managed care plans, a small increase in admissions rates between 1992 and 1995, shortened hospital stays, a lower inpatient hospital occupancy rate, a downsizing of hospital personnel, and lower rates of general inflation.[49]

The second largest health care expenditure is for physicians' services, which accounted for 20 percent of all health care costs (more than $217 billion) in 1999. From 1970 to 1999, the cost of physicians' services rose by almost 1,800 percent. From 1980 to 1990 alone, the cost of physicians' services rose by 300 percent.[50] By 1999, the average physician's salary in the Untied States was about $167,000 (see Table 12.5).

Physician organizations argue that high salaries are necessary to repay the high debts incurred by medical students. In 1996 the median educational debt of all medical school graduates was $71,500. Specifically, the debt was $65,000 at public and $92,000 at private medical schools. One-third of all graduates of private

TABLE 12.5 ■ Average Salaries of Practicing Physicians, 1999

SPECIALTY	SALARY
Anesthesiology	$203,326
Cardiology	$207,690
Emergency medicine	$157,286
Family practice	$122,625
General surgery	$190,273
Internal medicine	$127,366
Neurology	$149,309
Obstetrics/gynecology	$204,752
Oncology	$173,655
Pathology	$175,048
Pediatrics	$121,776
Psychiatry	$130,267
Radiology	$209,150

Source: Allied Physicians, "Physician Salary Surveys, 1999." Retrieved from the World Wide Web: http://www.allied-physicians.com/salary_surveys/physician-salaries.htm

medical schools currently have educational debts in excess of $100,000.[51] The problem of high physician salaries is aggravated by the growth in the number of expensive medical specialists. For example, in 1994 only 34 percent of the nation's physicians were in **primary care** specialties (e.g., family practice, internal medicine, obstetrics/gynecology, and pediatrics). Today roughly 65 percent of medical school graduates are specialists—a reversal of the ratio that existed 30 years ago.[52]

The high cost of prescription drugs is also driving up health care costs. Consumers pay more for their medicine in the United States than in any other country. Americans filled 40 percent more prescriptions in 1998 than in 1992, and the costs of these drugs increased from $50.7 billion in 1992 to $100.6 billion in 1999. Pharmaceutical drug expenditures were $5.5 billion in 1970; by 1999 they rose to $100.6 billion, an 1,800 percent increase. Drug costs rose 11 percent per year between 1992 and 1997, more than twice as fast as other health care expenses. Older Americans unprotected by Medicaid spend 10 percent of their total income on prescription drugs. Many of these people are exposed to financial catastrophe as a result of highly inflated drug prices. In fact, in recent years the manufacturers of the top 20 drugs have increased their profits at five times the average rate of Fortune 500 companies.[53]

In 1999 the drug industry spent $8.3 billion promoting its products—nearly half as much as the $17 billion it spent on research and development. Direct consumer advertising accounted for $1.3 billion of the total, with the rest being aimed at medical professionals. The advertising paid off. Posting huge increases in sales between 1993 and 1998 were heavily advertised drugs that included antihistamines (sales increases of $1.9 billion), antidepressants ($5 billion), cholesterol reducers ($3.4 billion), and antiulcer drugs ($2.7 billion).[54] Over a decade when health care costs almost doubled, prescription drug prices increased by a whopping 152 percent.[55]

 ## Cutting Health Care Costs

There are two aspects to cutting health care costs. The first involves cutting costs for governmental health care programs; the second involves lowering overall medical costs.[56] The rising costs of Medicare led the federal government to seek alternative ways to lower hospital costs, including the Diagnostic Related Group system (DRG). In 1983 Congress enacted the DRG form of medical payment. Although earlier Medicare rules had restricted the fees hospitals could charge, the government generally reimbursed them for the entire bill. This style of reimbursement was called retrospective (after-the-fact) payment. By contrast, DRGs are a form of **prospective payment system,** or payment before the fact; the federal government specifies in advance what it will pay for the treatment of 468 classified illnesses or diagnosis-related groups.[57]

Developed by health researchers at the Yale–New Haven Hospital, the DRG system was designed to enforce economy by defining expected lengths of hospital stays. This system provides a treatment and diagnostic classification scheme, using the patient's medical diagnosis, prescribed treatment, and age as a means for categorizing and defining hospital services. In other words, the DRG system determines the length of a typical patient's hospital stay and reimburses hospitals only for that period of time. (Exceptions to the DRG classification system are made for long hospital stays, certain kinds of hospital facilities, hospitals that are the only facility in a community, and hospitals that serve large numbers of poor people.) Additional costs beyond the DRG allotment must be borne by the hospital. Conversely, if a patient requires less hospitalization than the maximum DRG allocation, the hospital gets to keep the difference. Hospitals may not charge the patient more than the DRG allotment. Hence, patients not yet ready for discharge (e.g., patients who do not have appropriate aftercare services available) may be discharged—a situation that can result in patient dumping.

Managed Care

Managed care became a household word during the 1990s. About 81.3 million Americans are now enrolled in HMOs, up from 33.3 million in 1990. An estimated 89 million more are enrolled in PPOs, which cost more but allow patients more flexibility. HMOs have been embraced by the nation's large employers as a way to control health costs. But although managed care cut costs for most of the 1990s, by 1998–99 costs started climbing again, increasing by about 5 percent in 1998 and by more than 7 percent in 2000.[58]

Paul Schmolling Jr., Merrill Youkeles, and William Burger define **managed care** as "an umbrella for health care insurance systems that contract with a network of hospitals, clinics, and doctors who agree to accept fees for each service or flat payments per patient. The advantage to providers is that they are given a ready source of referrals."[59] (Figure 12.6 lists various types of managed care systems.)

FIGURE 12.6	Types of Managed Care Plans

- *Health maintenance organizations (HMO)*: A prepaid or capitated insurance plan in which individuals or their employers pay a fixed monthly fee for services rather than a separate charge for each visit or service.

- *Preferred provider organizations (PPO)*: A type of HMO in which an employer or insurance company contracts with a selected group of health care delivery providers for services at preestablished reimbursement rates. Consumers have the choice of whom to contact to provide the service. If a doctor is not on the provider list, higher out-of-pocket expenses will result.

- *Exclusive provider organization (EPO)*: A type of HMO in which members must get care only from the EPO doctors, who may treat only members of the plan.

- *Independent practice association (IPA)*: A type of HMO that has large numbers of independent doctors in private practice. Physicians are paid a fixed fee for treating IPA members but can also treat patients who are not members of the plan.

- *Network model*: Arrangement in which multispeciality groups of doctors have contracts with more than one HMO. Doctors work out of their own offices.

- *Point of service (POS)*: An option that can be offered by any type of HMO. If patients use doctors in their HMO network, and if referrals are made only by the primary care physician, only nominal fees are charged. If patients use doctors outside their HMO network, the cost is higher.

- *Physician–hospital organization (PHO)*: Organized group of doctors affiliated with a particular hospital who provide services to patients enrolled in their plan as they would in an HMO.

Source: Adapted from Naomi Brill and Joanne Levine, *Working with People,* 7th ed. (Boston: Allyn & Bacon, Needham, MA 2001).

Proponents of managed care argue that the system has effectively lowered health care costs without reducing the quality of health care services. They maintain that managed care encourages more efficient and less expensive medical care and that it can stress prevention over treatment. Because doctors reimbursed by managed care entities have little incentive to overtreat patients or to recommend unnecessary medical care, the health care system is expected to be more efficient.

There is evidence to suggest strongly that managed care systems can indeed slow the rise in health care costs, at least in the short term. For example:

- The per capita growth in health care expenditures was 2.7 percent in 1994, dropping from an average of 5 percent throughout the 1980s and early 1990s. Moreover, the per capita national expenditure on health care was $3,510 in 1994, only $100 more than in 1993 and half the increase of $200 from 1992 to 1993.

- Community hospital expenses grew only 2.9 percent in 1994 and 3.2 percent in 1995, a two-thirds drop from 9 percent in 1990 and a drop of five times from the 18 percent growth rate in 1981. For the first time, in 1994 hospital costs per case rose more slowly than the rate of inflation. The average length of stay in a hospital (5.7 days) dropped 4.2 percent from 1994 to 1995. For those 65 and over, the average length of a hospital stay (7.1 days) dropped by 6.6 percent. Moreover, the occupancy rate of hospitals dropped from 73.7 percent in 1978 to 59.7 percent by 1995. After increasing an average of 6.4 percent between 1978 and 1983, hospital employment decreased by 0.5 percent from 1993 to 1995.

- Physicians' salaries dropped on average 3.6 percent from 1993 to 1994—the first recorded drop in physicians' salaries in the history of the American Medical Association.[60] In areas of California where managed care dominates the market, some medical specialists reported declines of 30 percent in their income over 1994 and 1995.[61]

Managed care is clearly having an important impact in shaping medicine in the United States. On average, physicians received 83 percent of their 1992 gross practice incomes from third-party sources (e.g., governmental and private insurers). Of that amount, more than 40 percent came specifically from private managed care operations. In fact, broadly defined, private managed plans now cover two-thirds of all privately insured Americans. Jumping on the bandwagon, the federal and many state governments have encouraged (and, in some states, required) Medicare and Medicaid beneficiaries to join managed care plans. By 1995 there were 165 Medicare HMOs with 2.6 million members.[62] But although the number of Medicare HMOs had risen to 237 by 1998, more than 147 of them fully or partially abandoned the market by 2001. This leaves only 90 HMOs to continue serving seniors, and 37 of them are losing money. By 2001, nearly 934,000 Medicare beneficiaries were dropped from their HMOs, on top of the 700,000 that were dropped in the two previous years. Insurers have charged that the federal government's Medicare reimbursement rate is too low to keep pace with medical inflation and ensure the financial solvency of Medicare HMOs.[63]

Not surprisingly, the AMA has taken a position against managed care. AMA Vice President James Todd asked, "Whoever would have imagined that the noble practice of medicine would be shoved around by cutthroat competition in a rough and tumble marketplace? . . . Physicians want to be treated as professionals, not as commodities, not as medical merchandise to be bought and sold . . . by market traders who are more concerned with profits than patients."[64] Also not surprisingly, managed care's emphasis on primary care may result in a glut of 165,000 specialists.[65]

Critics of managed care (including HMOs) maintain that they are plagued with serious problems.[66] Indeed, managed care has not won the hearts and minds of the public. In a 1999 sur-

vey, only 46 percent of Americans said they were very confident their treatment would be based on their health care needs rather than on the cost of their care. Another national poll found that 61 percent of Americans agreed with the statement "I'm frustrated and angry about the state of the health care system in this country." In addition, only a third of people who had been ill in the previous year said they were completely happy or very happy about the care they received through their HMO.[67]

Seventy-two percent of physicians say the quality of care is worse under managed care. Some physicians have joined unions, and others have been forming networks to negotiate contracts with managed care. Still others have stopped taking HMO patients. Hospitals say they are being squeezed by slow and low payments from HMOs and cuts to Medicare. Many have had to cut staff. Nurses say that hospitals often are so short-staffed that patient care is being compromised. One study found that nearly 70 percent of nurses worry about inadequate staffing levels.[68]

Many HMOs are in financial trouble; the industry posted $1.25 billion in net losses in 1998. Some HMOs are raising premiums, cutting services, or even selling out. Several large managed care companies across the country have gone bankrupt, leaving state officials and consumers scrambling to find replacement coverage. For example, the last profitable year for Florida's HMOs was 1996, when they made a collective $45.3 million. In 1998 a majority of managed care companies in Florida, 21 of 35, lost a total of $55 million. Many of the nation's largest insurance companies have sold off their health insurance businesses as it has become harder to make a profit. Prudential sold its health insurance component to Aetna/U.S. Healthcare in 1998, after recording 1997 losses of $63 million in Florida alone.[69]

Managed care plans generally make access to specialists difficult for consumers. Plans do this by pressuring primary physicians not to refer or by limiting specialist care to one or two visits. Some managed care plans are reluctant to cover costly procedures or experimental treatments, especially those relating to cancer. Some plans refuse to pay for medical care clients receive while out of state, even if it was required in an emergency. Other enrollees complain that managed care forces them to use only primary care physicians, hospitals, and specialists that are on an approved list, which restricts their freedom of choice. And managed care operations sometimes do not provide the same level of benefits as Medicare, especially when it comes to home health care, physical therapy, and nursing home care.[70] Critics also note that the size of managed care operations has led to greater bureaucratization and impersonality.[71]

The managed care industry has become a target for some of the same lawyers that took on the tobacco industry. Lawyers have filed lawsuits under the federal racketeering statutes alleging that managed care companies have put profits above patient care. Legislation is also emerging in many states that would allow patients to sue their HMOs if they are denied needed care. Taken together, these developments diminish the ability of managed care corporations to curb the increases in medical care costs.

The Underinsured

The U.S. medical system provides good care for most people in the upper and upper middle classes, who are protected by adequate health insurance. Inadequate care, however, is the norm for some of those relying on this health care system. Although more than 70 percent of Americans are covered by private insurance plans,[72] gaps in private health insurance may include high copayments, limits on the length of hospital stays, dollar limits on payments to hospitals and physicians, exclusion of certain laboratory tests, refusal of coverage for office visits and routine health care, noncoverage for mental health services, refusal of coverage to persons who are found to be in poor health when applying for insurance, and a lack of coverage for dental and eye care. Because privately purchased health insurance has become almost unaffordable, the availability of health insurance may be a major factor in an individual's job search or decision to

continue in a job.[73] Moreover, employers may be reluctant to hire people with high-risk conditions, because of the negative effect on their insurance premiums. Finally, one of the most dramatic gaps is the frequent failure of private health insurance to cover catastrophic medical costs—those costs that could reduce a middle-class family to "medically indigent" status within only a few months.

 # AIDS and Health Care

The U.S. health care crisis is aggravated by the AIDS epidemic, which first surfaced during the presidency of Ronald Reagan. The Reagan administration initially saw the AIDS problem as being of little consequence. Indeed, expressing public concern for the suffering of homosexuals was a political liability—especially given that the Republican Party was actively courting the religious right, most of whose leaders saw AIDS as a divine punishment for the sin of homosexuality.[74] Unlike the Reagan and Bush administrations, the Clinton administration was not afraid to address the AIDS crisis. President Clinton pushed for full funding for the Ryan White Care Act, created the National Task Force on AIDS Drug Development, strengthened the Office of AIDS Research at the National Institutes of Health, and placed HIV/AIDS victims under the protection of the Americans with Disabilities Act.

The epidemiological data on AIDS is striking. Through June 1999, 753,907 cases of AIDS in the United States had been reported to the Centers for Disease Control (CDC); 438,795 AIDS-related deaths were reported by 2000. Another 431,924 were reported living with HIV or AIDS. Five states—New York, California, Florida, Texas, and New Jersey—account for more than 40 percent of HIV/AIDS cases. Among adults and adolescents with AIDS, three exposure categories account for 82 percent of U.S. AIDS cases: men who have sex with men (47 percent), injecting drug users (25 percent), and heterosexual sex partners of persons who are in high-risk groups or who have HIV/AIDS (10 percent) (see Table 12.6).[75]

In recent years, marked declines in new AIDS cases and AIDS deaths began in 1996 and continued into 1998 in association with the widespread use of potent combination antiretroviral therapies. However, the rates of decline in AIDS incidence and deaths slowed during the latter part of 1998 and 1999. In 1999 the numbers of cases and deaths each quarter stabilized or fluctuated slightly in most populations and geographic areas. By the end of 1999 AIDS prevalence was continuing to rise, with approximately 320,000 persons living with AIDS, although the rate of increase had slowed. Although the incidence of AIDS is leveling off among non-Hispanic whites, it is increasing among blacks and Hispanics. There is an upward trend among women who were infected with HIV through sexual contact, principally with drug-using partners.[76] Despite its relative slowing, AIDS is the second leading cause of death in men aged 25 to 44 and one of the top five causes of death in women of the same age group.[77]

AIDS is maldistributed within racial groupings (see Table 12.6). Of the 753,907 AIDS cases reported through June 1999, 300,851 occurred in non-Hispanic white males and 221,848 in African American men. Thus, although African American males make up only about 6 percent of the total U.S. population, they account for almost 30 percent of AIDS cases. The numbers are even more striking for women. African American women make up roughly 6 percent of the population, but they had 71,741 reported cases of AIDS, more than 2.5 times the number for white women (27,215).[78]

According to a recent Rand study, not all people with HIV are treated equally. Among adults with HIV in the United States, women receive inferior care compared to men, as do blacks and Hispanics compared to non-Hispanic whites. Uninsured and Medicaid-insured HIV victims receive inferior care compared to the privately insured. Patients infected through heterosexual, gay, or bisexual contacts receive superior care compared to patients infected through injection drug use. In sum, disparities in HIV care are frequently associated with insurance status, gender, race, ethnicity, exposure group, income, education, age, and even geographical region.[79]

The scope of the AIDS problem extends beyond U.S. borders. Globally, HIV/AIDS is spreading the most rapidly in developing countries (see

TABLE 12.6 ■ U.S. Male and Female Adult/Adolescent Cumulative AIDS Cases by Major Exposure Category and Race/Ethnicity (Major Population Groups), 2000

	NON-HISPANIC WHITE		NON-HISPANIC BLACK		HISPANIC	
EXPOSURE CATEGORY	*Male*	*Female*	*Male*	*Female*	*Male*	*Female*
Sex between men	220,156	NA	76,637	NA	46,996	NA
Injecting drug use	27,502	11,403	70,230	29,945	39,228	9,895
Sex between men and injecting drug use	24,422	NA	15,549	NA	7,473	NA
Hemophilia/coagulation disorder	3,753	1,815	1,056	1,273	574	543
Heterosexual contact:	5,375	10,896	16,027	27,203	6,288	11,641
Sex with injecting drug user	1,913	4,415	5,233	10,252	1,759	5,262
Sex with HIV-infected person, risk not specified	3,278	4,414	10,619	15,346	4,432	5,714

Source: National Center for HIV, STD and TB Prevention, Divisions of HIV/AIDS Prevention, "Mid-Year 2000 Edition, Vol. 12, No. 1 (December 6, 2000). Retrieved from the World Wide Web: http://www.cdc.gov/hiv/stats/hasrlink.htm

Table 12.7). The World Health Organization (WHO) estimated that by the year 2000 about 26.6 million people would be infected worldwide, of whom at least 4 million have already died. Asian and African countries have been hit the hardest; in South and Southeast Asia, the number of HIV infections rose from 1.5 to 2.5 million from 1993 to 1995.[80] Moreover, WHO estimates that in many developing countries, more than 60 percent of all new HIV infections occur in people under 25 years of age. Sixty percent of these new cases are females under the age of 21.[81]

Nowhere in the world has the impact of HIV/AIDS been more severe than in sub-Saharan Africa. At the regional level, more than 11 million Africans have already died, and another 25 million are living with HIV/AIDS (two-thirds of all the cases on earth). At the national level, the 21 countries with the highest HIV prevalence in the world are all in Africa. In Zimbabwe and

Botswana, one in four adults is infected. In at least 10 other African countries, prevalence rates exceed 10 percent. At the individual level, a child born in Zambia or Zimbabwe today is more likely than not to die of AIDS. In many other African countries, the lifetime risk of dying of AIDS is greater than one in three.[82]

Reforming U.S. Health Care

The U.S. health care system is driven by a combination of ideological and fiscal concerns. Primary among these ideological considerations is whether **health care access** should be a right or privilege. Conservatives generally believe that access to medical care is not a right but a privilege that must be earned through past or present

TABLE 12.7 ■ Regional HIV/AIDS Statistics, Worldwide 2000

REGION	ADULTS AND CHILDREN LIVING WITH HIV/AIDS	ADULTS AND CHILDREN NEWLY INFECTED WITH HIV	ADULT PREVALENCE RATE
Sub-Saharan Africa	25,300,000	3,800,000	8.8%
North Africa and the Middle East	400,000	80,000	0.2%
South and Southeast Asia	5,800,000	780,000	0.56%
East Asia and Pacific	640,000	130,000	0.07%
Latin America	1,400,000	150,000	0.50%
Caribbean	390,000	60,000	2.30%
Eastern Europe and Central Asia	700,000	250,000	0.35%
Western Europe	540,000	30,000	0.24%
North America	920,000	45,000	0.60%
Australia and New Zealand	15,000	500	0.13%
Total	36,100,000	5,300,000	1.10%

Source: UNAIDS, "Global Summary of the HIV/AIDS Epidemic." December 2000. Retrieved from the World Wide Web: http://www.unaids.org/wac/2000/wad00/files/WAD_epidemic_report.htm

labor force participation. Conservative democrats, in turn, believe that health care should be a right that is somehow tied to labor force participation, except in instances in which people are not linked to the workforce. Democratic socialists, grounded in a European tradition, argue that health care is a right that should be bestowed upon each individual at birth.

Another ideological engine driving debates about health care is the role of the private marketplace in the provision of medical care. Conservatives support the **commodification** of health care: They believe that the provision of medical services must be lodged squarely in the private marketplace. More specifically, health care should be provided by independent or quasi-independent medical facilities and by physicians who are either self-employed or employed by companies/organizations. Conservatives argue that medical institutions and drug companies should be free to establish the prices of health care and medical goods. They believe that in medical care, as with other commodities, increased competition lowers the price of goods and increases quality. Government regulation of the health care market is therefore seen as leading to more inefficiencies, lower quality or poorer service, and higher prices. Other conservatives, although they believe the private marketplace is the proper venue for the delivery of health care, also recognize that health care is a commodity that does not respond to market conditions in the same way as other commodities. For example, when a person is immobilized by cardiac arrest, it is unlikely that he or she will shop around for the best cardiac care prices. Likewise, most patients facing serious surgery will not choose a surgeon based only on price considerations. Thus, these conservatives believe that the health care marketplace must be somewhat regulated by government to ensure quality, price, and access.

Democratic socialists argue that health care is too important to be left to the vicissitudes of the marketplace. For them, health care should be removed from the context of a market in which decisions are made purely on economic terms. They believe that the marketplace is designed not to meet the needs of people but to maximize profits. Health care must therefore be socialized; that is, it should be free or heavily subsidized at the point of access, universal in its coverage, and administered and controlled by government.

In the past 30 years, most proposals designed to reform or transform health care in the United States have been linked either directly or indirectly to the U.S. political economy. Consequently, proposals for improving health care fall into three basic categories: (1) removing health care from the marketplace through socialized medicine; (2) maintaining the private health care marketplace while providing universal coverage through national health insurance; and (3) instituting incremental reforms designed to eliminate the more egregious features in the U.S. health care system.

Socialized Medicine

The most radical proposal for reforming the U.S. health care system involved the creation of a National Health Service (NHS). Drafted in the mid-1970s by left-wing health planners and members of Congress, and proposed in the late 1970s by Congressman Ronald Dellums (a social worker), the NHS would have established health care as a right of citizenship. As with the British model, it would have provided free (no fee at the point of access and no payments from third-party vendors) and comprehensive health care coverage, including diagnostic, therapeutic, preventive, rehabilitative, environmental, and occupational health services. To improve the maldistribution of medical services, the NHS would have provided free medical education in return for required periods of service in medically underserved areas.[83] The goal of the NHS was the elimination of private profit in the health care system, and under it a national commission would have been responsible for establishing a formulary of drugs, equipment, and supplies, with regional branches purchasing these goods in their inexpensive generic forms.[84]

Another proposal for restructuring U.S. health care as a **single-payer system** was the National Health Care Act of 1992. As in the Canadian model, states would have had responsibility for ensuring the delivery of health services, for paying all providers, and for planning in accordance with federal guidelines. Although this plan would have allowed the practice of private medicine, the act would have discontinued private health insurance coverage.[85] Supporters of this bill claimed that it would immediately reduce health care spending by 18 percent, and that a single payer approach would reduce the fraud endemic to a multiple-payer system.[86]

Supporters argue that socialized health care would allow for the coordination of health services and reduce profiteering by professionals and corporations. Moreover, they contend that the experience of other countries illustrates that a system incorporating strict budgeting, nationalization, and the elimination of the profit motive arrests the growth of health care costs and, in the end, will prove less expensive than the current privatized system.

National Health Insurance

Another strategy to restructure the United States' health care system is **National Health Insurance (NHI)**. According to Paul Starr, the United States was on the brink of establishing national health insurance several times during the twentieth century, but each time factors unique to the country's political and social institutions prevented its adoption.[87] In the 1930s, for example, NHI plans began to proliferate as part of Roosevelt's New Deal; but the idea was abandoned because of the strident opposition of the AMA—originally a supporter of NHI—and the fear that NHI's inclusion would jeopardize passage of the 1935 Social Security Act. President Harry Truman took up the NHI banner in the days following World War II, but by that time most middle-class and unionized workers were covered by private insurance plans. Moreover, the AMA again set its powerful lobbying machine into motion, this time equating national health insurance with socialized medicine and with Communism.[88]

One of the most comprehensive NHI plans was introduced in the 1970s by Senator Edward Kennedy (and successive coauthors). Supported by large segments of organized labor, the Kennedy plan included a presidentially appointed National Health Board charged with developing policy guidelines, managing the program, and planning and directing the yearly federal health budget. In addition, a national health insurance corporation would be developed to collect tax premiums from workers and disperse them to private insurance companies, which would process all claims. Under this system every American would have compulsory health insurance: Workers would be insured through their employers, the poor through a special federal insurance fund. The Kennedy plan would have eliminated the need for Medicare and Medicaid.[89]

The most recent incarnation of NHI occurred in the Health Security Act (HSA) proposed by President Clinton in 1993. Although the HSA was not a NHI plan in the strictest sense, it contained important components of national insurance. Clinton's bill was based partly on the ideas of the Jackson Hole Group, whose professionals reiterated the need for cost consciousness in health care and the need for substantial investment in outcome and evaluation research.[90]

To accomplish Clinton's health care goal, Hillary Clinton and Ira Magaziner led a 500-person task force charged with (1) extending medical insurance to the uninsured at a reasonable cost; (2) guaranteeing continued coverage when workers change jobs or get sick; (3) curbing and controlling steadily rising health care costs by developing health care networks; (4) addressing the problems of the insurance industry; (5) stopping drug companies from overinflating drug prices; (6) developing a basic core benefits package for every American; and (7) providing universal health care coverage. The result of this task force was the 1,342 page Health Security Act.

The HSA would have worked in the following manner. All citizens and legal immigrants were to get a card guaranteeing them a comprehensive lifelong package of health care benefits, including inpatient and outpatient medical care, prescription drugs, dental and vision care, long-term care, mental health services, and substance abuse treatment. Coverage would be continuous regardless of employment status. All participants would buy into large purchasing pools called Health Care Alliances. Each alliance would offer separate plans for consumers: (1) a **fee-for-service** option allowing consumers to choose their doctors; (2) a plan based on joining a network of doctors and hospitals; and (3) the choice of an HMO. Consumers would then select from three levels of cost-based benefit packages, although all plans would have a yearly out-of-pocket limit of $1,500 for an individual and $3,000 for a family. Low-income self-insurers would be charged based on a sliding scale. Those on public assistance would have their fees paid by Medicaid. Employers would have paid 80 percent of the premium of the standard benefit package; workers would pay the additional 20 percent. Employers would not be charged more than 7.9 percent of their payroll costs for insuring their workers.[91]

Despite a promising start, the HSA bill faltered almost from the moment of its inception. Opposition came from several quarters. Smaller health insurers felt they were being maneuvered out of the industry and took to the airwaves. Immediately, the Health Insurance Association of America (HIAA) broadcast $2 million worth of "Harry and Louise" commercials attacking the HSA as rationing health care under socialized medicine.[92] Within days HIAA claimed that more than 40,000 callers had phoned their 800 number to register complaints about health care reform.[93] On the congressional side, small business lobbyists argued that the costs of the employer mandate would bankrupt thousands of small companies. Within weeks, dozens of lobbyists ranging from pharmaceutical companies to tobacco companies to restaurants and labor unions besieged Congress. Anticipating the 1994 elections, health industry interest groups contributed $26 million to congressional campaigns.[94] Observers put the price tag on defeating the HSA at $100 million.[95] The conservative 104th Congress of 1994 killed the possibility of comprehensive health care reform.

Critics of NHI plans charge that they would modify payment mechanisms rather than encourage major changes in the health care system. Although NHI schemes would equalize the ability of patients to pay, they would not improve the accessibility or the quality of services. Furthermore, most NHI proposals call for coinsurance (copayments) in amounts that many poor people would not find affordable.[96] Contrary to what some critics claim, NHI schemes are not socialized medicine: Hospitals would remain private, doctors would continue to be private practitioners, and most plans would preserve a major role for private insurance companies.

Incremental Reform

Incremental reform of health care policy has proved more acceptable to the public and policymakers than sweeping reforms. This approach has generally focused on remedying the more troubling aspects of the private health care system and on fine-tuning public health care programs. One example of incremental reform was the Catastrophic Health Insurance Act.

In 1988 President Ronald Reagan signed the Catastrophic Health Insurance Act, the most sweeping reform of Medicare ever attempted. This legislation was designed to provide 33 million elderly and disabled Medicare beneficiaries with protection from catastrophic hospital, doctor, and outpatient drug costs. The new Medicare benefits were to be financed by two premiums. The first was applicable to all Medicare enrollees and would have been $4 per month in 1989, rising to $10.20 in 1993. The second, income-related premium was to be paid each year in conjunction with the federal income taxes paid by the 40 percent of Medicare enrollees with the highest incomes.[97] Because of consumer pressure (i.e., the elderly refused to support the self-financing part of the reforms) and the rising deficit, however, the Catastrophic Health Insurance Act was repealed by Congress even before it was implemented.[98]

After the 1994 defeat of the HSA, incremental reforms were the only politically viable alternative to current health care policy. One such reform was the Kennedy–Kassebaum bill (the Health Care Coverage Availability and Affordability Act) of 1996. Although federal tax law subsidizes employer-based health insurance, it does not provide the same subsidy for insurance purchased by individuals. Hence, almost 90 percent of those who have private health insurance obtain it through their employers. In 1985, to address this problem, Congress had passed the Consolidated Budget Reconciliation Act (COBRA), which permitted individuals leaving a company of 20 or more employees to continue their health insurance benefits for up to 18 months by paying 102 percent of the premium their employer had been paying. Although this had helped some people, others remained trapped in **job lock,** fearing that if they changed jobs they would be uninsurable because of a **preexisting condition.** Passage of the Kennedy–Kassebaum bill marked the first time any legislation had been enacted to protect people with preexisting medical conditions. This bill was expected to help about 25 percent of the Americans caught in job lock.[99] Although the Kennedy–Kassebaum bill was an important step, however, it did not address the critical issue of making health care insurance both accessible and affordable for all Americans. Nor did it address the fact that millions of Americans have no health coverage at all.

A conservative approach to incremental health care reform is based on the concept of the individual Medical Savings Account (MSA). The MSA is a form of self-insurance whereby individuals can purchase high-deductible health insurance while setting aside pretax dollars to pay for medical expenses. Opponents of MSAs fear, however, that these plans would appeal only to the healthy and wealthy, leaving those with less money and more health problems behind in an increasingly costly insurance pool.

Congress also passed legislation in 1996 to require insurers to pay for a 48-hour hospital stay following a vaginal birth and a 96-hour stay after a cesarean section. In addition, Congress passed an amendment designed to create some level of parity between mental health and physical health benefits. The amendment requires insurers to set the same levels for annual and lifetime caps on mental health benefits as on physical health benefits. However, the bill stipulates that plans are not prohibited from requiring preadmission screening before authorization of services; nor are they prohibited from restricting mental health coverage to only those services that are medically necessary.[100]

Other incremental reforms have been enacted on state levels. In Hawaii, employers are required to insure employees who work more than 20 hours a week.[101] A Health Rights program in Minnesota extends health care coverage to all noncovered low-income residents and charges them on a sliding-scale basis.[102] On the national level, it is likely that future incremental health care reforms may involve limiting malpractice awards, extending some form of coverage to the uninsured, and instituting some limitations on the power of managed care operations to shape health care.

Comparative Analysis: Health Care in Canada and Britain

Americans often overlook what is happening in other parts of the world. This section briefly explores medical systems in Canada (a single-payer system) and Great Britain (socialized medicine).

The Canadian Health Care System

The current Canadian health care system began more than 30 years ago when a hospital insurance plan in Saskatchewan evolved into a network of plans developed by Canada's 10 provinces and 2 territories.[103] In 1966 Canada passed the Medical Care Act (Medicare), which instituted a nationwide federal/provincial health insurance system that is publicly funded, privately delivered, and free at the point of access.[104] Each province is responsible for administering its own health care plan.[105] Although each of the 10 provinces and 2 territories has it own unique plan, all plans are essentially universal and comprehensive, covering all residents for inpatient and outpatient hospital and physician services. To receive federal funds, every plan must meet basic national eligibility standards:

1. *Universal coverage.* Every provincial resident must be covered under uniform terms and conditions.
2. *Portability.* Plans must be portable, in that they must cover residents who are temporarily away from home or who have moved to another province.
3. *Comprehensiveness.* All approved hospital and physicians' services must be covered, including medical and hospital care, mental health services, and prescription drugs for those over 65 and for those with catastrophic illnesses.
4. *No cost to patient at point of access.* Services must be free at point of access and include no financial barriers to care.
5. *Nonprofit administration.* Plans must be nonprofit and publicly administered.
6. *Freedom of choice.* Each Canadian is free to choose his or her provider.[106]

Unlike the U.S. system, the Canadian system is grounded in universal entitlement rather than linked to employment. Accordingly, all of Canada's 25 million residents are eligible for provincial health insurance, regardless of their employment status, except for people covered by other federal programs such as the military.[107] Questions arose in the 1980s about direct charges made to patients beyond the level paid by the provincial health care plan. The 1984 Canada Health Act eliminated all extra billing and user charges. Today virtually every Canadian is covered by a comprehensive medical and hospital plan with no copayment.[108]

General practitioners (GPs) make up the majority of physicians in Canada and provide most of the nation's health care. Specialists can be used only if a referral is received from the GP. Although patients may choose their primary-care physician, the choice is contingent upon whether the physician has openings for new patients. Patients also use the hospital in which the physician has admitting privileges. Besides providing free physician and hospital care, most provinces also cover the cost of travel and medical services if the treatment cannot be obtained in the area where the patient resides. Although covered health care is free at the point of access, some elements not covered include out-of-hospital drugs, dental care, eyeglasses, physical therapy, and chiropractic care not ordered by a medical doctor.[109]

Contrary to some misconceptions, the Canadian health care system is not a form of socialized medicine; instead, it is a social insurance model that mixes public funds with private health care delivery. Canada's single-payer model is based on the idea that provincial governments function as single-source payers of health care with a centralized locus of control. As such, Canada's provincial governments reimburse both hospitals and physicians on a prospective budgeting basis. Specifically, private physicians' fees are negotiated between the provincial governments and the medical associations. Reimbursements for physicians are on a fee-for-service basis. The salaries of physicians in Canada are generally lower than those of their U.S. counterparts. Because of budgetary problems, several provinces have limited payments to physicians who earn above a certain income by lowering the reimbursement rates.[110]

There are about 1,250 hospitals in Canada, of which 57 percent are run by religious orders or nonprofit organizations. Hospital reimbursements are made on a global prospective basis. In other words, hospitals operate on a negotiated but fixed yearly budget. As such, they must stay within the budgetary allotment granted by the province regardless of the number of patients seen in a year.[111]

Canada's Medicare system is paid for with a mixture of federal and provincial funds. Federal funds go to the provinces in the form of block grants and transfer payments. The provinces obtain funds to operate the medical system from general revenue taxes and, in the case of Alberta and British Columbia, from insurance premiums paid for by employers. Provinces that charge such premiums provide exemptions or subsidies for the aged, the unemployed, and the indigent.[112]

Critics of Canadian health care point to numerous problems facing the system. One of the most important is the question of funding. Cutbacks in government spending (from 1981 to 1992 the Canadian government cut transfer payments to the provinces by almost $8 billion), increasing demands for services, and the high cost of technology have made controlling costs the number one issue facing the Canadian health care system. The "cure" for these problems has been the replacement of federal support to the provinces with block grant transfers; a downsizing of the system, particularly the hospital sector (e.g., closing or merging hospitals, cutting staff, and shortening inpatient stays); and an increasing reliance on paraprofessional staff (e.g., replacing nurses with nursing attendants).[113]

Some critics have charged that Canada's prospective global budgeting system for hospitals has caused health care rationing. These critics argue that in order to cope with budgetary constraints, Canadian hospitals are closing down hospital wards during certain times of the year; filling up one-third of hospital beds with long-term elderly patients so as to keep high-volume (and expensive) traffic down; using cheaper medical materials; rushing medical procedures and thus jeopardizing accuracy; providing substandard hospital care; not investing in technology or capital improvements; and prioritizing illnesses into "urgent," "emergent," and "elective" categories, thereby causing artificial queues for treatment.[114] According to these critics, health care rationing is having a dramatic effect on Canada's medical system.[115]

Some health care analysts have suggested that the United States adopt a health care reform plan similar to the Canadian model.[116] They argue that a single-payer system allows for greater control of systemwide health care capacity—that is, supply, distribution, and costs—than does a fragmented insurance system in which no party has the overall authority for controlling the production and distribution of medical goods and services. Health care analysts also point to the uneven coverage provided to Americans under the current patchwork of private and public health insurance plans. In comparison to the universal, comprehensive, and publicly funded health care system that Canadians enjoy, most Americans are forced to purchase employer-based health insurance offering coverage that ranges from minimal to comprehensive, depending upon the type of policy. Moreover, a significant number of Americans fall through the cracks in health insurance: They receive no employment-based health insurance, they cannot afford to insure themselves, and they are ineligible for Medicaid or Medicare. Critics claim that a Canadian-style universal health care policy would ensure all Americans adequate medical care without regard to their ability to pay or the generosity of their employers.

Perhaps the most formidable argument for the United States' adopting a Canadian-style health care system is provided by an examination of leading health indicators and per capita health care spending. Before the Canadian Medicare system became operational in 1971, Canada lagged behind the United States in the important indicators of infant mortality and life expectancy. Impressive gains now place Canada ahead of the United States on both health indicators. Moreover, Canada has been able to achieve those gains while spending less of its GNP on health care than the United States. Although health care costs are rising in Canada, they are doing so at a slower rate than in the United States.[117]

Factors that influence lower health care costs in Canada include lower physician and administrative costs and less concern with malpractice litigation. In 1985 the per capita physician expenditure in Canada (calculated in U.S. dollars) was $202, compared with $347 in the United States. According to the *Journal of the American Medical Association*, the higher per capita expenditure in the United States is explained entirely by higher fees, because the per capita number of physician visits is actually lower in the United States than in Canada. Fees for procedures in the United States are more than three times as high as they are in Canada.

In addition, fees for evaluation and management services are about 80 percent lower in Canada. Part of the difference in fee structures may be related to the lower rates of malpractice litigation in Canada. Also, because Canadian health care is based on a single-payer system, overhead costs are lower.[118] In part, this is due to the significant portion of the U.S. health care budget that is spent on advertising and billing.[119] The single-payer system also lessens the paperwork load on physicians, thereby freeing them up to see more patients.

One indicator of the success of Canada's health care system is that the majority of Canadians are generally satisfied with it and show no inclination of giving it up.[120]

Britain's National Health Service

The National Health Service (NHS) is the most enduring aspect of the British Labour Party's postwar welfare state. The direct inspiration for the NHS was a 1944 white paper written for the wartime coalition government by Sir William Beveridge. The Beveridge Report maintained that a "comprehensive system of health care was essential to any scheme for improving living standards."[121]

After initial resistance from the British Medical Association, the National Health Service Act was passed in 1946 and took effect in 1948. In the words of the act, the aim was to promote "the establishment of a comprehensive health service designed to secure improvement in the physical and mental health of the people . . . and the prevention, diagnosis and treatment of illness."[122] The principle of freedom of choice was upheld in that people could either use the NHS or seek outside doctors. Doctors were guaranteed that there would be no interference in their clinical judgment, and they were free to take private patients while participating in the service. The main goal of the NHS was to provide free medical service to anyone in need. The NHS Act was based on a tripartite system: (1) hospital service with specialists; (2) general medical doctors, dentists, and eye doctors, maintained on a contractual basis; and (3) prevention and support systems, provided by local health departments.

Under the leadership of Minister of Health Anuerin Bevan, all Britain's hospitals were nationalized. Because most hospitals were owned by local governments or were heavily subsidized nonprofit institutions, nationalization was not difficult. General medical practitioners were brought into a new governmentally subsidized plan that provided universal basic medical care that was free at the point of access. This was not a major change, as physicians' services had been subsidized for industrial workers since before WWII. The NHS Act simply extended this coverage to the whole population. British physicians generally came to support the act because it guaranteed a steady income.

The NHS Act does not eliminate private medicine, and a small percentage of NHS hospital beds are reserved for private patients. As mentioned, general practitioners (GPs) and specialists are permitted to treat private patients while working in the NHS. Moreover, affluent patients are permitted to purchase private health insurance and private care. The major advantages of private care are more attractive hospital rooms and quicker service for elective surgery. About 15 percent of the British currently have private health insurance, which businesses often provide as a fringe benefit for upper-level management.

The backbone of the NHS is the GP. Every patient in Britain is registered with a GP who provides family care. Patients may change their GPs unless they are diagnosed with a chronic illness such as AIDS. GPs are paid by the NHS on the basis of an annual **capitation** fee (per-person fee) for each registered patient. Roughly half of a GP's income comes from capitation payments, with the rest made up by allowances for services such as contraceptive advice and immunization. The role of the GP is to provide primary medical care; GPs are forbidden to restrict their practice to any special client group. Individuals can register with any GP provided he or she is willing to accept them. GPs see almost 75 percent of their registered patients at least once a year; and, because mobility is relatively low in Britain, many people retain the same GP for a considerable period of time.[123]

The GP has wide professional latitude and equips his or her own office, hires staff, and may choose to work singly, in pairs, in groups, or in a government health center. Close to 50 percent of all GPs practice in groups of three or more. Health centers, part of the original National Health Service Act, mushroomed in the late 1960s and 1970s, and by 1975 there were 600 nationally. Sweeping changes in 1967 gave GPs increased benefits, including a higher capitation rate if they had a patient load of 2,500 to 3,500. In addition, extra remuneration was provided for each person on a doctor's list who was over 65, for night calls, for transients, for maternity care, for family planning services, and for certain preventive measures. GPs also receive partial reimbursement for secretaries, receptionists, and nurses, as well as for the rental costs of their offices. Extra payments are also provided for seniority, postgraduate education, and vocational training; for working in groups of three or more; and for practicing in underdoctored areas.[124]

The second tier of the British health care system is the physician consultant (specialist). Most referrals to consultants—except for accidents or emergency care—are made through GPs. Although employed by the government and under contract to a public hospital, a physician specialist is allowed a small private practice. In effect, patients in the community are served by GPs, whereas in the hospital they are under the care of specialists. As in the U.S. health care system, physician specialists are accorded greater prestige and remuneration.[125]

The NHS is funded from general taxes, with the proceeds divided among regional health authorities that plan local health services. The regions, in turn, divide their money among districts that pay for hospitals through global prospective budgets.[126] Health services under the NHS are relatively comprehensive, with hospital and primary medical care being free. However, there are significant patient charges for adult dentistry and eyeglasses and a charge for prescriptions (in 1996, between $5 and $6). Drug prices are agreed upon between the health department and the pharmaceutical industry according to a specific pricing formula based on company profits. In addition, government subsidies for medical education mean that students' direct educational costs are low.[127]

Critics complain that NHS hospital funds are doled out in a haphazard manner. For instance, considerable monies are spent on health care facilities in fast emptying city centers rather than in burgeoning population centers. One reform suggested to remedy this problem was the creation of "internal markets" whereby the distribution of NHS money would follow patients rather than the other way around. Another important problem was that hospitals received nothing extra for efficiently treating more patients at less cost; as a result hospitals had little incentive to improve efficiency.[128]

Another criticism of the NHS is that its funding is based not on the medical needs of consumers, but rather on how much the British treasury believes it can afford to spend on health care. The result is de facto health care rationing and long waiting lists for elective procedures—caused not by inefficiencies in the system but by limited resources. In addition, consumers complain of long waits in GP offices and of hospital buildings that are often in poor repair. There are also long waiting lists for elective surgeries such as hip replacements, routine treatment of varicose veins, and repairs of hernias. (There is believed to be little wait for urgent surgery.) Long waiting lists can be misleading to some extent, however, because they sometimes include people who have died, have moved, have already had their operations, or who have been kept waiting by consultants who want to secure more resources or private patients.[129]

Other critics charge that despite government efforts, there are serious shortages of doctors in certain parts of Britain. In addition, expenditures and resources under the NHS seem to be slanted toward hospitalization rather than toward primary, first-level care. Critics also complain about the lack of accountability of doctors and about strong unions that have supported restrictive practices and fought attempts to privatize support services.[130] Finally, other critics charge that the inequality in the British health system has resulted in higher disease and mortality rates for lower socioeconomic groups.

Under the original NHS Act, Parliament allocated money and power to local health authorities that managed the hospitals and contracted with specialists for services.[131] Passed in 1990, the National Health and Community Care Act was designed to reduce the long queues for the treatment of nonacute illnesses and procedures by introducing market efficiencies. Loosening the knot between funders and providers, this bill permitted some hospitals (called trust hospitals) to operate independently of the local health authority in setting fees, managing budgets, developing personnel packages, and purchasing goods. The theory was that independently managed hospitals would be more efficient than centrally planned ones. To further encourage efficiency, these trust hospitals were allowed to sell their services to any local health authority, private patients, or to private insurance companies. In addition, GPs with large practices were permitted to become fundholders of NHS grants from which they could purchase hospital or specialized services for their clients. It was expected that GPs would refer their patients to those hospitals or specialists that were the most efficient. Inefficient hospitals would get fewer referrals and thus would be forced to increase their quality of care while reducing costs.[132] Unfortunately, the hoped-for results have not been achieved.

Much of the reporting on the NHS in the U.S. press has tended to emphasize its flaws. Although some GPs express dissatisfaction with the system, however, the British people continue to use it in large numbers. For example, although 15 percent of Britons have private insurance, most use it as a supplement rather than as a substitute for the NHS.[133] Despite the criticisms, the NHS appears to be serving the majority of the British population as well as, and in some ways better than, the U.S. health care system. For instance, per capita health care expenditures are only 6 percent of Britain's GDP compared to more than 14 percent for the United States. Much of this lower cost is attributable to the success of GPs in keeping down hospital admission rates and to the relatively low administrative costs of the NHS. Notwithstanding the lower cost of the British health care system, most health indicators, such as life expectancy and infant mortality rates, are equivalent to or better than those found in the costlier U.S. health care system. Enoch Powell, a former British health minister, summed up the contradictions of the

NHS: "One of the most striking features of the NHS is the continual, deafening chorus of complaints which rises day and night from every part of it, a chorus only interrupted when someone suggests that a different system altogether might be preferable . . . it presents what must be a unique spectacle of an undertaking that is run down by everyone engaged in it."[134]

It is difficult to compare the quality of the Canadian and British health care systems with that of the system in the United States. For affluent or middle-class Americans with good health insurance, the U.S. system of health care may well provide the best medical care in the world; and for complex medical procedures involving sophisticated equipment and technology, U.S. health care is unequaled. Moreover, unlike the long queues characteristic of the U.K. and Canadian systems, the waiting period for surgery, tests, and other procedures is relatively short in the United States. Finally, physicians in this country are among the best trained in the world. However, the emphasis on costly equipment and technology is not without a price. A medical approach that emphasizes specific diseases over primary care and preventive medicine usually results in good care, but for fewer people. Health care systems that emphasize personal and primary care, accessibility, and free or inexpensive services often reach more people. Given that, the health care systems of Canada and Britain appear to distribute health resources more equitably than does the U.S. health care system.

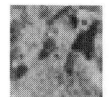 # Conclusion

The examination of health care in the United States raises important questions. What is this nation's responsibility for providing health care to all its citizens? How much high-tech medicine can our society realistically afford? How should U.S. medical resources be allocated? What, if any, limitations on personal freedom are permissible in the name of promoting health and preventing disease? These and other questions urgently require answers.

The U.S. health care system is facing an acute crisis. This crisis is grounded in the failure of the marketplace to curb health care expenditures, the system's overreliance on medical technology at the expense of providing primary health care services, the growth in health care administrative costs, and the large numbers of working people and their families who cannot afford health care coverage. Moreover, huge expenditures on health care in the United States are not producing greater longevity, lower rates of infant mortality, or any other indicators of improving public health.

The United States is one of the few industrialized countries that does not have a comprehensive plan for national health insurance or socialized medicine. Moreover, this is one of the few industrialized nations where medical expenses can cause poverty. Terri Combs-Orme suggests that a progressive reconstruction of the U.S. health care system must be grounded in the following principles:

1. Accessible health care should be a universal right of all Americans, not a privilege to be purchased or earned.
2. The quantity, quality, and accessibility of health care should be equal for all, not dependent on income or categorical status. No health care system should result in differential quantity, quality, or accessibility of care based on income, gender, age, or any other criterion.
3. Health care should not be linked to employment. A majority of Americans purchase health care insurance through their place of employment, but the fear of job loss or other issues not under their control undermines the security of this arrangement and limits their job mobility.
4. The quality, quantity, and accessibility of health care should not vary on a state-by-state basis.
5. A progressive health care system must balance the needs and rights of children and the elderly in a fair and rational way.
6. A comprehensive health care system should include coverage for and accessibility to long-term care for the elderly.[135]

If commodification and high costs are left unchecked, health care in the United States may someday be out of reach for the majority of citizens. Although the likely outcome of the U.S. health care crisis is unknown, the situation, left solely to the caprice of the marketplace, will undoubtedly worsen.

 # Discussion Questions

1. U.S. health care currently costs more than $1 trillion a year. Its cost has risen dramatically over the past 25 years in terms of the amount spent, the percentage of the GDP used for health care, and the per capita costs of health care. What are the main factors that have driven up health care costs? Can these factors be controlled? If so, how?
2. Striking increases in health care costs have occurred in the area of Medicaid and Medicare. What are the major factors contributing to the steep rise in Medicaid and Medicare costs? What can be done to stabilize these costs?
3. Some critics believe that Medicare and Medicaid costs cannot be brought under control without radical reform of the entire health care system. They argue that incremental reforms in the Medicare and Medicaid programs will have only a minuscule impact on the rise in federal and state expenditures for health care. Are these critics correct?

4. Evidence of the effectiveness of cost-controlling mechanisms such as DRGs has been mixed, although generally negative. Critics charge that not only has the DRG system failed to substantially reduce health care costs, but it has also led to a reduced level of patient care. Is the DRG system successful? If so, should it be a model for future health care reforms?

5. Many critics argue that there is a serious health care crisis in the United States. Describe the main characteristics of that crisis (e.g., health care costs, accessibility issues, uninsured populations, U.S. health indicators compared with those of other nations).

6. The AIDS epidemic is one of the most important public health issues facing the global community. Some critics insist that more money should be spent on basic AIDS research, outreach, and treatment. Other critics argue that AIDS is only one of many health care problems facing the United States and other countries around the world. They argue that the money spent on AIDS research should be in proportion to the numbers of people affected by the disease, which, in the United States, are relatively small when compared to the numbers of those suffering from cancer and heart disease. Is AIDS a significantly more important public health problem in this country than cancer, heart disease, or the effects of drugs, alcohol, and tobacco? Should the federal government spend proportionally more on AIDS research than on other diseases? If so, why?

7. Some health care analysts are calling for radical reform in the U.S. health care system. Many of these analysts insist that the nation's free market health care system should be replaced by a more cost-effective and comprehensive plan. Assuming that these health care analysts are correct, which of the health care systems described in this chapter would be the best model for the United States to emulate, and why?

8. Why has the United States not developed a health care system that is universal and publicly funded, like those of its industrial counterparts? Identify the forces and interests that are shaping health care policy in the United States. What, if anything, can be done to reform or radically transform U.S. health care?

 # Notes

1. Health Care Financing Administration, "President Clinton Announces Approximately 2.5 Million Children Have Enrolled in the State Children's Health Insurance Program, Praises the Decline in Uninsured, Urges Congress to Expand Coverage, Unveils New Funds for Outreach." September 29, 2000, Retrieved December 15, 2000, from the World Wide Web: http://www.hcfa.gov/init/092900wh.htm

2. Daniel Weinberg, "Press Briefing on 1995 Income, Poverty, and Health Insurance Estimates," Washington, DC: U.S. Bureau of the Census, Household Economic Statistics Division, September 26, 1996; and Jim Jefford Issues. Retrieved December 15, 2000, from the World Wide Web: http://jeffords.senate.gov/coverage.html

3. U.S. Census Bureau, Public Information Office, "Chances of Having Health Insurance Increase, Reversing 12-Year Trend, Census Bureau Says." Retrieved December 15, 2000, from the World Wide Web: http://www.census.gov/Press-Release/www/2000/cb00-160.html

4. Health Care Financing Administration, "President Clinton Announces."

5. Terri Combs-Orme, "Should the Federal Government Finance Health Care for All Americans? Yes," in Howard Jacob Karger

and James Midgley (eds.), *Controversial Issues in Social Policy* (Boston: Allyn & Bacon, 1993).

6. Irving J. Lewis and Cecil G. Sheps, *The Sick Citadel* (Boston: Oelgeschlager, Gunn, & Hain, 1983), p. 16.

7. Sumner A. Rosen, David Fanshel, and Mary E. Lutz (eds.), *Face of the Nation 1987* (Silver Spring, MD: NASW, 1987), p. 75.

8. Barbara Wolfe, "Changing the U.S. Health Care System: How Difficult Will It Be?" *Focus* 14, no. 2 (Summer 1992), p. 16.

9. David E. Rosenbaum, "Gloomy Forecast Touches Off Feud on Medicare Fund," *The New York Times* (June 6, 1996), pp. A1 and B14.

10. For a good historical analysis of the Medicare program, see Theodore R. Marmor, *The Politics of Medicare* (Chicago: Aldine, 1973).

11. U.S. House of Representatives, Committee on Ways and Means, *1996 Green Book* (Washington, DC: U.S. Government Printing Office, 1996), p. 896; Health Care Financing Administration, "1998 State Estimates—Medicaid—Personal Health Care." Retrieved December 16, 2000, form the World Wide Web: http://hcfa.hhs.gov/stats/nhe-oact/StateEstimates/Tables98/mcaid10.htm

12. Health Care Financing Administration, "Medicaid Eligibility." Retrieved December 17, 2000, from the World Wide Web: http://www.hcfa.gov/medicaid/meligib.htm

13. U.S. House of Representatives, *1996 Green Book*, p. 19.

14. Isaac Shapiro, Mark Sheft, Julie Strawn, Laura Summer, and Robert Greenstein, *The States and the Poor* (Washington, DC: Center on Budget and Policy Priorities, December 1991), p. 37.

15. Ibid., p. 17.

16. See S. Dentzer, "The War over That Other M Program," *U.S. News and World Report* (October 9, 1995), p. 71.

17. Children's Defense Fund, *The State of America's Children* (Washington, DC: Children's Defense Fund, 1987), pp. 110–118.

18. U.S. House of Representatives, *1996 Green Book*, p. 886.

19. Marilyn Ellwood, "The Medicaid Eligibility Maze: Coverage Expands, but Enrollment Problems Persist, Findings from a Five-State Study" (Washington, DC: Urban Institute December, 1999).

20. See Children's Defense Fund, *A Children's Defense Budget* (Washington, DC: Children's Defense Fund, 1988) p. 109; and Barbara Wolfe, "A Medicaid Primer," *Focus* 17, no. 3 (Spring 1996), pp. 1–6.

21. Health Care Financing Administration, "The State Children's Health Insurance Program: Preliminary Highlights of Implementation and Expansion." Retrieved July 2000 from the World Wide Web: http://www.hcfa.gov/init/wh0700.pdf

22. Kentucky Farm Bureau, "Summary of Master Tobacco Settlement," April 1, 1999. Retrieved December 17, 2000, from the World Wide Web: http://www.kyfb.org/FactTobSett040199.htm

23. National Governors' Association, "State Tobacco Settlement Spending at-a-Glance FY2000-01." Retrieved December 18, 2000, from the World Wide Web: http://www.nga.org/health/tobacco.asp

24. Richard Wolf and Martin Kasindorf, "Tobacco Money to Aid Local Problems," *USA Today* (November 22, 1999), p. A8.

25. See Health Care Financing Administration, "Actuarial Products, N.H.E. Projections, Table 1." Retrieved December 18, 2000, from the World Wide Web: http://www.hcfa.gov/stats/NHE-Proj/proj1998/tables/table1.htm

26. Paul Starr, *The Logic of Health-Care Reform* (Knoxville, TN: Grand Rounds Press, 1992), p. 45.

27. U.S. House of Representatives, *1996 Green Book*.

28. U.S. General Accounting Office, *U.S. Health Care Spending Trends, Contributing Factors, and Proposals for Reform* (GAO/HRD-91–102) (Washington, DC: U.S. General Accounting Office, 1991).

29. Michael Clemens, "Rising Costs Reflect Many Influences," *USA Today* (May 5, 1993), p. B2.

30. U.S. House of Representatives, *1996 Green Book*, p. 995.

31. See ibid.; and U.S. Department of the Census, *Statistical Abstract of the United States, 1991* (Washington, DC: U.S. Government Printing Office, 1991), p. 107.

32. Julie Appleby, "What Happens after the Band-Aids Run Out?" *USA Today* (December 8–10, 2000), pp. 1–2.

33. See Health Care Financing Administration, "Actuarial Products, N.H.E. Projections, Table 1"; and G. J. Schieber and J. P. Poullier, "International Health Care Spending: Issues and Trends," *Health Affairs* 10 (1991), p. 110.

34. Gerard F. Anderson, "Multinational Comparisons of Health Care," The Commonwealth Fund (October 1998). Retrieved December 18, 2000, from the World Wide Web: http://www.cmwf.org/programs/international/ihp_1998_multicompsurvey_299.asp#overview

35. Ibid.

36. Ibid.

37. Ibid.

38. Ibid.

39. Ibid.

40. Health Care Liability Alliance, "CBO Says Medical Liability Reform Will Save $1.5 Billion." Retrieved December 18, 2000, from the World Wide Web: http://www.hcla.org/html/hcla19980728.htm

41. R. Brook, C. J. Kamberg, and A. Meyer-Okaes, *Appropriateness of Acute Medical Care for the Elderly: Analysis of the Literature* (R3717) (Santa Monica, CA: Rand Corporation, 1989).

42. See U.S. Congressional Budget Office, *Projections of National Health Care Expenditures*. (Washington, DC: U.S. Congressional Budget Office, 1992). See also American Medical Association, *Trends in Health Care* (Chicago: American Medical Association, 1987).

43. Randolph D. Smoak, "Costs Hurt Doctors, Patients Alike," *USA Today* (May 5, 1993), p. A13.

44. Clemens, "Rising Costs Reflect Many Influences," p. B2.

45. Thomas A. Daschle, Rima J. Cohen, and Charles L. Rice, "Health Care Reform: Single-Payer Models," *American Psychologist* 48, no. 3 (March 1993), pp. 265–267.

46. See Paul Schmolling Jr., Merrill Youkeles, and William Burger, *Human Services in Contemporary America* (Pacific Grove, CA: Brooks/Cole, 1997); and "Doctors under the Knife," *Newsweek* (April 5, 1993), p. 29. See also Leon Ginsberg, *Social Work Almanac* (Washington,

DC: National Association of Social Workers, 1992), p. 123.

47. U.S. Congressional Budget Office, *Projections of National Health Care Expenditures*.

48. Kaiser Family Foundation, "Federal HIV/AIDS Spending: A Budget Chartbook." Retrieved December 19, 2000, from the World Wide Web: http://www.kff.org/content/1999/2149/

49. U.S. House of Representatives, *1996 Green Book*.

50. Health Care Financing Administration, "Actuarial Products, N.H.E. Projections, Table 2." Retrieved from the World Wide Web: http://www.hcfa.gov/stats/NHE-Proj/

51. Carl Bianco, "How Becoming a Doctor Works," Howstuffworks. Retrieved December 19, 2000, from the World Wide Web: http://www.howstuffworks.com/becoming-a-doctor11.htm

52. J. M. Colwill, "Where Have All the Primary Care Applicants Gone?" *The New England Journal of Medicine* 326 (1992), pp. 387–392.

53. Katherine van Wormer, *Social Welfare: A World View* (Chicago: Nelson-Hall, 1997), p. 412.

54. Nancy McVicar, "Drug Costs Go Up but Coverage Comes Down," *Sun-Sentinel* (February 23, 2000). Retrieved December 19, 2000, from the World Wide Web: http://www.sunsentinel.com/news/daily/detail/0,1136,27000000000116737,00.hNml

55. "Doctors under the Knife," p. 31.

56. John H. Goddeeris and Andrew J. Hogan, "Nature and Dimensions of the Problem," in John H. Goddeeris and Andrew J. Hogan (eds.), *Improving Access to Health Care: What Can the States Do?* (Kalamazoo, MI: W. E. Upjohn Institute for Employment Research, 1992), pp. 14–15.

57. Quoted in Marie A. Caputi and William A. Heiss, "The DRG Revolution," *Health and Social Work* 3, no. 6 (June 1984), p. 5.

58. McVicar, "Drug Costs Go Up."

59. Schmolling, Youkeles, and Burger, *Human Services in Contemporary America*, p. 54.

60. U.S. House of Representatives, *1996 Green Book*.

61. Stuart Schear, "The Ultimate Self-Referral: Medicare Reform, AMA-Style," *The American Prospect* 25 (March–April 1996), pp. 68–72.

62. Ellyn E. Spragins, "Simon Says, Join Us," *Newsweek* (June 19, 1995), pp. 55–58.

63. Vicki Lankarge, "Seniors Dropped from Medicare HMOs Shouldn't Rejoin Others, Weiss Warns," insure.com. November 14, 2000. Retrieved December 19, 2000, from the World Wide Web: http://www.insure.com/ health/medicare/fewoptions1100.html

64. Spragins, "Simon Says, Join Us," p. 68.

65. Ibid.

66. Howard Waitzkin, *The Second Sickness: Contradictions of Capitalist Health Care* (New York: Free Press, 1983), p. 220.

67. Nancy McVicar, "Medical Care Is There—If You Can Afford It," *Sun-Sentinel* (February 24, 2000). Retrieved December 19, 2000, from the World Wide Web: http://www.sun-sentinel.com/ news/daily/detail/0,1136,27500000000104840,00. html

68. Ibid.

69. Ibid.

70. Spragins, "Simon Says, Join Us."

71. Thomas H. Ainsworth, *Live or Die* (New York: Macmillan, 1983), p. 89.

72. John M. Herrick and Joseph Papsidero, "Uncompensated Care: What States Are Doing," in Goddeeris and Hogan, *Improving Access to Health Care*, pp. 139–140.

73. W. Greenberg, "Elimination of Employer-Based Health Insurance," in R. B. Helms (ed.), *American Health Policy: Critical Issues for Reform* (Washington, DC: AEI Press, October 1992), pp. 1–4.

74. Robert Searles Walker, *AIDS: Today, Tomorrow* (NJ: Humanities Press, New York, 1992), p. 134.

75. Centers for Disease Control, National Center for HIV, STD and TB Prevention, Divisions of HIV/AIDS Prevention "Mid-Year 2000 Edition," 12, no. 1. December 6, 2000, Retrieved December 19, 2000, from the World Wide Web: http://www.cdc.gov/hiv/stats/hasrlink.htm

76. Ibid.

77. Walker, *AIDS*, p. 134.

78. Centers for Disease Control, "Mid-Year 2000 Edition."

79. Martin Shapiro and Samuel Bozzette, "Privileged Treatment Inequities in HIV Care Demand Remedies for U.S. Health Care," 1999. Retrieved December 20, 2000, from the World Wide Web: http://www.rand.org/ publications/RRR/RRRfall99/privilege.html

80. World Health Report, "Executive Summary, 1995." Retrieved December 20, 2000, from the World Wide Web: www.who.ch/pro-grammes/whr/xsum95_e.htm

81. Quoted in Glendolyn Alex, Amy Ambler, Lisa Amundson, Nanette Biersdorfer, Tracy Milan, and Laila Narsi, "Social Issues III: Homosexuality and AIDS," unpublished paper, University of Houston Graduate School of Social Work, Houston, TX, Spring 1996.

82. World Bank, "World Bank Responds to HIV/AIDS Crisis in Africa: New Strategic Plan Calls for International Action on African AIDS Epidemic," News Release No. 2000/039/S. Retrieved December 20, 2000, from the World Wide Web: http://www.worldbank.org/ html/extme/039.htm

83. Ronald V. Dellums et al., *Health Services Act* (H.R.2969) (Washington, DC: U.S. Government Printing Office, 1979). For a good summary of the act, see Waitzkin, *The Second Sickness*, pp. 222–226.

84. Dellums et al., *Health Services Act.*

85. "Summary of S.2817, The National Health Care Act of 1992," *NASW–LA News* 16, no. 5 (September/October 1992), p. 2.

86. Daschle, Cohen, and Rice, "Health Care Reform," p. 267.

87. Paul Starr, *The Social Transformation of American Medicine* (New York: Basic Books, 1984).

88. Ibid.

89. Ibid.

90. Jeff Bingaman, Robert G. Frank, and Carrie L. Billy, "Combining a Global Health Budget with a Market-Driven Delivery System," *American Psychologist* 48, no. 3 (March 1993), pp. 271–272.

91. Diane M. DiNitto, *Social Welfare: Politics and Public Policy* (Boston: Allyn & Bacon, 1995), pp. 270–272.

92. Robin Toner, " 'Harry and Louise' Ad Campaign Biggest Gun in Health Care Battle," *San Diego Union-Tribune* (April 7, 1994), p. A7.

93. Sara Fritz, "Ads Are Designed to Counter Health Care Proposals," *Los Angeles Times* (May 15, 1993), p. A16.

94. Dana Priest, "The Slow Death of Health Reform," *Washington Post Weekly* (September 5–11, 1994), p. 11.

95. Douglas Frantz, "Lobbyists, Interest Groups Begin Costly Health Care Battle," *Los Angeles Times* (May 24, 1993).

96. Waitzkin, *The Second Sickness*, p. 218.

97. Spencer Rich, "Provisions of 'Catastrophic' Insurance Act," *Washington Post* (July 1, 1988), p. A21.

98. Ibid.

99. National Center for Policy Analysis, "Health Care Policy Brief," Dallas, TX, 1996.

100. C. Sabatino, "Kassebaum–Kennedy Health Insurance Bill Clears Congress: Medical Savings Accounts Limited to Demonstration Program," Families USA (Washington, DC: Families USA 1997).

101. Wolfe, "Changing the U.S. Health Care System," p. 17.

102. DiNitto, *Social Welfare*, p. 270.

103. W. Barnhill, "Canadian Health Care: Would It Work Here?" *Arthritis Today* 6, no. 6 (November–December 1992), p. 8.

104. Elaine Vayda and R. B. Deber, "The Canadian Health Care System: An Overview," *Social Science and Medicine* 18, no. 3 (1984), pp. 191–197.

105. I. Callaway, "Canadian Health Care: The Good, the Bad, and the Ugly," *Health Insurance Underwriter* (October 1991), pp. 18–35.

106. See Tracy Falwell, Suzy Carter, Jodie Daigle, Renee Mills, Lissa Cameron and Leticia Gonzalez-Castro, "International Health Care Systems Analysis: Canada, Britain, Germany, Sweden, France, Mexico and South Africa," unpublished paper, University of Houston Graduate School of Social Work, Houston, TX, April 30, 1996; and T. Mizrahi, R. Fasan, and S. Dooha, "National Health Line," *Health and Social Work* 18, no. 1 (1993), pp. 7–12.

107. Jonathan S. Rakich, "The Canadian and U.S. Health Care Systems: Profiles and Policies," *Hospital and Health Services Administration* 36, no. 1 (Spring 1991), pp. 26–27.

108. Falwell et al., "International Health Care Systems Analysis."

109. Barnhill, "Canadian Health Care," p. 19.

110. Ibid.

111. Ibid.

112. Rakich, "The Canadian and U.S. Health Care Systems," p. 32.

113. See Cynthia Crosson, "Canadian Health Care Is in Critical Condition," *National Underwriter* (January 20, 1992), p. 12; and van Wormer, *Social Welfare*, p. 419.

114. See Barnhill, "Canadian Health Care"; I. Munro, "How Not to Improve Health Care," *Reader's Digest* (September 1992), p. 21; and B. Gilray, "Standing Up for American Health Care," *Health Insurance Underwriter* (February 1992), p. 10.

115. Robert E. Moffitt, "Should the Federal Government Finance Health Care for All Americans?: No." In Howard Jacob Karger and James Midgley (Eds.), *Controversial Issues in Social Policy* (New York: Allyn and Bacon, 1993).

116. For example, David Himmelstein and Steffie Woolhandler, "A National Health Care Program for the United States: A Physicians' Proposal," *The New England Journal of Medicine* 320 (January 12, 1989), pp. 102–108; and Combs-Orme, "Should the Federal Government Finance Health Care for All Americans?"

117. Combs-Orme, "Should the Federal Government Finance Health Care for All Americans?"

118. van Wormer, *Social Welfare*, p. 419.

119. See Combs-Orme, "Should the Federal Government Finance Health Care for All Americans?" and "How Does Canada Do It? A Comparison of Expenditures for Physicians' Services in the United States and Canada," *Journal of the American Medical Association* 265, no. 19 (May 15, 1991), p. 2474.

120. W. Caragata, "Medicare Wars," *Maclean's* 108, no. 14 (1995), p. 4.

121. Ruth Levitt, *The Reorganised National Health Service* (London: Croom Helm, 1979), p. 15.

122. Quoted in ibid., p. 17.

123. Victor W. Sidel and Ruth Sidel, *A Healthy State* (New York: Pantheon, 1983), p. 144.

124. Ibid., pp. 144, 157–159.

125. Ibid., p. 172.

126. Ibid.

127. Sidel and Sidel, *A Healthy State*, p. 172.

128. "Nye Bevan's Legacy," *The Economist* (July 6, 1992), p. 12.

129. Ibid.

130. Ibid.

131. Levitt, *The Reorganised National Health Service*, p. 27.

132. "Nye Bevan's Legacy."

133. Ibid., p. 12.

134. Quoted in ibid., p. 12.

135. Combs-Orme, "Should the Federal Government Finance Health for All Americans?"

chapter 13

Mental Health and Substance Abuse Policy

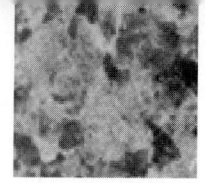

This chapter reviews the provision of mental health services to people with serious mental impairments. Before the rise of the community mental health movement, states were solely responsible for the care of their mentally disturbed residents. When the movement to improve mental health services through federal assistance to the states stalled, many who suffered from serious mental illness were left without care. This lack of adequate care was made worse by a series of legal decisions that reinforced the civil rights of mental patients while requiring the states to provide adequate services. As a result of these developments, many former mental patients are now living on the streets or in squalid single-room-occupancy hotels. In 1996 mental health advocates were encouraged by passage of the Mental Health Parity Act, which mandated that employers offer employees mental health benefits that were comparable to physical health care benefits. Despite this incremental reform, problems associated with chronic mental illness as well as with alcohol and drug abuse have become more prevalent. The lack of adequate support for substance abuse prevention and treatment efforts, coupled with the economic collapse of inner-city neighborhoods, left many urban areas subject to unprecedented levels of street violence and social deterioration. And while social workers in the public sector struggled to care for their seriously impaired clients, private practitioners prospered—although the more recent advent of managed care has attenuated their prospects.

Throughout the history of American social welfare, states have played a prominent role in mental health services. During the nineteenth century, social problems attributable to immigration, urbanization, and industrialization overwhelmed local poorhouses that had been established during the colonial era. Dorothea Dix championed the humane treatment of people with mental illness in the United States, and by the 1840s she was instrumental in convincing many states to construct special institutions to provide asylum to the emotionally deranged. In fact, Dix's leadership was so persuasive that

Congress passed legislation authorizing federal aid to the states for mental institutions. However, because President Franklin Pierce thought that the federal government should not interfere with the responsibility of the states to ensure social welfare, he vetoed the legislation in 1854.[1] It would not be until more than a century later that the federal government, through the Community Mental Health Centers Act, would assume a central role in determining mental health policy.

Consequently, mental health policy in the United States was articulated through the various states, which operated their own mental hospitals. Originally, state mental hospitals were intended to be self-sufficient communities offering good air, clean water, nutritious food, and healthful activities consistent with the dictates of "moral treatment." Considering the quality of life experienced by many Americans at that time, such refuges were sorely needed. Conditions in rural settings were no less dire than conditions in urban centers in the nineteenth century. Newspaper clippings from an immigrant community in Wisconsin, circa 1890, reveal the fate of vulnerable residents who failed to negotiate dispiriting social conditions.

The naked body of the wife of Fritz Armbruster, a woman who had worked in Best's Butcher Shop, was found frozen by the roadside near Albion, 6 miles from Black River Falls. She and her husband had separated, he living in town, she living alone in the house. Although no one had noticed that she had been suffering from any physical or mental disorder, 2 years ago, the loss of a child is said to have affected her very deeply and may have led to her becoming partially demented. The probability is that she rose in a fit of delirium and wandered away. . . .

Mr. Axel, a farmer living about 6 miles east of Kiel, Manitowoc County, cut his wife's throat a few days ago so that she might not recover and then killed himself. There were various rumors as to the cause of the tragedy such as domestic infelicity etc., but a few who had

dealings with Axel of late attributed the act to an aberration of mind. . . .

Milo L. Nichols, sent to the insane hospital a year or two ago after committing arson on Mrs. Nichols' farm is now at large . . . and was seen near the old place early last week. . . . He has proven himself a revengeful firebug.[2]

In response to these casualties, the state hospital served as a haven for the disturbed as well as protection for the community.

Admitted July 19, 1893. Town of Black River Falls. Norwegian. Married. Age 29. Seven children. Youngest 8 months. Housewife. Poor. First symptoms were manifested . . . when patient became afraid of everything and particularly of mediums. She is also deranged in religion and thinks everyone is disposed to persecute her and to injure her husband. . . .

Admitted January 20th, 1896. Town of Garfield. Age 52. Norwegian. Married. Two children, youngest 19 yrs old. Farmer. Poor. Illness began 10 months ago. Cause said to be his unfortunate pecuniary condition. Deluded on the subject of religion. Is afraid of injury being done to him. Relations say he has tried to hang himself. . . . September 29, 1896: Discharged . . . improved . . . Readmitted May 4, 1898: Delusion that he and his family are to be hanged or destroyed.[3]

An adverse social climate, coupled with the absence of welfare programs to cushion people against poverty, joblessness, inadequate housing, and illness, served to swell the population of state hospitals. By the 1920s the state hospital was an asylum in name only, and much of the care amounted to merely warehousing patients. In this milieu, some of the scientifically minded reformers of the Progressive Era found in the ideas of the eugenics movement a straightforward and surgically precise solution to the problem of state institutions being inundated by "mental defectives." Proponents of the eugenics movement who believed that the human race could be improved by selective breeding argued

that mental patients often suffered from hereditary deficiencies and that generational patterns of mental impairment should be eliminated by sterilization. In that adherents of eugenics were less concerned about the civil rights of individual mental patients than they were about the future of civilization, the fact that some patients might object was merely an inconvenience. In such instances, eugenicists obtained court permission to sterilize patients without their consent. Many patients, of course, lacked the mental capacity to comprehend sterilization and had no idea that the surgical procedures to which they were subjected would terminate their reproductive lives. By the 1930s 30 states had passed laws authorizing involuntary sterilization, and by 1935 20,000 patients had been sterilized, almost half of them in California. Involuntary sterilization of the feebleminded generated great controversy, eventually culminating in a Supreme Court decision, written by Oliver Wendell Holmes, that validated the practice. The case record upon which Holmes based his decision had been prepared by a social worker. Tragically, that case involved a young woman in Virginia who was sterilized, only to be judged psychologically normal years later.[4]

 # Mental Health Reform

More humane efforts to reform state institutions invariably involved the National Association for Mental Health (NAMH). Begun early in the twentieth century as an extension of the work of Clifford Beers, who had himself recovered after being hospitalized for mental illness, NAMH became critical of the custodial institutions operated by state governments. The issue of mental health attracted wide public attention during World War II, when approximately one in every four draftees was rejected for military service because of psychiatric or neurological problems.[5] In response to public outcry about mental health problems immediately after the war, Congress passed the Mental Health Act of 1946, which established the National Institute of Mental Health (NIMH). Accompanying the Mental Health Act was an appropriation for an exhaustive examination of the mental health needs of the nation. In 1961 NIMH released *Action for Mental Health,* a report that called for an ambitious national effort to modernize the U.S. system of psychiatric care.[6]

As David Mechanic observed, *Action for Mental Health* was a utopian vision of mental health care, the idealism of which conformed perfectly with a set of extraordinarily propitious circumstances. First, the postwar economy was booming, and, with cutbacks in military expenditures, a surplus existed that could be tapped for domestic programs. Second, a new generation of drugs—psychotropic medications—showed promise of being able to stabilize severely psychotic patients who before had been unmanageable. Third, a literature was emerging that was critical of the "total institution" concept of the state hospital and implied that noninstitutional— and presumably community—care was better. Finally, because of his experience with mental retardation as a family problem, President John F. Kennedy was supportive of programs that promised to improve mental health care.[7] These political and social circumstances did not go unnoticed by Dr. Robert H. Felix, a physician who had grown up with the Menninger family in Kansas and had developed a sharp critique of the state mental hospital as an institution for the care of emotionally disturbed patients. Felix was later to become director of NIMH. A primary architect of the community mental health movement, Felix was able to draw on his extensive experience in the Mental Hygiene Division of the U.S. Public Health Service as well as on the breadth of professional and political contacts that three decades of public service afforded.[8] Felix's objective was as simple as it was radical. He intended to pick up the banner last advanced by Dorothea Dix and reassert the role of the federal government in the nation's mental health policy. Through the community mental health movement, Felix would use federal legislation to reform the archaic state mental hospitals. The laws that enabled NIMH to reform mental health care

were the Community Mental Health Centers Acts of 1963 and 1965.

The Community Mental Health Centers Acts

Under the unusually advantageous circumstances of the postwar era, the first Community Mental Health Centers (CMHC) Act was passed by Congress and signed by President Kennedy on October 31, 1963. The enactment of CMHC legislation was not, however, without obstacles. To allay the American Medical Association's fears that the act represented socialized medicine, the CMHC Act of 1963 appropriated funds only for construction purposes. It was not until 1965, when the AMA was reeling from governmental proposals to institute federal health care programs for the aged and the poor, that funds were authorized for staffing CMHCs. Advocates of the CMHC Acts of 1963 and 1965 maintained that a constant target of the legislation was "to eliminate, within the next generation, the state mental hospital, as it then existed."

> *The strategy of the mental health leadership and their allies was to "demonopolize" the state role in the provision of mental health services and attempt to establish a triad of federal, state, and local support for mental health services. At this time, federal bureaucrats planned to blanket the whole country with comprehensive community mental health services. Their intention was not to federalize the total program through its financing, but to obtain a degree of control through the resulting federal regulations and standards.*[9]

The philosophical basis for transferring mental health care from the state hospital to the community was borrowed from public health, which had developed the concept of prevention. In adopting this formulation, proponents of community mental health presumed that services provided in the community would be superior to the warehousing of patients in state institutions. Prevention, according to the public health model, was of three types. **Primary prevention** efforts were designed to eliminate the onslaught of mental health problems. Certain psychiatric disturbances, such as depression and anxiety disorders, seemed to be caused by stress, which could be reduced by eliminating the source of stress. **Secondary prevention** consisted of early detection and intervention to keep incipient problems from becoming more debilitating. For example, screening schoolchildren for attention deficit disorders and providing corrective treatment could enhance a child's educational career and thereby enhance development throughout adolescence. **Tertiary prevention** consisted of "limiting the disability associated with a particular disorder, after the disorder had run its course." Typically, tertiary prevention activities sought to stabilize, maintain, and—when possible—rehabilitate those with relatively severe impairments.[10] It was clear to the community mental health activists that the state hospital addressed only tertiary prevention (and then poorly), whereas community mental health offered the prospect of combining primary and secondary intervention with a more adequate effort at tertiary prevention. The structure through which prevention would be operationalized was the community mental health center (CMHC).

According to the CMHC Acts, the United States was to be divided into catchment areas, each with a population of 75,000 to 200,000 persons.[11] Eventually, NIMH planned a CMHC for each catchment area, some 2,000 in all.[12] Programmatically, each CMHC was to provide all essential psychiatric services to the catchment area: inpatient hospitalization, partial hospitalization, outpatient services, 24-hour emergency services, and consultation and education for other service providers in the community. Soon after initial passage of the CMHC Act, child mental health as well as drug abuse and alcoholism services were added to the array of services provided. To make sure that patients were not lost between programs within the CMHC network, a **case management approach** was defined, whereby every case was

assigned to one professional who monitored the patient's progress throughout treatment. Financially, NIMH provided funding to disadvantaged catchment areas through matching grants over an eight-year cycle. At the end of the cycle, the catchment area was supposed to assume financial responsibility for the CMHC.[13] With this framework, mental health reformers believed that the CMHC was an effective alternative to the state hospital.

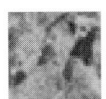 # Deinstitutionalization

Enthusiasm for community mental health reform ebbed when a series of circumstances that were beyond the control of the CMHC architects began to subvert the movement. Despite promising growth in the number of CMHCs during Johnson's presidency, the Nixon administration did not look favorably on CMHCs and impounded funds appropriated for mental health programs. Although funds were later released, the Nixon administration had clearly stated its disapproval of governmental mental health initiatives. Subsequent legislation to restore momentum to the flagging CMHC movement was crushed by a veto from President Ford. By the time a more sympathetic Carter administration assumed office, general economic problems were so serious that additional appropriations for mental health were not viable.[14] Still, at the end of Carter's term, 691 CMHCs continued to receive federal assistance. With the Omnibus Budget and Reconciliation Act of 1981, however, the Reagan administration collapsed all mental health funding into a block grant available to states for any mental health services they deemed fundable. As a result, the designation of CMHCs for direct receipt of federal funds ceased in 1981.[15]

In the meantime, however, many states had planned to shift responsibility for the mentally ill to the CMHCs. In fact, the community mental health movement had proved a timely blessing for officials in states where the maintenance of archaic state hospitals was an increasing economic burden. As states discharged patients from state institutions, they realized immediate savings; moreover, "the continuing fall in the numbers of patients to be housed provided state governments with plausible reasons for abandoning expensive schemes of capital investment designed to extend and (or) renovate their existing state hospital systems."[16] In all, 14 state hospitals were closed between 1970 and 1973. The prospect of substantial cost savings through the **deinstitutionalization** of patients received wide support. As governor of California, Ronald Reagan proposed closing all state hospitals by 1980.[17] Unfortunately, the transfer of patients from state institutions to settings in the community was not well planned. Through the mid-1970s, the deinstitutionalization movement was characterized by "severe fragmentation of effort and distribution of activity broadly throughout government with little effective coordination at the state or national level."[18] For purely economic reasons, then, state officials were strongly encouraged to facilitate deinstitutionalization regardless of whether or not alternative forms of care were available for those discharged from state hospitals. Ominously, by the end of the 1990s, 93 percent of the state psychiatric beds that had existed in 1955 had been lost to deinstitutionalization.[19]

Deinstitutionalization was further confounded by a series of judicial decisions in the mid-1970s that enhanced the civil rights of mental patients while at the same time requiring states to provide them with treatment. In **Wyatt v. Stickney,** Alabama District Court Judge Frank Johnson ruled that the state of Alabama was obliged to provide treatment to patients in state hospitals and ordered Governor Wallace and the state to appropriate millions of dollars for that purpose—a judgment with which the state subsequently failed to comply. Shortly thereafter, in **Donaldson v. O'Connor,** the Supreme Court determined that "the state could not continue to confine a mentally ill person who was not dangerous to himself or others, who was not being treated, and who could survive outside the hos-

pital." Finally, in **Halderman v. Pennhurst,** the Third District Court established that institutionalized patients deserved treatment in the "least restrictive alternative."

As a group, these rulings had a profound effect on institutional care for patients with mental impairments. Only persons dangerous to themselves or others could be hospitalized involuntarily. For those hospitalized, involuntarily or otherwise, states were obliged to provide adequate treatment in the manner that was least restrictive to the patient. These decisions promised to be enormously costly to state officials who were trying to curb mental health expenditures. To comply with the court decisions, states would have to pump millions of dollars into the renovation of institutions that had been slated to be closed. The solution, in many instances, was to use a narrow interpretation of *Donaldson* to keep emotionally disturbed people out of state institutions. In other words, judicial decisions, coupled with the fiscal concerns of state officials, provided a convoluted logic that served to justify first emptying state hospitals of seriously disturbed patients and then requiring the manifestation of life-threatening behavior for their rehospitalization. If people were not hospitalized in the first place, the states bore no obligation to provide the adequate, but expensive, treatment demanded by *Wyatt v. Stickney.* The criteria for hospitalization specified the most serious self-destructive behaviors; once admitted, however, patients were stabilized as quickly as possible and then discharged. As a result, those in greatest need of mental health services, patients who were seriously mentally ill, were often denied the intensive care they needed. The consequences for the mentally ill were substantial. In his interpretation of the legal decisions influencing mental health services, Alan Stone, a psychiatrist and a professor at Harvard Law School, observed that the true symbol of the Supreme Court *Donaldson* decision was a bag lady.[20] Thus, legal decisions favoring the mentally ill often proved illusory; in the name of enhancing the human rights of people with mental illness—but with no corresponding improvement in services—

they offered those people nothing more than the right to be insane.[21]

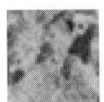

The Revolving Door

The shortfall of the community mental health movement, states' transfers of patients from mental hospitals, judicial decisions assuring patients of their civil rights, and the deinstitutionalization movement all combined to leave tens of thousands of former mental patients adrift. Although some former mental hospital patients were able to deal with community agencies in order to obtain mental health care, many of the seriously mentally ill were left to themselves.[22] By the late 1970s some 40,000 poor, chronically ill mental patients had been "dumped" in New York City. The 7,000 on the Upper West Side of Manhattan represented "the greatest concentration of deinstitutionalized mental patients in the United States."[23] Reporting in *Scientific American*, two mental health researchers described their experiences with deinstitutionalized patients:

> *Time and time again we see patients who were released from state hospitals after months or years of custodial care; who then survive [sic] precariously on welfare payments for a few months on the fringe of the community, perhaps attending a clinic to receive medication or intermittent counseling; who voluntarily returned to a hospital or were recommitted . . . who were maintained in the hospital on an antipsychotic medication and seemed to improve; who were released again to an isolated "community" life and who, having again become unbearably despondent, disorganized, or violent, either present themselves at the emergency room or are brought to it by a police officer. Then the cycle begins anew.[24]*

The high incidence of readmissions for psychiatric patients—the "revolving door"—had become an unavoidable problem in mental health.

In 1970 the ratio of readmissions per resident of a mental hospital was 1.4; in 1974 the ratio was 1.74; but by 1981 it had reached 2.83, double that of a decade earlier.[25] Through the mid-1980s the ratio of admissions per resident continued to edge up, and by 1986 it stood at 2.98.[26] By 1991, however, the ratio had fallen slightly to 2.88.[27]

Meanwhile, resources for state mental hospitals dwindled, leaving patient care uncertain. In an attempt to manage patients more cost-effectively, state mental institutions relied more heavily on psychoactive medication, sometimes with disastrous consequences. In California, for example, a federally funded group that oversees mental health care complained of unnecessary deaths of mental patients who had been left unsupervised after receiving medication:

> *The 28-year-old . . . patient died December 26, 1989, while he was locked in his dorm room . . . for 3 and one-half hours, the report charges. In addition to lithium and Valium, he was given Cogentin, which can cause vomiting, and Thorazine, which can suppress the body's natural coughing reflex. He suffocated on his own vomit and a piece of Christmas candy, the report said. The [other deaths] involved a 24-year-old patient who collapsed and died after he was given five different medications, and a 21-year-old man who had a fatal heart attack after he was given an injection of the psychiatric drug Haldol, the report said.[28]*

The first nationwide review of such deaths revealed that 142 psychiatric patients had died between 1988 and 1998 as a result of institutional abuses; 33 percent of the deaths were attributed to asphyxiation and 26 percent to cardiac problems. More than one-fourth were children.[29]

A coherent mental health policy had ceased to exist in the United States in the 1980s. By 1990, psychiatrist E. Fuller Torrey and his associates observed that "services for individuals with serious mental illness in the United States are a disaster by any measure used. Not since the 1820s have so many mentally ill individuals lived untreated in public shelters, on the streets, and in jails."[30] State hospitals had been divested of much of their responsibility for patients with serious psychiatric problems, but a complete system of CMHCs was not in place to care for many of those who had been deinstitutionalized.

As state hospitals converted from long-term custodial care to short-term patient stabilization, psychotropic medication came to be a routine form of treatment. But the psychopharmacological revolution, though consistent with the relatively orderly movement toward deinstitutionalization in the late 1960s, seemed incongruent with the psychiatric chaos of two decades later. Shown to stabilize psychotic patients until interpersonal treatment methods could be employed, the major tranquilizers—Prolixin, Thorazine, Haldol, Stelazine, to name a few—seemed clinically indicated within the controlled environment of the hospital. In a community setting, however, psychotropic medication became problematic. Once stabilized on major tranquilizers, patients frequently found the side effects of the medication—dry mouth, nervousness, torpor, lactation in women, impotence in men—unacceptable and stopped taking the medication.

Yet without medication such patients frequently decompensated, and without the regular supervision of psychiatric personnel, patients disappeared into inner-city ghettos or rural backwaters, adding to an already growing homeless population. Definitive data on the psychological condition of the homeless are difficult to generate, but a study of the homeless in Fresno, California, revealed that "34 percent were rated severely impaired and urgently in need of [psychiatric] treatment. An additional 33 percent were rated moderately impaired so that treatment would be of substantial benefit."[31] A Baltimore study found that 80 percent of the homeless were mentally ill, and most of these were also abusing illicit drugs and alcohol.[32] A HUD census of the homeless revealed that 62 percent had problems with alcohol abuse, 58 percent with drugs, and 57 percent with mental health.[33]

In the absence of mental health care, increasingly desperate former mental hospital patients turned to petty crime to gain income, thus clogging local courts. Commenting in 1991 on the surge in arrests of the mentally ill, one mental health worker became exasperated: "These people are forced to commit crimes to come to the attention of the police and get help."[34] By 2000 the Justice Department reported that 283,800, or 16 percent, of inmates in local and state correctional facilities suffered from mental disorders,[35] and another 550,000 were on parole.[36] Although the vast majority of mentally impaired inmates became little more than correctional ciphers, the circumstances of some received national attention. Of the 3,600 inmates on death row, approximately 10 percent are mentally retarded, a status recognized by only 13 of the 38 states permitting capital punishment; since 1976, 34 retarded inmates have been executed. As details about mentally impaired inmates became known, momentum grew to restrain capital punishment. For example, in 1995, Mario Marquez, who had an IQ of 60 and the aptitude of a seven-year-old, was executed in Texas for the murder of his niece. Hours before his execution he said, "I want to be God's gardener and take care of the animals." His attorney later said, "It was like talking to a five-year-old."[37]

Another telling incident involved a mentally ill African American who was mistaken for a man for whom an arrest warrant had been issued. Sharing only a last name and a common birth date, Kerry Sanders was rousted from sleeping on a Los Angeles park bench, arrested as Robert Sanders, and extradited to New York, where he was incarcerated for two years before the error was noticed. In the interim various attorneys, correctional officers, and social workers failed to recognize that the protests of Kerry Sanders were valid: He was not the man they had convicted. Yet a heavy dose of Haldol made him a convincing candidate for false imprisonment. It was not until a records clerk realized that Kerry Sanders was not the man for whom an arrest warrant was outstanding that he was released. Later, one of Kerry Sanders's prison doctors stated condescendingly, "He got medication, free meal, food, everything. He should say 'Thank you, for two years you guys treated me very nicely.'"[38]

By 2000 reformers were attempting to change judicial policy in regard to mentally ill convicts by creating special courts to deal with nonviolent offenders who had mental disorders. Paralleling special drug courts that had emerged in several metropolitan areas during the 1990s to contend with nonviolent drug abusers, the mental health court concept was advocated by the National Alliance for the Mentally Ill (NAMI). As of this writing the proposed legislation remained bottled up in Senate and House committees.

CMHCs under Siege

The discharge of patients from state mental hospitals imposed an enormous burden on the CMHCs. Because the seriously mentally ill were often unable to get care from hospitals, the CMHCs provided the only service these people received. A Philadelphia CMHC reported that 44 percent of its patients were chronically disturbed and that these patients consumed 70 percent of the mental health services provided.[39] CMHCs had to restructure their activities so as to focus on immediate care for seriously disturbed patients, with the result that "indirect" services, such as prevention and evaluation, were cut back. A study of 94 CMHCs showed that increasing demand for direct services to the seriously mentally disturbed began to skew mental health service delivery.[40] Thus, rather than being a mental health agency that provided a comprehensive range of services to all persons in a catchment area, the CMHC rapidly became an outpost for individuals with serious mental disturbances—a population that CMHCs were not intended to serve, at least not exclusively.

As client demand escalated, CMHCs faced significant cuts in federal funding. The Reagan administration moved to consolidate mental health funding in the form of block grants that were devolved to the states, but in the process reduced federal funding 21 percent.[41] With funding from the federal government diminishing, CMHCs became more dependent on the states, which had historically defined mental health care in the United States. CMHCs were able to compensate for federal reductions to some extent by obtaining more funding from government assistance programs. Significantly, nongovernmental sources, such as client fees and private insurance, continued to account for a relatively minor portion of CMHC operating expenses. Precisely how this reduction in federal funds affected the CMHC effort varied, of course, with individual programs. CMHCs in wealthier states, for example, were better able to weather the fiscal turmoil than were those in poorer states. Generally, however, CMHCs reduced staffing and programming through such strategies as layoffs and hiring freezes, staff reassignments, and internal reorganization.[42]

By the mid-1980s, CMHCs seemed to have made the necessary organizational adjustments to funding changes; but these were at the expense of staffing and programming needs that had been increasing. CMHCs were able to hire some new staff to make up for earlier reductions, but programming had stagnated completely. Eventually the morale of CMHC staff suffered, as mental health professionals could no longer see any relief from their inability to provide even minimal care to seriously mentally ill patients. In San Diego, for example, county officials decided to target scarce resources for only the most seriously disturbed, which drew this editorial response from a CMHC staff member:

> In the future . . . the community mental health clinics will provide little or no talking therapy to their thousands of clients. Instead, most patients will find their treatment limited to a 15-minute visit with a psychiatrist and a prescription for expensive psychotropic medications—bought, incidentally, at taxpayer expense.[43]

A decade after the devolution of mental health block grants to the states, CMHCs had adjusted by reducing professional staff; increasing caseloads; reorganizing and targeting **chronic care** services and services for people who were insured, and reducing services to children, adolescents, and the elderly who were uninsured.[44]

By 1990 mental health service delivery was diversifying. CMHCs maintained an important institutional role, yet no longer served as the focus of mental health reform as had been the case during the late 1960s and 1970s. CMHCs not only had failed to replace the state hospital system, but accounted for less than 5 percent of inpatient episodes. CMHCs were more visible in the realm of outpatient care, yet accounted for only 15.5 percent of visits, far below the 50.4 percent attributed to private practitioners.[45] Within two decades, not only had the steam gone out of the CMHC movement, but thousands of former mental patients had been left adrift. It was perhaps inevitable that more intrusive methods would evolve to care for them.

 ## Preventive Commitment

By the early 1990s, governmental mental health policy was in disarray. Deinstitutionalization had contributed to the homelessness problem, with at least 50 percent of the homeless being people with severe mental illness by the late 1980s.[46] When winter threatened the safety of some homeless people in New York City, a team of mental health workers were authorized to pick up those who posed a danger to themselves and to commit them to Bellevue Hospital for a three-week observation period, a policy referred to as **preventive commitment.** The first person picked up was Joyce Brown, who "was dirty, malodorous and abusive to passersby and defecated on herself."[47] To the chagrin of then Mayor Ed Koch, when Brown had been stabilized in Bellevue, attorneys from the American Civil Liberties Union challenged her involuntary commitment. The prospect that pending litigation might cancel the program led one supporter to observe that "for the severely mentally ill, liberty is not just an empty word but a cruel hoax."[48]

By late 1999, however, despite initial setbacks in preventive commitment, 41 states had authorized the practice.[49] The high number of treatment dropouts from outpatient therapy and the revolving door of hospitalization served to encourage local authorities to find some method for ensuring that seriously mentally ill persons would not deteriorate because of lack of intervention by mental health professionals. Preventive commitment provides for commitment of individuals who do not meet the statutory standard for involuntary hospitalization but who, it is asserted, are mentally ill, are unable to voluntarily seek or comply with treatment, and need treatment in order to prevent deterioration that would predictably result in dangerousness to self or others or grave disability.[50]

A tragic incident in early 1999 strengthened the cause of preventive commitment: In New York City a 32-year-old receptionist, Kendra Webdale, was pushed under a subway train and killed by a 29-year-old mental patient, Andrew Goldstein. During the two years prior to the incident, Goldstein not only experienced persistent hallucinations, but also acted violently, once assaulting a psychiatrist. Having been discharged from inpatient care, Goldstein had fared poorly in a basement apartment without a phone; he had sought residential services in a group facility to no avail, as there were no vacancies.[51] Within a year, the New York legislature enacted Kendra's Law, authorizing $30 million for preventive commitment.[52]

An increasingly popular mental health policy, preventive commitment nevertheless presents serious problems when there are inadequate resources to ensure that it is used properly. When a facility lacks adequate staff, preventive commitment can become a form of social control—as opposed to therapy—in which treatment "consists of mandatory medication and little else."[53] One authority on preventive commitment speculated that mental health professionals would have little choice but to use "forced medication" as "the treatment of choice" for those in preventive commitment and that they would have to "actually track down noncompliant patients at their place of residence or elsewhere and administer medication as part of a mobile outreach team."[54]

For those concerned with the civil rights of the mentally impaired, such an eventuality is nothing less than ghoulish, an exercise in state tyranny in the name of social welfare.[55] Even under conditions of adequate staffing, preventive commitment remains problematic. The side effects of psychoactive medications are so pronounced for many patients that they simply refuse to take the drugs, even under duress. Among the contraindications of psychoactive medications is **tardive dyskinesia,** permanent damage to the central nervous system resulting from long-term use of medications such as Prolixin and Stelazine. Because tardive dyskinesia is irreversible and is manifested by obvious symptoms—"protrusion of tongue, puffing of cheeks, puckering of mouth, chewing movements"[56]—the disorder raises a haunting specter: In an attempt to control psychological disturbances, psychiatry has created a host of physiological aberrations. Tardive dyskinesia appears after long-term use, sometimes even after medication is discontinued; so the number of mental patients with the disorder promises only to grow. In fact, one observer prophesied that the mental health problem in the coming decade would be tardive dyskinesia.[57] Unfortunately, critics of preventive commitment who cite the danger of tardive dyskinesia offer no economically or politically plausible alternative for the care of seriously mentally ill patients. As a result, preventive commitment—however troublesome—is likely to be an increasingly prominent feature of future mental health policy.

Mental Health Service Delivery

The Substance Abuse and Mental Health Services Administration (SAMHSA) of the Department of Health and Human Services oversees the federal Alcohol, Drug Abuse, and Mental Health block grants. These grants consolidate several separate or "categorical" programs established earlier, such as the CMHC Acts. Since 1981 all mental health expenditures have been in block grants to states. By using a block grant strategy, the federal government removed the power from federal agencies and transferred it to the individual states. Since the creation of mental health block grants, funding for mental health services has increased only incrementally, particularly in comparison with substantially greater funding for substance abuse services. During the mid-1990s the mental health block grant remained static; it began to increase slightly with the turn of the millennium, as shown in Table 13.1.

Static federal funding for mental health services signaled declining leadership in mental health reform. By the 1990s several states were exploring innovative methods for delivery of mental health services.[58] One approach involved the integration of services and payment through a capitation method, a strategy developed in several localities. Under a capitation method of payment, agencies are awarded a predetermined amount per client with which they must provide a range of services. Agencies are funded the capitation amount regardless of the actual cost of serving an individual client. Capitation in mental health care would mimic health maintenance organizations (HMOs), which have a successful track record in providing preventive and primary health care. "Mental health HMOs would centralize financing and delivery system responsibility, create financial incentives to reallocate resources from inpatient to outpatient settings, and reduce system fragmentation, as perceived by patients."[59] Such an arrangement has the advantage of being easy to administer, and it builds into the reimbursement scheme certain incentives that do not exist in other arrangements. Under a capitation reimbursement method, for example, agencies are encouraged to cut down on expensive services, such as hospitalization, because a surplus can be realized when the actual cost of care is below the capitation amount. "Money can be used to develop walk-in crisis centers, step-down units that provide intermediate care after an acute hospitalization, special case management programs for coordinating

TABLE 13.1 ■ SAMHSA Budget, by Activities (in thousands)

CATEGORY	FY 2000 APPROPRIATED	FY 2000 ESTIMATED	FY 2001 ESTIMATED
Research	$299,263	$296,675	$282,156
Capacity expansion	194,590	194,590	278,368
High-risk youth	7,000	7,000	7,000
Children's mental health	83,000	82,763	86,763
Protection and advocacy	25,000	24,903	25,903
Homeless formula grants	31,000	30,883	35,883
Mental health block grants	356,000	356,000	416,000
Substance abuse block grants	1,600,000	1,600,000	1,631,000
Program management	59,100	59,054	59,943
Total	$2,654,953	$2,651,868	$2,823,016

Source: "SAMHSA Budget" (Washington, DC: Substance Abuse and Mental Health Services Administration, 2000).

services and rehabilitation or special housing services."[60] In addition, agencies are penalized for neglecting to serve clients, because every capitated client represents a resource base for the agency.

An example of how a capitation method of payment could be used in mental health service delivery is the integrated mental health (IMH) concept being developed in New York State and Philadelphia. Capitated mental health care under IMH would have three major features. First, current **categorical grants**—Medicaid, Supplemental Security Income, Food Stamp Program, local funding—would be aggregated into a common fund from which capitation "premiums" would be paid. Second, a nonprofit planning and coordination agency would be established to oversee mental health care and in so doing negotiate contracts with providers, monitor performance, and evolve innovative programs. Third, particularly high-usage clients would be targeted for provision of less costly services in order to generate surpluses for less intensive services.[61]

The magnitude of cost savings that can be realized through IMH is illustrated by the deployment of a capitated system in two New York counties. In order to induce CMHCs to partici-

pate in the capitation arrangement, the counties established payment rates for levels of service for three types of patients: for "continuous patients," who had been hospitalized for some time, $39,000 per year; for "intermittent patients," who generally required intermediate care, two rates—$18,000 and $13,000; and for "outpatients," who needed the least intensive care, $5,000. State officials calculated that such payments would represent savings, because state hospital care exceeded $100,000 per patient annually. And indeed, by 1991–92 the continuous patient rate was reduced to $28,000; the intermittent rate was combined and lowered to $15,600; and the outpatient rate was increased to $11,600. Initial assessment of the program indicated cost savings and improved patient functioning. Participating CMHCs planned to use their revenue surpluses to extend mental health services to children and the elderly.[62]

The idea of integrating services through an arrangement such as the IMH is likely to become an important source of innovation in future mental health policy. Such an eventuality has significant implications for human service professionals, who may miss an important opportunity to shape mental health programs unless they are willing to sharpen their administrative skills. The capitation of mental health services, as might be suspected, places a premium on fiscal analysis, cost accounting, and strategic planning. In a policy environment in which capitation is an increasingly prevalent method of ensuring access to service while containing program costs, mental health administrators who are not knowledgeable about fiscal management may well lose control of programs to professionals from business and public administration.

Social workers have been reluctant to become managers in human service corporations;[63] yet case management services for people with serious mental illness "have enjoyed a rapid increase in prominence within the mental health system."[64] As conventionally structured, managed care in mental health has been subject to the same problems as managed physical health care, often attenuating services by limiting the number of therapeutic sessions. At worst a mental health corporation can collapse, as has Charter Behavioral Systems, leaving hundreds of patients adrift.[65] Regardless, unless mental health professionals increase their understanding of capitalism, they may find themselves working under the direction of business executives and using methods that are not optimal with respect to patients' well-being. Such a development is unlikely to be in the best interests of patients who are seriously emotionally disturbed. Indeed, the advent of managed care in mental health has contributed to the medicalization of psychiatry, particularly the use of psychoactive medications to control patient behavior, while reducing resources for less observable changes associated with talking therapy.[66]

In addition to the role that mental health professionals may play if mental health services are restructured, other issues emerge. If capitation becomes a primary vehicle for reimbursing providers, should government prefer nonprofit providers, ordinarily CMHCs, or for-profit providers, usually HMOs? As the commercialization of health care demonstrates, HMOs are quick to exploit new markets, and mental health delivery is no exception. But would HMOs continue to provide services to the chronically mentally ill, or would more disturbed patients become "refugees" from the HMOs that were once eager to recruit them?[67] Under either arrangement, is it reasonable to expect mentally impaired consumers to make wise choices in selecting a mental health provider? "Many clients receiving services in managed mental health care," cautioned one observer, "may have difficulty understanding and processing" the type of information they need to make a prudent choice in service provider.[68]

Questions about the ability of the mentally disturbed to make prudent decisions about their care notwithstanding, the comparative cost advantage of community-based services remains a compelling argument in favor of capitation. For example, the Threshold Jail Program, which provides care for mentally ill inmates, calculates a per diem of $26, compared to $70 for incarceration and $400 for mental hospital hospitalization. Although the program has been extant for only a few years, it has helped all of its 45 members avoid rearrest, an accomplishment that resulted in a grant of $495,000 from the state of Illinois.[69]

In Columbus, Ohio, another factor in the funding of mental health services emerged in 1996: the renewal of a property tax levy for mental health care. Local taxes accounted for about half of funding for local mental health care, but the levy for mental health and substance abuse was scheduled to end in 1996. Ominously, a renewal campaign that also increased the levy failed by less than 4 percent of the vote in 1995, so mental health advocates were hard pressed to succeed in the next election cycle. Through an intensive political campaign, the levy passed in 1996 by a safe margin, 61 percent to 39 percent, guaranteeing the continuation of local revenues.[70]

 # Parity for Mental Health Care

Although managed care defined much of the coverage for mental health care during the late 1980s and early 1990s, a reaction was building.

Under aggressive managed care plans, many who had received mental health services in the past found their options rationed—attenuated or eliminated altogether.[71] In response, a group of parents and relatives of the mentally ill organized NAMI and fought for extended mental health coverage.[72]

Advocates of extended mental health coverage were encouraged by the Clinton administration's proposed Health Security Act, a health care reform that might have placed mental health provision on a par with physical health services. The demise of the proposal left mental health advocates searching for a vehicle for obtaining parity. Health insurers opposed parity in mental health care, because it would increase the cost of premiums; the Congressional Budget Office projected that parity would raise premiums by 4 percent, or about $12 billion.[73] Given its aversion to increased health costs, to say nothing of its objections to government meddling in health care, few expected the conservative 104th Congress to move toward parity.

Yet, smarting from negative ratings associated with an overzealous conservative agenda, the 104th Congress suddenly reversed field in the closing days of the legislative session and in 1996 delighted mental health advocates by agreeing on legislation establishing parity for mental health care. Effective January 1, 1998, employers with more than 50 employees who offer any mental health coverage must include mental health benefits that are comparable to health benefits.[74] The consequences of legislatively mandating parity in mental health coverage were immediately disputed. Opponents warned of significant increases in health insurance premiums and the likelihood that employers would eliminate mental health coverage in order to dodge the parity mandate.[75] Defenders, on the other hand, minimized the implications for premium increases, noting that mental illness was, for the first time, being interpreted as a physiological disorder.

An evaluation of the Mental Health Parity Act released by the General Accounting Office in May 2000 tempered the enthusiasm of mental health advocates. Although 86 percent of employers surveyed were in compliance with the legislation, most—87 percent—had changed employee benefits so that mental health benefits were more restrictive. Significantly, only 3 percent reported that compliance had resulted in increased costs, and none had dropped mental health coverage altogether in response to mandated mental health parity.[76]

Parity for mental health care may have marked the end of the downsizing of mental health care, yet much remained to be done. The devolution of mental health care to the states beginning in the early 1980s, and the rationing of resources for mental health under managed care through the remainder of the decade, had effectively checked the expansion of mental health care; and the incarceration of mentally impaired offenders recalled the horrors against which Dorothea Dix had fought. Providing essential mental health services for poor people who evidence severe psychological disorganization remains a primary challenge to mental health advocates.

Substance Abuse

Mental health services are often associated with substance abuse. Human service professionals in direct services are familiar with clients who have chosen to anesthetize themselves from stress or misery with alcohol, tobacco, and other substances. Individuals' psychological problems are of course compounded by reliance on such substances, and these problems not only affect the families of substance abusers but also become more severe when addiction is manifested. Ordinarily, addiction is associated with alcohol and drugs, less often with tobacco. Substance abuse has become an important area of public policy not only because of the necessity for appropriations for treatment programs but also because of the enormous costs that substance abuse extracts from society. As these costs have escalated, substance abuse policy has attained a higher profile in domestic affairs.

The interaction of emotional difficulties, alcoholism, and substance abuse is reflected in social welfare policy and has been institutionalized in the Substance Abuse and Mental Health Services Administration. In recent years the federal SAMHSA budget has increased, but many critics would argue that it is still insufficient to address the mounting demands for substance abuse programs.

The consolidation of categorical grants into a federal block grant program under SAMHSA reflects the preference of many human service professionals for preventive programs that apply generically to all forms of substance abuse. This approach has been argued persuasively by Mathea Falco:

> *An estimated 18 million Americans are alcoholics and 55 million are regular smokers, compared to 5.5 million serious drug abusers. Each year alcohol causes 200,000 deaths from disease and accidents, while more than 400,000 Americans die from smoking. By contrast, deaths from all illicit drugs range from 5,000 to 10,000. The costs of health care and lost productivity caused by tobacco-related illnesses are estimated at $60 billion a year, and those attributed to alcoholism exceed $100 billion. For all illegal drugs, the National Institute of Drug Abuse sets the annual bill to society at $40 billion.*[77]

What is the logic in having separate preventive programs for tobacco, alcohol, and illegal drugs when effective prevention programs can be developed for all of them? In the light of diminishing resources for social programs, Falco's book *The Making of a Drug-Free America: Programs That Work*—a call for integrating prevention efforts—is compelling.

History of Substance Abuse

Although most societies have incorporated addictive substances into their religions or social conventions, the use of these substances is ordinarily circumscribed. For historical and demographic reasons, U.S. culture has been accepting of certain substances, ambivalent about some, and phobic about others. Tobacco, a crop the colonists were encouraged to cultivate by their European sponsors, has been a legal commodity since Europeans first settled in North America. Alcoholic beverages appear in most agrarian societies, and these are a fixture in American folklore. Still, the consequences of excessive alcohol consumption on family life led some religiously inspired Progressives to call for the prohibition of alcohol. From 1919 to 1933, the Eighteenth Amendment to the Constitution prohibited the manufacture and sale of alcoholic beverages in the United States. Cocaine was a common ingredient in many early patent medicines and in popular beverages such as Coca-Cola. Concern about quality in production, however, led to the Pure Food and Drug Act of 1906, which required that ingredients be listed on product labels. When the public learned that there was cocaine in some products, local jurisdictions prohibited their sale. Opium, imported with the Chinese laborers who built the western rail system, was initially ignored in this country until reports surfaced that women from upright families were frequenting "opium dens." The Hague Opium Convention of 1912, of which the United States was a leader, subsequently controlled the production and sale of opium internationally. In the United States, restrictions on the manufacture and sale of cocaine, heroin, and marijuana were first established through the 1914 Harrison Narcotic Act. Marijuana was effectively made illegal through the Marijuana Tax Act of 1937.[78]

Despite this legacy, governmental control of mind-altering substances is anything but consistent. Although the federal government wages a "drug war," some states, for all practical purposes, disregard marijuana possession. The sale and use of cocaine and heroin have become so essential to the economy of many poor inner-city communities that the police are ineffectual in controlling trade, able at best only to harass users.[79] During the 1980s cocaine was commonly used by young urban professionals (yuppies) as the drug of choice and glamorized by Hollywood. Meanwhile, a substantial market emerged in prescription drugs, such as Valium, which were available as widely as there were corrupt physicians willing to prescribe them.

Public intolerance of drug abuse escalated because of several factors. Continued carnage on the nation's highways because of drunk drivers led to the founding of Mothers Against Drunk Drivers (MADD), a voluntary group that fought aggressively for stiffer penalties for drivers under the influence of alcohol. The alcohol- and drug-related deaths of entertainers such as Janis Joplin, Jimi Hendrix, and Elvis Presley were sobering experiences for many young people. When sports stars Len Bias and Don Rogers died from cocaine overdoses, drug abuse took center stage in the United States. In the meantime, an ominous development served to underscore drug abuse as a public health problem, not simply as an individual moral problem. AIDS, initially associated with male homosexuals in this country, was increasingly prevalent among inner-city intravenous drug users (IDUs). Needle sharing among cocaine and heroin addicts was identified as a primary means of HIV transmission. Indiscriminate injections by IDUs quickly spread AIDS within the African American and Hispanic communities in major urban centers. When IDUs practiced unsafe sex, AIDS was passed to minority heterosexuals. As women who had contracted AIDS became pregnant, they bore infants who were HIV positive. By the early 1990s concerns about substance abuse drew together diverse groups of Americans. The anguish of the white suburban mothers of MADD was shared by black inner-city mothers with AIDS.

Alcohol Abuse

Americans steadily increased their consumption of alcohol from the end of World War II until the 1980s, when drinking began to decrease. By 1987 average per capita consumption was a little more than 2.5 gallons of alcoholic beverages a year.[80] However, that amount was not evenly distributed throughout the population. One-third of the adult population abstains from alcohol consumption; one-third of people who do drink consider their consumption to be light; and the remaining third are considered moderate to heavy drinkers. The 1999 National Household Survey on Drug Abuse revealed that 45 million Americans were binge drinkers on occasion and that 12.4 million were heavy drinkers.[81]

These statistics are directly related to serious social problems. Forty-eight percent of all convicted criminals used alcohol just before committing a crime, and 64 percent of offenses against public order are alcohol related.[82] Yet substance abuse services often are not available for drinkers who are subsequently incarcerated. In 1997 substance abuse services were available at 93.8 percent of federal correctional facilities but at only 60.3 percent of state prisons, 33.5 percent of jails, and 36.6 percent of juvenile facilities.[83]

Perhaps the most significant adverse consequence of alcohol consumption is highway accidents. The tragic death toll on U.S. highways provoked the establishment of MADD and demands for stronger penalties for drunk drivers as well as for public education campaigns to dissuade people from drinking while driving. This combination of motivators seemed to have a positive effect: Between 1982 and 1986 the number of inebriated drivers involved in fatal accidents dropped significantly. Even so, in 1987 approximately 23,000 people died in traffic accidents in which alcohol was implicated.[84] In 2000 Congress considered instituting a national standard of inebriation while driving.

Among the most pernicious effects of alcohol consumption is fetal alcohol syndrome (FAS), a physiological and mental deformation in infants caused by their mothers' ingestion of alcohol during pregnancy. FAS children exhibit behaviors that make them extraordinarily difficult to manage: limited attention span, slow response to stimuli, and an inability to incorporate a moral code. Because of these deficiencies, FAS children tend to have difficulty in the early socialization experiences of elementary school. Children with FAS frequently fail to understand complicated instructions; they tend to wander about, and they take the property of classmates without understanding the inappropriateness of such behavior. FAS is particularly difficult to diagnose in that its milder form, fetal alcohol effect (FAE), does not cause any physiological abnormality in facial structure. The National Institutes of Health estimated in 1990 that the incidence of FAS among children of heavy-drinking women was as high as 25 per 1,000 births and that the annual cost of coping with the disorder was almost one-third of a billion dollars.[85]

Although FAS has been recognized by pediatric researchers since 1973,[86] the syndrome was not widely known to the public until Michael Dorris's account of his adopted son's FAS condition was published in *The Broken Cord*. A novelist and the husband of award-winning author Louise Erdrich, Dorris wrote poignantly about his adoption of Adam, a Native American infant. Ignorant of Adam's condition, Dorris spent years consulting with teachers, having his son tested by psychologists, and transferring Adam to special schools. It was not until he visited an Indian reservation and a special education bus discharged a group of FAS children for school that Dorris learned about FAS from a friend. Suddenly Dorris understood that Adam was suffering from a permanent disorder brought about by his birth mother's drinking.

In *The Broken Cord* Dorris and Erdrich wrote movingly about the consequences of FAS. Both are Native Americans themselves, and their observations were as acute as they were controversial. Noting that as many as 25 percent of the children born on the Sioux Pine Ridge Reservation suffered from FAS, Dorris contended that Indian women's alcohol consumption during pregnancy represented a kind of genocide. In order to contain FAS, Dorris suggested that pregnant women who have previously given birth to FAS children and who demonstrate an inability to control their drinking be incarcerated until they give birth. Erdrich concurred, her rationale being that the health of the fetus had primacy over the mother's freedom to consume alcohol:

> *Knowing what I know now, I am sure that even when I drank hard, I would rather have been incarcerated for nine months and produce a normal child than bear a human being who would, for the rest of his or her life, be imprisoned by what I had done. And for those so sure, so secure, I say the same thing I say to those who would not allow a poor woman a safe abortion and yet have not themselves gone to adoption agencies and taken in the unplaceable children, the troubled, the unwanted: If you don't agree with me, then please, go and sit beside the alcohol-affected while they try to learn how to add.*[87]

The idea of restraining women during pregnancy to prevent fetal damage triggered a debate in the popular media. This controversy was fueled by two related issues. First, a rapid increase in the number of infants who tested positive for cocaine at birth raised the specter of a "biounderclass" consisting of a generation of minority children condemned to disability by maternal substance abuse.[88] Second, arrests of women for exposing their infants to substance abuse in utero enraged feminists who had watched the cutbacks in maternal health and social services during the 1980s. "It has become trendy," columnist Ellen Goodman observed acidly, "to arrest pregnant women for endangering their fetuses."[89] By the early 1990s an unstable truce had evolved between proponents of fetal health and women's rights. Clearly, both camps favored aggressive public education and early treatment for substance abuse before, during, and after pregnancy—but lack of funding made such initiatives unlikely.

As a result, the question of how to manage substance-abusing women during pregnancy has been passed down to program managers and clinical staff. As the number of infants testing positive for substance abuse increased, opposition to social control intervention on the basis that it violated women's rights became less tenable for human service professionals. Indeed, the possibility of compulsory treatment for pregnant drug abusers became an unavoidable issue when drug abuse was associated with the transmission of AIDS.[90] Compulsory treatment, of course, runs contrary to the individual liberties guaranteed by the Constitution, because it is possible only through some commitment procedure. Proponents of compulsory treatment and preventive commitment have argued that it is the only way to protect potential victims against the uncontrolled and hazardous behavior of addicts. Critics, on the other hand, insist that effective public education and treatment would make such draconian measures unnecessary.

The issue of alcohol abuse and pregnancy was highlighted in 1996, when a 35-year-old Wisconsin woman was charged with attempted murder for going on a drinking binge shortly before giving birth. Delivered by cesarean section, the infant appeared to suffer from FAS and was placed in foster care. In prosecuting the case, the district attorney presented witnesses who testified that the mother had stated her intent to kill the fetus by drinking. By the trial date the mother had been in recovery, pleaded innocent to the murder charge, and was trying to regain custody of her child. The case broke new ground in the legal status of an unborn child and a woman's maternal responsibility during pregnancy.[91] As of this writing the U.S. Supreme Court was deliberating the constitutionality of a South Carolina hospital's practice of providing data on pregnant mothers' substance abuse to law enforcement, after which the mothers were arrested for child abuse.[92]

This dilemma has serious implications for clients of substance abuse programs, as it does also for practitioners. Compulsory treatment is likely to deter some people from seeking treatment that they might have sought voluntarily, though perhaps at a later date. Compulsory treatment also places the practitioner in the role of social control agent, a role not conducive to building a client's trust. Compulsory treatment is likely to drive the substance abuse problem underground, further exacerbating the very problem it is intended to remedy. Without adequate investments in education and treatment, the future of substance abuse policy appears likely to be plagued by a series of such negatively reinforcing decisions.

Drug Abuse

By contrast with alcohol abuse, the prevalence of drug abuse is more difficult to ascertain be-cause the use of controlled substances—the focus of drug abuse—is illegal. It appears that general drug abuse has begun to decline after peaking during the 1979–80 period. In 1999 almost 15 million Americans reported use of illicit drugs, a significant decrease from the 25 million abusers estimated in 1979. Among younger Americans aged 12 to 17, drug abuse has been declining (from 11.4 percent in 1997 to 9.0 percent in 1999); that of young adults aged 18 to 25 has increased slightly (from 14.7 percent in 1997 to 18.8 percent in 1999). There is evidence that exposure to cocaine has decreased, but use of heroin has remained unchanged with an estimated 149,000 new heroin users in 1998. One-fourth of new heroin users are young and use methods other than injection.[93] Despite the reduction in the use of crack cocaine and the injection of heroin, hard drug abuse remains a serious health concern: As many as 25 percent of people who contract AIDS in this country are intravenous (IV) drug users.[94] A haunting scenario takes shape: IV drug users can no longer be thought of solely as tortured souls in the slow process of self-destruction; they have become transmitters of an epidemic that promises to be as costly as it is deadly.

The federal response to illicit drug use has been twofold, involving both interdicting the supply of illegal substances and reducing the demand through treatment and public education. Government strategies have oscillated wildly between the interdiction and prevention approaches. Before Ronald Reagan came to power, federal policy emphasized treatment and public education, assuming that these strategies would diminish demand. During the early 1970s, for example, two-thirds of federal appropriations for drug abuse were for treatment and education. A decade later, however, supply interdiction had superseded demand reduction as the prime strategy, consuming 80 percent of federal drug funds. Illegal drug use is considered in greater detail in Chapter 14.

For human service professionals an emphasis on prevention over interdiction would be a positive development in drug abuse policy. $500 million for school drug abuse prevention programs became available through the Drug Free Schools Act in the early 1990s. Applying the prevention trinity used in public health to drug abuse, it is evident that most treatment funding has been directed toward rehabilitating addicts (tertiary prevention) or treatment of abusers (secondary prevention). Limited primary prevention efforts have been field tested, but these are only now being widely adopted. Mathea Falco notes that not all have been equally effective. Life Skills Training (LST), developed in New York City, and STAR (Students Taught Awareness and Resistance), deployed in Kansas City, have been superior to DARE (Drug Abuse Resistance Education). But the real test of school prevention programs comes in poor neighborhoods where drug abuse is part of the community fabric. Programs such as the Westchester Student Assistance Program in New York, Smart Moves of the Boys and Girls Clubs, and the Seattle Social Development Project show promise; yet, upon evaluation, program graduates tend to report resistance to "soft" drugs—tobacco, alcohol, marijuana. Avoidance of "hard" drugs has not been clearly demonstrated through these programs.[95] This inability of prevention programs to produce resistance to hard drugs in high-risk neighborhoods may be due to methodological problems. High-risk youth who are susceptible to hard drug use are probably unlikely to complete a prevention program, nor are they good candidates to report hard drug usage through an outcome instrument. Instead, they are likely to be casualties of the research process for the same reasons they are casualties of substance abuse. Therefore, some researchers have contended that substance abuse prevention efforts will not be successful until a much more expansive definition of primary prevention—including social, economic, and institutional factors—is adopted.[96]

In the absence of major prevention initiatives, intervention strategies focus on treatment. Generally, employees with generous health insurance have been able to gain ready admission to drug abuse treatment programs. The poor, by contrast, have found treatment available irregularly, if at all. In response to the pervasive use of alcohol and drugs, treatment facilities expanded rapidly through the early 1980s. From 1978 to 1984 the number of hospital units treating alcohol and drug abusers increased 78 percent (from 465 to 829), and the number of beds in these facilities increased 62 percent (from 16,005 to 25,981). As Table 13.2 demonstrates, more resources have been committed to treatment for alcohol abuse than for drug abuse, though the difference has been declining.

Regardless, inpatient facilities provided only a fraction of treatment services to substance abusers. Perhaps half of the 5.5 million people currently using drugs would elect treatment if it were available, but that number is 1 million more than the number of available treatment slots.[97]

Although treatment lags behind demand, research continues to demonstrate the wisdom of investing in rehabilitation. Columbia University's Center on Addiction and Substance Abuse has reported that 32.3 percent of Medicaid hospitalization days were due to neonatal complications attributed to substance abuse. Cardiovascular and respiratory disorders associated with substance abuse accounted for another 31.4 percent of Medicaid hospitalization days. Significantly, when substance abuse was noted as a secondary diagnosis, the length of hospitalization doubled.[98] A comprehensive investigation of substance abuse treatment programs in California claimed savings of $7 for every $1 dollar in program costs. "Treatment is a good investment!" affirmed the California director of alcohol and drug programs. In a 1997 review of drug use treatment, SAMHSA reported that 12 months after treatment, illicit drug use dropped significantly: 48.2 percent for users of a primary drug (e.g., marijuana), 50.8 percent for crack, 54.9 percent for cocaine, and 46.6 percent for heroin.[99] As is often the case with addiction services, the subsequent question of long-term abstinence has not been thoroughly evaluated.

TABLE 13.2 ■ 1998 Treatment Episode Data

Primary Substance	1993	1994	1995	1996	1997	1998
	NUMBERS OF TREATMENT EPISODES					
Total	1,584,033	1,635,782	1,635,963	1,601,214	1,537,143	1,564,156
Alcohol	895,523	861,108	826,037	801,538	733,300	726,800
Alcohol only	542,629	506,693	477,814	458,838	413,267	411,575
Alcohol and drug	351,894	354,415	348,223	342,700	320,033	315,225
Opiates	206,865	231,674	236,613	232,242	236,055	233,507
Heroin	192,840	216,238	220,849	216,204	220,575	216,834
Other opiates	28,050	30,872	31,528	32,076	30,960	33,346
Cocaine	277,076	293,666	272,286	256,920	230,192	233,493
Smoked	201,216	217,344	202,865	190,143	169,724	170,493
Nonsmoked	75,860	76,322	69,421	66,777	60,405	63,002
Marijuana/hashish	111,265	139,670	170,974	192,103	198,079	208,671
Stimulants	28,907	45,167	63,217	52,893	68,048	70,618
Other drugs	21,262	21,497	20,792	18,968	17,571	19,270
	PERCENTAGES					
Alcohol	56.5	52.6	50.5	50.1	47.7	46.5
Alcohol	34.3	31.0	29.2	28.7	26.9	26.3
Alcohol and drug	22.2	21.7	21.3	21.4	20.8	20.2
Opiates	13.1	14.2	14.5	14.5	15.4	14.9
Heroin	12.2	13.2	13.5	13.5	14.3	13.9
Other opiates	1.8	1.9	2.0	2.0	2.0	2.1
Cocaine	17.5	18.0	16.6	16.0	15.0	14.9
Smoked	12.7	13.3	12.4	11.9	11.0	10.9
Nonsmoked	4.8	4.7	4.2	4.2	3.9	4.0
Marijuana/hashish	7.0	8.5	10.5	12.0	12.9	13.3
Stimulants	1.8	2.8	3.9	3.3	4.4	4.5
Other drugs	1.3	1.3	1.3	1.2	1.1	1.2

Source: 1998 Treatment Episode Data (Washington, DC: Substance Abuse and Mental Health Services Administration, 2000).

The extent to which substance abuse services will benefit from the 1996 legislation establishing parity of mental health services with health care remains to be seen. A major expansion of substance abuse treatment through employer insurance plans would inject substantial private resources into a service area that has been dominated by governmental programs and self-help groups. Yet because such insurance is connected to employment, it will not influence the treatment of abusers who are marginal to the labor market—those most impaired and most in need of intensive rehabilitation.

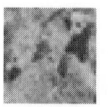

Private Practice and Mental Health Services

Mental health care has become an area in which social workers can emulate the success of psychiatrists and psychologists by establishing private practices. As a form of independent practice, private practice is influenced by the policies of the states regulating it, by professional associations, and by the insurance companies that pay clinicians for their services. Private social work practice in mental health has been controversial within the social work profession, as reflected in this depiction:

> *In increasing numbers, social workers are flocking to psychotherapeutic pastures, hanging out their shingles to advertise themselves as psychotherapists just as quickly as licensing laws will permit. For the most part, professional associations of social workers and schools of social work are active participants in the great transformation of social work from a professional corps concerned with helping people deal with their social problems to a major platoon in the psychotherapeutic armies.*[100]

Despite this kind of criticism, private practice continues to be an attractive vehicle for delivering clinical social services. Indeed, social workers employed in the for-profit sector, including private practice, reported a median income of $51,900, significantly more than the income of those working in the nonprofit sector, and second only to the median income of social workers employed by the federal government, $53,120.[101]

As Table 13.3 shows, social workers in for-profit settings are increasing in numbers beyond those in more traditional settings. Of all National Association of Social Workers (NASW) members, the number working in for-profit settings increased from 19.8 percent in 1988 to 27.9 percent in 1995.[102] A more recent subsample of NASW members indicated that in 2000 35 percent were employed in the private, for-profit sector.[103]

TABLE 13.3 ■ Primary Auspices of Working NASW Members

PRIMARY AUSPICES	1988		1991		1995	
	Numbers	*Percentages**	*Numbers*	*Percentages**	*Numbers*	*Percentages**
Public local	12,309	18.4%	15,368	18.5%	14,945	17.1%
Public state	11,937	17.9	12,461	15.0	11,359	13.0
Public federal	2,185	3.3	2,399	2.9	2,330	2.7
Public military	513	0.8	653	0.8	787	0.9
Private nonprofit	26,623	39.8	32,246	38.9	33,465	38.4
Private for profit	13,223	19.8	19,753	23.8	24,310	27.9
Total respondents	66,970		82,880		87,196	

Percentages do not total 100 because of rounding.

Source: Margaret Gibelman and Philip Schervish, *The Social Work Labor Force as Reflected in the NASW Membership* (Washington, DC: NASW, 1997), p. 69.

For some time, many mental health services have been delivered by psychiatrists and psychologists who work predominantly out of private offices. The upsurge of social workers' interest in private practice is such that today a large portion of students entering graduate programs in social work—as many as 80 percent[104]—do so with the expressed intent of establishing a private practice. Professional schools of social work are specifically equipped to prepare graduate students for private practice. "M.S.W. programs appear to offer more to the practitioner bound for private practice than to the social worker who would prefer to work in an agency setting," concluded researchers in a study of private and agency-based social workers.[105]

The current enthusiasm for private practice can be attributed to several factors. First, as mentioned, private practitioners often enjoy a prestige and income that set them apart from salaried professionals.[106] In addition, private practitioners work significantly fewer hours per week compared to colleagues in public and non-profit settings.[107] It is not surprising that social workers, who are mostly female and usually underpaid—social work salaries are significantly less than those of nurses or teachers[108]—would see private practice as a way to increase their earnings and status. In fact, women are more likely to engage in private practice than to work in traditional social service agencies; two-thirds of private practitioners are women.[109]

Private practitioners also have a degree of autonomy that is not available to professionals who are bound by the personnel policies of traditional agencies. Srinika Jayaratne and his associates found that "whereas 55 percent of the private practitioners report a high level of congruence between their expectations and their activities, only 18.3 percent of the agency practitioners do so."[110] This autonomy is important for experienced professionals who find continued supervision unnecessary or intrusive and who require some flexibility in their work schedules to make room for other priorities. Finally, private practice allows professionals to specialize in activities at which they are best instead of having to conform to organizational requirements

of the private agency or governmental bureaucracy. Again, 66.5 percent of private practitioners reported that they were able to do the things at which they excelled, whereas only 22.9 percent of agency practitioners said they could do so.[111]

The image of private practice that has emerged is one of freedom and opportunity, sans rules and regulations. This is somewhat misleading. Although private practice may involve comparatively fewer compliance requirements than does salaried employment, it is anything but unfettered. In actuality, private practice involves many policies with which practitioners must be familiar if they are to be successful. The policies that affect private practice originate primarily from three sources: the professional community (a private entity); a government regulatory authority (a public entity); and, because of the role of managed care, corporate firms. This situation is complicated by the provision of service through the marketplace of a capitalist economy that traditionally discriminates against groups that do not participate fully in the labor market—minorities, women, elderly people, people with disabilities. These groups frequently lack the resources to purchase the services provided by private practitioners. For this reason, private practice is not easily reconciled with the traditional values of the human service professions, which emphasize service to the community and to the disadvantaged. So it is paradoxical that private practice has become a popular method of social work practice, and this development remains controversial.

Private Practice in Social Work

The private practice of social work is a relatively recent phenomenon. The National Association of Social Workers did not officially sanction this form of service delivery for its members until 1964.[112] Before that, privately practicing social workers identified themselves as psychotherapists and lay analysts. Typically, they relied on referrals from physicians and psychiatrists,[113] and after World War II they began to establish "flourishing and lucrative" practices.[114] By 1991 10,458 NASW members were primarily involved in private practice, and another 9,325 indicated private practice as secondary employment.[115]

By 1987 all 50 states regulated social workers, with the majority of states requiring a master's degree in social work (M.S.W.). However, a social work license is not automatically awarded to those holding the M.S.W. degree. Many states require candidates for licensure to have two years of post–M.S.W. experience under the supervision of a **Licensed Certified Social Worker** (LCSW) and to pass an examination. Beyond these common requirements, states vary greatly in their regulatory practices. Maryland, for example, has a three-tier system: the LCSW for M.S.W.'s who have two years of post–M.S.W. experience and who have passed an examination; the Licensed Graduate Social Worker (LGSW) for newly graduated M.S.W.'s; and the Social Work Associate (SWA) for those with baccalaureate degrees in social work. To further complicate matters, new licensing legislation often allows candidates who have practiced professionally to become licensed without first meeting the requirements of the licensing legislation. This practice, called "grandfathering," is characteristic of new licensing legislation and, in that social work licensing is a relatively recent development in many states, there are many LCSWs in practice who would not otherwise meet the technical requirements for a license. Moreover, because some states exempt state employees from licensing requirements, many "social workers" in public welfare do not meet the licensing requirements necessary for the title of social worker. As a result, many social workers are licensed but have not met the requirements with which their colleagues must comply. Consequently, states often establish additional requirements for professionals to be eligible for vendorship. Special registries for clinical social workers may be used to identify LCSWs who are eligible for third-party payments.

Professional associations also designate practitioners who have expertise in particular areas. In social work the most common distinction is membership in the Academy of Certified Social Workers (ACSW). Requirements for the ACSW are two years of post–M.S.W. experience under the supervision of an ACSW and passage of an examination. These are similar to the requirements for the LCSW, but the two designations should not be confused. Because states have the legal authority to license professions, special distinctions established by professional associations are neither equivalent to nor a substitute for state licensure. Thus, it is common for experienced clinicians to list both LCSW and ACSW after their names as indications of professional competence. Recently the NASW (which administers the ACSW) also developed a "diplomate" designation, which identifies practitioners with skills above those required for the ACSW. Credentials such as the ACSW serve the function of distinguishing expertise among members of the professional community. But again, such credentials are determined by policies of the professional community and not by a public authority, as in the case of state licensure.[116]

Clinicians who successfully cultivate private practices stand to do quite well economically. Financial gain does not appear to be the sole motivation for social workers who enter private practice, however. In research on the motives of private social work practitioners versus social workers employed in agencies, Jayaratne and his associates concluded that stress reduction played an important part in the decision to go private. "Those in private practice reported fewer psychological and health strains, reported higher levels of performance, and, in general, felt better about their life circumstances," concluded the researchers. "On every measure, those in private practice scored significantly better than those in agency practice."[117]

Despite the popularity of private practice, it has provoked a great deal of controversy within the professional community. There are several aspects to this controversy, not the least of which is that many practitioners who have committed themselves to helping the disadvantaged by working in voluntary and governmental sectors view the instant popularity of private practice as antithetical to everything that is "social" about social work.

Donald Feldstein, head of the Federation of Jewish Philanthropies of New York, suggested years ago that private social work practice is similar to private medical practice in that it presents "new opportunities for rip-offs by the privileged." Private practice, he maintained, was replacing social decision making with market decision making. According to Feldstein, "Social decision making is preferable to marketing human services like soap. . . .The private practice of social work is still against everything that is social about the term social work."[119] Another critic impugned the motives of social workers in private practice:

> Over 15 years ago, when I first had exposure to private practitioners, they were objects of envy, never of nonacceptance. Obviously this envy has continued. For we see more social workers developing private practices. But why all the sham? Let's be honest enough to say it's usually done for the money.[120]

Defenders of private practice emphasize the benefits of the method for practitioners and clients. Why should social workers not enjoy the same professional freedom and responsibility as other professions that use private practice extensively; for instance, law, medicine, and psychiatry? Moreover, "some clients prefer the opportunity to choose their own practitioner and a service they consider more personal and confidential."[121] Concern for the client's perceptions means that practitioners must be concerned about their image. This is evident in one privately practicing social worker's description of her office:

> It is decorated with comfortable chairs, built-in book cases, soft lighting, etc., and is arranged in such a way as to offer several different possibilities for seating. It is commensurate with most of the socio-cultural levels of my client group and provides him or her the opportunity for free expression without being overheard. . . . Dealing with only one socio-cultural client group allows me to provide physical surroundings which facilitate the client's identification with the worker.[122]

On the surface, then, private practice often provokes strong responses from welfare professionals, who perceive private practitioners as avoiding efforts by the voluntary and governmental sectors to advance social equity. On the other hand, some private practitioners believe that their work offers them an opportunity not only to enhance their status but also to provide mental health services to a middle class that the profession has neglected.

Beneath this surface issue, there are more substantive problems raised by private practice. Perhaps the most important of these is "preferential selection," the practice of selecting certain clients for service while rejecting others. In an era of specialization, professionals will refer to other providers clients with problems that are inappropriate for their practice. An important finding of Jayaratne's research was that private practitioners do not perceive their clients in the same way that agency-based social workers do. The latter "were significantly more likely to agree with the statement that 'my personal values and those of my clients differ greatly' than those in private practice."[123] Preferential selection becomes an issue when private practitioners elect to serve less troubled clients (who are able to pay the full cost of care) while referring multiproblem clients (who are unable to pay the practitioner's fee for service directly or through insurance) to agencies of the voluntary sector. Such "creaming" of the client population places an enormous burden on public agencies, which are left to carry a disproportionate share of chronically disturbed and indigent clients. In effect, then, the public sector absorbs the losses that private practitioners would suffer if they served this population. Preferential selection has become so pronounced that researchers have facetiously identified it as a syndrome. According to Franklin Chu and Sharland Trotter, the commercialization of private practice contributes to the **YAVIS syndrome**—the tendency of clients of private practitioners to be *young, attractive, verbal, intelligent,* and *successful.* One might add *W* to the syndrome, because the clients also tend to be disproportionately white.[124] Consequently, clients of private practitioners are less likely to be poor, unemployed, old, and uneducated.

The Business of Private Practice

Aside from preferential selection, another set of issues relates directly to the business nature of private practice. Because private practice is a business, economic considerations figure prominently in a professional's activities. Robert Barker, an authority on private social work practice, explains how economic factors shaped a new practice he established with a colleague: "We hired a good secretary, employed interior decorators to redo our offices and waiting room. We hired an investment counselor and established retirement accounts and insurance programs. Most of all we became more serious about getting our clients to meet their financial obligations."[125]

The market nature of private practice, coupled with economic entrepreneurship, presents the possibility of questionable accounting practices, such as the creation of "uncollectible accounts," the use of "deliberate misdiagnosis," and the practice of "signing off." These practices involve income derived from third-party sources, usually health insurance. As private practitioners become more dependent on insurance reimbursement, these questionable accounting practices become important for the professional community at large.

Health insurance frequently covers outpatient psychiatric care at a **usual, customary and reasonable (UCR)** rate that is determined by the insurance companies. The UCR is what the therapist charges, not necessarily what he or she expects to collect from cash-paying clients. The practice of charging a fee higher than what is expected to be collected is termed holding an "uncollectible account," and it is frequently used with third-party fee payment arrangements. This practice is encouraged because insurance coverage rarely covers all of the practitioner's fee but leaves a certain percent to be paid by the client. For example, a social worker may have a UCR of $50 per session. The client may have insurance paying only 50 percent of the UCR, which leaves the client responsible for the remaining $25. If the client is unable to pay $25 per session but can afford $10, a clinician will bill the insurance company directly, using an assignment of benefits procedure, for $50. Meanwhile, the client pays $10 per session, as opposed to the implied obligatory contractual amount of $25. Although the therapist may collect a total of $35 per session and not the UCR of $50, it may be economical to prefer that amount over an extended period of treatment or possibly until the client can afford the full amount of the copayment. At question here is a professional practice that is contrary to the implied contractual relationship among the client, the clinician, and the third-party payer. Yet it is in the interest of the clinician to establish this as a regular accounting procedure; the clinician depends on income from fees and may fear that the insurance company will lower the UCR if a significant number of billings (usually 50 percent) are below the customary rate.

A second questionable practice is **deliberate misdiagnosis,** an intentional error in client assessment on the part of clinicians. In a survey of clinical social workers, 70 percent of whom had engaged in private practice, Stuart Kirk and Herb Kutchins found that 87 percent of practitioners frequently or occasionally used a less stigmatizing, or "mercy," diagnosis to avoid labeling their patients. On the other hand, clinicians also frequently misdiagnose in order to collect insurance payments.

Seventy-two percent of the respondents are aware of cases where more serious diagnoses are used to qualify for reimbursement. At least 25 percent of the respondents . . . indicated that the practices occurred frequently. Since reimbursement is rarely available for family problems, it is not surprising that 86 percent are aware of instances when diagnoses for individuals are used even though the primary problem is in the family. The majority of respondents said that this occurred frequently.[126]

Of course, such "overdiagnosis" is unethical, because it places the economic benefit of the clinician before the service needs of the client. Still, overdiagnosis continues to be a prevalent practice. Kirk and Kutchins suggest that "reimbursement systems, which have become increasingly important for psychiatric treatment for the last decade, are undoubtedly a major factor in encouraging over-diagnosis."[127] The undesirable consequences of a reimbursement-driven diagnosis system are multiple. First, of course, is the possibility that clients will be done harm, particularly if confidentiality is breached and the diagnosis becomes known to others outside the therapeutic relationship. Second, if the prevalence of severe mental disorders is overreported, public officials may make errors in program planning as a result. Third, and perhaps most important, overdiagnosis violates the "professionals' obligation to their profession to use their knowledge and skill in an ethical manner."[128] To be sure, individual digressions can be reported to professional and governmental bodies for investigation; but a greater problem exists for practitioners as a whole. Widespread misdiagnosis violates the social contract between the professional community and the state, and thus threatens to "corrupt the helping professions."[129] For these reasons, ethical problems associated with the relationship between diagnosis and reimbursement are of greater concern to the professional community.[130]

Finally, there is the practice of signing off. Signing off has become important because some insurance covers only services provided by psychiatrists or psychologists. In other instances, insurance will reimburse at a higher rate when the services are provided by a psychiatrist or psychologist than when they are rendered by a social worker. The sign-off practice is one in which, in order to maximize reimbursement, the psychiatrist or psychologist signs the insurance claim even though the services were provided by a social worker. In some instances psychiatrists and psychologists may recruit social workers, paying them half the fees charged to insurance companies and pocketing the difference. Signing off is a type of fee splitting, and it is "unethical because it allows practitioners to refer clients not to the professional most suitable for the client's needs, but to the person who pays the highest fee."[131]

In a community in which many private practitioners compete for a limited number of paying clients, aggressive business practices are likely to exacerbate questions about the ultimate concern of practitioners—whether it is the client's welfare or the clinician's income. Although the question is not ordinarily couched in such crude terms, the behavior of private practitioners may not be lost on the client population. Because clients usually seek services voluntarily, their impressions of practitioners are important; negative perceptions will eventually hurt practitioners as their clients seek services elsewhere. When unfavorable impressions emerge as a result of the practices described, practitioners will be prudent to take corrective action. Although the ethical code of the professional community can be a source for such action, much remains at the discretion of the individual practitioner.

Private practice is literally *private*, and practitioners enjoy "substantial discretion in conducting their activities."[132] Economic and other considerations may encourage private practitioners to engage in unethical or questionable practices. In such instances, other practitioners are obliged to report allegations of violations to the state licensing board or the professional association. Ultimately, it is in the interest of the professional community to address questionable practices of practitioners, and this includes the unethical business practices of private practitioners. When the media report that "routine falsification of insurance billings and other peculiarities of the mental health professions have caused acute anxiety among insurance companies . . . [who] now think they have little control over what they are paying for," more government regulation is probably not far behind.[133] In other instances the consequences are acutely embarrassing for the professional community, as when a leading proponent of third-party reimbursement for social workers in Kentucky was found guilty of insurance fraud and ordered to return $37,000 to Blue Cross–Blue Shield.[134]

The Future of the Private Sector

In response to the adverse circumstances besetting the profession, many human service professionals have turned to private practice as a way of securing their economic and professional objectives. Private practice gives program administrators a chance to maintain their direct service skills, educators the opportunity to continue contact with clients, and clinicians with families the freedom to combine professional practice and attention to family life. More important, private practice may prove an adjunct to agency activities. "By fostering part-time practice," researchers have noted, "the profession can keep its main focus on agency services where there is a commitment to serve persons without regard to their ability to pay and where there can be a basis for social action and reform."[135]

As the growth of managed care illustrates, much of private practice is a result of larger social forces. Ellen Dunbar, executive director of the California chapter of NASW, observed that "The major overriding trend that engulfs all others is that social work along with other service professions is becoming more commercial . . . [and] more an integral part of the free enterprise system."[136] In fact, the commercialization of social work attracted wide attention as the profession became more immersed in private practice. "There is concern," reported *Newsweek* magazine, "that too many social workers are turning their backs on their traditional casework among the poor to practice therapy." *Newsweek* wondered at the consequences of "an apparent middle-class therapy explosion at the expense of public welfare and grassroots service."[137] How social work will reconcile its commitment to social justice with the new opportunities presented by private practice remains a central question before the professional community.

The interest in alternative methods of service delivery represents an implicit criticism of traditional ways in which social agencies provide services. First, traditional agencies place constraints on employee discretion and professional autonomy. Second, rigid agency policies make few allowances for the demands of an employee's family life and community involvements. Third, the demands of increasing caseloads compounded by diminishing resources make traditional agencies a less desirable setting in which to practice. Although nonprofit agencies have been superior to governmental programs in the quality of services provided, these traditional auspices of service delivery are beginning to merge. Consequently, social work in smaller, voluntary agencies is not very different from the "proletarianized" work in larger, public agencies.[138] To the extent that traditional agencies become less desirable as contexts in which to practice, innovative models of service delivery surface.

As researchers on private practice have noted, rather than criticizing professionals who have opted for the private sector, the social work community should make it a priority to reform the means of service provision through traditional agencies. "The goal should be to make agency practice good for the health and well-being of the practitioner, because the ultimate beneficiary would be the client," Jayaratne and his colleagues comment.[139] Stan Taubman, who has held direct practice and administrative positions and who couples county employment with private practice, states the matter succinctly: "Private practice isn't keeping social workers out of public services. Public services are."[140]

One service delivery innovation has been **Employee Assistance Plans** (EAPs). Since the 1970s, social workers have been involved in EAPs that provide a range of services to workers, a population often neglected by traditional welfare programs.[141] By the late 1980s, occupational social welfare had become a popular specialization within social work, with graduate schools offering special curricula on the subject, a national conference inaugurated for specialists in the field, and a special issue of *Social Work* dedicated to it.[142] Although studies of EAPs are scarce,[143] there is evidence that occupational social work is likely to expand, particularly when located within the corporation. In a modest study of 23 "private-sector, management-sponsored" EAPs, Shulamith Straussner found that in-house programs demonstrated notable advantages over those contracted out. For example, EAPs located within the corporation cost one-third as much as contracted-out services. In-house EAPs proved adaptable to management priorities, developing "short-term programs to deal with company reorganization or retrenchment, special health concerns . . . [and] other organizational needs." Significantly, union representatives approved in-house EAPs twice as frequently as they did contracted-out programs.[144] These findings suggest that EAPs that are managed by employers are perceived by management and unions as superior to services provided by an external agency. If corporate executives and labor leaders develop personnel policies consistent with these findings, welfare professionals will find the business community a hospitable setting in which to practice. In that event, occupational social work within the corporation may become as prevalent an auspice of practice as the voluntary and governmental sectors are.

Another service delivery innovation is employee ownership. Curiously, human service professionals have frequently advocated employee ownership as a method for empowering clients, yet fail to see comparable benefits for themselves. For example, Cooperative Home Care Associates (CHCA) of New York City has been co-owned by some 170 employees since its inception in 1985. CHCA offers above-average wages as well as health and vacation benefits and has, as a result, served as a vehicle out of poverty for many workers who had been on public assistance.[145]

An as yet unexplored innovation for human service professionals is the Employee Stock Option Plan (ESOP). Through ESOPs workers gain ownership of a firm by gradually acquiring stock, the acquisition of which is granted certain tax advantages. By 1990 ESOPs had been used to leverage the transfer of 11,000 companies to 12 million employees. Workers had used ESOPs to purchase wholly or in part several large corporations, such as J. C. Penney, Kroger's, Avis, and United Airlines.[146] Inexplicably, human service professionals had not used ESOPs to gain control over the organizations that employ them. In part this can be explained by the fact that the traditional auspices of practice have been the nonprofit and governmental sectors: It may seem implausible for Department of Social Service employees to seek ownership of the local welfare department or for professionals hired by the local Family Service Agency to acquire that organization. Nevertheless, recent trends in privatization make employee ownership more probable.

In the absence of employee ownership alternatives, some private practitioners have undertaken competitive strategies vis-à-vis managed care corporations. In New York, 230 therapists belonging to the American Mental Health Alliance won a contract to serve 370,000 union members; Access Behavioral Care, Inc., a therapist-owned practice in Philadelphia, has served 3 million people since its creation in 1995; and Psych Management Inc., a proprietary firm of psychiatrists, has served more than 100,000 clients through Blue Cross–Blue Shield.[147] In other instances, private clinicians have reacted defensively. The Virginia, California, New Jersey, and District of Columbia chapters of the American Psychological Association have sued HMOs for restricting the number of therapeutic sessions, limiting out-of-network referrals, and purging provider lists.[148] It remains to be seen if social workers will join psychologists in challenging the prerogatives of managed care firms.

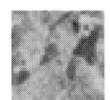

Conclusion

This chapter examined the provision of mental health services to the seriously mentally impaired and substance abuse policy. Both mental health and substance abuse policy are complex issues that speak to the various disconnects that characterize American social welfare policy. The mental health system is characterized by the devolution of mental health services to the states. Unfortunately, states are unwilling to pick up the costs for mental health services. Moreover, the aftermath of deinstitutionalization is still very evident with regard to homelessness and substance abuse. Beyond alcohol abuse is the problem of the war on drugs and the continued under-investment in treatment. It is unlikely that the new Bush administration will address most of these knotty issues.

 ## Discussion Questions

1. In the early 1980s funding for community mental health centers (CMHCs) was converted to mental health block grants. To what extent did your community evolve complete CMHCs? What has happened to them since the 1980s? What priorities have been established through the mental health block grant system? How has this changed mental health services in your community?

2. The misuse of psychoactive medication has been implicated in several undesirable consequences. Has tardive dyskinesia become a significant problem among mental health patients in your community? If so, what is being done to prevent it? Are more or fewer mental patients going through the "revolving door"?

3. The effects of substance abuse on innocent people present difficult policy dilemmas for decision makers. What policies could be put in place to prevent the birth of infants with FAS or AIDS? How could the rights of mothers be protected? What should be the role of human service professionals in such cases?

4. Prevention and treatment of substance abuse vary from locality to locality. What has your community done to dissuade young people from substance abuse? Have these initiatives been successful? According to what indicators?

5. What resources has your community committed to dealing with substance abuse? Have these resources been adequate? Which organizations support or oppose increasing treatment for substance abuse?

6. How many of the students in your social work program are planning on establishing themselves as clinical entrepreneurs? To what extent are social workers in your community engaged in private practice? How has managed care attenuated their economic viability?

 ## Notes

1. Jean Quam, "Dorothea Dix," *Encyclopedia of Social Work*, 18th ed. (Silver Spring, MD: NASW, 1987), p. 921.
2. Michael Lesy, *Wisconsin Death Trip* (New York: Pantheon, 1973), p. 33.
3. Ibid.
4. Stephen Gould, "Carrie Buck's Daughter," *Natural History* (July 1984), pp. 85–92.
5. Walter Trattner, *From Poor Law to Welfare State* (New York: Free Press, 1974), p. 175.
6. Joint Commission on Mental Illness and Health, *Action for Mental Health* (New York: Basic Books, 1961).
7. David Mechanic, *Mental Health and Social Policy* (Englewood Cliffs, NJ: Prentice-Hall, 1969), pp. 59–60.
8. Henry Foley, *Community Mental Health Legislation* (Lexington, MA: D.C. Heath, 1975), pp. 13–14.
9. Ibid., pp. 39, 40.

10. Bernard Bloom, *Community Mental Health* (Monterey, CA: Brooks/Cole, 1977), pp. 74–75.

11. National Institute of Mental Health, *Community Mental Health Centers Program Operating Handbook* (Washington, DC: U.S. Department of Health, Education, and Welfare, 1971), pp. 2–6.

12. Foley, *Community Mental Health Legislation*, p. 126.

13. The description of CMHCs is derived from the *Community Mental Health Centers Policy and Standards Manual*, 1988; see National Institutes of Health, *Community Mental Health Centers Program Operating Handbook*, (Washington, DC: Department of Health, Education, & Welfare, 1989).

14. Bloom, *Community Mental Health*, pp. 46–56.

15. U.S. Census Bureau, *Statistical Abstract of the United States*, 108th ed. (Washington, DC: U.S. Government Printing Office, 1987), p. 104.

16. Andrew Scull, *Decarceration* (Englewood Cliffs, NJ: Prentice-Hall, 1977), p. 71.

17. Ibid., p. 69.

18. Donald Stedman, "Politics, Political Structures, and Advocacy Activities," in James Paul, Donald Stedman, and G. Ronald Neufeld (eds.), *Deinstitutionalization* (Syracuse, NY: Syracuse University Press, 1977), p. 57.

19. E. Fuller Torrey and Mary T. Zdanowicz, "Deinstitutionalization Hasn't Worked," *Washington Post* (July 9, 1999), p. A29.

20. Alan Stone, *Law, Psychiatry, and Morality* (Washington, DC: American Psychiatry Press, 1984), pp. 116, 117.

21. Jean Isaac Rael, " 'Right' to Madness: A Cruel Hoax," *Los Angeles Times* (December 14, 1990), p. E5.

22. Uri Aviram, "Community Care of the Seriously Mentally Ill," *Community Mental Health Journal* 26, no. 1 (February 1990), pp. 23–31.

23. Peter Koenig, "The Problem That Can't Be Tranquilized," *The New York Times Magazine*, (May 21, 1978), p. 15.

24. Ellen Bassuk and Samuel Gerson, "Deinstitutionalization and Mental Health Services," *Scientific American* 238, no. 2 (February 1978), p. 18.

25. Steven Segal, "Deinstitutionalization," *Encyclopedia of Social Work*, 18th ed. (Silver Spring, MD: NASW, 1987), p. 378.

26. Per September 22, 1988, conversation with Joanne Atay, research associate, author of Division of Biometry and Applied Sciences, *Additions and Resident Patients at End of Year, State and County Mental Hospitals, by Diagnosis and State* (Rockville, MD: National Institute of Mental Health, 1988).

27. Steven Segal, "Deinstitutionalization," *Encyclopedia of Social Work*, 19th ed. (Washington, DC: NASW, 1995), p. 706.

28. "State Blamed for 3 Deaths at Mental Hospitals," *Los Angeles Times* (October 2, 1991), p. A4.

29. Eric Weiss, "Mental Patients' Deaths Probed," *Washington Post* (October 11, 1998), p. A28.

30. Cited in Glenn Yank, David Hargrove, and King Davis, "Toward the Financial Integration of Public Mental Health Services," *Community Mental Health Journal* 8, no. 2 (April 1992), p. 99.

31. Joseph Sacks, John Phillips, and Gordon Cappelletty, "Characteristics of the Homeless Mentally Disordered Population in Fresno County," *Community Mental Health Journal* (Summer 1987), p. 114.

32. "Survey of Homeless Shows Mental Illness and Addiction," *The New York Times* (September 10, 1989), p. 16.

33. "Homeless in America: A Statistical Profile," *The New York Times* (December 12, 1999), p. K3.

34. Hector Tobar, "Mentally Ill Turn to Crime in a Painful Call for Help," *Los Angeles Times* (August 26, 1991), p. A1.

35. Edward Walsh, "16% of State, Local Inmates Found Mentally Ill," *Washington Post* (July 12, 1999), p. A6.

36. Kari Lydersen, "For Jailed Mentally Ill, a Way Out," *Washington Post* (June 28, 2000), p. A3.

37. Raymond Bonner and Sara Rimer, "Executing the Mentally Retarded Even as Laws Begin to Shift," *The New York Times* (August 7, 2000), p. 1.

38. Benjamin Wieser, "My Name Is Not Robert," *The New York Times Magazine* (August 6, 2000), p. 34.

39. A. Anthony Arce and Michael Vergare, "Homelessness, the Chronic Mentally Ill and Community Mental Health Centers," *Community Mental Health Journal* (Winter 1987), p. 9.

40. Judith Larsen, "Community Mental Health Services in Transition," *Community Mental Health Journal* (Winter 1987), pp. 19, 20.

41. Trevor Hadley and Dennis Chulhane, "The Status of Community Mental Health Centers Ten Years into Block Grant Financing," *Community Mental Health Journal* (April 1993), p. 96.

42. Larsen, "Community Mental Health Services in Transition," p. 22.

43. Donald Woolson, "Policy Makes Short Shrift of Mentally Ill," *Los Angeles Times* (November 2, 1986), p. C4.

44. Hadley and Chulhane, "The Status of Community Mental Health Centers," p. 97.

45. Ronald Manderscheid and Mary Sonnenschein (eds.), *Mental Health, United States, 1994* (Rockville, MD, Substance Abuse and Mental Health Administration, 1994), pp. 38, 37.

46. Community for Creative Non-Violence, *Homelessness in America* (Washington, DC: CCNV, 1987).

47. Josh Barbanel, "Homeless Woman to be Released after Being Forcibly Hospitalized," *The New York Times* (January 19, 1988), p. 8.

48. Charles Krauthammer, "How to Save the Homeless Mentally Ill," *The New Republic* (February 8, 1988), p. 23.

49. Paul Stavis, "Treatment by Cooperation," *Washington Post* (August 19, 1999), p. A21.

50. "Developments in Mental Disability Law: 1986," *Clearinghouse Review* (January 20, 1987), p. 1148. Quoted in Ruta Wilk, "Involuntary Outpatient Commitment of the Mentally Ill," *Social Work* (March–April 1988), p. 133.

51. Michael Winerip, "Bedlam in the Streets," *The New York Times Magazine* (May 23, 1999).

52. Stavis, "Treatment by Cooperation," p. A21.

53. "Developments in Mental Disability Law: 1986," *Clearing House Review* (October 1988), p. 43; and Wilk, "Involuntary Outpatient Commitment" (note 50 above), p. 134.

54. Wilk, "Involuntary Outpatient Commitment," p. 136.

55. See, for example, Thomas Szasz, *The Myth of Mental Illness* (New York: Harper & Row, 1961) and David Ingleby (ed.), *Critical Psychiatry: The Politics of Mental Health* (New York: Pantheon, 1980).

56. *Physician's Desk Reference* (Oradell, NJ: Medical Economics Company, 1986), p. 2014.

57. Harris Chaiklin, "The New Homeless and Service Planning on a Professional Campus," 53rd Chancellor's Colloquium (Baltimore, MD: University of Maryland, December 4, 1985), p. 10.

58. Glenn Yank, David Hargrove, and King Davis, "Toward the Financial Integration of Public Mental Health Services," *Community Mental Health Journal* 28, no. 2 (April 1992), pp. 2–12.

59. Jon Christianson and Muriel Linehan, "Capitated Payments for Mental Health Care: The Rhode Island Programs," *Community Mental Health Journal* 25, no. 2 (Summer 1989), p. 122.

60. A. P. Schinnar, A. B. Rothbard, and T. R. Hadley, "Opportunities and Risks in Philadelphia's Capitation Financing of Public Psychiatric Services," *Community Mental Health Journal* 25, no. 4 (Winter 1989), p. 256.

61. Ibid., pp. 257–258.

62. Phyllis Marshall, "The Mental Health HMO: Capitation Funding for the Chronically Mentally Ill. Why an HMO?" *Community Mental Health Journal* 28, no. 2 (April 1992), pp. 9–14.

63. David Stoesz, "Human Service Corporations: New Opportunities for Administration in Social Work," *Administration in Social Work* (Fall 1993), pp. 8–16.

64. Charles Rapp and Ronna Chamberlain, "Case Management Services for the Chronically Mentally Ill," *Social Work* (September–October 1985), p. 417.

65. Barry Meier, "A Price Too High?" *The New York Times* (February 16, 2000), p. C1.

66. T. M. Luhrman, *Of Two Minds: The Growing Disorder in American Psychiatry* (New York: Knopf, 2000).

67. R. Thomas Riggs, "HMOs and the Seriously Mentally Ill—a View from the Trenches," *Community Mental Health Journal* 32, no. 3 (June 1966), p. 214.

68. Patricia Backlar, "Managed Mental Health Care: Conflicts of Interest in the Provider/Client Relationship," *Community Mental Health Journal* 32, no. 2 (April 1996), p. 104.

69. Kari Lydersen, "For Jailed Mentally Ill, a Way Out," *Washington Post* (June 28, 2000), p. A3.

70. Janenne Allen and Richard Boettcher, "Passing a Mental Health Levy," *Journal of Community Practice* 7, no. 3 (2000).

71. Charles Hall, "What Price Peace of Mind?" *Washington Post* (April 23, 1996), p. A7.

72. Agnes Hatfield, "The National Alliance for the Mentally Ill: A Decade Later," *Community Mental Health Journal* 27, no. 2 (April 1991), pp. 89–106.

73. Robert Samuelson, "Mental Health's Gray Areas," *Washington Post Weekly* (June 10–16, 1996), p. 5.

74. Helen Dewar and Judith Havemann, "Conferees Expand Insurance for New Mothers, Mentally Ill," *Washington Post* (September 20, 1996), p. A1.

75. Stuart Auerbach, "The Cost of Increased Coverage," *Washington Post Weekly* (September 30–October 6, 1996), p. 19.

76. "Mental Health Parity" (Washington, DC: General Accounting Office, May 10, 2000).

77. Mathea Falco, *The Making of a Drug-Free America* (New York: Times Books, 1992), p. 24.

78. Mathea Falco, *Winning the Drug War* (New York: Priority Press, 1989), pp. 19–20.

79. David Simon and Edward Burns, *The Corner: A Year in the Life of an Inner-City Neighborhood* (New York: Broadway Books, 2000).

80. *Alcohol and Health: Seventh Special Report to the U.S. Congress* (Washington, DC: U.S. Government Printing Office, 1990), p. 14.

81. "1999 National Household Survey on Drug Abuse" (Washington, DC: Substance Abuse and Mental Health Services Administration, 2000).

82. *Alcohol and Health: Sixth Special Report to the U.S. Congress* (Washington, DC: Department of Health and Human Services, 1987), p. 13.

83. *1997 Survey of Correctional Facilities* (Washington, DC: Substance Abuse and Mental Health Services Administration, 1997).

84. *Alcohol and Health: Seventh Special Report to the U.S. Congress,* p. 165.

85. Ibid., pp. 140, 139.

86. Ibid., p. 139.

87. Louise Erdrich, "Foreword," in Michael Dorris, *The Broken Cord* (New York: Harper & Row, 1989), p. xviii.

88. Charles Krauthammer, "The Horror of Addicted Newborns," *San Diego Tribune* (July 31, 1992), p. B7.

89. Ellen Goodman, "Community Begs Off, but Prosecutes Mom," *Los Angeles Times* (February 9, 1992), p. B9.

90. Department of Health and Human Services, *Compulsory Treatment of Drug Abuse* (Washington, DC: U.S. Government Printing Office, 1989).

91. Edward Walsh, "In Case against Alcoholic Mother, Underlying Issue Is Fetal Rights," *Washington Post* (October 7, 1996), p. A4.

92. Charles Lane, "Court Hears Drug-Test Arguments," *Washington Post* (October 5, 2000), p. A10.

93. "1999 National Household Survey on Drug Abuse."

94. Carl Leukefeld and Frank Tims, "An Introduction to Compulsory Treatment for Drug Abuse: Clinical Practice and Research," in *Compulsory Treatment of Drug Abuse: Research and Clinical Practice* (Rockville, MD: Department of Health and Human Services, 1988), p. 2.

95. Falco, *The Making of a Drug-Free America,* Chaps. 3 and 4.

96. Derek Mason, Mark Lusk, and Michael Gintzler, "Beyond Ideology in Drug Policy: The Primary Prevention Model," *Journal of Drug Issues* 22, no. 4 (Fall 1992), pp. 81–89.

97. Barry Bearak, "Road to Detox: Do Not Enter," *Los Angeles Times* (September 30, 1992), p. A1.

98. Center on Addiction and Substance Abuse, *The Cost of Substance Abuse to America's Health Care System* (New York: Center on Addiction and Substance Abuse, 1993), pp. 33, 42.

99. *National Treatment Improvement Evaluation Study* (Washington, D.C.: Substance Abuse and Mental Health Services Administration, 1997).

100. Harry Specht and Mark Courtney, *Unfaithful Angels* (New York: Free Press, 1994), p. 8.

101. "1999 Full-Time Social Work Income" (Washington, DC: NASW, Practice Research Network, 2000).

102. Margaret Gibelman, *Who We Are: A Second Look* (2nd ed.) (Washington, DC: NASW, 1996), p. 69.

103. National Association of Social Workers, "Data on Practice Auspice" (Washington, DC: NASW, August 2000).

104. Philip Brown and Robert Barker, "Confronting the 'Threat' of Private Practice," *Journal of Social Work Education* 31, no. 1 (Winter 1995), p. 106.

105. Srinika Jayaratne, Kristine Siefert, and Wayne Chess, "Private and Agency Practitioners: Some Data and Observations," *Social Service Review* 62 (June 1988), p. 331.

106. Margaret Gibelman and Philip Schervish, *What We Earn: 1993 NASW Salary Survey* (Washington, DC: NASW, 1993), pp. 25, 27.

107. Diane Vinokur-Kaplan, Srinika Jayaratne, and Wayne Chess, "Job Satisfaction and Retention of Social Workers in Public Agencies, Non-Profit Agencies and Private Practice," *Administration in Social Work* 18, no. 3 (1994), p. 103.

108. Gibelman and Schervish, *What We Earn*, p. 32.

109. Vinokur-Kaplan, Jayaratne, and Chess, "Job Satisfaction," p. 103.

110. Ibid., p. 329.

111. Ibid.

112. Although Mark Courtney notes that a de facto private practice can be identified much earlier: "Psychiatric Social Workers and the Early Days of Private Practice," *Social Service Review* (June 1992), pp. 95–105.

113. M. A. Golton, "Private Practice in Social Work," *Encyclopedia of Social Work* (Silver Spring, MD: NASW, 1973), p. 949.

114. Walter Trattner, *From Poor Law to Welfare State* (New York: Free Press, 1974), p. 250.

115. Gibelman, *Who We Are*, pp. 65, 73.

116. For details on state licensure and professional certification, see Robert Barker, "Private and Proprietary Services," *Encyclopedia of Social Work*, 18th ed., Silver Spring, MD: NASW, 1987).

117. Srinika Jayaratne, Mary Lou Davis Sacks, and Wayne Chess, "Private Practice May Be Good for Your Health and Well-Being," *Social Work* 36 (May 1991), pp. 226–227.

118. Jae-Sung Choi, "Members' Views on the California Licensing System for Social Work Practice" (Sacramento: NASW, California Chapter, 1990), p. 6.

119. Donald Feldstein, "Debate on Private Practice," *Social Work* 22, no. 3 (1977), p. 3.

120. Ibid., p. 4.

121. Patricia Kelley and Paul Alexander, "Part-Time Private Practice: Practical and Ethical Considerations," *Social Work* 30, no. 3 (May–June 1985), p. 255.

122. N. T. Edwards, "The Survival of Structure and Function in Private Practice," *Journal of the Otto Rank Association* 13 (1979), pp. 12, 15.

123. Jayaratne, Sacks, and Chess, "Private Practice May Be Good for Your Health," pp. 228–229.

124. Franklin Chu and Sharland Trotter, *The Madness Establishment* (New York: Grossman, 1974), p. 61.

125. Robert Barker, *The Business of Psychotherapy* (New York: Columbia University Press, 1982), p. xi.

126. Stuart Kirk and Herb Kutchins, "Deliberate Misdiagnosis in Mental Health Practice," *Social Service Review* 62 (June 1988), p. 230.

127. Ibid., p. 234.

128. Ibid., pp. 232, 234–235.

129. Ibid., p. 235.

130. Kimberly Strom, "Reimbursement Demands and Treatment Decisions: A Growing Dilemma for Social Workers," *Social Work* 37 (September 1992), p. 18.

131. Robert Barker, *Social Work in Private Practice* (Silver Spring, MD: NASW, 1984), p. 113.

132. Kirk and Kutchins, "Deliberate Misdiagnosis in Mental Health Practice," p. 232.

133. Kathy Sawyer, "Insuring the Bureaucracy's Mental Health," *Washington Post* (April 10, 1979), p. A8.

134. " 'Signing Off' Fraud Charge Warns Kentucky Clinicians," *NASW News* 32, no. 6 (June 1987), p. 1.

135. Kelley and Alexander, "Part-Time Private Practice," p. 254.

136. Ellen Dunbar, "Future of Social Work," *NASW California News* 13, no. 18 (May 1987), p. 3.

137. David Gelman, "Growing Pains for the Shrinks," *Newsweek* (December 14, 1987), p. 71.

138. Michael Fabricant and Steven Burghardt, *The Welfare State Crisis and the Transformation of Social Service Work* (Armonk, NY: M. E. Sharpe, 1992).

139. Jayaratne, Davis Sacks, and Chess, "Private Practice May Be Good for Your Health," p. 229.

140. Stan Taubman, "Private Practice! Oh No!" *NASW California News* (March 1991), p. 8.

141. See Sheila Akabas, Paul Kurzman, and Norman Kolben (eds.), *Labor and Industrial Settings: Sites for Social Work Practice* (New

York: Council on Social Work Education, 1979); Martha Ozawa, "Development of Social Services in Industry: Why and How?" *Social Work* 25 (November 1980), pp. 86–93; and Dale Masi, *Human Services in Industry* (Lexington, MA: D. C. Heath, 1982).

142. "Social Work in Industrial Settings," *Social Work* 33 (January–February 1988), p. 65.

143. But see J. Decker, R. Starrett, and J. Redhorse, "Evaluating the Cost-Effectiveness of Employee Assistance Programs," *Social Work* 31 (September–October 1986), p. 83.

144. Shulamith Straussner, "Comparison of In-House and Contracted-Out Employee Assistance Programs," *Social Work* 33 (January–February 1988), p. 53.

145. Francis Lappe and P. M. Dubois, *The Quickening of America: Rebuilding Our Nation, Remaking Our Lives* (San Francisco: Jossey-Bass, 1994).

146. Ibid.

147. Nancy Jeffrey, "A New Balancing Act for Psychotherapy," *Wall Street Journal* (January 5, 1998).

148. Lucette Lagnado and Nancy Jeffrey, "Psychologists Sue over Managed Care," *Wall Street Journal* (December 11, 1998).

chapter 14

Criminal Justice

This chapter provides an overview of crime and corrections in the United States, beginning with the history of U.S. criminal justice. Chapter sections explore the roles of various governmental jurisdictions in criminal justice; recent data on crime and justice expenditures; important developments and issues that include juvenile justice, the underclass and crime, the War on Drugs, and the "new penology"; and the future of criminal justice in this country.

All societies respond to norm-defying behavior through sanctions, though there is considerable variation among the penalties societies apply to specific behaviors. In Western cultures irrational deviance is usually understood as a mental health matter, whereas anormative behavior on the part of a rational actor falls under the purview of law enforcement. In either case, deviance is of interest to human service professionals, because clients often present anormative activity. Deviance is also an issue of social justice, because poor people and minorities of color are disproportionately represented among those incarcerated in mental or correctional institutions.

History of U.S. Criminal Justice

Modern criminal justice in the United States can be traced to the faith in social science that originated in the West in the eighteenth century. Before the advent of classical criminology, justice was predicated on vengeance: Illegal acts brought the wrath of authority on the deviant. In premodern societies in which deviance was understood to be a product of evil influences, vicious and barbaric methods were justified as ways to excise Satan or to maintain archaic social structures. Thus, mutilation, torture, and capital punishment were often employed, some-

times in grotesque public displays, in order to rid society of malevolent influences.

Modern criminology dates from the Enlightenment of the eighteenth century and its notion that humankind was capable of producing the methods for its own perfectibility. The radical jurist and philosopher Jeremy Bentham (1748–1832) contended that scientific methods could be the vehicle for "the rational improvement of the condition of men." Accordingly, Bentham successfully advocated a series of reform laws in Great Britain, including several pertinent to penal institutions.[1] In the United States, Cesare Beccaria applied Bentham's utilitarian philosophy to corrections, arguing that crime could be measured in its severity, that prevention was more important than punishment, that the purpose of punishment was deterrence (not revenge), and that incarceration should segregate prisoners so as not to exacerbate lawlessness.[2] Thus, liberal, humanistic values in criminal justice can be traced to the earliest thinkers in criminology.

Nevertheless, the early American colonists had imported traditional European thinking about crime and its control. Jails were a fixture of all settlements of any size, and justice was often swift and uncompromising. In 1776, in response to the dungeonlike facilities that typified colonial America, the Quakers established the Philadelphia Society for Alleviating the Miseries of Public Prisons.[3] During the following decades, institutional reformers such as Dorothea Dix sought to make jails and almshouses more humane. Unfortunately, the reformer's accomplishments were often subverted. An influx of immigrants, many of whom were unable to adjust to the American experience, became incarcerated in mental and correctional institutions. An American ethos of rugged individualism left little room for compassion, particularly when adults were concerned. In 1854 President Franklin Pierce vetoed legislation that would have involved the federal government in institutional care for people with mental illness, effectively leaving institutional control of deviants in the hands of the states.

Midway through the nineteenth century, an unlikely pioneer in U.S. corrections emerged. In 1841 a Boston shoemaker, John Augustus, agreed to supervise petty criminals, post bail, and report to the courts on his progress with the offenders' rehabilitation. The services provided by Augustus were less expensive than prison, and many of his charges seemed to benefit from rehabilitation—all the more so because Augustus used his own money. Thus, a modest shoemaker began what was to become a nationwide system of probation.[4]

Some early criminologists sought more direct applications of emerging sciences to the study of crime. The Italian psychiatrist Cesare Lombroso, for example, proposed the existence of a "criminal type," a construct of inferior intelligence, exaggerated physical features, and a taste for amoral activities—including tattooing. The idea that a criminal could be physiologically identifiable and criminal behavior genetically transmitted has preoccupied some criminologists ever since Lombroso. For example, in 1913 Charles Goring studied English convicts, and during the 1920s Earnest Hooton evaluated American criminals; both concluded that prisoners were "organically inferior" to their law-abiding compatriots.

The notion of a genetic origin of deviant behavior was popularized by the eugenics movement shortly after the turn of the twentieth century. Proponents of natural selection, some of them esteemed scientists and jurists, convinced state legislators to pass legislation allowing for involuntary sterilization of "mental defectives." By the mid-1950s more than 58,000 mental patients and convicts had been forcibly sterilized.[5] The practice of involuntary sterilization abated during the Civil Rights movement when it became recognized that many of the victims were women and minorities of color. That most victims of the eugenics movement were disadvantaged populations was not coincidental. Race suffused the thinking of eugenicists, as Lombroso illustrated when he wrote in 1871 that "Only we white people have reached the most perfect symmetry of bodily form."[6]

The suggestion that crime was organically determined generated a firestorm of criticism during the 1960s when it was pointed out that an increasing number of criminals were minorities of color, the same populations that had been victimized by oppressive social policies. Despite this recognition, the contention that criminogenic behavior is hereditary continues to surface in the popular literature. A well-known popularization of genetically transmitted deviance was *The Bell Curve* (1994) by Richard Herrnstein and Charles Murray. The authors contended that, to a significant extent, poverty is hereditary; as a result, many social program expenditures are wasteful. Herrnstein and Murray argued that U.S. society is becoming stratified by intellectual ability, with a "cognitive elite" overseeing a degenerative underclass.[7] Another review of research on genetically transmitted crime revealed that heredity had a slightly positive influence on criminal behavior; however, the researcher suspected that future research would be more productive if it focused on the interaction between environment and genetic attributes.[8]

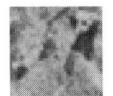 # The Criminal Justice System

The U.S. criminal justice system is similar to education and mental health in that states and localities provide a significantly larger portion of services than the federal government. The Constitution, of course, reserves public functions to the states unless they are ceded to the federal government; in the case of criminal justice, this means that state and local government expenditures exceed those of the federal government by a factor of four.[9] During the 1980s expenditures for criminal justice more than doubled, a fact that warrants clarification. Much of the increase was attributable to corrections (as opposed to police protection and judicial and legal costs) which, on a per capita basis, increased from $30.34 in 1980 to $123.40 in 1992, an increase of 306 percent. Moreover, there was considerable variation in state expenditures. In 1992, for example, the per capita cost of criminal justice in the District of Columbia was $1,184.60; that of nearby West Virginia was $117.30.[10] In summary, more resources were allocated to locking up inmates than to police protection or legal services; and wealthier jurisdictions spent substantially more than poorer ones on criminal justice.

Similarly, both rates of crime and types of offense have varied over time. From 1987 to 1997 crime decreased 2.5 percent, as shown in Table 14.1.

Crime dropped significantly from the early 1990s to the end of the decade; in 1999, 10 percent fewer violent crimes were committed than in 1998.[11] The reasons for this are unclear. Demographers have noted that younger, more crime-prone people are aging and are less likely to be violent as a result; the Clinton administration cited its crime policies. In all likelihood, the proliferation of a drug economy in inner cities, the easy availability of firearms, and escalating gang violence contribute to an increasing murder rate. Indeed, differentiating urban from rural locales reveals that even though violent crime has dropped in both, the crime rate in cities not only is higher than in rural areas, but also is well above the levels of 1969.[12] Nonetheless, the reduction in violent crime in cities, associated with a reduction in cocaine use, has sparked a renaissance of some neighborhoods.[13]

But how accurate are crime figures? Traditionally, crime data have been aggregated by the FBI from the reports of state and local law enforcement agencies in the form of the Uniform Crime Report (UCR). Since 1973, however, an annual National Crime Survey (NCS) has been conducted as an alternative to the UCR. By 1990

TABLE 14.1 ■ Crime and Crime Rates, by Type of Offense: 1987–1997

YEARS	NUMBER OF OFFENSES (IN THOUSANDS)					
	Total	*Murder*	*Rape*	*Robbery*	*Assault*	*Property Crime*
1987	13,509	20	92	518	855	12,025
1988	13,923	21	93	543	910	12,537
1989	15,251	22	95	578	952	12,605
1990	14,476	23	103	639	1,055	12,656
1991	14,873	25	107	688	1,093	12,961
1992	14,438	24	109	672	1,127	12,506
1993	14,145	25	106	660	1,136	12,219
1994	13,990	23	102	619	1,113	12,123
1995	13,863	22	98	581	1,099	12,064
1996	13,494	20	96	536	1,037	11,805
1997	13,175	18	96	498	1,022	11,540
PERCENT CHANGE						
1987 to 1997	−2.5%	−9.4%	5.5%	−3.8%	19.6%	−4.0%
1994 to 1995	−0.9	−7.3	−4.6	−6.1	−1.3	−0.6
1995 to 1996	−2.7	−8.8	−1.3	−7.8	−5.6	−2.1
1996 to 1997	−2.4	−7.6	−0.1	−7.0	−1.4	−2.2

Source: Adapted from U.S. Census Bureau, *Statistical Abstract of the United States, 1999* (Washington, DC: U.S. Government Printing Office, 1999), p. 214.

it was evident that quite different portraits of crime were emerging from the two compilations. With regard to burglary and auto theft, shortly after its inception the NCS reported significantly higher rates than the UCR, but the path of both surveys merged by the late 1980s. With regard to larceny and assault, the NCS and UCR diverged significantly over time, failing to merge.

In the case of rape, the results were even more perplexing. In 1973 the UCR rape rate was 24 per 100,000 population; the NCS rate was more than 50 percent higher at 38. By 1990 the surveys had reversed: The UCR reported more than 105 rapes per 100,000 population, but the NCS had dropped to 24. According to the UCR, rape had increased fourfold in 17 years, but the NCS documented a reduction of 50 percent. The data indicated that law enforcement authorities were escalating their campaign against sexual assault; at the same time, households were reporting a significant decline in rape. In their attempt to sort out the differences in UCR and NCS rape rates, Gary Jensen and Maryaltani Karpos speculated that an escalating UCR documentation led law enforcement to take rape more seriously, the results eventually yielding a suppression in the rape rate reported by the NCS.[14] If this explanation endures, it is rather dramatic evidence of the possibility of the deterrence of crime when victims, in this case women, press upon law enforcement, primarily men, the import of specific types of crime.

The Jensen and Karpos interpretation of the sharp downturn in rape has policy implications as well. For example, in 1994 the Violence Against Women Act (VAWA) was passed, and in the following year $26 million was allocated to the states, the first of $800 million over a five-year period.[15] During the period when the UCR documented reductions in rape, the incidence of child abuse—a different indicator of domestic violence—continued to climb. Thus, while domestic violence against women seemed to be diminishing, violence directed at children escalated. If law enforcement *is* effective at containing rape, then a case can be made for diverting funding to reduce domestic violence targeted at abused children.[16]

The disposition of offenders varies, of course. Those who have not been convicted of violent offenses and who have no previous criminal record are likely to be granted probation. Those who have been convicted of offenses under local or state jurisdiction may be jailed or imprisoned in facilities that have often been determined to violate minimal human standards of care. Federal convicts, on the other hand, may be incarcerated in prisons that are qualitatively better, some of which have a decidedly pleasant ambiance. Having served time for good behavior, many prisoners earn early release and go on parole, during which they must report regularly to a supervising officer. These various statuses are depicted in Table 14.2. In less than two decades the numbers of incarcerated offenders more than tripled.

Prisons have been a signal concern in criminal justice, both because of the cost of incarceration and because of what imprisonment rates say about the preponderance of serious precipitating offenses. Among the nations of the world the incarceration rate of the United States is second only to that of Russia. Russia imprisons 687 inmates per 100,000 population; the United States, 682. The rates for other nations are strikingly lower: South Africa 321, Canada 115, France 90, and Japan 39.[17] Beyond these figures, the United States passed a benchmark coinciding with the new millennium in 2000, when 2 million people were behind bars.[18] In this population, gender and race emerge prominently: Roughly 90 percent of inmates are men,[19] and two-thirds are minorities of color. Virtually half of all inmates are African American.[20]

Juvenile Justice

Juvenile justice is a significant feature of U.S. criminal justice for several reasons. Young deviants are good candidates for becoming adult deviants, in which case they become subject to the adult criminal justice system. Because the majority of adult offenders were also known to the juvenile justice system, it stands to reason

TABLE 14.2 ▪ Adults on Probation, in Jail or Prison, or on Parole

YEAR	TOTAL	PROBATION	JAIL	PRISON	PAROLE
1980	1,840,400	1,118,097	182,288	319,598	220,438
1981	2,006,600	1,225,934	195,085	360,029	225,539
1982	2,192,600	1,357,264	207,853	402,914	224,604
1983	2,475,100	1,582,947	221,815	423,898	246,440
1984	2,689,200	1,740,948	233,018	448,264	266,992
1985	3,011,400	1,968,712	254,986	487,953	300,203
1986	3,239,400	2,114,621	272,735	526,436	325,638
1987	3,459,600	2,247,158	294,092	562,814	355,505
1988	3,714,100	2,356,483	341,893	607,766	407,977
1989	4,055,600	2,522,125	393,303	683,367	456,803
1990	4,348,000	2,670,234	403,019	743,382	531,407
1991	4,535,600	2,728,472	424,129	792,535	590,442
1992	4,762,600	2,811,611	441,781	850,566	658,601
1993	4,944,000	2,903,061	455,500	909,381	676,100
1994	5,141,300	2,981,022	479,800	990,147	690,371
1995	5,355,100	3,077,861	499,300	1,078,541	679,421
1996	5,475,000	3,161,030	510,400	1,127,528	676,045
1997	5,690,700	3,261,888	557,974	1,185,800	685,033

Source: Adapted from U.S. Census Bureau, *Statistical Abstract of the United States, 1999* (Washington, DC: U.S. Government Printing Office, 1999), p. 233.

that diverting youngsters from juvenile crime may well keep them out of the adult criminal justice system. From a crime prevention standpoint, reaching young people early, when their understanding of themselves in relation to social norms is still being formed, is a more plausible strategy than attempting to intervene with adult offenders, who have a less malleable sense of themselves vis-à-vis social institutions.

The first institution for juvenile delinquency was the New York City House of Refuge established in 1825. Massachusetts followed suit with a boys' facility established in 1847 and one for girls in 1854.[21] These institutions paralleled other institutions designed to care for neglected children, such as Charles Loring Brace's New York Children's Aid Society, established in 1853. Such

institutions were not known for indulging children; furnishings were spartan, the discipline harsh, and escapes common. The orphanage/asylum for children became the subject of scathing parody under the pen of Charles Dickens. During the Progressive Era reformers contended that youth should be adjudicated separately from adults, and the first juvenile court was established in Chicago in 1899.[22]

Institutional care for adolescent deviants remained virtually unchanged until the 1960s, when critics of warehousing children advocated for community alternatives. In 1972 Congress passed the Juvenile Justice and Delinquency Prevention Act, a measure that intended, in part, to remove children who were "status offenders" from the more serious deviants who had actually committed felonies or violent crimes. According to Jerome Miller, a youth service advocate, the act ultimately failed. However, it gave impetus to those who were proponents of noninstitutional care for delinquents.

In 1969 Miller assumed the directorship of the Massachusetts Division of Youth Services (DYS), a position that was to become symbolic of correctional reform in the United States. A social worker, Miller had been an officer in the U.S. Air Force, trained in the Menninger Clinic, and earned a doctorate at Catholic University. His initial plan, to seek incremental reforms in Massachusetts, faded as the structural flaws of state juvenile justice became more apparent. All of the personnel positions were filled through political patronage, and very few human service professionals could be found at DYS. Staff routinely resorted to cruel and inhumane treatment—such as breaking fingers of escapees, smearing feces on incorrigibles, and placing miscreants in solitary confinement—that would have been unconstitutional in an adult institution. As Miller learned during his first months on the job, rather than instituting changes, staff and administration subverted attempts to make DYS more amenable to reform. The institutional conspiracy of DYS was becoming as evident as it was implacable. At the same time, Miller was becoming aware of a compelling research finding: The longer children were institutionalized in DYS facilities, the *more* likely they were to become more serious adult offenders. As Miller saw it, not only were his reforms being disregarded, but also he was managing an institution that made youth *worse.* This seemed especially counterproductive when it became evident that the vast majority of adolescents in DYS institutions were not violent felons but teens who had a knack for getting into trouble.

Miller responded to the intransigence of DYS staff with the most radical of plausible solutions: If DYS was not amenable to reform and continued to damage adolescents, the most conscionable act would be simply to close it down. Thus, over a period of months, Miller and a hand-picked staff discharged the children to alternative community-based care programs. With the exception of a handful of violence-prone adolescents, all of the youth were removed from DYS by the end of Miller's tenure in the 1970s.

The consequences of such an abrupt transformation were predictable. Legislators objected to closing DYS facilities, particularly when an institution was in a legislator's district and thereby an employer of constituents. Law-and-order activists condemned Miller for turning loose on the Massachusetts public the next generation of felons. Researchers recorded a different experience. Using recidivism as an outcome measure, Lloyd Ohlin and Bob Coates of Harvard's Center for Criminal Justice found that in districts of the state in which strong community-based alternatives had been deployed, recidivism was markedly lower.[23]

Eventually the Massachusetts experiment was to become a benchmark in juvenile justice in the United States, a case study used by several prominent professional schools. In writing a postscript on the experience, Miller targeted the indiscriminate labeling of youthful deviants by human service professionals who were oblivious to the fates their judgment brought on young offenders: "Our prisons and reform schools are filled with fabricated aliens made yet more alien by those who should know better, but who insufficiently understand the subjects of their research beyond narrow methodological parameters or highly controlled settings which demean and impoverish human experience."[24]

Incarceration as the intervention of choice for youthful offenders continues to be a source of disagreement within juvenile justice. Research on conventional as well as innovative programs yields mixed outcomes. An analysis of the closing of Maryland youth detention facilities revealed that youth who were not institutionalized had higher recidivism rates—although this held only for crimes against property, not for crimes against persons or involving drugs.[25]

Early proponents of another initiative, boot camps, promised that discipline, exercise, and routine would deter adolescents from future offending. At boot camp "inmates would receive physical training, military discipline, and drug abuse treatment, all under the direction of military personnel and with the aim of preparing them for a life that would combine . . . the requirement of regular drug tests and the opportunity for gainful employment."[26] By 1993 boot camps had been established in 25 states, but just as rapidly enthusiasm faded. A study of Georgia facilities commissioned by the Justice Department concluded that boot camps failed to deter young offenders.[27] In 1994 Connecticut closed its National Guard boot camp, citing "rampant gang activity, assaults on weaker inmates, marijuana use, sexual activity, and gambling."[28] An analysis of boot camps in 8 states concluded that alumni of boot camps were neither more nor less likely to commit future offenses.[29]

Despite the lack of success of boot camps, elected officials redoubled their efforts to contain what was perceived as an explosion in the number of juveniles who were engaged in violent crime. Many resorted to treating juvenile offenders as adults. Since 1992, 45 states have altered adjudication of juveniles in order to facilitate treating them as adults. "As a result, the number of youths under 18 held in adult prisons, and in many cases mixed in with adult criminals, has doubled in the last 10 years or so, from 3,400

in 1985 to 7,400 in 1997. Of the juveniles incarcerated on any given day, one in 10 are in adult jails or prisons."[30]

Many youth advocates objected to increasing the severity of punishment for adolescents, citing evidence that some violent juvenile crime was abating. As Table 14.3 shows, juvenile arrests have changed dramatically since 1980. Murder, rape, and robbery peaked during the mid-1990s but have since dropped back to levels proximate to those of 1980. On the other hand, arrests for sale and possession of illegal drugs show alarming increases; although arrests for selling drugs began to decline late in the 1990s, arrests for possession continue to climb.

Within a context of high juvenile crime and rampant drug use, Boston juvenile authorities imposed an innovation that sparked the interest of criminologists across the country. Under Operation Night Light, an aggressive initiative targeting high-risk youth, Boston juvenile authorities precipitated a reduction in youth homicides, which numbered 70 from 1992 through 1995, to zero from 1996 through 1998. As one journalist described the effort, "Juvenile law enforcement in Boston has become a community-

TABLE 14.3 ▪ Juvenile Arrests for Selected Offenses

OFFENSE	1980	1985	1990	1991	1992	1993	1994	1995	1996	1997
Violent crime	77,220	75,077	97,103	95,677	118,358	122,434	125,141	123,131	104,455	99,342
Murder	1,475	1,384	2,661	2,626	3,025	3,473	3,114	2,812	2,184	1,873
Rape	3,668	5,073	4,971	4,766	5,451	5,490	4,873	4,556	4,228	4,102
Robbery	33,529	31,833	34,944	35,632	42,639	44,598	47,046	47,240	39,788	36,059
Assault	33,504	36,787	54,527	52,653	67,243	68,873	70,108	68,523	58,255	57,308
Weapons violations	21,203	27,035	33,123	37,575	49,903	54,414	52,278	46,506	40,145	39,001
Drug abuse	86,685	78,660	66,300	58,603	73,232	90,618	124,931	149,236	148,783	154,540
Drug sale	13,004	14,846	24,575	22,929	25,331	27,635	32,746	34,077	32,558	30,642
Drug possession	73,681	63,814	41,725	35,674	47,901	62,983	92,185	115,159	116,225	123,898

Source: Adapted from U.S. Census Bureau, *Statistical Abstract of the United States, 1999* (Washington, DC: U.S. Government Printing Office, 1999), p. 222.

sized octopus that embraces teenagers who are temporarily troubled and ensnares (without necessarily jailing) those who are chronically violent."[31] Subsequently, several cities have attempted to replicate the Boston model.

The War on Drugs

By the 1980s, events had propelled the control of drug abuse to a top priority in U.S. criminal justice. The deterioration of inner cities had been accompanied by an alarming degree of social dysfunction. Illegal drugs were not only prevalent in the poorest minority neighborhoods but had also become an essential, if not the predominant, part of the local economy. As gangs vied over turf and ever more profitable drug peddling, violence exploded. Drive-by shootings became commonplace in larger cities. Gang-bangers invaded previously neutral territory—hospitals, mortuaries, cemeteries—in pursuit of enemies. Innocent people became victims of a rash of holdups, car-jackings, and seemingly random shootings. In response, President Reagan declared war on drugs.

Logically, two strategies dominated the War on Drugs: government interdiction of supplies, aimed at eliminating the substance, or treatment programs deployed to diminish the demand for illegal drugs. Appropriations for drug control increased substantially during the 1980s, but much of the funding was allocated for interdiction and comparatively less for treatment. For example, federal funds for law enforcement increased from $800 million in 1981 to $1.9 billion in 1986; yet funding for prevention, education, and treatment decreased from $404 million in 1981 to $338 million in 1985, a 40 percent drop when adjusted for inflation.[32] More recently, the 2001 budget of the Office of National Drug Control (ONDC) proposed $420 million for prison construction and $327.5 million for interdiction compared to $127.0 million for treatment. Astonishing many drug policy analysts, the Clinton administration proposed $1.6 billion to eliminate coca production in Colombia.[33]

Despite massive infusions of funds for the Drug Enforcement Administration (DEA) and the Coast Guard, by the late 1980s most analysts agreed that supply interdiction had failed. Experts contended that emphasizing law enforcement would not solve the nation's drug problem. "It would be naive to assume that this well-meant legislative effort will be an end to our drug dilemma," concluded the late Sidney Cohen, former director of the Division of Narcotic Addiction and Drug Abuse of the National Institute of Mental Health:

> We have not yet come to understand the resolute, determined, amoral nature of the major traffickers or their enormous power. Perhaps we do not even recognize that, for tens of hundreds of thousands of field workers, collecting coca leaves or opium gum is a matter of survival. At the other end of the pipeline is the swarm of sellers who could not possibly earn a fraction of their current income from legitimate pursuits. If they are arrested, they are out after a short detention. If not, many are waiting to take their place.[34]

If efforts to reduce the propagation of coca in South and Central America proved futile, attempts to reduce street trafficking were similarly unsuccessful. A kilogram of cocaine wholesaled in Miami for $60,000 in 1981; by the late 1980s, the cost had plummeted to $10,000.[35] The price of cocaine was so low that crack houses were able to offer cocaine free to new customers, charging regulars as little as $2.[36]

To compound the problem, the application of interdiction at the street level, where drugs were sold, led to arrests of users and petty distributors, swelling already overcrowded prisons. Between 1980 and 1990 the number of federal prisoners incarcerated for the violation of drug laws increased from 1,945 to 9,804.[37] By 1997 drug abuse accounted for more arrests than any other offense.[38] Thus, the focus on interdiction and enforcement proved perverse. To contain drug use through law enforcement, the country was imprisoning thousands of addicts at enormous cost, yet funding for prevention and treatment lagged far behind allocations for incarceration. Most ironic, drug treatment for incarcerated addicts was virtually nonexistent.

The mismatch between the needs of drug addicts and the eligibility requirements of social programs was captured by journalist Barry Bearak, who followed a group of junkies in New York City. Scavenging what funds he had left, one junkie decided to have himself admitted to a detox program. After a full day's bouncing from one welfare agency to another seeking eligibility for "special" Medicaid, which would pay for the detox services, Georgie, a middle-aged Hispanic man, found himself in a line for public assistance only a few minutes before closing time. While Georgie waited, a friend who had come with him also to get into detox was shooting up in the rest room:

> The line moved slowly. Georgie's turn finally came a few minutes before 5 p.m. It was a short discussion. He had been in the wrong spot. He needed to be at the Application Desk, back over by Table Five where he had started.
>
> He hurried across the big room. "Can I ask you a question?" he said to a clerk.
>
> "I'm sorry," she answered, her fingers busy in a file drawer. "I need to get this out of the way."
>
> Georgie spoke up with more urgency: "I want to get into detox."
>
> The woman turned to face him now. "You came too late," she said, shaking her head. "We're not giving out any more appointments."
>
> "We've been getting the runaround all day."
>
> She eyed him more carefully, looking over his sweaty face. She spoke slowly and distinctly for the junkie's benefit. "When you come back in, all they'll give you is an appointment," she said. "You won't get emergency Medicaid. Then, with an appointment, you have to come back in a week or so and see an interviewer. Then, after they have reviewed the case, the client is contacted by mail, and that takes three weeks or a month."
>
> Georgie took this in and was stunned. "So the mumbo jumbo about getting on Medicaid the same day is bull——?" he said without anger, but with resignation.
>
> "That's right. The only way to get on is with HIV [the AIDS virus]." At last, good news. His face brightened. "Well, I'm HIV," he said.
>
> The clerk took a step back from him. "You'd have to be able to prove it with a certified letter from your doctor," she said.
>
> With that, Georgie was beaten. His shoulders sagged. And the clerk knew she could shift her attention back to the end-of-the-day filing.[39]

How Georgie came to drug addiction is speculative, of course; yet many social observers cite social and economic conditions in the poorest inner-city neighborhoods that conspire to make self-administered anesthesia desirable for many adolescents. By the early 1990s, for the first time, the number of young African Americans who were neither in school nor employed exceeded 50 percent in every section of the United States.[40] During the 1980s the combination of reductions in governmental assistance to cities through social programs and the prevalence of drug trafficking had a pronounced effect on inner-city neighborhoods. Gradually, once squalid but quiet urban neighborhoods began to echo with gunfire as rival gangs fought over turf; areas in many industrial cities virtually imploded.[41] The "wilding" of New York City teenagers who savagely beat a female jogger was replicated when a gang of Boston youths raped and murdered a young mother.[42] Gang killings in Los Angeles soared 69 percent during the first eight months of 1990.[43] In 1992 Los Angeles reported more than 800 drug-related homicides.[44] Gang-related murders in the nation's capital, which reached a three-year high in 1990, led a police department spokesperson to quip, "At the rate we're going the next generation is going to be extinct."[45]

Observers of urban poverty described a serious deterioration in inner-city communities of the 1980s as contrasted with those of the 1960s. When Claude Brown returned to Harlem 20 years after the publication of his *Manchild in the Promised Land*, he was shocked by the casual viciousness of gang members toward their victims.[46] "In many if not most of our major cities, we are facing something very like social regression," wrote New York's Senator Daniel Patrick Moynihan. "It is defined by extraordinary levels of self-destructive behavior, interpersonal violence, and social class separation intensive in some groups, extensive in others."[47] In the socioeconomic vacuum that had developed in the poorest urban neighborhoods, the sale and consumption of drugs became central to community life. The toll this conversion has taken on young African Americans is astonishing. As of 1988, 43 percent of those convicted of drug trafficking were African American. In New York, Hispanics and African Americans accounted for 92 percent of arrests for drug offenses in 1989. In 1990 the Sentencing Project, a criminal justice reform organization, reported that one-fourth of all African Americans between the ages of 20 and 29 were incarcerated, on parole, or on probation. Yet the Sentencing Project data scraped only the top of what was a very large statistical iceberg.

In *Search and Destroy: African-American Males in the Criminal Justice System,* Jerome Miller identified the frequency with which young African American males were likely to run afoul of the law, reporting that

> on an average day in 1991, more than four in ten (42%) of all the 18-35-year-old African-American males who lived in the District of Columbia were in jail, in prison, on probation/parole, or being sought on arrest warrants; on an average day in Baltimore, 56% of all its young African-American males were in prison, jail, on probation/parole, on bail, or being sought on arrest [emphasis original].[48]

According to Miller, incarceration was damaging enough, but simply arresting all these young men inflicted substantial harm—because most employment applications inquire about an arrest record, and research demonstrates that employers avoid candidates with arrest records.

For Miller the War on Drugs was just another "moral panic," the sort of melodrama that an insecure middle class creates in order to retain its social standing. A moral panic is manifested by the emergence of policies and professionals

that seek to reestablish social control over a phantom threat. In the case of the War on Drugs, conservative politicians and law enforcement officers convinced the public that the nation suffers from a new generation of violent minority youth that must be held in check. The evidence presented for the law-and-order agenda consisted largely of the arrest rates for violent and repeat offenders; yet Miller contended that most "violent" offenses represented the overcharging of miscreants by overzealous police, and most "repeat" offenders were rearrested for drug-related offenses. Not coincidentally, Miller contended, blacks were the target of the War on Drugs. For 1991, he noted, "the national incarceration rate in state and federal prisons was 310 per 100,000. For white males it was 352 per 100,000. For black males ages 25–29 it stood at an incredible 6,301."[49] Many of the arrests were drug related, a category that was increasing dramatically among African American youth. Per 100,000 population, drug arrests for black youth increased from 683 in 1985, to 1,200 in 1989, to 1,415 in 1991.[50] The racial disparity in juvenile drug arrests is shown in Figure 14.1.

The social consequence of the arrest and incarceration of so many black youths, Miller alleged, was the cultivation of an oppositional

FIGURE 14.1 Racial Bias in Arrest Rates

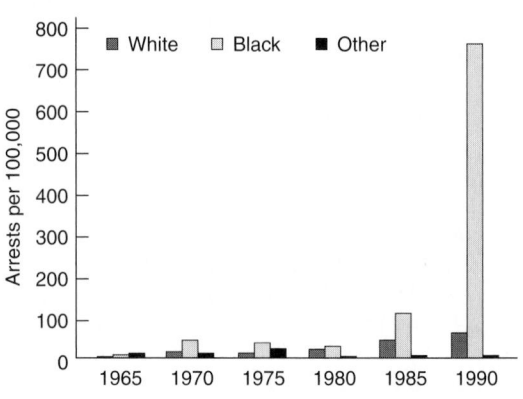

Source: Adapted from Jerome Miller, *Search and Destroy* (New York: Cambridge University Press, 1996).

culture, replete with violence, in which engaging the criminal justice system was "something of a puberty rite, a transition to manhood."[51] Drawing an Orwellian conclusion, Miller predicted that jails would soon morph into "simple internment camps" for minority youth who were refugees from an alienating culture.

Other observers also documented the grim circumstances of poor minority families in urban centers. A common denominator of these portrayals was drug-related violence that seemed to metastasize throughout inner-city communities, extracting a horrifying toll on minority populations. The effect on African American family life was depicted poignantly by Alex Kotlowitz, who followed the daily activities of two youngsters, Lafayette and Pharaoh Rivers. The boys ventured out of their mother's apartment in one of Chicago's housing projects at the risk of being shot by drug dealers.[52] In New York City a popular elementary school principal, Patrick Daly, was shot to death while walking through a drug-infested neighborhood searching for a nine-year-old who had left school in tears after a fight.[53] During the summer of 1992, drug-related street violence in Baltimore reached the point where the state chapter of the National Association for the Advancement of Colored People formally requested that the governor of Maryland declare a state of civil emergency and call out the National Guard to restore order in the city.

By 2000 drug abuse had stabilized, yet the war on drugs continued amid escalating controversy. Since 1985 the United States had invested $300 billion in attempting to control the drug trade, but the results were hotly disputed.[54] Most of the arrests for drug abuse occurred at the local level, and the number of offenders quickly clogged the courts.[55] High demand for drugs fueled international drug cartels, with those in nearby Mexico and Colombia provoking diplomatic tensions around extradition and interdiction.[56] More fundamental issues emerged as the right expressed concern about involvement of the military in nondefense activities[57] and the left proposed legalization of drugs as a more realistic alternative.[58] In a bit of understatement, the nation's third drug policy czar, Barry McCaffrey, concluded, "Serious challenges remain."[59]

The Underclass and "Moral Poverty"

The contention that "crime" was largely a bourgeois contrivance to maintain control over hostile minority youth, as argued by liberals like Jerome Miller, was challenged by conservative crime theorists of the 1980s. Conservatives argued that the chronic poor suffered from problems qualitatively different from those of the temporarily poor. The latter lacked basic resources, and the provision of cash benefits was a prudent response to their circumstances. The chronic poor, however, evidenced a "behavioral" poverty that differentiated them from the transient poor. The behaviorally poor engaged in habits—teen pregnancy, drug abuse, petty theft, unmarried parenthood, and welfare dependency—that not only ensured continual destitution, but also subverted the intent of well-intended social programs.[60] Behavioral poverty precipitated and maintained the underclass.

Accordingly, in their 1996 book *Body Count*, William Bennett, John DiIulio Jr., and John Walters argued that the upsurge in crime could be attributed to "moral poverty":

> *the poverty of being without loving, capable, responsible adults who teach right from wrong; the poverty of being without parents and other authorities who habituate you to feel joy at others' joy, pain at others' pain, satisfaction when you do right, remorse when you do wrong; the poverty of growing up in the virtual absence of people who teach morality by their own everyday example and who insist that you follow suit. In the extreme, moral poverty is the poverty of growing up severely abused and neglected at the hands of deviant, delinquent, or criminal adults.*[61]

To substantiate their argument, Bennett, DiIulio, and Walters cited data on the behavior of state prisoners in 1991. For that year 45 percent of prisoners were on probation or parole when they committed their latest offense. During community supervision in the previous 17 months, the 162,000 probation violators committed some 6,400 murders, 7,400 rapes, 10,400 assaults, and 17,000 robberies. During community supervision of the previous 13 months, the 156,000 parole violators committed some 6,800 murders, 5,500 rapes, 8,800 assaults, and 22,500 robberies. "Together, probation and parole violators committed 90,639 violent crimes while 'under supervision' in the community."[62]

> At the core of the crime wave is a new category of "super-predators"—radically impulsive, brutally remorseless youngsters, including ever more preteenage boys, who murder, assault rape, rob, burglarize, deal deadly drugs, join gun-toting gangs, and create serious communal disorders. They do not fear the stigma of arrest, the pains of imprisonment, or the pangs of conscience. They perceive hardly any relationship between doing right (or wrong) now and being rewarded (or punished) for it later.[63]

Bennett, DiIulio, and Walters averred that much of the increase in crime could be attributed to a proliferation of drugs that had become so extensive as to represent de facto normalization of drug abuse. The severe damage associated with heroin and cocaine justified increasing drug interdiction efforts and getting tough with street criminals who peddle drugs. Regarding treatment, Bennett, DiIulio, and Walters noted that funding increases for treatment had not been accompanied by a significant decrease in the number of addicts seeking rehabilitation, as shown in Figure 14.2.

Although existing treatment capacity was serving only half the nation's addicts, the authors of *Body Count* proposed few changes other than eliminating bureaucratic waste in order to extend treatment resources. Beyond that, little could be done, given the poor track record of treatment programs in getting addicts into recovery. For many addicts treatment was a cyclical experience, not an end to their substance abuse; the authors concluded. They cited the California Civil Addict Program, which reported that more addicts eventually died after receiving treatment (27.7 percent) than became drug free (25 percent).[64]

The conservative prescription for moral poverty was as extensive as it was sometimes implausible. Bennett, DiIulio, and Walters advocated reinforcing work as opposed to unconditional welfare, removing young children from dysfunctional homes, and encouraging adoption as an alternative to foster care. Although public policy might prove instrumental in reducing "criminogenic" influences, it was less apropos, if not irrelevant, as a vehicle for other suggestions, such as limiting children's TV time or reasserting the importance of religious values in daily life.[65]

Subsequently, DiIulio moderated his position about juvenile delinquents, recognizing the environmental deficits that contributed to their misconduct. In researching programs that served delinquents, DiIulio found that religious groups were often the most effective in treating delinquents.[66] DiIulio has become an advocate of "charitable choice," the contracting out of social services through community-based religious

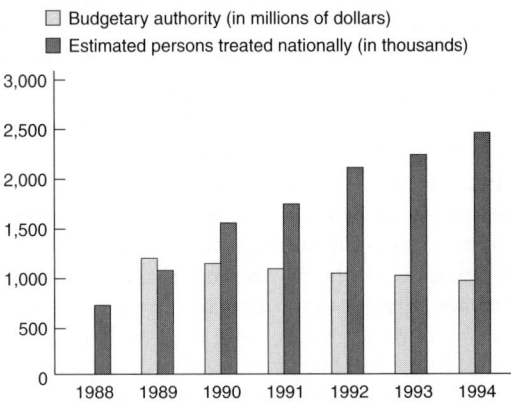

FIGURE 14.2   Federal Drug Treatment Spending and Number of Persons Treated, 1988–1994

Source: Table adapted from William Bennett, John DiIulio Jr., and John Walters, *Body Count* (New York: Simon & Schuster, 1996), p. 174.

organizations. By conceding that the compassion of religious intercession is more effective than to punishment through incarceration, Di-Iulio has reversed his earlier position with respect to juvenile delinquency.[67]

To the extent that social and economic factors—particularly the skewing of opportunities of minority youth who become adult offenders—are associated with crime, an argument can be made for environmental influences in criminal conduct; and this argument leads to a liberal orientation to criminal justice. This is the logic that John Hagan has adopted in developing the concept of the "social embeddedness" of crime. In reviewing research on juvenile delinquency and adult offenders, Hagan noted the interaction of family and environment in the transmission of criminal behavior. Poor neighborhoods generate delinquents, often from families in which a parent has been an offender. Such intergenerational transmission of crime can be attributed to heredity; but, as noted earlier in this chapter, the relationship is too weak to be anywhere near conclusive. Consequently, Hagan takes a more direct, and more useful, route in explaining how poor communities harbor crime-prone families that produce delinquents, many of whom become adult criminals. In poor communities, Hagan contends, two developmental paths evolve for children. Kids from working families with effective adult supervision are socialized in school and through early employment into a world in which there is the likelihood of success. By contrast, children from families in which an adult is an offender are more likely to encounter the juvenile justice system; and not only does that system label them as delinquent, but the punishment of juvenile offenders—incarceration or its surrogates—also interferes with kids' completing school or building a sound foundation for future employment. Essentially, young people from families with adult offenders are doubly burdened. As Hagan writes,

> *involvements of parents in crime likely provide youths with more promising connections to illegal than legal labor markets. As well, contacts with criminal friends are more likely to integrate youths into the criminal under-world than into referral networks for legal employment. And youthful delinquent acts are likely to distance actors further from the job contacts that initiate and sustain legitimate occupational careers.*[68]

So oriented, it is understandable how delinquency-prone youth could find gang involvement a natural progression in socialization. Drug-related gang activities, frequently targeted by law enforcement, bring arrests and sentences that label youngsters and disrupt education and employment. Before the end of high school, a delinquent has accumulated sufficient negative attributes to subvert any interest in conventional rewards. In place of education and employment, gang activity alternates with incarceration, producing a vicious circle. Measures of the intractability of the delinquent's circumstance can be found in the "oppositional culture" that flourishes among poor minority youth. The popularization of vulgar gangsta' rap, a pattern of claiming the loyalty of young women by impregnating them, and "dissing" enemies (including authority figures)—even at the risk of bodily harm—are all part of the capitulation that young minority males make in the face of overwhelming odds militating against traditional means of success. Oppositional culture reproduces itself in children born to young minority women whose aspirations have been sabotaged. Such children experience little that is nurturing or dependable, least of all fathers—given that their fathers, knowing the tentativeness of life on the streets, expect to be dead or incarcerated well before their offspring reach adolescence. The scenario is as tragic as it is "embedded" in the social reality of its perpetrators and victims.

The evolution of liberal policies that divert youth from delinquency and subsequently prevent adult lawlessness has been advocated eloquently by William Julius Wilson. Mainstreaming the underclass, Wilson argues, requires enhanced educational opportunity; the realization of educational standards in inner-city schools; an increase in earned income tax credits for poor working families; and, in the end, a WPA-type public employment program. Eventually, improved educational and employment opportunities will overcome current inducements to engage in lawlessness.

> As more people become employed, crime, including violent crime, and drug use will subside; families will be strengthened and welfare receipt will decline significantly; ghetto-related culture and behavior, no longer sustained and nourished by persistent joblessness, will gradually fade.[69]

Thus, Wilson reiterates a major finding from the research on opportunity and crime: Lawlessness declines as rates of employment and marriage rise.

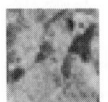 # Legalization of Drugs

During the 1980s, seemingly endless retreats in the war on drugs led some analysts to propose legalizing controlled substances.[70] Drug legalization had been a standard demand among libertarians, who argue that individuals should have the freedom to engage in any activity so long as it does not harm others. Then, during the Reagan presidency, a small number of leaders representing law, economics, and politics complemented the libertarian position with their own arguments. Noting the massive sums pumped into law enforcement and the meager results demonstrated by interdiction and treatment, proponents of legalization argued that U.S. policy on substance abuse was at best naive and at worst counterproductive. They contended that the current policy was little more than a replication of Prohibition's futile effort to ban alcohol from U.S. culture. A more mature and pragmatic policy would be to admit that certain substances were part of contemporary lifestyles and simply to regulate them, much as tobacco and alcohol are regulated. Legalizing drugs would enable substantial sums to be freed from law enforcement and put toward abuse prevention and treatment programs. Legalization would decriminalize drug use, thereby cutting the prison population significantly and, by de-

stigmatizing users, making it more likely that users would enter treatment. Additional revenues could be raised by government because illegal substances would be available legitimately and taxed accordingly. Advocates of legalization questioned the claims of the defenders of the status quo who argued that prevention, treatment, and interdiction were effective strategies that would show positive results in the long run. Legalization of drugs, claimed its adherents, could produce substantial results immediately.

Momentum toward legalizing drugs reached its peak during the mid-1980s and then flagged. Public policy scholars raised questions for which there were no ready answers. Should all drugs be legalized? Or should legalization be limited to soft drugs, such as marijuana and minor tranquilizers, while restrictions on hard drugs were maintained? Should availability be unlimited, or should age restrictions apply, as they do now with tobacco and alcohol? If there were taxes on drugs and restrictions on their purchase, would not the government still have to fund law enforcement, regulate product safety, and maintain a taxing authority in order to contain an illicit market? If the government were to attempt to counter a black market by supplying drugs directly, it would be in the contradictory position of supplying drugs while also offering treatment for users of those same drugs.[71]

Further confounding the issue of drug legalization was the firestorm of controversy over crack cocaine. Proponents of legalization visualized drugs as substances analogous to tobacco and alcohol: People dependent on marijuana, heroin, and many psychedelics could use their drugs discreetly, they contended, without disrupting society. The proliferation of crack cocaine, however, presented a completely different picture. Not only was crack implicated in violent incidents, but the craving for it was more intense than that for many other drugs. The prospect of legalizing a substance over which users seemed to have so little control and which, moreover, was connected to homicides, addicted infants, and community destruction seemed inconsistent with the vision implied by drug legalization.

By the 1990s the legalization of drugs had drifted to the margin of the substance abuse debate, although it was still advocated by a small coterie of prominent people, such as New Mexico's Governor Gary Johnson and financier George Soros. Despite obvious contradictions represented by the status of tobacco and alcohol, few suggested that other substances should be legalized. In fact, pressure increased to contain the use of tobacco and alcohol. Municipalities expanded the areas they designated as smoke-free, and stricter standards and fines were established for driving under the influence of alcohol. Increasingly, authorities came to believe that soft drugs served a "gateway" function, introducing young users to more addictive substances. Rather than loosening of the regulation of such substances, continued restrictions were called for.[72] Finally, the most limited form of legalization—allowing physicians to prescribe certain substances for addicts—faltered when the country that had pioneered this strategy, Great Britain, halted the practice.[73]

If a consensus had begun to emerge about not legalizing controlled substances, there was far less unanimity about how to reclaim neighborhoods in which drugs had become central to social and economic life. Aggressive action by law enforcement officers appeared to have reached an apex, then degenerated in the face of a lawless netherworld—as when, for example, DEA agents raided the wrong house and critically wounded a San Diego man in a drug bust gone wrong. The practice of handing down severe sentences for even first-time offenders began to lose its luster as a strategy when the cost of incarceration proved to exceed by far the value of taking small-time drug traffickers off the street. The seizure of property belonging to persons who had been implicated in drug transactions became a small scandal when newspapers reported that innocent people had lost belongings to overzealous law enforcement officers.[74] The promise of paramilitary boot camps for first-time offenders who had been convicted of drug-related crimes, although it looked like an appealing solution to a public frustrated by increasing numbers of crime-prone youth,

failed to demonstrate any long-term changes in behavior.[75]

In the last decade of the twentieth century, many inner-city neighborhoods were more lethal for minority Americans than they had been at any time in the nation's history. Children learned that they could make hundreds of dollars a day carrying crack between dealers, easily eclipsing the income of conventionally employed adults in the community. This made a joke of the work ethic; no one with any self-respect would consider a dead-end job paying the minimum wage. Young men who had little hope of finding a good job traded their future for quick wealth and community notoriety in the drug trade. Drug-related violence made a mockery of already fragile community institutions. Gang members were shot to death in funeral homes, schools, even hospitals. Most tragically, infants born of crack-addicted mothers writhed and screamed at birth as they experienced withdrawal, only to be diagnosed later with HIV. Unwanted, many suffered in group homes and died at an early age.

While academics debated the finer points of drug legalization, the quality of life for the urban poor grew increasingly desperate. What had once been a grim struggle to reconcile meager income with daily living requirements had become a frantic scramble for safety. At best, the drug scourge forced inner-city residents to sharply curtail their expectations. At worst, it terminated expectations altogether. Eventually, the degradation of life attributed to the proliferation of drugs entered the popular media, clashing with cherished images of America. For too many of the urban poor, the American dream had not just faded from memory; it had been replaced by an antithetical image—the American nightmare.

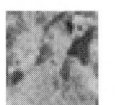 # The "New Penology"

While academics debated the merits of the legalization of drugs, the public was growing increasingly intolerant of crime. Since the mid-1980s the nation has seen a significant increase in prison construction, the passage of new laws requiring incarceration of repeat offenders, and the reinstitution of capital punishment in some states. Approaching the end of the twentieth century, the United States boasted an incarcerated population that exceeded 2 million. In 1970 the number of inmates in state and federal correctional facilities was 96.7 per 100,000 population; by 1993 the number had more than tripled, at 352.9;[76] by 1997 it had more than quadrupled, to 445.[77] In 1994 the Violent Crime Control and Law Enforcement Act introduced the "three strikes" penalties for repeat offenders and increased the number of federal crimes to which the death penalty applies.[78] The number of prisoners under the death sentence soared. In 1980 688 inmates were on death row; by 1993 that number had increased to 2,727; by 1997 3,335 awaited execution. Of these, 43.7 percent were nonwhite;[79] the number of minority people of color with death sentences thus were more than double their proportion of the general population.

The rapid expansion in correctional facilities led criminologists Malcolm Feeley and Jonathan Simon to identify the advent of a "new penology." In contrast to the old penology that focused on individual rehabilitation (via probation or parole) or deterrence (via incarceration), the new penology eschewed these for the efficient management of large populations of high-risk offenders. The mission of criminal justice, contended Feeley and Simon, was "managerial, not transformative";[80] the social function of criminal justice was "rabble management,"[81] or controlling "unruly groups."[82]

As a managerial phenomenon, the new penology required a method for classification and incarceration, and the federal sentencing guidelines incorporated in the 1984 Comprehensive Crime Control Act (implemented on November 1, 1987) served just that purpose. The U.S. Sentencing Commission established an elaborate system of 258 categories for determining the punishment for an offense according to its severity and the offender's previous convictions.[83] The guidelines generated controversy

when it became evident that drug sentences varied considerably according to the type of substance and the race of the offender. For example, regular cocaine is considered less serious than crack cocaine; crack cocaine is used most widely by African Americans; thus, drug offenses by black offenders yield longer sentences. An appellate judge in Minnesota determined that the average sentence for African Americans was more than twice as long as that for whites.[84] Racial disparities in sentencing infuriate some federal judges, because the guidelines provide little latitude for the court to tailor the punishment to fit the crime.

The use of sentencing guidelines was consistent with the new penology, contended Feeley and Simon. In its new configuration, the purpose of criminal justice was not to arbitrate punishment in relation to lawlessness, but to incapacitate large numbers of high-risk offenders selectively. Accordingly, prisons became warehouses for the offenders who were judged to represent the highest risk to society. Because a high-risk designation is positively associated with race and indigence, the new penology functioned to regulate the most troublesome— and allegedly dangerous—elements of the underclass, and drug involvement served to identify those among the underclass who presented the highest risk. Thus, within the contemporary urban milieu, the new penology became an instrument of racial and class oppression.

It could be argued that in the United States prisons have historically served as institutions of last resort for incorrigible populations that have proved difficult to socialize. In that respect the large numbers of African Americans who dominate the prisons today are little different from the Irish or Italian immigrant inmates who disproportionately populated correctional facilities decades ago. If there is a qualitatively different aspect to contemporary corrections, however, it lies in the merging of systems management with the rapid expansion of the correctional corporations. The fundamental difference between the old, government-maintained penology and the new, corporate-managed penology is that the latter has a financial stake in an expanding correctional market, whereas the incentives under the old penology were such that the state attempted to limit criminal justice expenditures.

Thus, an analysis of corrections produced by Steven Donziger for the National Criminal Justice Commission targeted the emerging "prison–industrial complex." According to Donziger, the prison–industrial complex consisted of an "iron triangle" of "government bureaucrats, private industry leaders, and politicians who work together to expand the criminal justice system."[85] In the United States in 1996 there were 21 companies with annual revenues exceeding $250 million, managing some 88 prisons in which 50,000 inmates were incarcerated—a twentyfold increase in the number of inmates managed by for-profit correctional firms since 1984.[86] The passage of the "three strikes" legislation targeting repeat offenders, the war on drugs, and the consequences of the sentencing guidelines provided the prison–industrial complex with a more than adequate supply of inmates. Because most inmates were nonviolent offenders, incarceration in the minimum- and medium-security facilities that were favored by for-profit firms proved ideal. Contrasted to the archaic prisons typical of the old penology, the facilities managed by for-profit firms were not only more adequate with regard to basic amenities, but also more likely to provide educational and other services as methods to maintain a compliant population. The prison–industrial complex is not without its detractors, however. Prison guard unions have emerged as staunch critics of for-profit corrections, because a primary means by which for-profit firms reduce their costs is hiring staff who are less expensive than state correctional officers—who benefit from state civil service regulations and higher pay. Although prisoners tend to benefit from correctional facilities managed by for-profit firms, the new penology brings with it a classic conflict between labor (prison guards) and management (CEOs).

 # The Future of Criminal Justice

With the expansion of correctional facilities in response to escalating crime, calls for reform of the criminal justice system have become increasingly shrill. Among the most prominent reforms are community policing, victim assistance, harsher sentences, and death sentence reviews. Competing views of criminal justice have driven these policy changes.

Community policing. Conceived in Houston, community policing reassigned law enforcement officers from patrol cars and specialty units, which had isolated them from the public, to beats on the streets of high-crime areas. As mayors and the public noted the benefits of community policing,[87] the reform spread, eventually becoming a prominent feature of federal crime policy. President Clinton promised federal funding to deploy 100,000 more police officers to combat crime, and in 1995 the attorney general boasted that the Clinton administration had placed more than 25,000 police officers in the Community Oriented Policing Services (COPS) program.[88]

Victim assistance. Created through the 1984 Victims of Crime Act, the Justice Department's Office for Victims of Crime receives funds derived from settlements of federal civil cases and makes grants for two purposes: victim compensation and victim assistance. In 1996 the program allocated $528.9 million among 2 million beneficiaries. Because the program is not well known, outreach efforts have been undertaken to alert prospective recipients about the availability of assistance.[89]

Harsher sentences. As a result of crimes committed by repeat offenders, particularly sexual offenses, jurisdictions have stiffened sentencing. Since its inception in the mid-1990s, California's "three strikes" law has resulted in a doubling of sentences for second-time offenders and mandates sentences of 25 years to life for third-time offenders, even those convicted of nonviolent crimes.[90] In response to the murders of Megan Kanka and Polly Klaas, the Violent Crime Control and Law Enforcement Act of 1994 included mandatory registration of sexual offenders with local law enforcement, information that is available to the public.[91]

Death sentence review. During the 1990s, an increasing number of death penalty convictions were reversed, some within days if not hours of scheduled executions. To dramatize the prospect of executing an innocent person, the Northwestern University Law School convened a conference on the issue in November 1998, featuring more than 30 former death row inmates.[92] In a related development, the introduction of DNA evidence resulted in the release of 70 inmates, including 8 from death row, who had been wrongfully convicted.[93] In 1999 the governor of Illinois announced a moratorium on executions, because so many of the state's death row inmates had been found innocent.[94] Finally, an exhaustive study of capital punishment revealed that two-thirds of death sentences had been reversed on appeal, suggesting that the sentencing process was rife with irregularity.[95]

If conservatives defined criminal justice policy through the 1980s and 1990s, two developments marked the possibility of an ideological shift. About 95 percent of current inmates locked up during the past two decades—585,000 by 2000—will require some type of reentry service if they are to avoid notoriously high recidivism rates: Of state prisoners, for example, 62 percent are rearrested within three years, and 41 percent are reincarcerated.[96] Yet, apart from experimental pilot demonstrations such as drug courts, comparatively little attention has been directed at services for ex-cons. Among the most successful services is the Delancey Street Foundation, a nonprofessional residential program, conceived in San Francisco in 1971. Delancey Street boasts that 90 percent of its graduates become productive citizens, although its capacity is limited to only 1,000 residents.[97]

In the late 1990s charges of police misconduct, latent since the Los Angeles riot that was precipitated by the acquittal of officers charged with beating Rodney King, resurfaced. The brutality of New York police who shot and and sodomized African immigrants appalled the nation, as did the wholesale corruption within the Los Angeles Police Department. Several officers from an elite Los Angeles antigang unit were charged with stealing drugs from an evidence locker, planting guns on suspects, even shooting unarmed gang members. Still incomplete, investigation of the scandal has resulted in the overturning of 100 convictions, further inquiry into the conduct of 70 police officers, and the certain prospect of millions of dollars in civil litigation.[98]

 # Conclusion

Despite a burgeoning population of Americans intimately acquainted with the criminal justice system, the prospect of radical reform appears dim. Other than driving down unemployment through its economic policies and encouraging community policing, the Clinton presidency was unwilling to propose any viable alternative to prison expansion. As a result, the prison–industrial complex has metamorphosed as it expands to process and capitalize on the legions of young black men sentenced and placed in its care. Despite the enormous institutional and psychological costs associated with incarceration, momentum has yet to build in the direction of community-based services. Thus, criminal justice remains one of the greatest institutional challenges facing American social policy.

Discussion Questions

1. Crime varies considerably in terms of both the nature of offenses and the characteristics of offenders. How prevalent is crime in your community? What are the primary offenses? Who are the offenders?

2. State and local governments vary regarding the management of juvenile delinquency. Does your community have a juvenile court? Are its deliberations open to the public? What are the usual offenses that bring a youth to juvenile court?

3. Many communities are building new correctional facilities. Is your community upgrading corrections? To what extent do new facilities reflect the new penology? Are for-profit correctional firms active in your state? If not, should they be? Should they be allowed to contract to manage probation and parole?

4. Legalization of drugs has become a heated issue. What are the implications of drug legalization for substance abuse programs? How could drug legalization be structured in your state? How would substances be taxed? How would tax revenues from legalization be allocated?

5. In many poor urban communities, drug-related street violence has escalated to unprecedented heights. How has your community balanced resource allocations for supply interdiction versus resources for demand reduction? To what extent is substance abuse treatment available to inmates in local correctional facilities? Have specific neighborhoods in your community organized to contain and reduce drug trafficking? Which agencies have supported such initiatives?

6. As the war on drugs has failed to live up to its promise, more attention has been focused on prevention, particularly among children. What models have agencies in your community adopted to prevent substance abuse among kids? How much money has been allocated for prevention programs? What is the track record of the prevention programs adopted in your community?

 # Notes

1. *Encyclopedia of Sociology* (Guilford, CT: Dushkin Publishing Group, 1974).

2. D. Stanley Eitzen and Doug Timmer, *Criminology* (New York: Wiley, 1985), pp. 15–16.

3. Phyllis Day, *A New History of Social Welfare* (Englewood Cliffs, NJ: Prentice-Hall, 1989), p. 181.

4. Ibid., p. 182.

5. Jerome Miller, *Search and Destroy: African–American Males in the Criminal Justice System* (New York: Cambridge University Press, 1996), p. 207.

6. Quoted in ibid., p. 185.

7. Richard Herrnstein and Charles Murray, *The Bell Curve* (New York: Free Press, 1994).

8. Glenn Walters, "A Meta-Analysis of the Gene–Crime Relationship," *Criminology* 30, no. 4 (1992), pp. 8–16.

9. *Justice Expenditures and Employment Abstracts* (Washington, DC: U.S. Department of Justice, 1992).

10. *Sourcebook of Criminal Justice Statistics, 1994* (Washington, DC: Congressional Information Services, 1995), Tables 1.7 and 1.8.

11. Peter Slevin, "Violent Crime Down 10% in 1999," *Washington Post* (August 28, 2000), p. A2.

12. David Vise and Lorraine Adams, "Despite Rhetoric, Violent Crime Climbs," *Washington Post* (December 5, 1999), p. A3.

13. Pam Belluck, "Blighted Areas Are Revived as Crime Rate Falls in Cities," *The New York Times* (May 29, 2000), p. 1.

14. Gary Jensen and Maryaltani Karpos, "Research on the Behavior of Rape Statistics," *Criminology* 31, no. 4 (1993), p. 382.

15. *Annual Report of the Attorney General of the U.S.* (Washington, DC: Department of Justice, 1995), p. 4.

16. Lela Costin, Howard Karger, and David Stoesz, *The Politics of Child Abuse in America* (New York: Oxford University Press, 1996).

17. "Behind Bars," *Washington Post* (June 3, 2000), p. A9.

18. "Nation's Prison Population Climbs to Over 2 Million," *Washington Post* (August 10, 2000), p. A4.

19. U.S. Census Bureau, *Statistical Abstract of the United States, 1999* (Washington, DC: U.S. Government Printing Office, 1999), p. 231.

20. David Masci, "Prison-Building Boom," *Issues in Social Policy* (Washington, DC: Congressional Quarterly, 2000), p. 138.

21. Day, *A New History of Social Welfare*, p. 180.

22. James Leiby, *A History of Social Welfare and Social Work in the United States* (New York: Columbia University Press, 1978), p. 147.

23. Jerome Miller, *Last One over the Wall* (Columbus, OH: Ohio State University, 1991), p. 222.

24. Ibid., p. 243.

25. Denise Gottfredson and William Barton, "Deinstitutionalization of Juvenile Offenders," *Criminology* 31, no. 4 (1993), pp. 98–117.

26. James Q. Wilson and John DiIulio Jr., "Crackdown," *The New Republic* (July 10, 1989), p. 54.

27. Rhonda Cook, "Georgia's Prison Boot Camps Don't Work, Study Says," *San Diego Union Tribune* (May 8, 1994), p. A32.

28. "Connecticut Suspends Gang-Riddled Youth Boot Camp," *San Diego Union Tribune* (June 12, 1994), p. A6.

29. Doris Mackenzie et al., "Boot Camp Prisons and Recidivism in Eight States," *Criminology* 33, no. 3 (1995), p. 78.

30. Margaret Talbot, "The Maximum Security Adolescent," *The New York Times Magazine* (September 10, 2000), p. 42.

31. Blaine Harden, "Boston's Approach to Juvenile Crime Encircles Youths, Reduces Slayings," *Washington Post* (October 23, 1997), p. A3.

32. Mathea Falco, *Winning the Drug War* (New York: Priority Press, 1989), pp. 26–27.

33. Barry McCaffrey, *The Office of National Drug Control's Fiscal Year 2001 Budget* (Washington, DC: ONDC, March 23, 2000).

34. Sidney Cohen, "The Drug-Free America Act of 1986," *Drug Abuse and Alcoholism Newsletter* (San Diego, CA: Vista Hill Foundation, 1987), pp. 1–3.

35. Falco, *Winning the Drug War*, p. 29.

36. Barry Bearak, "A Room for Heroin and HIV," *Los Angeles Times* (September 27, 1992), p. A18.

37. "Drug Policy: It's Time to Try Something Very Different," *Los Angeles Times* (January 4, 1993), p. B6.

38. U.S. Census Bureau, *Statistical Abstract of the United States, 1999*, p. 222.

39. Bearak, "Road to Detox: Do Not Enter," *Los Angeles Times* (September 30, 1992), p. A18.

40. John Kasarda, "Industrial Restructuring and the Consequences of Changing Job Locations," in Reynolds Farley (ed.), *Changes and Challenges: America 1990* (New York: Russell Sage Foundation, 1995), Table 5.15.

41. Christopher Jencks, "Deadly Neighborhoods," *The New Republic* (June 13, 1988), p. 18; Juan Williams, "Hard Times, Harder Hearts," *Washington Post* (October 2, 1988), p. C4.

42. "Eight Boston Teenagers Charged in Savage Slaying of Young Mother," *Los Angeles Times* (November 21, 1990), p. A4.

43. Louis Sahagun, "Gang Killings Increase 69%, Violent Crime Up 20% in L.A. County Areas," *Los Angeles Times* (August 21, 1990), p. B8.

44. Jesse Katz, "County's Yearly Death Toll Reaches 800," *Los Angeles Times* (January 19, 1993), p. A23.

45. Gabriel Escobar, "Slayings in Washington Hit New High, 436, for 3rd Year," *Los Angeles Times* (November 24, 1990), p. A26.

46. Claude Brown, *Manchild in the Promised Land* (New York: Macmillan, 1965); Claude Brown, "Manchild in Harlem," *The New York Times* (September 16, 1984), p. 16.

47. Daniel Patrick Moynihan, *Came the Revolution* (San Diego: Harcourt Brace Jovanovich, 1988), p. 291.

48. Miller, *Search and Destroy*, pp. 7–8.

49. Ibid., p. 54.

50. Ibid., p. 85.

51. Ibid., p. 99.

52. Alex Kotlowitz, *There Are No Children Here* (New York: Doubleday, 1991).

53. Barry Bearak, "Brooklyn Neighborhood Grieves for Its Mr. Chips," *Los Angeles Times* (December 19, 1992), p. A6.

54. Glenn Frankel, "The Longest War," *Washington Post Weekly* (July 7, 1997), p. 6.

55. David Simon and Edward Burns, "Too Much Is Not Enough," *Washington Post* (September 7, 1997), p. C1.

56. Pamela Frank, "Drugs across the Border: A War We're Losing," *Washington Post Weekly* (September 29, 1997), p. 27.

57. Jim McGee, "Military Seeks Balance in Delicate Mission: The Drug War," *Washington Post* (November 29, 1996).

58. George Soros, "The Drug War 'Cannot Be Won,'" *Washington Post* (February 2, 1997).

59. Barry McCaffrey, "National War on Drugs Symposium" (Washington, DC: Georgetown University, October 4, 2000).

60. Michael Novak, *The New Consensus on Poverty and the Family* (Washington, DC: American Enterprise Institute, 1987).

61. William Bennett, John DiIulio Jr., and John Walters, *Body Count* (New York: Simon & Schuster, 1996), p. 56.

62. Ibid., p. 105.

63. Ibid., p. 27.

64. Ibid., pp. 175–176.

65. Ibid., Chap. 5.

66. Jim Wallace, "With Unconditional Love," *Sojourners* (October 1997).

67. James Traub, "The Criminals of Tomorrow," *The New Yorker* (November 4, 1996).

68. John Hagan, "The Social Embeddedness of Crime and Unemployment," *Criminology* 31, no. 4 (1993), p. 469.

69. William Julius Wilson, *When Work Disappears* (New York: Knopf, 1996), p. 238.

70. Ethan Nadelmann, "The Case for Legalization," *The Public Interest* 92 (1988), pp. 3–17.

71. James Jacobs, "Imagining Drug Legalization," *The Public Interest* 101 (Fall 1990), pp. 27–34.

72. Falco, *The Making of a Drug-free America*, p. 100.

73. Jacobs, "Imagining Drug Legalization," p. 30.

74. Jim Newton, "Seizure of Assets Leaves Casualties in War on Drugs," *Los Angeles Times* (October 14, 1992), p. A1; David Savage, "Drug-Case Forfeitures Will Be Reviewed," *Los Angeles Times* (January 16, 1993), p. A2.

75. David Lamb, "Last Shot to Salvage Their Lives," *Los Angeles Times* (January 17, 1993), p. A1.

76. U.S. Census Bureau, *Statistical Summary of the United States* (Washington, DC: U.S. Census Bureau, 1995), Table 349.

77. U.S. Census Bureau, *Statistical Abstract of the United States, 1999*, p. 231.

78. *Annual Report of the Attorney General of the U.S.*

79. U.S. Census Bureau, *Statistical Abstract of the United States, 1999*, p. 233.

80. Malcolm Feeley and Jonathan Simon, "The New Penology," *Criminology* 30, no. 4 (1992), p. 452.

81. Miller, *Last One over the Wall*, p. 76.

82. Feeley and Simon, "The New Penology," p. 455.

83. Mary Flaherty and Joan Biskupic, "Justice by the Numbers," *Washington Post Weekly* (October 14–20, 1996), p. 88.

84. Mary Flaherty and Joan Biskupic, "Rules Often Impose Toughest Penalties on Poor, Minorities," *Washington Post* (October 9, 1996), p. A26.

85. Steven Donziger, "The Prison–Industrial Complex," *Washington Post* (March 17, 1996), p. C3.

86. Ibid., p. C3.

87. Janet Vinzant and Lane Crothers, "Street-Level Leadership: The Role of Patrol Officers in Community Policing," *Criminal Justice Review* 19, no. 2 (Autumn 1994), pp. 56–71.

88. *Annual Report of the Attorney General of the U.S.*

89. Sharon Walsh, "Crime Does Pay . . . Its Victims," *Washington Post* (February 2, 1997), p. A1.

90. Rene Sanchez, "A Movement Builds Against 'Three Strikes' Law," *Washington Post* (February 18, 2000), p. A3.

91. Hans Selvog, "Moral Panic and Sex Offenders" (Richmond, VA: Virginia Commonwealth University School of Social Work, 2000).

92. Mary Cooper, "Death Penalty," in *Issues in Social Policy* (Washington, DC: Congressional Quarterly, 2000).

93. Brooke Masters, "DNA Testing in Old Cases Is Disputed," *Washington Post* (September 10, 2000), p. A1.

94. Bob Herbert, "Criminal Justice Breakdown," *The New York Times* (February 14, 2000), p. A27

95. Brooke Masters, "A Death Sentence, Then a Reversal," *Washington Post Weekly* (June 19, 2000), p. 34.

96. Peter Slevin, "Life After Prison," *Washington Post* (April 24, 2000), p. A1.

97. Ray Rivera, "On Delancey Street," *The Santa Fe New Mexican* (October 19, 1997).

98. William Booth, "In L.A. Police Scandal, 4 Go on Trial for Faking Cases," *Washington Post* (October 14, 2000), p. A3.

chapter 15

Child Welfare Policy

This chapter examines the evolution of child welfare policy in the United States. Child protective services, foster care, adoption, and Head Start have been the focus of child welfare policy since the 1960s. The devolution of welfare to the states through the Personal Responsibility and Work Opportunity Reconciliation Act of 1996 has introduced questions about the prospects of poor children whose mothers are entering the labor market.

In U.S. social welfare, the condition of children is inextricably linked to the status of their families. Because the United States has failed to establish a family policy that ensures basic income, employment, and social service supports to parents, parents frequently have difficulty in caring for their children. As families are less able to care for their children, the demand for child welfare services escalates. The commitment that national governments make toward reducing poverty among children varies considerably. Among industrialized nations, the United States fares poorly indeed. The Luxembourg Study, which rated the extent to which nations deploy income assistance to lift children out of poverty, found that the United States ranked last, as indicated in Table 15.1.

In the United States in recent years, the proportion of children living in poverty, the proportion of children in single-parent households, the percentage of mothers in the workforce, and the birthrate of women in minority groups have all remained high. In 1995, 14.7 million children were living in poverty in this country, a signifi-

TABLE 15.1 ■ Child Poverty in Seventeen Developed Countries before and after Government Assistance

COUNTRY	BEFORE ASSISTANCE	AFTER ASSISTANCE	PERCENTAGE OF CHILDREN LIFTED OUT OF POVERTY
United States	26%	22%	17%
Australia	20	14	29
Canada	23	14	40
Ireland	30	12	60
Israel	24	11	54
United Kingdom	30	10	67
Italy	12	10	17
Germany	9	7	24
France	25	7	74
Netherlands	14	6	55
Norway	13	5	64
Luxembourg	12	4	65
Belgium	16	4	77
Denmark	16	3	79
Switzerland	5	3	35
Sweden	19	3	86
Finland	12	3	78

Source: *Kids Count 1996* (Baltimore: Annie E. Casey Foundation, 1996), p. 17.

cant increase from the 10.2 million poor children in 1974.[1] Although child poverty diminishes when family incomes increase during economic expansion, improvement slowed between the 1993–95 period, when 1.2 million children per year were lifted out of poverty, and the 1995–98 period, when only 400,000 per year rose from the ranks of the poor.[2] More troubling, the Children's Defense Fund has reported that the number of children in families with incomes less than half of the poverty line increased sharply during the late part of the 1990s.[3]

Poverty has adverse consequences for infants, contributing to insufficient prenatal care and high infant mortality. This fact explains, in part, the relatively high infant mortality rate of the United States: 7.3 deaths per 1,000 live births, compared to Sweden's 3.5, Japan's 4.3, Germany's 5.3, the United Kingdom's 6.1, and Canada's 6.3.[4] Despite the chronically poor showing of child welfare in the United States relative to other industrialized nations, the most recent federal accounting that included such variables as violent crime, poverty, mortality, teen pregnancy, and overall health, indicated that U.S. children were faring somewhat better than in the past.[5]

Although an increase in a broad range of family and child welfare services might be expected in view of the chronic negligence that has typified the nation's care for its children, the societal response has been extremely varied. As Jeanne Giovannoni notes, "at best we have a hodgepodge of funding and regulatory mechanisms, and we rely predominantly on market mechanisms dictating both the amount and variety of care available."[6] Others have been less charitable. Alvin Schorr, a veteran welfare scholar, has observed, "From the 1960s on, child welfare suffered a series of blows that left [conventional] ideology and the program in shambles."[7]

A classification of child welfare services completed by the Child Welfare League of America identified nine diverse components: services in the home, day care, homemaker services, foster care, adoption, group home care, institutional care, protective services, and services to unmarried parents.[8] Of these, protective services, foster care, and adoption are most frequently identified as being related exclusively to child welfare and, therefore, are the focus here.

Child welfare services are often controversial, because they sanction the intervention of human service professionals in family affairs that are ordinarily assumed to be private matters and the prerogative of parents. This dilemma places extraordinary demands on child welfare professionals, who are mandated to protect the best interests of the child while not intruding on the privacy of the family.[9] Recently, this conundrum has become more pronounced: Advocates for child welfare services demand more programs, but traditionalist groups attempt to cut programs that they see as designed to subvert the family. Ironically, much of this argument could be defused if the United States adopted a family policy that helped parents care for children more adequately, thus reducing the need for the more intrusive child welfare interventions. For the moment, however, the adoption of any family policy is unlikely, and child welfare policy remains among the more controversial components of U.S. in American social welfare.

History of U.S. Child Welfare Policy

Although many states established orphanages during the eighteenth century, current child welfare policy in the United States has its origins in the 1870s.[10] The large number of child paupers led Charles Loring Brace, founder of New York's Children's Aid Society, to move thousands of children from deleterious urban conditions in New York City to farm families in the Midwest. Eventually, criticism of Brace's methods, which were divisive of family and community, contributed to more preventive approaches to children's problems. By the beginning of the twentieth century, most large cities had children's aid societies that practiced the "boarding out" of children (the payment of a fee for child rearing) to sponsors in the community.[11] The boarding out of children until adoption (except in the case of children with disabilities, who were unlikely to be adopted) was the forerunner of today's foster care and adoption programs in the United States.

Protective services for children began with one of the more unusual incidents in American social welfare. In 1874 a New York church worker, Etta Wheeler, discovered that an indentured nine-year-old child, Mary Ellen, was being tied to a bed, whipped, and stabbed with scissors. On investigating what could be done for Mary Ellen, Wheeler spoke with the director of the New York Society for the Prevention of Cruelty to Animals (NYSPCA) on behalf of the child. Although it was subsequently believed that intervention on behalf of Mary Ellen was predicated on her status as an animal warranting protection, rather than as a child, a careful review of the case indicated that Mary Ellen's case was adjudicated consistently with legal precedents involving abused children.[12] The following year, the New York Society for the Prevention of Cruelty to Children was established.[13] By 1922, 57 societies for the prevention of cruelty to children had been established to protect abused youngsters.[14]

Child welfare proved an effective rallying issue for Progressives, who advocated intervention on the part of the federal government. In 1909 James E. West, a friend of President Theodore Roosevelt and later head of the Boy Scouts of America, convinced Jane Addams and other welfare leaders to attend a two-day meeting on child welfare. This first White House Conference on Children focused attention on the plight of destitute families, agency problems with the boarding out of children, and the importance of home care. The conference proved so successful that it was subsequently repeated every 10 years—with the exception of 1981, when the conference was canceled by the Reagan administration. The White House Conference on Children served as a model for legitimating and attracting attention to social welfare needs. One significant product of the White House Confer-

ence on Children was the call to establish a federal agency to "collect and exchange ideas and information on child welfare." With an initial appropriation of $25,640, the U.S. Children's Bureau was established in 1912 under the auspices of the Department of Commerce and Labor.[15] Instrumental in the early years of the Children's Bureau were Lillian Wald, of New York's Henry Street Settlement House, and Florence Kelley, an alumna of both the Henry Street Settlement and Hull House. Julia Lathrop, a former resident of Hull House, was the bureau's first director.[16]

Because of the economic circumstances of poor families, child labor emerged as a primary concern of early child welfare advocates. The absence of public relief meant that families were compelled to work at whatever employment might be available, however wearing and demeaning. Children worked full shifts in coal mines and textile mills; women labored in sweatshops. Neither were protected from dangerous or unhygienic working conditions. Under the guidance of Florence Kelley, the National Consumer League fought for children and women using a dual strategy. First, the league lobbied for reform in the working conditions of women through regulation of sweatshops and factories, and for ending the exploitation of children by prohibiting child labor. Second, it advocated ameliorating the grinding poverty of many families by means of a family subsidy that would make such deplorable work less necessary. For Kelley, the family subsidy was a preventive measure with which she was quite familiar; in Illinois in 1911, she had successfully lobbied for passage of the Funds for Parents Act. This act was a precursor of the Aid to Dependent Children program, part of the original Social Security Act of 1935.[17]

Before the Great Depression, welfare advocates could boast of a series of unprecedented initiatives designed to improve the conditions of poor families in the United States. The Children's Bureau Act of 1912 established a national agency to collect information on children. The Child Labor Act of 1916 prohibited the interstate transportation of goods manufactured by children. The Maternity and Infancy Act of 1921 assisted states in establishing programs that dramatically reduced the nation's infant and maternal mortality rates. Yet these hard-won successes, were constantly at risk of being subverted. The Supreme Court ruled the Child Labor Act unconstitutional in 1918, and the Maternity and Infancy Act was terminated in 1929, when Herbert Hoover and Congress refused further appropriations.[18] Child and family welfare initiatives remained unsuccessful until the Social Security Act of 1935 ushered in a complete set of welfare policies.

The Social Security Act addressed child welfare in two of its provisions. Title IV introduced the Aid to Dependent Children program, which provided public relief to needy children through cash grants to their families. Title V reestablished Maternal and Child Welfare Services (which had expired in 1929) and expanded the mandate of the Children's Bureau, whose goal was now to oversee a new set of child welfare services "for the protection and care of homeless, dependent, and neglected children, and children in danger of becoming delinquent."[19] Significantly, both family relief and child welfare services were to be administered by the states through public welfare departments. As a result, as of 1935 the provision of child welfare services shifted largely from the private, voluntary sector to the public, governmental sector.

Within public welfare, the responsibility for child welfare has shifted between the federal and state governments. Since 1935 the state and federal governments have shared responsibility for social services provided to families, but the role of the federal government has changed with respect to income maintenance benefits to poor families. From 1935 until 1996, federal and state government shared the funding and administration of the AFDC program. With devolution of public assistance to the states through the Personal Responsibility and Work Opportunity Reconciliation Act (PRWORA), however, the federal government limited its role to one of funding and limited oversight. PRWORA instituted a block grant program, Temporary Assistance to Needy Families (TANF), that is primarily under the control of state government. Consistent with the residual conception of welfare, primary responsibility for children rests with their parent(s) with state intervention as a backup.

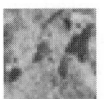

Protective Services for Children

Through the Social Security Act, states proceeded to develop services to children independently of one another and within the relatively loose specifications of the act. In the absence of a centralized authority that would ensure standardized care throughout the United States, child welfare services varied greatly from state to state and even within states. In the two decades following the passage of the Social Security Act, child welfare services had become established within U.S. social welfare, but with a high degree of fragmentation.

In the 1960s the status quo in child welfare was upset by increasing reports of child abuse and neglect. A pediatrician, C. Henry Kempe, identified nonaccidental injuries to children as the "battered child syndrome." As more states began to address the problem, child welfare advocates built a compelling case for a national standard for child protective services. This lobbying led to the passage of the Child Abuse Prevention and Treatment Act of 1974, which established the National Center for Child Abuse and Neglect within the Department of Health and Human Services and presented a model statute for state child protective programs. All 50 states eventually enacted the model statute, which, among its provisions, specified the following:

- a standard definition of child abuse and neglect
- methods for reporting and investigating abuse and neglect
- immunity for those reporting suspected injuries inflicted on children
- prevention and public education efforts to reduce incidents of abuse and neglect

As a result of these national standards, the National Center for Child Abuse and Neglect was able—for the first time—to report trends in child abuse and the need for protective services for children. Alarmingly, the data collected by the National Center revealed a dramatic increase in reports of child abuse; these more than doubled between 1976 and 1986, when reports of child abuse numbered 2 million.[20] In 1991 Chicago's National Committee for the Prevention of Child Abuse reported that 1,383 children died as a result of abuse, 50 percent more than the number reported in 1986.[21] Most troubling was that reports of child abuse continued to climb through the mid-1980s, while at the same time expenditures for child protective services were decreasing.[22]

Increases in child abuse reports and decreases in expenditures led to a crisis in child welfare services. The magnitude of this crisis was mapped in 1987 by Douglas Besharov, an authority on child welfare policy:

> Of the 1,000 children who die under circumstances suggestive of parental maltreatment each year, between 30 and 50 percent were previously reported to child protective agencies. Many thousands of other children suffer serious injuries after their plight becomes known to authorities. . . . Each year, about 50,000 children with observable injuries severe enough to require hospitalization are not reported [emphasis original].[23]

Stories of child abuse fatalities began to appear with greater frequency in the media. Shortly before Thanksgiving of 1987, the report of the beating death of a six-year-old girl under the care of a middle-class couple in Greenwich Village in New York City became a feature story in *Newsweek*.[24] Unfortunately, incidents of child abuse were too often associated with child welfare programs mandated to protect children. In Kansas City, 25 percent of the children in foster care were found to have been abused.[25] During the spring of 1988, National Public Radio broadcast a report of two Illinois state "social workers" who had been dismissed for failure to make home visits and for falsification of records associated with the deaths of two children who had been reported as victims of child abuse.[26] In Baltimore, a group of current and former foster children won a decision in the Fourth District Court of Appeals after charging that 20 administrators and caseworkers of the Baltimore City Department of Social Services had failed "to adequately monitor and protect children in foster care."[27] Such litigation placed child welfare personnel in a double bind: They were faced with increasing demands for services, yet did not have adequate staff resources to respond effectively. "If you take children out of the home, you're snatching them. If you leave them in the home [and they're abused], you didn't protect them," complained Jim Bell of the Massachusetts Department of Social Services. "We try to deal the best we can in that environment and protect the [case]workers. We don't want them hanging out there all alone."[28]

One consequence of this disintegration of children's services was a volatile debate over the definition of child *abuse and neglect*. One solution to the widening disparity between dwindling resources for children's services and increasing reports of abuse and neglect, of course, would be to redefine the criteria in accordance with which emergency services for children were deployed. If conservatives could promulgate a more restrictive definition of *abuse and neglect*, they would benefit directly, in that such a change would effectively subvert demands for greater funding for children's services and parents would retain wider latitude for their behavior in the home. Contending that *confirmed* reports of child abuse had consistently declined since implementation of the Child Abuse Prevention and Treatment Act, Besharov argued for a more restrictive definition.[29] Countering this claim, David Finkelhor of the University of New Hampshire's Family Research Laboratory noted that annual data from the American Humane Association indicated fairly steady rates of validated abuse and neglect, from 40 to 43 percent of all reports. Because more specific research on the nature of general abuse and sexual abuse suggested increasing incidence, Finkelhor argued for more resources for child protection.[30]

The rapid deterioration of child welfare services led children's advocates to call for more funding of social services. But proposals for increased support for child welfare services did not go unchallenged. Ambiguity in the definition of what constituted child abuse and neglect had contributed to incidents in which child welfare workers appeared to disregard parental rights in their eagerness to protect children. Perhaps the most notorious instance of such overzealousness occurred during the summer of 1984, when social workers from the Vermont Department of Social and Rehabilitation Services and the state police rounded up 112 children from "a radical Christian sect" and detained them for three days to search for indications of abuse. When the American Civil Liberties Union threatened to sue the state on behalf of the religious community, state officials reconsidered, and the children were returned to their parents.[31] Similar but less newsworthy incidents enraged parents who, feeling unjustly accused, formed VOCAL (Victims of Child Abuse Laws) in an attempt to restore traditional parental rights in the face of what they perceived to be the intrusiveness of the state.

Conservative scholars contributed to the grassroots indignation that fueled VOCAL. Sociologists Bridgitte and Peter Berger contended that social services such as child welfare were the vehicle through which middle-class professionals evangelized among lower-class clients. In disputes between professionals and parents over parents' versus children's rights, the Bergers' recommendation was to "trust parents over against experts."[32] With momentum building during the 1980s, the 3,000 members of VOCAL took their complaints into the public arena. In Arizona, for example, VOCAL held up a $5.4-million appropriation for child protective services.[33]

Further distracting public attention from child maltreatment, during the 1980s some family therapists suggested that therapy could "recover memories" of childhood abuse. By the end of the decade, showcase trials of child day care providers, teachers, clergy, and parents resulted in a series of convictions based on incidents that had been previously forgotten but were later retrieved during clinical treatment. Later, as appeals raised questions about the veracity of allegations, the "recovered memory" movement came under scrutiny. By the time a Wenatchee, Washington, minister and his wife were found innocent in 1996 of charges that they had run a satanic cult that abused children, judgments for most of the perpetrators convicted in earlier trials had been reversed on appeal.[34]

While academics, policy wonks, and therapists debated definitional, ideological, and clinical aspects of child maltreatment, child protective services continued to deteriorate. New York City's child welfare services became the focus of scrutiny in the cases of a series of children who died despite having been active child protection cases. In 1992 five-year-old Jeffrey Harden died from broken ribs and burns caused by scalding water. Although Jeffrey's family had been known to child welfare authorities for 18 months, intervention by four different caseworkers failed to identify the risk to the child. By the time of his death, all four workers had left the agency.[35]

During Thanksgiving 1995, young Elisa Izquierdo was beaten to death by her demented mother. Despite repeated calls by neighbors and school officials, the city's child protection workers had failed to prevent her murder. Within a year, four-year-old Nadine Lockwood had starved to death. Again, child welfare workers had failed to confirm Nadine's deteriorating health even though neighbors had complained about her neglect. An investigation into the Child Welfare Administration showed the magnitude of agency failure: In a fifth of reported cases, workers failed to interview all of the children in the family; in two out of five cases, workers ignored previous reports of child abuse; almost one-fifth of cases were closed despite the risk of future abuse. Following the exposé, Mayor Rudolph Giuliani announced plans to restructure child welfare in the city.[36] Despite the appointment of a new commissioner of children's services, Nicholas Scoppetta,[37] a subsequent report found that 40 percent of abused and neglected children were returned home and mistreated again.[38]

Although New York City provided the headlines, virtually every major metropolitan area featured at least one scandal involving a child who died while under the care of protective services. A poignant case involved Brianna Blackmond, whose case was mismanaged by the District of Columbia's Department of Child and Family Services (DCFS): Having been removed from her addict mother's care, the toddler was returned after a series of snafus and died as a result.[39] The case attracted wide attention, because DCFS's inadequate care of the district's children had resulted in placement of the agency under a court-appointed receiver. After several years, the staff were upgraded until virtually all were M.S.W.'s, yet the agency continued to show serious performance problems,[40] chief among them high caseloads and high turnover.[41] By 2000 a deteriorating work environment had resulted in "foster care panic," in which DCFS workers removed children from parents, leading the *Washington Post* to accuse social workers of "flight from professional judgment and responsibility." "Social workers are abandoning their training as well as the children and families they've been hired to serve," the paper intoned.[42] Six months later the General Accounting Office reported that DCFS had failed to investigate 1,200 cases of suspected neglect and abuse within 30 days, among other structural problems.[43] Soon, the reporting of DCFS children placed with families outside the district was so poor that Maryland suspended accepting DCFS children for foster care. Meanwhile, another case was unnecessarily delayed, and a judge issued an order for the DCFS receiver to appear in court. The receiver ignored the order; this led to her arrest, handcuffing, and quick retreat to a restroom to dodge reporters.[44] More composed, the receiver announced that she would legally challenge the judge's authority to hold her accountable, a statement that was widely derided.[45] As the entire spectacle occurred in the nation's capital, congressional Republicans convened hearings to investigate misfeasance on the part of DCFS as well as the judgment of the receiver.[46] Eventually the receiver apologized to the court, paid fines that included reimbursement of parties inconvenienced by her absence at the hearing, and subsequently resigned. None of this reflected well on child welfare professionals, who appeared inept under the scrutiny of the federal lawmakers responsible for oversight of federal child welfare policy.

Tragically, the deaths of children due to abuse and neglect were not a local problem but one that had become nationwide. By the mid-1990s the U.S. Advisory Commission on Child Abuse and Neglect concluded that some 2,000 children were dying of abuse and neglect annually,[47] far above the 1,111 deaths counted by the National Center on Child Abuse and Neglect.[48] In rating the child homicide rates for industrial nations, a British researcher concluded that the child fatality rate of the United States was double that of the second most lethal nation for children, Australia.[49] Indeed, the rate of reported as well as confirmed cases of abuse and neglect in the United States were more than double those of the United Kingdom or Canada.[50]

Regardless of increases in injury and death to children due to abuse and neglect, child welfare professionals were fancying a new approach to serving at-risk families, "family preservation." Initially demonstrated in the late 1970s through the Homebuilders program, family preservation called for the provision of intensive services for a brief period, usually six weeks, by a worker assigned four to six cases. Services provided ranged from crisis intervention to home repair to child day care—all intended to stabilize the family and prevent out-of-home placement of a child.

Family preservation was greeted enthusiastically by child welfare professionals because of the multiple benefits it offered. Foremost, by keeping a family intact, this approach avoided out-of-home placement of a child who had been abused or neglected. Because of the high cost of out-of-home placement, family preservation thus offered financial benefits: The cost of mounting a family preservation program was quickly recovered through savings from the reduction in out-of-home placements. Finally, in valuing family unity over child removal, family preservation allied child welfare agencies with conservative traditionalists who placed family rights over those of children.

The relationship between family preservation and child protective services was oblique but nonetheless consequential. Child welfare professionals understood family preservation as a preventive strategy that could preclude the most dramatic disposition of child protective services, out-of-home placement. As family preservation captured the allegiance of child welfare professionals, the focus on child protection began to lapse. Even as fatalities due to child abuse mounted, children's advocates pressed for policy changes focusing on family preservation. Consequently, when the 1993 Clinton economic package was passed, it included $930 million for family support and preservation services over five years, but only a footnote reference to child protective services.[51]

Despite policies intended to ameliorate child abuse, the number of confirmed cases of maltreated children has climbed steadily, more than quadrupling from 10 per 1,000 in 1976 to 47 in 1996.[52] In 1994 the number of children who had been victimized by abuse and neglect exceeded 2 million, an increase of 27 percent since 1990. Of the 2.9 million reports of maltreatment in 1994, 56 percent were unsubstantiated, and 38 percent were substantiated.[53] Between 1986 and 1993 the number of children who were seriously injured increased from 143,000 to 570,000. Yet despite increased injuries to children, fewer cases were investigated; 44 percent of cases were investigated in 1986, but only 28 percent were so disposed in 1993.[54] The types of maltreatment inflicted on children are shown in Table 15.2. Girls, 52.3 percent of victims, were more likely to be maltreated than boys, 46.7 percent. Although the majority of abused children, 56.4 percent, were white, African American children were disproportionately overrepresented at 26.4 percent of victims. The vast majority of perpetrators were parents, as shown in Table 15.3.

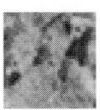

Foster Care for Children

TABLE 15.2 ■ Victims by Type of Maltreatment

TYPE OF MALTREATMENT	PERCENTAGE OF VICTIMS*
Neglect	52.9%
Physical	25.5
Other	14.8
Sexual	13.8
Emotional	4.7
Unknown	4.1
Medical	2.5

*Total exceeds 100 percent because some states report multiple types of maltreatment.

Source: U.S. Department of Health and Human Services, National Center on Child Abuse and Neglect, *Child Maltreatment 1994: Reports from the States to the National Center on Child Abuse and Neglect* (Washington, DC: U.S. Government Printing Office, 1996) pp. 2–5.

TABLE 15.3 ■ Perpetrators

TYPE OF PERPETRATOR	PERCENTAGE*
Parents	79.2%
Other relatives	9.9
Noncaretakers	4.7
Child care providers	1.3
Foster parents	0.6
Facility staff	0.4
Unknown	3.8

Note: Total is less than 100 percent due to rounding.

Source: U.S. Department of Health and Human Services, National Center on Child Abuse and Neglect, *Child Maltreatment 1994: Reports from the States to the National Center on Child Abuse and Neglect* (Washington, DC: U.S. Government Printing Office, 1996) pp. 2–10.

When parents are unable to care for their children, foster care is often used to provide alternative care. As an extension of the practice of boarding out children, most foster care in the United States is at no cost to the parents, and children are placed in the homes of other families. There is an important relationship between child protective services and foster care in U.S. social welfare. Foster care is primarily a service for victims of child abuse; more than half of children in foster care were placed there by child protective service workers. The second most prevalent reason for child foster care is the "condition or absence of the parent," accounting for about 20 percent of foster care placements.[55]

As in the case of protective services, foster care for children was not coordinated under the provisions of the Social Security Act. States adopted separate policies and, unfortunately, took few measures to monitor children in foster care. During the early 1960s a series of studies began to document a disturbing development: Rather than being a temporary arrangement for child care, foster care had become a long-term experience for many youngsters, with 70 percent of children in foster care for more than one year.[56] Not only had states planned poorly for the reunification of children with their original families, but in many instances child welfare agencies lost track of foster care children altogether. During the summer of 1992, the District of Columbia's Department of Human Services (DHS) was rocked by a foster care scandal when it was reported that the department had literally no idea of the location of one out of every four children it had placed in foster care.[57]

In response to the deterioration of children's services, several "family preservation" demonstration projects were begun. As discussed earlier, these efforts offered intensive services to families in order to prevent children from being placed in foster care or to effectively reunite children with their biological parents. The demonstrations seemed to be cost-effective. In Virginia, 14 pre–foster care placement service projects concluded that family functioning improved in 69 percent of the families receiving intensive support services. Moreover, the cost of support services was $1,214 per child, substantially less than the cost of foster care ($11,173) or residential care ($22,025) over the average length of time (4.6 years) a child was in these out-of-home settings.[58] As a result of these field experiments, "permanency planning" became a central feature of the Adoption Assistance and Child Welfare Act of 1980.

Permanency planning is "the systematic process of carrying out, within a brief time-limited period, a set of goal-directed activities designed to help children live in families that offer continuity of relationships with nurturing parents or caretakers and the opportunity to establish lifetime relationships."[59] The Child Welfare Act was an ambitious effort, and one expert heralded it as making it "possible to implement at state and local levels a comprehensive service delivery system for children."[60] As a result of permanency planning, the number of children in foster care plummeted. In 1977 500,000 children were in foster care; by 1983 the number had dropped to 251,000. Welfare workers swiftly removed children from foster care and reunited them with their biological families under the rationale that community support services would assist parents. Early research on family preservation services indicated cost savings; but some families needed extensive service costing as much as $2,600. As caseloads expanded, public agencies struggled to pay for necessary services. An analysis of a model family reunification program found that deficits in agency resources—gaps in service, large caseloads and high worker turnover, and inadequate family preparation, among others—presented problems in more than half of all cases. The researchers were "unaware of any reported successful permanency planning program that has high caseloads as a program component."[61]

Tragically, inadequate resources sometimes created a vicious circle: When biological parents received few support services, they were less able to care for their children, thereby contributing to the need for child protective services. In the absence of intensive support services, permanency planning for many children meant a revolving door—placement in foster care, reunification with the biological parent(s), and then a return to foster care. In 1982 43 percent of children had been in multiple placements, but by 1983 53.1 percent had been in more than one placement; 20.1 percent had been placed twice, 24.2 percent three to five times, and 8.8 percent six or more times.[62] The National Association of Social Workers newsletter reported the instance of a four-year-old New York boy who was placed in 37 different homes in two months and described another child who had been placed in 17 homes in 25 days.[63]

In large measure, the permanency planning movement faltered because of lack of support services to families. Not long after passage of the Adoption Assistance and Child Welfare Act of 1980, Ronald Rooney observed prophetically that "if the promise of permanency planning is to be realized, those who allocate funds must provide money for a continuum of services that are delivered from the point of entry into foster care and include programs designed to prevent the removal of children from their homes."[64] Yet in 1981 an important source of family support services, Title XX, was cut 21 percent. For 1992 the Title XX appropriation, $2.8 billion, was $100 million less than the amount funded in 1981, despite a 58 percent increase in reports of child abuse and neglect since that time.[65] And the decline in gross appropriations for Title XX reveals only a small part of the defunding of the program: Once inflation is factored in, it can be seen that between 1977 and 1992 Title XX actually lost $3.2 billion, or 55.4 percent of its funding.[66] A decade after the early permanency planning demonstration projects, Theodore Stein feared that the movement was being subverted by budget cuts and a reliance on crisis services in child welfare.[67]

Limited funding for child welfare under Title XX induced states to become more dependent on other federal sources of revenue. Because it was funded completely by the federal government and did not require any state matching funds, Title XX was the optimal funding source for child welfare program administrators, but it had one important limitation: Revenues were capped. Other available federal assistance included Title IV-B of the Social Security Act, which allocated a fixed amount of funds for children's services and required a 25 percent state matching contribution. Title IV-E of the Social Security Act was not capped, but federal funds did require a matching state contribution ranging from 25 to 50 percent. Moreover, the two programs that child welfare program administrators looked to under Title IV-E, foster care and adoption assistance, were reserved for poor children who would have been eligible for welfare had they stayed at home. In other words, beyond Title XX,

child welfare administrators could try to address increases in service demand through other federal programs; but Title IV-B funds were capped and required a state match, and open-ended Title IV-E funds were earmarked for welfare children in addition to requiring a state match.

Under these circumstances, Byzantine patterns of service funding evolved during the 1980s as child welfare officials strove for matching formulae that optimized federal reimbursement. Imaginative program managers from affluent states first matched federal requirements for welfare children in order to capture Title IV-E funds, then funded the state match for IV-B funds, reserving Title XX funds to the extent possible for nonwelfare children. Program managers from states unwilling to meet the federal matching requirements had little choice but to use scarce Title XX funds, sometimes for welfare children. Table 15.4 shows trends in three sources of federal revenues for children's services from 1986 to 1998. The rapid expansion of funds for foster care of welfare children under Title IV-E, an open-ended entitlement, contrasts with capped funding under Title IV-B and Title XX,[68] creating the risk that states may be induced to place poor, and disproportionately minority, children in foster care rather than helping them stay at home by funding in-home support services.

To compound the problems faced by foster care workers, quality foster care placements became scarce. A declining standard of living forced many women into the job market, thus restricting the pool of families with a parent at home to supervise children[69]—a requisite for desirable foster care. Soon the shortage of foster homes became critical. In the mid-1980s the director of the Illinois Department of Children and Family Services pleaded for 1,000 new foster parents to prevent the collapse of the state's foster care program.[70] In an investigation into the death of one foster care child, a Virginia grand jury cited "the acute shortage of suitable shelter for the 6,000 neglected, abused, and disabled children" in the state as a factor contributing to the child's death.[71] Thus, by the late 1980s, with permanency planning beset with multiple problems, foster care was an unreliable

TABLE 15.4 ▪ Federal Funding for Child Welfare, Foster Care, and Adoption (dollars in millions)

YEAR	IV-B CHILD WELFARE	IV-B/2 SAFE AND STABLE FAMILIES	IV-E FOSTER CARE	IV-E INDEPENDENT LIVING	IV-E ADOPTION
1986	$198	–	$ 605	–	$ 55
1987	223	–	793	$45	74
1988	239	–	891	45	97
1989	247	–	1,153	50	111
1990	253	–	1,473	60	136
1991	274	–	1,819	70	175
1992	274	–	2,233	70	220
1993	295	–	2,547	70	272
1994	295	$ 60	2,607	70	325
1995	292	150	3,050	70	411
1996	277	225	3,114	70	485
1997*	292	240	3,243	70	571
1998*	292	255	3,360	70	661
1999*	292	275	3,551	70	772

*Estimated

Source: U.S. House of Representatives, Ways and Means Committee, *1998 Green Book* (Washington, DC: U.S. Government Printing Office, 1998), p. 731.

way of serving many of the most endangered children in the United States.

Nevertheless, reversing the decline of the early 1980s, some 442,000 children were in foster care by 1992. With passage of the Family Support and Preservation Program in 1993, extended by the Promoting Safe and Stable Families Act, policymakers gave priority to supporting troubled families in order to prevent foster care placements. As a result the number of children in foster care fell once again, well below what it had been in the late 1970s. But as the century ended, foster care placements were rising again. Despite support services, parents experienced difficulty caring for troubled children, who had problems associated with the cocaine epidemic. In 1998 the foster care caseload passed 300,000 and was projected to rise to 341,000 by 2002.[72]

Compounding the challenges surrounding foster care is the welfare reform legislation en-acted in 1996, which requires unrealistic labor market participation rates on the part of welfare recipients (50 percent by 2002) and allows states to institute time limits of less than two years. Hundreds of thousands of poor welfare families have been and will be deleted from public assistance rolls. In 1996 the Congressional Budget Office projected that 2 to 4 million children would be kicked out of the social safety net if the federal five-year lifetime limit on receipt of welfare was implemented.[73] Many liberals feared that termination of public aid would leave poor parents unable to care for their children and induce many to consider foster care as a regrettable but necessary recourse. Thus, welfare reform would increase the number of children in foster care. Yet, several years after federal welfare reform, there was no clear evidence that children had been adversely affected by welfare reform, at least as indicated by rates of child abuse and foster care.[74]

Several issues have emerged to dampen enthusiasm about foster care as a solution for children from very troubled families. Although many mothers negotiate return of their children who had been placed in foster care, some overcoming the considerable hurdles associated with drug abuse,[75] others experience protracted difficulties. In some instances children who have been placed in foster care are returned to mothers who are poor candidates for resuming care. A celebrated case involved Cornelious Pixley, a two-year-old African American toddler who had been placed with a white policewoman after his mother was convicted of murdering his infant sister. Following a judge's order that Cornelious be returned to his mother, the foster mother challenged the decision with the assistance of child advocacy organizations. The challenge was based not only on the mother's homicide conviction, but also on her violation of probation as well as her difficulty stabilizing her household. Eventually, custody was remanded to the foster mother.[76]

Too often, foster care has emerged as the catalyst of family dramas that become the grist of journalistic accounts of a child welfare system that "is infected with mistrust, backbiting and second-guessing," hardly the ambiance that builds public confidence. One reporter summarized his impression of child welfare:

> As soon as a complaint is received, a virtual industry of social workers, lawyers, judges and administrators goes to work, and no matter how pure the intentions are, the process often deteriorates into chaos. A central goal of child welfare is permanence and stability for the child, but cases routinely become so mired in complications, and legalities, and indecision, and nastiness, and the necessity of trying to understand a specific moment of horror in the larger context of societal issues, that the focus can shift from the search for permanence to the mere passage of time. Months pass. Years pass. Rather than resolution, there is drift, so much that nationally, on average a third of the children entering foster care will be there in excess of two years, creating, instead of stability, an ambiguity that can be damaging.[77]

Increasing demand for foster parents and homosexual rights collided in a controversy about the suitability of gays and lesbians as parents. A Texas child welfare supervisor ordered the removal of a foster child from a lesbian foster parent, arguing that the state's antisodomy statutes defined homosexual households as unacceptable.[78] The *Washington Post*'s Colbert King undoubtedly spoke for many when he observed, "I couldn't care less what those [foster] parents look like as long as they are strong in themselves and are giving that kid the sense of security, belonging and love that every child on this earth needs."[79]

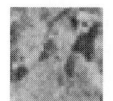 # Adoption

From the standpoint of permanency planning, adoption has become an important child welfare service. In the early 1980s the Children's Bureau noted that 50,000 "hard-to-adopt" children were waiting for homes. Many of these children were of minority origin, had disabilities, or were older and had been in foster care for several years.[80] Because such children posed a financial burden for adoptive parents, the Adoption Assistance and Child Welfare Act of 1980 provided subsidies to adoptive parents. In 1983 6,320 children were being subsidized each month at a cost of $12 million.[81] By 1996 the adoption assistance program had mushroomed to 113,000 cases, with maintenance payments totaling $302 million;[82] by 2002 the caseload is projected to be 229,000 with federal payments of $1.1 billion—a doubling of cases and tripling of allocations in only six years.[83] Providing incentives for parents to adopt hard-to-adopt children clearly supported the concept of permanency planning, as "90 percent of subsidized adoptions involve foster parents whom the subsidy has enabled to adopt children with whom they had formed a relationship . . . and most of these are minorities or have special needs."[84] Moreover, subsidized adoption proved cost-effective, costing 37 percent less than foster care.

Still, adoption is not without controversy. Because children come from a variety of racial and cultural groups, questions have been raised about transcultural adoption. Should agencies give consideration to maintaining the cultural identity of children placed for adoption by finding them homes in their birth culture? This question was at the heart of the Indian Child Welfare Act of 1978. Native Americans were disturbed that "25 to 35 percent of all American Indian children [were] separated from their families and placed in foster homes, adoptive homes, or institutions."[85] The fact that 85 percent of such placements were in non-Indian families and left the children "without access to their tribal homes and relationships" raised the specter of partial cultural genocide.[86] To reinforce the cultural identity of Native American children, the Indian Child Welfare Act provided for

> minimal Federal standards for the removal of Indian children from their families and the placement of such children in foster or adoptive homes which will reflect the unique values of Indian culture, and for assistance to Indian tribes in the operation of child and family service programs.[87]

Equally important, the Indian Child Welfare Act established tribes, rather than state courts, as the governing bodies responsible for Indian foster children.

A similar argument for culturally appropriate placement of children was advanced during the 1980s by the National Association of Black Social Workers (NABSW). Noting an unacceptably high percentage of black children placed with white families, NABSW contended that cross-racial adoptions deprived individual children of their racial identity and would eventually result in a degree of cultural genocide for the black community. Research on cross-racial adoption, however, consistently found that African American children did not suffer adverse consequences from growing up in white families. In 1996 President Clinton signed legislation forbidding interference in child placement for reasons based on race, except by Indian tribes.[88]

Although provisions to reinforce the cultural identity of children have unquestionable merit in a pluralistic society, the circumstances of many racial and cultural minorities leave the implementation of such policies in doubt.[89] Without basic health, education, and employment supports, many minority families are likely to have difficulty adopting children. For example, the number of African American children available for adoption far outstrips the number of African American families able to adopt children, despite the fact that African American families "adopt at a rate 4.5 times greater than white or Hispanic families."[90]

Changes in family composition further cloud the picture. The pool of adoptive families has diminished with the increase in the number of female–headed households. The combination of low wages for women and a shortage of marriageable men means that mothers are encouraged to maintain small families, not to expand them through adoption. In the mid-1980s Esther Wattenberg of the University of Minnesota Center for Urban and Regional Affairs suspected that

> the remainder of the [twentieth century] will be dominated by a sorting out of "the best interests of the child" in the extraordinarily complex family relationships that develop out of extending family boundaries to stepparents, several sets of grandparents, and an assortment of new siblings from remarried families that join and unjoin family compositions.[91]

 # Head Start

In response to concerns about the lack of educational preparation of poor children, Head Start was incorporated in the Economic Opportunity Act of 1964. The first Head Start programs were established in poor communities a year later. Intended to compensate for a range of deficits displayed by poor children, Head Start offered health and dental screening, nutrition, and socialization experiences in addition to preschool academic preparation. Of the Great Society programs, Head Start was one of a few that captured the imagination of the nation. Despite wide public support, however, participation in Head Start was somewhat uneven, as Table 15.5 shows. Significantly, it was not until 1995 that the enrollment of Head Start eclipsed that of 1966; today, fewer than half of eligible children participate in the program.[92]

During the 1980s, when government assistance to the poor was restrained, many poor families dispatched both parents to the labor market to stabilize family income, and this increased the need for Head Start. Even the Deficit Reduction Act of 1990, which held spending for most social programs in check, provided for modest increases in Head Start.[93] In large measure this funding reflected a growing appreciation that Head Start was a proven investment in human capital. Award-winning author Sylvia Ann Hewlett noted that "Head Start ($3,000 a year per child) is much less expensive than prison ($20,000 a year per inmate)."[94] The 1996 welfare reform act, which required recipients of family cash assistance to participate in the labor market, increased Head Start enrollments even further.

Since its inception, Head Start has largely become a prekindergarten program for the minority poor. Sixty-two percent of children enrolled are age four, and almost 30 percent are age three; 36 percent are African American, 25 percent are Hispanic, 4 percent are Native American, and 3 percent are Asian. Thirteen percent of Head Start children have disabilities.[95] Few dispute the value of Head Start programming for at-risk children, persistent questions about the long-term benefits of the program notwithstanding. Rather than subverting Head Start, research on such questions has become central to the growing conservative critique of public education.

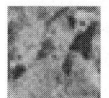

Emerging Issues in Child Welfare

Changes in the economic and social circumstances of families in the United States have broadened the scope of the issues that have traditionally defined child welfare policy. Of these changes, three are likely to shape child welfare in the future: day care, maternal and child health, and teenage pregnancy.

Day Care

Day care for children has risen in importance as more and more parents with children work. In 1998 families in which both parents worked exceeded more than half of all married couples with children, up from 33 percent in 1976.[96] At the same time the number of working mothers with young children has skyrocketed; in 1947 only 12.0 percent of mothers with children under age six worked outside the home, but by 1996 62.3 percent did.[97] The need for child day care is felt both by middle-income families, in which both parents work in order to meet the income requirements of a middle-class lifestyle, and by low-income families, in which a parent is encouraged or required to participate in a welfare-to-work program. Yet the child care available is

TABLE 15.5 ▪ Head Start: Participation and Federal Funding, Selected Years (dollars in millions)

FISCAL YEAR	ENROLLMENT	BUDGET AUTHORITY
1965 (summer only)	561,000	$96.4
1970	477,400	325.7
1975	349,000	403.9
1980	376,300	735.0
1985	452,080	1,075.0
1990	548,470	1,552.0
1995	750,077	3,534.1

Source: U.S. House of Representatives, Ways and Means Committee, *1998 Green Book* (Washington, DC: U.S. Government Printing Office, 1998) p. 1010.

often unreliable, expensive, and of questionable quality. Thus, by 1994, almost twice as many children were cared for in a family home as in organized child care facilities.[98] Although poor families typically find family care of their children less expensive than organized child care, on average child care costs consume 17 percent of their income.[99] Even then, available child care often does not conform to the work schedules of parents. A study of New York City families found that half had to patch together day care from multiple providers. Low wages fail to attract the more skilled providers to the day care field, leading the Children's Defense Fund to observe ruefully that "despite their higher levels of education, child care providers are paid less than animal caretakers, bartenders, or parking lot and amusement park attendants."[100]

The crisis in child day care received nationwide attention in 1986 when two Miami children, unsupervised because their mother had to work and could not locate child care, climbed into a clothes dryer in which they "tumbled and burned to death."[101] This incident was cited in the introductory remarks to a proposed $375 million Child Care Services Improvement Act. An indicator of the severity of the day care crisis was that the legislation was sponsored by Orrin Hatch, a conservative senator noted for his prior opposition to social welfare legislation.[102]

The primary programs assisting parents with child care are the federal dependent care tax credit, the child care tax credit, the Child Care and Development Block Grant, and Title XX. The dependent care tax credit allows families to deduct 30 percent of up to $2,400 spent on child day care for a given year; the child care tax credit is available to families with incomes below 85 percent of a state's median income. As "tax expenditures"—de facto allocations the Internal Revenue Service creates by not taxing income spent for a specific purpose—the child care tax credit is budgeted at $20.4 billion for 2000, the largest form of federal assistance for child care.[103] Unfortunately, only a small portion of the child care tax credit is refundable, allowing poor families a cash refund for child care expenses. With passage of the 1996 welfare reform

act, several child care programs were consolidated under the Child Care and Development Block Grant, funding for which was set at $2.4 billion for 2000.[104] Under Title XX states are able to purchase day care for poor families; but as of 1995, for example, only $414 million, or 14.8 percent, of the $2.8 billion in Title XX funds was expended for child care.[105]

Maternal and Child Health

Maternal and child health has emerged as an issue among child welfare advocates as younger poor women give birth to low-birth-weight babies for which they have received inadequate prenatal care. Low birth weight is a concern because such infants have a higher incidence of developmental disabilities, some of which are permanent and eventually require institutional care. The relationship between low birth weight and developmental disabilities, long recognized by public health officials, resurfaced in *Hunger in America*, a 1985 report by the Physician Task Force on Hunger in America funded through the Harvard University School of Public Health. The task force noted that "low birth-weight is the eighth leading cause of death in the United States." Efforts to sustain premature and low-birth-weight infants are expensive and, even when successful, often cannot forestall "long-term growth and developmental problems." Infants born small and premature suffer 25 percent more major neurological problems and 117 percent more minor neurological problems than do normal infants.[106]

Despite such documentation, the incidence of low birth weight among infants in the United States is relatively high, comparable to that of many poorer nations; that among African Americans parallels the rate of many African nations. Low birth weight in minority infants is of particular concern, because it relates to lack of adequate prenatal care: Since 1970 the rate of late or no prenatal care among African Americans has been more than twice the rate for whites.[107] Moreover, the percentage of low-birth-weight infants born to nonwhite teenagers is alarming, ranging from a low of 15.3 percent in Hawaii to a high of 32.9 percent in Mississippi.[108] Given the relatively high number of teen pregnancies in the nonwhite population, these figures translate to a disturbing reality: Substantial numbers of nonwhite infants in the United States are born with serious neurological deficits.

The primary federal program to enhance prenatal care for low-income families is WIC, the Special Supplemental Nutrition Program for Women, Infants, and Children. Under WIC, low-income pregnant and nursing women and their young children are eligible for food coupons through which they may obtain especially nutritious foods. While the WIC program would seem a logical method for addressing the low-birth-weight problem of infants born to poor women, participation in the WIC program is not at desirable levels. Nationwide, only about half of the people financially eligible to participate in WIC do so.[109] Participation and expenditures for WIC are listed in Table 15.6.

Teen Pregnancy

Problems relating to maternal and infant health are exacerbated by the sharp rise in the numbers of adolescent females having children. Out-of-wedlock births became an important family issue in the 1980s, when the incidence of unwed motherhood increased so rapidly that by 1983 half of all nonwhite births were outside of marriage.[110] Even though the absolute number of births to teenagers declined between 1973 and 1991, the decline in the total number of adolescent females meant that the teen pregnancy rate was increasing substantially.[111] Most troubling was that the percentage of unmarried teenage mothers was rising so rapidly that by 1984 it was triple what it had been 25 years before.[112] As Table 15.7 shows, despite a continued high rate, particularly among African Americans, increases in the number of unmarried teens giving birth began to slow, then reverse, during the 1990s.

This increase in childbearing among very young unmarried women poses a serious problem for public policy for two basic reasons. First, teenage mothers are more likely to drop out of school and thus to fail to gain skills that would make them self-sufficient. Adolescent mothers, particularly those who are African American or Hispanic, are apt to have less command of basic skills. Poor skill development represents an especially critical problem when the skills in question are parenting skills. Second, teenage mothers are more likely to have to depend on welfare, the benefits of which are at levels lower than the actual cost of raising children. This combination of inadequate skill development and dependence on public welfare presents the specter of poor teenagers bearing poor children in an endless cycle of hopelessness. The consequences are particularly tragic for the children, who have little prospect of escaping the poverty trap. Reductions in the numbers of working African American and

TABLE 15.6 ▪ WIC Participation and Spending (dollars in millions)

| YEAR | PARTICIPATION IN THOUSANDS | | | | SPENDING IN CONSTANT DOLLARS |
	Women	*Infants*	*Children*	*Total*	
1980	411.0	507.0	995.0	1,913.0	$1,413.2
1985	665.0	874.0	1,600.0	3,138.0	2,173.8
1990	1,035.0	1,412.5	2,069.4	4,516.9	2,572.3
1995	1,576.8	1,817.3	3,500.1	6,894.2	3,544.5

Source: U.S. House of Representatives, Ways and Means Committee, *1998 Green Book* (Washington, DC: U.S. Government Printing Office, 1998), p. 1002.

TABLE 15.7 ■ Number and Rate of Births to Unmarried Women

AGE OF MOTHER	NUMBER OF BIRTHS			RATES PER 1,000 UNMARRIED WOMEN		
	All Races	*White*	*Black*	*All Races*	*White*	*Black*
1980:						
Under 15	9,024	3,166	5,691	NA	NA	NA
15–19	262,777	130,417	126,278	27.6	18.5	87.9
15–17	121,900	58,705	60,548	20.6	12.0	68.8
18–19	140,877	71,712	65,728	39.0	24.1	118.2
20–24	237,265	118,445	114,538	40.9	25.1	112.3
25–29	99,583	46,722	47,594	34.0	21.5	81.4
1993:						
Under 15	11,467	4,868	6,293	NA	NA	NA
15–19	357,432	213,080	133,031	44.5	33.6	102.4
15–17	152,212	87,032	60,412	30.6	22.1	76.8
18–19	205,220	126,048	72,619	66.9	52.4	141.6
20–24	438,538	283,538	159,598	69.2	54.2	142.2
25–29	233,776	139,905	84,604	57.1	46.7	94.5
1995:						
Under 15	11,441	5,196	5,876	NA	NA	NA
15–19	375,738	236,546	127,241	44.4	35.5	92.8
15–17	161,140	98,415	57,766	30.5	23.6	68.6
18–19	214,598	138,131	69,475	67.6	55.4	131.2
20–24	432,003	271,466	145,134	70.3	58.0	127.7
25–29	228,614	143,006	75,815	56.1	48.7	84.8

Source: U.S. House of Representatives, Ways and Means Committee, *1998 Green Book* (Washington, DC: U.S. Government Printing Office, 1998), pp. 1247–1248.

Hispanic males who are marriageable means that many of these children have little hope that their mother will marry and thus pull them out of poverty—which had been the most prevalent way for mothers to become independent of public welfare.[113] The loss of buying power of the income support provided by Aid to Families with Dependent Children (now TANF) has meant that public assistance does not provide an adequate economic base for poor children.[114]

In response to the high teen pregnancy rate, the Clinton administration moved on several fronts. The 1996 welfare reform act required that unmarried teen parents live at home or in a supervised setting in order to receive cash assistance; in addition, states were encouraged to establish Second Chance homes for pregnant teens. Fifty million dollars was made available to states for initiating abstinence education programs. In 1999 HHS Secretary Donna Shalala announced a national campaign to prevent teen pregnancy, focusing on the role of local nonprofit organizations in pregnancy prevention. These, initiatives, in conjunction with strengthened child support enforcement, were credited with helping sustain a steady decline in black teen pregnancy, which in 1999 fell for the eighth straight year.[115]

Conclusion: The Future of Child Welfare

After a half century of federal legislation, many child welfare advocates had become pessimistic about the care provided to youngsters in the United States. Hopes for using the family as the primary institution for child welfare had faded in the absence of economic and social supports to keep families intact. Lacking such supports, most families were reliant on the labor market to generate income to meet essential needs. Although some of the benefits of unprecedented prosperity and low unemployment began to trickle down to poor families by the end of the twentieth century, many welfare and working poor families continued to struggle. The 1996 imposition of welfare time limits cast a long shadow over poor families. In the absence of a coherent national family policy, poor families were less able to care for children; as a result, child welfare services—such as protective services, foster care, and adoption—have attempted to compensate for severe family deficits.

During the 1990s two strategies emerged in child welfare: the concept of child support assurance as a way to address income maintenance for poor families, and the idea of a children's authority as a way to restructure child welfare. As early as 1991 the National Commission on Children recommended the deployment of a demonstration program to test an enhanced child support enforcement and insurance scheme. Irwin Garfinkel, a social work professor at Columbia University, proposed a child support enforcement and assurance program (CSEAP) to replace family welfare. The CSEAP would reform child support in three ways: (1) The amount of child support would be calculated as a percentage of the absent parent's income; (2) support payments would be automatically withheld from paychecks; and (3) a minimum benefit to children would be provided by the federal government.[116] A federal CSEAP initiative with these components, Garfinkel reasoned, could replace most of the highly stigmatized family welfare program. The CSEAP concept is not without its critics, however. One critic opposed the idea because it placed the federal government in the same awkward position it has had with cash welfare—namely, subsidizing broken families.[117]

Meanwhile, states were experimenting with various methods for stretching their dollars to do more for children. Gradually, these efforts evolved into a potent critique of the traditional ways in which children's services had been delivered. "What's needed is a complete overhaul of children's services, bringing together public and private organizations to meet the comprehensive needs of children, adolescents, and parents," stated Stanford University's Michael Kirst.[118] Noting that many children from problem families were known to several separate health and human services agencies—none with sufficient resources to substantively help any one child—children's advocate Sid Gardner called for collaborative efforts among service providers: "In fact, we are ultimately failing our children not only because we haven't invested in them, but also because as communities we have failed to work together to hold ourselves accountable for the substantial resources we do invest—and for the outcomes of our most vulnerable residents."[119] Social worker Bonnie Bernard of the Far West Laboratory for Educational Research and Development observed that collaboration or restructuring, however defined, targets power relations. "True restructuring means the redistribution of policymaking power, not only from the central office administration to the local school," but to professionals and ultimately to consumers and their communities.[120] In 1996 Lela Costin, Howard Karger, and David Stoesz proposed that in every jurisdiction children's services be restructured and placed under a Children's Authority, a local body that would provide a comprehensive array of services under performance-based management.[121]

Discussion Questions

1. Much of child welfare—protective services, foster care, adoptions—is funded through a complex array of categorical programs. How does your welfare department optimize reimbursement through these funding sources? As a result of reimbursement systems, what are the priorities for children's services? How would you reconcile discrepancies between categorical funding priorities and community needs?

2. Maintaining the cultural identity of minority children who receive foster care and adoption services is a heated issue in child welfare. When there are too few minority families for the children needing foster care and adoption, what should be the policy of the welfare department in placing minority children? How consistent is your answer with current child welfare policy in your community?

3. Providing preschool programs for children is an increasingly important issue as more mothers enter the workforce. How adequate are day care provisions in your community? Who is responsible for the oversight of day care? To what extent are the needs of low-income families considered in day care arrangements? What percentage of families eligible for Head Start actually participate in this program in your community?

4. Among health-related child welfare concerns are infant mortality and low birth weight. How do the statistics in your community compare with the state and national incidence of these two important indicators of child welfare? What are the incidences of infant mortality and low birth weight for children of teenage and minority mothers in your community? What plans does your community have for improving the health status of infants of minority and low-income families?

5. What is the plausibility of reforming child welfare by instituting a child support enforcement and assurance program or consolidating existing services under a Children's Authority? If you favor one of these, how would you convince the public that it constitutes real welfare reform?

Notes

1. U.S. House of Representatives, Ways and Means Committee, *1998 Green Book* (Washington, DC: U.S. Government Printing Office, 1998), p. 1245.

2. Kathryn Porter and Wendell Primus, "Changes since 1995 in the Safety Net's Impact on Child Poverty" (Washington, DC: Center on Budget and Policy Priorities, 1999), p. v.

3. Arloc Sherman, "Extreme Child Poverty Rises Sharply in 1997" (Washington, DC: Children's Defense Fund, 1999), p. 2.

4. Marc Miringoff and Marque-Luisa Miringoff, *The Social Health of the Nation* (New York: Oxford University Press, 1999), pp. 52, 53.

5. Dale Russakoff, "Report Shows Children's Well-Being Is Improving," *Washington Post* (July 14, 2000), p. A1.

6. Jeanne Giovannoni, "Children," *Encyclopedia of Social Work,* 18th ed. (Silver Spring, MD: NASW, 1987), p. 247.

7. Alvin Schorr, "The Bleak Prospect for Public Child Welfare," *Social Service Review* 74, no. 1 (March 2000), p. 125.

8. Alfred Kadushin, "Child Welfare Services," *Encyclopedia of Social Work*, 18th ed. (Silver Spring, MD: NASW, 1987), p. 268.

9. Dale Russakoff, "Assessing an Ambiguous Threat: Parents," *Washington Post* (January 19, 1998), p. A1.

10. Walter Trattner, *From Poor Law to Welfare State* (New York: Free Press, 1974), p. 100.

11. Ibid., pp. 106–107.

12. Sallie Watkins, "The Mary Ellen Myth," *Social Work* 35 (November 1990), p. 503.

13. Diana DiNitto and Thomas Dye, *Social Welfare* (Englewood Cliffs, NJ: Prentice-Hall, 1987), p. 153.

14. Kathleen Faller, "Protective Services for Children," *Encyclopedia of Social Work*, 18th ed. (Silver Spring, MD: NASW, 1987). p. 386.

15. Trattner, *From Poor Law to Welfare State*, pp. 181, 183.

16. James Leiby, *A History of Social Welfare and Social Work in the United States* (New York: Columbia University Press, 1978), pp. 148–149.

17. June Axinn and Herman Levin, *Social Welfare* (New York: Harper & Row, 1982), p. 159.

18. Trattner, *From Poor Law to Welfare State*, p. 186.

19. Axinn and Levin, *Social Welfare*, pp. 224–228.

20. Barbara Kantrowitz et al., "How to Protect Abused Children," *Newsweek* (November 23, 1987), p. 68.

21. Sandra Evans, "Increase in Baby Killings Attributed to Family Stress," *Washington Post* (June 23, 1992), p. A1.

22. Faller, "Protective Services for Children," pp. 387, 389.

23. Douglas Besharov, "Contending with Overblown Expectations," *Public Welfare* (Winter 1987), pp. 7, 8.

24. Kantrowitz et al., "How to Protect Abused Children," p. 68.

25. "Foster Care: Duty v. Legal Vulnerability," *NASW News* (July 1988), p. 3.

26. "Social Workers' Neglect," *All Things Considered* (Washington, DC: National Public Radio, April 15, 1988). *NASW News* later reported that the employees cited in this broadcast were not professional social workers but employees of the state.

27. "High Court Review Urged on Foster Care Liability," *NASW News* (July 1988), p. 3.

28. Ibid.

29. Douglas Besharov, "Right versus Rights: The Dilemma of Child Protection," *Public Welfare* 43 (1985), pp. 19–46.

30. David Finkelhor, "Is Child Abuse Overprotected?" *Public Welfare* 48 (1990), pp. 22–29.

31. Fox Butterfield, "Sect Members Assert They Are Misunderstood," *The New York Times* (June 24, 1984), p. 16.

32. Bridgitte Berger and Peter Berger, *The War over the Family* (Garden City, NY: Doubleday, 1983), p. 213.

33. Besharov, "Contending with Overblown Expectations," p. 8.

34. William Claiborne, "Child Sex Ring or Witch Hunt: Charges Divide Town," *Washington Post* (November 14, 1995), p. A1; "A Northwest Town's Nightmare Continues," *Washington Post Weekly* (June 24–30, 1995), p. 31; Lela Costin, Howard Karger, and David Stoesz, *The Politics of Child Abuse in America* (New York: Oxford University Press, 1996).

35. Douglas Besharov with Lisa Laumann, "Child Abuse Reporting," *Society* (May/June 1996), p. 43.

36. David Stoesz and Howard Karger, "Suffer the Children," *Washington Monthly* (June 1996), p. 20.

37. Dale Russakoff, "Protector of N.Y. City's Children Knows the System Well," *Washington Post* (December 19, 1996), p. A3.

38. Rachel Swarns, "Court Experts Denounce New York's Child Agency," *The New York Times* (October 22, 1997), p. A19.

39. Scott Higham and Sari Horwitz, "Brianna's Death Motivates House Probe of D.C. Agency," *Washington Post* (May 6, 2000), p. B1.

40. *"LaShawn A. V. Williams:* A Progress Report" (Washington, DC: Center for the Study of Social Policy, March 7, 2000).

41. Sari Horwitz and Scott Higham, "Foster Care Caseloads 'Horrible,'" *Washington Post* (March 27, 2000), p. A1.

42. "'Foster Care Panic,'" *Washington Post* (March 1, 2000), p. A16.

43. Scott Higham and Sari Horwitz, "GAO Study Faults D.C. Child Care," *Washington Post* (September 20, 2000), p. A1.

44. Scott Higham and Sari Horwitz, "D.C. Child Welfare Official Arrested," *Washington Post* (August 15, 2000), p. A1.

45. Sari Horwitz and Scott Higham, "Child Welfare Chief Drops Lawsuit," *Washington Post* (August 24, 2000), p. B3.

46. Sari Horwitz and Scott Higham, "DeLay Lambastes Foster Care in D.C.," *Washington Post* (September 21, 2000), p. A1.

47. Costin, Karger, and Stoesz, *The Politics of Child Abuse in America.*

48. U.S. Department of Health and Human Services, National Center on Child Abuse and Neglect, *Child Maltreatment 1994: Reports from the States to the National Center on Child Abuse and Neglect* (Washington, DC: U.S. Government Printing Office, 1996).

49. Costin, Karger, and Stoesz, *The Politics of Child Abuse in America.*

50. Jane Waldfogel, *The Future of Child Protection: How to Break the Cycle of Abuse and Neglect* (Cambridge: Harvard University Press, 1998).

51. Costin, Karger, and Stoesz, *The Politics of Child Abuse in America.*

52. Miringoff and Miringoff, *The Social Health of the Nation,* p. 75.

53. U.S. Department of Health and Human Services, *Child Maltreatment 1994,* p. ix.

54. Barbara Vobejda, "HHS Study Finds Sharp Rise in Child Abuse," *Washington Post* (September 19, 1996), p. A8.

55. Theodore Stein, "Foster Care for Children," *Encyclopedia of Social Work,* 18th ed. (Silver Spring, MD: NASW, 1987), pp. 641–642.

56. Ibid., p. 643.

57. Keith Harriston, "D.C. Foster Children Are Missing," *Washington Post* (August 6, 1992), p. C1.

58. Children's Defense Funds, *A Children's Defense Budget* (Washington, DC: Children's Defense Fund, 1988), p. 179.

59. Anthony Maluccio and Edith Fein, "Permanency Planning: A Redefinition," *Child Welfare* (May–June 1983), p. 197.

60. Duncan Lindsey, "Achievements for Children in Foster Care," *Social Work* (November 1982), p. 495.

61. Peg Hess, Gail Folaron, and Ann Jefferson, "Effectiveness of Family Reunification Services," *Social Work* 37 (July 1992), pp. 306, 310.

62. Stein, "Foster Care for Children," p. 641.

63. "Foster Care Duty v. Legal Vulnerability," p. 3.

64. Ronald Rooney, "Permanency Planning for All Children?" *Social Work* (March 1982), p. 157.

65. Children's Defense Fund, *A Children's Defense Budget,* p. 54.

66. U.S. House of Representatives, *1992 Green Book* (Washington, DC: U.S. Government Printing Office, 1992), p. 830.

67. Stein, "Foster Care for Children," p. 649.

68. Title XX amounts are not included in the table because the federal government does not collect data on how much is expended by states for child welfare.

69. Esther Wattenberg, "The Fate of Baby Boomers and Their Children," *Social Work* (January–February 1986), pp. 85–93.

70. Kantrowitz et al., "How to Protect Abused Children," p. 71.

71. Mary Jordan, "Foster Parent Scarcity Causing Crisis in Care," *Washington Post* (July 20, 1986), p. A9.

72. U.S. House of Representatives, *1998 Green Book,* p. 733.

73. David Stoesz, "Welfare Behaviorism," *Society* (Spring, 1997), p. 33.

74. Somini Sengupta, "No Rise in Child Abuse Seen in Welfare Shift," *The New York Times* (August 10, 2000), p. 1.

75. Dale Russakoff, "One Child's Chaotic Bounce in Mother Government's Lap," *Washington Post* (January 18, 1998); "Against the Odds, a Failed Mother Returns to Her Children," *Washington Post* (January 20, 1998), p. A1.

76. Steve Vogel, "Md. Custody Debate: Did Law Force Judge to Return Child to Killer?" *Washington Post* (January 1, 1998), p. B1; Manuel Perez-Rias, "Pixley Denied Custody of Son," *Washington Post* (January 12, 2000), p. A1.

77. David Finkel, "'No Say Goodbye to Diane'," *Washington Post Magazine* (May 4, 1997), pp. 10–11.

78. Sam Verhovek, "Homosexual Foster Parent Sets Off a Debate in Texas," *The New York Times* (November 30, 1997), p. 20.

79. Colbert King, "What Every Child Needs," *Washington Post* (March 11, 2000), p. A19.

80. Elizabeth Cole, "Adoption," *Encyclopedia of Social Work,* 18th ed. (Silver Spring, MD: NASW, 1987), p. 70.

81. U.S. House of Representatives, Committee on Ways and Means, *Background Material and*

Data on Programs within the Jurisdiction of the Committee on Ways and Means (Washington, DC: U.S. Government Printing Office, 1985), p. 494.

82. U.S. House of Representatives, Committee on Ways and Means, *1994 Green Book* (Washington, DC: U.S. Government Printing Office, 1994), p. 599.

83. U.S. House of Representatives, *1998 Green Book*, p. 733.

84. Cole, "Adoption," p. 71.

85. Ronald Fischler, "Protecting American Indian Children," *Social Work* (September 1980), p. 341.

86. Evelyn Lance Blanchard and Russell Lawrence Barsh, "What Is Best for Tribal Children?" *Social Work* (September 1980), p. 350.

87. Fischler, "Protecting American Indian Children," p. 341.

88. Spencer Rich, "Wage Bill Includes Provisions Intended to Increase Adoptions," *Washington Post* (August 10, 1996), p. A4.

89. Patricia Hogan and Sau-Fong Siu, "Minority Children and the Child Welfare System," *Social Work* (November–December 1988), pp. 312–317.

90. Cole, "Adoption," p. 70.

91. Wattenberg, "The Fate of Baby Boomers and Their Children," p. 24.

92. Children's Defense Fund, *The State of America's Children, 1991* (Washington, DC: Children's Defense Fund, 1991), p. 44.

93. Paul Leonard and Robert Greenstein, *One Step Forward: The Deficit Reduction Package of 1990* (Washington, DC: Center on Budget and Policy Priorities, 1990), p. 34.

94. Sylvia Ann Hewlett, *When the Bough Breaks* (New York: HarperCollins, 1992), p. 300.

95. U.S. House of Representatives, *1998 Green Book*, p. 1011.

96. "Two-Income Families Now a Majority," *Richmond Times-Dispatch* (October 24, 2000), p. A3.

97. U.S. House of Representatives, *1998 Green Book*, p. 661.

98. Ibid., p. 666.

99. Ibid., p. 671

100. Children's Defense Fund, *The State of America's Children, 1988* (Washington, DC: Children's Defense Fund, 1988), p. 207.

101. Ibid., p. 214.

102. Ibid., p. 32; also National Association of Social Workers, "1986 Voting Record" (Silver Spring, MD: NASW, 1987).

103. U.S. House of Representatives, *1998 Green Book*, pp. 439–440.

104. Ibid., p. 684.

105. Ibid., pp. 714, 720.

106. Physician Task Force on Hunger in America, *Hunger in America* (Cambridge, MA: Harvard University Press, 1985), p. 65.

107. Miringoff and Miringoff, *The Social Health of the Nation*, p. 52.

108. Children's Defense Fund, *The Health of America's Children* (Washington, DC: Children's Defense Fund, 1987), p. 72.

109. Ibid., p. 84.

110. Michael Novak (ed.), *The New Consensus on Family and Welfare* (Washington, DC: American Enterprise Institute, 1987), p. 135.

111. U.S. House of Representatives, *1998 Green Book*, p. 1245.

112. Lisbeth Schorr, *Within Our Reach* (Garden City, NY: Doubleday, 1988), p. 13.

113. William Julius Wilson, "American Social Policy and the Ghetto Underclass," *Dissent* (Winter 1988), pp. 80–91.

114. David Ellwood, *Poor Support: Poverty and the American Family* (New York: Basic Books, 1988), p. 58.

115. "Preventing Teenage Pregnancy" (Washington, DC: U.S. Department of Health and Human Services, August 8, 2000).

116. Irwin Garfinkel, "Bringing Fathers Back In: The Child Support Assurance Strategy," *The American Prospect* (Spring 1992), p. 75.

117. Mickey Kaus, *The End of Equality* (New York: Basic Books, 1992).

118. Michael Kirst, "Improving Children's Services," *Phi Delta Kappan* (April 1991), p. 616.

119. Sid Gardner, "Failure by Fragmentation," *California Tomorrow* (Fall 1989), p. 19.

120. Bonnie Benard, "School Restructuring Can Promote Prevention," *Western Center News* (December 1991), p. 8.

121. Costin, Karger, and Stoesz, *The Politics of Child Abuse in America* (note 34 above).

chapter 16

Housing Policies

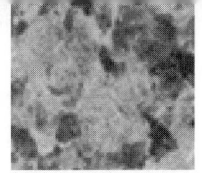

Housing is a topic that has recently fallen out of favor with the media. Despite limited coverage in the press, however, housing problems affect millions of Americans. Persistent problems include a lack of low-income affordable housing, dilapidated and dangerous housing, and high numbers of homeless people. Although housing discussions have frequently focused on homelessness, finding and maintaining adequate and affordable housing is also problematic for people on public assistance, for the working poor, and for a large section of the supposedly stable middle class. This chapter examines the problems of housing in the United States, with particular emphasis on low-income housing, housing affordability, homelessness, and proposals for housing reform.

Overview of Housing Legislation

Federal housing legislation began in 1937. As Table 16.1 illustrates, this legislation developed into a tangle of laws that often evolved in conflicting directions.

In 1990 Congress passed the Cranston–Gonzales National Affordable Housing Act, the first new piece of legislation in more than a decade to address the housing needs of low- and moderate-income people. This act authorized a new indirect approach to housing in the form of block grants to state and local governments. The 1990 legislation had six specific goals: (1) to decentralize housing policy by allowing states to design and administer their own housing programs; (2) to use nonprofit sponsors to help develop and implement housing services; (3) to link housing assistance more closely with social services; (4) to facilitate home ownership for low- and moderate-income people; (5) to preserve existing federally subsidized housing units; and (6) to initiate cost sharing among federal, state,

and local governments and nonprofit organizations.[1] The legislation introduced the HOME investment partnerships block grant program, the Homeownership and Opportunity for People Everywhere (HOPE) program, and the national home ownership trust demonstration.

The centerpiece of the National Affordable Housing Act was the HOME program, designed to increase the supply of affordable housing for low-income families by providing federal grants to state and local governments. All states and more than 300 local jurisdictions receive HOME funds. Ninety percent of HOME-assisted units in a jurisdiction must be affordable for families with incomes below 60 percent of the area median, with the remaining units being affordable for families with incomes up to 80 percent of the median. The HOME program allows states and communities some flexibility in addressing their local housing needs: Matching federal/state HOME program funds can be used for tenant-based rental assistance; property acquisition or rehabilitation; or, in some cases, new construction. Providing an opportunity for local innovation, at least 15 percent of HOME funds must be used for projects sponsored by Community Housing Development Organizations (CHDOs) or neighborhood-based nonprofit groups.[2]

A second major component is the HOPE program, which was designed to facilitate home ownership by low-income families through the sale of publicly owned or held homes to current residents or other low-income households. The HOPE program has four components: (1) HOPE I finances the sales of public housing apartments to residents; (2) HOPE II finances the sales to low-income persons of other apartment buildings held by the federal government (such as property acquired from failed savings and loan associations); (3) HOPE III finances the sale of single-family homes owned by federal, state, or local governments; and (4) HOPE IV represents an effort to combine social services with housing assistance for elderly and disabled households that would otherwise be unable to live independently.[3]

TABLE 16.1 ▪ Historical Highlights of Pre-1990 Housing Legislation

Housing Act of 1937	The United States had no national housing policy before the Housing Act of 1937. The objective of the act was to "provide financial assistance to the states and political subdivisions thereof for the elimination of unsafe and unsanitary housing conditions, for the eradication of slums, for the provision of decent, safe and sanitary dwellings for families of low income, and for the reduction of unemployment and the stimulation of business activity, to create a United States Housing Authority and for other purposes."[1]
Housing Act of 1949 (amended the 1937 act)	This amendment called for federal money for slum clearance and urban redevelopment and for the creation of a public authority charged with building and administering 135,000 low-income housing units annually for six years. In addition, the Housing Act of 1949 included the goal of providing a decent home and a suitable living environment for every family.[2] Specifically, this bill required each locality to develop a plan for urban redevelopment that contained provisions for "predominantly residential dwellings." The wording of this bill was interpreted by localities to mean that only one-half of new construction was to be devoted to low-income housing. Inadvertently, the federal government created a policy that encouraged urban redevelopment at the expense of existing low-income housing.
Housing Act of 1954 (amended the 1949 act)	"Urban development" was changed to urban renewal, and localities were required to submit a master plan for removing urban blight and for community development. The act removed the requirement that new federally subsidized urban construction be "predominantly residential," clearing the way for massive slum clearance projects. It also allowed localities to more easily lease or sell land and to avoid the construction of public housing. This led to charges that cities were insensitive to the needs of long-term low-income residents. Using renewal projects, localities tried to revitalize inner cities by attracting middle- and upper-income families at the expense of displaced poor families. From 1949 to 1963, urban renewal projects removed about 243,000 housing units and replaced them with 68,000 units, of which only 20,000 were for low-income families.[3]
Demonstration Cities and Metropolitan Development Act (Model Cities)	Passed in 1966, this act was part of President Lyndon Johnson's Great Society effort. In large part, it focused on issues of deteriorated housing and blighted neighborhoods. The Model Cities legislation promised to "concentrate public and private resources in a comprehensive five-year attack on social, economic, and physical problems of slums and blighted neighborhoods."[4] The Model Cities act and virtually all neighborhood development acts were superseded by the Housing and Community Development Act of 1974.
The Housing and Community Development Act of 1974	This was a wide-ranging bill that included provisions for urban renewal, neighborhood development, model cities, and water and sewer projects; there were neighborhood and facility grants, public facilities and rehabilitation loans, and urban beautification and historic preservation grants.[5] Although spending priorities were determined at the national level, each community was required to submit a master plan, including specific reference to its low-income housing needs. The amount allocated for fiscal years 1978 to 1980 was almost $11 billion, and more than 1,800 communities received entitlement grants in the first two years of the program.[6]
Home Mortgage Disclosure Act	This 1976 act was concerned with the problem of mortgage redlining. Housing observers had argued that a major cause of community deterioration was "lending strikes," or redlining, by financial institutions. Redlining is defined as "an outright refusal of an insurance company, bank, or other financial institution to provide its services solely on the basis of the location of the property in question. The term is derived from the practice of marking in red the area on a map that is to be avoided by those responsible for the distribution of the services of that institution."[7] As a result of this policy, families seeking to purchase a home in a redlined neighborhood might be denied a mortgage loan, insurance, or other

TABLE 16.1 ■ Continued

	necessary services. In 1976 President Gerald Ford signed the HMDA, which required virtually every bank or savings and loan association to disclose where it made its loans each year. Although useful for community groups trying to pressure local banks into greater neighborhood involvement the law was almost useless in cities without active community organizations.
Community Reinvestment Act of 1977	Significantly broader than the HMDA, the CRA established the principle that each bank and savings institution has an obligation to make loans in every neighborhood of its service area. Virtually all lending institutions are covered under the CRA, and the law requires the federal government to annually evaluate the performance of each lending institution. Primary enforcement involves control by federal regulatory agencies over new bank charters, and over bank growth, mergers, relocations, and acquisitions. Although the CRA works well in theory, only a handful of the estimated 250 or more challenges brought under the CRA have resulted in punitive action against lenders. Mainly, the power of the CRA rests with the ability of community groups to win commitments directly from lending institutions, usually in the form of negotiated settlements. It is estimated that $7.5 billion has been committed by banks and savings associations to low-income communities as the result of negotiated CRA agreements.

1. Quoted in Charles S. Prigmore and Charles R. Atherton, *Social Welfare Policy: Analysis and Formulation* (Lexington, MA: D.C. Heath, 1979), pp. 146–147.

2. Robert Morris, *Social Policy of the American Welfare State,* 2nd ed. (New York: Longman, 1985), p. 131.

3. Ibid., p. 132.

4. Barbara Habenstreit, *The Making of America* (New York: Julian Messner, 1971), p. 46.

5. Richard Geruson and Dennis McGrath, *Cities and Urbanization* (New York: Praeger, 1977), pp. 6–7.

6. Ibid., p. 40.

7. National Training and Information Center, *Insurance Redlining: Profits v. Policyholders* (Chicago: NTIC, 1973), p. 1.

The linkage between housing and social services was strengthened by the Family Sufficiency program of the 1990 housing act. Specifically, this program called for public housing authorities (PHAs) to help residents obtain coordinated social services designed to assist them in gaining employment. Participating families must complete these programs or risk losing their housing assistance. In return, as a participant's income increased, the money that would normally go toward a higher rent (calculated at 30 percent of income) was set aside in a special escrow account to be used for the purchase of a home. The legislation also included modest funds to create "Family Investment Centers" that provided social services in or near public housing projects.[4]

In 1998 President Clinton signed the Quality Housing and Work Responsibility Act of 1998 (QHWRA), in some ways the housing equivalent of the 1996 PRWORA. In line with the PRWORA, the federal government devolved its responsibility as the primary agent for publicly assisted housing to 3,400 semiautonomous local PHAs. With input from public housing residents, these strengthened PHAs determine rents, admissions policies, and what (if any) social services are provided. The QHWRA also ties workforce participation into housing benefits. For example, (1) PHAs are permitted to consider prospective tenants' employment history when deciding whether to admit them; (2) TANF recipients who do not fulfill their work requirement can lose Section 8 or public housing benefits; and (3) PHAs are encouraged to recruit "good" working-class families to act as role models for welfare-dependent families (the legislation decreases the percentage of public housing units earmarked for very low-income families from 75 to 70 percent). The QHWRA also mandates that low-income tenants take personal responsibility for moving into better living conditions (e.g., a single family home).[5] The QHWRA was an attempt by the federal government to align housing programs with other social welfare reforms that emphasize work, personal responsibility, and local autonomy.

The Federal Government and Low-Income Housing Programs

For many families the cost of housing represents the single largest expenditure in the household budget. It is a fixed cost that is often paid before food, clothing, and health care bills. For poor families, the precious little that remains after rent or mortgage payments is used to buy necessities for the rest of the month. The important impact of housing costs on family finances has helped encourage the federal government's involvement with low- and non-low-income housing programs. Table 16.2 provides an overview of key HUD (Department of Housing and Urban Development) and FmHA (Farmers Home Administration) programs relating to the housing problems of low-income households.

Despite its importance, governmental assistance for housing was never provided as an entitlement to all households that qualify for aid. Hence, unlike income maintenance programs such as SSI and the former AFDC, housing programs are not automatically provided to all eligible applicants. Congress appropriates funds yearly for various new commitments, most of which run 5 to 50 years. Because funding levels are usually low, however, only a portion of eligible applicants actually receive assistance. For example, in 1998, 14 million poor households were

eligible for housing assistance, but only 4.1 million actually received it.[6] Of the poor households that did receive housing assistance, about one-third lived in government-run housing projects; two-thirds rented from private landlords under Section 8.[7] (Figure 16.1 lists statistics about public housing as of the mid-1990s.) Moreover, contrary to popular myth, fewer than one-quarter of all TANF families receive any form of housing assistance.[8]

The low level of funding for housing programs has resulted in long waiting lists for public housing and rent subsidies. The Council of Large Public Housing estimated that waiting lists for public housing nationwide include 2.35 million households, many of whom will wait two or more years before getting a unit. Between 1996 and 1998 the average wait for Section 8 housing assistance vouchers rose from 26 to 28 months. Only one-third of poor renter households receive federal, state, or local government subsidies. The remaining two-thirds are placed on waiting lists. As a result, many poor families resort to temporary shelters or inadequate housing arrangements. Some people on long waiting lists are forced to live on the streets.[9]

Despite the overwhelming need for housing assistance, federal housing programs were cut back sharply in the 1980s and 1990s. For example, during the mid-1970s housing assistance was extended to as many as 400,000 new families a year. Under the Reagan administration that number was slashed to 40,000. For FY 1997, for the first time since the federal government had become involved in housing, the federal budget reduced the number of new families receiving housing assistance to zero.[10] From 1996 to 1998 Congress prohibited HUD from issuing new housing vouchers, which resulted in a loss to 51,000 families who could have received housing assistance. Because housing assistance is not an entitlement program, when PHAs use up their vouchers, they must wait until the next congressional approval.

In 1996 HUD had a budget of $19.5 billion—a decrease of 22 percent from 1993. After 1996 HUD's budget increased steadily, and by 1999 it had a budget of $25.5 billion, the same amount

TABLE 16.2 ■ Overview of HUD and Farmers Home Administration Programs

HUD Section 8	In 1999 this HUD program provided subsidized rental payments to almost 3 million families. Section 8 is based on a voucher system that allows low-income tenants to occupy existing and privately owned housing stock. The voucher is a subsidy that covers the difference between a fixed percentage of a tenant's income (30 percent) and the fair market rent of a housing unit. The HUD subsidy goes directly to the local PHA, which then pays the landlord, provided that the unit meets quality standards. Contract terms for subsidies last for 5 to 15 years. About half of Section 8 is project based, meaning that tenants have to live in specific apartments. The other half is tenant based, allowing tenants to take their subsidies and move. Section 8 also provides funds for new construction and for substantial and moderate rehabilitation of existing units.[1]
HUD Public Housing	Public housing was established by the U.S. Housing Act of 1937 and is restricted to households with incomes too low to pay for suitable private housing.[2] The income of most families in public housing is less than 25 percent of the area median income. About one-half of the families rely primarily on public assistance (TANF, SSI, and General Assistance) for their income; the other half rely mostly on earned incomes, pensions, or Social Security. Residents pay 30 percent of their monthly adjusted income on rent. There are more than 13,000 public housing developments (most are low-rise) in 3,400 localities. Contrary to popular myth, fewer than 10 percent of public housing units are severely degraded.[3]
FmHA Section 202: Housing for the Elderly and Handicapped	This program provides financing to nonprofit organizations wanting to build housing for elderly people or residents with disabilities. In 1974 Section 202 was tied to Section 8, so instead of providing only low-interest loans to build apartments, it also provides rental subsidies. By 1998 there were 6,200 Section 202 projects housing 330,000 elderly and disabled residents.[4]
FmHA Sections 235 and 236: Below-Market Interest Rate Program	Section 236 provides developers with low-interest loans in return for construction of moderately priced rental housing. This program was designed to provide housing for those whose incomes were too high to qualify for public housing but too low to meet the rental costs of unsubsidized housing. Section 235 also provides low-income families with subsidized and low-interest mortgages to enable them to purchase a home. In 1988 almost 150,000 units were subsidized under this program; an additional 400,000 units existed where the mortgages were paid off, where the purchasers had graduated to unsubsidized interest rates as their incomes rose, or where the owners had defaulted.[5]
FmHA Section 502	This is the largest FmHA program. It makes low-interest loans available for home purchases in rural areas. In 1994 some 765,000 rural families had borrowed almost $20 billion under the Section 502 program.
FmHA Section 504	Section 504 provides grants or low-interest loans to low-income families for home repairs.
Other FmHA Programs	FmHA operates a rental housing program much like Section 236 and a rural rental assistance program that provides subsidies to tenants. The FmHA also has a number of smaller, special-purpose programs, such as Sections 514 and 515, which provide housing for migrant workers.
The Low-Income Housing Tax Credit (LIHTC)	Created as part of the Tax Reform Act of 1986, the LIHTC program is currently the largest rental housing construction program in the United States. It is esti-

(continued)

TABLE 16.2 ▪ Continued

The Low-income Housing Tax Credit (LIHTC) *(continued)*	mated that the program has produced nearly 1 million affordable units since its inception. The LIHTC is designed to subsidize the construction or rehabilitation of housing for low-income families. Support is given to private investors in the form of a tax credit that is cashed in over a 10-year period. In exchange, rents must be maintained at affordable levels. Under the supervision of the U.S. Internal Revenue Service, 54 state and local housing finance agencies administer the LIHTC program.

1. Paul A. Leonard, Cushing N. Dolbeare, and Edward B. Lazere, *A Place to Call Home: The Crisis in Housing for the Poor* (Washington, DC: Center on Budget and Policy Priorities and Low-Income Housing Information Service, April 1989), pp. 76–80.

2. Ibid.

3. National Low-Income Housing Coalition, NLIHC Background on Housing Issues. Retrieved December 26, 2000, from the World Wide Web: http://www.handsnet.org/nlihc/backgrd2.htm#pubhsg

4. Ibid; and Housing and Urban Development, "Use of Section 202 Projects to Support Assisted Living Activities for Frail Elderly and People with Disabilities: Directive Number: 98-12." Retrieved from the World Wide Web: http://www.hud.gov/local/atl/atl9812.html

5. National Low-Income Housing Coalition, NLIHC Background on Housing Issues.

as in 1993.[11] Low-income housing has historically been one of the most unpopular issues on the domestic policy agenda. Because of the department's close association with public housing, HUD has become one of the more unpopular federal agencies.[12] Beyond the public's skepticism, HUD suffers from other problems. For one, housing poor people is expensive. In 1996 HUD spent more than $6,000 a year to house a poor family. By comparison, it cost Medicare $5,000 a year to provide health care to an elderly person.[13]

The United States spends less on housing assistance than any other Western industrial democracy. Not only does the U.S. government fail to adequately assist poor people with housing, but most housing subsidies benefit the nonpoor. The $66 billion that the government now "spends" (does not receive) because of mortgage interest and property tax deductions is about four times as much as it spends on low-income housing, and more than two-thirds of the benefits of those tax deductions go to families with incomes above $75,000 a year. In 1995 homeowners with incomes above $100,000 a year received a total of $28.9 billion in federal tax deductions for mortgage interest payments. In comparison, the 1996 HUD budget was only $19 billion.[14] More than 80 percent of homeowners with incomes over $90,000 receive these tax breaks, whereas only 10 percent of homeowners earning between $10,000 and $20,000 get any benefit from such deductions.[15] Cushing Dolbeare sums up the problem: "Benefits from federal programs are so skewed that *the total of all the assisted housing payments ever made under all HUD assisted housing programs, from the inception of public housing in 1937 through 1980, was less than the costs to the federal government of housing-related tax expenditures in 1980 alone* [emphasis original]."[16]

 **Issues in Housing Policy**

The equity represented by home ownership is the cornerstone of wealth for most U.S. families. Between 1995 and 1998 the value of Americans' primary residences climbed 20 percent, from $7.8 trillion to $9.4 trillion.[17] Home owners have capitalized on soaring prices when they sell. The Federal Reserve Board estimated that the average capital gain on a home sale has exceeded $25,000 from 1995 to 2000. With sales of existing

---

FIGURE 16.1   Facts about Conventional Public Housing

Total number of households: 1,250,000

Average household size: 2.4 persons

Race/ethnicity of households:

37% non-hispanic white

47% non-hispanic black

13% Hispanic

3% Asian

1% Native American

Age of household head: 7% under 25

Household composition:

49% families with children

34% elderly

9% disabled

8% other

Median household income: $6,420

Average household monthly rent: $169

Number of public housing developments: 13,741

Public housing is concentrated in high-poverty areas. In 1995, almost 70 percent of public housing was located in neighborhoods where the median household income was under $20,000.

Sources: Tenant data from "Characteristics of Households in Public Assisted Housing," PD&R Recent Research Results, HUD, December 1995. Public housing development data from HUD System for Management Information, September 1995.

homes running at roughly 4.5 million annually, realized capital gains amounted to as much as $560 billion in the second half of the 1990s.

Trends in U.S. Housing

The following represent some highlights of the often contradictory U.S. housing trends:

- The national home ownership rate reached a new annual high of 67.7 percent in 2000 and continues to climb across all geographic regions, age groups, and racial/ethnic groups. Home sales and the value of residential construction reached new highs in 2000.

- Although persistent disparities between whites and minorities of color narrowed only slightly (minority home ownership was at 48.2 percent in 2000), minorities still accounted for nearly 40 percent of the net growth in the number of owners in the second half of the 1990s. Rapid household growth, combined with climbing ownership rates, has boosted the minority presence in home-buying markets. On the other hand, millions of very low-income households still lack adequate affordable housing, and losses of subsidized units are rising.

- Home equity remains an especially important source of wealth for low-income and minority households. In 1998, among non-elderly homeowners with incomes under $20,000, half held 69 percent or more of their net household wealth in home equity. By comparison, among homeowners with incomes of $50,000 to $60,000, half held 38 percent or less of their net wealth in home equity. For half of non-Hispanic black home owners, home equity accounted for 57 percent or more of their net wealth. For half of Hispanic homeowners, the share was even higher at 71 percent or more. Among half of non-Hispanic white homeowners, though, the contribution of home equity to wealth was 40 percent or less.

- Urban sprawl continues to increase. As employment decentralizes, families are able to live and work at greater distances from the urban core. As a result, low-density metro counties have witnessed explosive job and housing growth in recent years, whereas activity in high-density counties has been limited.

- The South and West are continuing to grow. Between 1990 and 1998 new construction added 25 percent or more to the **housing stocks** of 21 metropolitan areas in the South and West. No metropolitan area in the Northeast and only two in the Midwest experienced housing stock growth of this magnitude.

- The exodus from central cities continues. Although most cities in the South and West registered gains, the movement away from many localities in the Northeast and Midwest pushed national net out migration from larger cities to 1.2 million households between 1997 and 1999. In fact, between 1997 and 1999 more than half a million households with incomes of $60,000 or more left these cities for suburban or nonmetropolitan areas. From 1990 to 1997 job growth in the lower-density fringe of metro areas was 19 percent, compared with only 4 percent in the high-density core.

- Mortgage innovations (e.g., low down payments, adjustable rate mortgages, and flexible underwriting standards) have resulted in increased home ownership for low-income first-time home buyers. Loans to low-income buyers in metro areas increased by 55 percent between 1993 and 1998, compared with a 40 percent increase in loans to high-income borrowers. However, many of these mortgage innovations are risky adjustable rate mortgages that are inflation sensitive.

- Record numbers of very low-income households are spending more than half their incomes on housing. About 500,000 very low-income renters and nearly as many very low-income owners earning at least the equivalent of the full-time minimum wage spend this much for housing.

- From 1993 to 1999 the rise in home prices exceeded the general inflation rate. Moreover, house price appreciation became much more uniform across the country as the longest expansion in U.S. history shored up housing markets nationwide.

- Growth in loans for manufactured homes has also kept markets strong; these loans increased 173 percent between 1993 and 1998, rising from 3.5 percent to 6.2 percent of all home purchase loans.

- Five states—Florida, California, Georgia, North Carolina, and Texas—account for about 40 percent of **housing starts** nationwide.

- There was a 13 percent increase in the supply of second homes in the 1990s. Using the broadest definition of second homes—homes held for seasonal or occasional use—the number of units added over the decade exceeded 700,000.

- Low-income households that have already attained home ownership are largely insulated from escalating costs and have enjoyed rising incomes. Nevertheless, the number of very low-income homeowners facing severe housing cost burdens continued to increase through the late 1990s.

- Houses are larger today than in the past. The size of newly constructed single-family homes rose from a median of 1,385 square feet in 1970 to 2,000 square feet in 1998, an increase of 44 percent. The median square footage of all homes in the United States for 1997 was 1,702 square feet, up from 1,583 in 1985.

- In 1940 fewer than 8 percent households were one-person households. In 1997 almost 25 percent of households consisted of one person. The increase in the number of people living alone has been accompanied by the growing number of multifamily units such as condominiums and apartment buildings. Detached single-family homes still dominate the housing stock, but that dominance today is less than in the past. Only 10 percent of 1940 households resided in structures with five or more units. This share of the market almost doubled by 1990, with about 18 percent of households residing in structures with five or more units.

- In 1940 almost half of all housing units lacked complete plumbing facilities. The percentage of households without complete plumbing dropped from 36 percent in 1950 to 17 percent in 1960. In 1940 three-fourths of households used either coal/coke or wood to heat their homes. By 1990 fewer than 1 percent of households heated their homes with coal/coke, and only about 4 percent with wood. More than three-fourths of households now rely on either utility-based gas or electricity to heat their homes.[18]

Problems in Home Ownership

Beginning in the 1970s, many people were forced to spend a higher percentage of their income on housing than they could reasonably afford. Some of these people became so financially overextended that they became vulnerable to mortgage default or eviction—or lacked the necessary cash for purchasing other necessities.

Between 1967 and 1991 the median income for home owners rose only slightly (in constant 1989 dollars), from $28,011 to $32,320, while the median home price went from $56,466 to $67,672. During that same period the total annual cost of home ownership rose from $4,727 to $7,806. In 1967 the median annual mortgage payment was $3,400; by 1991 it had risen to $5,245. Perhaps more important, between 1967 and 1991[19] the total cost of home ownership as a percentage of income for first-time buyers rose from 17.1 to 31.3 percent.

The increase in the price of single-family homes is even sharper when costs are not adjusted for inflation. In 1970 the average new single-family home sold for $26,600; in 2000 it sold for $201,000. For existing single-family homes the price went from $25,700 to $179,400 (see Table 16.3). The median price of housing also varies widely by city and region. For example, from 1985 to 1989 the median price of an existing single-family home in Los Angeles went from $118,700 to $218,000; in New York and Boston it rose from $134,000 to $186,000; and in Providence, Rhode Island, it rose from $67,500 to $131,000.[20]

As a result of these and other factors, home ownership rates for very low-income families with children has dropped by more than 20 percent since 1985.[21] Some 45 percent of very low-income households are home owners. More than half of these households are headed by females or include at least one elderly member. In addition, nearly one-quarter are headed by minorities. Unlike very low-income renters, who tend to live in central cities, very low-income home owners are more often found in suburban neighborhoods (47 percent) and in nonmetropolitan areas (27 percent). Nearly 60 percent of very low-income home owners pay more than 30 percent of their incomes for housing; 10 percent pay more than 50 percent. Faced with these high payment burdens, some poor owners defer basic upkeep. From 1984 to 1993 a million very low-income owners spent an average of less than $250 on home maintenance and/or replacements each year. Partly as a result, by 1995 an estimated 1.1

TABLE 16.3 ■ Average U.S. Housing Prices, Mortgage Rates, and Median Family Income in Non-Inflation-Adjusted Dollars; Selected Years

PERIOD	NEW SF HOMES*	EXISTING SF HOMES	MORTGAGE RATES	MEDIAN INCOME
1970	$ 26,600	$ 25,700	8.35%	$ 9,867
1975	42,600	39,000	9.21	13,719
1980	76,400	72,800	12.95	21,023
1985	100,800	86,000	11.74	27,735
1990	149,800	118,600	10.04	35,353
1995	158,700	139,000	7.85	39,558
2000	201,100	179,400	8.02	40,816

*SF = single family

Source: Data from U.S. Department of Housing and Urban Development, *U.S. Housing Market Conditions* (Washington, DC: HUD, Office of Policy Development and Research, November 2000).

million very low-income home owners lived in substandard housing. Making necessary improvements is difficult even for low-income owners, who are often equity rich but cash poor. Low incomes often prevent these home owners from being able to refinance their mortgages or qualify for home equity loans or lines of credit.[22]

Factors such as mortgage instruments also play an important role in determining housing affordability for low-income home owners. Many poor and first-time home buyers lack adequate credit, have a sketchy credit history, or do not have the down payment or qualifying income required for a conventional mortgage. One way for low-income home buyers to qualify has been to use a variety of inflation-sensitive mortgage instruments, including variable or adjustable rate mortgages (ARMs). These ARMs often include a low initial interest rate, sometimes four or more percentage points below fixed rates. Although most ARM mortgages are capped, they can fluctuate seven or more percentage points above the initial loan rate. Thus, a family with an ARM-based home loan might originate a mortgage at 4 percent, but by the fifth year of an inflationary spiral the interest rate could climb to 11 percent, resulting in a huge increase in mortgage payments. ARMs protect lending institutions against inflation, but they make home ownership more tenuous—because the home-owner no longer has the security of predictable fixed payments for the life of the mortgage.[23]

As with second-chance car financing firms and alternative telephone and cellular phone companies, the home-buying market has developed a secondary poverty industry. This industry takes several forms. For one, strict underwriting regulations have spawned the creation of a subprime lending industry. Subprime lenders specialize in loans to borrowers with blemished credit histories, reaching traditionally underserved markets. The subprime lending boom in low-income minority areas—areas sometimes subject to **redlining** by conventional lenders—is noteworthy because of the higher rates and fees these lenders charge. Between 1993 and 1998 subprime lenders increased their share of home purchase loans in metropolitan areas from 1 to

5 percent, helping nearly a half million families buy homes. In neighborhoods that are both low income and minority, subprime lenders' share of loans to home buyers soared from 2 to 15 percent in only five years. Growth in the subprime lender share of refinance loans in metro areas has been even more dramatic. In 1998 subprime specialists captured 46 percent of the refinance market in low-income minority areas and 30 percent in high-income minority areas—but only 18 percent in low-income predominantly white areas and 6 percent in high-income white areas.[24]

Another secondary poverty-related industry involves owner financing. In this instance an individual or a company purchases a home at its market (or below market) value and then resells it to a low-income buyer who cannot qualify for a conventional home mortgage because of a poor credit history or a low income. Because the owners finance the property, there is no requirement for a third-party appraisal and they can charge whatever price and set whatever interest rate they choose. Typically, these properties are sold well above market value with a high interest rate. A substantial down payment is required, so the seller is protected. Should the low-income buyer miss a payment or two, foreclosure is swift and sure.

Problems in Rental Housing

The robust economy of the late 1990s did little to relieve the housing problems of low-income renters. Renters in the bottom quarter of the income distribution saw their real incomes decline between 1996 and 1998, while rents increased by 2.3 percent.[25]

Although welfare-to-work programs have met with some success, working households cannot always afford suitable housing. In 1997 3.9 million very low-income households living in unsubsidized rental housing had salaries equal to or exceeding the equivalent of full-time employment at the federal minimum wage. More than two-thirds of these households paid 30 percent or more of their incomes for housing (the accepted HUD standard is 30 percent), and 25 percent paid more than 50 percent. Among very low-income working households, unsubsidized renters face particular hardships, with 71 percent shouldering high housing cost burdens (costs exceeding 50 percent of household income). These working poor renting families tend to be young, to be headed by a single person or a single parent, and to reside in the nation's central cities.[26]

According to HUD estimates, the number of very low-income households facing severe housing problems—paying more than half of their incomes for housing and/or living in severely inadequate units—set a record in 1997. In that year about 5.4 million very low-income renters receiving no housing assistance had severe housing problems. At the same time, 4.6 million very low-income home owners had severe housing problems, with 4.3 million devoting more than half their incomes to cover costs.[27]

The incidence of housing problems in rural areas is often overlooked. In 1997 about 1 in 10 rural owners and 1 in 5 rural renters spent more than half their incomes for housing. Roughly a third of very low-income owners and an even larger share of very low-income renters faced high cost burdens. Rural households are also more likely than urban families to live in severely inadequate housing. Meanwhile, only 17 percent of very low-income rural renters received housing subsidies, compared with 28 percent of very low-income urban renters. Federal funding for loans and grants specifically targeted to rural households has been slashed, and assistance has shifted from direct loans, providing deeply subsidized assistance, to guaranteed loans serving rural residents with higher incomes.[28]

Problems in Finding Affordable Housing. If finding affordable housing is difficult for poor and moderate-income home owners, it has reached crisis proportions for low-income renters. There are four major reasons for the affordability gap in rental housing: (1) Real incomes of very low-income renter households have been dropping; (2) the number of renter households has been increasing; (3) the number of low-cost unsubsidized rental units is dropping, and governmental housing assistance has not compensated for these losses; and (4) rents have increased.

The standard benchmark for "affordability" is that households should pay no more than 30 percent of their after-tax income for housing. Households paying between 30 and 50 percent for housing have moderate cost burdens; households paying more than 50 percent have severe cost burdens. Almost 30 million U.S. households pay more than 30 percent of their income for housing.[29]

Evidence of the crisis in affordable rental housing is provided by the relationship of the fair market rent (FMR) to monthly minimum wage income and public assistance benefits. The FMR, a HUD designation, is an amount equal to or more than what is paid for rent by 45 percent of recent movers. The FMR is the monthly amount needed to rent privately owned, decent, safe, and sanitary rental housing of a modest (nonluxury) nature with suitable amenities. The national median "housing wage," based on each county's housing wage (wage required to rent a two-bedroom unit at the FMR), is $12.47 an hour—more than twice the federal minimum wage of $5.15 an hour. This means that on average there must be more than two full-time minimum wage workers to enable a household to afford a two-bedroom housing unit at the FMR.[30]

Some states have recognized that the federal minimum wage is insufficient and have passed legislation mandating higher standards. Still, in no state with a minimum wage greater than the federal minimum wage does the increase equal the two-bedroom housing wage for that state. In no county, metropolitan area, or state is the minimum wage, federal or state, as high as the corresponding housing wage for a one-, two-, or three-bedroom housing unit at the FMR. In 32 percent of counties, 54 percent of metro areas, and 44 percent of states, the housing wage is at least twice the federal minimum wage. In three states—New Jersey, New York, and Hawaii—the housing wage is more than three times the minimum wage. An examination of state, metropolitan, and local data illustrates that a substantial number of renters cannot afford the cost of basic rent. In 46 percent of states, 54 percent of all metro areas, and 49 percent of all local jurisdictions, 40 percent or more of renters cannot afford the FMR for a two-bedroom unit.[31]

As mentioned earlier, when poor households live in adequate housing, they usually pay for it by spending an excessive percentage of their income on rent. Hence, many of these households have little left over for other necessities such as heat, food, clothing, and health care. Some of these families find themselves in a "heat or eat" situation. Little research has been done on the health effects of rent burdens; but Dr. Alan Meyers, a pediatrician at Boston Medical Center, studied 200 poor children and found that only 3 percent of children whose families received rent subsidies were underweight for their age. For children whose families were on the subsidized housing wait list, in contrast, 22 percent were underweight for their age. After examining the records of 11,000 poor children, Meyers found that children were most likely to be underweight in the 90 days after the coldest month of the year; this finding bolstered his theory that families make the choice of whether to "heat or eat."[32]

The Shortage of Affordable Housing Units. Severe housing problems are related to the dwindling supply of affordable unsubsidized housing units available to very low-income households. Recent losses of units to either rising rents or demolition have intensified the housing problems of the more than 70 percent of very low-income renters who receive no rent subsidies. Between 1993 and 1995, for example, the number of unsubsidized units affordable by very low-income households dropped 8.6 percent—a decrease of nearly 900,000 units. At the same time, the number of units affordable by extremely low-income households—those with incomes less than 30 percent of the area median—fell by 16 percent.[33] Many affordable units were abandoned, were converted into condominiums, or became unaffordable because of cost increases.

In light of housing affordability problems, it is important to preserve the limited supply of federally subsidized rental housing. By 1999, however, 90,000 subsidized units had been lost as private owners opted out of HUD programs or prepaid their subsidized mortgages to capitalize on higher rents. Based on historical trends, 10 to 15 percent of the remaining project-based as-sisted units with contracts expiring in coming years will be at risk of loss. For current tenants of properties whose owners opt out or prepay their mortgages, HUD has been offering vouchers to make up for the gap between new, higher rents and 30 percent of tenant incomes.[34]

Physical conditions in the subsidized housing market are hardly better. Although demand for public housing is strong, more than 60,000 seriously distressed units are slated for demolition. More than 27,600 units had been torn down by the end of 1999. Despite HUD's replacement goal of 45 percent, only 7,273 units had been built or rehabilitated as of late 1999. Hence, while demolition has proceeded apace, an equal number of replacement units has not been provided.[35]

As the largest federal rental production program, tax credits have supported the construction of more than 1 million affordable units for people earning 60 percent or less of area median incomes. Keeping tax credit–assisted units in the affordable stock is gaining new urgency, because the compliance periods (periods during which rents must be kept affordable) for the first 23,000 units built under the program are set to expire in 2002. Worse, fewer of these subsidized units are being added each year, because the tax credit is not inflation adjusted. In fact, the number of units receiving tax credit allocations fell from a high of 117,099 in 1994 to just 67,822 in 1998.[36]

Several other factors have converged to deplete low-income housing stock. For one, the commercial renovation of central-city downtown areas is problematic for the poor. Developments consisting of new office buildings, large apartment complexes, shopping areas, and parking lots often replace low-income housing bordering on downtown areas. Traditionally affordable (and often run-down) apartment buildings, cheap single room occupancy (SRO) hotels, rooming houses, and boardinghouses are razed as new office buildings and shopping complexes are erected. Displaced longtime residents are forced to find housing in more expensive neighborhoods; to double up with family or friends; or, in some cases, to become homeless.

The loss of SRO housing units has fueled the homelessness problem. In the past SROs were home to many poor individuals (including those suffering from substance abuse and mental illnesses) who were not living in public or low-income subsidized housing. But between 1970 and the mid-1980s, an estimated 1 million SRO units were demolished. San Francisco lost 43 percent; Los Angeles lost more than 50 percent; New York lost 87 percent; and Chicago experienced the total elimination of its SRO housing units and hotels. These demolitions left many poor individuals homeless, particularly those suffering from mental illness and substance abuse.[37]

According to George Sternlieb and Jones Hughes, there is evidence that "a new town may be evolving in town."[38] This new town, or "gentrified" neighborhood, is a major component of an urban renaissance taking place in many U.S. cities. Attracted by old houses amenable to restoration; good transportation facilities; and close proximity to employment and artistic, cultural, and social opportunities, young professionals and white-collar workers have begun to resettle the poor, aging, and usually heavily minority sections of central cities in the process called **gentrification.**

Although the renovation of central-city areas, as in New York's SoHo district, often makes a neighborhood more attractive (and potentially a tourist attraction), the effect on the indigenous—and often poor—population can be devastating. As homes become renovated, the prices of surrounding homes may increase. Although low-income home owners may be able to command a high resale price for their homes, they may find few suitable places to move to. Furthermore, as neighborhoods become affluent, property taxes are likely to rise, thus creating a burden on existing low-income home owners. Previously affordable rental housing may undergo huge rent increases as neighborhoods become more desirable, thereby driving out older and poorer tenants and shutting out new low-income residents. Although gentrification has been selective, with the main demographic movement continuing to be suburban, it has had a striking impact on some central-city neighborhoods.

The conversion of apartment buildings into condominiums represents another threat to the poor. As a consequence of tax breaks and income shelters, previously affordable rental housing is rapidly being turned into condominiums. Whether initiated by tenants or by developers, condominium conversion represents a serious depletion of good-quality rental stock. Because units in these conversions may cost $50,000 or more, low-income tenants can rarely afford the benefits of condominium living; and although renters are often offered a separation fee when a building undergoes conversion, this amount may barely cover the costs of moving, much less make up for the difference between renters' current rent and a higher alternative rent.

Overcrowded and Deficient Housing. Problems of overcrowding and structural inadequacy affect a significant number of U.S. households. HUD defines a housing unit as overcrowded if there is an average of more than one person per room. According to this definition, almost 3 million households live in overcrowded conditions, sometimes as a result of families' doubling up to avoid becoming homeless. In 1995 HUD classified 2 million housing units as seriously inadequate. "Inadequate" housing is housing with severe physical deficiencies; for example, it may lack hot water, electricity, or a toilet or may have neither a bathtub nor shower. Years of neglect have led to a serious backlog of repairs among 1.1 million assisted and 350,000 unassisted HUD-insured units. A study estimates that restoring systems in these buildings to adequate working condition would have cost $4.2 billion in 1995. In the suburbs both owners and renters make up substantial shares of households suffering from inadequate housing. That is, the number of suburban households living in these conditions equals that in central cities, but a larger share are home owners.[39]

Lead paint is one of the principal problems in units needing rehabilitation. The Centers for Disease Control and Prevention notes that lead poisoning is one of the most common and devastating environmental diseases that affect young children, causing developmental and behavior problems. Children are exposed to lead poisoning by living in older homes with peeling, chipping, and flaking paint. According to the National Low-Income Housing Coalition, almost 9 percent of all children under age six—1.7 million children—suffer from lead poisoning. The rate of lead poisoning for children between ages one and two is more than 11.5 percent. In many poor urban communities, well over half the children are affected by exposure to lead hazards. Because low-income families often occupy poorly maintained older homes, their children are four times more likely to have lead poisoning than children in high-income families. Lead was banned from residential paint in 1978, but more than half of the housing stock in the United States still contains some lead paint.[40]

Other Factors Affecting Housing

Another problem affecting affordable housing is property taxes—the heart of local revenue gathering. The escalating costs of providing governmental services have resulted in significant increases in property taxes, which landlords generally pass along to renters in the form of higher rents. In response, many states have tried to reduce property tax burdens for low-income households. The most common form of property tax relief occurs through **circuit breaker programs.** A typical circuit breaker program is activated when taxes exceed a specified proportion of a home owner's income; in most such programs, low-income households are sent a yearly benefit check in which all or part of the property tax is refunded. Circuit breaker programs for low-income renters operate in a similar manner. Typically, in other words, a portion of the rent paid by a low-income household is considered to represent the property tax passed on by the landlord and is thus refunded by the state or local government. Although circuit breaker programs can provide some relief, they are often restricted to the elderly or disabled. For example, although 31 states and the District of Columbia have circuit breaker programs, 21 states restrict eligibility to elderly and disabled households. Twenty-seven of these 31 states

cover both renters and home owners; 6 states restrict eligibility to home owners.[41]

Housing costs also are aggravated by high utility rates. Nationwide, the average family pays about $1,300 in utility bills. However, in many parts of the country, especially the Northeast and the Midwest, an average family may pay considerably more, because of high heating costs. Low-income consumers spend anywhere from 13 to 44 percent of their total household income on utilities, whereas average-income Americans spend only 4 percent.[42] Thus, increases in home energy bills disproportionately affect the poor. In some cases the result is utility shutoffs. For example, it is estimated that in 1984 more than 1.4 million households had their natural gas shut off because of delinquent payments.[43]

In 1981, to mitigate the effects of the federal deregulation of oil prices and the large oil price increases of the 1970s, Congress passed the Low-Income Home Energy Assistance Program (LIHEAP). This legislation permits states to offer three types of assistance to low-income households: (1) funds to help eligible households pay their home heating or cooling bills; (2) allotments for low-income weatherization; and (3) assistance to households during energy-related emergencies. States are required to target LIHEAP benefits to households with the lowest incomes and with the highest energy costs relative to their income and family size. In 1999 LIHEAP served 4.3 million households and spent about $1.4 billion, considerably less than its $2.2 billion expenditure in 1992; between 1985 and 1999 LIHEAP experienced a 48 percent funding decline.[44]

Housing discrimination is another barrier facing the poor. This discrimination takes two forms: racial discrimination and discrimination against families with children. Although illegal, racially based discrimination in housing is still prevalent. In addition, many landlords and real estate agents refuse to rent to families with children. Often these families, even when they do find housing, are required to pay higher rents, provide exorbitant security deposits, or meet qualifications not required of renters without children.[45] Discrimination against families with children continues, even though Congress has banned such discrimination since 1988.[46]

 # Homelessness

Homelessness can be defined simply as a lack of housing. As such, it represents both a simple and a complex problem. Specifically, homeless people are not a homogeneous group. For some individuals homelessness is a lifestyle choice, the freedom to roam without being tied down to one place. For others, particularly people with mental illness and chronic alcoholism, homelessness reflects the deterioration of an overburdened public mental health system. The breakdown in the mental health system is aggravated by an influx of previously healthy people who, when reduced to economic deprivation and homelessness, develop symptoms of mental disturbance. For other people homelessness is rooted in cuts in federally subsidized housing programs and in the cost income squeeze of the housing market. Finally, large numbers of people experience homelessness as a result of the inability of public assistance benefits to keep pace with the cost of living, especially in the area of housing and utilities. Despite the variety of causes, almost all forms of homelessness are tied to poverty. In that sense, homelessness is a manifestation of poverty.

The actual number of homeless people in the United States is difficult to ascertain for several reasons. First, definitions of homelessness vary from study to study, and different methods for counting homeless people yield different results. Second, many of the homeless are "hidden" in that they live in campgrounds, automobiles, boxcars, caves, tents, boxes, or other makeshift housing. Or they may live temporarily with family members or friends. Such arrangements make it nearly impossible for agencies to count every person who is without stable housing. Studies of how many people are homeless on any given day or week (point-in-time studies) or of

how many have experienced homelessness over a given time period (prevalence counts) are more feasible. These studies measure the magnitude of homelessness and therefore present an account of the number of people who experience homelessness over a time, not an exact number of homeless people. Most studies count people who are homeless in a given community by tracking people who use the services of soup kitchens and shelters.

Third, the homeless population is often undercounted in federal surveys for political reasons. Specifically, if the true extent of homelessness were acknowledged, then local, state, and federal authorities would have to target more services and funds for the homeless. For example, the U.S. Census Bureau estimated in 1990 that the homeless population was only 228,000.[47] In contrast, Joel Blau, using figures from the National Alliance to End Homelessness, argued that on any given night some 735,000 Americans are homeless; over the course of a year, between 1.3 and 2 million people experience homelessness.[48] Other advocacy organizations claim that about 3 million people are homeless.[49]

Characteristics of the Homeless Population

Although homelessness has been a long-standing problem in most large urban areas, it has been propelled onto center stage by media images of bag ladies, mentally ill people, chronic alcoholics, street people, and uprooted families. These images may make for interesting copy, but popular stereotypes obscure both the extent of homelessness and the true nature of the problem. Homeless people are the poorest of the poor. They include single-parent families and, occasionally, two-parent families. They are people who work but who earn too little to afford housing. They are women and children escaping from domestic violence. They are runaway youngsters or youngsters who have been thrown out. They are unemployed people—some who are looking for work, and some who have never worked. The homeless include retired people on small fixed incomes, many of whom have lost their cheap

SRO hotel rooms to gentrification; school dropouts; drug addicts; disabled and mentally ill people lost in a maze of outpatient services; people who have worn out their welcome with family or friends; young mothers on welfare who remain on long waiting lists for public housing; families who have lost their overcrowded quarters. The list below summarizes data from the National Survey of Homeless Assistance Providers and Clients conducted by the Census Bureau in 1996 for 12 federal agencies. Released in a 1999 HUD report, this survey interviewed representatives of almost 12,000 homeless programs and more than 4,000 clients. It is the most comprehensive study conducted on the homeless population to date. The picture it paints is indeed bleak.

- *Families.* Sixty percent of homeless women had children ages 0 to 17; 65 percent of these women lived with at least one of their minor children. Forty-one percent of homeless men had children ages 0 to 17; 7 percent of these men lived with at least one of their minor children. Most of these homeless children were young; 20 percent were ages 0 to 2, 22 percent were ages 3 to 5, 20 percent were ages 6 to 8, 33 percent were ages 9 to 17, and age was not given for 5 percent. Parents reported that 45 percent of the 3- to 5-year-olds attended preschool and that 93 percent of school-age children (ages 6 to 17) attended school regularly. Fifty-one percent of children were in households receiving AFDC, 70 percent were in households receiving food stamps, 12 percent were in households receiving SSI, and 73 percent received Medicaid.

- *Gender and marital status.* Seventy-seven percent of the homeless were male and 23 percent were female. Most homeless clients (85 percent) were single (that is, they did not have any of their children with them); 50 percent never married; 7 percent were married; 14 percent were separated; 26 percent were divorced; 4 percent were widowed.

- *Race.* Forty-one percent of the homeless were non-Hispanic white, 40 percent African American, 10 percent Hispanic, and 8 percent Native American; 1 percent were other races.

- *Age.* Ten percent of the homeless were between the ages of 17 and 24; 81 percent were 25 to 54; and 9 percent were 55 and older.

- *Education.* Thirty-seven percent of the homeless had less than a high school education; 36 percent had completed high school; and 28 percent had some education beyond high school.

- *Food intake.* Twenty-eight percent of the homeless said they sometimes or often did not get enough to eat (compared with 12 percent of poor U.S. adults); 20 percent ate one meal a day or less. Thirty-nine percent of the homeless said that in the previous 30 days they had been hungry but unable to afford food (compared with 5 percent of poor Americans); 40 percent had gone without anything to eat for a day or longer in the previous 30 days because they could not afford food (compared to 3 percent of poor Americans).

- *Chemical dependency and mental illness.* Thirty-eight percent of the homeless reported indicators of alcohol use problems; 26 percent reported indicators of drug use problems; 39 percent reported indicators of mental health problems. Sixty-one percent reported indicators of one or more of these problems.

- *Physical health.* Three percent of the homeless reported having HIV/AIDS; 3 percent reported tuberculosis; 26 percent reported acute infectious conditions such as a cough, cold, bronchitis, pneumonia, tuberculosis, or sexually transmitted disease other than AIDS. Eight percent reported acute noninfectious conditions such as skin ulcers, lice, or scabies; 46 percent reported having chronic health conditions such as arthritis, high blood pressure, diabetes, or cancer. Fifty-five percent had no medical insurance.

- *Crime.* Thirty-eight percent of the homeless claimed someone had stolen money or things from them; 22 percent had been physically assaulted; 7 percent had been sexually assaulted.

- *Income.* Single homeless clients reported a mean income of $348 in the previous 30 days, an amount only 51 percent of the 1996 federal poverty level of $680 a month for one person. Clients in family households reported a mean income of $475 during the previous 30 days, an amount only 46 percent of the 1996 federal poverty level of $1,023 a month for a family of three. Single homeless clients had only 12 percent of the median monthly income of all U.S. households in 1995 ($2,840), and homeless families only 17 percent.

■ *Work.* Forty-four percent of the homeless had done paid work during the previous month. Twenty percent had worked in a job lasting at least three months; 25 percent worked at a temporary or day labor job; and 2 percent earned money by peddling or selling personal belongings. Three percent reported more than one source of earned income; 21 percent received income from family members or friends; 1 percent received child support. Eight percent reported income from panhandling in the previous 30 days.

■ *Public assistance.* Thirty-seven percent of the homeless received food stamps; 52 percent of households received AFDC; 11 percent received SSI; and 9 percent received General Assistance. Six percent of homeless veterans received veteran-related disability payments, and 2 percent received veteran-related pensions. Thirty percent received Medicaid, and another 7 percent received medical care from the Department of Veterans Affairs.

■ *Locations.* Although there are homeless clients in every type of community, 71 percent were in central cities; 21 percent were in the suburbs and urban fringe areas; and 9 percent were in rural areas.

■ *Shelter and food.* Within the week previous to the interview, 31 percent of the homeless had slept on the streets or in other places not meant for habitation; 66 percent used an emergency shelter, transitional housing program, or program offering vouchers for emergency accommodation. Thirty-six percent used soup kitchens, and 10 percent used other homeless assistance programs (e.g., drop-in centers, food pantries, outreach programs, mobile food programs).

■ *Episodes of homelessness.* Forty-nine percent of clients were in their first episode of homelessness; 34 percent had been homeless three or more times. Single homeless clients and clients in families were equally likely to be in their first homeless episode, but single clients were more likely than clients in families to have been homeless three times or more. For 28 percent of homeless clients, the current episode had lasted three months or less, but for 30 percent it had lasted more than two years. Clients in families were more than twice as likely as single clients to have been homeless for three months or less; single clients were almost three times as likely as clients in families to be in homeless spells that had lasted more than two years.

■ *Veterans.* Thirty-three percent of male homeless clients were veterans. Forty-seven percent of veterans had served during the Vietnam era, and 57 percent had served since the Vietnam era. Many had served in more than one time period. Thirty-three percent of the male veterans were stationed in a war zone, and 28 percent were exposed to combat.

■ *Childhood.* Twenty-seven percent of homeless clients had lived in foster care or in a group home or other institutional setting for part of their childhood; 25 percent reported childhood physical or sexual abuse; 21 percent reported childhood experiences of homelessness; 33 percent reported running away from home; and 22 percent reported being forced to leave home.

■ *Homeless services.* There are about 40,000 homeless assistance programs offered at about 21,000 locations in the United States. Food pantries, estimated at close to 9,000, are the most common type of program. Emergency shelters are next with an estimated 5,700 programs, followed closely by transitional housing programs (4,400), soup kitchens and other distributors of prepared meals (3,500), outreach programs (3,300), and voucher distribution programs (3,100). On an average day in February 1996, emergency shelters expected 240,000 program contacts, transitional housing programs expected 160,000, permanent housing programs expected 110,000, and voucher distribution programs expected 70,000. Expected contacts include those made by both homeless and other people who use services. Forty-nine percent of all homeless assistance programs are located in central cities, 32 percent in rural areas, and 19 percent in suburban areas. Because central-city programs serve more clients, a larger share of program contacts occur there.[50]

Trends in Homelessness

As noted earlier, homelessness and poverty are inextricably linked. Because poor families have limited resources that can cover only a portion of their basic needs, they often must make difficult choices between housing and food, clothing, or health care. Housing costs absorb the greatest percentage of a poor family's income, which can leave low-income families only a paycheck away from living on the streets if faced with a serious crisis. Families who have moved from welfare to work under the 1996 welfare reform law are not doing as well as projected, because of inadequate work supports and low wages. Most TANF recipients who enter the labor market do so with jobs that pay slightly above poverty wages. Moreover, the full effects of the five-year TANF lifetime cap have yet to be felt and could lead to even greater numbers of homeless people in coming years.

Lack of affordable health care can cause many struggling families to spiral into homelessness when a serious illness or injury causes extended absence from work, job loss, or depletion of savings to pay for health care. Mental illness and drug and alcohol addiction also play a role. The increasing number of mentally ill homeless individuals is not entirely due to the deinstitutionalization of mentally ill patients from mental hospitals; rather, homelessness results because mentally ill people experience difficulty in accessing supportive housing along with treatment services. People who are both poor and addicted also face a high risk of homelessness.

Domestic violence has been linked to homelessness for many female–headed households. Specifically, many poor women are forced to choose whether to stay in an abusive relationship or become homeless. A study conducted in 1990 by the Ford Foundation found that 50 percent of homeless women and children were fleeing domestic violence; another survey, by the U.S. Conference of Mayors, found that domestic violence was a primary cause of homelessness.[51]

Another disturbing trend is the rise of homeless youth. Domestic violence (physical and sexual abuse) accounts for a growing number of homeless youth under the age of 18. The estimated number of homeless or "unaccompanied" youth on the streets each year is approximately 300,000. According to the National Coalition for the Homeless, "Because of their age, homeless youth have few legal means by which to earn enough money to meet basic needs. Many . . . find that exchanging sex for food, clothing, and shelter is their only chance for survival on the streets."[52]

Attempts to Address Homelessness

On July 22, 1987, President Ronald Reagan signed the Stewart B. McKinney Homeless Assistance Act into law. The McKinney Act created more than 20 separate programs to be administered by nine federal agencies. Some of the services provided by the act include emergency food and shelter, job training, mental health care, transitional and permanent housing, education, health care services, substance abuse treatment, and veterans' assistance services. In 1990 Congress amended the act to remove requirements that kept homeless children from attending school, including proof of immunization, former school records, and proof of residency. The federal government spent more than 1.28 billion in 1999 on programs to help the homeless[53] (See Table 16.4.)

Apart from the McKinney Act, several broader proposals have emerged for alleviating the problem of homelessness. In 1987 Chester Hartman proposed a nine-point solution for ending homelessness: (1) Massively increase the number of new and rehabilitated units offered to lower-income households; (2) lower the required rent/income ratio in government housing from

TABLE 16.4 ■ Federal Expenditures on Selected Homeless Programs, 1999

PROGRAM	1999 FEDERAL EXPENDITURES (IN MILLIONS)
HUD Homeless Assistance Program	$ 975.0
Emergency Food and Shelter Program	100.0
Health Care for the Homeless	79.6
Projects for Assistance in Transition from Homelessness	26.0
Education for Homeless Children and Youth	28.8
Runaway and Homeless Youth Programs	73.6
Homeless Veterans Reintegration Project	3.0
	Total: $1,286.0

Source: National Coalition for the Homeless, "FY95–FY00 Funding for Homeless Assistance Programs" (2000). Retrieved from the World Wide Web http://nch.ari.net/appchart.html

30 to 25 percent; (3) arrest the depletion of low-income housing through neglect, abandonment, conversion, and sale; (4) preserve the SRO hotels; (5) establish a national "right to shelter"; (6) require local governments to make available properties that can be used as shelters and second-stage housing; (7) create legislation that gives tenants reasonable protection from eviction; (8) provide governmental assistance to home owners facing foreclosure; and (9) provide suitable residential alternatives for mentally ill people.[54]

The "Federal Plan to Help End the Tragedy of Homelessness," prepared in the 1990s under the auspices of the Interagency Council for the Homeless, provides a set of objectives aimed at reducing homelessness: (1) Increase the participation of homeless families and individuals in mainstream programs that provide income support, social services, health care, education, employment, and housing; agencies should monitor these programs to gauge their impact on homelessness. (2) Improve the efficiency and effectiveness of homelessness-targeted programs in addressing the multiple needs of homeless persons. (3) Increase the availability of support services in combination with appropriate housing. (4) Improve access to quality, affordable, and permanent housing for homeless families and in-

dividuals. (5) Develop strategies for preventing homelessness by improving the methods for identifying families and individuals at risk of imminent homelessness; change current policies that may contribute to homelessness; and propose other initiatives to prevent people from becoming homeless.[55]

Homelessness cannot be eradicated unless basic changes are made in federal housing, income support, social services, health care, education, and employment programs. Benefit levels for these programs must be made more adequate; the erosion of welfare benefits must be stopped; residency and other requirements that exclude homeless persons must be changed; and programs (including outreach) must be made freely available to the homeless and the potentially homeless. Moreover, a real solution to the homeless problem must involve the provision of permanent housing for those who are currently or potentially homeless. Federal programs and legislation must be coordinated and expanded to provide decent, affordable housing, coupled with needed services, for *all* poor families. Finally, both the states and the federal government must intervene directly in the housing market by controlling rents, increasing the overall housing stock, limiting speculation, and providing income supports.

Housing Reform

The housing crisis faced by low-income people has led to numerous suggestions for housing reform. Some conservative critics argue that low-income housing assistance should be abolished, thus allowing the law of supply and demand to regulate rents and, eventually, to drive down prices. Free market economic philosophy suggests that as rents increase, demand will slacken, and eventually rents will drop. Another argument is that government intervention in housing should occur only through the supply side. In other words, the government should stimulate production of rental housing by offering financial incentives such as tax breaks to builders, entrepreneurs, and investors. If rental housing is made more profitable, more units will be built, and the increase in the housing stock will lower prices.

Some liberal critics contend that because housing is a necessity and the demand is relatively inelastic, marketplace laws should not be allowed to dominate. For example, the National Low-Income Housing Coalition has called for

- guaranteeing housing assistance to people who need it
- ending homelessness by linking housing with services to support recovery and self-sufficiency
- providing a permanent and adequate supply of affordable housing
- preserving and improving federally assisted affordable homes for people with low incomes
- providing the opportunity for resident control of housing
- preserving neighborhoods and ending displacement
- ending economic and racial segregation through affirmative housing programs and the enforcement of fair housing laws

- reforming federal tax laws to give priority to aiding people with the greatest housing needs
- providing the financing needed to preserve, build, and rehabilitate housing[56]

Several housing reforms have been either tried or proposed in recent years. The first involved the Clinton administration's plan to collapse and convert all HUD funds into state block grants. Although not implemented, this approach was known as the "blueprint," and called for the conversion of the public housing program into a **voucher** system. HUD would provide local authorities with block granted funds to provide vouchers to public housing tenants. The tenants would then be free to stay in public housing or to use their vouchers to rent private apartments. The vouchers would be worth the difference between 30 percent of a tenant's income and the total rent in private housing, up to a predetermined ceiling.[57]

Liberals argued that public housing was not designed to be competitive in the private real estate market. Instead, it was developed to provide cheap housing for those who lacked other alternatives and was unlikely to attract people who did not require subsidization.[58] In addition, the residential mobility that HUD claimed would result from privatizing public housing was predicated on unrealistic beliefs—the beliefs that affordable, private rental housing is available, housing antidiscrimination laws are respected in the private market, landlords are willing to rent to low-income families of color who have children, and landlords are willing to participate in a governmental program.[59]

Much of the innovation in housing in recent years has come from the nonprofit sector. There are now more than 2,000 nonprofit housing groups that have built or renovated more than half a million housing units, most of them since 1990. These nonprofits operate with a combination of government subsidies and private contributions. They also get help from two important foundations—the Local Initiatives Support Corporation and the Enterprise Foundation. According to Jason De Parle, the nonprofits' "impressive track records address the fear that more subsidized housing would mean more government-financed slums."[60]

One of the largest efforts has been mounted by the Enterprise Foundation. Started by Jim and Patty Rouse in 1982, the Enterprise Foundation is a national nonprofit housing and community development organization directed by distinguished national business and community development leaders. Its goals are, first, "to build a national movement to change the way life is lived in low income neighborhoods. Second, to demonstrate ourselves what can be done, and third, to communicate what works and to advocate it."[61] Specifically, the Enterprise Foundation assists community-based nonprofit organizations and state and local governments in developing affordable housing and community services by brokering low-interest loans, grants, and equity to finance affordable housing; helps with linking residents to human services; and helps train people to be effective community leaders.[62] By 1999 the Enterprise Foundation had built 100,000 affordable homes, the results of leveraging $3 billion in equity from 170 corporate investors. Operating with field offices in 17 cities and with a network of 1,100 community organizations throughout the country, Enterprise and its subsidiaries have helped 30,000 low-income people find work and helped thousands of those people find affordable community child care.[63]

Although nonprofit housing organizations like the Enterprise Foundation are making an important impact on the country's housing problem, they have limitations. For example, many of the housing groups focus their attention on the less needy—those with incomes at 50 percent of the median. This occurs in part because no one group knows how to house large numbers of the poorest people, especially those on public assistance. If the poorest people are grouped together too tightly, neighborhoods may collapse. If they are spread out in the suburbs, the new neighbors complain. Perhaps more importantly, the scope and pace of building or renovating under nonprofits is inadequate to meet the need. Nonprofits are building

or renovating about 50,000 units a year, and at that rate it would take a century to house the 5 million families with rent burdens.[64]

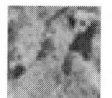 # Conclusion

The housing crisis is grounded in issues of availability and affordability. It is a structural problem that is based on the failure of incomes to keep pace with housing costs; an overdependence on credit to build and buy houses; a profit-making system that drives home ownership, development, and management; and the failure of states and the federal government to intervene actively in the housing market through more and higher subsidies or stricter regulation. Driven by the profit motive, speculation has forced up the price of rental and residential property faster than income growth. As a profit is made by each link in the housing chain (real estate agents and developers, lenders, builders, materials producers, investors, speculators, landlords, and home owners), renters and home buyers are forced to pay the costs. Put another way, the cost of every rental unit or home reflects the profits made by all the parties who have come directly or indirectly into contact with the property.

The provision of adequate low- and moderate-income housing is an important challenge facing modern society. The poor have difficulty finding decent affordable housing; blue-collar workers and the lower middle class are caught in the cost/income squeeze and are having a difficult time buying and holding onto their homes. In an economic downturn, this "affordability squeeze" can result in increased mortgage foreclosures, higher rates of property tax and delinquency defaults, more evictions and homelessness, more overcrowding and doubling up of families, decreases in the consumption of other important necessities, deteriorating neighborhoods, increased business failures, higher rates of unemployment in the building trades, and the collapse of some financial institutions.

Past and current government programs have had minimal impact on the crisis in affordable housing. Current housing programs are seriously underfunded, fragmentary, and without clear or focused goals. Because the federal government has often been viewed as an arbiter of last resort, some housing advocates contend that the government has the responsibility to ensure that adequate housing becomes a right rather than a privilege, and that healthy, sound, and safe neighborhoods become a reality.

An adequate housing policy for the United States must address cost burden, overcrowding, and housing quality. It must also provide opportunities for true housing choice and an end to the discriminatory patterns that have led to de facto housing segregation in U.S. society. The nation will not have achieved the 1949 housing goal of "a decent home and suitable living environment for every American family" until all households have the opportunity to live in adequate housing located in safe neighborhoods.

 # Discussion Questions

1. From 1937 until the present, the history of federal housing policy been marked by evolving priorities and programmatic shifts. Describe the dominant trends in federal housing policy from 1937 onward and show how those trends led to the creation of current housing policies. What, if any, ideas and programs in current housing policies have their roots in earlier federal policies? In what direction has federal housing policy evolved? What is the current emphasis in federal housing policy?

2. According to some critics, federal low-income housing policy is marked by severe inadequacies. Describe the more serious shortcomings in federal low-income housing policy and discuss alternative policies to rectify those shortcomings.

3. Home ownership is an important variable in U.S. society because it is equated with the growth of assets. For example, after paying rent for 30 years a poor family has nothing to show except 360 rental receipts. By contrast, another poor family will at least have its home as a major asset after paying off a 30-year mortgage. What are some of the obstacles standing in the way of home ownership for poor people? What policies can be developed to help poor families overcome these barriers?

4. What are some of the most significant problems facing poor people in finding affordable rental housing of decent quality? What federal or state policies can be implemented to help poor families find such housing?

5. HUD has created a series of guidelines by which to evaluate whether a particular housing unit has "severe" physical deficiencies. Are HUD's criteria adequate? If not, what other criteria should be added to HUD's guidelines?

6. Homelessness has been described by some commentators as just another housing problem. Others argue that homelessness is primarily a manifestation of poverty. Still others contend that homelessness has psychological roots and should be seen as a social or human service problem. Where do you stand on the issue? Will the homeless problem be solved if people are simply given adequate shelter and decent jobs? Or is homelessness for many a manifestation of deeper psychosocial problems? If so, what programs, if any, should be developed for the homeless?

7. Several proposals have been offered to eradicate the problem of homelessness. Which of these programs (or combination of programs) has the best chance of eradicating homelessness?

8. Many experts argue that for low-income people, both renters and home owners, the housing situation has reached crisis proportions. Do you agree? If so, why? Moreover, what kinds of housing policies are needed to defuse this crisis and stabilize the housing market for low-income families? Should housing be considered a right and thus be removed from the grip of the marketplace?

 # Notes

1. Edward B. Lazere, Paul A. Leonard, Cushing N. Dolbeare, and Barry Zigas, *A Place to Call Home: The Low-Income Housing Crisis Continues* (Washington, DC: Center on Budget and Policy Priorities and Low-Income Housing Information Service; December 1991), pp. 45–47.
2. Charles S. Prigmore and Charles R. Atherton, *Social Welfare Policy: Analysis and Formulation* (Lexington, MA: D. C. Heath, 1979), pp. 48–50.
3. National Training and Information Center, *Insurance Redlining, Profits v. Policyholders* (Chicago: NTIC, 1973), p. 1.
4. Ibid., pp. 52–53.
5. Center for Community Change, "Solutions," 1999. Retrieved December 29, 2000, from the World Wide Web: http://www.community-change.org/pahcrisis2.html
6. Habitat for Humanity, "U.S. Affordable Housing Statistics" (2000). Retrieved December 29, 2000, from the World Wide Web: http://www.habitat.org/how/stats.html
7. U.S. Census Bureau, "1993 American Housing Survey." Retrieved December 29, 2000, from the World Wide Web: http://www.census.gov/ftp/pub/hhes/www/ahs.html
8. Sharon Parrott, *The Cato Institute Report on Welfare Benefits: Do Cato's Numbers Add Up?* (Washington, DC: Center on Budget and Policy Priorities, 1996).
9. National Coalition for the Homeless, "Why are People Homeless?" June 1999, retrieved December 29, 2000, from the World Wide Web: http:/nch.ari.net; see also Laura Waxman, *A Status Report on Hunger and Homelessness in America's Cities: 1995* (Washington, DC: U.S. Conference of Mayors, 1995); and Children's Defense Fund, *The State of America's Children, 1991* (Washington, DC: Children's Defense Fund, 1991).
10. National Coalition for the Homeless.
11. U.S. Department of Housing and Urban Development, "Waiting in Vain: Update on America's Rental Housing Crisis." Retrieved December 29, 2000, from the World Wide Web: http://www.hud.gov/houscris.html
12. National Academy of Public Administration, "Renewing HUD: Study Recommends Major Changes in Housing Agency," *Journal of Housing* (1994), pp. 22–28.
13. Jason De Parle, "Slamming the Door," *The New York Times Magazine* (October 20, 1996), pp. 52–58, 94, 105–106.
14. P. Dreier, "The New Politics of Housing," *Journal of American Planning Association* 63, no. 1 (1997), pp. 6–15.
15. National Low-Income Housing Coalition, NLIHC Background on Housing Issues. Retrieved December 29, 2000, from the World Wide Web: http://www.handsnet.org/nlihc/backgrd1.htm#needs
16. Quoted in Lazere et al., *A Place to Call Home: The Low-Income Housing Crisis Continues*, p. 69.
17. Joint Center for Housing Studies at Harvard University, *The State of the Nation's Housing: 2000*. Retrieved December 29, 2000, from the World Wide Web: http://www.gsd.harvard.edu/jcenter/Publications/State%20of%20the%20Nation%27s%20Housing%202000/Text/Executive%20Summary.html
18. Ibid; also Ohio Association of Realtors, "Better, Bigger Homes Available for Today's Buyers." Retrieved December 29, 2000, from the World Wide Web: http://www.ohiorealtors.org/news/prez_col/0403.html; George Sternlieb and

James W. Hughes, "Housing in the United States: An Overview," in George Sternlieb, James W. Hughes, Robert W. Burchell, Stephen C. Casey, Robert W. Lake, and David Listokin (eds.), *America's Housing* (New Brunswick, NJ: Rutgers University, Center for Urban Policy Research, 1980), pp. 5–7; Sumner M. Rosen, David Fanshel, and Mary E. Lutz (eds.), *Face of the Nation, 1987* (Silver Spring, MD: NASW, 1987), p. 68; and Joint Center for Housing Studies of Harvard University, *The State of the Nation's Housing, 1992* (Boston: Joint Center for Housing Studies of Harvard University, 1992), p. 12.

19. Joint Center for Housing Studies of Harvard University, *The State of the Nation's Housing, 1992*, pp. 28–31.

20. U.S. Census Bureau, *Statistical Abstract of the United States, 1991* (Washington DC: U.S. Government Printing Office, 1991), pp. 715–717.

21. Habitat for Humanity, "Poverty Housing Defeats Families." Retrieved December 29, 2000, from the World Wide Web: http://www.habitat.org/Why/HW_Articles/Poverty_Housing.html

22. Joint Center for Housing Studies at Harvard University, *The State of the Nation's Housing: 2000.*

23. U.S. Department of Housing and Urban Development, *U.S. Housing Market Conditions,* August 1996.

24. Joint Center for Housing Studies at Harvard University, *The State of the Nation's Housing: 2000.*

25. Ibid.

26. Ibid.

27. Ibid.

28. Ibid.

29. National Low-Income Housing Coalition, NLIHC Background on Housing Issues.

30. National Low-Income Housing Coalition, *Out of Reach* (Washington, DC: NLIHC, September 2000).

31. Ibid.

32. Tracy L. Kaufman, *Out of Reach: Can Americans Pay Rent?* (Washington, DC: NLIHC, 1996), p. 57.

33. Joint Center for Housing Studies at Harvard University, *The State of the Nation's Housing: 2000.*

34. Ibid.

35. Ibid.

36. Ibid.

37. National Coalition for the Homeless, "Why Are People Homeless?" (June 1999); NCH Fact Sheet #1. Retrieved December 29, 2000, from the World Wide Web: http://nch.ari.net

38. George Sternlieb and James W. Hughes, "Back to the Central City: Myths and Realities," in Sternlieb et al. (eds.), *America's Housing,* p. 173.

39. Habitat for Humanity, "U.S. Affordable Housing Statistics" (2000); Joint Center for Housing Studies at Harvard University, *The State of the Nation's Housing: 2000.*

40. National Low-Income Housing Coalition. NLIHC Background on Housing Issues.

41. Ibid., pp. 43–44.

42. Carol Biedrzycki, "Residential and Low-Income Electric Customer Protection," Texas Ratepayers' Organization to Save Energy, Inc., Austin, TX. Retrieved December 29, 2000, from the World Wide Web: http://www.ncat.org/liheap/pubs/txreport.htm

43. Center on Budget and Policy Priorities, *Smaller Slices of the Pie* (Washington, DC: CBPP, November 1985), p. 33.

44. Senator Paul Wellstone, "Senate Coalition Taking Offensive in Anticipated LIHEAP Funding Fight," March 25, 1999. Retrieved December 29, 2000, from the World Wide Web: http://wellstone.senate.gov/liheap7.htm; U.S. House of Representatives, Committee on Ways and Means, *1992 Green Book* (Washington, DC: U.S. Government Printing Office, 1992), pp. 1697–1702.

45. Senator Paul Wellstone.

46. Children's Defense Fund, *The State of America's Children, 1992* (Washington, DC: Children's Defense Fund, 1992) p. 38.

47. Quoted in Diana M. DiNitto, *Social Welfare: Politics and Public Policy* (Boston: Allyn & Bacon, 1995), p. 87.

48. Joel Blau, *The Visible Poor: Homelessness in the United States* (New York: Oxford University Press, 1992), p. 124.

49. Ibid.; and Brent McCarthy, Heather McClellan, Terry Moore, Jorge Morales, and Andrea Pucciarello, "Social Welfare in the Clinton Era," unpublished paper, University of Houston,

Graduate School of Social Work, Houston, TX, April 25, 1996.

50. U.S. Department of Housing and Urban Development, *Homelessness: Programs and the People They Serve* (Washington, DC: December 1999).

51. National Coalition for the Homeless, "Domestic Violence and Homelessness" (April 1999), NCH Fact Sheet #8. Retrieved December 30, 2000, from the World Wide Web: http://nch.ari.net

52. Ibid.

53. National Low-Income Housing Coalition, *1996 Advocate's Resource Book* (Washington, DC: NLIHC, 1996).

54. Chester Hartman, "The Housing Part of the Homelessness Problem," in Boston Foundation, *Homelessness: Critical Issues for Policy and Practice* (Boston: Boston Foundation, 1987), pp. 17–19.

55. National Low-Income Housing Coalition, *1996 Advocate's Resource Book.*

56. See National Low-Income Housing Coalition. NLIHC Background on Housing Issues; and National Low-Income Housing Coalition, *1995 Advocate's Resource Book* (Washington, DC: NLIHC, 1995).

57. McCarthy et al., "Social Welfare in the Clinton Era," pp. 23–25.

58. R. Stanfield, "Vouching for the Poor," *National Journal* 18, no. 27 (1995), pp. 1094–1098.

59. E. Mulroy and P. Ewalt, "Is Shelter a Private Problem?" *Social Work* 41 (1996), pp. 125–128.

60. De Parle, "Slamming the Door," p. 94.

61. Quoted in Len Lazarick," Enterprise Foundation Brings Entrepreneurial Spirit to Social Causes," *The Business Monthly* (December 1999). Retrieved December 30, 2000, from the World Wide Web: http://www.bizmonthly.com/news1999/december/enterprise.html

62. The Enterprise Foundation. Retrieved December 30, 2000, from the World Wide Web: http://www.entrprisefoundation.org/

63. Len Lazarick, "Enterprise Foundation Brings Entrepreneurial Spirit to Social Causes."

64. De Parle, "Slamming the Door."

chapter 17

The Politics of Food Policy and Rural Life

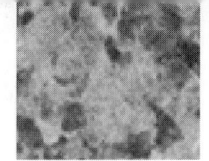

The policies related to the production and distribution of food form an important part of the U.S. welfare state. This chapter examines the federal response to hunger and the government's attempts to distribute foodstuffs to the poor. Topics considered include the Food Stamp Program, WIC and other food programs, U.S. farm policy, the plight of farmworkers in the United States, and the overall problems of food production and distribution. Although the issues around food may initially seem disparate, they are tied together in a complex mosaic that is basic to the well-being of the nation.

Hunger in the United States

One of the most striking aspects of poverty in the United States is hunger. The terms *hunger* and *malnutrition* conjure up images of emaciated Third World children with bloated bellies, skinny arms, and protruding eyes. Americans often think of hunger as a distant phenomenon that pertains mainly to developing countries. Hunger does exist in this country, however, although often in more subtle ways. People with inadequate food may eat only once a day or skip meals for several days; they may be subject to chronic malnutrition; women may bear low-birth-weight babies, and babies may be at risk from high infant mortality rates. Crossing age, race, and gender lines, hunger in the United States affects children, the elderly, the unemployed and the underemployed, homeless people, people with disabilities, and both two-parent and single-parent families. The single common thread connecting these diverse groups to the problem of hunger is poverty.

Cheap and plentiful food is a tradition in this country. Americans spend a smaller percentage of their income on food than any other nation, and we feed much of the world with our surpluses. Consumers, retailers, restaurants, and farmers throw away one-quarter of the U.S. food

stock (almost 100 billion pounds of edible food) each year. Yet data collected by the federal government show that almost 12 percent of U.S. households either suffer from hunger or worry about going hungry. This is double the rate of any other industrialized nation.[1] The U.S. Department of Agriculture relies on poverty statistics to determine the extent of hunger in the United States. USDA data show that only 12 percent of households with incomes below the poverty line have an adequate level of basic nutrition.[2]

Children who are denied an adequate diet are at a greater risk than other low-income children of not reaching their full potential as individuals. Undernourished youngsters have trouble concentrating and bonding with other children and are more likely to suffer illnesses that cause them to be absent from school. They consistently perform more poorly on standardized tests. Poor performance early in school is a major risk factor for dropping out of school in later years. Studies also have shown that even mildly undernourished children may potentially suffer brain, cognitive, and psychological impairment that, if not corrected, can be irreversible. Recent research conducted by the Center on Hunger, Poverty and Nutritional Policy at Tufts University found compelling evidence that improved nutrition can modify and even reverse these effects. John Cook and Katie S. Martin found that millions of poor children have substandard intakes of important major nutrients. Analysis of government data revealed major differences between poor and nonpoor children's intakes of 10 out of 16 essential nutrients.

Cook and Martin also found that millions of poor children suffer from chronic undernutrition, the underconsumption of essential nutrients and food energy.[3] Intake of these nutrients is considered crucial to sound health and normal development. Inadequate food energy intake (caloric intake) can cause problems with attention, concentration, learning, and other important daily activities. For children who have not eaten breakfast, the educational value of a morning spent in the classroom may be lost. Repeated episodes of inadequate food energy intake can lead to cumulative deficits in learning, lower academic achievement, higher rates of school failure, and cognitive impairment.[4] Poor children also are at risk of nutrient deficiencies that can lead to serious health problems, including growth failure, physical weakness, anemia, and stunting. Several of these problems can lead to irreparable damage to young children.

The Face of American Hunger

The following data give a picture of who is hungry in the United States.

- According to a 1995 national USDA survey, hunger existed in 4.2 million households—4.1 percent of all U.S. households. These households had one or more persons that reported experiencing reduced food intake because of a lack of financial resources. Nearly 20 percent of the households (817,000 of the 4.2 million) had one or more members who experienced severe hunger. In some of these households (332,000), children experienced reduced food intake; where no children were present, adults experienced a prolonged lack of food. The lower a household's income, the higher the chance of experiencing hunger.

- According to a 1999 USDA study, 31 million Americans are food insecure. This means that they are either hungry or unsure of where their next meal will come from. Women and children make up 75 percent of that population. Four million children under the age of 12 are going hungry. More than one-half (54 percent) of families with children seeking emergency food assistance are single-parent households.

- Of those hungry in the United States, 47 percent are non-Hispanic white, 32 percent are African American, 15 percent are Hispanic, 3 percent are Native American, and 3 percent are other.

- Sixteen percent of the nation's hungry are 65 and older, 46 percent are between the ages of 18 and 65, and 38 percent are under 18.

- In 1999 approximately 12 million children were food insecure. Ten million U.S. children are malnourished. Of the more than 21 million emergency food recipients served by the Second Harvest network in 1999, more than 8 million were children. One in five people in a soup kitchen line is a child. Forty-six percent of food recipient households with children include at least one child under age five. In 1999, 9 percent of food recipient households reported that children had missed meals in the past month because they lacked food or the means to obtain food. Requests for emergency food assistance rose by 18 percent in 1999, and in the cities 61 percent of the requests came from families with children.

- Greater numbers of Americans throughout the country are going to food pantries and soup kitchens for basic food necessities. A study by the U.S. Conference of Mayors found that in 1999 21 percent of requests for emergency food aid went unmet, because local feeding organizations lacked adequate food resources. Catholic Charities reported that during 1998 the demand for emergency assistance rose an average of 38 percent among reporting agencies. Requests for emergency food assistance increased by 22 percent in Los Angeles in 1999.

- Thirty-six percent of people served by emergency food centers have a high school diploma or equivalent. Forty percent have not completed high school; only five percent have attended college or received a college degree.[5]

 # Governmental Food Programs

The politics of food—or of the way food is distributed in U.S. society—is a complex phenomenon. Like all resources in a free market society, food is a commodity that is bought and sold. In a pure market sense, those who cannot afford to purchase food are unable to consume it. Left to the caprice of the marketplace, many poor people would face malnutrition or even starvation. This problem is particularly acute in an urban society, in which most people lack gardening skills and in any case have no access to land. Providing the poor with access to food is a redistributive function of the welfare state. The obligation of the government to provide food to the poor is similar to the obligation to provide economic opportunity: When either or both are unavailable in adequate quantities, it is the responsibility of the welfare state to respond.

The federal government's response to hunger and malnutrition has consisted of several major programs: (1) the Food Stamp Program, (2) the commodity distribution program, (3) the National School Lunch and Breakfast programs, (4) the Special Milk program, (5) the Special Supplemental Nutrition Program for Women, Infants, and Children (WIC), (6) the Child and Adult Care Food Program, (7) the Summer Food Service Program, and (8) the Meals on Wheels and Congregate Dining programs.

A Short History of Food Stamps and a Description of the Program

In 1933, Congress established the Federal Surplus Relief Corporation, an agency designed to distribute surplus commodity foods as well as coal, mattresses, and blankets. In 1939, Congress established a food stamp program. This was terminated in 1943, when a commodity food distribution program was reestablished. A pilot food stamp program began during the presidency of John F. Kennedy, and in 1964 the current Food Stamp Act was passed. Figure 17.1 describes the current eligibility rules for the Food Stamp Program.

Although the Food Stamp Program (FS) is fully funded by the federal government and administered by the USDA, state and local welfare agencies qualify applicants and provide them with stamps. Administrative costs are shared by federal, state, and local governments. Recipients are given an allotment of stamps based on family size and income, with eligibility requirements and benefits determined at the federal level. Food stamp eligibility is based on a means test. Recipients originally had to pay a set price (depending on family size and income) for their stamps, with the amount to be paid less than the face value of the stamps. For example, this enabled some people to purchase $75 worth of food stamps for $35; the difference between the amount paid and the face value of the stamps was called a "bonus." This system proved unwieldy, however, because many poor people could not afford to purchase any stamps. In 1977 purchase requirements were dropped, and national participation rates rose by 30 percent.

Food Stamps: Who Is in the Program and What Does It Cost?

In 2000 17 million people (down from 27.5 million in 1995) received FS benefits at a cost of $17 billion (down from $24.6 billion in 1995). The average benefit in 2000 was $72.77 a month per person. In 1999, the FS program was characterized by the following:

- FS benefits accounted for more than one-fifth of the average participating household's monthly income.

- Almost 56 percent of FS households contained children; 68.5 percent were single female–headed households; 15.1 percent were headed by married parents. The average FS family contained 3.3 persons. Thirty-nine percent of FS recipients were nonelderly adults; 34 percent were children in single-parent households; 13 percent were children in multiple-adult households; and 9.4 percent were elderly adults. More than 26 percent of FS households contained disabled persons. Among adult participants, 71 percent were women.

- The average household with children received $234 a month in FS benefits ($274 for a married couple household). The average monthly FS benefit per household was $162. More than 81 percent of benefits went to households with children.

| **FIGURE 17.1** | Food Stamp Eligibility Guidelines 2000–2001 |

Resources

Households may have $2,000 in countable resources, such as a bank account, or $3,000 in countable resources if at least one person is age 60 or older. However, certain resources are not counted, such as a home and lot, the resources of people who receive Supplemental Security Income (SSI), and the resources of people who receive Temporary Aid to Needy Families (TANF).

Income

Households must meet income tests unless all members are receiving Title IV (TANF) assistance, SSI, or in some places General Assistance. Most households must meet both the gross and net income tests, but a household with an elderly person or a person who is receiving certain types of disability payments has to meet only the net income test. "Gross income" means a household's total, nonexcluded income, before any deductions have been made. "Net income" means gross income minus allowable deductions. Households, except those noted, that have income over the amounts listed in Table 17.1 (see p. 469) cannot get food stamps.

Deductions

Allowable deductions are the following:

A 20 percent deduction from earned income.

A standard deduction of $134 for all households.

A dependent care deduction when needed for work, training, or education–but not more than $200 for each child under age two and not more than $175 for each other dependent.

Medical expenses for elderly or disabled members that are more than $35 for the month, if they are not paid by insurance or someone else.

Legally owed child support payments.

Excess shelter costs that are more than half of the household's income after the other deductions. Allowable costs include the cost of fuel to heat and cook with, electricity, water, the basic fee for one telephone, rent or mortgage payments, and taxes on the home. The amount of the shelter deduction cannot be more than $300 unless one person in the household is elderly or disabled.

Legal Immigrants and Rules on Work

Citizenship/Alien Status

U.S. citizens and many noncitizens may be eligible for food stamps. For example, refugees, asylees, Cubans, Haitians, Amerasians, and persons whose deportation has been withheld may be eligible for seven years after they enter the United States or are granted status. Persons legally admitted for permanent residence may be eligible if they have 40 qualifying quarters of Social Security work coverage or they have a U.S. military connection. Refugees, asylees, Cubans, Haitians, Amerasians, persons whose deportation has been withheld, parolees, persons legally admitted for permanent residence, and battered aliens may be eligible if they were legally living in the United States on August 22, 1996, and were 65 on that date or are now receiving disability payments or are under the age of 18. Native Americans who cross the Canadian or Mexican borders are eligible, as are certain Hmong and Highland Laotians and their spouses and children.

Even if some members of a household are not eligible, those who are may be able to get food stamps. A number of states have their own programs to provide benefits to immigrants who do not meet the regular Food Stamp Program eligibility requirements.

| **FIGURE 17.1** | Continued |

Work

With some exceptions, able-bodied adults between 16 and 60 must register for work, accept suitable employment, and take part in an employment and training program to which they are referred by the food stamp office. Failure to comply with these requirements can result in disqualification from the program. In addition, able-bodied adults between 18 and 50 who do not have any dependent children can get food stamps only for 3 months in a 36-month period if they do not work or participate in a workfare or employment and training program other than job search. This requirement can be waived in some locations.

Source: Adapted from Food and Nutrition Service, USDA, "Eligibility, 2000–2001." Retrieved from the World Wide Web: http://www.fns.usda.gov/fsp/MENU/APPS/ELIGIBILITY/ELIG.HTM

■ The largest proportion of FS participants were non-Hispanic whites (40.6 percent), more than one-third were African Americans (36.1 percent), and 18.1 percent were Hispanic.[6] Tables 17.1 and 17.2 provide an overview of the FS program benefits.

Special Supplemental Nutrition Program for Women, Infants, and Children (WIC)

The WIC program was enacted on September 26, 1972. This program originally began as a two-year pilot program to provide nutritional counseling and supplemental foods to pregnant and breast-feeding women, infants, and young children at nutritional risk. The goal of the program is to address areas of child development that are most affected by poor health and inadequate nutrition, including impaired learning.[7] Specifically, the twin goals of WIC are (1) to enrich the food intake of participants by providing them with food or with coupons or food cards that they redeem at local grocery stores, and (2) to educate mothers, individually and in group classes, on how to prevent nutritional difficulties.

TABLE 17.1 ■ Income Guidelines and Benefits for Food Stamps, 2000

HOUSEHOLD SIZE	MAXIMUM GROSS MONTHLY INCOME (130% OF POVERTY)	MAXIMUM NET MONTHLY INCOME (100% OF POVERTY)	MAXIMUM ALLOTMENT LEVEL
1	$ 905	$ 696	$130
2	1,219	938	238
3	1,533	1,180	341
4	1,848	1,421	434
5	2,162	1,633	515
6	2,476	1,905	618
7	2,790	2,146	683
8	3,104	2,388	781
Each additional member	+315	+242	+98

Source: U.S. Department of Agriculture, Food and Nutrition Service, "Frequently Asked Questions." Retrieved October 6, 2000, from the World Wide Web: http://www.fns.usda.gov/fsp/menu/faqs/faqs.htm

TABLE 17.2 ▪ Food Stamps Statistics, Selected Years, 1975–1995 (participants and cost figures in millions)

YEAR	TOTAL COST OF FS	NUMBER OF PARTICIPANTS	PERCENTAGE OF POPULATION USING FS	AVERAGE MONTHLY BENEFITS PER PERSON
1975	$ 4,624	16.3	7.6%	$ 21.40
1978	5,573	14.4	6.5	26.80
1981	11,812	20.6	9.0	39.50
1984	13,275	20.9	8.8	42.70
1987	13,535	19.1	7.8	45.80
1990	17,686	20.0	8.0	59.00
1991	21,012	22.6	9.0	63.90
1993	23,653	26.9	9.3	67.97
1995	20,500	26.7	8.9	71.50
2000	16,956	17.1	6.0	72.77

Source: U.S. Department of Agriculture, Food and Nutrition Service, "Food Stamp Participation and Costs." Retrieved November 22, 2000, from the World Wide Web: http://www.fns.usda.gov/pd/fssummar.htm

WIC is not an entitlement program; that is, Congress does not set aside funds to allow every eligible individual to participate in the program. WIC is a federal grant program for which Congress authorizes a specific amount of funds each year. WIC is administered at the federal level by USDA's Food and Nutrition Service (FNS) and at the state level by 87 state WIC agencies. WIC operates through 2,000 local agencies in 10,000 clinic sites, in 50 state health departments, 32 Indian tribal organizations, American Samoa, the District of Columbia, Guam, Puerto Rico, and the Virgin Islands. There are approximately 46,000 authorized WIC retailers. Each state receives cash grants and is responsible for developing, implementing, and monitoring its WIC program.[8] Income eligibility is less restrictive than for public assistance programs; federal guidelines target families whose pretax income is at or below 185 percent of the federal poverty line. Eligibility is limited to pregnant women (through pregnancy and up to six weeks after birth or after pregnancy ends—one in four new mothers participates in WIC); breast-feeding women (up to the infant's first birthday); non-breast-feeding postpartum women (up to six months after the birth of an infant or after pregnancy ends); infants (up to the first birthday—WIC serves 45 percent of all U.S. infants); and children up to their fifth birthday.

Qualified beneficiaries receive supplemental foods each month in the form of actual food items or, more often, are given vouchers for the purchase of specific items in retail stores. Items that may be included in a food package include milk, cheese, eggs, infant formula, cereals, and fruits and vegetables. The USDA requires food packages that provide specific types and amounts of food appropriate for six categories of participants: (1) infants from birth to 3 months; (2) infants from 4 to 12 months; (3) women and children with special dietary needs; (4) children from one to five years of age; (5) pregnant and nursing mothers; and (6) postpartum nursing mothers. In addition to receiving food benefits,

WIC participants also receive nutritional counseling.[9] In 2000 WIC served roughly 7 million women and children and cost $3.94 billion.[10]

Other Food Programs

Augmenting the Food Stamp Program and WIC are a range of programs targeting various constituencies.

After-school snacks. Snacks are available to children and teenagers in after-school programs through the National School Lunch Program and the Child and Adult Care Food Program (discussed below). The Child Nutrition Reauthorization Act of 1998 enhances nutrition benefits for all children—with a special emphasis on older children—by authorizing reimbursement for snacks served to children through age 18 (and to individuals, regardless of age, who are determined by the state agency to be mentally or physically disabled) who participate in organized after-school programs.[11]

National School Lunch Program. The NSLP provides lunches and the opportunity to practice skills learned in classroom nutrition education. The NSLP is a federally assisted meal program operating in more than 96,000 public and nonprofit private schools and residential child care institutions.

School districts and independent schools that take part in the lunch program get cash subsidies and donated commodities from the USDA for each meal they serve. In return, they must serve lunches that meet federal requirements, and they must offer free or reduced-price lunches to eligible children. Children from families with incomes at or below 130 percent of the poverty level are eligible for free meals. Those between 130 percent and 185 percent of the poverty level are eligible for reduced-price meals, for which students

can be charged no more than 40 cents. Children from families with incomes over 185 percent of poverty pay a full price, though their meals are still subsidized to some extent. Local school food authorities set their own prices for full-price meals, but most operate their meal services as nonprofit programs.

In 1997 more than 26.3 million children received lunches daily through the NSLP. Since the program began, more than 170 billion lunches have been served. In 1999 Congress appropriated $5.46 billion for the NSLP.[12]

School Breakfast Program. The SBP provides breakfasts to promote learning readiness and healthy eating behaviors. Some 7.4 million children in more than 72,000 schools and institutions use the SBP, a federal program that provides states with cash assistance for nonprofit breakfast programs in schools and residential child care institutions. The program is administered at the federal level by the USDA through its FNS. State education agencies and local school food authorities administer the program at the local level.

Children whose families meet income criteria may receive free or reduced-price breakfasts. Those from families with incomes at or below 130 percent of the federal poverty level are eligible for free meals. Children whose family income is between 130 percent and 185 percent of the poverty level are eligible for reduced-price meals. Those from families over 185 percent of poverty pay a full price, although their meals are still subsidized to some extent. Schools may not charge more than 30 cents for a reduced-price breakfast. Schools set their own prices for breakfasts served to students who pay the full meal price, though they must operate their meal services as nonprofit programs. In 1999 Congress appropriated $1.35 billion for the School Breakfast Program. In 1999 an average of 7.3 million children participated daily; of those, 6.3 million received their meals free or at a reduced price.[13]

Special Milk Program. The SMP offers milk to children who lack access to other meal programs. The program provides milk to children in schools and child care institutions that do not participate in other federal child nutrition meal service programs. When local school officials offer free milk under the program, any child from a family that meets income guidelines for free meals and milk is eligible. Each child's family must apply annually for free milk eligibility. In 1999 more than 7,100 schools and residential child care institutions participated, along with 1,300 summer camps and 518 nonresidential child care institutions. Congress appropriated $18 million for the SMP in 1999.[14]

Summer Food Service Program. The SFSP serves meals and snacks to low-income children during long school vacations. The FNS administers the SFSP at the federal level; state education agencies administer the program in most states, although in some areas the state health or social service department or an FNS regional office may be designated. Locally, SFSP is run by approved sponsors, including school districts, local government agencies, camps, or private nonprofit organizations. Sponsors provide free meals to a group of children at a central site, such as a school or a community center.

States approve SFSP meal sites as open, enrolled, or camp sites. Open sites operate in low-income areas where at least half of the children come from families with incomes at or below 185 percent of the federal poverty level, making the children eligible for free and reduced-price school meals. Children 18 and younger may receive free meals and snacks through SFSP. Meals and snacks are also available to persons with disabilities who are over age 18 but who participate in school programs for mentally or physically disabled people. Congress appropriated $294.4 million for SFSP in 1999.[15]

Child and Adult Care Food Program. CACFP provides meals and snacks to infants, young children, and impaired adults who receive day care. Public, private nonprofit, and some for-profit adult day care facilities that provide structured, comprehensive services to functionally impaired nonresident adults may participate in CACFP. Children age 12 and younger are eligible to receive up to two meals and one snack each day at a day care home or center through CACFP. Children who reside in homeless shelters may receive up to three meals a day. Migrant children age 15 and younger, and persons with disabilities regardless of their age, are also eligible for CACFP. In 1999 USDA reimbursed $1.6 billion to institutions participating in CACFP; 2.6 million children and 62,500 adults were served meals.[16]

Food distribution. Food distribution programs are designed to (1) strengthen the nutrition safety net through commodity distribution and other nutrition assistance to low-income families, emergency feeding programs, Indian reservations, and the elderly and (2) strengthen U.S. agriculture. More than a billion pounds of food is provided to 26 million schoolchildren a year.

Although some of the low-income elderly receive food stamps, they can also be served by Meals on Wheels and the Congregate Meal Dining program. Meals on Wheels was begun in 1972 and was designed to improve nutrition for the elderly. Various community agencies arrange the daily delivery of meals to elderly persons living at home, and aged persons who receive food stamps can use them to purchase the meals. (Others are asked to make a donation.) The Congregate Meal Dining program provides meals at such places as senior citizen centers.

Other federal food programs include the Emergency Food Assistance Program, which provides funds to local agencies through a national board of charitable organizations. This national charitable board, in part consisting of the United Way, the Salvation Army, and Catholic Charities, distributes funds to local charities, soup kitchens, shelters, and other organizations that deal with hunger and homelessness. The federal government also provides funding to help subsidize emergency food agencies and to help pay for the storage and distribution of federal surplus food commodities.

Have the Food Programs Worked?

Because WIC is a discretionary rather than an entitlement program, it can serve only as many people as its budget allows. Consequently, it is estimated that only 46 percent of those eligible receive WIC benefits.[17] Moreover, many counties have no WIC program; many others turn people away or have long waiting lists.[18] Although states *may* provide additional funds for WIC, only a minority of them do so.[19]

According to USDA studies, WIC saves lives and improves the health of nutritionally at-risk women, infants, and children. The results of studies conducted by FNS and other nongovernment entities demonstrate that WIC is one of the nation's most successful and cost-effective nutrition intervention programs. Some highlights of the findings are that WIC improves diet and diet-related outcomes; improves infant feeding practices; improves immunization rates and regular medical care; improves cognitive development; and improves preconceptional nutritional status. USDA research has also shown that the WIC program is playing an important role in improving birth outcomes and thus in containing health care costs. USDA reports found that Medicaid-eligible pregnant women in five states who participated in WIC during their pregnancies had longer pregnancies, fewer premature births, lower incidence of low-birth-weight infants, fewer infant deaths, and a greater likelihood of receiving prenatal care. Health care savings ranged from $1.77 to $3.13 for each dollar spent on WIC.[20]

The Food Stamp Program. The number of participants in the Food Stamp Program grew dramatically from 1989 (19 million) to 1994 (28 million) but has declined steadily since then. In September 1997 about 62 percent of eligible people in the United States received food stamps. In 1999 participation in FS declined to 17.7 million cases, the lowest level since 1979. The 33 percent decline from 1994 to 1999 was far greater than could be explained by an improving economy and welfare reform. Specifically, between 1995 and 1997, the number of people in poverty dropped by roughly 1 million people—or less than 3 percent. But the number leaving food stamps fell by more than 4 million people—a 15 percent drop over the same period. From 1993 to 1998 the number of children living in poverty declined by nearly 13.4 percent, whereas the number of children receiving food stamps declined by 28.6 percent, nearly three times as much. In 1994 94 percent of eligible children were receiving food stamps; by 1998 the participation rate decreased to 75 percent for eligible children living in small families.[21]

Despite a strong economy, the level of food security among U.S. households changed little from 1995 to 2000. For example, in 1998 nearly 10 million people lived in households that experienced hunger. Moreover, the number of Americans who are food insecure has remained constant at approximately 31 million people, and the demand nationwide at hunger relief agencies is up.[22]

Welfare reform and welfare-to-work programs are not working if working people cannot afford to buy enough food. Hunger relief agencies report that since the early 1990s the greatest increase in hunger has been among the working poor. Thirty-nine percent of emergency food recipient households (those served in charity soup kitchens, food pantries, and emergency shelters) have at least one adult working. Of working people in emergency food recipient households, 49 percent are working full time (40 hours or more per week). According to the U.S.

Conference of Mayors, 37 percent of people requesting emergency food assistance in U.S. cities are employed.[23]

A 1999 General Accounting Office (GAO) study on food stamps found that even though food stamp and welfare caseloads have declined, the need for food assistance has not diminished. Rather, needy individuals and families are increasingly relying on sources other than food stamps, such as food banks, soup kitchens, and emergency pantries. These findings are corroborated by other data. A Wisconsin study found that more than one-third of former welfare recipients had problems paying for food despite a high incidence of employment. Fewer than half of the former recipients reported having more money than when they were receiving public assistance, and 68 percent reported that they were "barely making it." A South Carolina Department of Social Services study reported that after leaving TANF 17 percent of former welfare recipients had no way to buy food some of the time. This is twice the number of families who reported such problems while receiving assistance. An analysis of former welfare recipients in Massachusetts found that 18 percent of families leaving the rolls were back on welfare after three months, and 21 percent were back after a year; and the same study found that food insecurity increased for many families after they went off welfare. Forty percent of the families interviewed did not have enough food or enough of the right kinds of food after being off welfare for one year. More than 20 percent of families who remained off welfare after one year used food banks or had to borrow money to buy food. In short, as poor Americans transition from welfare to work and their benefits are cut or reduced, they are finding their meager wages insufficient to meet basic needs, including child care, transportation, and housing costs. As a result, working poor families may cut their food budget or turn to a local charity for aid.[24]

Food stamp participation also is hampered by excessive red tape. The organization Second Harvest reviewed the application process for food stamps in all 50 states and the District of Columbia. They found that:

- More than half (29) of the states and the District of Columbia have food stamp applications 10 to 36 pages long—much longer than necessary.
- Food stamp applications are difficult to read and complete, and they include excessive and invasive questions—often with little or no legal connection to the Food Stamp Program.
- The average length of a state food stamp application is 12 pages; the two longest state forms are in Minnesota (36 pages) and West Virginia (33 pages). Ten other states have applications between 19 and 28 pages long. Most food stamp applications are longer than the applications for a federal firearms permit, a federal home mortgage loan, or a school bus driver's license.
- Only 15 states have two-part applications in which the first part, generally shorter, may be used to initiate the process and begin the accrual of benefits once certified.
- Food Stamp applications in 49 of the 50 states and the District of Columbia contain certification statements that must be signed by the applicant (under penalty of perjury) that are written at the ninth- to twelfth-grade reading level. Some state food stamp applications require applicants to provide accurate information (under penalty of perjury) using terms that many are unlikely to understand, such as liquid assets, deemed income, deprivation factor, and so forth.
- Some applications require information regarding children's income and bank accounts; income from baby-sitting; charity and gifts from churches and synagogues; income from panhandling, bingo, and plasma donation; and garage sale receipts.[25]

 # Farming in the United States

The 1980s were a tumultuous time for farmers in the United States, and in many places the period rivaled the Great Depression of the 1930s.[26] Agricultural members of the American Bankers Association estimated that 3.8 percent of all farmers filed for bankruptcy in 1985 alone.[27] A 1985 USDA study of 1.7 million farms indicated that 214,000 were in serious financial difficulty, with 38,000 classified as technically insolvent.[28] Other farm indicators were equally bleak. In 1981 the total asset value of U.S. agriculture was $1 trillion; by 1985 it had shrunk to $692 billion, a 30 percent drop and the steepest fall since the Great Depression. Although U.S. farms had declined in number by a modest 16,000 between 1978 and 1982, between 1982 and 1987 they declined by 151,000, or at a rate of about 30,000 annually.[29]

In spite of these dire conditions, in the late 1980s U.S. farmers made a relative comeback—due in part to the worldwide 1987–88 drought, which depleted the grain reserves of many nations. By early 1990 farmland prices in the United States had risen, and farm exports increased to 148.5 million tons. Real net cash farm income went up from $48.5 billion in 1987 to about the same level as had prevailed in the mid-1970s. More importantly, the farm debt stabilized.[30] On the other hand, the growth in farm equity was still trailing the 3 to 4 percent rate of general inflation.[31]

Historically, farmers had demanded that agricultural commodity price supports be set at parity levels: an equal ratio between farm prices and input/output costs.[32] In 1942, Congress established the price support levels at 90 percent of parity. From 1942 to 1953, average prices paid to farmers were at 90 to 100 percent of parity, thereby raising market prices, ensuring a secure income for farmers, reducing the need for excessive debt, and encouraging stabilization in the price of grain.

By the end of World War II, however, powerful corporations, academics, and free traders had begun to wage war on the farm parity program. Soil conservation, supply management, and parity were characterized as socialist ideas that interfered with a free market economy. Grain companies called for lower prices to help them sell abroad, arguing that expanded exports and food aid programs would compensate farmers for lower commodity prices. Industrialists

maintained that lower food prices would translate into cheaper labor costs, and agribusiness believed that lowered commodity prices would result in more production, thereby increasing the use of their products.

Ultimately the small farmer lost to this powerful coalition, and farm parity was terminated in 1953. As a result, the purchasing power of net farm income decreased even as exports rose. Held constant in 1967 dollars, the purchasing power of net farm income dropped from an annual average of $25 billion in 1942–52 (the years of farm parity) to an average of $13.3 billion in 1953–72. In 1952 net farm income was greater than total farm debt; by 1983 net farm income was less than farm interest payments.[33]

Not all farmers were affected equally by the farming crisis of the mid-1980s. For instance, although almost one-sixth of all U.S. farming households suffered net income losses in 1984[34] and many middle-sized farmers (with farms in the 80- to 500-acre range) were forced to abandon farming, very small farms endured, and very large farms were becoming more and more dominant in U.S. agriculture. In 1984 more than two-fifths of all U.S. farms had total annual sales of less than $10,000, accounting for only 2 percent of all farm sales. These farms experienced an overall net loss of income. By contrast, farms with sales exceeding $500,000 a year earned an average income of $219,000. Finally, in 1984 three-fifths of the total income of farming families (a proportion that is growing) came from nonfarm employment.[35]

Family farming embodies many of this nation's most cherished traditional values—hard work, independence, strong family life, close-knit communities, and democratic institutions. For many rural families farming is not a vocation but a way of life. Work on the land, often a legacy from parents or grandparents, creates a commitment both to a specific place and to the family heritage.[36] This psychological connection to farming means that many farmers see themselves as farmer–caretakers. Financial failure may therefore leave farmers not only with a sense of personal failure but also with feelings of shame for having failed both their families and their heritage. This situation can result in emotional disturbances ranging from stress and depression to self-destructive or aggressive behavior.[37] The Reverend Paul Tidemann, a Lutheran minister who studied the farm crisis of the 1980s, reported that "The loss of a farm . . . is not the same as a loss of a job. It signals the loss of a personal and family connection to the land. It prompts a sense of betrayal, in many cases, of generations of farmers, past, present, and future."[38]

The Current State of U.S. Farming

Family farms in the United States are rapidly being replaced by corporate farms. This trend spans all agricultural sectors. Corporate agriculture is a system wherein the farm owner, the farm manager, and the farm worker are different people. This system represents a dramatic shift from the historic structure of Midwest and Great Plains agriculture, in which individual farmers make the decisions and reap the profits. Industrial agriculture encourages large-scale, highly specialized farms where uniformity is emphasized over quality—and where many costs are shifted from the farm operation to society. In North Carolina in 1995, for example, a 25-million-gallon hog manure spill at a factory farm killed thousands of fish, destroyed crops, and severely damaged a local river. A new hog operation in Utah will raise 2.5 million hogs a year, producing more waste than the entire city of Los Angeles.[39] Corporatization leads to closed markets where prices are fixed not by open, competitive bidding but by negotiated contracts. Producers who don't produce in large volumes are discriminated against in price or other terms of trade. Under these conditions, many smaller farmers who don't participate in "vertical integration" are forced out of business because they have no place to sell their products.

An integral part of corporate farming is vertical integration, whereby agricultural corporations control all aspects of production, including raising, owning, slaughtering, and marketing livestock or agricultural products. One example of vertical integration is ConAgra, the largest distributor of agricultural chemicals in North America and one of the largest fertilizer producers. ConAgra owns more than 100 grain elevators, 2,000 railroad cars, and 1,100 barges, and it is the largest of the three corporations that mill 80 percent of North America's wheat. ConAgra is also the largest turkey producer and the fourth largest broiler producer, producing its own poultry feed as well as other livestock feed. The corporation hires growers to raise its birds and then processes them in its own facilities. This poultry can then be purchased as fryers, under the name of Country Skillet, or in further processed foods such as TV dinners and pot pies under the labels of Banquet and Beatrice Foods (owners of Swift, Butterball Turkeys, Hunt's, Peter Pan, and Orville Redenbacher). ConAgra is the second largest food processor in the United States and the fourth largest in the world.[40]

The Face of U.S. Farming

The following items highlight the important current trends in U.S. agriculture.

- *Dwindling farms.* Of all the occupations in this country, farming today is facing the greatest decline. There are 1.91 million farms remaining in the United States; between 1993 and 1997, the number of mid-sized family farms dropped by 74,440. Between 1978 and 1998, some 300,000 U.S. farms disappeared. In 1920 the United States had over 925,000 black-operated farms; by 1999 there were fewer than 18,500. The rate of agricultural loss by black farmers is more than twice that of losses by other farmers. Small farms operated by hobby farmers now account for 35 percent of all farms.

- *Dwindling incomes.* In 1999 the average farm with annual gross sales between $50,000 and $250,000 had a net income of only $23,159. More than 80 percent of a farmer's gross income is eaten up by expenses. The median weekly income of a small farmer in 1998 was $447, a little more than $23,000 a year. Most family farmers must work jobs off the farm to make ends meet.

In 1999 88 percent of the average farm operator's household income came from nonfarm sources. Even in the farm-based counties of the middle border states (Minnesota, North Dakota, South Dakota, Iowa, Kansas, and Nebraska), a 1989 study by the Center for Rural Affairs found that 48 percent of all earned income came from nonfarm employment, 27 percent of that income from self-employment.

■ *The graying of U.S. farms.* Half of all current farmers are likely to retire in the next decade. Nearly half of all farmers are older than 55—the average age is 53—and just 8 percent are younger than 35. U.S. farmers over age 55 control more than half the farmland; since 1987 the number of entry-level farmers replacing them has fallen by 30 percent and now makes up only 10 percent of all farmers. These trends suggest an almost total absence of a new generation of beginning farmers.

■ *Consolidation and control.* Nearly half of all U.S. land is farmland (more than 1 billion acres). Only 4 percent of landowners hold 47 percent of this farmland. In California, the nation's largest agricultural producer, 3 percent of California farms control 60 percent of the market. Nationwide the figures are similar—7 percent of U.S. farms received 60 percent of the net cash farm income in 1992. One study estimates that in 2000 about 50,000 of the largest farms in the United States will account for 75 percent of agricultural production.

■ *Women and farming.* Ownership and control in U.S. agriculture also have distinct gender biases. Of those who control U.S. farmland, only 4 percent are women. Women tend to own smaller farms; the average size of properties held by men is one-third larger than that of farms held by women.

■ *Crop prices.* The farmer's share of each food dollar has dropped steadily over the past half century, from 41 cents in 1950 to only 20 cents in 1999. Adjusted for inflation, the price a farmer received for corn in 1999 was the lowest in 25 years. Since 1985 farm prices have dropped steadily for commodities such as corn, wheat, and soybeans: In 1999 those prices were 35 to 50 percent lower than in 1985.

■ *Corporate farming.* Five corporations control 87 percent of all beef processing, and four corporations control 56 percent of all pork processing. Forty producers now control one-third of all hogs raised in the United States. Since 1986 the number of hog operations has declined by 72 percent—a loss of more than 247,500 operations. Of the remaining hog operations, 2 percent control nearly half of all hog inventory. Four meatpacking companies control an estimated 79 percent of cattle slaughter; five companies control 78 percent of the sheep slaughter industry. Since 1980 the major players' share of control in the beef industry has grown from 36 percent to 87 percent; it has risen from 32 percent to 56 percent in the hog industry. Two percent of farms produce 50 percent of agricultural product sales.

Ninety-eight percent of all poultry is produced by large corporations, and only four companies dominate 49 percent of production. These companies control everything from the laying of eggs to the marketing of chicken meat. One company grows, kills, and processes 40 million birds a week—more than most countries produce. Farmers who are contract growers for these large companies absorb most of the risks while reaping little of the profits.

Four companies control 71 percent of flour milling, four companies control 74 percent of wet corn milling, four companies control 76 percent of soybean crushing, and four companies control 89 percent of the cereal market. The largest companies are Archer Daniels Midland (ADM), Cargill, and ConAgra.

■ *Rural health and food quality.* Many rural residents are exposed to excessive odors from factory farms and often suffer from nausea, vomiting, coughing, and headaches. The factory farms' extreme confinement and increased levels of production of animals intensify the opportunity for contamination of meat and poultry with bacteria such as E. coli and salmonella, which can cause human illness and death. Crowded livestock conditions lead to a reliance on antibiotics to maintain animal health; this practice, in turn, contributes to the development of antibiotic-resistant bacteria. Antibiotic-resistant bacteria in animals can be passed on to humans through the food supply.

- *Farm subsidies.* Large farms receive nearly twice as much in government payments as do small farms. A General Accounting Office study found that one-third of farm subsidies go to the largest 1 percent of producers and that another third goes to 80 percent of farmers (those with sales under $100,000).

- *Efficiency.* Despite the trends of bigness and commercialization, the cost per unit for agricultural production is no better in larger commercial operations than in family farms. Factory farms add many real costs, such as increased use of fossil fuels, environmental damage, health threats, and threats to the safety of the food supply. The optimum efficiency for raising hogs is reached on a farrow-to-finish operation with just 150 sows.[41]

Farmworkers

Essential to the multibillion-dollar U.S. fruit and vegetable industry are the efforts of millions of farmworkers. Because agricultural production depends on the influx of seasonal labor, each year anywhere from 3 to 5 million families leave their homes to follow the crops. The wages and conditions they labor under are by all measures scandalous.

Who Are America's Farmworkers?

The following is an overview of U.S. farmworkers in 1997–98.

- *Demographics.* Eighty-one percent of farmworkers were foreign born, with the majority (77 percent) being Mexican born. About 19 percent of farmworkers were born in the United States. U.S.-born whites accounted for just 7 percent of

all farmworkers; U.S.-born Hispanics, African Americans, and other minorities of color made up the remaining 12 percent. The average age of farmworkers was 31, and half were under 29 years of age. Eighty percent of farmworkers were men; 50 percent were married; and slightly less than half were parents.

- *Education and language.* Eighty-four percent of farmworkers spoke Spanish, and farmworkers typically had completed six years of education. Twenty percent had completed less than three years of schooling; only 15 percent had completed high school. Only 10 percent of farmworkers spoke or read English fluently.

- *Labor and conditions.* Sixty percent of all farmworkers held just one U.S. farm job per year; during the course of the year, they spent roughly half their time doing farm work. Fifty-six percent of all farmworkers migrated within the United States or internationally. Farmworkers earned $5.94 an hour on average. About 20 percent reported being covered by unemployment insurance, but only 3 percent had employer-provided health insurance. Seventy-seven percent of farmworkers were paid by the hour and 20 percent by the piece.

- *Wages.* The purchasing power of farm wages declined by more than 10 percent (from $6.89 to $6.18 an hour) between 1989 and 1998. That is, farmworkers lost 11 percent of their purchasing power in that decade. By 1998 the average farm wage was just 48 percent of the average industrial wage.

- *Legal status.* Fifty-two percent of farmworkers lacked work authorization; 24 percent were legal permanent residents; and 22 percent were U.S. citizens.

- *Poverty.* Most farmworkers (about 60 percent) were poor, and the proportion is trending upwards. Overall, the farmworker population was very poor, with 61 percent living below the poverty line. Nearly 75 percent of farmworker families had incomes of less than $10,000 a year. The median income of individual farmworkers was less than $7,500 a year. This is particularly striking given that the 1.5 percent of U.S. farms with the highest sales employ more than half of the farm labor.

■ *Use of social services.* Despite their poverty, few farmworkers use social services. In 1997–98 just 20 percent of farmworkers reported using unemployment insurance. Likewise, only 10 percent reported using WIC benefits. The use of Medicaid and food stamps had declined to between 10 and 13 percent of the farmworker population.

■ *Assets.* Few farmworkers had assets. By 1997 fewer than 44 percent of farmworkers owned a vehicle (down from 49 percent in 1994–95). Because more than half of farmworkers did not own a vehicle, many were forced to pay for rides to work. Home ownership also had declined. In 1994–95 one-third of all farmworkers owned or were buying a house; by 1998 that number was only 14 percent.

■ *Women.* Women farmworkers had lower personal incomes than men. The median income for women farmworkers was between $2,500 and $5,000; for men it was between $5,000 and $7,500. Only 1 in 10 women earned more than $10,000 in farm work, whereas 2 in 10 men did.

■ *Regional earnings.* Farm earnings also varied by region. In the Midwest workers had the lowest median farm earnings (between $1,000 and $2,500), and 37 percent had earnings of less than $500 a year. Workers in the Northeast and the Southeast earned slightly more. Median farm earnings in those regions were between $2,500 and $5,000. Workers in the Western states had the highest earnings, although their farm incomes were still relatively low.[42]

Housing is a vital necessity for farmworkers. In 1997 21 percent of all farmworkers received free housing from their employers, 7 percent rented from employers, 47 percent rented privately, and 18 percent owned their own homes. More than 35 percent of farmworker housing in eight major agricultural labor states (California, Florida, Texas, Washington, Colorado, Michigan, New York, and Ohio) lacked inside running water. It is estimated that one-third of U.S. farm laborers work in fields without drinking water, hand-washing facilities, or toilets. And at the end of the workday, many farmworkers do not have a home to go to. The number of farmworkers needing housing exceeds the available housing units. In 1980, for example, housing was available for only about one-third of the estimated 1.2 million migrant farm workers who needed it. In addition, migrant farmworkers face barriers in obtaining private housing. For example, rural communities may not have enough rental units available—or they may be unwilling to rent to migrant farmworkers because they cannot provide deposits, qualify for credit checks, or make long-term rental commitments.[43]

Education is also problematic for the families of migrant farmworkers. Constant mobility makes it hard for the children of farmworkers to complete their education. Children who move often are two and a half times more likely to repeat a grade than children who do not move. Changing schools is emotionally difficult for children, and youngsters are more likely to drop out of school if they change schools four or more times; educators who work with migrant children say that 55 percent of these children graduate nationwide. Migrant children also face intense economic pressure to drop out of school.[44]

Child labor is yet another problem. The Department of Labor found that most seasonal agricultural workers are married and/or have children. Often, the family's poverty requires that all able family members work. In fact, agriculture is the only industry that allows workers under the age of 16: The Fair Labor Standards Act sets age 12 as the legal limit for farm work, with exemptions available for children as young as 10 or 11. An estimated 43,000 children accompanied by family members, and an additional 55,000 unaccompanied minors, are involved in farm labor. Moreover, about 250,000 children migrate each year, approximately 90,000 of them across an international border. When children work in the fields, occupational injury presents an even more significant risk for them than for adults because of the youngsters' lack of experience.[45]

The health problems experienced by farm-workers are staggering. One of the many health risks they face is the exposure to pesticides, herbicides, and fungicides. National estimates of the number of farmworkers, farmers, and their families potentially exposed to toxic chemicals range from 3.2 to 4 million people. The Environmental Protection Agency (EPA) has estimated that each year there are 300,000 acute illnesses and injuries attributable to the occupational use of pesticides. Children work and play in the fields, and thus are exposed to the same occupational hazards as adults. Evidence has shown that, because of their lower weight and higher metabolism, children are more susceptible than adults to the toxic effects of toxic chemicals. One study found that 48 percent of children had worked in fields still wet with pesticides; 36 percent had been sprayed either directly or indirectly (by drift); and farm operators had sprayed 34 percent of the children's homes in the process of spraying nearby fields. A 1988 study of 460 farmworkers in Washington State found that 89 percent did not know the name of a single chemical to which they had been exposed; 76 percent had never received any information on appropriate protection measures.[46]

As a result of the exposure to pesticides, farmworkers frequently suffer stomach ailments, headaches, rashes, burns, and other toxic chemical–related problems. Many die from cancer, and too often workers' babies are born with severe birth defects. Many families must sleep, bathe, and cook near the fields where they work and have no option but to use water that may be contaminated with toxic chemicals. A 1990 study of migrant children working on farms in western New York found that more than 40 percent had been sprayed while in the fields.[47] The following statistics illustrate some of the health and safety problems faced by farmworkers.

- Agriculture is the most dangerous occupation in the United States; between 1979 and 1983 about 23,800 children and adolescents were injured, and 300 died from their injuries. Forty-eight out of every 100,000 agricultural workers died of unintentional work-related injuries in 1988.

- One study found that about 34 percent of migrant children were infected with intestinal parasites and/or suffered severe asthma, chronic diarrhea, vitamin A deficiency, chemical poisoning, or continuous bouts of otitis media leading to hearing loss. Other commonly reported health problems included lower height or weight, respiratory disease, skin infections, and undiagnosed congenital and developmental problems. Researchers found a 10.9 percent rate of chronic health conditions among migrant children, compared to the national rate of 3 percent. The majority of pre-school-age children of farmworkers are not appropriately vaccinated for their age level.

- The life expectancy of migrant farmworkers is 49 years, compared to the U.S. average of 75 years.

- Water-related parasitic infections afflict migrant farmworker adults and children an average of 20 times more often than the general population.

- Farmworkers suffer from the highest rate of toxic chemical injuries of any group of workers in the United States.

- More than any other workers, farmworkers suffer and die from heat stress and dehydration.

- Health centers rank alcohol and drug abuse as the fourth largest health problem among adult patients of migrant health centers.

- Death rates from influenza and pneumonia are as much as 20 percent and 200 percent higher, respectively, for farmworkers than the national average.

- In a study conducted by the CDC, 44 percent of farmworkers screened had positive TB tests.

- It is estimated that as few as 33 percent of female farmworkers receive prenatal care during the first trimester of pregnancy, even though many migrant pregnancies are classified as high-risk with multiple indicators. The infant mortality rate among migrants is 125 percent higher than in the general population.[48]

In the 1960s the difficult conditions faced by farmworkers led to the emergence of the United Farm Workers union (UFW) in California, a movement led by the charismatic César Chávez. At its peak in the 1970s, the UFW had about 120,000 workers under contract, and between 1966 and 1980 it obtained two 40 percent wage increases in the grape industry, among other gains. But during the 1980s contracts began to expire and successive Republican administrations stacked the California Agricultural Labor Relations Board with pro-industry members, effectively gutting the law that had created the board. In the midst of a hostile political climate and internal differences, the UFW went into a decade-long slump. By the middle 1990s the UFW had only about 20,000 workers under contract in California, Texas, and Florida.

The 1980s saw the rise of independent labor contractors as key players in the farm industry. Hired by growers, these middlemen round up laborers and deliver them to the fields. Contractors pay less than growers, offer few benefits, and provide little job security. They also have a reputation for mistreating farmworkers and cheating them out of part of their wages. Contractors shield large growers from labor actions and legal claims, distancing them from the actual hiring of workers. If a judgment comes down against a labor contractor, the contractor often vanishes or puts the businesses into bankruptcy, only to emerge in a new place or under a new name. The labor subcontracting system is an important obstacle to improving the welfare of farmworkers. One demand being passed by farmworker activists is the creation of legislation that would make growers legally responsible for their workers, regardless of whether they use contractors.

 ## Governmental Farm Policies

President Ronald Reagan signed the Food Security Act into law in 1985. This legislation was distinctive in three ways: (1) It was the most complicated farm bill ever passed; (2) it cost the federal government more than previous farm bills had (about $80 billion from 1986 to 1990); and (3) the price supports, at least in terms of parity, were lower than they had been in previous legislation.[49] The 1985 farm bill operated in the following way: A target price for each commodity was set by Congress and the secretary of agriculture; if prices fell below that level, participating farmers received a subsidy from the government. This system was connected to the Commodity Credit Corporation (CCC) loan rates. For example, in 1986 the CCC loan rate—in effect, the price to buyers—for a bushel of corn was $1.92, and the target price was $3.03. On 7 billion bushels of corn, the difference cost almost $8 billion in subsidies. Even so, the USDA estimated that the target price was 17 cents less per bushel than it actually cost farmers to raise the corn.[50] Farmers were therefore losing money on every harvested bushel and were forced to borrow money to cover their losses. Grain corporations and foreign buyers were thus being allowed to purchase corn at per bushel prices more than $1.00 below the cost of production. Federal policy was subsidizing the grain corporations at the expense of farmers, taxpayers, and the general public.

In 1990 Congress passed a five-year farm bill that made important changes in policies affecting farmers, consumers, and the environment. In particular, the 1990 farm bill reduced the number of acres for which farmers could receive deficiency payments, permitted planting flexibility, and maintained the market-oriented loan rates contained in the 1985 farm bill. The bill also contained features that improved the quality of U.S. grain, continued the protection of fragile wetlands, created new incentives to help farmers prevent the contamination of ground and surface water on 10 million acres, created incentives to help farmers use fewer toxic chemicals and required farmers who used hazardous chemicals to keep records of their use, helped farmers meet environmental laws, established the first-ever national "organically grown" label, and provided a significant rural development aid package.[51] It was estimated that this bill would cost $40 billion over five years, in contrast to the $80 billion price tag on the 1985 farm bill.

On April 4, 1996, President Bill Clinton signed the Federal Agricultural Improvement and Reform (FAIR) Act into law, replacing the 1990 farm bill. This legislation enjoyed broad support both from Republicans, who wanted an agricultural free market, and from urban liberals, who wanted to end farm subsidies. The 1996 farm bill was based on a similar ideological premise as the PRWORA of the same year: Namely, it was designed to wean farmers off governmental subsidies in the same way that TANF attempted to wean welfare recipients off public assistance. For free marketers, subsidy-dependent farmers were all too similar to subsidy-dependent welfare recipients.

The heart of the FAIR Act is the "Freedom to Farm" commodity program, which replaces traditional farm subsidies (i.e., those that reimburse farmers when market prices drop) with a system of fixed annual payments that decline over seven years. This legislation has fundamentally changed farm policy by severing the connection between subsidies and current farm prices. The act provides for AMTA (Agricultural Market Transition Act) payments to be given annually to farmers in descending amounts from 1996 to 2002. The government delivers these payoffs to all farmers who grow wheat, feed grains, cotton, rice, and soybeans/oilseed. The total payments of $36 billion decline over a seven-year period—from $5.6 billion in 1996 to 5.4 billion in 1997, 5.5 billion in 1998, 5.3 billion in 1999, 5.1 billion in 2000, and $4 billion in the remaining years, thus ending the open-ended entitlement of previous legislation. The government provides these payments regardless of that year's actual crop performance or the income of individual farmers. Ironically, the first year of payments happened to be a great crop year, so most farmers were paid when they actually didn't need the money.[52] The success was not long lived, however. In 1998 production grew, demand fell, and prices declined. The price of a bushel of wheat at the Chicago Board of Trade dropped from $7.16 in 1996 to less than $3.00 in 1998.[53]

The 1996 farm bill, nominally a program that was supposed to save taxpayers money, cost more than the legislation it replaced.[54] Unlike TANF, AMTA did not hold: Congress retreated from the AMTA spending caps and approved emergency relief payments. In 1998 Clinton vetoed a bill for $4 billion in emergency farm spending because he wanted $7 billion. At that point farmers had already received $5 billion in subsidies months ahead of schedule. In 1999 Congress approved another $9.3 billion in emergency funding. Critics believe that the goal of making farmers self-reliant and less dependent on government subsidies has not been achieved. Proponents argue that reforms in trade, taxation, and regulation are needed in order for this policy to reach its potential.[55]

Sustainable Agriculture

The environmental challenges facing the United States are greater than at any time in the nation's history. Global environmental threats such as climate change; stratospheric ozone depletion; and the loss of biological diversity (through accelerating extinctions of species), forests, and fish stocks affect all countries regardless of their stage of economic development.

In June 1993 President Bill Clinton appointed 25 leaders from business, government, environmental, civil rights, and Native American organizations to the Council on Sustainable Development. Their charge was to transform the idea of sustainable development into a concrete plan of action. As a benchmark, the council adopted the definition of sustainable development proposed by the United Nations Brundtland Commission in 1987. This stated that **sustainable development** must "meet the needs of the present without compromising the ability of future generations to meet their own needs." The final vision statement of the council noted that: "Our vision is of a life-sustaining earth. We are committed to the achievement of a dignified, peaceful, and equitable existence. We believe a sustainable United States will have an economy that equitably provides opportunities for satisfying livelihoods and a safe, healthy, high quality of life for current and future generations. Our nation will protect its environment, its natural resource base, and the functions and viability of natural systems on which all life depends."[56]

Sustainable development theories also address the crisis of farmland mismanagement in the United States and abroad. Farming and related activities are the foundation of the U.S. food and fiber industry, which provides jobs for 20 percent of the workforce and contributes $820 billion to the GNP. Moreover, the nearly 1 billion acres of land in agricultural production is responsible for feeding, clothing, and housing 280 million people in the United States and millions more abroad. Yet, every minute, the United States loses 3 acres of productive farmland to urban sprawl—shopping malls, housing subdivisions, and the like. Since the first Earth Day in 1970, the United States has lost more than 40 million acres of farmland to development. In North Carolina and Florida alone, 283,000 acres of cropland disappear each year. In California 100,000 acres disappear. Net cropland losses in the United States between 1982 and 1992 covered an area the size of New Jersey.[57]

Urbanization is a leading cause of the loss of cropland. The spread of roads, buildings, and industrial parks consumes precious farmland. Cropland is also being lost because of the depletion or diversion of irrigation water. In many water-scarce areas, water is supplied from nonrenewable aquifers. If farmers deplete the water stock or if it is siphoned off by large cities, agricultural land will either be abandoned or become less productive. Although irrigated land accounts for only 16 percent of all cropland worldwide, it supplies 40 percent of the world's grain.[58]

Each year the United States loses 2 billion tons of topsoil to wind and water erosion. As many as 1 billion tons wash into nearby waterways, carrying away natural nutrients and the fertilizers and pesticides contained in the soil. This erosion damages water quality, fish and wildlife habitat, and recreational opportunities. Farmers spend an estimated $8 billion on fertil-

izers and $6 billion on fuel each year. Thus, the use of fertilizers, toxic chemicals, and fuel strains already tight farm budgets as well as threatening the environment. The overuse and misapplication of fertilizers and fuel threatens both the land and the farmers' profitability.[59]

For some years the impressive success of the intensified agriculture that began in the 1960s led to a complacent attitude toward cropland loss. Specifically, some people believed that farm yields were rising so quickly that they more than compensated for any loss of arable land. By 1984, however, the growth in crop yields had slowed down. This trend was intensified in the 1990s as the amount of productive U.S. cropland per person fell to less than one-sixth the size of a soccer field. With global grain production falling, the world has consumed half its grain reserves since 1987, reducing them to an all-time low.[60] Moreover, the shrinking supply of cropland and the slowing of yield increases comes on the brink of the largest projected increase in food demand in history. In 25 years farmers will be required to feed 2.2 billion more people than they do today; yet most governments continue to allow land that could be used to grow food to be developed or washed away by erosion.[61]

Sustainable development is seen by many as an alternative to environmental degradation. According to social worker Richard Estes, the concept of sustainable development has succeeded in uniting differing theoretical and ideological perspectives into a single conceptual framework.[62] In an ecological context, sustainable development promotes a process whereby natural resources are replenished and future generations continue to have adequate resources to meet their needs.[63] Although sustainable development is an important concept, however, its wide use by different groups in the development process gives some pause for concern. For example, some groups use the term *sustainable development* to designate a radical restructuring of society with regard to environmental development and economic growth. Others simply use the idea of sustainable development to signal a change in attitudes and emphasis. Such different approaches are sometimes labeled "dark green strategies" versus "light green strategies." Although some policy analysts claim that sustainable development can be the basis for a new developmental and ecological paradigm, others caution that it can be a concept not yet fully developed.[64]

Conclusion

The production, distribution, and consumption of food have historically been rooted in political economy. Through various forms of legislation, the U.S. government has traditionally responded to the needs of diverse groups that have an interest in food—farmers, consumers, the poor or their advocates, food distributors, grain traders, and the Third World and wealthier countries that depend on U.S. food production.

The federal government has responded to these interests by creating a patchwork quilt of policies and programs. One of the most important of these is the Food Stamp Program, an ingenious strategy that helps keep food affordable for low-income consumers, helps stabilize farm prices, slows down agricultural surpluses by subsidizing consumption, and allows food merchants and distributors to increase their profits by ensuring a volume of subsidized consumers. The nation's food problems persist, however. These problems, which are serious for many poor people and farmers, have reached crisis proportions for others—including the very poor, farmworkers, and marginal farmers. Tragically, many farmers in the United States now profit from food stamps not because the program helps them control surplus farm goods but because it provides them with coupons. It is a sad commentary when the producers of food are unable to purchase what they grow.

Discussion Questions

1. The Food Stamp Program is currently the single most important federal program for combating hunger. Nevertheless, there are serious questions as to why close to 40 percent of those eligible for food stamps are not enrolled. Why has the federal government not been more aggressive in promoting food stamps? What changes, if any, could be made in the program to make it more accessible to greater numbers of eligible people?

2. WIC and the Food Stamp Program are similar in many respects. What are the specific differences between these programs? Is it necessary for WIC to be a separate program? If so, why?

3. There are serious questions as to the effectiveness of U.S. food programs for the poor. What alternatives, if any, are there to the matrix of food programs that currently make up the nutritional safety net?

4. The farming situation in America has historically been economically volatile. For example, farming was reasonably good in the 1970s, after which it spun into a depression in the early and mid-1980s. What programs and policies, if any, should be implemented to stabilize the U.S. farming?

5. Some claim that sustainable development should be the basis for a new developmental and ecological paradigm. Is sustainable development a theory that is viable enough to serve as the basis for a series of policies? Why or why not?

6. The problem of how to deal fairly with farmworkers in the United States is both difficult and chronic. What are some possible solutions for promoting equity and fairness for farmworkers in this country?

Notes

1. A. A. Skolnick, "More Children Cry as Congress Shakes Its Head," *Journal of the American Medical Association* 274, no. 10 (1995), p. 783.
2. C. Aikens, "One in Six Struggle with Chronic Hunger," *Oakland Post* (April 19, 1995), p. 6.
3. John T. Cook and Katie S. Martin, "Differences in Nutrient Adequacy among Poor and Non-Poor Children (Summary of Findings)," Tufts University School of Nutrition—Center on Hunger, Poverty & Nutrition Policy, March 1995.
4. Ibid.
5. Uri Feinstein Center for a Hunger Free America, "Help Us End Hunger in the United States," 2000, retrieved January 2, 2001, from the World Wide Web: http://www.uri.edu/volunteer/endhunger/; Peter Eisinger, *Toward an End to Hunger in America* (Washington, DC: Brookings Institution, 1999); Second Harvest, "Who's Hungry?" 2000, retrieved January 2, 2001, from the World Wide Web: http://www.secondharvest.org/whoshungry/working_poor.html; Second Harvest, "Childhood Hunger," 2000, retrieved January 2, 2001, from the World Wide Web: http://www.secondharvest.org/childhunger/childhunger.html
6. U.S. Department of Agriculture, Food and Nutrition Service, "Characteristics of Food Stamp Households: Fiscal Year 1999," July 2000. Retrieved January 2, 2001, from the World Wide Web: http://www.fns.usda.gov/oane/menu/Published/fsp/FILES/adv99char.PDF
7. Illa Tennison, "WIC Policy Analysis," unpublished paper, University of Missouri–Columbia School of Social Work, 1987, p. 5.
8. Ibid.
9. U.S. House of Representatives, Committee on Ways and Means, *1992 Green Book* (Washington, DC: U.S. Government Printing Office, 1992), p. 1687.
10. U.S. Department of Agriculture, Food and Nutrition Service, "WIC Program Participation and Costs," November 22, 2000. Retrieved January 2, 2001, from the World Wide Web: http://www.fns.usda.gov/pd/wisummary.htm

11. U.S. Department of Agriculture, Food and Nutrition Service, "Nutrition Assistance Programs," February 6, 2000. Retrieved January 2, 2001, from the World Wide Web: http://www.fns.usda.gov/fns/
12. Ibid.
13. Ibid.
14. Ibid.
15. Ibid.
16. Ibid.
17. See U.S. House of Representatives, *1992 Green Book*, p. 1688; and Kristin Cotter, "Texas WIC: Strategy for Outreach Policy," unpublished paper, University of Houston Graduate School of Social Work, Houston, TX, fall 1996.
18. Children's Defense Fund, *The State of America's Children, 1988* (Washington, DC: Children's Defense Fund, 1988), p. 186.
19. Isaac Shapiro and Robert Greenstein, *Holes in the Safety Nets* (Washington, DC: Center on Budget and Policy Priorities, 1988), pp. 33–34.
20. U.S. Department of Agriculture, Food and Nutrition Service, "How WIC Helps," May 15, 2000. Retrieved January 3, 2001, from the World Wide Web: http://www.fns.usda.gov/wic/CONTENT/howwichelps.htm
21. U.S. Department of Agriculture, Food and Nutrition Service, "Reaching Those in Need: Food Stamp Participation Rates in the States," July 2000. Retrieved January 3, 2001, from the World Wide Web: http://www.fns.usda.gov/oane/menu/Published/fsp/FILES/FSPart2000sum.HTM
22. Ibid.
23. Second Harvest, "Who's Hungry?"
24. Second Harvest, "Who We Are," December 2000. Retrieved January 3, 2001, from the World Wide Web: http://www.secondharvest.org/whoshungry/who_we_serve.html
25. Second Harvest, "State-by-State Review of Food Stamp Applications," November 2000. Retrieved January 4, 2001, from the World Wide Web: http://www.secondharvest.org/policy/food_stamp_study.html
26. M. Drabenstott and M. Duncan, "Another Troubled Year for U.S. Agriculture," *Journal of*

the American Society of Farm Managers and Rural Appraisers 49, no. 1 (1985), pp. 58–66.

27. Cited in Joanne Mermelstein, "Criteria of Rural Mental Health Directors in Adopting Farm Crisis Programming Innovation," unpublished Ph.D. dissertation in Public Policy Analysis and Administration, St. Louis University, 1986, p. 3.

28. Ibid.

29. "U.S. Farm Sector, in Annual Checkup, Shows Strong Pulse," *Farmline* (December–January 1991), p. 2.

30. Ibid., pp. 4–5; also see Jim Ryan and Ken Erickson, "Balance Sheet Stable in 1992," *Agricultural Outlook 46* (January–February 1992), pp. 29–30.

31. Ryan and Erickson, "Balance Sheet Stable," p. 29.

32. U.S. Department of Agriculture, "History of Agricultural Price Support and Adjustment Programs, 1933–84," *Bulletin No. 485* (Washington, DC: Economic Research Service, 1984), pp. 8–9.

33. Steve Little, "Parity: Survival of the Family Farm," unpublished paper, University of Missouri–Columbia School of Social Work, 1986, pp. 8–9.

34. Mary Ahearn, "Financial Well-Being of Farm Operators and Their Households," U.S. Department of Agriculture, *Report No. 563* (Washington, DC: Economic Research Service, September 1986), p. iii.

35. Ibid.

36. Mermelstein, "Criteria of Rural Mental Health Directors" (note 27 above), pp. 5–6.

37. Ibid., p. 7.

38. Quoted in John M. Herrick, "Farmers' Revolt! Contemporary Farmers' Protests in Historical Perspective: Implications for Social Work Practice," *Human Services in the Rural Environment* 10, no. 1 (April 1986), p. 9.

39. Center for Rural Affairs, "Corporate Farming and Industrialization," 2000. Retrieved January 4, 2001, from the World Wide Web: http://www.cfra.org/Issues.htm#Corporate

40. Andrew Nelson, "From a Lifestyle to a Business, Small Farming in Transition: A Case Study Analysis of Small Farming in the Upper Midwest," Grinnell College Prairie Studies Program and the Office of Senator Byron Dor-

gan. August 11, 2000. Retrieved January 4, 2001, from the World Wide Web: http://www.grinnell.edu/CPS/Student%20Projects/Nelson_Farm.htm

41. Andrew Nelson, "From a Lifestyle to a Business;" Larry Keller, "Family Farming an Endangered Career," October 30, 2000, from CNN.com. Retrieved January 4, 2001, on the World Wide Web: http://fyi.cnn.com/2000/fyi/news/10/30/family.farms/; Center for Rural Affairs, "Corporate Farming and Industrialization"; Farm Aid, "Family Farm Numbers," 2000. Retrieved January 4, 2001, from the World Wide Web: http://www.farmaid.org/org/farm/facts.asp; Farm Aid, "Factory Farming," 2000. Retrieved January 5, 2001, from the World Wide Web: http://www.farmaid.org/org/farm/factory.asp; Farm Aid, "Questions and Answers," 2000. Retrieved January 5, 2001, from the World Wide Web: http://www.farmaid.org/org/farm/q_a.asp

42. U.S. Department of Labor, "Findings from the National Agricultural Workers Survey (NAWS) 1997–1998," Research Report No. 8, March 2000. Retrieved January 5, 2001, from the World Wide Web: http://www.dol.gov/dol/asp/public/programs/agworker/report_8.pdf; and Richard Mines, Susan Gabbard, and Anne Steirman, "A Profile of U.S. Farm Workers, Demographics, Household Composition, Income and Use of Services" (April 1997), U.S. Department of Labor, Office of the Assistant Secretary for Policy, prepared for the Commission on Immigration Reform, retrieved January 5, 2001, from the World Wide Web: http://www.dol.gov/dol/asp/public/programs/agworker/report/major.htm

43. See V. A. Wilk, *The Occupational Health of Migrant and Seasonal Farmworkers in the United States* (Washington, DC: Farmworkers Justice Fund, 1985); Juan Ramos and Celia Torres, "Migrant and Seasonal Farm Workers," *Encyclopedia of Social Work*, 18th ed. (Silver Spring, MD: NASW, 1987), p. 151; and National Center for Farmworker Health, *Facts about America's Farmworkers* (Washington, DC: National Center for Farmworker Health, 1996).

44. Wilk, *Occupational Health*.

45. Ibid; and Bureau of Primary Health Care, "The Children's Health Initiative, Migrant and

Seasonal Farmworker Children: The Current Situation and the Available Opportunities," Health Resources and Services Administration, October 24, 1997. Retrieved January 5, 2001, from the World Wide Web: http://www.bphc.hrsa.gov/mhc/MIGRANT.HTML

46. Bureau of Primary Health Care, "The Children's Health Initiative."

47. Gary Huang, "Health Problems among Migrant Farmworkers' Children in the U.S." ERIC Digests, January 1, 1993. Retrieved January 5, 2001, from the World Wide Web: http://www.ed.gov/databases/ERIC_Digests/ed357907.html

48. Ibid.

49. Ibid.

50. G. Kaye Kellogg, "The Crisis of the Family Farm in America Today," unpublished paper, University of Missouri–Columbia School of Social Work, 1987, pp. 9–10.

51. U.S. Government, "Conference Committee Approves Five-Year Farm Bill," news release, Washington, DC, October 16, 1990.

52. Ford C. Runge and Stuart Kimberly, "Agricultural Policy Reform in the United States: An Unfinished Agenda" (Washington, DC: Center for International Food and Agricultural Policy, October 1996), pp. 1–30.

53. James Bovard, "Farmers Harvest Bumper Crop in Beltway," *Wall Street Journal* (October 21, 1998), pp. 1, 2.

54. American Farmland Trust, "1996 Farm Bill Review," 1996. Retrieved January 5, 2001, from the World Wide Web: http://farm.fic.niu.edu/aft/fbreview.html

55. R. A. Wirtz, "Farm Crisis: Here We Go Again?" *fedgazette*. Retrieved January 5, 2001, from the World Wide Web: http://www.minneapolisfed.org/pbus/fedgaz/99–10/cover.html

56. The Council on Sustainable Development, "Sustainable America: A New Consensus," 1995. Retrieved January 5, 2001, from the World Wide Web: http://www.whitehouse.gov/WH/EOP/pcsd/info/highlite.html

57. Vir Singh, "World Wide Cropland Losses," *Earth Times* (November 20, 1996). Retrieved January 6, 2001, from the World Wide Web: http://www.earthtimes.org/romesummitvirsinghnov13.htm

58. Ibid.

59. American Farmland Trust, "Why Save Farmland?" 1996. Retrieved January 6, 2001, from the World Wide Web: http://farm.fic.niu.edu/aft/aftwhysave.html

60. American Farmland Trust, "What's Happening to America's Agricultural Resources?" 1996. Retrieved January 6, 2001, from the World Wide Web: http://farm.fic.niu.edu/aft/aftwhathap.html

61. Ibid.

62. Richard Estes, "Toward Sustainable Development: From Theory to Praxis," *Social Development Issues* 15, no. 3 (1993), pp. 1–22.

63. Katherine van Wormer, *Social Welfare: A World View* (Chicago: Nelson-Hall, 1997).

64. James Midgley, *Social Development: The Development Perspective in Social Welfare* (London: Sage, 1995).

chapter 18

The American Welfare State in International Perspective

Various schemes have evolved as shorthands to depict the mutual relationships of nations and, by inference, their comparative levels of development. In recent times a three-part classification has enjoyed extensive use: a First World, consisting of the industrial nations of the capitalist West; a Second World, made up of the communist nations that constructed political economies as an alternative to the market-dominated First World; and a Third World, comprising nations that were former colonies of the First World and later achieved independence, often through revolutions of liberation. This tripart formulation became prevalent after the Second World War as the cold war intensified. Many developing nations adopted the slogans of revolution, if not outright insurrection, in order to shed the influences of First World colonial nations. The Second World viewed the Third World as a theater of independence, an arena in which the exploitation of capitalism would be summarily ended and the colonized nations would be brought into the communist sphere of influence. On the defensive, the First World deployed foreign aid, technical assistance, cultural exchange, and, on occasion, diplomatic subterfuge to neutralize Second World incursions into the Third World. In several regions—Central America, Southeast Asia, and sub-Saharan Africa—the First and Second Worlds recruited insurgents who acted as their surrogates, engaging the opposition in armed conflict at considerable cost in arms and human life.

With the fall of the Berlin Wall in 1989, the Three World formulation lost utility. Foremost, the collapse of the Soviet Union and its Warsaw Pact satellites halved the scale of the Second World. The remaining communist nations—the People's Republic of China, North Korea, and Cuba—posed no immediate threat to the First World and were unlikely to serve as models for Third World nations. At the same time, some nations of the Third World had been transformed substantially from their colonial era status. Several Arab nations, despite feudal forms of governance, had prospered through oil exports, achieving levels of income that mirrored those of industrial nations. And despite the absence of natural resources, a handful of nations in Southeast Asia—Hong Kong, South Korea, Taiwan, Singapore—experienced such consistently high levels of growth that they became known as the "Four Tigers."

Tragically, many Third World nations lost ground. By the end of the millennium, several of the nations of sub-Saharan Africa and Southeast Asia were significantly less developed than they had been a generation earlier, when they achieved independence from the First World. Nations such as Cambodia, Bangladesh, Afghanistan, Somalia, and Sierra Leone had lost so much capital, their infrastructure had deteriorated to such an extent, and their polity had become so unstable that development analysts began to speculate about the emergence of a Fourth World. Further confounding the prospects of Fourth World nations, the end of the cold war led the affluent industrial nations of the First World, particularly the United States, to expend relatively *less* on foreign aid than they had during the Soviet threat.

 ## Typologies of Welfare States

The welfare states of the industrialized West vary structurally. With his colleague Charles Lebeaux, Harold Wilensky sought to summarize the differences between the European and American welfare states by constructing a typology of social welfare systems. The typology contrasts **residual welfare** with **institutional welfare**. The residualist approach is concerned with providing a minimal safety net for the poorest sections of the population rather than catering for the population as a whole. Wilensky and Lebeaux believed that social policy in the United States is essentially residualist in nature. On the other hand, the institutional approach, which typifies European social welfare, seeks to provide a variety of social programs for the whole population and to combine economic and social

489

objectives in an effort to enhance the well-being of all.[1]

These ideas were developed by the British social policy writer Richard Titmuss. Titmuss agreed that the residual approach typified social welfare in the United States and that an institutional approach was dominant in Europe. However, Titmuss noted that some countries did not fall into the residual and institutional dichotomy. For this reason he added a third category to the typology, which he called the industrial performance model. He believed that this approach characterized social policy in the former Soviet Union and communist Eastern European countries.[2]

Several subsequent attempts have been made to construct typologies of welfare states that go beyond Wilensky and Lebeaux's twofold category. One of the first was by Norman Furniss and Timothy Tilton, who provided a threefold classification that encompassed what they called the "positive state," the "social security state," and the "social welfare state." The United States exemplified the first, Britain the second, and Sweden the third.[3]

Canadian writer Ramesh Mishra, who has written extensively about international social welfare, retained the twofold approach developed by Wilensky and Lebeaux; but he stressed the efforts of some countries to forge strong alliances among government, labor, and business in order to reach a consensus on social welfare issues. This approach is known as corporatism. In corporatist societies, social welfare is integrated into the economy and other institutions of society. Countries such as Sweden, Austria, and Australia are typical of the corporatist approach. Mishra used the term *integrated welfare state* to connote the corporatist approach. On the other hand, Britain and the United States were noncorporatist in that they did not integrate social and economic policy or seek to forge a consensus around welfare issues. For this reason, Mishra called them *differentiated welfare states*. Mishra was one of the first writers to suggest that Britain was not, as Titmuss believed, like the rest of Europe but rather more like the United States in its approach to social welfare.[4]

Gosta Esping-Andersen's typology also recognized the corporatist type when classifying welfare states. However, Esping-Andersen grouped countries somewhat differently from Mishra. In addition to the corporatist category (Italy, Japan, France, and Switzerland), Esping-Andersen identified two other types, the liberal welfare state (Australia, Britain, and the United States) and the social democratic welfare state (Austria, the Netherlands, and the Scandinavian countries).[5] More recently, Norman Ginsburg (1992) constructed a fourfold typology comprising the social democratic welfare state (typified by Sweden), the social market welfare state (Germany), the corporate market welfare state (United States), and the liberal collectivist welfare state (Britain).[6] However, of the various typologies of welfare states that have been developed by social policy investigators, Esping-Andersen's is perhaps the most widely accepted.[7]

Although the typologies differ from one another, they use similar criteria when classifying countries. All place emphasis on *government* social programs and neglect the role of voluntary organizations and other nonstatutory activities in social welfare. The typologies also reveal the normative preferences of the authors. That is, although the typologies are intended to classify countries for analytical purposes, it is clear that they give expression to beliefs about the desirability of the role of government in social welfare. Analysts who favor extensive government involvement in social welfare have represented countries with extensive public programs more favorably in the typologies than countries that do not place as much emphasis on government involvement. For this reason, it is not surprising that most of the typologies depict the United States negatively in comparison to European welfare states.

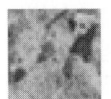 # American Exceptionalism

The apparent unwillingness of the United States to emphasize government social welfare programs has been described by Edwin Amenta and Theda Skocpol as "welfare exceptionalism."[8] These authors have also summarized explanations of the country's reluctance to create an institutional European-style welfare state. One such explanation is that the racial, ethnic, and religious diversity of the United States has prevented the emergence of a comprehensive welfare state. In European nations people are more united and have a stronger sense of civic responsibility; in contrast, the pursuit of separate interests by a great number of different groups in the United States mitigates against the emergence of a single national system of provision that caters to all citizens.

Another explanation is based on the country's high degree of political decentralization, which impedes the emergence of strong central political institutions. Combined with a high degree of diversity, the tradition of decentralization creates cleavages in U.S. society that effectively prevent the emergence of a strong, centralized, and comprehensive welfare state. It has also been noted that the United States does not have a long tradition of bureaucratic government that can support centralized welfare programs. Some have claimed that this is because of the absence of a feudal tradition. Developing this idea, others have pointed to the unique role of the courts in policymaking in this country, the separation of the executive and legislative branches, and the role of powerful political interest groups—all of which impede the emergence of a strong, centralized welfare state.

Another explanation stresses the role of the unique individualist culture of the United States, pointing out that the ideology of individualism is far stronger here than in Europe and that it is fundamentally antithetical to state welfare. It has also been argued that trade unions are weaker in the United States than in Europe and that the political left, which has played a major role in the emergence of the European welfare states, has not been strong in this country.

The notion of **welfare state exceptionalism** offers interesting insights into social policy in the United States, it can be criticized. For example, the idea that the United States is a wel-

fare laggard is based largely on a comparison of social programs such as health insurance and family allowances. The absence of these programs is usually emphasized by those claiming that the United States does not have a comprehensive welfare state. Although it is true that government health care and family income maintenance programs are poorly developed in the United States, the role of indirect support for families through tax relief and tax deductions for medical expenses is often ignored, as is the significance of Medicare and state and local health care programs.

In addition, the United States has excelled in other social fields. During the nineteenth century it led the world in the development of public education; and it still compares favorably with many other countries in terms of access to education, particularly at the tertiary (college and university) level. The United States is also a pioneer in some aspects of environmental protection; and although environmental concerns are not always regarded as an integral part of social policy, the impact of the environment on human well-being should not be underestimated.[9] Comparative studies have also shown that when particular social programs such as retirement pensions are compared, the United States fares quite well.[10] In addition, recent historical research reveals that in the late nineteenth century, the United States was ahead of other Western countries in developing income maintenance programs for veterans and for women with children. At the turn of the century, no other industrializing country had introduced mother's pensions, and none came as close to creating a "maternal" rather than "paternal" welfare state.[11]

Another problem is that comparisons between Europe and the United States are often characterized by strong personal biases. For example, a strong pro-British bias pervades Titmuss's writings. He has been criticized for presenting his arguments in a way that ensures the moral superiority of the institutional welfare state model.[12] It is also apparent that the European countries have widely varied welfare systems and that not all European welfare states are centralized, comprehensive, or highly activist. Studies of welfare policies in other parts of the world also have shown the U.S. welfare state in more favorable terms. For example, unlike the United States, Australia did not until recently have a universal social security system, and it relied extensively on means-tested social programs.[13]

Nevertheless, it is difficult to reach the conclusion that the United States is one of the world's welfare leaders. Despite its extensive educational and social security provisions, the country does not compare favorably to the other industrial nations in the extent, comprehensiveness, or coverage of its welfare system. In fact, its position has deteriorated in recent years as social programs were retrenched under the Reagan, Bush, and Clinton administrations.

Although many social policy writers in the United States have complained about their country's comparatively low level of welfare provision, however, others are not disturbed by these findings. *Welfare pluralists,* as they are known, claim that unfavorable comparisons between the United States and other countries are based on the idea that state involvement in social welfare is a good thing. They reject this assertion and do not believe that social needs should be met primarily by the government. Instead of relying only on the state for social welfare, welfare pluralists argue that people can enhance their well-being through their own efforts, through the help of neighbors or their families, by purchasing services on the market, or by obtaining help from voluntary organizations.[14] They point out that in the United States people make effective use of nongovernmental agencies, and that international comparisons should not be limited to government social programs. They also point out that although the United States may lag behind in public welfare provision, people enjoy exceptionally high standards of living and unequaled opportunities. This is why the country remains a magnet for immigrants from all over the world—who come not to receive government handouts but to share in the American dream.

 # The Welfare State in Transition

As a result of the globalization of capital, welfare states—however they are classified—have made structural adjustments to remain competitive. Welfare states grew steadily during the relatively stable economic period of the 1950s to the early 1970s; but by the mid-1970s most industrial economies began to experience high inflation, high rates of unemployment, sluggish economic growth, and unacceptably high levels of taxation. During this difficult period Western governments were forced to reassess their overall economic strategies, including the resources allocated to welfare activities. Hence, beginning in the early 1970s, most Western governments either cut welfare programs or arrested their growth.[15]

All Western nations are experiencing a crisis rooted in the need to compete in a new global economy.[16] According to conservative policy analysts, national survival in the new economic order can be achieved only if government cuts costs and becomes more efficient. In addition, these analysts argue for the creation of government policies that encourage the accumulation of the capital necessary for investment, industrial modernization, and corporate growth. Conservatives maintain that this precondition for economic survival is possible only when government freezes or lowers personal and corporate tax rates. The subsequent loss of tax revenue, however, often results in heavy governmental debt, cuts in all services (including social services), a deterioration of the infrastructure, and myriad social problems.

The general emphasis on efficiency and profitability also leads to industrial reorganization, which in turn leads to rapidly changing production technologies that displace workers and result in plant closures and downsizing. Thus, the effects of conservative policy changes are exacerbated as cuts in governmental services coincide with the increased demand for social services by victims of the global-based economic changes. In other words, Western industrial nations face a two-pronged assault on the welfare state: (1) the impact of the global economy on government spending, and (2) an increase in the use of social services by workers dislocated by global economic changes.

Western industrialized nations pursued liberal social policies after World War II.[17] In the United States, most presidents following Franklin D. Roosevelt tolerated—and in some cases even promoted—a liberal social welfare agenda. Although the general belief in the United States was that people should adjust to the market rather than the other way around, the social consensus also dictated that the nation should strengthen human capital in order to make people more economically competitive.[18] Thus, social welfare programs were developed to increase human capital through education, employment, health, and housing. The belief was that as human capital increased, the dependent person (or at least his or her children) would eventually be able to compete in a free market. For those who could not compete because of serious deficits (such as disabilities or old age), a system of social insurance or public assistance was developed to ensure a minimum level of subsistence. Thus, the dual focus of the welfare state was (1) to create programs to increase human capital and (2) to create programs to subsidize people unable to participate in the workforce. Even conservative presidents like Richard Nixon acquiesced to this welfare consensus.

But a more conservative welfare consensus emerged during the 1980s. This new consensus called for (1) making welfare benefits conditional on employment and other norms; (2) transforming open-ended entitlements to discretionary programs; (3) containing the growth of the governmental sector while retaining (in curtailed form) fundamental programs that affect the elderly and the working poor; (4) replacing government with other institutions, such as families and community-based organizations; and (5) contracting out services and benefits to the private sector. In effect, ideologues of the new right argued that the liberal welfare state was a failed social experiment.[19] During the 1990s the conservative critique of the welfare state, introduced first by Margaret Thatcher in the United Kingdom and Ronald Reagan in the United States, prompted a reassessment of public welfare within liberal circles, with the result that Bill Clinton and Tony Blair (nominal liberals) essentially continued the conservative vector in social policy. Most recently, the implications of this trend have been explored by Anthony Giddens, who contends that this represents a "third way" in social policy.[20]

The retrenchment of the U.S. welfare state, once the exemplar of protection against insecurities related to poverty and illness, is enormously ironic. Reductions in welfare benefits have contributed to the formation of an "underclass" within the most prosperous of nations. Thus, in the major cities of the West, communities of squatters can be found, people whose poverty is not unlike that seen in the shantytowns that have been characteristic of the developing world. If the globalization of capital has resulted in the internationalization of prosperity, it has also produced an international class of paupers.

 # Ranking National Development

Various frameworks have been proposed to gauge the progress of nations. Among the first was the Gini coefficient, a figure denoting the extent to which the distribution of income diverges from perfect equality. Gini coefficients range from a value of 0 when the distribution of income is equal, to a value of 1 when the distribution is unequal. Nations with high degrees of **income inequality** have Gini coefficients in the 0.50 to 0.70 range; while those with relatively equal distributions have coefficients ranging from 0.20 to 0.35.[21] These values are then multiplied by 100 to produce the Gini index. Critics of the Gini coefficient cite the limitations of a portrait of development that is based solely on income. Other indicators, such as longevity, education, opportunity, and environment, should be included, they claim. Although this argument has obvious merit, defenders of the Gini coefficient cite its value when the disparity between the rich and poor has become such a chasm. By way of illustration, two-thirds of the world's population survives on less than $1 per day; "the assets of the world's 358 billionaires exceed the combined annual incomes of countries with 45 percent of the world's people."[22]

The Weighted Index of Social Progress

A rather more ambitious assessment of the progress of nations has been undertaken by Richard Estes, a social work professor in the United States.[23] For 1970, 1980, 1990, and 1995 Estes has ranked the social progress of nations according to their performance along 46 variables that are grouped in 10 subindices: education, health, women, defense, economic factors, demography, geography, political participation, cultural diversity, and welfare. Containing so many variables, Estes's scheme is much more sophisticated than the Gini coefficient. At the same time, Estes's formulation contains assumptions that are open to question. In the classic American liberal tradition, for example, Estes assumes that military expenditures are inversely related to social progress. As another example, the welfare subindex consists of the foundations of the modern welfare state, another assumption of liberal ideology.[24] Estes's 1995 ranking of the social progress of nations is shown in Table 18.1.

Estes's analysis is as informative about international development as it is controversial. The top slots are reserved for the well-articulated welfare states of central and northern Europe. Of urgent concern are those nations at the bottom of the ranking; their conditions have worsened to such a degree that they generate negative numbers, essentially indicating reverse development. For the most part these are developing nations

that have experienced internal strife, armed conflict that has further detracted from an already precarious developmental status.

In some respects, however, Estes's classification invites skepticism. Canada and the United States fall relatively far down the scale in Estes's ranking: The United States is ranked 27 and Canada 31. The ranking of Bulgaria above the United States spurred a *New York Times* reporter to examine various development indexes. She reported that Nicholas Eberstadt of the American Enterprise Institute, a moderate–conservative policy institute in Washington, D.C., dismissed such rankings on the basis that "they pivot on arbitrary evaluations about which there is no universal consensus." In rebuttal, Estes acknowledged that "The present social situation in Bulgaria is miserable, but in terms of responding to basic human needs, Bulgaria enjoys the legacy of social provision that characterized all of the states and partners of the former Soviet Union, i.e., high literacy, high access to at least basic health care, guaranteed housing, guaranteed income support during old age and other periods of income loss, and so on."[25] The discrepancies between Estes's scale and the UN Human Development Index, discussed below, reflect different criteria in measuring development.

Because Estes has undertaken this exercise each decade, the longitudinal transformation of nations has become evident. Between 1970 and 1992 many nations have experienced substantial change in their progress. Notably, the former satellite nations of the Soviet Union have plummeted, primarily as a result of the removal of the artificial supports of command economies and their replacement with capitalism. Of the former Warsaw Pact nations, only Hungary, the former Czechoslovakia, and Poland have been able to avoid free fall since the collapse of the Soviet Union. Another group of nations have lost ground because of war. By 1990 Lebanon, Cambodia, Afghanistan, Somalia, and Ethiopia had fallen a considerable distance from their rankings two decades earlier. The price of ending apartheid in South Africa also appears to have been a dramatic drop.

TABLE 18.1 ■ Estes Weighted Index of Social Progress (WISP), 1995

RANK	NATION	SCORE	RANK	NATION	SCORE
1	Denmark	98.4	40	Korea, Republic of	72.8
2	Norway	95.6	41	Taiwan	72.6
3	Austria	93.2	42	Costa Rica	72.1
4	Sweden	93.1	43.5	Uruguay	71.2
5	France	91.9	43.5	Russian Federation	71.2
6	Finland	90.8	45	Croatia	68.7
7	Luxembourg	90.7	46	Mauritius	68.1
8	Ireland	89.1	47	Argentina	67.9
9	Poland	88.5	48	Belarus	67.6
10	Germany	88.1	49	Armenia	67.5
11	Italy	87.9	50	Panama	66.0
12	Netherlands	87.8	51	Moldova	65.6
13	Iceland	87.5	52	Singapore	65.1
14	Hungary	87.2	53	Thailand	63.8
15	Slovenia	86.9	54.5	Cuba	62.6
16	Belgium	86.8	54.5	Colombia	62.6
17	United Kingdom	86.4	56.5	Kyrgyz Republic	61.8
18	Portugal	86.2	56.5	Tunisia	61.8
19	Spain	85.8	58	Venezuela	61.5
20	Japan	85.5	59	South Africa	61.3
21	New Zealand	85.3	60	Jamaica	61.0
22	Czech Republic	84.4	61	Brazil	60.0
23	Switzerland	83.1	62	Trinidad and Tobago	59.3
24	Australia	82.6			
25	Greece	82.1	63	Albania	59.0
26	Bulgaria	82.0	64	Paraguay	58.4
27	United States	79.9	65	Mexico	57.9
28	Estonia	79.8	66	Uzbekistan	57.7
29	Slovak Republic	79.6	67	Ecuador	56.7
30	Ukraine	78.1	68	Jordan	55.6
31	Canada	77.8	69	El Salvador	55.5
32	Hong Kong	77.7	70	Georgia	55.3
33	Chile	76.7	71	Lebanon	55.2
34	Lithuania	75.4	72	Macedonia	55.0
35	Romania	74.9	73	Kuwait	54.7
36	Cyprus	74.8	74	Malaysia	54.5
37	Yugoslav Republic	74.1	75	Algeria	54.3
38	Israel	73.7	76	Dominican Republic	53.8
39	Latvia	73.5			

(continued)

TABLE 18.1 ■ Continued

RANK	NATION	SCORE	RANK	NATION	SCORE
77	Honduras	53.1	115	India	29.3
78.5	Philippines	52.8	116	Congo	28.7
78.5	Sri Lanka	52.8	117	Gabon	28.6
80	Turkey	52.4	118	Togo*	27.8
81	Azerbaijan	52.1	119	Madagascar*	26.9
82	Peru	51.9	120	Zambia*	25.4
83	Libya	50.8	121	Kenya	24.9
84	Kazakhstan	50.3	122	Ghana	24.8
85	Fiji	50.2	123	Senegal	23.8
86	Bahrain	49.6	124	Haiti*	22.8
87	Egypt	49.2	125	Cameroon	22.4
88	Mongolia	49.1	126	Tanzania*	22.0
89	Guyana	48.7	127	Benin*	21.8
90	Saudi Arabia	48.3	128	Papua New Guinea	21.1
91	Syria	46.6			
92	Qatar	45.6	129	Malawi*	21.0
93	Iran	45.5	130	Pakistan	20.4
94	Morocco	45.3	131	Cambodia*	19.2
95	Botswana*	44.3	132	Comoros*	18.2
96.5	Namibia	43.3	133	Nepal*	17.6
96.5	Indonesia	43.3	134	Burundi*	17.5
98	Bolivia	42.4	135	Mali*	16.5
99	Viet Nam	41.4	136	Sudan*	16.3
100	Swaziland	40.9	137	Central African Republic.*	15.5
101	Tajikistan	40.4			
102	Lesotho*	40.1	138	Gambia*	14.6
103	Suriname	39.8	139	Mauritania*	13.4
104	Korea, People's Democratic Republic	39.2	140	Bhutan*	12.7
			141	Djibouti*	11.8
			142	Nigeria	10.8
105	Turkmenistan	38.3	143	Yemen*	10.6
106	China	37.7	144	Zaire*	9.9
108	Oman	35.7	145.5	Cote d'Ivoire	9.5
109	Guatemala	33.7	145.5	Lao*	9.5
110	Nicaragua	33.5	147	Rwanda*	8.5
111.5	Zimbabwe	32.5	148	Guinea*	8.1
111.5	Iraq	32.5	149	Uganda*	7.7
113	Myanmar*	30.3	150	Guinea Bissau*	6.8
114	Bangladesh*	29.7	151	Burkina Faso*	6.5

TABLE 18.1 ▪ Continued

RANK	NATION	SCORE	RANK	NATION	SCORE
152	Eritrea	6.3	157	Liberia*	− 5.3
153	Niger*	5.0	158	Somalia*	− 7.4
154	Ethiopia*	1.2	159	Sierra Leone*	− 7.5
155	Chad*	0.8	160	Afghanistan*	− 10.8
156	Mozambique*	− 3.1	161	Angola*	− 24.7

*Officially classified by the United Nations as among "Least Developing Countries" (LDC).

Source: Richard Estes, *Trends in World Social Development: The Social Progress of Nations* (New York: Praeger, 1997).

Several developing nations have increased their ranking position by 10 or more. South Korea and Singapore (and probably Taiwan and Hong Kong, had data for those countries been available in 1970) have vaulted from Third World to First World membership. Another subgroup consisting of Jordan, Indonesia, and Libya has also prospered, largely as a result of authoritarian leadership. Of course, Estes's 1995 ranking, fails to capture more recent events that would change nations' rankings. Political instability, coupled with the ongoing effects of the demise of the Soviet Union, probably drops Albania into the sixth if not the seventh decile. Uncertainty about a change in leadership compounded by famine would place North Korea (PDR) well below its 1995 position. Genocide in Rwanda and Burundi could well drop these nations into the last decile, accompanying Sierra Leone, Afghanistan, and Angola as among the most hopeless places on earth.

The Human Development Index

Since 1990 the United Nations has published the Human Development Index (HDI) as a register of the development of nations. The HDI is a composite of three variables: life expectancy, educational attainment, and income. A nation's HDI score, an average of the sum of the three variables, has a maximum possible value of 1. The HDI for nations in 1997 is indicated in Table 18.2.

In constructing the HDI, researchers arbitrarily designated the 45 nations with HDI scores above .800 as high in human development. Nations classified as medium, between .799 and .500, numbered 94. The 35 countries below .499 were identified as low in human development.

The HDI demonstrates that nations with somewhat lower incomes are nonetheless able to sustain longevity and mount educational programs. Despite a per capita GDP that is 63 percent that of Italy's, Greece claims comparable longevity and a comparable percentage of the population enrolled in educational programs. Similarly, Cuba's per capita GDP is one-third that of Saudi Arabia, yet Cubans enjoy greater longevity and more educational opportunity than Saudis. Still, the HDI is a less than optimal classification. An important qualification is that nations evidence significant variations internally that are not registered by the national HDI score. Ordinarily, national capitals, industrial cities, and ports elevate a nation's HDI score; rural and remote areas have a depressive affect. Although the "medium" developing nations rank higher than those ranked "low," the rural areas of the "medium" HDI-scoring nations tend to parallel those nations that rank lowest.

To address important issues related to social progress, the UN has developed other indices to assess national development. A Human Poverty Index incorporates nations' percentages of people not expected to reach age 40, their percentages of illiterate adults, the resources they have

TABLE 18.2 ■ Human Development Index, 1997

RANK	NATION	HDI	LIFE EXPECTANCY (YEARS)	GROSS SCHOOL ENROLLMENT (PERCENT)	PER CAPITA GDP (IN DOLLARS)
1	Canada	.932	79.0	99%	$22,480
2	Norway	.927	78.1	95	24,450
3	United States	.927	76.7	94	29,010
4	Japan	.924	80.0	85	24,070
5	Belgium	.923	77.2	100	22,750
6	Sweden	.923	78.5	100	19,790
7	Australia	.922	78.2	100	20,210
8	Netherlands	.921	77.9	98	21,110
9	Iceland	.919	79.0	87	22,497
10	United Kingdom	.918	77.2	100	20,730
11	France	.918	78.1	92	22,030
12	Switzerland	.914	78.6	79	25,240
13	Finland	.913	76.8	99	20,150
14	Germany	.906	77.2	88	21,260
15	Denmark	.905	75.7	89	23,690
16	Austria	.904	77.0	86	22,070
17	Luxembourg	.902	76.7	69	30,863
18	New Zealand	.901	76.9	95	17,410
19	Italy	.900	78.2	82	20,290
20	Ireland	.900	76.3	88	20,710
21	Spain	.894	78.0	92	15,930
22	Singapore	.888	77.1	73	28,460
23	Israel	.883	77.8	80	18,150
24	Hong Kong	.880	78.5	65	24,350
25	Brunei	.878	75.5	72	29,773
26	Cyprus	.870	77.8	79	14,201
27	Greece	.867	78.1	79	12,769
28	Portugal	.858	75.3	91	14,270
29	Barbados	.857	76.4	80	12,001
30	South Korea	.852	72.4	90	13,590
31	Bahamas	.851	73.8	74	16,705
32	Malta	.850	77.2	78	13,180
33	Slovenia	.845	74.4	76	11,800
34	Chile	.844	74.9	77	12,730
35	Kuwait	.833	75.9	57	25,314
36	Czech Republic	.833	73.9	74	10,510

TABLE 18.2 ▪ Continued

RANK	NATION	HDI	LIFE EXPECTANCY (YEARS)	GROSS SCHOOL ENROLLMENT (PERCENT)	PER CAPITA GDP (IN DOLLARS)
37	Bahrain	.832	72.9%	81%	$16,527
38	Antigua and Barbuda	.828	75.0	76	9,692
39	Argentina	.827	72.9	79	10,300
40	Uruguay	.826	73.9	77	9,200
41	Qatar	.814	71.7	71	20,987
42	Slovakia	.813	73.0	75	7,910
43	United Arab Emirates	.812	74.8	69	19,115
44	Poland	.802	72.5	77	6,520
45	Costa Rica	.801	76.0	66	6,650
46	Trinidad and Tobago	.797	73.8	66	6,840
47	Hungary	.795	70.9	74	7,200
48	Venezuela	.792	72.4	67	8,860
49	Panama	.791	73.6	73	7,168
50	Mexico	.786	72.2	70	8,370
51	St. Kitts and Nevis	.781	70.0	78	8,017
52	Grenada	.777	72.0	78	4,864
53	Dominica	.776	74.0	77	4,320
54	Estonia	.773	68.7	81	5,240
55	Croatia	.773	72.6	67	4,895
56	Malaysia	.768	72.0	65	8,150
57	Colombia	.768	70.4	71	6,810
58	Cuba	.765	75.7	72	3,100
59	Mauritius	.764	71.4	63	9,310
60	Belarus	.763	68.0	80	4,850
61	Fiji	.763	72.7	80	3,990
62	Lithuania	.761	69.9	75	4,220
63	Bulgaria	.758	71.1	70	4,010
64	Suriname	.757	70.1	71	5,161
65	Libya	.756	70.0	92	6,697
66	Seychelles	.755	71.0	61	8,171
67	Thailand	.753	68.8	59	6,690
68	Romania	.752	69.9	68	4,310
69	Lebanon	.749	69.9	76	5,940
70	Western Samoa	.747	71.3	66	3,550
71	Russian Federation	.747	66.6	77	4,370
72	Ecuador	.747	69.5	73	4,940

(continued)

TABLE 18.2 ■ Continued

RANK	NATION	HDI	LIFE EXPECTANCY (YEARS)	GROSS SCHOOL ENROLLMENT (PERCENT)	PER CAPITA GDP (IN DOLLARS)
73	Macedonia	.746	73.1	70%	$ 3,210
74	Latvia	.744	68.4	71	3,940
75	St. Vincent and Grenada	.744	73.0	78	4,250
76	Kazakhstan	.740	67.6	76	3,560
77	Philippines	.740	68.3	82	5,520
78	Saudi Arabia	.740	71.4	56	10,120
79	Brazil	.739	66.8	80	6,480
80	Peru	.739	68.3	78	4,680
81	St. Lucia	.737	70.0	74	5,437
82	Jamaica	.734	74.8	63	3,440
83	Belize	.732	74.7	72	4,300
84	Paraguay	.730	69.6	64	3,980
85	Georgia	.729	72.7	71	1,960
86	Turkey	.728	69.0	61	6,350
87	Armenia	.728	70.5	72	2,360
88	Dominican Republic	.726	70.6	66	4,820
89	Oman	.725	70.9	58	9,960
90	Sri Lanka	.721	73.1	66	2,490
91	Ukraine	.721	68.8	77	2,190
92	Uzbekistan	.720	67.9	76	2,529
93	Maldives	.716	64.5	74	3,690
94	Jordan	.715	70.1	66	3,450
95	Iran	.715	69.2	72	5,817
96	Turkmenistan	.712	65.4	90	2,109
97	Kyrgyzstan	.702	67.6	69	2,250
98	China	.701	69.8	69	3,130
99	Guyana	.701	64.4	64	3,210
100	Albania	.699	72.8	68	2,120
101	South Africa	.695	54.7	93	7,380
102	Tunisia	.695	69.5	70	5,300
103	Azerbaijan	.695	69.9	71	1,550
104	Moldova	.683	67.5	70	1,500
105	Indonesia	.681	65.1	64	3,490
106	Cape Verde	.677	68.9	77	2,990
107	El Salvador	.674	69.1	64	2,880

TABLE 18.2 ▪ Continued

RANK	NATION	HDI	LIFE EXPECTANCY (YEARS)	GROSS SCHOOL ENROLLMENT (PERCENT)	PER CAPITA GDP (IN DOLLARS)
108	Tajikistan	.665	67.2	69%	$ 1,126
109	Algeria	.665	68.9	68	4,460
110	Viet Nam	.664	67.4	62	1,630
111	Syria	.663	68.9	60	3,250
112	Bolivia	.652	61.4	70	2,880
113	Swaziland	.644	60.2	73	3,350
114	Honduras	.641	69.4	58	2,220
115	Namibia	.638	52.4	82	5,010
116	Vanuatu	.627	67.4	47	3,480
117	Guatemala	.624	64.0	47	4,100
118	Solomon Islands	.623	71.7	46	2,310
119	Mongolia	.618	65.8	55	1,310
120	Egypt	.616	66.3	72	3,050
121	Nicaragua	.616	67.9	63	1,997
122	Botswana	.609	47.4	70	7,690
123	Sao Tome and Principe	.609	64.0	57	1,851
124	Gabon	.607	52.4	60	7,550
125	Iraq	.586	62.4	51	3,197
126	Morocco	.582	66.6	49	3,310
127	Lesotho	.582	56.0	58	1,860
128	Myanmar	.580	60.1	55	1,199
129	Papua New Guinea	.570	57.9	37	2,564
130	Zimbabwe	.560	44.1	68	2,350
131	Equatorial Guinea	.549	50.0	64	1,817
132	India	.545	62.6	55	1,670
133	Ghana	.544	60.0	42	1,640
134	Cameroon	.536	54.7	43	1,890
135	Congo	.533	48.6	68	1,620
136	Kenya	.519	52.0	50	1,190
137	Cambodia	.514	53.4	61	1,290
138	Pakistan	.508	64.0	43	1,560
139	Comoros	.506	58.8	39	1,530
140	Laos	.491	53.2	55	1,300
141	Democratic Republic of Congo	.479	50.8	39	880

(continued)

TABLE 18.2 ■ Continued

RANK	NATION	HDI	LIFE EXPECTANCY (YEARS)	GROSS SCHOOL ENROLLMENT (PERCENT)	PER CAPITA GDP (IN DOLLARS)
142	Sudan	.475	55.0	34	1,560
143	Togo	.469	48.8	61	1,490
144	Nepal	.463	57.3	59	1,090
145	Bhutan	.459	60.7	12	1,467
146	Nigeria	.456	50.1	54	920
147	Madagascar	.453	57.5	39	930
148	Yemen	.449	58.0	49	810
149	Mauritania	.447	53.5	41	1,730
150	Bangladesh	.440	58.1	35	1,050
151	Zambia	.431	40.1	49	960
152	Haiti	.430	53.7	24	1,270
153	Senegal	.426	52.3	35	1,730
154	Cote d'Ivoire	.422	46.7	40	1,840
155	Benin	.421	53.4	42	1,270
156	Tanzania	.421	47.9	33	580
157	Djibouti	.412	50.4	21	1,266
158	Uganda	.404	39.6	40	1,160
159	Malawi	.399	39.3	75	710
160	Angola	.398	46.5	27	1,430
161	Guinea	.398	46.5	28	1,880
162	Chad	.393	47.2	29	970
163	Gambia	.391	47.0	41	1,470
164	Rwanda	.379	40.5	43	660
165	Central African Republic	.378	44.9	26	1,330
166	Mali	.375	53.3	25	740
167	Eritrea	.346	50.8	27	820
168	Guinea–Bissau	.343	45.0	34	861
169	Mozambique	.341	45.2	25	740
170	Burundi	.324	42.4	23	630
171	Burkina Faso	.304	44.4	20	1,010
172	Ethiopia	.298	43.3	24	510
173	Niger	.298	48.5	15	850
174	Sierra Leone	.254	37.2	30	410

available in the form of health services and safe water, and their percentages of underweight children under age five. A Gender-Related Development Index reflects life expectancy, adult literacy, school enrollment, and income for women.

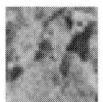 ## Capability Poverty

The idea that development is a multifaceted phenomenon has eclipsed a more circumscribed notion based on simple economic parameters. Using the HDI as a basis, development researchers began to evolve a more inclusive and dynamic understanding of authentic progress and to promulgate the idea of "capability poverty." The philosophical rationale for capability poverty was stated fully by Amartya Sen, who noted two profound historical truths: There are no records of famine within democratic societies, nor are there instances of war waged between them. Rather, these most severe events can be attributed to nondemocratic decision making that excludes large groups of people, who then bear the brunt of flawed policies. Sen's contention that freedom was a precondition of development, not a by-product to be enjoyed long after industrialization, earned him the Nobel Prize in economics in 1998.

The capability approach to development advocates "the expansion of the 'capabilities' of persons to lead the kind of lives they value—and have reason to value," Sen proposed, "Greater freedom enhances the ability of people to help themselves and also to influence the world, and these matters are central to the process of development."[26] Logically, however, deprivation of elemental requirements of survival subverts the possibility of full social participation, as do inadequate institutions that deny education, health, and recreation to subgroups. In constructing his argument for a "support-led process," Sen diverged with proponents of an economic model in which health, education, and labor benefits were viewed as being secondary. He contended that

the success of the support-led process as a route [to development] does indicate that a country need not wait until it is much richer (through what may be a long period of economic growth) before embarking on rapid expansion of basic education and health care. The quality of life can be vastly raised, despite low incomes, through an adequate program of social services. The fact that education and health care are also productive in raising economic growth adds to the argument for putting major emphasis on these social arrangements in poor economies, without *having to wait for "getting rich" first.*"[27]

Sen's pathbreaking work was soon elaborated by his colleague, Martha Nussbaum. In *Women and Human Development* Nussbaum states the philosophical rationale for an absolute standard of social justice for the most chronically oppressed among the world's poor: women. "The core idea is that of the human being as a dignified free being who shapes his or her own life in cooperation and reciprocity with others, rather than being passively shaped or pushed around by the world in the manner of a 'flock' or 'herd' animal," contends Nussbaum. "A life that is really human is one that is shaped throughout by these human powers of practical reason and sociability."[28] Thus, optimal development is not only freedom from want but also the full enjoyment of a range of social and political opportunities. Nussbaum lists 10 elements of a capability approach to development:

1. Life: enjoying full longevity.
2. Bodily health: having good health, including reproductive freedom.
3. Bodily integrity: appreciating freedom of movement, security from assault, and pleasure in sexual relations.
4. Senses, imagination, and thought: using the mind to explore rational and emotive bases for life as well as to advance their enhancement.

5. Emotions: enjoying attachments to others that are not controlled nor censored by others.
6. Practical reason: forming a conception of what is desirable and planning one's life.
7. Affiliation: respecting and living with others without fear of discrimination.
8. Other species: living in harmony with all features of the environment.
9. Play: enjoying activities that are entertaining and rejuvenating.
10. Control over one's environment: owning property and engaging politically in order to prosper.[29]

So formulated, the capability approach to development provides a blueprint for achieving and maintaining progress. This approach is particularly compelling in an era of rapid international changes attributable to shifts in capital, production, and labor. "Especially in an era of rapid economic globalization, the capabilities approach is urgently needed to give moral substance and moral constraints to processes that are occurring all around us without sufficient moral reflection," Nussbaum concludes. "It may be hoped that the capabilities list will steer the process of globalization, giving it a rich set of human goals and a vivid sense of human waste and tragedy, when choices are pondered that would otherwise be made with only narrow economic considerations in view."[30]

 # International Aid

Historically, the most developed nations (in other words, the more advanced welfare states) have endeavored to advance development by redistributing wealth to the developing world. The traditional means of this redistribution has been intergovernmental transfers, though with increasing frequency other intermediaries are being employed. Table 18.3 summarizes the recent performance of the industrialized nations and demonstrates several trends in international aid. Foremost, nations with the largest economies, notably Japan and the United States, rank in the last tier in terms of aid as a percentage of GNP, contributing significantly less than other, smaller industrialized nations. Indeed, the Scandinavian welfare states have consistently demonstrated international citizenship superior to that of the more laissez-faire economies. Compounding this pattern has been a downward trend in allocations for international aid. During the decade depicted by the data, international aid from national governments dropped in 14 of the 20 nations. This retreat from aid has contributed to a reassessment of international assistance. As governments have donated less, reliance has increased on private **NGOs** (nongovernmental organizations) and on **quangos** (quasi-NGOs) such as the World Bank, the International Monetary Fund, and regional development banks.

 # Global Capital

The foundation for global markets was laid after World War II with an international agreement for currency stabilization and debt financing that was negotiated at Bretton Woods, New Hampshire. The Bretton Woods agreement established the International Monetary Fund (IMF), an international agency accountable to its member nations. With the expansion of capital to overseas markets during the 1960s, the IMF initiated a program of Special Drawing Rights (SDRs) or loans that encouraged expansionary policies in developing nations. This program, however, collided with the acute economic contraction of the 1970s due to the oil embargo, driving much of the developing world into severe debt. Subsequent IMF policies to restructure debt payments have stressed "conditionalities," or internal economic reforms, often requiring controversial reductions in domestic spending for health, education, and related social programs.

TABLE 18.3 ▪ Net Official Development Assistance Disbursed, 1986–1987 and 1997

RANK	NATION	TOTAL (IN MILLIONS)	PERCENTAGE OF GNP		HDI RANK
			1986–87	*1997*	
1	Denmark	$1,637	.88%	.97%	15
2	Norway	1,306	1.13	.86	2
3	Netherlands	2,947	.99	.81	8
4	Sweden	1,731	.87	.79	6
5	Luxembourg	95	.17	.55	17
6	France	6,307	.58	.45	11
7	Canada	2,045	.48	.34	1
8	Switzerland	911	.30	.34	12
9	Finland	379	.48	.33	13
10	Belgium	764	.48	.31	5
11	Ireland	187	.23	.31	20
12	Germany	5,857	.41	.28	14
13	Australia	1,061	.40	.28	7
14	United Kingdom	3,433	.29	.26	10
15	Austria	527	.19	.26	16
16	New Zealand	154	.28	.26	18
17	Spain	1,234	.08	.23	21
18	Japan	9,358	.30	.22	4
19	Italy	1,266	.37	.11	19
20	United States	6,878	.21	.09	3

Source: Adapted from United Nations *Human Development Report, 1999* (New York: Oxford University Press, 2000).

The World Bank, also accountable to its member nations, provides resources to enhance infrastructure, initially through the International Bank for Reconstruction and Development (IBRD). Following the dramatic success of the Marshall Plan that rebuilt postwar Europe, the World Bank instituted the International Development Association (IDA) in 1960 to redirect activities to developing nations. Focusing on the poorest nations, World Bank aid is often in the form of credits, long-term loans that are interest free.[31]

Both the IMF and World Bank presume that international markets will be a means for development—a strategy that, though markedly successful for industrialized nations, has been less so for developing nations. With the demise of state socialism, international markets have, nonetheless, become the primary means for economic growth of the Third World. Two entities have facilitated this growth: The General Agreement on Tariffs and Trade (GATT), established in 1947, enjoyed only modest success in reducing tariffs until 1967, but in that year impediments against international trade were cut drastically. And in 1995 the World Trade Organization (WTO) was created to accelerate the emergence of global markets, augmenting

GATT. Since then membership in GATT/WTO has increased dramatically. Between 1980 and 1999 the number of GATT member nations increased from 85 to 134.[32]

The rapid expansion of international capital, during a period of retrenchment in governmental foreign aid, has highlighted the role of private sources of aid for international development. Figure 18.1 shows the dramatic shift in assistance to the developing world.

The Future

Although the unprecedented expansion of global markets has furthered economic growth internationally, the benefits have not been evenly distributed. Since the 1970s, the per capita GDP of the most developed one-third of nations has increased significantly; in contrast, that of the middle third has dropped from 12.5 to 11.4 percent and that of the lowest third fell 3.1 to 1.9 percent. "Such findings are of great concern," observed authors of the World Bank's development report, "because they show how difficult it is for poor countries to close the gap with their wealthier counterparts."[33]

Critics of global capitalism perceived such disparities as more than the inevitable consequences of international markets, however. Citing a crushing debt burden that required some Third World nations to repay international lenders sums that exceeded their nation's annual economic growth, as well as the imposition of program restructuring as a condition for future loans, opponents of international capital took to the streets in a series of demonstrations. In 1999 demonstrators seriously hampered WTO meetings in Seattle; several months later attempts to disrupt meetings of the World Bank in Washington, D.C., were less successful. High on the demonstrators' lists of demands were debt relief for developing nations and a restructuring of international aid organizations in order to make assistance more just. In demanding a restructuring of global finance, many demonstrators pointed to the $1 *trillion* traded daily by currency speculators, on which a trivial tax of .001 percent would generate $3 billion each day that could be put to work in development projects.[34]

Given the infeasibility of deconstructing the organizations at the top of the global financial empire, development strategists have focused their energies on nongovernmental organizations. Jessica Mathews, a senior fellow at the U.S. Council on Foreign Relations, has contended that NGOs provide a bond among peoples whose relations have been abraded by the competitiveness of international markets and the retraction of aid from industrialized governments.

At a time of accelerating change, NGOs are quicker than governments to respond to new demands and opportunities. Internationally, in both the poorest and richest countries, NGOs, when adequately funded, can outper-

FIGURE 18.1   Private Capital Flows to Developing Countries

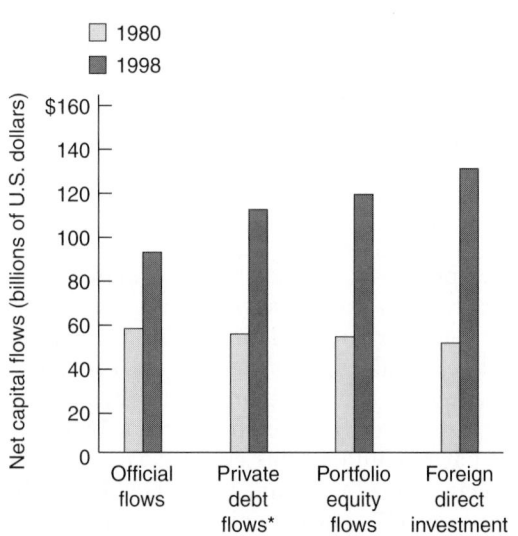

*Include loans and bonds. South Korea is included in the figures for developing countries.

Source: World Bank, *Global Development Finance* (Washington, DC: World Bank, 1999).

form government in the delivery of many public services. Their growth, along with that of the other elements of civil society, can strengthen the fabric of many still-fragile democracies.[35]

During recent decades hundreds of NGOs have emerged to facilitate development in the Third World. As is typical of voluntary ventures, these initiatives have both positive and negative features. On the positive side, their aggregate budgets and staffs eclipse the projects of many governmental projects; on the negative side, they tend to be fragmented, any coordination being a product of volition. Three NGOs that either have become well established in development circles or show promise of breaking new ground are Habitat for Humanity, the Grameen Development Bank, and First Nations Development Institute.

Habitat for Humanity. Established by Millard Fuller in 1976, Habitat for Humanity is a Christian organization that enlists volunteer labor and donated supplies to build housing for the world's homeless. On a budget of about $20 million, Habitat for Humanity had constructed tens of thousands of homes in areas from rural sub-Saharan Africa to *colonias* in Latin America to ghettos in the United States. Not operated as a welfare program, Habitat for Humanity requires that future home buyers provide sweat equity in constructing houses for others before they become eligible for one themselves. Home purchase is then arranged through zero-interest loans.

Grameen Development Bank. In 1976, economics professor Muhammad Yunus made a small loan to a woman peasant in Bangladesh so that she could purchase materials for making bamboo stools. Pioneering a peer lending strategy whereby small groups of peasants receive a loan for which the entire group is responsible, the Grameen Bank not only enhanced the productivity of poor people but also reinforced solidarity. Soon, borrowers whom commercial banks had written off as too risky demonstrated a repayment rate above 95

percent. By 2000 the Grameen Bank boasted 1,148 branches, 2.4 million members, and cumulative disbursements exceeding $3 billion.[36] Unique to the Grameen Bank is a social compact, "the 16 decisions," to which members must subscribe in order to become members. Addressing issues ranging from sanitation to birth control, education, and nutrition, the "16 decisions" provide a moral scaffolding for the bank's social architecture. Not a welfare program, Grameen Bank loans are interest bearing; the expectation is that, once repaid, they will make the borrower's loan group eligible for larger loans in the future.

First Nations Development Institute. Established in 1979 by Rebecca Adamson, a Cherokee Indian who wanted to end forever the dependence of Native Americans on the federal government, First Nations Development Institute (FNDI) has become an advocate for indigenous peoples worldwide. In addition to organizing community development banks on reservations in the United States, FNDI has advocated the rights of Aborigines in Australia as well as nomads of the Kalahari Desert. The FNDI paradigm integrates four components—community, nature, subsistence, and culture—into a unity that is antithetical to the exploitive, individualistic model typical of the industrial West. In so doing, FNDI eschews welfare, associating it with the demise of traditional kinship patterns: "The government welfare systems, superimposed on a complex and existing system of giving, sharing and reciprocity has facilitated the breakdown of the kinship system," contends FNDI Vice President Sherry Salway Black, an Oglala Sioux.[37] In advocating for the world's indigenous populations, or first peoples, FNDI serves a population that is often neglected by traditional development projects.

NGOs cannot, of course, be expected to replace military forces or compensate for government inaction in the face of genocide. History will be a harsh judge on the West for its diffidence at Srebrenica,[38] and it will be condemning of the West's utter disinterest in the ongoing slaughter in the Congo,[39] to say nothing of its complicity in the butchery in Sierra Leone.[40] An unanswered question is whether NGOs can address the infrastructure deficits that were once the province of industrialized governments or their international intermediaries. By way of illustration, consider these situations:

- Equatorial Guinea, an African backwater best known through Robert Klitgaard's scathing caricature of corruption, *Tropical Gangsters*,[41] has been blessed by the discovery of a large oil field, yet has virtually no civic infrastructure through which to ensure that oil revenues become translated into national development.[42]
- The HIV infection rate for adults exceeds 20 percent in five nations in sub-Saharan Africa, constituting an epidemic that rivals the Black Death of fourteenth-century Europe; yet international efforts to contain the disease have been inexplicably delayed, resulting in the preventable infection of millions of adults and children.[43]
- The widening digital divide—the disparity in access to computer technology between industrialized nations and the developing world—is furthering the gap between rich and poor nations. For example, the United States and Canada boast 1,396 Web servers, compared to 142 for Europe, 22 for Latin America, and 11 for Asia.[44]

As these circumstances suggest, the emerging issues in international development demand innovative solutions, and they demand them urgently. That urgency should rule out any complacency on the part of those favoring traditional strategies.

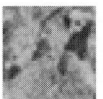

Conclusion

Nations vary developmentally both as individual entities and as clusters. Thus, the United States is more developed than Niger, just as the countries of the industrialized West are more affluent than those of sub-Saharan Africa. At the same time, countries and regions influence one another, contributing to the dynamism of international relations. A common tendency in the West has been to regard the welfare states of North America and western Europe as ideals to which the developing nations should aspire.

Yet a series of events has challenged this assumption. First, since the 1980s the welfare states of the West have retrenched, reducing their fiscal commitments to social programs. Second, among developing nations, subgroups have emerged. The oil embargo of the 1970s highlighted a small group of nations, the oil-exporting countries, that have comparatively high per capita income despite relatively low industrialization. Another subgroup consists of Southeast Asian nations that have prospered by aggressively pursuing capitalist strategies of development. As for the nations of sub-Saharan Africa: Most of them are worse off today than when they achieved independence during the 1960s, a tragedy that has been exacerbated by the HIV/AIDS epidemic. Third, international development agencies, such as the United Nations and the International Monetary Fund, have begun to explore alternative scenarios to prosperity—scenarios, such as sustainable development, that are often contrary to the alienating individualism and narcissistic consumption characteristic of the traditional welfare state.

 # Discussion Questions

1. Which framework or index, if any, best measures international social development?

2. Is examining a nation's material conditions the best way to evaluate social develop-

ment? If not, what other indicators should be used?

3. What are the main reasons that some Third World countries are less developed now than before they achieved independence?

4. Which welfare state typology provides the best explanation for the development of welfare states?

5. Compared to those of other nations, is the U.S. welfare state really "exceptional"? Why or why not?

6. How much inherent validity is reflected in national development rankings?

7. In the light of international data, how important to development is foreign aid?

 # Notes

1. Harold Wilensky and Charles Lebeaux, *Industrial Society and Social Welfare* (New York: Russell Sage Foundation, 1965).

2. Richard M. Titmuss, *Social Policy: An Introduction* (London: Allen & Unwin, 1971).

3. Norman Furniss and Timothy Tilton, *The Case for the Welfare State* (Bloomington, IN: Indiana University Press, 1977).

4. Ramesh Mishra, *The Welfare State in Crisis* (Brighton, England: Wheatsheaf Books, 1984).

5. Gosta Esping-Andersen, *Three Worlds of Welfare Capitalism* (Cambridge, England: Polity Press, 1990).

6. Norman Ginsburg, *Divisions of Welfare: A Critical Introduction to Comparative Social Policy* (London: Sage, 1992).

7. These typologies seek to classify the social welfare systems of the industrial societies and do not refer to the developing countries of the Third World. Attempts to construct comprehensive typologies that include the developing countries are still preliminary. See James Midgley, "Models of Welfare and Social Planning in Third World Countries," in Brij Mohan (ed.), *New Horizons in Social Welfare and Policy* (Cambridge, MA: Schenkman, 1985), pp. 89–108; and Stewart MacPherson and James Midgley, *Comparative Social Policy and the Third World* (New York: St. Martin's Press, 1987).

8. Edwin Amenta and Theda Skocpol, "Taking Exception: Explaining the Distinctiveness of American Public Policies during the Last Century," in Francis C. Castles (ed.), *The Comparative History of Public Policy* (New York: Oxford University Press, 1989), pp. 292–333.

9. Wilensky's comparative analysis of 64 countries rated the United States high in education and environmental protection but stated that this was at the expense of traditional social programs. See Harold Wilensky, *The Welfare State and Equality* (Berkeley: University of California Press, 1975). See also Arnold J. Heidenheimer, Hugh Heclo, and Carolyn Teich Adams, *Comparative Public Policy* (New York: St. Martin's Press, 1975), p. 258.

10. In 1975 Wilensky (*The Welfare State and Equality*, p. 105) noted that the United States "allocates a larger fraction of its total welfare spending to pensions than any of the twenty-two richest nations [in the world]." However, more recent expenditure data from the OECD show that although U.S. pension expenditures remain comparatively high, the United States is by no means a world leader. See Organization for Economic Cooperation and Development (OECD) *Social Expenditure, 1960–1990* (Paris: OECD, 1995).

11. Theda Skocpol, *Protecting Soldiers and Mothers: The Political Origins of Social Policy in the United States* (Cambridge, MA: Harvard University Press, 1992).

12. Robert Pinker, *The Idea of Welfare* (London: Heinemann, 1979).

13. M. A. Jones, *The Australian Welfare State: Growth Crisis and Change* (Sydney: Allen & Unwin, 1980); Terry Carney and Peter Hanks, *Social Security in Australia* (Melbourne: Oxford University Press, 1994).

14. See Martin Rein and Lee Rainwater (eds.), *Public/Private Interplay in Social Protection* (Armonk, NY: M. E. Sharpe, 1986); Sheila Kamerman, "The Mixed Economy of Welfare," *Social Work* 29 (1983), pp. 5–11; David Stoesz, "A Theory of Social Welfare," *Social Work* 34 (1989), pp. 101–107; Neil Gilbert and Barbara Gilbert, *The Enabling State: Modern Welfare Capitalism in America* (New York: Oxford University Press, 1989); Richard Rose, "Common Goals but Different Roles: The State's Contribution to the Welfare Mix," in R. Rose and R. Shiratori (eds.), *The Welfare State East and West* (New York: Oxford University Press, 1986), pp. 13–39.

15. Howard Glennester and James Midgley (eds.), *The Radical Right and the Welfare State* (London: Wheatsheaf Books, 1991).

16. See Barry Bluestone and Bennett Harrison, *The Deindustrialization of America* (New York: Basic Books, 1982); Samuel Bowles, David Gordon, and Thomas E. Weisskopf, *Beyond the Wasteland* (Garden City, NY: Doubleday, 1983); Bennett Harrison and Barry Bluestone, *The Great U-Turn* (New York: Basic Books, 1988); Robert Reich, *Tales of a New America* (New York: Times Books, 1987); and Lester C. Thurow, *The Zero-Sum Solution* (New York: Simon & Schuster, 1985).

17. See Charles Atherton, "The Welfare State: Still on Solid Ground," *Social Service Review* 63 (Fall 1989), pp. 167–179; and Joel Blau, "Theories of the Welfare State," *Social Service Review* 63 (March 1989), pp. 226–237.

18. Atherton, "The Welfare State."

19. Martin Anderson, "Welfare Reform," in Peter Duignan and Alvin Rabushka (eds.), *The United States in the 1980s* (Stanford, CA: Hoover Institution, 1980), pp. 145–164; George Gilder, *Wealth and Poverty* (New York: Basic Books, 1981); Lawrence Mead, *Beyond Entitlement* (New York: Free Press, 1986); and Charles Murray, *Losing Ground* (New York: Basic Books, 1984).

20. Anthony Giddens, *The Third Way* (London: Polity Press, 2000).

21. Michael Todaro, *Economic Development* (White Plains, NY: Longman, 1994), p. 140.

22. United Nations, *Human Development Report* (New York: Oxford University Press, 1996), p. 2.

23. Richard Estes, *Trends in World Social Development: The Social Progress of Nations* (New York: Praeger, 1997).

24. Ibid.

25. Barbara Crossette, "Is Life Better in Bulgaria?," *The New York Times* (September 7, 1997).

26. Amartya Sen, *Development as Freedom* (New York: Knopf, 1999), p. 18.

27. Ibid., pp. 48–49.

28. Martha Nussbaum, *Women and Human Development* (New York: Cambridge University Press, 2000), p. 72.

29. Ibid., pp. 78–80.

30. Ibid., p. 105.

31. Todaro, *Economic Development*, pp. 476–481.

32. World Bank, *Entering the 21st Century* (Washington, DC: World Bank, 2000), pp. 6–7.

33. Ibid., p. 18.

34. David Stoesz, Charles Guzzetta, and Mark Lusk, *International Development* (Boston: Allyn & Bacon, 1999), pp. 260–261.

35. Jessica Mathews, "The Age of Nonstate Actors," *Foreign Affairs* 76, no. 1 (January/February 1997), p. 63.

36. Grameen Foundation, *Grameen Connections* 3, no. 3 (Washington, DC: Grameen Foundation, Summer 2000), p. 3.

37. Cited in Stoesz et al., *International Development*, p. 191.

38. Chuck Sudetic, *Blood and Vengeance* (New York: Penguin, 1999).

39. Peter Gourevitch, *We Wish to Inform You That Tomorrow We Will Be Killed with Our Families* (New York: Farrar, Straus & Giroux, 1998).

40. Ryan Lizza, "Where Angels Fear to Tread," *The New Republic* 223, no. 4 (July 24, 2000).

41. Robert Klitgaard, *Tropical Gangsters* (New York: Basic Books, 1990).

42. Norimitsu Onishi, "Oil Riches, and Risks, in Tiny African Nation," *The New York Times* (July 23, 2000).

43. Barton Gellman, "The World Shunned Signs of Coming Plague," *Washington Post* (July 5, 2000).

44. Anthony Faiola and Stephen Buckley, "Poor in Latin America Embrace Net's Promise," *Washington Post* (July 9, 2000), p. A25.

Glossary

Absolute Poverty. A measurement and classification of poverty that is based on the minimal standard of living (including food, shelter, and clothing) necessary for survival.

Acute Care. Health care in which a patient is treated for an acute (immediate and severe) episode of illness.

Affirmative Action. Programs designed to redress past or present discrimination against minorities (including women) through criteria for employment, promotion, and educational opportunities that give these groups preferential access to such resources or opportunities.

Ageism. Age-based discrimination against elderly persons.

Alleviative Approach to Poverty. Strategies designed to ease the suffering of the poor rather than to eliminate the causes of poverty. Examples include AFDC, SSI, and the Food Stamp Program.

All-Payer System. The imposition of uniform prices on medical services, regardless of the payee.

Ambulatory Care. Health services provided without the patient's being admitted. Care provided by ambulatory care centers, hospital outpatient departments, physicians' offices, and home health care services falls under this heading.

Ancillary Services. Professional charges for X rays, laboratory tests, and other similar patient services.

Area Poverty. Economic depression in particular geographic regions.

Block Grant. A method of funding social programs by which the federal government makes monies available to states for a wide range of services, including social services. Block grants usually allow states more freedom by diminishing or eliminating federal program regulations. Block grants are usually fixed in terms of the amount available.

Brown v. Board of Education of Topeka, Kansas. Landmark 1954 U.S. Supreme Court decision ruling that "separate but equal" facilities in education were inherently unequal.

Bureaucratic Disentitlement. The denial of benefits to eligible recipients by agents of public agencies.

Bureaucratic Rationality. The ordering of social affairs by governmental agencies.

Capitalism. An economic system in which most of the production and distribution of goods and services occurs under private auspices.

Capitation. Method of payment in which a care provider is paid a fixed amount for each person served regardless of the actual number of clients or the nature of services delivered.

Case Management. The process by which all related matters of a case are managed by a single professional, often a social worker.

Categorical Grant. A method of funding social services through which the federal government makes available to the states monies that must be spent for very narrowly specified service needs.

Charity Organization Society (COS). A voluntary organization active in the late nineteenth and early twentieth centuries that attempted to coordinate private charities and promote a scientific approach to philanthropy.

Chronic Care. Long-term care of individuals with long-standing, persistent diseases or conditions.

Chronic Unemployment. The rate of unemployment attributable to persons who have persistent trouble finding work because of an absence of low-skilled jobs or because they have severe deficiencies in basic social and work skills.

Circuit Breaker Programs. Tax rebate programs designed to relieve the low-income, elderly, or disabled homeowner or renter from the burden of property or utility taxes.

Clinical Entrepreneurs. An interest group within U.S. social welfare that is associated with private practice and the provision of social welfare in the private marketplace.

Clinical or Critical Pathways. A "map" of preferred treatment/intervention activities.

Comprehensive Major Medical Insurance. A policy designed to provide the protection offered by both a basic and a major medical health insurance policy.

Commercialization. The consequence of subjecting social welfare to the marketplace; includes advertising for services, marketing services, and pricing services.

Commodification. The placing of social needs formerly met in the public sector (e.g., health care, counseling services) within the private market sector.

Commonweal. The general good, or the public welfare.

Communitarianism. Political philosophy that strives to seek a middle ground between conservatism and liberalism. Communitarians are often socially liberal, although they maintain that freedom must have its bounds. They are in favor of moral education.

Comparable Worth. The idea that workers should be paid equally when they do different types of work that require the same level of skill, education, knowledge, training, responsibility, and effort.

Conservatism. An American ideology emphasizing the role of the marketplace and the private sector in meeting both human and social welfare needs.

Corporate Sector. That part of the mixed welfare economy consisting of large, for-profit human service corporations.

Corporate Social Responsibility. The concept that corporations should be held accountable for practices and decisions that adversely affect the communities in which they do business; also, the responsibility of corporations to promote the general well-being of society.

Cost-of-Living Adjustments (COLAs). Adjustments designed to keep income maintenance and social insurance benefits in line with inflation. COLAs affect Food Stamps, Social Security, and SSI benefits.

Cost Shifting. Charging one group of patients more in order to make up for underpayment by others.

Culture of Poverty. According to one theoretical school, the concept that poverty is transmitted intergenerationally and that certain of its traits are found across diverse cultures and societies.

Curative Approach to Poverty. An approach designed to rehabilitate the poor through attacking the causes of poverty, such as illiteracy, poor nutrition, or lack of employment.

Cyclical Unemployment. A type of unemployment attributable to swings in economic performance, such as recessions.

Decommodification. A welfare approach that, through generous social programs, allows people to opt out of the labor force without a significant loss of income, jobs, or general welfare; also, the outcome of social programs that take needs formerly met through the marketplace (e.g., health care or personal social services) and turn them into public utilities (i.e., needs met by the public sector).

De Facto Segregation. Racial segregation that is not legally mandated by the state but that characterizes school systems and residential housing patterns.

Deinstitutionalization. The removal, in the late 1960s and 1970s, of many mentally ill or mentally retarded patients from state institutions and their placement in community settings.

Deliberate Misdiagnosis. Intentional distortion of a diagnosis in order to avoid labeling a client or for the purpose of collecting insurance payments.

Democratic Capitalism. The type of political economy characteristic of the United States, with a democratic polity and a capitalist economy.

Dependency Ratio. The number of workers required to pay into the Social Security system to support one retired worker living on Social Security.

Diagnostic Related Groups (DRGs). A prospective form of payment for Medicare-incurred charges. Specifically, DRGs are a classification scheme whereby hospitals are reimbursed only for the maximum number of days an illness or surgical procedure is designated to take.

Discouraged Workers. Those who have stopped seeking work out of frustration with their poor employment prospects.

Disentitlement. The removal of an entitlement status for a group of people. Specifically, the PRWORA disentitled poor beneficiaries from receiving lifetime benefits.

Donaldson v. O'Connor. Court decision ruling that mental patients could not be confined unless they were dangerous to themselves or others, and that they should not be confined unless they are being treated and cannot survive without hospitalization.

Dual Labor Market. A labor market divided into two classes of workers. See Primary Labor Market and Secondary Labor Market.

Durable Medical Equipment. Items of medical equipment owned or rented that are placed in the home of an insured patient to facilitate treatment and/or rehabilitation.

Earned Income Tax Credit (EITC). A federal program that functions somewhat like a negative income tax. Specifically, qualified working families or single people receive a tax rebate from the federal government that exceeds the taxes they paid.

Electronic Benefit Transfers (EBT). The attempt by the federal government to use technology in the delivery of benefits. This can include automatically depositing public assistance benefits into the savings accounts of re-

cipients, the use of debit cards in food stamp benefits, and so forth.

Emergency Assistance Funds. Special needs payments that can be made under the AFDC program for extraordinary needs such as homelessness prevention, fuel or utility bills, and burial.

Emergency Assistance Program. A program that operates under AFDC and is intended to provide short-term cash assistance to families in crisis.

Employee Assistance Plans. Social services provided by companies for their employees in recognition that many personal problems are either directly related to, or have an impact on, the workplace.

Employee Retirement Income Security Act of 1974 (ERISA). Act regulating the majority of private pension and welfare group benefit plans in the United States; also called the Pension Reform Act.

Entitlements. Governmental resources (cash or in-kind) to which certain groups are entitled, based on their ability to meet the established criteria. Entitlement programs have open-ended resources in that people cannot be denied benefits because of governmental resource constraints.

Equal Rights Amendment (ERA). An act that if passed would give women the same rights under the law as men.

Establishment of Paternity. Identification of the fathers of the children of unwed mothers; required in order to aid states in their efforts to collect child support.

Family Cap. Usually, the policy that recipient mothers will not receive any (or only partial) benefits for any children born while they are on public assistance.

Fee-for-Service. A method of reimbursement based on payment for services rendered. Payment may be made by an insurance company, the patient, or a government program such as Medicare or Medicaid.

Feminization of Poverty. A social trend marked by the increasing frequency of poverty among women. It is thought to be related to the high incidence of women relying on governmental aid, the low wages that characterize traditional female employment, occupational segregation, and family decomposition (divorce, desertion, or death).

Fill-the-Gap. An AFDC benefit method used by some states in which countable income (i.e., labor market income) does not result in a dollar-for-dollar reduction in the AFDC payment a family receives.

Fiscal Year (FY). A budgetary rather than a normal year. Government and social service agencies' fiscal years often begin on July 1 rather than January 1.

Frictional Unemployment. The rate of unemployment, usually about 3 percent, considered inevitable for a viable economy.

Functional Welfare. A social welfare–related concept that holds that social service benefits should be justified in relation to productivity. Usually a standard of conforming conduct is required on the part of recipients in exchange for benefits.

Gatekeeper. A primary care physician responsible for overseeing and coordinating all aspects of a patient's medical care. In order for a patient to receive a specialty care or hospital admission, the gatekeeper must preauthorize the visit.

General Assistance (GA). State or locally run programs designed to provide basic benefits to low-income people who are ineligible for federally funded public assistance programs.

Gentrification. Resettlement of existing low-income neighborhoods by middle- and upper-class homeowners or investors. This development can result in forcing poor and indigenous residents out of their neighborhoods.

Global Budget. A regional or nationwide cap on private and public health care spending.

Governmental Sector. That part of the mixed welfare economy consisting of social programs administered by government, particularly the federal government.

Great Society. A series of social welfare programs (including community development, training and employment, and health and legal services) enacted between 1963 and 1968 during the administration of President Lyndon Baines Johnson; formerly called the War on Poverty.

Greening/Greens. An environmental orientation to social policy. Greening often incorporates an environmental awareness with a social justice perspective.

Gross Domestic Product (GDP). A measure of the total output of goods and services produced by a country's economy.

Gross National Product (GNP). A measure of the total domestic and foreign output claimed by residents of a country. It is made up of the Gross Domestic Product (GDP) and of incomes accruing to foreign residents.

Halderman v. Pennhurst. Court decision ruling that institutionalized patients were entitled to treatment in the least restrictive possible environment.

Health Care Access. A patient's ability to obtain medical care. Access is determined by the availability of medical services, the location of health care facilities, transportation, hours of operation cost of care, and so forth.

Health Insurance Purchasing Cooperative (HIPC). A governmental or quasi-governmental entity established to purchase bulk health insurance for businesses and individuals.

Health Maintenance Organizations (HMOs). Membership organizations that typically provide comprehensive health care. Members usually pay a regular fee and are thus entitled to free (or minimal-cost) hospital care and physicians' services.

Home Health Care. Full range of medical and other health-related services, such as physical therapy, nursing, counseling, and social services, that are delivered in the home of a patient by a provider.

Homophobia. The fear of (and subsequent discrimination against) homosexuals on the basis of their sexual preference.

Housing Starts. Number of new houses begun in a given period.

Housing Stock. The number of currently available houses.

Human Capital. Productive investments that are embodied in humans. These include education, training, skills, experience, knowledge, and health. Increases in human capital result from expenditures on education, job training, and medical care.

Human Service Executives. An interest group within U.S. social welfare that is associated with human service corporations and advocates the provision of social welfare through large-scale for-profit programs.

Human Services. A concept equivalent to social welfare.

Iatrogenic Diseases. Diseases that are directly caused by medical intervention.

Ideological State Apparatus. The means (e.g., education, the print media, the family, television, and tradition) by which the primary ideology of a society is promulgated and maintained.

Ideology. A set of socially sanctioned assumptions, usually unexamined, explaining how the world works and encompassing a society's general methods for addressing social problems.

Income Distribution. The pattern of how income is distributed among the various socioeconomic classes in a society.

Income Inequality. The unequal distribution of income across socioeconomic classes.

Income Maintenance Programs. Social welfare programs designed to contribute to or supplement the income of an individual or family. These programs are usually means-tested and thus based on need.

Indian Child Welfare Act of 1978. Legislation that restored child placement decisions to the individual tribes.

Individual Development Accounts. Savings accounts designed and subsidized by individual states that allow low-income people to amass assets for specific purposes such as home purchase, education, or starting a small business.

In-Kind. Noncash goods or services provided by the government that function as a proxy for cash; for example, food stamps, Section 8 housing vouchers, and Medicare.

Inpatient Care. Care given in a hospital, nursing home, or other medical institution.

Institutional Welfare. A conception of welfare holding that governmental social programs that assure citizens of their basic needs (for food, housing, education, income, employment, and health) are essential to an advanced economy. Such programs are considered a right of citizenship.

Job Lock. Individuals' inability to change jobs because they would lose crucial health benefits.

Job Opportunities and Basic Skills (JOBS). Program created in the Family Support Act of 1988. The bill required a portion of a state's welfare caseload (usually AFDC mothers) to participate in a work or training program.

Keynesian Economics. An economic school that proposes government intervention in the economy through such activities as social welfare programs to stimulate and regulate economic growth.

Liberalism. A primary American ideology that advocates government intervention in the market in order to ensure the provision of basic goods, services, and rights to disenfranchised populations who are otherwise unable to obtain them.

Libertarians. A small but influential group that advocates more individual responsibility and a very limited role for government in social and economic affairs.

Licensed Certified Social Worker. A social worker holding the Master of Social Work degree who has practiced for two years under supervision and who has passed an examination. Twenty-nine states license social workers.

Managed Care. The organization of networks of health care providers (e.g., doctors, clinics, and hospitals) into cost-effective systems. Institutions or individual health care providers who are in managed care systems agree to accept set fees for each service or flat payments per patient. HMOs are one example of managed care.

Managed Competition. A hybrid health care system combining free market forces and governmental regulation, in which health care is organized to encourage competition among health care providers. Specifically, employers and other consumers form large purchasing networks that accept bids for health care from HMOs or other health plans. The competition among health care providers for contracts is intended to foster quality and lower costs.

Manpower Development and Research Corporation (MDRC). A well-known research organization that has done significant studies in various areas of social welfare policy. MDRC is best known for its research and demonstration projects in the area of workfare.

Market Rationality. The ordering of human affairs by corporate institutions within the marketplace.

Means Test. Test of income and assets designed to determine whether an individual or household meets the economic criteria necessary for receiving governmental cash transfers or in-kind services.

Medigap. Private health insurance plans that supplement Medicare benefits by covering some costs not paid for by Medicare

Milliken v. Brady. A 1974 U.S. Supreme Court decision that ruled that school busing across city-suburban boundaries to achieve integration was not required unless the segregation had resulted from official action.

Mixed Welfare Economy. An economy in which governmental, private nonprofit, and private for-profit providers of social welfare coexist within the same society.

National Association of Social Workers (NASW). The major national organization of professional social workers.

National Health Insurance. Various insurance-based proposals that incorporate comprehensive health coverage for the entire nation.

Neoconservatism. A recent American ideology, based on conservatism, that recognizes the necessity for social welfare but designs social programs so that they are compatible with the requirements of a market economy and traditional values.

Neoliberalism. A recent American ideology, based on liberalism, that assumes that universal social programs such as those advanced by liberals are implausible because of current social, political, and economic limitations. Neo-

liberals opt for more modest changes in social welfare programs.

New Deal. The name given to the massive Depression-era social and economic programs initiated under the presidency of Franklin Delano Roosevelt.

NGO. A nongovernmental organization (private or voluntary) that plans, delivers, or funds social services.

Occupational Segregation. The domination of low-wage sectors of the labor market by a minority group. For example, women are thought to be occupationally segregated in "pink-collar" jobs, as secretaries, receptionists, typists, and so forth.

Office of Economic Opportunity (OEO). The federal agency that was charged with the responsibility for designing and implementing the Great Society programs.

Oligopolization. The process through which a small number of organizations effectively control a market.

Omnibus Budget Acts. Inclusive budgets passed by Congress.

Pay-Go. A system for determining federal budgetary allocations that emerged out of the 1991 Omnibus Budget Reconciliation Act. In short, funding for any new program (or enhanced funding for an existing program) must come from reallocating existing money.

Per Capita Income. A determination of income based on dividing the total household income by the number of family members.

Permanency Planning. A strategy for helping foster children to live in families that offer continuity of relationships and the opportunity to establish lifetime relationships.

Personal Social Services. A term most often used by the British to denote social services that are delivered on a face-to-face basis (e.g., counseling and rehabilitation services).

Personal Responsibility and Work Opportunity Reconciliation Act of 1996 (PRWORA). The comprehensive act passed in 1996 that created the TANF program, limited benefits to both legal and illegal immigrants, changed the qualifications for SSI, and established the precedent that government no longer had the responsibility for maintaining the poor indefinitely. In effect, it disentitled the poor from income support programs.

Play-or-Pay. A proposed health insurance plan in which employers would either provide their employees with private health insurance or be obliged to pay into a government pool whose funds would be used to provide health coverage for otherwise noncovered citizens.

Plessy v. Ferguson. The 1896 U.S. Supreme Court decision that formally established the "separate but equal" doctrine in race relations.

Pluralism. The character, climate, or practices of a heterogeneous society in which many competing interest groups help to shape social policies.

Policy Framework. A systematic process for examining a specific policy or a set of policies.

Policy Institute. A private organization, funded by contributions and government contracts, that researches social problems and proposes social policies.

Political Action Committees (PACs). Organizations, usually associated with special interest groups, that divert campaign contributions to candidates running for public office in order to influence their later decisions on public policy.

Political Economy. The blending of economic analysis with practical politics. In effect, political economy views economic activity within a political context.

Political Practice. A method of social work practice in which social workers advance their priorities either by assisting those in political office or by running for office themselves.

Poverty Line. A yearly cash income threshold (based on family size) set by the federal government to determine if an individual or household can be classified as poor. Sometimes called the poverty threshold or poverty index.

Posttransfer Poor. The individuals or families who remain under the poverty line even after receipt of public assistance.

Preexisting Condition. A physical condition of an insured person that existed prior to the issuance of his/her policy or his/her enrollment in a health plan.

Preferential Selection. The selection of clients for treatment according to the organizational needs of the provider as opposed to the needs of the client; usually used to describe the practice of private providers who prefer insured clients with less severe problems.

Pretransfer Poor. Individuals or households who are under the poverty line before receiving public assistance funds.

Preventive Approach to Poverty. Social welfare strategies (e.g., social insurance programs) designed to prevent people from becoming poor.

Preventive Commitment. The institutionalization of persons who do not meet the requirements for involuntary hospitalization but who are likely to deteriorate without inpatient care.

Primary Care. Basic or general health care rendered by general practitioners, family practitioners, internists, obstetricians, and pediatricians.

Primary Labor Market. The full-time jobs that provide workers with an adequate salary, a career track, and benefits.

Primary Prevention. Efforts designed to eliminate the causes of social problems.

Private Practice. The provision of clinical services through the marketplace by individual practitioners or small groups of practitioners.

Privatization. The ownership or management of social services by the private sector, either nonprofit agencies or proprietary corporations. Privatization of public assistance involves attempts by individual states to have for-profit corporations manage the delivery of their public assistance benefits.

Professional Monopoly. The right to exclusive practice granted an occupational group in exchange for its promise to hold the welfare of the entire community as its ultimate concern.

Progressive Era. A period in the United States from the late 1800s to World War I, when progressive activists stressed the need for morality, ethics, and honesty in social, political, and economic affairs. The Progressive movement advocated numerous progressive reforms. It was also successful in establishing progressive legislation, including the progressive income tax.

Proprietary.   Defined by provision of services on a for-profit basis.

Prospective Payment System (PPS).   A payment method that establishes rates, prices, or budgets before services are rendered and costs are incurred.

Preferred Provider Organization (PPO).   Organization that uses primary care physicians as gatekeepers; a form of managed care.

Public Choice School.   A school of political economy that suggests that because interest group demands inevitably lead to budget deficits, government should therefore limit concessions to these groups as much as possible.

Public Policy.   Policies designed by government that contain a goal, a purpose, and an objective. Public policy may also incorporate a standing plan of action toward a specific goal.

Public Transfer Programs.   Programs such as AFDC, SSI, and Social Security that transfer money from the governmental sector to families or individuals who either are entitled to it or have earned it.

Quangos.   Quasi-nongovernmental organizations that have some affiliation with government but are predominately private.

Racism.   Discrimination against or prejudicial treatment of a racially different group.

Radical Social Work.   Social work informed by the belief that the political economy is incapable of incremental reform and that the system must be challenged through various means to advance social justice.

Rationalization.   Measures designed to make an organization or agency as efficient and cost-effective as possible.

Redlining.   In the area of housing, the refusal of mortgage or insurance companies to provide services in selected neighborhoods thought to be high-risk areas for defaults or excessive claims.

Reciprocity.   The requirement that a client demonstrate a specific activity or standard of conduct in order to obtain welfare benefits.

Relative Poverty.   A measurement and classification of poverty that is based on and related to the standard of living enjoyed by other members of a society.

Residual Welfare.   A conception of welfare holding that the family and the market are the individual's primary sources of assistance but that governmental "safety net" programs may provide temporary help.

Secondary Labor Market.   Jobs that are characterized by irregular, seasonal, or part-time employment and that pay relatively low hourly wages, provide no benefits, and offer no career track.

Secondary Prevention.   Early detection and intervention to keep incipient problems from becoming more debilitating.

Self-Reliance School.   A relatively new school of political economy advocating low-technology and local solutions to social problems.

Settlement Houses.   Organizations that began in the late nineteenth century as an attempt to bridge the class differences marking U.S. society. Based on the residence of middle-class volunteers in immigrant neighborhoods, settlement houses emphasized the provision of social services as well as reform activities.

Sexism.   Discrimination against women based solely on their gender. Sexism can also be directed at men.

Single-Payer System.   A centralized system of health care payment in which the government assumes responsibility for the costs (but not the delivery) for health services. People choose their doctor and hospital, and the government pays the bill according to a fixed-fee schedule. Coverage is often universal and is rights based rather than employment based. Canada is the best-known example of a single-payer system.

Social Insurance.   A system that compels individuals to insure themselves against the possibility of indigence. Similar to private insurance, social insurance programs set aside a sum of money that is held in trust by the government to be used in the event of a worker's death, retirement, disability, or unemployment. Individuals are entitled to social insurance benefits on the basis of their previous contributions to the system.

Socialism. A school of political economy that attributes the need for social welfare to the social problems caused by capitalism. Socialists advocate restructuring the political economy—in the case of the United States, capitalism—as the most direct way of promoting social welfare.

Social Justice. An ideal of equity and fairness in all areas of social, political, and economic life, as well as the provision of basic necessities to all without regard to their participation in the market; an objective of liberals and progressives.

Social Services. Programs designed to increase human capital by ameliorating problems in psychosocial functioning, providing necessary goods and services outside normal market mechanisms, and providing cash supplements to make up for the lack of market income.

Social Stratification. The vertical segmentation of the population according to income, occupation, and status.

Social Wage. A term used to refer to the additional "wage" a worker receives as part of the universal benefits paid out by a welfare state (e.g., health care coverage or housing loans).

Social Welfare Policy. The regulation of the provision of benefits to people who require assistance in meeting their basic life needs, such as needs for employment, income, food, health care, and relationships.

Sociopolitical Planning. Methods for anticipating program needs that are interactive, involving groups likely to be affected by a program.

Spells of Poverty. Periods of time (often limited) during which individuals or families fall below the poverty line.

Standardization. The reduction of services to a common denominator in order to lower provider costs.

Structural Unemployment. The rate of unemployment attributable to long-lasting and deep maladjustments in the labor market.

Supply-Side Economics. A school of political economy that proposes reductions in social programs so that tax dollars can be reinvested in the private sector to capitalize economic growth.

Sustainable Development. A theory that stresses the need to develop an appropriate balance between material needs and future resource availability. It calls for a form of balanced economic development.

Swann v. Charlotte-Mecklenburg Board of Education. A 1971 U.S. Supreme Court ruling that approved court-ordered busing to achieve racial integration in school districts with a history of discrimination.

Tardive Dyskinesia. Permanent damage to the central nervous system, evidenced by involuntary movements, that is caused by psychotropic medication.

Technomethodological Planning. Methods of anticipating program requirements using databases from which projections of future program needs can be derived.

Temporary Aid for Needy Families (TANF). The part of the Personal Responsibility and Work Opportunity Reconciliation Act (PRWORA) that replaced the AFDC program. It is a block grant program based on workfare, time-limited benefits (a maximum of five years), and strict work participation rates. The TANF program was instituted in 1996.

Tertiary Prevention. Efforts to limit the effects of a disorder after it has become manifest.

Think Tanks. Policy institutes.

Time Limits. The length of time a recipient (or a recipient's family) is allowed to remain on welfare. The federal government has instituted a five-year lifetime cap on benefits; several states have set shorter caps.

Traditionalism. A social movement that gained increased strength during the 1970s. Traditionalists seek to make social policy conform with their conservative social and religious values.

Traditional Providers. An interest group within American social welfare; associated with voluntary nonprofit agencies, traditional providers promote local institutions as a preferred method of solving social problems.

Underclass. The lowest socioeconomic group in society, characterized by chronic poverty;

that is, its members are poor regardless of the economic circumstances in the society at large.

Underemployed. Individuals who are working at jobs in which their skills are far above those required for the position; also, those who are employed part time when their desire is to be employed full time.

Unemployment. The condition of individuals more than 16 years old who are looking for work.

Usual, Customary, and Reasonable (UCR). Accepted fee established by a majority of practitioners in a given community for a given procedure. The UCR is defined by insurance companies to determine the proper level of payment for covered procedures.

Voluntary Sector. The part of the mixed welfare economy that consists of private, nonprofit agencies.

Vouchers. A system of government-issued coupons that allows lower-income consumers to choose freely between various services. Vouchers are sometimes made available for education, social services, rental assistance, or other benefits.

War on Poverty. See Great Society.

Welfare Behaviorism. The attempts of public officials to modify (by instituting specific social policies) the behavioral patterns of low-income people, especially welfare beneficiaries.

Welfare Bureaucrats. Interest groups within American social welfare associated with governmental social programs that advocate the provision of social welfare through large-scale public social programs.

Welfare Capitalism. An advanced system of social welfare existing in progressive capitalist countries.

Welfare Dependency. The economic dependence of a family or individual on governmental welfare services, especially cash grants.

Welfare State. A state in which the national government ensures essential goods, services, and opportunities to residents as a right of citizenship.

Welfare State Exceptionalism. The differences between the U.S. welfare system and those of other welfare states, especially those of western Europe.

Workfare. A system begun in the late 1960s whereby AFDC recipients were required either to work or to receive work training (sometimes in the form of higher education). The concept of workfare underlies the welfare reform bills passed in 1988 and in 1996.

Work Participation Rates. The percentage of individuals on public assistance that states are required to have in the workforce under TANF guidelines.

Working Poor. Families or individuals who are in the workforce (full- or part-time) but who are still at or below the poverty line.

Wyatt v. Stickney. The court decision requiring states to provide adequate levels of treatment to hospitalized mental patients.

YAVIS Syndrome. The tendency of clinicians to prefer clients who are young, attractive, verbal, intelligent, and successful.

Index

 # Photo Credits

p. 1: © Hulton-Deutsch Collection/CORBIS; p. 28: © AP/Wide World Photos; p. 39: © AP/Wide World Photos; p. 55: © AP/Wide World Photos; p. 111: © AP/Wide World Photos; p. 142: © Amy Etra/PhotoEdit; p. 164: © AP/Wide World Photos; p. 205: © AP/Wide World Photos; p. 251: © Arthur Grace/Stock Boston; p. 271: © Bob Daemmrich/The Image Works; p. 319: © AP/Wide World Photos; p. 358: © Fritz Hoffmann/The Image Works; p. 392: © Steven Hansen/Stock Boston; p. 415: © Hannah Gail/CORBIS; p. 438: © Bettmann/CORBIS; p. 464: © CORBIS; p. 488: © Ilene Perlman/Stock Boston.